LIFE OF JAMES BUCHANAN

Fifteenth President of the United States
BY
GEORGE TICKNOR CURTIS
IN TWO VOLUMES
Vol. I

Editor's note: apologies for the floating numbers throughout the book. Although efforts have been taken to remove them, in order to leave dates intact for ease of readability, not all could be removed. Thank you for your understanding.

PREFACE.

Notwithstanding the proverbial tendency of biographers to contract what Macaulay has called "the disease of admiration," no one who can lay claim to any strength of mind need allow the fear of such an imputation to prevent him from doing justice to a public man whose life, for whatever reason, he has undertaken to write. But that my readers may judge of the degree of my exposure to this malady, a frank explanation of the circumstances under which I came to write this work is due both to them and to myself. In the summer of 1880, the executors and the nearest surviving relatives of Mr. Buchanan asked me to allow them to place in my hands the whole collection of his private papers, with a view to the preparation of a biographical and historical work concerning his public and private life. This duty could not have been undertaken by me, without an explicit understanding that I was to treat the subject in an entirely independent and impartial spirit. To be of much value, the work, as I conceived, must necessarily be, to some extent, a history of the times in which Mr. Buchanan acted an important part as a public man. Moreover, although I had been for far the greater part of this period an attentive observer of public affairs, I had no special interest in Mr. Buchanan's fame, and was never personally known to him. I could have no object, therefore, of any kind, to subserve, save the truth of history; nor did the representatives ivof Mr. Buchanan desire me, in assuming the office of his biographer, to undertake that of an official eulogist. I have sought for information, aside from the papers of the late President, in many quarters where I knew that I could obtain it; but the opinions, inferences and conclusions contained in these volumes are exclusively my own, excepting in the few instances in which I have expressly quoted those of other persons. No one has exercised or endeavored to exercise the slightest influence over what I have said of Mr. Buchanan, and I acknowledge and have felt no loyalty to his reputation beyond the loyalty that every man owes to justice and to truth.

I have thought it proper to say this much concerning my relations to the family of Mr. Buchanan, for two reasons. The President, by his will, appointed as his biographer a personal friend, the late Mr. William B. Reed of Philadelphia, in whom he had great confidence, and who was a very accomplished writer. But Mr. Reed was prevented by private misfortunes from doing anything more than to examine Mr. Buchanan's voluminous papers, and to prepare two introductory chapters of the intended Life. Of these I could make no use, as they did not accord with my method of treating the subject. After Mr. Reed had surrendered the task which he had undertaken, the papers were placed in the hands of the late Judge John Cadwallader of Philadelphia, another personal friend of the President. This gentleman died before he had begun to write the proposed work; and when the papers, which had been placed in his hands by the executors, came into mine, along with another large collection from Wheatland, I had to subject them to an entirely new arrangement and classification, before anything could be done. In resorting to a stranger as the biographer of Mr. Buchanan, his executors and friends did what circumstances had rendered unavoidable. The only assurance I can give is that I have had no reason to be otherwise than strictly faithful vto what I believe to be the truth concerning the whole of Mr. Buchanan's career.

The other reason for a candid explanation of my relation to this subject will occur to every one. Mr. Buchanan's administration of the Government during the four years which preceded the commencement of our civil war, is a topic upon which friends and foes have widely differed. But no unprejudiced person who now examines the facts can doubt that, in many minds, injustice has been done to him. Perhaps this was inevitable, considering that a sectional civil war, of vast magnitude and attended with great bitterness, followed immediately after his retirement from office, when a political party which had been in opposition to his administration came for the first time into the full control of the Federal Government. It was in the nature of things—or rather, I should say, it was in the nature of man—that those who succeeded to the Government should have charged upon the outgoing administration that they had been remiss in their public duty; and that under the example of men in high places, there should have grown up a popular belief that Mr. Buchanan favored the secession of the Southern States, either purposely, or by lack of the proper energy to meet it in its incipient stages. Charges of this kind found popular credence in a time of unexampled excitement; and since the war was ended, there have been, and doubtless there still are, many persons who regard President Buchanan as a man who could have saved the country from a frightful civil war, if he had had the wish and the energy to nip Secession in the bud.

Such, at all events, were the reproaches with which many of his countrymen pursued him into retirement, and continued to follow him to his grave. Denied as he was a hearing while he lived, because the perils and turmoils of the immediate present unfitted men to look dispassionately back into the past, he may well have desired that in some calmer time, when he had gone viwhere there is neither ignorance, nor prejudice, nor rancor, some one should "read his cause aright to the unsatisfied." To that better time he looked forward with an undoubting faith in the ultimate justice of his country. I believe that the time which he anticipated has come; and that nothing more than a proper examination of the facts is now needed, to insure for him all the vindication that he could ever have desired.

In regard to this and to every other part of his life, I have found it an interesting task to trace the history of a man whose public and private character were always pure, whose patriotism was co-extensive with his whole country, whose aims were high, and who was habitually conscientious in the discharge of every obligation. My estimate of his abilities and power as a statesman has risen with every investigation that I have made; and it is, in my judgment, not too much to say of him as a President of the United States, that he is entitled to stand very high on the catalogue—not a large one—of those who have had the moral courage to encounter misrepresentation and obloquy, rather than swerve from the line of duty which their convictions marked out for them.

I must say a few words in explanation of my method of describing important public transactions, the interest in which attaches both to the events and to an individual who has borne a chief part in them. There are two modes of historical writing. One is to make a narrative of the course of a foreign negotiation, for example, or of any other public action, without quoting despatches or documents. The other, which scarcely rises above the dignity of compilation, is to let the story be told mainly by the documents. But in biography, where the interest centres for the nonce in some principal actor, I conceive that the better course is to unite the two methods, by so much of description as is needful to illustrate the documents, and by so much of quotation as is needful to give force to the viinarrative. It often happens, however, that the private letters which a person in high official station receives or writes, are quite valuable to the elucidation of official papers and official acts, as they certainly may render a description more lively than it would be without them. The collection of Mr. Buchanan's papers is exceedingly rich in private correspondence, both with persons towards whom he stood in official, and with other persons towards whom he stood in only social, relations; and I have drawn largely upon these materials. Whether I have accomplished the object at which I have aimed, the reader will judge. It is for me to do no more than to apprise him that I have endeavored to write for his instruction and his entertainment, as well as to render justice to the person whose life I have described. To vindicate in all things the public policy of the party with which he acted, has not been my aim. I have only sought to exhibit it in its true relation to the history of the times. Sincerity and strength of conviction were as characteristic of those to whom Mr. Buchanan was politically opposed, as they were of his political associates.

It is perhaps almost superfluous for me to say that it would have been impracticable for me within the limits of these two volumes to give an account of every debate in Congress in which Mr. Buchanan took part, or of every transaction with which he was connected as a foreign minister, as Secretary of State, or as President. Such of his speeches as I have quoted at length have been selected because of the interest that still attaches to the subject, or some part of it, or because they illustrate his powers as a debater; and in making selections or quotations from his diplomatic papers, I have been unavoidably confined to those which related to critical questions in our foreign relations. It was equally impracticable for me to touch upon the connections which he had with numerous political persons in the course of a public life of forty years. I have drawn a necessary line, and have drawn it between those with whom he stood in some important official relation, or who occupied important public positions, and those who belong in the category of politicians more or less prominent and active, with whom all very eminent public men have more or less to do; including the former and excluding the latter. But of course I have varied this rule in the case of friends who stood in personal rather than political relations with him.

It remains for me to give a description of the materials of which I have made use, and to make the customary acknowledgments to those who supplied them.

Any man who has been in public life for a long period of time, and has attained to the highest public stations, must necessarily have accumulated a vast amount of materials of the highest importance to the elucidation of his own history and of the history of the times in which he has acted. Mr. Buchanan had a habit of preserving nearly everything that came into his hands. The mass of his private correspondence is enormous. I can hardly specify the number of letters that I have had to read, in order to form an adequate idea of the state of the public mind in the opposite sections of the Union during the period when he first had to encounter the secession movement. My recollection of the condition of public opinion at such junctures was pretty vivid, but I could not venture to trust to it without examining the best evidence; for undoubtedly the best evidence of public opinion was to be found in the private letters which at such periods reached the President from all quarters of the country. Many hundreds of such letters have been examined, in order to write, and to write correctly, a very few pages. Mr. Buchanan had also another habit of great utility. Although he did not always keep a regular diary or journal, he rarely held an important conversation, or was engaged in a critical transaction, without writing down an account of it with his own hand immediately afterward. These extremely valuable memoranda will be found to throw great light upon many matters that have hitherto been left in obscurity, or have been entirely misrepresented. He was also an indefatigable letter-writer; and of those of his own letters of which he did not keep copies, he procured many from his correspondents after his retirement to Wheatland. He wrote freely, easily, and I should think rapidly. His familiar letters rarely received or required much correction; but his official productions were polished with great care.

The principal mass of these papers, along with the public documents which were connected with them, was collected by Mr. Buchanan himself, in the interval between his retirement from the Presidency and his death. This collection was placed in my hands by his brother and executor, the Rev. Edward Y. Buchanan, D.D., of Philadelphia. Another large collection came to me from Mr. and Mrs. Henry E. Johnston, the present possessors of Wheatland. Mrs. Johnston enriched the collection of papers which were sent to me from Wheatland, by adding to them a great quantity of her uncle's letters to herself, of which she kindly permitted me to take copies.

From James Buchanan Henry, Esq., nephew of the President, and for some time his private secretary, and from Miss Buchanan, daughter of the Rev. Dr. Buchanan, I have received interesting contributions, which have found their place in my work.

Next to these, the immediate relatives of President Buchanan, I am indebted to the Hon. Jeremiah S. Black, Attorney-General and afterwards Secretary of State during Mr. Buchanan's Presidency, for important information. I am under like obligations to Brinton Coxe and Joseph B. Baker, Esqs., of Philadelphia, friends of the late President.

And finally, from my own valued friend of many years, Samuel L. M. Barlow, Esq., of New York, I have received two very interesting contributions, which are quoted and credited xin their appropriate places. I am also under a similar obligation to W. U. Hensel, Esq., of Lancaster, and to George Plumer Smith, Esq., of Philadelphia. Nor should I omit to mention the name of Hiram B. Swarr, Esq., co-executor with Dr. Buchanan, and the confidential lawyer of the late President, at Lancaster, as one who has very materially aided my researches.

New York, May 1, 1883.

Central America—The Monroe Doctrine, and the Clayton-Bulwer Treaty 619

LIFE OF JAMES BUCHANAN.

CHAPTER I.

1791–1820.

BIRTH AND PARENTAGE—EARLY EDUCATION AND COLLEGE LIFE—STUDY OF THE LAW—ADMISSION TO THE BAR—SETTLES IN LANCASTER—A VOLUNTEER IN THE WAR OF 1812—ENTERS THE LEGISLATURE OF PENNSYLVANIA—EARLY DISTINCTION—PROFESSIONAL INCOME—RETIRES FROM PUBLIC LIFE—DISAPPOINTMENT IN LOVE—RE-ENTERS PUBLIC LIFE—ELECTED TO CONGRESS.

Autobiography, when it exists, usually furnishes the most interesting and reliable information of at least the early life of any man. Among the papers of Mr. Buchanan, there remains a fragment of an autobiography, without date, written however, it is supposed, many years before his death. This sketch, for it is only a sketch, ends with the year 1816, when he was at the age of twenty-five. I shall quote from it, in connection with the events of this part of his life, adding such further elucidations of its text as the other materials within my reach enable me to give.

The following is the account which Mr. Buchanan gives of his birth and parentage:

"My father, James Buchanan, was a native of the county Donegal, in the kingdom of Ireland. His family was respectable; but their pecuniary circumstances were limited. He emigrated to the United States before the date of the Definitive Treaty of Peace with Great Britain; having sailed from —— in the brig Providence, bound for Philadelphia, in 1783. He was then in the twenty-second year of his age. Immediately after his arrival in Philadelphia, he proceeded to the house of his maternal uncle, Mr. Joshua Russel, in York county. After spending a short time there, he became an assistant in the store of Mr. John Tom, at Stony Batter, a 2country place at the foot of the North Mountain, then in Cumberland (now in Franklin county.)

"He commenced business for himself, at the same place, about the beginning of the year 1788; and on the 16th of April, in the same year, was married to Elizabeth Speer. My father was a man of practical judgment, and of great industry and perseverance. He had received a good English education, and had that kind of knowledge of mankind which prevented him from being ever deceived in his business. With these qualifications, with the facility of obtaining goods on credit at Baltimore at that early period, and with the advantages of his position, it being one of a very few spots where the people of the western counties came with pack horses loaded with wheat to purchase and carry home salt and other necessaries, his circumstances soon improved. He bought the Dunwoodie farm for £1500 in 1794, and had previously purchased the property on which he resided at the Cove Gap.

"I was born at this place on the 23d of April, 1791, being my father's second child. My father moved from the Cove Gap to Mercersburg, a distance of between three and four miles, in the autumn of 1796, and began business in Mercersburg in the autumn of 1798. For some years before his death, which occurred on the 11th of June, 1821, he had quite a large mercantile business, and devoted much of his time and attention to superintending his farm, of which he was very fond. He was a man of great native force of character. He was not only respected, but beloved by everybody who approached him. In his youth, he held the commission of a justice of the peace; but finding himself so overrun with the business of this office as to interfere with his private affairs, he resigned his commission. A short time before his death, he again received a commission of the peace from Governor Hiester. He was a kind father, a sincere friend, and an honest and religious man.

"My mother, considering her limited opportunities in early life, was a remarkable woman. The daughter of a country farmer, engaged in household employment from early life until after my father's death, she yet found time to read much, and to reflect deeply on what she read. She had a great fondness for poetry, and could repeat with ease all the passages in her favorite authors which struck her fancy. These were Milton, Pope, Young, Cowper, and Thomson. I do not think, at least until a late period of her life, she had ever read a criticism on any one of these authors, and yet such was the correctness of her natural taste that she had selected for herself, and could repeat, every passage in them which has been admired.

"She was a sincere and devoted Christian from the time of my earliest recollection, and had read much on the subject of theology; and what she read once, she remembered forever. For her sons, as they successively grew up, she was a delightful and instructive companion. She would argue with them, and often gain the victory; ridicule them in any folly or 3eccentricity; excite their ambition, by presenting to them in glowing colors men who had been useful to their country or their kind, as objects of imitation, and enter into all their joys and sorrows. Her early habits of laborious industry, she could not be induced to forego—whilst she had anything to do. My father did everything he could to prevent her from laboring in her domestic concerns, but it was all in vain. I have often, during the vacations at school or college, sat in the room with her, and whilst she was (entirely from her own choice) busily engaged in homely domestic employments, have spent hours pleasantly and instructively in conversing with her. She was a woman of great firmness of character and bore the afflictions of her later life with Christian philosophy. After my father's death, she lost her two sons, William and George Washington, two young men of great promise, and a favorite daughter. These afflictions withdrew her affections gradually more and more from the things of this world—and she died on the 14th of May, 1833, at Greensburg, in the calm but firm assurance that she was going home to her Father and her God. It was chiefly to her influence that her sons were indebted for a liberal education. Under Providence, I attribute any little distinction which I may have acquired in the world to the blessing which He conferred upon me in granting me such a mother."

The parents of Mr. Buchanan were both of Scotch-Irish descent, and Presbyterians. At what time this branch of the Buchanan family emigrated from Scotland to Ireland is not known; but John Buchanan, the grandfather of the President, who was a farmer in the county of Donegal in Ireland, married Jane Russel, about the middle of the last century. She was a daughter of Samuel Russel, who was also a farmer of Scotch-Presbyterian descent in the same county. James Buchanan, their son, and father of the President, was brought up by his mother's relatives. Elizabeth Speer, the President's mother, was the only daughter of James Speer, who was also of Scotch-Presbyterian ancestry, and who emigrated to Pennsylvania in 1756. James Speer and his wife (Mary Patterson) settled at first on a farm ten miles from Lancaster, and afterwards at the foot of the South Mountain between Chambersburg and Gettysburg. It is told in some memoranda which now lie before me, that in 1779, James Speer left the "Covenanted Church," on account of difficulties with Mr. Dobbins, his pastor, and was afterwards admitted to full communion in the Presbyterian congregation under the care of the Rev. John Black. This incident 4sufficiently indicates the kind of religious atmosphere in which Mrs. Buchanan grew up; and the letters of both parents to their son, from which I shall have occasion to quote frequently, afford abundant evidence of that deep and peculiar piety which characterized the sincere Christians of their denomination. They were married on the 16th of April, 1788, when Mrs. Buchanan was just twenty-one, and her husband twenty-seven. Eleven children were born to them between 1789 and 1811. James, the future President, was born April 23d, 1791.

Of his early education and his college life, he gives this account:

"After having received a tolerably good English education, I studied the Latin and Greek languages at a school in Mercersburg. It was first kept by the Rev. James R. Sharon, then a student of divinity with Dr. John King, and afterwards by a Mr. McConnell and Dr. Jesse Magaw, then a student of medicine, and subsequently my brother-in-law. I was sent to Dickinson College in the fall of 1807, where I entered the junior class.

"The college was in a wretched condition; and I have often regretted that I had not been sent to some other institution. There was no efficient discipline, and the young men did pretty much as they pleased. To be a sober, plodding, industrious youth was to incur the ridicule of the mass of the students. Without much natural tendency to become dissipated, and chiefly from the example of others, and in order to be considered a clever and a spirited youth, I engaged in every sort of extravagance and mischief in which the greatest proficients of the college indulged. Unlike the rest of this class, however, I was always a tolerably hard student, and never was deficient in my college exercises.

"A circumstance occurred, after I had been a year at college, which made a strong and lasting impression upon me. During the September vacation, in the year 1808, on a Sabbath morning, whilst I was sitting in the room with my father, a letter was brought to him. He opened it, and read it, and I observed that his countenance fell. He then handed it to me and left the room, and I do not recollect that he ever afterwards spoke to me on the subject of it. It was from Dr. Davidson, the Principal of Dickinson College. He stated that, but for the respect which the faculty entertained for my father, I would have been expelled from college on account of disorderly conduct. That they had borne with me as best they could until that period; but that they would not receive me again, and that the letter was written to save him the mortification of sending me back and having me rejected. Mortified to the soul, I at once determined upon my course. Dr. John King was at the time pastor of the congregation to which my 5parents belonged. He came to that congregation shortly after the Revolution, and continued to be its pastor until his death. He had either married or baptized all its members. He participated in their joys as well as their sorrows, and had none of the gloomy bigotry which too often passes in these days for superior sanctity. He was, I believe, a trustee of the college, and enjoyed great and extensive influence wherever he was known. To him I applied with the greatest confidence in my extremity. He gave me a gentle lecture—the more efficient on that account. He then proposed to me, that if I would pledge my honor to him to behave better at college than I had done, he felt such confidence in me that he would pledge himself to Dr. Davidson on my behalf, and he did not doubt that I would be permitted to return. I cheerfully complied with this condition; Dr. King arranged the matter, and I returned to college, without any questions being asked; and afterwards conducted myself in such a manner as, at least, to prevent any formal complaint. At the public examination, previous to the commencement, I answered without difficulty every question which was propounded to me. At that time there were two honors conferred by the college. It was the custom for each of the two societies to present a candidate, and the faculty decided which of them should have the first honor, and the second was conferred upon the other candidate as a matter of course. I had set my heart upon obtaining the highest, and the society to which I belonged unanimously presented me as their candidate. As I believed that this society, from the superior scholarship of its members, was entitled to both, on my motion we presented two candidates to the faculty. The consequence was, that they rejected me altogether, gave the first honor to the candidate of the opposite society, and the second to Mr. Robert Laverty, now of Chester county, assigning as a reason for rejecting my claims that it would have a bad tendency to confer an honor of the college upon a student who had shown so little respect as I had done for the rules of the college and for the professors.

"I have scarcely ever been so much mortified at any occurrence of my life as at this disappointment, nor has friendship ever been manifested towards me in a more striking manner than by all the members of the society to which I belonged. Mr. Laverty, at once, in the most kind manner, offered to yield me the second honor, which, however, I declined to accept. The other members of the society belonging to the senior class would have united with me in refusing to speak at the approaching commencement, but I was unwilling to place them in this situation on my account, and more especially as several of them were designed for the ministry. I held out myself for some time, but at last yielded on receiving a kind communication from the professors. I left college, however, feeling but little attachment towards the Alma Mater."

In regard to the danger of his expulsion from the college, which Mr. Buchanan has frankly recorded in his autobiographical 6fragment, I find no other reference to it. But I have seen in the note-books of his studies and in the notes which he kept of lectures that he attended, abundant proof that he was, as he says, "a tolerably hard student." He seems to have had a strong propensity to logic and metaphysics, and of these studies there are copious traces in his own handwriting. The incident which he relates concerning his disappointment in not receiving one of the highest of the college honors at his graduating "commencement," is thus touched upon in a letter from his father:

Mercersburg, September 6, 1809.

Dear Son:—

Yours is at hand (though without date) which mortifies us very much for your disappointment, in being deprived of both honors of the college, especially when your prospect was so fair for one of them, and more so when it was done by the professors who are acknowledged by the world to be the best judges of the talents and merits of the several students under their care. I am not disposed to censure your conduct in being ambitious to have the first honors of the college; but as it was thought that Mr. F. and yourself were best entitled to them, you and he ought to have compounded the matter so as to have left it to the disposition of your several societies, and been contented with their choice. The partiality you complain of in the professors is, no doubt, an unjust thing in them, and perhaps it has proceeded from some other cause than that which you are disposed to ascribe to them.

Often when people have the greatest prospects of temporal honor and aggrandizement, they are all blasted in a moment by a fatality connected with men and things; and no doubt the designs of Providence may be seen very conspicuously in our disappointments, in order to teach us our dependency on Him who knows all events, and they ought to humble our pride and self-sufficiency...... I think it was a very partial decision, and calculated to hurt your feelings. Be that as it will, I hope you will have fortitude enough to surmount these things. Your great consolation is in yourself, and if you can say your right was taken from you by a partial spirit and given to those to whom it ought not to be given, you must for the present submit. The more you know of mankind, the more you will distrust them. It is said the knowledge of mankind and the distrust of them are reciprocally connected......

I approve of your conduct in being prepared with an oration, and if upon delivery it be good sense, well spoken, and your own composition, your audience will think well of it whether it be spoken first, or last, or otherwise......

7We anticipate the pleasure of seeing you shortly, when I hope all these little clouds will be dissipated.

From your loving and affectionate father,

James Buchanan.

Following Mr. Buchanan's sketch of his early life, we come to the period immediately after he graduated from Dickinson College.

I came to Lancaster to study law with the late Mr. Hopkins, in the month of December, 1809, and was admitted to practice in November, 1812. I determined that if severe application would make me a good lawyer, I should not fail in this particular; and I can say, with truth, that I have never known a harder student than I was at that period of my life. I studied law, and nothing but law, or what was essentially connected with it. I took pains to understand thoroughly, as far as I was capable, everything which I read; and in order to fix it upon my memory and give myself the habit of extempore speaking, I almost every evening took a lonely walk, and embodied the ideas which I had acquired during the day in my own language. This gave me a habit of extempore speaking, and that not merely words but things. I derived great improvement from this practice.

It would seem that young Buchanan remained at home with his parents after he had graduated until the month of December, when he went to Lancaster and entered himself as a student at law, in the office of Mr. Hopkins. The following letters from his parents give all that I am able to glean respecting the period of his law pupilage, and the choice of a permanent residence after he had been admitted to practice, which was, it seems, in November, 1812.

[FROM HIS FATHER.]

March 12, 1810.

...... I am very glad to hear you are so well pleased with Lancaster, and with the study of the law.

...... I hope you will guard against the temptations that may offer themselves in this way, or any other, knowing that without religion all other things are as trifles, and will soon pass away...... Your young acquaintances often talk of you, and with respect and esteem. Go on with your studies, and endeavor to be eminent in your profession.

Mr. Buchanan was admitted to the bar in the year which saw the commencement of the war with Great Britain, under the Presidency of Mr. Madison. His early political principles 8were those of the Federalists, who disapproved of the war. Yet, as the following passages in his autobiography show, he was not backward in his duty as a citizen:[1]

The first public address I ever made before the people was in 1814, a short time after the capture of Washington by the British. In common with the Federalists, generally, of the Middle and Southern States, whilst I disapproved of the declaration of war under the circumstances in which it was made, yet I thought it was the duty of every patriot to defend the country, whilst the war was raging, against a foreign enemy. The capture of Washington lighted up a flame of patriotism which pervaded the whole of Pennsylvania. A public meeting was called in Lancaster for the purpose of adopting measures to obtain volunteers to march for the defence of Baltimore. On that occasion I addressed the people, and was among the first to register my name as a volunteer. We immediately formed a company of dragoons, and elected the late Judge Henry Shippen our captain. We marched to Baltimore, and served under the command of Major Charles Sterret Ridgely, until we were honorably discharged. This company of dragoons was the avant courier of the large force which rushed from Pennsylvania to the defence of Baltimore. Mr. Buchanan's entrance into public life is thus described by himself:

In October, 1814, I was elected a member of the House of Representatives, in the Legislature, from the county of Lancaster. The same principles which guided my conduct in sustaining the war, notwithstanding my opposition to its declaration, governed my course after I became a member of the Legislature. An attack was threatened against the city of Philadelphia. The General Government was nearly reduced to a state of bankruptcy, and could scarcely raise sufficient money to maintain the regular troops on the remote frontiers of the country. Pennsylvania was obliged to rely upon her own energies for the defence, and the people generally, of all parties, were ready to do their utmost in the cause.

Two plans were proposed. The one was what was called the Conscription Bill, and similar to that which had been rejected by Congress, reported in the [State] Senate by Mr. Nicholas Biddle, by which it was proposed to divide the white male inhabitants of the State above the age of eighteen into classes of twenty-two men each, and to designate one man by lot from 9the numbers between the ages of eighteen and forty-five of each class, who should serve one year, each class being compelled to raise a sum not exceeding two hundred dollars, as a bounty to the conscript. This army was to be paid and maintained at the expense of the State, and its estimated cost would have been between three and three and one-half million of dollars per annum. The officers were to be appointed by the Governor, by and with the advice and consent of the Senate.

The other was to raise six regiments under the authority of the State, to serve for three years, or during the war, and to pass efficient volunteer and militia laws.

[Here the narrative changes to the third person.]

"On the 1st of February, 1815, Mr. Buchanan delivered his sentiments in regard to the proper mode of defending the Commonwealth, on the bill entitled 'An act for the encouragement of volunteers for the defence of this Commonwealth.' He said: 'Since, then, the Congress have deserted us in our time of need, there is no alternative but either to protect ourselves by some efficient measures, or surrender up that independence which has been purchased by the blood of our forefathers. No American can hesitate which of these alternatives ought to be adopted. The invading enemy must be expelled from our shores; he must be taught to respect the rights of freedom.'

"Again, speaking of the Conscription Bill, he said: 'This law is calculated to be very unjust and very unequal in its effects. Whilst it will operate as a conscription law upon the poor man in the western parts of the State, where property is not in danger, it will be but a militia law with the rich man in the eastern part of the State, whose property it contemplates defending. The individuals in each class are, to be sure, to pay the two hundred dollars in proportion to their comparative wealth, as a bounty to the substitute or conscript. It will, therefore, be just in its operation among the individuals composing each class, but how will it be with respect to entire classes? Twenty-two men in the city of

Philadelphia, whose united fortunes would be worth two million dollars, would be compelled to pay no more than twenty-two men in the western country, who may not be worth the one-thousandth part of that sum.'

"After Mr. Buchanan had stated that he would have voted for the Enlistment Bill, had he not been necessarily absent when it passed the House, he said: 'After all, I must confess, that in my opinion an efficient volunteer and militia bill, together with the troops which can be raised under the Voluntary Enlistment Bill, will be amply sufficient for the defence of the city of Philadelphia. We need not be afraid to trust to the patriotism or courage of the people of this country when they are invaded. Let them have good militia officers, and they will soon be equal to any troops of the world. Have not the volunteers and militia on the Niagara frontier fought in such a manner as to merit the gratitude of the nation? Is it to 10be supposed that the same spirit of patriotism would animate the man who is dragged out by a conscription law to defend his country, that the volunteer or militiaman would feel? Let us, then, pass an efficient militia law, and the Volunteer Bill which is now before us. Let us hold out sufficient inducement to our citizens to turn out, as volunteers. Let their patriotism be stimulated by self-interest, and I have no doubt that in the day of trial there will be armies of freemen in the field sufficiently large for our protection. Your State will then be defended at a trifling comparative expense, the liberties of the people will be preserved, and their willingness to bear new burdens be continued.'

"The bill having passed the Senate, was negatived in the House, on the 3d of February, 1815, by the decisive vote of 51 to 36. It was entitled 'An act to raise a military force for the defence of this Commonwealth.' The Senate and the House thus differed in regard to the best mode of defending the Commonwealth; the one being friendly to the Conscription Bill, and the other to the Voluntary Enlistment and Volunteer Bill. All agreed upon the necessity of adopting efficient means for this purpose. Before any final action was had upon the subject, the news of peace arrived, and was officially communicated by Governor Snyder to the Legislature on the 17th February, 1815."

So open and decided was I in my course in favor of defending the country, notwithstanding my disapproval of the declaration of war, that I distinctly recollect that the late William Beale, the shrewd, strong-minded, and influential Democratic Senator from Mifflin county, called upon me, and urged me strongly during the session to change my [political] name, and be called a Democrat, stating that I would have no occasion to change my principles. In that event, he said he would venture to predict that, should I live, I would become President of the United States. He was mistaken, for although I was friendly to a vigorous prosecution of the war, I was far from being a "Democrat" in principle.

[FROM HIS FATHER.]
September 22, 1814.
Dear Son:—

I received your letter of the 9th ult. from Baltimore, which stated that you were then honorably discharged. This news was very gratifying, as at that moment we received accounts that the British were making their attack on Baltimore, both by sea and land, and consequently our forebodings with respect to your fate were highly wound up......

You say you are in nomination for the Assembly. I am not certain that it will be to your advantage, as it will lead you off from the study and practice of the law. If by your industry and application you could become eminent at the bar, that would be preferable to being partly a politician and partly a lawyer. However, you must now be directed by circumstances and the counsel of your friends.

11...... The Assembly has passed a law for the benefit of the poor, which in fact prevents them from paying any debts, as they hold all under cover of the reserve made them in the law. So much for popularity at the expense of justice.

October 21, 1814.

Dear Son:—

I received yours by Mr. Evans, informing me you were elected to the Assembly. The circumstances of your being so popular amongst your neighbors as to give you a majority over Isaac Wayne, who, I suppose, was one of the highest on your ticket, is very gratifying to me, and I hope your conduct will continue to merit their approbation. But above all earthly enjoyments, endeavor to merit the esteem of heaven; and that Divine Providence who has done so much for you heretofore, will never abandon you in the hour of trial. Perhaps your going to the Legislature may be to your advantage, and it may be otherwise. I hope you will make the best of the thing now. The feelings of parents are always alive to the welfare of their children, and I am fearful of this taking you from the bar at a time when perhaps you may feel it most......

There is now every prospect of a continuation of the war. The terms offered us by the British are such that no true American could comply with, or submit to them...... News has just come to this place that Lord Hill has arrived with 16,000 men.

From your loving father,

J. B.

January 20, 1815.

...... I am glad to find you are well pleased at being a member of the Legislature. Perhaps it may have the effect you mention, that of increasing your business hereafter. I am glad to hear that you mean to proceed with caution, and speak only when you are well prepared for the subject you mean to speak upon. You are young, consequently deficient in experience; therefore you must supply that defect by watchfulness and application, never forgetting that every gift you may possess flows from that Being who has always been your friend, and will continue to be so, if you are in your duty.

February 24, 1815.

Dear Son:—

I expect you are now engaged in repealing many of those laws which have been enacted for prosecuting the war with vigor. As the olive-branch has been presented to us, it will change all our plans, and we will again be permitted to return in peace to our different occupations, and ought to thank heaven for the blessing. This night we are to illuminate this place in consequence of peace. Those who have seen the treaty say it is dishonorable to America; that there are none of those points gained for which we declared war.

12June 23, 1815.

...... You appear to hesitate about going to the Legislature again, and I am both unable and unwilling to advise you on that point; but as it appears your business has not decreased by being there last winter, I would have no objection to your going another session, as it would afford you another opportunity of improvement, and perhaps the people of your district may some time elect you to Congress. Could you not get an active young man as a student that could keep your office open in your absence, and do a little business for you?......

You may expect to have many difficulties and dangers to encounter in your passage through life, especially as your situation becomes enviable; but I hope you will always depend upon the protection of that kind Providence, who has dealt so kindly with you, to shield you from the shafts of malicious enemies.

Your mother and the family send their kind love to you, and believe me your loving father,

J. B.

The next event in his life of which I find any mention in his autobiography, was the delivery of an oration before the Washington Society of Lancaster, July 4, 1815, of which he speaks as follows:

On the 4th of July, 1815, I delivered the oration before the Washington Association of Lancaster, which has been the subject of much criticism. There are many sentiments in this oration which I regret; at the same time it cannot be denied that the country was wholly unprepared for war, at the period of its declaration, and the attempt to carry it on by means of loans, without any resort to taxation, had well nigh made the Government bankrupt. There is, however, a vein of feeling running throughout the whole oration—of which, as I look back to it, I may be excused for being proud—which always distinguishes between the conduct of the administration and the necessity for defending the country. Besides, it will be recollected that this oration was not delivered until after the close of the war. I said: "Glorious it has been, in the highest degree, to the American character, but disgraceful in the extreme to the administration. When the individual States discovered that they were abandoned by the General Government, whose duty it was to protect them, the fortitude of their citizens arose with their misfortunes. The moment we were invaded, the genius of freedom inspired their souls. They rushed upon their enemies with a hallowed fury which the hireling soldiers of Britain could never feel. They taught our foe that the soil of freedom would always be the grave of its invaders."

I spoke with pride and exultation of the exploits of the navy, and also of the regular army during the last year of the war. The former "has 13risen triumphant above its enemies at home, and has made the proud mistress of the ocean tremble. The people are now convinced that a navy is their best defence."[2]

In the conclusion there is a passage concerning foreign influence which must be approved by all. "Foreign influence has been, in every age, the curse of Republics. Her jaundiced eye sees all things in false colors. The thick atmosphere of prejudice, by which she is forever surrounded, excludes from her sight the light of reason; whilst she worships the nations which she favors for their very crimes, she curses the enemies of that nation, even their virtues. In every age she has marched before the enemies of her country, 'proclaiming peace, when there was no peace,' and lulling its defenders into fatal security, whilst the iron hand of despotism has been aiming a death-blow at their liberties." And again, "We are separated from the nations of Europe by an immense ocean. We are still more disconnected from them by a different form of government, and by the enjoyment of true liberty. Why, then, should we injure ourselves by taking part in the ambitious contests of foreign despots and kings?"

[FROM HIS FATHER.]

July 14, 1815.

No doubt you will have many political enemies to criticise your oration, but you must take the consequences now. It is a strong mark of approbation to have so many copies of it published. I hope to see one of them.

I am busily engaged with my harvest. I am very glad I did not purchase goods as I proposed, as they have fallen greatly in price.

September 1, 1815.

...... Myself and the family are very anxious to see you, yet I am glad that your business is so good that you cannot, with propriety, leave it, yet you must always make your calculations to come as often as you can. Have you agreed to your nomination for the Legislature another session? You know your own situation best. If you think proper to take another seat, it has my approbation. I have read your oration, and I think it well done. Perhaps it is a little too severe, and may hurt the feelings of some of your friends, who have been friendly, independent of politics. I have lent it to a few people who have asked for it, and they all speak well of your performance.

14Oct. 19, 1815.

...... It appears from the Lancaster Journal, you are again elected. I wish you may end the next session with the same popularity as a statesman that you gained in the last session. Mr. Buchanan's own account of his second term of service in the Legislature is thus given:

I was again elected a member of the House of Representatives in the State Legislature in October, 1815. The currency at that period was in great disorder throughout the Middle, Western, and Southern States, in consequence of the suspension of specie payments occasioned by the war. On the 20th of December, 1815, a resolution was adopted by the House of Representatives, instructing the Committee on Banks, "to inquire into the causes of the suspension of specie payments by the banks within this Commonwealth; and also, whether any or what measures ought to be adopted by the Legislature on this subject." This committee was composed of Mr. McEuen, of the city; Milliken, of Mifflin; Stewart, of Fayette; and Dysart, of Crawford. On the 12th of January, 1816, Mr. McEuen made a report which concluded with a recommendation that a law should be passed, obliging the banks to pay interest on balances to each other monthly, at the rate of six per cent. per annum, after the 1st of March; also, obliging the banks refusing to pay specie for their notes after the 1st of January, 1817, to pay interest at the rate of eighteen per cent. per annum from the time of demand; and forfeiting the charters of such banks as should refuse to redeem their notes in specie after the 1st of January, 1818. A bare majority of the committee had concurred in the report. The minority had requested me to prepare a substitute for it, and offer it as soon as the report was read. This substitute concluded with a resolution, "that it is inexpedient at this time for the Legislature to adopt any compulsory measures relative to the banks." The original report and the substitute were postponed, and no action was ever had afterwards upon either.

The substitute states the following to have been the causes of the suspension of specie payments in Pennsylvania:

1. The blockade by the enemy of the Middle and Southern seaports, the impossibility of getting their productions to market, and the consequent necessity imposed upon them to pay in specie to New England the price of the foreign merchandise imported into that portion of the Union.

2. The large loans made by banks and individuals of this and the adjacent States to the Government to sustain the war, and the small comparative loans made in New England, which were paid by an extravagant issue of bank notes. These latter bore but a small proportion to the money expended there. To make up this deficiency, the specie of the Middle and Southern States was drawn from the vaults of these banks, 15and was used by the New England people in commerce, or smuggled to the enemy.

3. The great demand for specie in England.

4. The recent establishment of a number of new banks throughout the interior of Pennsylvania, which drew their capital chiefly from the banks in Philadelphia and thereby

weakened them, compelled them first to suspend specie payments. These new banks, in self-defence, were therefore obliged to suspend.

5. The immense importation of foreign goods at the close of the war, and the necessity of paying for them in specie, have continued the suspension.

During this session, and whilst the debates on the subject were proceeding in Congress, I changed my impression on the subject of a Bank of the United States, and became decidedly hostile to such an institution. In this opinion I have never since wavered, and although I have invested much of the profits of my profession in stocks, and was often advised by friends to buy stock in this bank, I always declined becoming a stockholder. Whilst the bill was pending in Congress, I urged Mr. Holgate and other influential Democrats in the House to offer instructions against the measure, but could not prevail with them. I recollect Mr. H. told me that it was unnecessary, as our Democratic Senators in Congress would certainly vote against the measure without any instructions.

Mr. Buchanan appears to have left the Legislature at the end of the session of 1815–16, with a fixed determination to devote himself exclusively to the practice of his profession. He says:

After my second session in the Legislature, I applied myself with unremitting application to the practice of the law. My practice in Lancaster and some of the adjoining counties was extensive, laborious, and lucrative. It increased rapidly in value from the time I ceased to be a member of the Legislature. During the year ending on the 1st of April, 1819, I received in cash for professional services $7,915.92, which was, down to that time, the best year I ever experienced.[3]

16Among his professional employments at this period, I find the following modest allusion to a cause in which he gained great distinction:

During the session of the Legislature of 1816–17 I alone defended the Hon. Walter Franklin and his associates on articles of impeachment against them before the Senate; and during the session of 1817–18, I defended the same judges on other articles, and had for associates Mr. Condy and Mr. Hopkins. I never felt the responsibility of my position more sensibly than, when a young man between 25 and 26 years of age, I undertook alone to defend Judge Franklin; and although he was anxious I should, again the next year, undertake his cause without assistance, yet I insisted upon the employment of older and more experienced counsel.

As the impeachment case referred to in the close of this sketch was the occasion of Mr. Buchanan's early distinction at the bar, a brief account of it may be here given. It was a prosecution instituted from political motives, and was a lamentable exhibition of party asperity. Judge Franklin was the president judge of the court of common pleas for a judicial district composed of the counties of Lancaster, Lebanon, and York. His associates were not lawyers. At a period of great political excitement, which had continued since the close of the war with Great Britain, there arose a litigation in Judge Franklin's court which grew out of one of the occurrences of the war. In July, 1814, the President had made a requisition on the Governor of Pennsylvania for the services of certain regiments of militia. The troops were called and mustered into the Federal service. Houston, a citizen of Lancaster, refused to serve; he was tried by a court-martial, held under the authority of the State, convicted, and sentenced to pay a fine. For this he brought an action in the common pleas against the members of the court-martial and its officer who had collected the fine. On the trial, Judge Franklin ruled that when the militia had been mustered into the service of the United States, the control of the State and its power to punish were ended. The plaintiff, therefore, recovered a verdict. Judge Franklin was subjected to this impeachment for ruling a point of law on which the Judges of the Supreme Court of the United States afterwards differed.

17In a diary kept by a gentleman who watched this impeachment with the deepest interest, I find the following allusion to Mr. Buchanan's argument:

"This argument was conducted with great ingenuity, eloquence, and address. It made a deep impression. It will tend very much to raise and extend the reputation of Mr. Buchanan, and will have, I hope, a favorable effect upon his future prospects as a lawyer and a politician."

The impression produced by Mr. Buchanan's argument was so strong, that the managers of the impeachment asked for an adjournment before they replied to it. His defence was made upon the sound doctrine that "impeachment" of a judge for a legal opinion, when no crime or misdemeanor has been committed, is a constitutional solecism. The respondent was acquitted, and his advocate acquired a great amount of reputation for so young a man.

With an honorable and distinguished professional career thus opening before him, a favorite in society both from his talents and his character, young, high-spirited and full of energy, it seemed that happiness had been provided for him by his own merits and a kind Providence. But there now occurred an episode in his life which cast upon him a never-ending sorrow. He became engaged to be married to a young lady in Lancaster, who has been described to me, by persons who knew her, as a very beautiful girl, of singularly attractive and gentle disposition, but retiring and sensitive. Her father, Robert Coleman, Esq., a wealthy citizen of Lancaster, entirely approved of the engagement. After this connection had existed for some time, she suddenly wrote a note to her lover and asked him to release her from the engagement. There is no reason to believe that their mutual feelings had in any degree changed. He could only reply that if it was her wish to put an end to their engagement, he must submit. This occurred in the latter part of the summer of 1819. The young lady died very suddenly, while on a visit to Philadelphia, on the 9th of the December following, in the twenty-third year of her age. Her remains were brought to her father's house in Lancaster, on the next Saturday, just one week from the day on which she left home. "The funeral," says the diary already quoted from, "took place the next day, 18and was attended by a great number of the inhabitants, who appeared to feel a deep sympathy with the family on this distressing occasion."

From the same source, I transcribe a little obituary notice, which was published in a Lancaster paper on the 11th of December, and which the diary states was written by Mr. Buchanan:

"Departed this life, on Thursday morning last, in the twenty-third year of her age, while on a visit to her friends in the city of Philadelphia, Miss Anne C. Coleman, daughter of Robert Coleman, Esquire, of this city. It rarely falls to our lot to shed a tear over the mortal remains of one so much and so deservedly beloved as was the deceased. She was everything which the fondest parent or fondest friend could have wished her to be. Although she was young and beautiful, and accomplished, and the smiles of fortune shone upon her, yet her native modesty and worth made her unconscious of her own attractions. Her heart was the seat of all the softer virtues which ennoble and dignify the character of woman. She has now gone to a world where in the bosom of her God she will be happy with congenial spirits. May the memory of her virtues be ever green in the hearts of her surviving friends. May her mild spirit, which on earth still breathes peace and good-will, be their guardian angel to preserve them from the faults to which she was ever a stranger—

"'The spider's most attenuated thread

Is cord, is cable, to man's tender tie
On earthly bliss—it breaks at every breeze.'"
The following letter, written by Mr. Buchanan to the father of the young lady, is all that remains of written evidence, to attest the depth of his attachment to her:
[JAMES BUCHANAN TO ROBERT COLEMAN, ESQ.]
Lancaster, December 10, 1819.
My dear Sir:

You have lost a child, a dear, dear child. I have lost the only earthly object of my affections, without whom life now presents to me a dreary blank. My prospects are all cut off, and I feel that my happiness will be buried with her in the grave. It is now no time for explanation, but the time will come when you will discover that she, as well as I, have been much abused. God forgive the authors of it. My feelings of resentment against them, whoever they may be, are buried in the dust. I have now one request to make, and, for the love of God and of your dear, departed 19daughter whom I loved infinitely more than any other human being could love, deny me not. Afford me the melancholy pleasure of seeing her body before its interment. I would not for the world be denied this request. I might make another, but, from the misrepresentations which must have been made to you, I am almost afraid. I would like to follow her remains to the grave as a mourner. I would like to convince the world, and I hope yet to convince you, that she was infinitely dearer to me than life. I may sustain the shock of her death, but I feel that happiness has fled from me forever. The prayer which I make to God without ceasing is, that I yet may be able to show my veneration for the memory of my dear departed saint, by my respect and attachment for her surviving friends.
May Heaven bless you, and enable you to bear the shock with the fortitude of a Christian. I am, forever, your sincere and grateful friend,
James Buchanan.
There is among Mr. Buchanan's papers a letter written to him by one of his friends, shortly after the death of Miss Coleman, which shows how this affliction immediately affected him, and how it was regarded by persons of high social standing in Pennsylvania, who were not prejudiced by erroneous beliefs in regard to the circumstances which led to the breaking of the engagement.
[AMOS ELLMAKER TO MR. BUCHANAN.]
December 20, 1819.
Dear Sir:—

I hear you have left Lancaster, and have not heard where you have gone to; but I take it for granted the absence will be short. I am writing, I know not why, and perhaps had better not. I write only to speak of the awful visitation of Providence that has fallen upon you, and how deeply I feel it. The thought of your situation has scarcely been absent from my mind ten days. I trust your restoration to your philosophy and courage, and to the elasticity of spirits natural to most young men. Yet time, the sovereign cure of all these, must intervene before much good can be done. The sun will shine again—though a man enveloped in gloom always thinks the darkness is to be eternal. Do you remember the Spanish anecdote? A lady, who had lost a favorite child, remained for months sunk in sullen sorrow and despair. Her confessor, one morning, visited her, and found her, as usual, immersed in gloom and grief. "What!" says he; "have you not forgiven God Almighty?" She rose, exerted herself, joined the world again, and became useful to herself and friends.

20Might I venture to hint advice? It would be to give full scope (contrary to common advice on similar occasions), I say to give full vent and unrestrained license to the feelings and thoughts natural in the case for a time—which time may be a week, two weeks, three weeks, as nature dictates—without scarcely a small effort during that time to rise above the misfortune; then, when this time is past, to rouse, to banish depressing thoughts, as far as possible, and engage most industriously in business. My opinion is that too early an effort to shake off a very heavy affliction is often, if not always, dangerous. An early effort is futile, and worse—an unavailing struggle renders the mind cowardly, and sinks the spirits deeper in gloom. The true way to conquer is to run away at first. The storm which uproots the firmest oak passes harmlessly over the willow.

Forgive all this talk; it opens in my own bosom a wound which a dozen years have not cicatrized, and brings to my recollection a dark period of my own days, the remembrance of which yet chills me with horror.

Two of your cases here may be tried. If they are, I will endeavor to assist your colleague, Mr. Elder, for you, and for your benefit. This is our court week for the civil list......

Mrs. E—— talks much of you, and if she knew I was writing, would have me add her kindest message—indicative of the interest she feels. Farewell.

Amos Ellmaker.

In the course of Mr. Buchanan's long subsequent political career, this incident in his early life was often alluded to in partisan newspapers, and in that species of literature called "campaign documents," accompanied by many perversions and misrepresentations. These publications are each and all unworthy of notice. On one occasion, after he had retired to Wheatland, and when he had passed the age of seventy, he was shown by a friend a newspaper article, misrepresenting, as usual, the details of this affair. He then said, with deep emotion, that there were papers and relics which he had religiously preserved, then in a sealed package in a place of deposit in the city of New York, which would explain the trivial origin of this separation.[4] His executors found these papers inclosed and sealed separately from all others, and with a direction upon 21them in his handwriting, that they were to be destroyed without being read. They obeyed the injunction, and burnt the package without breaking the seal. It happened, however, that the original of the letter addressed by Mr. Buchanan to the young lady's father, before her funeral, was not contained in this package. It was found in his private depositaries at Wheatland; and it came there in consequence of the fact that it was returned by the father unread and unopened.

It is now known that the separation of the lovers originated in a misunderstanding, on the part of the lady, of a very small matter, exaggerated by giddy and indiscreet tongues, working on a peculiarly sensitive nature. Such a separation, the commonest of occurrences, would have ended, in the ordinary course, in reconciliation, when the parties met, if death had not suddenly snatched away one of the sufferers, and left the other to a life-long grief. But under the circumstances, I feel bound to be governed by the spirit of Mr. Buchanan's written instruction to his executors, and not to go into the details of a story which show that the whole occurrence was chargeable on the folly of others, and not on either of the two whose interests were involved.

Among the few survivors of the circle to which this young lady belonged, the remembrance of her sudden death is still fresh in aged hearts. The estrangement of the lovers was but one of those common occurrences that are perpetually verifying the saying, hackneyed by everlasting repetition, that "the course of true love never did run smooth." But it ran, in this case, pure and unbroken in the heart of the survivor, through a long and varied life. It became a grief that could not be spoken of; to which only the most distant allusion could be made; a sacred, unceasing sorrow, buried deep in the breast of a man who was formed for domestic joys; hidden beneath manners that were most engaging, beneath strong social tendencies, and a chivalrous old-fashioned deference to women of all ages and all claims. His peculiar and reverential demeanor towards the sex, never varied by rank, or station, or individual attractions, was doubtless in a large degree caused by the tender memory of what he had found, or fancied, in her whom he had lost in his early days by such a cruel fate. If her 22death had not prevented their marriage, it is probable that a purely professional and domestic life would have filled up the measure alike of his happiness and his ambition. It is certain that this occurrence prevented him from ever marrying, and impelled him again into public life, after he had once resolved to quit it. Soon after this catastrophe, he was offered a nomination to a seat in Congress. He did not suppose that he could be elected, and did not much desire to be. But he was strongly urged to accept the candidacy, and finally consented, chiefly because he needed an innocent excitement that would sometimes distract him from the grief that was destined never to leave him.[5] Great and uninterrupted, however, as was his political and social success, he lived and died a widowed and a childless man. Fortunately for him, a sister's child, left an orphan at an early age, whom he educated with the wisest care, filled to him the place of a daughter as nearly and tenderly as such a relative could supply that want, adorning with womanly accomplishments and virtues the high public stations to which he was eventually called.

23

CHAPTER II.

1820–1824.

MONROE'S ADMINISTRATION—EMINENT MEN IN CONGRESS—NOTICES OF WILLIAM LOWNDES AND JOHN RANDOLPH OF ROANOKE—JOHN SARGEANT—BUCHANAN BECOMES A LEADING DEBATER—BANKRUPT BILL—CUMBERLAND ROAD—THE TARIFF.

In the autumn of 1820, Mr. Buchanan was elected a Representative in Congress for a district composed of the counties of Lancaster, York, and Dauphin. He was nominated and elected as a Federalist. He took his seat on the 3d of December, 1821.

Of course a young man of nine-and-twenty, who had been for two terms a member of the Legislature of his native State, and had been somewhat active in that body, was already possessed of some powers as a debater. But his political principles, as a national statesman, were yet to be formed. The "Federalism" of the period in which Mr. Buchanan came into public life, and which was professed by those among whom he grew up, chiefly consisted in an opposition to the war of 1812 and to some of the measures of the Administration which conducted it. In the five years which followed the peace of 1815, the sharper lines which had separated the Federal and the Republican (or Democratic) parties, and their distinctive organizations, almost disappeared. Mr. Monroe, who succeeded Mr. Madison, was elected President, for the term commencing March 4, 1817, by a majority of 109 out of 217 electoral votes. At his second election, for the term commencing March 4, 1821, his majority was 118 out of 235. This near approach to unanimity evinces almost an obliteration of party distinctions. Mr. Monroe's personal popularity and the general confidence that was reposed in him had a considerable influence in producing what 24was called "the era of good feeling," which prevailed while he administered the government. The Federalists, who had been strongest in the North and the East, were conciliated by his first Inaugural, while his strength was not weakened among the Republicans (or Democrats) of the South. In truth, it was not until the war was over and some of the animosities which it caused had begun to fade, that the attention of men began to be directed to questions of internal administration, which would involve an exploration of the Federal powers and a discussion of policies applicable to a state of peace.

When Mr. Buchanan entered Congress there was no sectionalism to disturb the repose of the country. The Cabinet was a fair representation of the different sections, its members being from Massachusetts, New York, Georgia, South Carolina, Ohio, and Maryland. It remained the same, with one exception only, until Mr. Monroe went out of office in 1824.[6] It is not easy to trace among the public men of this period any fixed political doctrines such as afterwards came to distinguish the opposing parties. All that can be said is, that in the Middle States those who had been Republicans had a strong tendency to the Virginia principles of State Rights; but what these were, beyond a general tendency to watch and prevent undue expansion of the Federal powers, it would be difficult now to say. In Congress, most of the Eastern representatives were Free Traders, while those of the Middle States were in favor of moderate protection. Among the Southern members there was a disposition to follow a liberal policy in the administration of the government, which was aided by the ability and ambition of Mr. Calhoun, the Secretary of War. But among the members, chiefly confined to the Southwestern States, there was a compact knot of men who were called "Radicals," in the political nomenclature of that period. It is hard to define them, but their distinctive policy appears to have been a steady resistance to all expenditures of public money, and a persistently strict construction of the Constitution. Thus there cannot be said to have been any well-defined parties at this period, such as the country has since been 25accustomed to. But they began to be formed on the questions relating to finance and the development of the internal resources of the country, which arose during Mr. Monroe's Presidency, and continued to a later period. Men who had been Federalists and men who had been Republicans, during the previous administrations, passed into the one or the other of the subsequent parties, which assumed new designations, without much real historical connection with the old parties that had preceded them.

The personal composition of the two Houses of Congress at this time presents many interesting names. In the Senate, Rufus King, who had been a Senator during Washington's Administration, and Nathaniel Macon, who had been a Representative at the same time, gave a flavor of the formative period of the Republic. John Galliard and William Smith (of South Carolina) and James Brown (of Louisiana) were also among the older members. A somewhat younger class of men numbered among them Martin Van Buren, who succeeded General Jackson as President.

Mr. Buchanan always considered it one of the great advantages of his life that he had the benefit, at this early period, of the society of Mr. King and Mr. Macon, and he always spoke in the most grateful terms of their personal kindness to him. The members of the House of Representatives, with one exception, General Smith of Maryland, were younger men. They are spoken of in the following paper, which I find in Mr. Buchanan's handwriting, and in which he has recorded his impressions of that beau-ideal of a statesman, William Lowndes, of South Carolina, by whose early death, in 1822, the country lost one of the ablest, most accomplished and purest men it has ever produced:[7] "I entered the House of Representatives with George McDuffie and Joel R. Poinsett of South Carolina, Andrew Stevenson of Virginia, John Tod of Pennsylvania, John Nelson of Maryland, Reuben H. Walworth and Churchill C. Cambreleng of New York, and Benjamin Gorham of Massachusetts. They were all able and promising men, having already attained high distinction in their respective States.

26"Among those who had served in former Congresses, Mr. William Lowndes of South Carolina was the foremost in ability and influence. Next to him stood Mr. Sergeant of Pennsylvania, Mr. McLane of Delaware, Mr. Philip P. Barbour of Virginia, Mr. Baldwin of Pennsylvania, Mr. Tracy of New York, and John Randolph of Roanoke. Neither Mr. Clay nor Mr. Webster was a member of Congress at this period. Mr. Lowndes did not take his seat until December 21st, nearly three weeks after the beginning of the session. In the meantime, the new members of the House awaited his arrival in Washington with much interest. He, with Mr. Calhoun and Mr. Cheves, had constituted what was termed the 'Galaxy' of young men whom South Carolina sent to the House to sustain the war of 1812 with Great Britain, and he ranked the first among them.

"Mr. Lowndes had been unanimously nominated in December, 1821, by the Legislature of South Carolina, as a candidate for the Presidency to succeed Mr. Monroe. To this he made no direct response. In a letter to a friend in Charleston, after stating that he had not taken and never would take a step to draw the public eye upon him for this high place, he uttered the memorable sentiment: 'The Presidency of the United States is not, in my opinion, an office to be either solicited or declined.' And such was the general conviction of his candor and sincerity that no man doubted this to be the genuine sentiment of his heart. Fortunate would it have been for the country had all future aspirants for this exalted station acted in accordance with this noble sentiment. At the time, as Mr. Benton truly observes, 'he was strongly indicated for an early elevation to the Presidency— indicated by the public will and judgment, and not by any machinery of individual or party management, from the approach of which he shrank as from the touch of contamination.'[8]

"When Mr. Lowndes took his seat in the House, it was apparent to all that his frail and diseased frame betokened an early death, though he was then only in the forty-first year of his age. He was considerably above six feet in height, and was much stooped in person. There was nothing striking in his countenance to indicate great and varied intellectual powers. As a speaker he was persuasive and convincing. Though earnest and decided in the discussion of great questions, he never uttered a word which could give personal offence to his opponents or leave a sting behind. His eloquence partook of his own gentle and unpretending nature. His voice had become feeble and husky, and when he rose to speak, the members of the House, without distinction of party, clustered around him so that they might hear every word which fell from his lips. Towards his antagonists he was the fairest debater ever known in Congress. It was his custom to state their arguments so strongly and clearly that John Randolph, on one occasion, exclaimed: 'He will never be able to answer himself.' He possessed all the varied information necessary to the character of a great American statesman; 27and this, not merely in regard to general principles, but to minute practical details.

"On one occasion it became his duty, as Chairman of the Committee on Commerce, in the House, to present a history of the origin, progress and character of our trade with the East Indies. This he did with such fulness and precision that Mr. Silsbee, a well-informed and much-respected member of the House, and afterwards a Senator from Massachusetts, declared in his place, that although he had been engaged in that trade for many years, the gentleman from South Carolina had communicated to the House important information and shed new light on the subject which had never been known to him. On another occasion, two young members made a wager that Mr. Lowndes could not promptly state the process of manufacturing a common pin. On propounding the question to him, he at once stated the whole process in minute detail.

"Mr. Lowndes' great influence,—for he was the undisputed leader in the House—arose in no small degree from the conviction of its members that he never had a sinister or selfish purpose in view, but always uttered the genuine sentiments of his heart. Mr. Lowndes had not the least jealousy in his nature. In his social intercourse with his fellow-members he was ever ready and willing to impart his stores of information on any subject, without feeling the least apprehension that these might be used to anticipate what he himself intended to say, or in debate against himself. His health continuing to decline, he resigned his seat in the House, and by the advice of his physicians, embarked in October, 1822, from Philadelphia in the ship Moss, with his wife and daughter, for London. He died on the passage, on the 27th of that month, and was buried at sea.

"His death was announced in the House of Representatives on the 21st of January, 1823, by Mr. James Hamilton, his successor. This was the first occasion on which such honors had been paid to the memory of any one not a member of the House at the time of his decease. Among the eulogies pronounced was one by John W. Taylor, of New York, who had been the Speaker of the House during the session immediately preceding. He had been an active and able opponent of Mr. Lowndes throughout the debates and proceedings on the Missouri question, which had for two years convulsed the House and the country, until its settlement at the close of the last session. Coming from a political antagonist, it so graphically presents the true character of Mr. Lowndes, that I am tempted to copy a portion of it. After referring to his death, as 'the greatest misfortune which had befallen the Union' since he had held a seat in its councils, he proceeds: 'The highest and best hopes of this country looked to William Lowndes for their fulfillment. The most honorable office in the civilized world—the Chief Magistracy of this free people—would have been illustrated by his virtues and talents. During nine years' service in this House, it was my happiness to be associated with him on many of its most important committees. He never failed to shed new light on all subjects to which he applied his vigorous and discriminating mind. 28His industry in discharging the arduous and responsible duties constantly assigned him, was persevering and efficient. To manners the most unassuming, to patriotism the most disinterested, to morals the most pure, to attainments of the first rank in literature and science, he added the virtues of decision and prudence, so happily combined, so harmoniously united, that we knew not which most to admire, the firmness with which he pursued his purpose or the gentleness with which he disarmed opposition. His arguments were made not to enjoy the triumph of victory, but to convince the judgment of his hearers; and when the success of his efforts was most signal, his humility was most conspicuous. You, Mr. Speaker, will remember his zeal in sustaining the cause of our country in the darkest days of the late war.'

"The whole House, with one accord, responded to the truthfulness of these sentiments so happily expressed by Mr. Taylor. And yet, strange to say, the published debates of Congress contain but a meagre and imperfect sketch, and offer no report at all of the speeches of this great and good man. His fame as a parliamentary speaker, like that of the great commoner, Charles James Fox, must mainly rest upon tradition now fast fading away. The editors of the National Intelligencer truly remark that, 'of all the distinguished men who have passed periods of their lives in either House of Congress, there is certainly no one of anything like equal ability who has left fewer traces on the page of history or on the records of Congress than William Lowndes, the eminent Representative in Congress for several years of the State of South Carolina.' The reason which they assign why so few of his eloquent speeches are to be found on record is attributable, in part, to his unfeigned diffidence, which placed less than their true value upon his own exertions, and in part to an objection which he had, on principle, to the practice of writing out speeches for publication, either before or after the delivery. Little or no reliance could be placed on the reporters of that day. The art even of shorthand writing was almost unknown in this country, and the published sketches prepared by the so-called reporters, were calculated to injure rather than to elevate the character of the speaker.

"How much has been lost to the country by the scruples of Mr. Lowndes may be imagined from the 'little gem' of a speech written out by him at the personal request of Mr. Silsbee, then a member of the House, on the bill for the relief of the family of Commodore Perry, but never published until more than twenty years after his death. It does not appear in the annals of 1821 that he made any speech on this occasion. It may be added, to show the incapacity of the reporters of that day, that there is no other mention of his speech against the bankrupt bill, commenced on February 21st, and concluded on March 5th, 1822, though listened to with rapt attention by the House, except that he did speak on these two days. From physical exhaustion he was unable to say all he had intended on this important subject. His name does not even appear in the index as a speaker on this bill.

"I have written much more than I should otherwise have done, to repair 29injustice done to the character of the ablest, purest, and most unselfish statesman of his day."[9]

Of John Randolph and John Sergeant, Mr. Buchanan thus records his recollections:

John Randolph of Roanoke was the most conspicuous, though far from the most influential member of the House, when I first took my seat. He entered the House in 1799, and had continued there, with the exception of two terms, from that early period. His style of debate was in perfect contrast to that of Mr. Lowndes. He was severe and sarcastic, sparing neither friend nor foe, when the one or the other laid himself open to the shafts of his ridicule. He was a fine belles-lettres scholar, and his classical allusions were abundant and happy. He had a shrill and penetrating voice, and could be heard distinctly in every portion of the House. He spoke with great deliberation, and often paused for an instant as if to select the most appropriate word. His manner was confident, proud, and imposing, and pointing, as he always did, his long forefinger at the object of attack, he gave peculiar emphasis to the severity of his language. He attracted a crowded gallery when it was known he would address the House, and always commanded the undivided attention of his whole audience, whether he spoke the words of wisdom, or, as he often did, of folly. For these reasons he was more feared than beloved, and his influence in the House bore no proportion to the brilliancy of his talents. He was powerful in pulling down an administration, but had no skill in building anything up. Hence he was almost always in the opposition, but was never what is called a business member. To me he was uniformly respectful, and sometimes complimentary in debate. I well remember Mr. Sergeant putting me on my guard against Mr. Randolph's friendship."

"Mr. Sergeant entered the House in December, 1815, and had continued to be a member since that day. As a lawyer, he stood in the front rank among the eminent members of the bar of Philadelphia, at a period when its members were greatly distinguished throughout the country for ability and learning. His personal character was above reproach. From his first appearance he maintained a high rank in the estimation of the House. As a debater, he was clear and logical, and never failed to impart information. His fault was that of almost every member of Congress who had become a 30member after a long and successful training at the bar. He was too exhaustive in his arguments, touching every point in the question before the House without discriminating between those which were vital and those which were subordinate. His manner was cold and didactic, and his prolixity sometimes fatigued the House. In his social intercourse with the members, he was cold but not repulsive. The high estimation in which he was held, arose from the just appreciation of his great abilities, and of his pure and spotless private character. There was nothing ad captandum about him. He was regarded by his constituents in Philadelphia with pride and affection, who generally spoke of him as 'our John Sergeant.'" The first debate in which Mr. Buchanan took part related to a bill, introduced by General Smith of Maryland, making appropriations for the Military Establishment. This discussion, which took place on the 9th and 11th of January, 1822, was an excited one, from the inner motive of the opposition to the bill, which was aimed at the supposed aspirations of Mr. Calhoun, the Secretary of War. In reference to the Secretary Mr. Buchanan said: "I have no feeling of partiality for the Secretary of War, nor of prejudice against him. I view him merely as a public character, and, in that capacity, I conscientiously believe that he has done his duty." After a sharp reply from Mr. Randolph, the bill was passed by a very large majority, the members of the so-called "Radical" party alone voting against it. There very soon occurred another debate which is of greater importance, since it marks the direction which Mr. Buchanan's mind was beginning to take on the subject of Federal powers and State Rights. This was the occasion of the introduction of a Bankrupt bill.

Prior to this time, Congress had but once exercised the constitutional power "to establish uniform laws on the subject of bankruptcies throughout the United States." This was in the Bankrupt law of 1800, which was repealed in 1804. Of the power of Congress to legislate on the subject of "bankruptcy" there can of course be no doubt, since it is expressly conferred. But there has always been a doubt respecting the true construction of the terms "bankruptcy" and "bankrupt." Following the English system, the Act of 1800 rejected the idea that these terms include all "insolvents," of all occupations, and confined the meaning to "traders," or mercantile insolvents. Here, 31therefore, was one very serious question in interpretation to be encountered; for although the measure, of which some account is now to be given, contemplated, as it was first introduced, none but commercial insolvents, it finally turned upon an amendment which would have made it applicable to all classes of insolvent debtors. In either aspect, too, it brought into view the contrasted functions of the Federal and the State courts, in the enforcement and collection of private debts.

The close of the war, in 1815, was followed by extensive financial embarrassment among the commercial classes. The merchants of Philadelphia suffered severely during the five years which succeeded the peace, and it was by one of their Representatives, Mr. John Sergeant, that a bankrupt bill, retrospective as well as prospective in its operation, was introduced in the House, on the 11th of December, 1821. On the 22d of January, 1822, the debate was opened by Mr. Sergeant, as Chairman of the Judiciary Committee. His speech was exceedingly able, and even pathetic, for he spoke for a large class of ruined men. The discussion continued until the 12th of March, Mr. Sergeant standing almost alone in advocacy of the bill, in opposition to George Tucker and Philip P. Barbour of Virginia, and to Mr. Lowndes of South Carolina. The latter, although opposed to the bill, did not accord with the strict constructionists of Virginia. Thus far, the proposed measure included only commercial insolvents. But on the 12th of March, a member from Kentucky offered an amendment that included all insolvent debtors, which was adopted. This, of course, changed the aspect of the whole subject, and whether so intended or not, finally defeated the bill. Mr. Buchanan spoke in opposition to the bill on the day the amendment was adopted. He did not question the power of Congress to pass a bankrupt law. Nor did he contend that the "bankruptcy" referred to in the Constitution, necessarily included only commercial insolvents. But there is very perceptible in his speech on this occasion a tendency to that line of politics which he afterwards adopted and always adhered to, and which may be described as a forbearance from exercising Federal powers of acknowledged constitutional validity, in modes and upon occasions which may lead to an absorption of State jurisdictions. 32Thus he said: "The bill, as it stood before the amendment, went far enough. It would, even then, have brought the operation of the law and the jurisdiction of the Federal Courts into the bosom of every community. The bill as it now stands will entirely destroy the symmetry of our system, and make those courts the arbiters, in almost every case, of contracts to which any member of society who thinks proper to become a bankrupt may be a party. It will at once be, in a great degree, a judicial consolidation of the Union. This was never intended by the friends of the Constitution...... The jurisdiction of Federal Courts is now chiefly confined to controversies existing between the citizens of different States. This bill, if it should become a law, will amount to a judicial consolidation of the Union."

Of the general tenor of this sweeping measure, Mr. Buchanan said:

"Let a bankrupt be presented to the view of society, who has become wealthy since his discharge, and who, after having ruined a number of his creditors, shields himself from the payment of his honest debts by his certificate, and what effects would such a spectacle be calculated to produce? Examples of this nature must at length demoralize any people. The contagion introduced by the laws of the country would, for that very reason, spread like a pestilence, until honesty, honor, and faith will at length be swept from the intercourse of society. Leave the agricultural interest pure and uncorrupted, and they will forever form the basis on which the Constitution and liberties of your country may safely repose. Do not, I beseech you, teach them to think lightly of the solemn obligation of contracts. No government on earth, however corrupt, has ever enacted a bankrupt law for farmers; it would be a perfect monster in this country, where our institutions depend altogether upon the virtue of the people. We have no constitutional power to pass the amendment proposed by the gentleman from Kentucky; and if we had, we never should do so, because such a provision would spread a moral taint through society which would corrupt it to its very core."

The next important discussion in which Mr. Buchanan took part was on a bill relating to the Cumberland Road. Before he entered Congress, a national turnpike had been built by the Federal Government, extending from Cumberland in the State of Maryland to Wheeling in the State of Virginia. It crossed a narrow part of Maryland, passed through a corner of Pennsylvania, and touched but a small part of Virginia. The principal 33interest felt in this work was in the Western States. It encountered much opposition in Pennsylvania, where a turnpike road had been built, under State authority, from Philadelphia to Pittsburgh, which was kept in repair by tolls, and which paid a small dividend to its stockholders. A national road, supported by the Federal Government, and taking the travel from the Pennsylvania road was considered in that State as a grievance. Moreover, whenever the question of appropriating money for the continued support of this national road, or the alternative of imposing tolls, arose in Congress, the question of constitutional power to establish such means of communication necessarily arose at every stage of the legislation. That legislation is of interest now, inasmuch as the course taken by Mr. Buchanan illustrates the development of his opinions upon the constitutional question.

Of the last appropriation for continuing the Cumberland Road, there remained a balance in the Treasury of less than $10,000. In the General Appropriation Bill of this session (1822), provision was made for the repair of the road. A member from New Jersey moved to increase the amount. On this amendment there was an animated discussion, in which Mr. Buchanan appears to have considered that this public work was so beneficial to the general prosperity of the Union, that Congress might well appropriate the money needed for its support. "The truth is," he said, "we are all so connected together by our interests, as to place us in a state of mutual dependence upon each other, and to make that which is for the interest of any one member of the Federal family beneficial, in most instances, to all the rest. We never can be divided without first being guilty of political suicide. The prosperity of all the States depends as much upon their Union, as human life depends upon that of the soul and body." It is quite obvious that this kind of reasoning was, however true in the general, too broad and sweeping to justify the appropriation of money from the Federal Treasury for a public work which could claim no other than an incidental and remote relation to the prosperity of all the States. Every appropriation of money by Congress must rest upon some specific power of the Federal Constitution; and although Congress has a specific power "to regulate commerce among the several States," and while it may be admitted that commerce includes intercourse, it has been from the first, and still is, a serious question whether this grant of the power of commercial regulation includes a power to establish and maintain the means by which commerce is carried on, and by which intercourse may be facilitated, unless such means fall within the designation of "post-roads," and are established, primarily at least, for the transmission of mails. The appropriation proposed for the continued support of the Cumberland Road failed, and then came the question, in a separate bill, of imposing tolls for the support of the road. Mr. Buchanan voted for this bill, as did most of his colleagues from Pennsylvania, and it passed both Houses. But on the 4th of May (1822), the President, Mr. Monroe, returned the bill with a very long message, stating his objections to it. From this voluminous message, we may extract, although with some difficulty, two positions; first, that in Mr. Monroe's opinion, Congress had no power to raise money by erecting toll-gates and collecting tolls, and that the States cannot individually grant such a power to Congress by their votes in Congress, or by any special compact with the United States; secondly, that Congress having an unlimited power to raise money by taxation general and uniform throughout the United States, its absolute discretion in the appropriation of the money so raised is restricted only by the duty of appropriating to the purposes of the common defence, and of general, not local, benefit. The first of these positions will be conceded by every one. The second admits of some doubt. Its soundness depends upon the true interpretation of the first of the enumerated powers of the Federal Constitution, that which contains the grant of the taxing power.[10] This is not the place to enter upon the discussion of controverted questions of constitutional interpretation. But all students of the Federal Constitution are aware that the grammatical construction of the clause to which Mr. Monroe referred, admits of, and has been claimed to admit of, two interpretations. Read by itself, and without reference to the other enumerated powers, this clause has been supposed by some persons to grant an unlimited power to tax for any purpose that in the judgment of Congress will promote the general welfare of the United States, provided only that the taxation is uniform. On the other hand, it has been contended that the clause is not a broad, independent, and specific power to tax for any object that will promote the general welfare of the United States, but that it is limited to the promotion of the general welfare through the exercise of some one or more of the other enumerated powers of the Constitution, each of which must receive its own scope from a just interpretation before the people of the United States can be taxed for the means of exercising that power. Viewed in the latter sense, the clause contains a grant of the power of taxation, general and universal in its nature, but limited as to its objects by the objects of each of the other enumerated powers. Viewed in the former sense, it becomes a separate and independent power to tax for any object that will promote the general welfare, without reference to the exercise of any of the specific powers of the Constitution which form the objects for which the Federal Government was created. Mr. Monroe's veto message on this occasion was sustained in the House by a vote of 68 to 72, and the bill consequently failed. The vote of the House, however, is to be considered as a concurrence in Mr. Monroe's objection that Congress cannot establish toll-gates and collect tolls, and not as an affirmance of the general views which he expressed on the taxing power. But upon Mr. Buchanan this message produced a strong effect. It was the first time that his mind had been brought sharply to the consideration of the questions in what mode "Internal Improvements," as they were called, can be effected by the General Government, and consequently he began to perceive the dividing line between the Federal and the State powers. Although he had voted for the bill imposing tolls upon the Cumberland Road, influenced probably by the desire to diminish its injurious competition with the Pennsylvania road, he took occasion at the next session to retract the error of which he had been convinced by Mr. Monroe's message. When a bill was introduced at the next session, making an appropriation for the preservation and repair of the Cumberland Road, he moved 36as an amendment that the United States retrocede the road to the three States through which it passed, on condition that they would keep it in repair and collect no more tolls than such as would be necessary for that purpose. Being now convinced that Congress could not impose the tolls, he thought the only alternative was to cede the road to the States, since it could not be supported from the Federal Treasury without producing inequality and injustice. His amendment was rejected and the bill was passed.[11] A precedent was thus established for the support of the road by Congress. The subject will again recur in 1829 and 1836. In Mr. Buchanan's speech in 1829 will be found the expression of his more matured constitutional views on the whole subject of Internal Improvements.[12]

The 17th Congress, which commenced its session in December, 1822, and terminated in March, 1823, witnessed a protracted discussion on the doctrine of "protection," which extended into the 18th Congress. The tariff of 1823–4 was the second measure of that kind after the war. At that period the prevalent doctrine in the New England States was Anti-protectionist. The city of Boston was represented by Mr. Benjamin Gorham, a lawyer of remarkable ability, the immediate predecessor of Mr. Webster. His speech against the new tariff was replied to by Mr. Buchanan; and if the reply is a fair indication of the speech against which it was directed, Mr. Gorham's language must have been vehement.[13] Mr. Buchanan said:

"The gentleman from Massachusetts has declared this bill to be an attempt, by one portion of the Union for its own peculiar advantage, to impose ruinous taxes on another. He has represented it as an effort to compel the agriculturists of the South to pay tribute to the manufacturers of the North; he has proclaimed it to be a tyrannical measure. He has gone further, and boldly declared that the people of the South should resist such a law, and that they ought to resist it. The gentlemen from Massachusetts and Georgia (Mr. Tattnall) have proclaimed it tyranny, and tyranny which ought to be resisted. I confess I never expected to hear inflammatory speeches of this kind within these walls which ought to be sacred to union; I never expected to hear the East counselling the South to resistance, that we might thus be deterred from prosecuting a measure of policy, urged upon us by the necessities of the country. It was by a combination between the cotton-growers of the 37South and the manufacturers of the North, that the introduction of coarse cottons from abroad has been in effect prohibited by the high rates of duties. It is ungenerous, then, for the South and the East to sound the tocsin of alarm and resistance when we wish indirectly to benefit the agriculturists and manufacturers of the Middle and

Western States by the imposition of necessary duties. If I know myself, I am a politician neither of the East nor of the West, of the North nor of the South; I, therefore, shall forever avoid any expressions, the direct tendency of which must be to create sectional jealousies, sectional divisions, and, at length, disunion—that worst and last of all political calamities. I will never consent to adopt a general restrictive system, because the agricultural class of the community would then be left at the mercy of the manufacturers. The interest of the many would thus be sacrificed to promote the wealth of the few. The farmer, in addition to the premium which he would be compelled to pay the manufacturer, would have also to sustain the expenses of the Government. If this bill proposed a system which leads to such abuses, it should not receive my support. If I could, for a single moment, believe in the language of the gentleman from Georgia—that this bill would compel the agricultural to bow down before the manufacturing interest—I should consider myself a traitor to my country in giving it any support."

In the subsequent Congress, Mr. Buchanan spoke twice on the subject of the tariff, namely, March 23d and April 9th, 1824. But the foregoing extract from his speech in February, 1823, is sufficient to show how moderate and just his views were on the subject of protection.

When Mr. Buchanan entered Congress in December, 1821, his professional income was the largest that he ever received. He had then been eight years at the bar, and his emoluments from his profession, which were less than $1,000 for the first year, had become more than $11,000 for the year 1821–2. They then fell off somewhat rapidly, and in the year 1828 they amounted to only a little more than $2,000.

38

CHAPTER III.

1824–1825.

ELECTION OF JOHN QUINCY ADAMS—THE "BARGAIN AND CORRUPTION"—UNFOUNDED CHARGE—GENERAL JACKSON'S ERRONEOUS IMPRESSION—HIS CORRESPONDENCE WITH MR. BUCHANAN.

I now approach one of those periods of intense political excitement which it becomes every one who has to write of them to treat in an entirely impartial and judicial spirit. The subject of this chapter is the Presidential election of 1824,[14] and Mr. Buchanan's connection with it. The famous "coalition" between Mr. John Quincy Adams and Mr. Clay, is a topic that involves so much that is personal, that one must needs divest one's self of all preconceived opinions, and must regard the whole matter with that indifference which the present age already feels, and which is solicitous only to do no injustice to individual reputations. At the same time, the whole case should be plainly stated; for it touches a provision of the Constitution, by which its framers supplied a means for filling the office of President, in the event of there being no choice through the electoral colleges.

In the year 1824, there were 261 electoral votes in the Union, a majority being 131. The candidates at the popular election were General Jackson, Mr. John Quincy Adams, Mr. Crawford, and Mr. Clay. Neither of them was the candidate of a distinctively organized political party. General Jackson was a member of the Senate, from the State of Tennessee. Mr. Adams was Secretary of State, under President Monroe. Mr. Crawford, who had formerly been a Senator from Georgia, was not in any public position. Mr. Clay was a Representative 39from Kentucky, and was chosen Speaker of the House at the beginning of the session. Neither of these candidates having received a majority of the electoral

28

votes, the election of a President devolved on the House of Representatives, in which body each State would have one vote. But as the Constitution required that the choice of the House be confined to the three highest candidates on the list of those voted for by the electors, and as Mr. Clay was not one of the three, he was excluded. He and his friends, however, had it in their power to make either General Jackson or Mr. Adams President; and Mr. Clay at all times had great control over his friends. How he would cast his vote, and how he would lead his followers who were members of the House to cast theirs, became therefore an intensely exciting subject of speculation both in Washington and throughout the country. For a short time it was supposed that Mr. Clay and the other members from Kentucky would be governed by a resolution adopted by both branches of the Legislature of that State, requesting their members of Congress to vote for General Jackson. This resolution had been adopted in the Kentucky House of Representatives on the 31st of December (1824), by a majority of 73 to 11; and in the Senate of the State it was adopted by a vote of 18 to 12. It spoke what was the undoubted wish of the people of Kentucky, whose first choice for the office of President was Mr. Clay himself, but whose preference for General Jackson to Mr. Adams was explicitly declared by their Legislature.[15] General Jackson had received the unanimous electoral votes of eight States: New Jersey, Pennsylvania, North Carolina, South Carolina, Tennessee, Mississippi, Indiana, and Alabama. Mr. Adams had received the unanimous electoral votes of the six New England States. If the Representatives of these various States in Congress should vote as their States had voted, it would require but five additional States to elect General Jackson, while seven would be needed to elect Mr. Adams. Of the remaining States which had not unanimously given their electoral votes to General Jackson or to Mr. Adams, it appears that General Jackson 40received one of the electoral votes of New York, Mr. Adams received twenty-six, and Mr. Crawford five. Delaware had given one of its electoral votes to Mr. Adams and two to Mr. Crawford. General Jackson had seven of the electoral votes of Maryland, Mr. Adams three, and Mr. Crawford one. Virginia had given all of her electoral votes, twenty-four, to Mr. Crawford. Louisiana had given three of her electoral votes to General Jackson, and two to Mr. Adams. The electoral votes of Illinois had gone two for General Jackson, and one for Mr. Adams. Which of these doubtful States would be won in the great contest for General Jackson, and which for Mr. Adams, was now the all-absorbing topic, and the result depended very much upon the course of Mr. Clay.

Among the scandals which hung around this election, it was afterward said that Mr. Buchanan, while the matter was pending before the House of Representatives in the winter of 1824–5, had, as an agent or friend of Mr. Clay, approached General Jackson and sought to secure his promise to make Mr. Clay Secretary of State, in consideration of his receiving Mr. Clay's vote and influence in the House. There was not much intrinsic probability in this imputation, for the relations between Mr. Clay and Mr. Buchanan were not such as would naturally have led to the selection of the latter as Mr. Clay's agent in such a negotiation, even if Mr. Clay had been capable of making such an attempt to obtain from General Jackson a promise to make him Secretary of State, while the election of a President was pending in the House. But inasmuch as General Jackson, nearly twenty years afterward, was quoted in support of this statement, it is proper that I should lay before the reader Mr. Buchanan's own explicit account of what actually took place. It will be seen hereafter that General Jackson, who always believed that there had been a corrupt political bargain between Mr. Clay and Mr. Adams, was led afterwards to think that Mr. Buchanan had at the time of the election entertained the same belief, and yet that Mr. Buchanan had refrained from denouncing the bargain as he should have done, because he had himself made the same kind of attempt for Mr. Clay, in the conversation which he had with General Jackson before the election took place. Mr. Buchanan's own account of his interview 41with General Jackson shows very clearly that, instead of seeking an interview with General Jackson for the purpose of proposing to him to make a bargain with Mr. Clay about the office of Secretary of State, his sole object was to obtain from General Jackson a denial of a prevailing rumor that he had said he would continue Mr. Adams in that office, if elected President.

At the time of this occurrence, Mr. Buchanan was a comparatively young member of Congress, in the beginning of his fourth session. Speaking of himself in the third person, he says in a memorandum now before me, "He [Buchanan] had never personally known either General Jackson or Mr. Clay until about the opening of this Congress, when the one took his seat as a Senator from Tennessee, and the other was elected Speaker of the House. Having great confidence in the sound political principles and exalted character of General Jackson, and greatly preferring him to any of the other candidates, he [Buchanan] had taken a very active part before the people of Pennsylvania in securing for him their electoral vote. Still, he was at the same time a warm admirer of Mr. Clay."

The prevalent rumor that General Jackson had said he would continue Mr. Adams in the office of Secretary of State, in case of his election to the Presidency, was supposed to derive some color of probability from their known friendly relations, and from the defence which Mr. Adams had made of the General's conduct in the Seminole war. It was a rumor that greatly disturbed General Jackson's friends and supporters in Pennsylvania. They regarded Mr. Adams' constitutional views as much too latitudinarian for the leading position in General Jackson's cabinet; and they feared that the General's announcement of such a purpose would stand in the way of his election by the House of Representatives. Mr. Buchanan fully shared this anxiety of his Pennsylvania constituents and political friends; and with the approbation and advice of a leading gentleman among this class of General Jackson's supporters, Mr. Buchanan determined to ascertain from the General himself whether there was any foundation for the rumor.[16] He first 42endeavored to obtain the information from Major Eaton, the colleague of General Jackson in the Senate, and his most intimate friend. Major Eaton declined to make the inquiry. Mr. Buchanan then determined to make it himself. What follows is from Mr. Buchanan's own account of the interview, which lies before me in his handwriting:

Calling at the General's lodgings in "the Seven Buildings," Mr. Buchanan accompanied him, on his own invitation, in a walk as far as the War Department, where the General had to call on public business. After a suitable introduction and reference to the rumor afloat, Mr. Buchanan requested him to state whether he had ever declared that in case he should be elected President he would appoint Mr. Adams Secretary of State. To this he replied by saying that whilst he thought well of Mr. Adams, he had never said or intimated that he would or would not make this appointment. With this answer, Mr. Buchanan was entirely satisfied, and so expressed himself. The object of his mission was thus accomplished. The General's answer was positive and emphatic. It made a deep and lasting impression on his only auditor, who requested permission to repeat it, and he gave it without reserve.

This, however, was not the whole of the conversation; and in order to explain how this conversation became afterwards distorted into the appearance of an application by Mr. Buchanan to General Jackson on behalf of Mr. Clay, it is necessary to advert to something which took place between Mr. Buchanan and Mr. Philip S. Markley, another Representative from the State of Pennsylvania, before Mr. Buchanan spoke to General Jackson. Mr. Markley had been a devoted advocate of Mr. Clay for the Presidency. He urged Mr. Buchanan to see General Jackson, and to persuade him either to say that Mr. Clay should be Secretary of State, or to remain absolutely silent as between Mr. Clay and Mr. Adams; "for then," as he remarked, "the friends of Mr. Clay would be placed upon the same footing with the friends of Mr. Adams, and fight them with their own weapons." If Mr. Buchanan had made any proposition to General Jackson respecting Mr. Clay, there might have been some foundation for the subsequent charge that Mr. Buchanan approached the General as an emissary of Mr. Clay. But, in point of fact, Mr. Buchanan did nothing of the kind. After the General had given him the assurance that he had 43never said he would or would not appoint Mr. Adams Secretary of State, and before they parted, Mr. Buchanan mentioned, as an item of current news, what he had heard Mr. Markley say. It does not appear to have produced upon General Jackson, at the time, any impression that Mr. Buchanan wished him to hold out any encouragement to the friends of Mr. Clay that in the event of his election he would make Mr. Clay Secretary of State. On the contrary, from what General Jackson said in answer to Mr. Buchanan's sole inquiry, it is apparent that Mr. Buchanan obtained the only answer that he sought to obtain, namely, that the General had not said that he would or would not appoint Mr. Adams as his Secretary of State. Mr. Buchanan continues his account of the interview as follows:

"When I parted from the General, I felt conscious that I had done my duty, and no more than my duty, towards him and my party, as one of his most ardent and consistent political friends. Indeed the idea did not enter my imagination at the time that the General could have afterwards inferred from any thing I said, that I had approached him as the emissary of Mr. Clay, to propose to elect him President, provided that he (the General) would agree to appoint him Secretary of State. It is but justice to observe that the General stated, in his subsequent publication, that I did not represent myself to be the friend and agent of Mr. Clay. Surely, if Mr. Clay had desired or intended to have made such a bargain, he would have selected as his agent an old political and personal friend. Events passed on," Mr. Buchanan continues; "then came the letter of Mr. George Kremer to the Columbian Observer, of the 25th of January, 1825, charging the existence of a corrupt bargain between Messrs. Adams and Clay; his avowal of its authorship, the appeal of Mr. Clay to the House of Representatives against the charges it contained, the report of the Committee on the subject, and, on the same day, the election of Mr. Adams as President of the United States by the House of Representatives; Mr. Adams receiving the vote of thirteen States, including that of Kentucky, General Jackson of seven States, and Mr. Crawford of four States. During all the debates and proceedings of the House, on Mr. Clay's appeal against the charges of Mr. Kremer, it was never intimated to me, in the most distant manner, by any human being, that I was expected to be a witness to sustain this charge, or had any connection with the subject more than any other member of the House.

"The conduct of General Jackson, after his defeat, was admirable. He bore it with so much dignity and magnanimity, and perfect self-control, as to elicit strong commendations, even from his political opponents. At President Monroe's levee, on the evening of the election, where he and Mr. Adams were both present, it was repeatedly remarked, from the courtesy and kindness 44of his manner and conversation, contrasted with the coldness and reserve of Mr. Adams, that a stranger might have inferred he had been the successful and Mr. Adams the defeated candidate."

The election of Mr. Adams by the House of Representatives was followed after the adjournment of Congress by a correspondence between Mr. Buchanan and General Jackson, commencing in the spring of 1825 and extending to August, 1827. This correspondence shows, first, the terms on which General Jackson and Mr. Buchanan parted in Washington in the spring of 1825; and in the next place it fixes the time and mode in which the idea was first presented to the mind of General Jackson that Mr. Buchanan came to him in December, 1824, as a friend of Mr. Clay. The reader will observe that, while the election of Mr. Adams was a recent event, while the country was ringing with the charge of a "corrupt coalition" between Mr. Adams and Mr. Clay, and down to the 29th of January, 1827, during the whole of which period General Jackson's mind was peculiarly excited by what he may have believed concerning the means by which his rival had become President, there is no trace in this correspondence of any feeling on his part that Mr. Buchanan had ever been in any way connected with the supposed bargain, or with any effort to make a similar bargain between General Jackson and Mr. Clay, or that Mr. Buchanan knew of any important fact that would tend to support the charge of a bargain between Mr. Adams and Mr. Clay. It was not until the summer of 1827, nearly three years after the conversation between General Jackson and Mr. Buchanan, that the General appears to have had an erroneous impression of Mr. Buchanan's purpose in seeking that interview.

[MR. BUCHANAN TO GENERAL JACKSON.]
May 29, 1825.
My Dear General:—

I write this letter from Mercersburg, being now on a visit to my mother and the family. I have no news of any importance to communicate, but both inclination and duty conspire to induce me to trouble you occasionally with a few lines, whilst you must be gratefully remembered by every American citizen who feels an interest in the character of his country's glory.

45You have imposed additional obligations upon me by the uniform kindness and courtesy with which you have honored me.

In Pennsylvania, amongst a vast majority of the people, there is but one sentiment concerning the late Presidential election. Although they submit patiently, as is their duty, to the legally constituted powers, yet there is a fixed and determined resolution to change them as soon as they have the constitutional power to do so. In my opinion, your popularity in Pennsylvania is now more firmly established than ever. Many persons who heretofore supported you did it cheerfully from a sense of gratitude, and because they thought it would be disgraceful to the people not to elevate that candidate to the Presidential Chair, who had been so great a benefactor of the country. The slanders which had been so industriously circulated against your character had, nevertheless, in some degree affected their minds, although they never doubted either your ability or patriotism, yet they expressed fears concerning your temper. These have been all dissipated by the mild prudence and dignity of your conduct last winter, before and after the Presidential election. The majority is so immense in your favor that there is little or no newspaper discussion on the subject. I most sincerely and fervently trust and hope that the Almighty will preserve your health until the period shall again arrive when the sovereign people shall have the power of electing a President.

There never was a weaker attempt made than that to conciliate the good opinion of Pennsylvania in favor of the administration by the appointment of Mr. Rush, although no appointment could have produced the effect desired; yet, if the President had selected Mr. Sergeant, he would have chosen a man who had been his early and consistent friend, and one whose character for talents and integrity stands high with all parties in this State. Mr. Rush was a candidate for the office of elector on the Crawford ticket. I verily believe his appointment will not procure for the administration, out of the city of Philadelphia, twenty new friends throughout the State. In that city their additional strength is limited to John Binns and a few of his devoted followers.

I hope Mrs. Jackson, ere this, has been restored to her accustomed health. When I left her, I felt some apprehensions in relation to the issue of her disease. Please to present to her my kindest and best respects, and believe me to be ever your sincere friend,
James Buchanan.

[GENERAL JACKSON TO MR. BUCHANAN.]
Hermitage, June 25, 1825.
Dear Sir:—

I have the pleasure to acknowledge the receipt of your kind letter of the 29th ult., which has just reached me.

That respect which I formed for your character on our first acquaintance increased with our friendly intercourse, and to you was only extended what I viewed a debt due to your merit as a gentleman of intelligence and urbanity. 46It is, therefore, a source of much gratification to me to receive a letter from you, detailing the friendly feelings of the citizens of Pennsylvania toward me.

It is gratifying to hear, through you, that the confidence and support which the majority of the citizens of Pennsylvania expressed for me, by their vote on the Presidential question, will not be withdrawn by the artful and insidious efforts of my enemies. This is another evidence of the firmness and indulgence of the freemen of Pennsylvania. This organized plan of calumny and slander, levelled against me by the unprincipled and wicked, will not owe its defeat to any effort of mine, unless it be that which always attends truth and a conscious rectitude of conduct, when submitted to an untrammelled and honest public. The continued good opinion, therefore, of my fellow-citizens of Pennsylvania, lays me under additional obligations, whilst it connects my name with another guaranty of the wisdom of our government—I mean in furnishing to posterity another example of the weakness of demagogues when endeavoring to advance to power upon the destruction of innocence.

It is much to the honor of the good citizens of Pennsylvania that they calmly submit to the legally constituted power; this all good citizens will do, who love a government of laws, although they show much disapprobation at the means by which that power was obtained, and are determined to oppose the men who obtained power by what they believe illicit means. The great constitutional corrective in the hands of the people against usurpation of power, or corruption by their agents, is the right of suffrage; and this, when used with calmness and deliberation, will prove strong enough. It will perpetuate their liberties and rights, and will compel their representatives to discharge their duties with an eye single to the public interest, for whose security and advancement government is constituted.

I have not yet been so fortunate as to fall in with Mr. Frazer, although I have made inquiry for him. Should I meet with him, be assured it will be a gratification to me to extend to him those attentions due to any of your friends.

I regret very much that the bad health of Mrs. J. prevented me from passing through your hospitable town. I assure you, could we have done so, it would have afforded Mrs. J. and myself much pleasure. Mrs. J.'s health is perfectly restored. So soon as I got her to breathe the mountain air of Pennsylvania, she mended by the hour.

We are also blessed, in this section of the country, with the promise of fine crops. Our cotton promises a good crop. This is six days earlier than ever known in this section of country.

Mrs. J. joins me in kind salutations to you, with our best wishes for your happiness.

Your friend,

Andrew Jackson.

47[GENERAL JACKSON TO MR. BUCHANAN.]

Hermitage, April 8, 1826.

Dear Sir:—

I received, by due course of mail, your friendly letter of the 8th ult., transmitting a resolution passed by the Convention at Harrisburg, in which it is declared "that their confidence in me is unimpaired." This resolution adds another to the many obligations which I owe to the Republicans of Pennsylvania, and which shall be cherished as long as the feelings of gratitude and the sentiments of patriotism have a place in my heart. What greater consolation could be offered to my declining years than the reflection that my public conduct, notwithstanding the difficulties through which it has led me, can still be honored with testimonials so distinguished as this from the enlightened and patriotic Pennsylvanians; I desire no greater.

I have noted your remarks relative to Mr. Molton C. Rogers—every information I have received concerning him corroborates your account of him, and I have no doubt he fully merits the high character he sustains.

We have received the result of the Panama question in the Senate. From the whole view of the subject I have been compelled to believe that it is a hasty, unadvised measure, calculated to involve us in difficulties, perhaps war, without receiving in return any real benefit. The maxim that it is easier to avoid difficulties than to remove them when they have reached us, is too old not to be true; but perhaps this and many other good sayings, are becoming inapplicable in the present stage of our public measures, which seem to be so far removed from our (illegible) that even the language of Washington must be transposed in order to be reconciled to the councils of wisdom. I hope I may be wrong—it is my sincere wish that this Panama movement may advance the happiness and glory of the country—but if it be not a commitment of our neutrality with Spain, and indirectly with other powers, as, for example, Brazil, I have misconstrued very much the signification of the anathemas which have been pronounced upon the Assembly at Verona, as well as the true sense of the principles which form international law. Let the primary interests of Europe be what they may, or let our situation vary as far as you please from that which we occupied when the immortal Washington retired from the councils of his country, I cannot see, for my part, how it follows that the primary interests of the United States will be safer in the hands of others than in her own; or, in other words, that it can ever become necessary to form treaties, alliances, or any connections with the governments of South America, which may infringe upon the principles of equality among nations which is the basis of their independence, as well as all their international rights. The doctrine of Washington is as applicable to the present, as to the then primary interests of Europe, so far as our own peace and happiness are concerned, and I have no hesitation in saying, so far as the true interests of South America are concerned—maugre the discovery of Mr. Adams, that if Washington was now with us, 48he would unite with him in sending this mission to Panama. No one feels more for the cause of the South Americans than I do, and if the proper time had arrived, I trust that none would more willingly march to their defence. But there is a wide difference between relieving them

from a combination of league powers, and aiding them in forming a confederation which can do no good, as far as I am apprised of its objects, and which we all know, let its objects be the best, will contain evil tendencies.
Believe me to be, with great respect,
Your obedient servant,
Andrew Jackson.
[GENERAL JACKSON TO MR. BUCHANAN.]
Hermitage, Oct. 15, 1826.
Mr Dear Sir:—

I was very much gratified on the receipt of your letter of the 21st ult., which reached me yesterday, and thank you for the information it contains. I want language to express the gratitude I feel for the unsolicited, but generous support of the great Republican State of Pennsylvania—did I lack a stimulus to exert all my faculties to promote the best interests of my country, this alone would be sufficient. Who could abandon the path of Republican virtue when thus supported by the voluntary approbation of the enlightened and virtuous citizens of such a State as Pennsylvania? I answer, none whose minds have been matured in the schools of virtue, religion and morality.
I am happy to learn that Mr. Cheves has become your neighbor and a citizen—he is a great blessing to any society—he has a well-stored mind of useful information, which he will employ to the benefit of his country and the happiness of the society to which he belongs. Please present me to him respectfully.
I regret to learn that the drought has visited your section of country, and your crops are not abundant; still, so long as we have a supply of breadstuffs and other substantials, we ought to be thankful and happy. When we contrast our situation with Ireland and England, we ought to view ourselves as the chosen people of God, who has given us such a happy government of laws and placed us in such a climate and fertile soil. We ought not only to be thankful, but we ought to cherish and foster this heavenly boon with vestal vigilance.
Mrs. J. joins me in kind salutations and respects to you.
I am, very respectfully, your friend,
Andrew Jackson.
49[GENERAL JACKSON TO MR. BUCHANAN.]
Hermitage, Jan. 29, 1827.
Dear Sir:—

Your favor of the 19th has been before me for some time, but observing in the papers the obituary notice of your brother, whose illness took you from the city, I have delayed acknowledging its receipt until advised of your return. I pray you to accept my sincere condolence for the serious loss you have sustained in the death of your brother.
I suspect the Administration begins to perceive the necessity of public confidence, without which it is an arduous undertaking to execute the solemn duties confided by the Constitution to the Chief Magistrate. The Panama "bubble" and the loss of the trade with the British West Indies are the result of this defect in the Cabinet, for it cannot be supposed that such reputed diplomatists would have committed errors so obvious, had not some influence stronger than the public good operated upon their minds. My hope, however, is that the wisdom of Congress may remedy these blunders, and that my friends the "factious opposition" may, in your own language, never forget the support due to the country.

I had predicted, from the movements of (illegible) and Rochester, that the Panama subject was done with, and that the charge of "factious opposition" would be hushed, but it appears I was mistaken. —— is to be the theatre on which these mighty projects are to be unfolded. Alas! what folly and weakness!

Present me to my friend Mr. Kremer, and believe me,

Very respectfully, your obedient servant,

Andrew Jackson.

In the spring of 1827, Mr. Carter Beverley, of Virginia, was on a visit to General Jackson at the "Hermitage." The conversation turned on the incidents which preceded the election of Mr. Adams, and General Jackson gave some account of his interview with Mr. Buchanan in December, 1824, speaking of Mr. Buchanan, however, not by name, but as "a leading member of Congress." Mr. Beverley wrote an account of this conversation to a friend in North Carolina, who published his letter. Mr. Beverley afterward wrote to General Jackson, saying that his letter was not intended for publication, but asking if its statements were correct. General Jackson, without seeing Mr. Beverley's published letter, then wrote an answer to Mr. Beverley, which was published, and in which he stated that "a leading member of Congress" had, as the agent or confidential friend of Mr. Clay, proposed to him to engage to make Mr. Clay Secretary of State, and that he emphatically declined to do so. Subsequently, in another publication, General Jackson gave the name of Mr. Buchanan as the member who had thus approached him. The public was thus (in 1827) electrified by a statement, coming from General Jackson himself, that Mr. Clay, who had been charged with purchasing his appointment by Mr. Adams as Secretary of State, by his promise to make Mr. Adams President, had attempted, through Mr. Buchanan, to negotiate the same kind of corrupt bargain with General Jackson, on the like promise to make General Jackson President. It is very easy to see how this mistake first arose in the General's mind. Recollecting the information which Mr. Buchanan had given him of the over-zealous and imprudent conversation of Mr. Markley, who was a known partisan of Mr. Clay,—information which Mr. Buchanan assigned as a reason why the General should disavow the rumor that he had promised to appoint Mr. Adams Secretary,—General Jackson had evidently come to misunderstand the object of Mr. Buchanan in mentioning what Mr. Markley had said. It must be remembered that at this time (1827) there was an angry and excited controversy going on, respecting the supposed bargain between Mr. Clay and Mr. Adams; that Mr. Clay was publishing, and that General Jackson was publishing; that General Jackson undoubtedly believed that there had been an improper understanding between Mr. Adams and Mr. Clay, and it was very natural for him to take up the idea that Mr. Buchanan, by mentioning what Mr. Markley had said, stood ready, as a friend of Mr. Clay, to propose and carry out a similar bargain with himself. Apart from Mr. Buchanan's denial, there seems to be an intrinsic improbability that one who had been an earnest supporter of General Jackson in the popular election, and who feared that even a rumor of his intended appointment of Mr. Adams would injure the General in the House of Representatives, and who knew that it would greatly injure him in Pennsylvania, if it were not contradicted, should have exerted himself to get from the General a promise to make Mr. Clay Secretary of State. Promises, or rumors of promises, in regard to this appointment, were the very things which Mr. Buchanan was interested to prevent. It was very unfortunate that General Jackson did not afterwards and always see, that the mention by Mr. Buchanan of Mr. Markley's wishes, was intended to present to his (the General's) mind the importance of his denial of the rumor that he had said he would appoint Mr. Adams. In all that scene of intrigue—and apart from any thing said or done by the principal persons concerned in that great struggle, there was intrigue—General Jackson acted with the rigid integrity that belonged to his character. Mr. Buchanan acted with no less integrity. He wished to prevent General Jackson's cause from being injured in the House and in the country, by unfounded rumors with which the heated atmosphere of Washington was filled; and he could have had no motive for seeking to make Mr. Clay Secretary of State, at the expense of exposing General Jackson to the same kind of rumor in regard to Mr. Clay which he was anxious to counteract in regard to Mr. Adams.

After the publication of General Jackson's letter to Mr. Beverley, Mr. Buchanan wrote to a friend as follows:

[MR. BUCHANAN TO MR. INGHAM.]

Lancaster, July 12, 1827.

Dear Sir:—

I received yours yesterday evening, and hasten to give it an immediate answer. With you, I regret the publication of General Jackson's letter to Mr. Beverley. It may do harm, but cannot do good. The conversation which I held with the General will not sustain his letter, although it may furnish a sufficient reason for his apprehensions. My single purpose was to ascertain from him whether he had ever declared he would appoint Mr. Adams Secretary of State in case he were elected President. As to the propriety and policy of propounding this question to him, I had reflected much, and had taken the advice of a distinguished Jackson man, then high in office in Pennsylvania. I had no doubt at the time that my question, if answered at all, would be answered in the negative; but I wished it to come from himself that he stood uncommitted upon this subject.

In my interview with the General (which, by the way, was in the street), I stated the particulars of a conversation between Philip S. Markley and myself, as one reason why he should answer the question which I had propounded. Out of my repetition of this conversation the mistake must have arisen. This conversation would be one link in the chain of testimony, but of itself it is altogether incomplete.

52How General Jackson could have believed I came to him as an emissary from Mr. Clay or his friends to make a corrupt bargain with him in their behalf, I am at a loss to determine. He could not have received the impression until after Mr. Clay and his friends had actually elected Mr. Adams, and Adams had appointed Clay Secretary of State. Although I continued to be upon terms of the strictest intimacy with General Jackson whilst he continued at Washington, and have corresponded with him occasionally since, he has never adverted to the subject. From the terms of his letters to me, I never could have suspected that he for a moment supposed me capable of becoming the agent in such a negotiation. The idea that such was his impression never once flitted across my mind. When regularly called upon, I need not tell you that I shall speak the truth. If the matter be properly managed, it will not injure General Jackson; but I can readily conceive that such a course may be taken in relation to it by some of our friends, as will materially injure his prospects.

From your friend,

James Buchanan.

At about this time, Mr. Clay publicly disclaimed all knowledge respecting the interview between Mr. Buchanan and General Jackson, and the latter then wrote to Mr. Buchanan the following explanatory letter:

[GENERAL JACKSON TO MR. BUCHANAN.]

Hermitage, July 15, 1827.

Dear Sir:—

You will see from the enclosed publication of Mr. Clay repelling the statement made by me respecting the propositions said to have been made by his friends to mine and to me, and intended to operate upon the last election for President, that it becomes necessary for the public to be put in possession of the facts. In doing this you are aware of the position which you occupy, and which, I trust, you will sustain when properly called on. Ever since the publication, and the inquiry before the House of Representatives in January and February, 1825, questions have been propounded from various sources calculated to draw from me the information I had upon that unpleasant subject. Many, no doubt with sinister views, placing me in selfish connection with the facts from my accustomed silence, have sought to fortify the character of Mr. Clay. But in a number of cases, where inquiry seemed to be prompted by a frank and generous desire to obtain the truth, I felt myself bound to answer in a corresponding spirit, and accordingly the statement made by you to me has been on several occasions repeated, as it was to Mr. Beverley, who visited me at my house, where he found a number of his friends and relatives.

53Having remained all night, in the morning, conversing on politics, the question so often put to me before was asked by Mr. Beverley. It was answered. Mr. Beverley went to Nashville and wrote to his friend in North Carolina, who it appears published his letter. On the 15th of May last, he wrote me from Louisville, requesting to be informed whether the statement made by him was correct, and observing that his letter was not intended for publication. Not having seen the letter, as published, there was no safe alternative for me but that adopted, of making the statement, as you will see in the enclosed paper.

I shall now, in reply to Mr. Clay's appeal, give my authority, accompanied by the statement you made to Major John H. Eaton and to Mr. Kremer, and leave Mr. Clay to his further inquiries. He cannot be indulged by me in a paper war, or newspaper discussion. Had his friends not voted out Mr. McDuffie's resolutions when Mr. Clay threw himself upon the House, the truth or falsehood of these statements would have been made manifest, and the public mind now at rest upon the subject. That they did, will appear, reference being had to the National Journal of the 5th of February, 1825. You will recollect that Mr. McDuffie moved to instruct the Committee to inquire whether the friends of Mr. Clay had hinted that they would fight for those who paid best, and whether overtures were said to have been made by the friends of Mr. Clay, offering him the appointment of Secretary of State for his influence, and to elect Mr. Adams, and whether his friends gave this information to the friends of General Jackson and hinted that if the friends of Jackson would close with them, &c., &c., giving the Committee the power to examine on oath.

I have no doubt, when properly called on, you will come forth and offer me the statement made to Major Eaton, then to Mr. Kremer, and then to me, and give the names of the friends of Mr. Clay who made it to you.

I will thank you to acknowledge the receipt of this letter on its reaching you.

I have the honor to be, with great respect,

Your obedient servant,

Andrew Jackson.

Early in August, 1827, Mr. Buchanan published a card in the Lancaster Journal, embodying the recollections which I have given, but which it is not necessary to reproduce; and after a brief but inconclusive reply from Mr. Markley, the matter passed out of the public mind. Later in the same year (1827) Mr. Clay published an elaborate vindication of his conduct, in the course of which he thus refers to Mr. Buchanan:

"In General Jackson's letter to Mr. Beverley, of the 6th of June last, he admits that in inferring my privity to the proposition which he describes as borne by Mr. Buchanan, he may have done me injustice; and, in his address to the public of the 18th of July last, giving up the name of this gentleman as his only witness, he repeats that he possibly may have done me injustice, in assuming my authority for that proposition. He even deigns to honor me with a declaration of the pleasure which he will experience if I should be able to acquit myself! Mr. Buchanan has been heard by the public; and I feel justified in asserting that the first impression of the whole nation was, as it is yet that of every intelligent mind unbiased by party prejudice, that his testimony fully exonerated me, and demonstrated that General Jackson, to say no more, had greatly misconceived the purport of the interview between them. And further: that so far as any thing improper was disclosed by Mr. Buchanan touching the late Presidential election, it affected General Jackson and his friends exclusively. He having manifestly injured me, speculation was busy, when Mr. Buchanan's statement appeared, as to the course which the General would pursue, after his gratuitous expression of sympathy with me. There were not wanting many persons who believed that his magnanimity would prompt him publicly to retract his charge, and to repair the wrong which he had done me. I did not participate in that just expectation, and therefore felt no disappointment that it was not realized. Whatever other merits he may possess, I have not found among them, in the course of my relations with him, that of forbearing to indulge vindictive passions. His silent contemplation of, if not his positive acquiescence in, the most extraordinary interpretation of Mr. Buchanan's statement that ever was given to human language, has not surprised me. If it had been possible for him to render me an act of spontaneous justice by a frank and manly avowal of his error, the testimony now submitted to the public might have been unnecessary.

[MR. BUCHANAN TO MR. INGHAM.]

Lancaster, August 9, 1827.

Dear Sir:—

Ere this can reach you, you will have seen General Jackson's letter to the public, in which he has given up my name. It will at once strike you to be a most extraordinary production as far as I am concerned. My statement will appear in the Lancaster Journal to-morrow, which I shall send you. I have not suffered my feelings to get the better of my judgment, but have stated the truth in a calm and temperate manner. If General Jackson and our editors shall act with discretion, the storm may blow over without injuring [any one]. Should they, on the contrary, force me to the wall and make it absolutely necessary for the preservation of my own character to defend myself, I know not what may be the consequence.

I have stated the conversation between Markley and myself in as strong terms as the truth would justify, but no stronger. It is in your power to do much to give this matter a proper direction. Indeed I would suggest to you the propriety of an immediate visit to Philadelphia for that purpose. My friends are very indignant, but I believe I can keep them right.

You will perceive that General Jackson has cited Mr. Eaton as a witness. I have treated this part of his letter with great mildness. In a letter to me, which I received day before yesterday, the General intimates that George Kremer would confirm his statement. This letter is imprudent, and, in my opinion, an improper one. It is well it has fallen into the hands of a political friend.

You will discover that your knowledge concerning my conversation with General Jackson was nearly correct. The friend who wrote me the letter of the 27th December, 1824,

referred to in my communication, was Judge Rogers, then Secretary of State [of Pennsylvania].
From your sincere friend,
Mr. Ingham.   James Buchanan.
[MR. BUCHANAN TO GENERAL JACKSON.]
Lancaster, August 10, 1827.
Dear Sir:—

I received your letter of the 15th ultimo on Tuesday last. Your address to the public also reached me upon the same day, in the Cincinnati Advertiser. This communication made it necessary for me to publish in detail the conversation which I held with you concerning the Presidential election on the 30th December, 1824. I shall enclose to you in this letter that part of the Lancaster Journal containing it. I regret, beyond expression, that you believed me to be an emissary from Mr. Clay, since some time before the first Harrisburg convention which nominated you, I have ever been your ardent, decided, and, perhaps without vanity I may say, your efficient friend. Every person in this part of the State of Pennsylvania is well acquainted with the fact. It is, therefore, to me a matter of the deepest regret that you should have supposed me to be the "friend of Mr. Clay." Had I ever entertained a suspicion that such was your belief, I should have immediately corrected your impression.
I shall annex to this letter a copy of that which I wrote to Duff Green, on the 16th of October last. The person whom I consulted in Pennsylvania was the present Judge Rogers of the Supreme Court—then the Secretary of State of this Commonwealth.
The friends of the Administration are making great efforts in Pennsylvania. We have been busily engaged during the summer in counteracting them. Success has, I think, hitherto attended our efforts. I do not fear the vote of the State, although it is believed every member of the State administration, except General Bernard, is hostile to your election. Your security will be in the gratitude and in the hearts of the people.
Please to present my best respects to Mrs. Jackson, and believe me to be, very respectfully, your friend,
James Buchanan.
56This subject of Mr. Buchanan's connection with the Presidential election of 1824–5, and its incidents, passed out of the public mind, after the publication of the letters which I have quoted. But it was again revived when Mr. Buchanan became a candidate for the Presidency in 1856. All that it is needful to say here is, that for nearly three years after the election of 1824–5, no impression seems to have existed in the mind of General Jackson that Mr. Buchanan's interview with him in December, 1824, had any purpose but that which Mr. Buchanan has described; but that in 1827, General Jackson, in the heat of the renewed controversies about the supposed bargain between Mr. Adams and Mr. Clay, took up the erroneous idea that Mr. Buchanan could, if he were to declare the truth, make it apparent that Mr. Clay or his friends had attempted to effect the same kind of bargain with General Jackson, which attempt was indignantly repelled. A candid examination of the facts is all that is needful to convince any one that the General was in error in 1827, and that he was equally in error at a much later period. When he became President, and for a long time thereafter, his confidence in Mr. Buchanan was manifested in so many ways that one is led to believe that his view in 1827 of Mr. Buchanan's conduct in the matter of the Presidential election of 1824–5 was an exceptional idiosyncrasy, resulting from the excitement which his mind always felt in regard to that event, and which was strongly renewed in him in 1827.

It will be necessary to advert to this subject again, because, when Mr. Buchanan was a candidate for the Presidency in 1856, the whole story was revived by persons who were unfriendly to him, and who then made use of a private letter which was extracted from General Jackson in 1845, in a somewhat artful manner, when he was laboring under a mortal illness. But an account of this political intrigue belongs to the period when it was set on foot.

57

CHAPTER IV.
1825–1826.

BITTER OPPOSITION TO THE ADMINISTRATION OF JOHN QUINCY ADAMS—BILL FOR THE RELIEF OF THE REVOLUTIONARY OFFICERS—THE PANAMA MISSION—INCIDENTAL REFERENCE TO SLAVERY.

The circumstances attending the election of Mr. Adams led to the formation of a most powerful opposition to his administration, as soon as he was inaugurated. The friends of General Jackson, a numerous and compact body of public men, representing a much larger number of the people of the Union than the friends of Mr. Adams could be said to represent, felt that he had been unfairly deprived of the votes of States in the House of Representatives which should have been given to him. Especially was this the case, they said, in regard to the State of Kentucky, whose Legislature had plainly indicated the wish of a majority of her people that her vote in the House should be given to General Jackson; and when it was announced that Mr. Adams, who had received the unanimous electoral vote of only six States, had obtained the votes of thirteen States in the House, while General Jackson had obtained but seven, and when Mr. Clay had been appointed by Mr. Adams Secretary of State, there was a bitterness of feeling among the supporters of General Jackson, which evinced at once a fixed determination to elect him President at the end of the ensuing four years.

In regard to the state of parties, viewed apart from the merely personal element of leadership and following, there was not much, in the beginning of Mr. Adams's administration, to distinguish its supporters from its opponents. In the course, however, of that administration, those who defended it from the fierce assaults of the opposition, began to take the name of National Republicans, while the opponents of the administration began to call themselves Democrats. Included in the 58opposition were the political friends and followers of Mr. Calhoun, and the political friends and followers of General Jackson; the latter being distinctly known and classified as "Jackson men." In the Senate there was a number of older men, who were not likely to form an active element of parliamentary opposition or defence; such as Mr. Silsbee of Massachusetts, Mr. Dickerson of New Jersey, Mr. Samuel Smith of Maryland, Mr. William Smith of South Carolina, Mr. Macon of Georgia, Mr. Rowan of Kentucky, and Mr. Hugh L. White of Tennessee. The opposition in the Senate was led by a younger class of men: Mr. Van Buren of New York, Mr. Woodbury of New Hampshire, Mr. Tazewell of Virginia, Mr. Hayne of South Carolina, Mr. Berrien of Georgia, and Mr. Benton of Missouri.[17] But it was not in the Senate that the great arena of debate between the assailants and the defenders of this administration was to be found during the first year or two of its term. In the House, at the opening of the 19th Congress, which began its session in December, 1825, there was an array of combatants—ardent, active and able debaters. Of these, composing the leaders of the opposition, were Mr. Buchanan, Samuel D. Ingham, William C. Rives, James K. Polk, John Forsyth, George McDuffie, Edward Livingston, William Drayton, William S. Archer, Andrew Stevenson, Mangum, Cambreleng, and Louis

McLane. The eccentric John Randolph was also one of the leaders of the opposition. The leading friends of the administration were Webster, Sprague, Bartlett, John Davis, Edward Everett, Burgess, Taylor, Letcher, Wright, Vinton, and Henry L. Storrs.

Before the opposition had marshalled their forces for an attack upon the administration, a debate occurred in the House of Representatives upon a subject that did not involve party divisions. A bill was introduced by a Pennsylvania member for the relief of the surviving officers of the Revolution. It proposed an appropriation of only one million of dollars, and it was confined strictly to the cases of the Revolutionary officers to whom half-pay for life had been granted by Congress in 591780, who had afterwards accepted a commutation of five years' full pay, in lieu of half-pay for life, and who were paid in certificates that were never worth more than one-fifth of their nominal value, and which were soon depreciated to about one-eighth. The passage of this measure depended upon the prudence and skill of those who favored it. The mover, Mr. Hemphill of Pennsylvania, and Mr. Dayton, had advocated the bill in speeches of much discretion, and there was a good prospect of its adoption. In this state of things, an untoward amendment was offered by a member from Massachusetts, which proposed to increase the appropriation. This had a manifest tendency to defeat the bill; and at this crisis Mr. Buchanan came forward to restate the case of the officers, and to replace the measure on its true footing. He said:

"It is with extreme reluctance I rise at this time to address you. I have made no preparation to speak, except that of carefully reading the documents which have been laid upon our tables; but a crisis seems to have arrived in this debate, when the friends of the bill, if ever, must come forward in its support. I do not consider that the claim of the officers of the Revolution rests upon gratitude alone. It is not an appeal to your generosity only, but to your justice. You owe them a debt, in the strictest sense of the word; and of a nature so meritorious, that, if you shall refuse to pay it, the nation will be disgraced. Formerly, when their claim was presented to Congress, we had, at least, an apology for rejecting it. The country was not then in a condition to discharge this debt without inconvenience. But now, after forty years have elapsed since its creation, with a treasury overflowing, and a national debt so diminished, that, with ordinary economy, it must, in a very few years, be discharged, these officers, the relics of that band which achieved your independence, again present themselves before you, and again ask you for justice. They do not ask you to be generous—they do not ask you to be grateful—but they ask you to pay the debt which was the price of your independence. I term it a debt; and it is one founded upon a most solemn contract, with which these officers have complied, both in its letter and in its spirit, whilst you have violated all its obligations.

"Let us spend a few moments in tracing the history of this claim. It arose out of the distresses of the Continental Army, during the Revolutionary War; and the utter inability of the government, at that time, to relieve them. What, sir, was the situation of that army, when it lay encamped at the Valley Forge? They were naked, and hungry, and barefoot. Pestilence and famine stalked abroad throughout the camp. The first blaze of patriotism which had animated the country, and furnished the army with its officers, had begun to die away. These officers perceived that the contest would be 60long, and bloody, and doubtful. They had felt, by sad experience, that the depreciated pay which they received, so far from enabling them to impart assistance to their wives and children, or hoard up anything for futurity, was not sufficient to supply their own absolute and immediate wants. Placed in this situation, they were daily sending in their resignations, and abandoning the cause of their country. In this alarming crisis, Washington earnestly recommended to Congress to grant the officers half-pay, to commence after the close of the contest, as the only remedy for these evils, within their power. The country was not then able to remunerate the officers for the immense and unequal sacrifices which they were making in its cause. All that it could then do was to present them a prospect of happier days to come, on which hope might rest. With this view, Congress, in May, 1778, adopted a resolution allowing the officers who should continue in service until the end of the war, half-pay for seven years. This resolution produced but a partial effect upon the army. The time of its continuance was to be but short; and there were conditions annexed to it, which, in many cases, would have rendered it entirely inoperative.

"In August, 1779, Congress again acted upon this subject, and resolved, 'That it be recommended to the several States to grant half-pay for life to the officers who should continue in the service to the end of the war.' This recommendation was disregarded by every State in the Union, with one exception; and I feel proud that Pennsylvania was that State. She not only granted half-pay for life to the officers of her own line, but she furnished them with clothing and with provisions. Thus, when the General Government became unable to discharge its duty to her officers and soldiers, she voluntarily interposed and relieved their distresses. General Washington, when urging upon Congress the necessity of granting to the officers half-pay for life, pointed to those of the Pennsylvania line as an example of the beneficial consequences which had resulted from that measure.[18]

"Congress at length became convinced of the necessity of granting to the Continental officers half-pay for life. Without pay and without clothing, they had become disheartened and were about abandoning the service. The darkest period of the Revolution had arrived, and there was but one ray of hope left to penetrate the impending gloom which hung over the army. The officers were willing still to endure privations and sufferings, if they could obtain an assurance that they would be remembered by their country, after it should be blessed with peace and independence. They well knew Congress could not relieve their present wants; all, therefore, they asked was the promise of a future provision. Congress, at length, in October, 1780, resolved, 'That half-pay for life be granted to the officers in the army of the United States who shall continue in service to the end of the war.'

"Before the adoption of this resolution, so desperate had been our condition, that even Washington apprehended a dissolution of the army, and had begun to despair of the success of our cause. We have his authority for declaring that, immediately after its adoption, our prospects brightened and it produced the most happy effects. The state of the army was instantly changed. The officers became satisfied with their condition, and, under their command, the army marched to victory and independence. They faithfully and patriotically performed every obligation imposed upon them by the solemn contract into which they had entered with their country.

"How did you perform this contract on your part? No sooner had the dangers of war ceased to threaten our existence—no sooner had peace returned to bless our shores, than we forgot those benefactors to whom, under Providence, we owed our independence. We then began to discover that it was contrary to the genius of our Republican institutions to grant pensions for life. The jealousy of the people was roused, and their fears excited. They dreaded the creation of a privileged order. I do not mean to censure them for this feeling of ill-directed jealousy, because jealousy is the natural guardian of liberty.

"In this emergency, how did the Continental officers act? In such a manner as no other officers of a victorious army had ever acted before. For the purpose of allaying the apprehensions of their fellow-citizens, and complying with the wishes of Congress, they consented to accept five years' full-pay in commutation for their half-pay for life. This commutation was to be paid in money, or securities were to be given on interest at six per cent., as Congress should find most convenient.

"Did the government ever perform this their second stipulation to the officers? I answer, no. The gentleman from Tennessee was entirely mistaken in the history of the times, when he asserted that the commutation certificates of the officers enabled them to purchase farms, or commence trade, upon leaving the army. Congress had not any funds to pledge for their redemption. They made requisitions upon the States, which shared the same fate with many others, and were entirely disregarded. The faith and the honor of the country, whilst they were intrusted to thirteen independent and jealous State sovereignties, were almost always forfeited. We then had a General Government which had not the power of enforcing its own edicts. The consequence was that, when the officers received their certificates, they were not worth more than about one-fifth of their nominal value, and they very soon fell to one-eighth of that amount.

"Let gentlemen for a moment realize what must then have been the situation and the feelings of these officers. They had spent their best days in the service of their country. They had endured hardships and privations without an example in history. Destitute of everything but patriotism, they had lived for years upon the mere promise of Congress. At the call of their country, they had relinquished half-pay for life, and accepted a new promise of five years' full-pay. When they had confidently expected to receive this recompense, 62it vanished from their grasp. Instead of money, or securities equal to money, which would have enabled them to embark with advantage in civil employments, they obtained certificates which necessity compelled most of them to sell at the rate of eight for one. The government proved faithless, but they had, what we have not, the plea of necessity, to justify their conduct.

"In 1790, the provision which was made by law for the payment of the public debt, embraced these commutation certificates. They were funded, and the owner of each of them received three certificates; the first for two-thirds of the original amount, bearing an interest immediately of six per cent.; the second for the remaining third, but without interest for ten years; and the third for the interest which had accumulated, bearing an interest of only three per cent.

"What does this bill propose? Not to indemnify the officers of the Revolution for the loss which they sustained in consequence of the inability of the government, at the close of the war, to comply with its solemn contract. Not, after a lapse of more than forty years, to place them in the situation in which they would have been placed had the government been able to do them justice. It proposes to allow them even less than the difference between what the owners of the commutation certificates received under the funding system, and what these certificates when funded were worth upon their face. My colleague has clearly shown, by a fair calculation, that the allowance will fall considerably short of this difference. If the question now before the committee were to be decided by the people of the United States instead of their Representatives, could any man, for a moment, doubt what would be their determination?

"I hope my friend from Massachusetts will not urge the amendment he has proposed. Judging from past experience, I fear, if it should prevail, the bill will be defeated. Let other classes of persons who think themselves entitled to the bounty of their country present their claims to this House, and they will be fairly investigated. This is what the surviving officers of the Revolution have done. Their case has been thoroughly examined by a committee, who have reported in its favor; and all the information necessary to enable us to decide correctly is now in our possession. I trust their claim will be permitted to rest upon its own foundation. They are old, and for the most part in poverty; it is necessary, if we act at all, that we act speedily, and do them justice without delay. In my opinion, they have a better claim to what this bill contemplates giving them, than any of us have to our eight dollars per day. Gentlemen need apprehend no danger from the precedent; we shall never have another Revolutionary war for independence. We have no reason to apprehend we shall ever again be unable to pay our just debts. Even if that should again be our unfortunate condition, we shall never have another army so patient and so devoted as to sacrifice every selfish consideration for the glory, the happiness, and the independence of their country. I shall vote against the proposed amendment because I will do no act which may have a tendency to defeat this bill."

63Mr. Buchanan used to relate, in after years, that at this juncture, the friends of the bill were dismayed by the course of Mr. Everett, who was then a young member from Massachusetts, and who wished to make and insisted upon making a rhetorical speech. The friends of the bill remonstrated with him, that all had been said that needed to be said; and that the only thing to be done was to vote down the amendment, after which the bill was almost certain to be passed. But Mr. Everett persisted, and made his speech while the amendment was pending.[19] He "demanded" of the House to pass the bill, and by passing it as proposed to be amended by his colleague to give the survivors of the Revolution "all they ask and more than they ask." The consequence was that the appropriation was increased. Then a member from New York moved to extend its provisions to every militia-man who had served for a certain time. Then other amendments embraced widows and orphans, artificers and musicians, the troops who fought at Bunker Hill, the troops raised in Vermont, those of the battles of Saratoga and Bennington, and of the Southern battles. The enemies of the original measure promoted this method of dealing with it, and finally, when thus loaded down with provisions not at all germane to its real principle, it was recommitted to the Committee and was therefore lost.

The first important subject of contention on which the opposition 64put forth their strength against the administration of Mr. Adams related to what was called "The Panama Mission." In his Message of December, 1825, the President made the following announcement:

"Among the measures which have been suggested to the Spanish-American Republics by the new relations with one another resulting from the recent changes of their condition, is that of assembling at the Isthmus of Panama, a Congress at which each of them should be represented, to deliberate upon objects important to the welfare of all. The republics of Colombia, of Mexico, and of Central America, have already deputed plenipotentiaries to such a meeting, and they have invited the United States to be also represented there by their ministers. The invitation has been accepted, and ministers on the part of the United States will be commissioned to attend at those deliberations, and to take part in them, so far as may be compatible with that neutrality from which it is neither our intention nor the desire of the other American States that we should depart."

It was, beyond controversy, the constitutional prerogative of the President, as the organ of all intercourse with foreign nations, to accept this invitation, and to name Ministers to the proposed Congress. The Senate might or might not concur with him in this step, and might or might not confirm the nominations of the proposed Ministers. He sent to the Senate the names of John Sergeant of Philadelphia, and Richard C. Anderson of Kentucky, as the Ministers of the United States to the proposed Congress at Panama. The Senatorial opposition, led by Mr. Benton and Mr. Tazewell, after a long discussion in secret session, took a vote upon a resolution that it was inexpedient to send Ministers to Panama. This was rejected by a vote of 24 to 19; and the nominations were then confirmed by a vote of 27 to 17 in the case of Mr. Anderson, and by a vote of 26 to 18 in the case of Mr. Sergeant. The diplomatic department having thus fully acted upon and confirmed the proposed measure, it remained for the House of Representatives to initiate and pass the necessary appropriation. The turn that was given to the subject in the House gave rise to an animated debate on a very important constitutional topic, in which Mr. Buchanan, although opposed to the Mission, asserted it to be the duty of the House to make the appropriation, now that the Senate had confirmed the appointment of the Ministers. This 65debate began upon a resolution reported by the Committee on Foreign Affairs, that "in the opinion of the House it is expedient to appropriate the funds necessary to enable the President of the United States to send Ministers to the Congress of Panama." To this resolution, Mr. McLane of Delaware had moved an amendment, which, if it had been adopted, would have placed the House of Representatives in the anomalous attitude of annexing, as a condition of its grant, instructions as to the mode in which the diplomatic agents of the United States were to act in carrying out a foreign mission. Mr. Buchanan, who was in favor of the amendments, was also in favor of making the appropriation necessary to enable the President to send the Mission; and in support of this constitutional duty of the House, he made an argument on the 11th of April (1826) which drew from Mr. Webster the compliment that he had placed this part of the subject in a point of view which could not be improved.[20] Mr. Buchanan said: "I know there are several gentlemen on this floor, who approve of the policy of the amendments proposed, and wish to express an opinion in their favor; and who yet feel reluctant to vote for them, because it is their intention finally to support the appropriation bill. They think, if the amendments should be rejected, consistency would require them to refuse any grant of money to carry this mission into effect. I shall, therefore, ask the attention of the committee, whilst I endeavor to prove that there would not, in any event, be the slightest inconsistency in this course.

"I assert it to be a position susceptible of the clearest proof, that the House of Representatives is morally bound, unless in extreme cases, to vote the salaries of Ministers who have been constitutionally created by the President and Senate. The expediency of establishing the mission was one question, which has already been decided by the competent authority; when the appropriation bill shall come before us, we will be called upon to decide another and a very different question. Richard C. Anderson and John Sergeant 66have been regularly nominated by the President of United States to be Envoys Extraordinary and Ministers Plenipotentiary 'to the Assembly of American nations at Panama.' The Senate, after long and solemn deliberation, have advised and consented to their appointment. These Ministers have been created—they have been called into existence under the authority of the Constitution of the United States. That venerated instrument declares, that the President 'shall have power, by and with the advice and consent of the Senate, to make treaties, provided two-thirds of the Senators present concur: and he shall nominate, and, by and with the advice and consent of the Senate, shall appoint Ambassadors, other public Ministers and Consuls, Judges of the Supreme Court, and all other officers of the United States, whose appointments are not herein otherwise provided for, and which shall be established by Law.' What, then, will be the question upon the appropriation bill? In order to enable our Ministers to proceed upon their mission, the President has asked us to grant the necessary appropriation. Shall we incur the responsibility of refusing? Shall we thus defeat the mission which has already been established by the only competent constitutional authorities? This House has, without doubt, the physical power to refuse the appropriation, and it possesses the same power to withhold his salary from the President of the United States. The true question is, what is the nature of our constitutional obligation? Are we not morally bound to pay the salaries given by existing laws to every officer of the Government? By the act of the first May, 1810, the outfit and salary to be allowed by the President to Foreign Ministers are established. Such Ministers have been regularly appointed to attend the Congress at Panama. What right then have we to refuse to appropriate the salaries which they have a right to receive, under the existing laws of the land?

"I admit there may be extreme cases, in which this House would be justified in withholding such an appropriation. 'The safety of the people is the supreme law.' If, therefore, we should believe any mission to be dangerous, either to the existence or to the liberties of this country, necessity would justify us in breaking the letter to preserve the spirit of the Constitution. The same necessity would equally justify us in refusing to grant to the President his salary, in certain extreme cases, which might easily be imagined.

"But how far would your utmost power extend? Can you re-judge the determination of the President and Senate, and destroy the officers which they have created? Might not the President immediately send these Ministers to Panama; and, if he did, would not their acts be valid? It is certain, if they should go, they run the risk of never receiving a salary; but still they might act as Plenipotentiaries. By withholding the salary of the President, you cannot withhold from him the power; neither can you, by refusing to appropriate for this mission, deprive the Ministers of their authority. It is beyond your control to make them cease to be Ministers.

"The constitutional obligation to provide for a Minister, is equally strong as that to carry into effect a treaty. It is true, the evils which may flow 67from your refusal may be greater in the one case than the other. If you refuse to appropriate for a treaty, you violate the faith of the country to a foreign nation. You do no more, however, than omit to provide for the execution of an instrument which is declared by the Constitution to be the supreme law of the land. In the case which will be presented to you by the appropriation bill, is the nature of your obligation different? I think not. The power to create the Minister is contained in the same clause of the Constitution with that to make the treaty. They are powers of the same nature. The one is absolutely necessary to carry the other into effect. You cannot negotiate treaties without Ministers. They are the means by which the treaty-making power is brought into action. You are, therefore, under the same moral obligation to appropriate money to discharge the salary of a Minister, that you would be to carry a treaty into effect.

"If you ask me for authority to establish these principles, I can refer you to the opinion of the first President of the United States—the immortal Father of his Country—who, in my humble judgment, possessed more practical wisdom, more political foresight, and more useful constitutional knowledge, than all his successors.

"I have thus, I think, established the position, that gentlemen who vote for the amendments now before the committee, even if they should not prevail, may, without inconsistency, give their support to the appropriation bill."

Sound as this was, it is a little remarkable that Mr. Buchanan should not have considered that the duty of voting the necessary appropriation precluded the House of Representatives from dictating what subjects the Ministers were to discuss or not to discuss. Those who favored the proposed amendments founded themselves on the legal maxim that he who has the power to give may annex to the gift whatever condition he chooses. This was well answered by Mr. Webster, that in making appropriations for such purposes the House did not make gifts, but performed a duty. The amendments were rejected on the 21st of April, and on the following day the Panama Appropriation Bill was passed, Mr. Buchanan voting with the majority.[21]

Some of the topics incidentally touched upon in the discursive 68debate on this Panama Mission are of little interest now. But one may be referred to, because it related to the dangerous topic of slavery. An apprehension was felt by those who were opposed to this measure, and by Mr. Buchanan, among others, that the Spanish-American Republics, more particularly Mexico and Colombia, might concert measures at this proposed Congress to seize the West India Islands, and raise there the standard of emancipation and social revolution. Those who entertained this apprehension, therefore, did not wish to see the moral and political influence of this proposed Congress increased by the participation of the United States in its proceedings. It may have been an unfounded fear; but in truth, excepting in so far as the objects of this assembly were understood and explained by the American Administration itself, very little was known of the purposes entertained by its original projectors. It was certainly not unnatural, in the then condition of our own country, and of the West Indies, in regard to the matter of slavery, that public men in the United States should have been cautious in regard to this exciting topic. At all events, it was introduced incidentally, in the discussion on the proposed Mission, and Mr. Buchanan thus expressed himself upon it:

"Permit me here, for a moment, to speak upon a subject to which I have never before adverted upon this floor, and to which, I trust, I may never again have occasion to advert. I mean the subject of slavery. I believe it to be a great political and a great moral evil. I thank God, my lot has been cast in a State where it does not exist. But, while I entertain these opinions, I know it is an evil at present without a remedy. It has been a curse entailed upon us by that nation which now makes it a subject of reproach to our institutions. It is, however, one of those moral evils, from which it is impossible for us to escape, without the introduction of evils infinitely greater. There are portions of this Union, in which, if you emancipate your slaves, they will become masters. There can be no middle course. Is there any man in this Union who could, for a moment, indulge in the horrible idea of abolishing slavery by the massacre of the high-minded, and the chivalrous race of men in the South. I trust there is not one. For my own part I would, without hesitation, buckle on my knapsack, and march in company with my friend from Massachusetts (Mr. Everett) in defence of their cause."[22]
70
CHAPTER V.
1827–1829.

GREAT INCREASE OF GENERAL JACKSON'S POPULARITY—"RETRENCHMENT" MADE A POLITICAL CRY—DEBATE ON THE TARIFF—BUCHANAN ON INTERNAL IMPROVEMENTS—THE INTERESTS OF NAVIGATION—THE CUMBERLAND ROAD AGAIN DISCUSSED—INELIGIBILITY OF A PRESIDENT.

The 20th Congress, which assembled in December, 1827, opened with a great increase in the forces of the opposition. The elections in the autumn of 1826 evinced an extraordinary growth of General Jackson's popularity. Mr. Adams found himself in a minority in both branches of Congress. In the House, the opponents of his administration numbered 111 members, its friends 94. It is quite probable, however, that but for the indiscretion of certain members who have ranked as friends of the administration, the angry and criminating discussion of the subject of "retrenchment," which was deprecated by the wisest men of the opposition, but into which they were forced, would not have occurred. It was precipitated by the defiant attitude of two or three members who should have allowed the cool leaders of the opposition to strangle it, as they were at first disposed to do. But once commenced, it drew into bitter strife the excited elements of party and personal warfare, and went on through nearly a whole session with little credit to some who participated in it, but in the end to the great and not altogether just damage of the administration.

It happened that on the 22d of January (1828) a member from Kentucky, Mr. Chilton, an earnest "Jackson man," who had formerly been a clergyman but was now a politician, introduced in the House certain resolutions instructing the Committee of Ways and Means to report what offices could be abolished, what salaries reduced, and other modes of curtailing the expenses of the government. It is apparent that this could not have 71been a step taken by concert with the leaders of the opposition. A party that was daily growing in strength, and that was almost morally certain to overthrow the party of the administration, and to elect the next President, could have had no motive for shackling themselves with a legislative measure reducing the number of offices or the salaries of the officers that must be retained. They could not know in advance how they could carry on the government, and it would be mere folly for them to put laws on the statute-book framed while they were not charged with the duties of administration, and suggested only as a topic for exciting popular discontent against those who were responsible neither for the existing number of offices nor for the salaries paid to them. "Retrenchment," as a popular cry, was not a movement which the leading men of the opposition in the House of Representatives either needed or desired to initiate. Mr. McDuffie, the chairman of the Committee of Ways and Means, and a vehement opponent of the administration, objected to Mr. Chilton's resolutions at the outset. So did Mr. Buchanan; and the latter often said, in subsequent years, that they would have been crushed out of all consideration, if the friends of the administration had left them in the hands of its opponents. They were moved by an inconsiderable member, who was one of the stragglers of the opposition forces, and they were met by administration members who were about equally inconsiderable, in a tone of challenge and defiance. In vain did Mr. McDuffie and Mr. Buchanan contend that the present was no time to discuss the expenditures of the government. In vain did the most considerable and important friends of the administration deprecate an unprofitable, intolerant, and useless debate. The mover of the resolutions would not be silenced, and the few indiscreet supporters of the administration, who demanded that their discussion should go on, would not permit them to receive their proper quietus by the application of "the previous question." Never was a deliberative body drawn, in spite of the unwillingness of its best members on both sides, into a more unseemly and profitless discussion.

Among the friends of General Jackson who deprecated and endeavored to put a stop to this discussion was Mr. Edward Livingston of Louisiana, the oldest member of the House, and 72a person of great distinction. He made an earnest appeal to the House to end the whole matter by referring the resolutions to a committee without further debate. This was not acceded to by the friends of the administration, who wished to continue the discussion. Mr. Edward Everett, then a young member from Massachusetts, moved an adjournment after Mr. Livingston's effort to terminate the whole discussion, in order to make a speech, which he delivered on the 1st of February. Mr. Buchanan said in reply to him: "This debate would have ended on Thursday last, after the solemn appeal for that purpose, which was made to the House by the venerable gentleman from Louisiana, had not the gentleman from Massachusetts himself prevented it by moving an adjournment. That gentleman ought to know that he can never throw himself into any debate without giving it fresh vigor and importance."

In the course of this speech, Mr. Buchanan made some allusion to the alleged "bargain and corruption" by which Mr. Adams had been made President; and he thus touched upon the only important consideration that could be said to belong to the circumstances of that election:

"Before, however, I commence my reply to that gentleman, I beg leave to make a few observations on the last Presidential election. I shall purposely pass over every charge which has been made, that it was accomplished by bargain and sale or by actual corruption. If that were the case, I have no knowledge of the fact, and shall therefore say nothing about it. I shall argue this question as though no such charges had ever been made. So far as it regards the conduct which the people of the United States ought to pursue, at the approaching election, I agree entirely with the eloquent gentleman from Virginia [Mr. Randolph] (I cannot with propriety call him my friend), that it can make no difference whether a bargain existed or not. Nay, in some aspects in which the subject may be viewed, the danger to the people would be the greater, if no corruption had existed. It is true, that this circumstance ought greatly to influence our individual opinions of the men who now wield the destinies of the Republic; but yet the precedent would be at least equally dangerous in the one case as in the other. If flagrant and gross corruption had existed, every honest man would start from it with instinctive horror, and the people would indignantly hurl those men from the seats of power, who had thus betrayed their dearest interests. If the election were pure, there is, therefore, the greater danger in the precedent. I believe, in my soul, that the precedent which was established at the last Presidential election, ought 73to be reversed by the people, and this is one of my principal reasons for opposing the re-election of the present Chief Magistrate.

"Let us examine this subject more closely. General Jackson was returned by the people of this country to the House of Representatives, with a plurality of electoral votes. The distinguished individual who is now the Secretary of State, was then the Speaker of this House. It is perfectly well known, that, without his vote and influence, Mr. Adams could not have been elected President. After the election, we beheld that distinguished individual, and no man in the United States witnessed the spectacle with more regret than I did, descending—yes, Sir, I say descending—from the elevated station which you now occupy, into the cabinet of the President whom he had elected.

"'Quantum mutatus ab illo.'

"In the midnight of danger, during the darkest period of the late war, 'his thrilling trump had cheered the land.' Although among the great men of that day there was no acknowledged leader upon this floor, yet I have been informed, upon the best authority, that he was 'primus inter pares.' I did wish, at a future time, to see him elevated still higher. I am one of the last men in the country who could triumph over his fallen fortunes. Should he ever return to what I believe to be correct political principles, I shall willingly fight in the same ranks with him as a companion—nay, after a short probation, I should willingly acknowledge him as a leader. What brilliant prospects has that man not sacrificed!

"This precedent, should it be confirmed by the people at the next election, will be one of most dangerous character to the Republic. The election of President must, I fear, often devolve upon this House. We have but little reason to expect that any amendment, in relation to this subject, will be made to the Constitution in our day. There are so many conflicting interests to reconcile, so many powers to balance, that, when we consider the large majority in each branch of Congress, and the still larger majority of States, required to amend the Constitution, the prospect of any change is almost hopeless. I believe it will long remain just as it is. What an example, then, will this precedent, in the pure age of the

Republic, present to future times! The people owe it to themselves, if the election must devolve upon this House, never to sanction the principle that one of its members may accept, from the person whom he has elected, any high office, much less the highest in his gift. Such a principle, if once established, must, in the end, destroy the purity of this House, and convert it into a corrupt electoral vote. If the individual to whom I have alluded, could elect a President and receive from him the office of Secretary of State from the purest motives, other men may, and hereafter will, pursue the same policy from the most corrupt. 'If they do these things in the green tree, what shall be done in the dry?' "This precedent will become a cover under which future bargains and corrupt combinations will be sanctioned, under which the spirit of the Constitution will be sacrificed to its letter."

74It is not needful to describe the topics of this discussion. Mr. Chilton's resolutions, after being somewhat amended, were sent to a Select Committee on Retrenchment. The result was a majority and a minority report, of which six thousand copies were printed and circulated through the country. I turn from this subject to matters of more importance.

Mr. Buchanan's position in this Congress required him to exert his powers as a debater more than ever before. The House of Representatives was at this time a body in which real debate was carried on upon some subjects, however the discussion on "retrenchment" may be characterized. Its discussions on the tariff, commencing on the 4th of March and terminating on the 15th of May, were conducted with great ability. Among the best speeches on the tariff bill of this session, there is one by Mr. Peleg Sprague of Maine, and one by Mr. Buchanan. Both exhibit a great deal of research. Mr. Buchanan's speech, begun in Committee of the Whole on the 2d of April, in answer to Mr. Sprague, is an excellent specimen of business debate. The details on which these two gentlemen differed, and on which the debate between them and others chiefly turned, are of little interest now; nor does any tariff debate afford much development of permanent principles. So varying are the circumstances which from time to time give rise to an application of the doctrines that are indicated by the terms "free-trade" and "protection." Still there may be found in this tariff speech of Mr. Buchanan, matter which is of some interest in his personal history as an American statesman, because it shows that he had now risen to the rank of a statesman, and because it gives his general views of what had at this time become known as "the American System."

Mr. Buchanan, on this occasion, felt that he was combating a disposition to favor certain interests at the expense of others. In the debate on the tariff of 1824, when Mr. Clay developed his views on the subject of protection, and Mr. Webster found fault with the details of a measure which he said could not be properly characterized as an American System, Mr. Buchanan had shown that while he was ready to accede to a tariff for the incidental protection of our own manufactures, he was not disposed to carry the doctrines of protection so far as to injure the 75agricultural classes; but that in imposing the duties necessary to defray the expenses of the government, he should take care to benefit indirectly both the manufacturing and the producing interests. In 1828 the proposed alterations of the tariff aimed at a more uniform operation of the customs duties upon all the great interests of the country. A motion made by Mr. Sprague, to strike from the bill an additional duty of five cents per gallon on molasses, and twenty-five dollars per ton on hemp, led to a discussion on the navigating interests, as affected by such an amendment, and the whole subject of what was meant by protection and "the American system" came up afresh. The following extracts from Mr. Buchanan's speech afford fair specimens of his manner of dealing with this subject:

I shall cheerfully submit to the public judgment whether the bill, although I dislike the minimum principle which it contains, does not afford sufficient protection to the manufacturers of woolens. I think it does; but I wish to be distinctly understood, in relation to myself, that I always stand ready, in a fair spirit, to do everything in my power to promote the passage of a just and judicious tariff, which shall be adequate for their protection; and that, for the sake of conciliation, and to effect this purpose, I am willing to sacrifice individual opinion to a considerable extent.

What, Sir, is the American System? Is it the system advocated by the gentleman from Maine, which would build up one species of domestic industry at the expense of all the rest, which would establish a prohibition and consequent monopoly in favor of the woolen manufacturer whilst it denied all protection to the farmer? Certainly not. The American System consists in affording equal and just legislative protection to all the great interests of the country. It is no respecter of persons. It does not distinguish between the farmer who plows the soil in Pennsylvania and the manufacturer of wool in New England. Being impartial, it embraces all. There is, in one respect, a striking difference between the farmer, the merchant, and the manufacturer. The farmer eating the bread of toil, but of independence, scarcely ever complains. If he suffers, he suffers in silence; you rarely hear him, upon this floor, asking redress for his grievances. He relies with that confidence which belongs to his character upon the justice of his country, and does not come here with importunate demands. The case is different in regard to the manufacturer and the merchant. When they feel themselves aggrieved—when they require the aid of your legislation, then complaints ring throughout the country, from Georgia to Maine. They never cease to ask, until they obtain. And shall this contented and uncomplaining disposition of the great agricultural interest, be used as an argument upon this floor against affording it relief? I trust not.

76The gentleman from Maine has shown himself to be a true disciple of the Harrisburg Convention School. Even that convention, although the chief objects of their regard appeared to be wool and woolens, recommended further protection to iron, hemp, flax, and the articles manufactured from them, and to domestic distilled spirits. The gentleman from Maine has moved to strike from the bill additional duties which it proposes upon the importation of foreign hemp and molasses; and in his speech, he has argued against any additional duties either upon iron, or steel, or flax, or foreign spirits. In his opinion, therefore, the American System can embrace no other interest except that of the growers and manufacturers of wool.

[Here Mr. Sprague explained. He said his observations upon the other items, besides those he had moved to strike from the bill, were only intended to illustrate what would be their effect on the navigating interest.]

Mr. Buchanan resumed. I perceive, from the gentleman's explanation, I did not misunderstand his argument. If this be the American System, I should like to know it as soon as possible; for then I shall be opposed to it. I venture to assert that, if those with whom the gentleman from Maine usually acts upon this floor have embraced the opinions which he has avowed, it is a vain, a culpable waste of time to proceed further with this discussion. Let the bill at once go to the tomb of all the Capulets. If the New England manufacturer must be protected, whilst the Pennsylvania farmer is abandoned—if this be the American System, instead of being a mourner at its funeral, I shall rejoice that it has met the fate which it deserved, and has been consigned to an early grave.

The Legislature of Pennsylvania has given us what, in my opinion, is the correct version of the American System. They have declared that "the best interests of our country demand that every possible exertion should be made to procure the passage of an act of

Congress imposing such duties as will enable our manufacturers to enter into fair competition with foreign manufacturers, and protect the farmer, the growers of hemp and wool, and the distiller of spirits from domestic materials, against foreign competition. The people of Pennsylvania do not ask for such a tariff as would secure to any one class, or to any section of the country, a monopoly. They want a system of protection which will extend its blessings, as well as its burdens, as equally as possible over every part of the Union; to be uniform in its operation upon the rich as well as the poor." They have therefore instructed their Senators, and requested their Representatives, "to procure, if practicable, the establishment of such a tariff as will afford additional protection to our domestic manufactures, especially of woolen and fine cotton goods, glass, and such other articles as, in their opinion, require the attention of Congress, so as to enable our citizens fairly to compete with foreign enterprise, capital, and experience, and give encouragement to the citizens of the grain-growing States, by laying an additional duty upon the importation of foreign spirits, flax, china ware, hemp, wool, and bar iron."

77This resolution speaks a language which I am proud to hear from the Legislature of my native State.

If it be the disposition of a majority of the members of this committee to strike out of the bill iron, hemp, foreign spirits and molasses, no Representative from the State of Pennsylvania, who regards either the interest or the wishes of his constituents, will dare to vote for what would then remain. The time has forever past when such a measure could have received our sanction. We shall have no more exclusive tariffs for the benefit of any one portion of the Union. The tariff of 1824 partook much of this character; it contained no additional duty on foreign spirits or molasses, and only added five dollars per ton to the duty on foreign hemp. So far as the grain-growing States expected to derive peculiar benefits from that measure, they have been, in a great degree, disappointed.

What was the course which gentlemen pursued in relation to the woolen bill of the last session? I endeavored to introduce into it a small protection for our hemp and domestic spirits. We were then told that my attempt would endanger the fate of the bill; that the period of the session was too late to introduce amendments; and that if we would then extend protection to the manufacturers of wool, a similar protection should, at a future time, be extended to the agricultural interest of the grain-growing States. My respectable colleague [Mr. Forward] has informed the committee that he voted for the bill of the last session under that delusion. How sadly the picture is now reversed! When an interest in New England, which has been estimated at 40,000,000 of dollars, is at stake, and is now about to sink, as has been alleged, for want of adequate protection, it seems that gentlemen from that portion of the Union would rather consign it to inevitable destruction than yield the protection which the present bill will afford to the productions of the Middle and Western States. If they are prepared to act upon a policy so selfish, let them at once declare it, and not waste weeks upon a bill which can never become a law. The gentleman from Maine endeavored to sustain his motives by attempting to prove that, if the duties proposed by the bill should be imposed upon hemp and molasses, it would injure, nay, probably destroy the navigation of the country. Indeed he pronounced its epitaph. It is gone! Five cents per gallon upon molasses, and twenty-five dollars per ton upon hemp will sink our navigating interest; will sweep our vessels from the ocean! When I compare the storm of eloquence and of argument which the gentleman has employed to strike out hemp and molasses from this bill, with the object to be attained, he reminded me—

"Of ocean into tempest tost
To waft a feather or to drown a fly."

An additional duty of five cents per gallon on molasses and twenty-five dollars per ton upon hemp will consign the navigation of the country to inevitable and almost immediate destruction! This is the kind of argument which the gentleman has thought proper to address to the committee.

The gentleman from Maine has said that our navigation goes abroad unprotected to struggle against the world; and he has expatiated at length upon this part of the subject. I trust I shall be able to prove, without fatiguing the committee, that no interest belonging to this or any other country ever received a more continued or a more efficient protection than the navigation of the United States. I heartily approve this policy. I would not, if I could, withdraw from it an atom of the protection which it now enjoys. I shall never attempt to array the great and leading interests of the country against each other. I am neither the exclusive advocate of commerce, of manufactures, or of agriculture. The American System embraces them all. I am the advocate of all. When, therefore, I attempt to show to the committee the protection which has been extended by this government to its navigation, I do it in reply to the argument of the gentleman from Maine, and not in a spirit of hostility to that important interest.

Mr. Buchanan then entered upon an elaborate historical examination of the care for the interests of our navigation that had been exerted by Congress from 1789 to the time when he was speaking.[23] On the subject of the navy, as likely to be affected by measures that were complained of for a tendency to depress the commercial marine, he said:

"The gentleman from Maine has used a most astonishing argument against any further protection to hemp and flax and iron. We ought not further to encourage our farmers to grow flax and hemp, nor our manufacturers to produce iron. And why? Because you will thus deprive the navigating interest of the freight which they earn, by carrying these articles from Russia to this country. Can the gentleman be serious in contending that, for the sake of affording freight to the ship-owners, we ought to depend upon a foreign country for a supply of these articles? This argument strikes at the root of the whole American System. Upon the same principle we ought not to manufacture any article whatever at home, because this will deprive our ships of the carriage of it from abroad. This principle, had it been adopted in practice, would have left us where we were at the close of the American Revolution. We should still have been dependent upon foreign nations for articles of the first necessity. This argument amounts to a proclamation of war, by our navigation, against the agriculture and manufactures of the country. You must not produce, because we will then lose the carriage, is the sum and substance of the argument. Am I then to be seriously told, that for the purpose of encouraging our ship-owners, our farmers ought to be deprived of the markets of their own country, for those agricultural productions which they can supply in abundance? I did not expect to have heard such an argument upon this floor.

"By encouraging domestic industry, whether it be applied to agriculture or manufactures, you promote the best interests of your navigation. You furnish it with domestic exports to scatter over the world. This is the true American System. It protects all interests; it abandons none. It never arrays one against another. Upon the principles of the gentleman, we ought to sacrifice all the other interests of the country to promote our navigation. This is asking too much.

"The gentleman from Maine seems to apprehend great danger to the navy from the passage of this bill. He appears to think it will fall with so much oppression upon our navigation and fisheries, that these nurseries of seamen for the navy may be greatly injured, if not altogether destroyed.

"In regard to the value and importance of a navy to this country, I cordially agree with the gentleman from Maine. Every prejudice of my youth was enlisted in its favor, and the judgment of riper years has strengthened and confirmed those early impressions. It is the surest bond of our Union. The Western States have a right to demand from this government that the mouth of the Mississippi shall be kept open, both in war and in peace. If you should not afford them a free passage to the ocean, you cannot expect to retain them in the Union; they are, therefore, as much, if not more, interested in cherishing the navy than any other portion of the Republic. The feeling in its favor contains in it nothing sectional—it is general. We are all interested in its preservation and extension. Unlike standing armies, a navy never did, nor ever will, destroy the liberties of any country. It is our most efficient and least dangerous arm of defence.

"To what, then, does the argument of the gentleman lead? Although iron, and hemp, and flax, and their manufactures, are essential to the very existence of a navy, yet he would make us dependent for them upon the will of the Emperor of Russia, or the King of Sweden. A statesman would as soon think of being dependent on a foreign nation for gunpowder, or cannon, or cannon-balls, or muskets, as he would for the supply of iron, or flax, or hemp, for our navy. Even if these articles could not be produced as cheaply in this as in other countries, upon great national principles, then domestic production ought to be encouraged, even if it did tax the community. They are absolutely necessary for our defence. Without them, what would become of you, if engaged in war with a great naval power? You would then be as helpless as if you were deprived of gunpowder or of cannon. Without them, your navy would be perfectly useless. Shall we, then, in a country calculated by nature above all others for their production, refuse to lend them a helping hand? I trust not.

"The gentleman from Maine has said much about our fisheries, and the injurious effects which the present bill will have upon them. From this argument, 80I was induced again to read the bill, supposing that it might possibly contain some latent provision, hostile to the fisheries, which I had not been able to detect. Indeed, one might have supposed, judging merely from the remarks of the gentleman, without a reference to the bill, that it aimed a deadly blow against this valuable branch of our national industry. I could find nothing in it, which even touched the fisheries. They have ever been special favorites of our legislation. I shall not pretend to enumerate, because the task might seem invidious, the different acts of Congress affording them protection. They are numerous. The gentleman has, in my opinion, been very unfortunate in his complaints that they have not been sufficiently protected. From the origin of this government, they have been cherished, in every possible manner, by our legislation. For their benefit we have adopted a system of prohibitions, of drawbacks, and of bounties, unknown to our laws in relation to any other subject. They have grown into national importance, and have become a great interest of the country. They should continue to be cherished, because they are the best nurseries of our seamen. I would not withdraw from them an atom of the protection which they have received; on the contrary, I should cheerfully vote them new bounties, if new bounties were necessary to sustain them. They are the very last interest in the country which ought to complain.

"The gentleman, whilst he strenuously opposed any additional protection to domestic iron, and domestic hemp, surely could not have remembered, that the productions of the fisheries enjoy a monopoly of the home market. The duties in their favor are so high as to exclude foreign competition. We do not ask such prohibitory duties upon foreign iron, flax, or hemp. We demand but a moderate increase; and yet the fisheries, which are protected by prohibitory duties, meet us and deny to us this reasonable request."

That Mr. Buchanan's opposition to the administration of Mr. John Quincy Adams was not carried on in the spirit of a partisan is evinced by his action on an appropriation asked for to enable the Executive to continue and complete a system of surveys, preparatory to a general plan of internal improvements. There was much opposition to this appropriation, especially on the part of those who denied the power of the General Government to make such public works as were then classed as "internal improvements." Mr. Buchanan met their objections as follows:

Mr. Buchanan expressed his dissent from the opinions avowed by the two gentlemen who had preceded him. The true question ought to be distinctly stated. The act of 1824 sanctioned the policy, not of immediately entering upon a plan of internal improvement, but of preparing for it, by 81obtaining surveys, plans, and estimates in relation to the various roads and canals that were required throughout the country. The sum of $30,000 had been appropriated, not for a single year, but for a specific purpose, which purpose had not yet been accomplished. Many surveys were now in progress, which were not more than half completed, and the question was whether the House would withdraw the means of completing them. A discussion of the general policy of the plan was out of place on an appropriation bill. Whatever might be decided as to carrying such a system of internal improvement into effect, these surveys were of great advantage to the American people. Should that system never be adopted, this mass of information could not fail to be useful. The constitutional question of power did not fairly arise on a proposal to employ the engineers already at the disposal of the War Department, in a particular manner.

Should the time ever arrive when we have more in the Treasury than we know what to do with, the argument of the gentleman from Virginia [Mr. Barbour] might have some force. But the question now was, whether the House would arrest these surveys? Mr. B., for one, would not do it. He would give the administration the sum now asked, and would hold them responsible for its application.

There is no more interesting part of Mr. Buchanan's early Congressional career than his course on the subject of the Cumberland Road. We have seen that when he first had occasion to act on this subject as a member of Congress, he was inclined to accept the doctrine that Congress had power to establish this road, and to levy tolls for its support. But he had not then closely examined this subject. Mr. Monroe's message vetoing the Cumberland Road bill of 1822 produced in Mr. Buchanan's mind a decided change. At a subsequent session, he endeavored, but without success, to have the road retroceded to the States through which it passed, on condition that they would support it by levying tolls.[24] In 1828–29 he renewed this effort, and on the 29th of January, 1829, he made an elaborate speech upon the whole subject, which is of sufficient interest and importance to warrant its reproduction entire. As a constitutional argument it is valuable; and for its independent attitude towards the people of his own State, it is exceedingly creditable to him as a public man.

82Mr. Buchanan said that the bill and the amendment now before the committee presented a subject for discussion of the deepest interest to the American people. It is not a question (said Mr. B.) whether we shall keep the road in repair by appropriations; nor whether we shall expend other millions in constructing other Cumberland roads—these would be comparatively unimportant; but it is a question upon the determination of which, in my humble judgment, depend the continued existence of the Federal Constitution in anything like its native purity. Let it once be established that the Federal Government can enter the dominion of the States; interfere with their domestic concerns; erect toll-gates over all the military, commercial, and post-roads within their territories,

56

and define and punish, by laws of Congress, in the courts of the United States, offences committed upon these roads,—and the barriers which were erected by our ancestors with so much care, between Federal and State power, are entirely prostrated. This single act would, in itself, be a longer stride towards consolidation than the Federal Government have ever made; and it would be a precedent for establishing a construction for the Federal Constitution so vague and so indefinite, that it might be made to mean anything or nothing.

It is not my purpose, upon the present occasion, again to agitate the questions which have so often been discussed in this House, as to the powers of Congress in regard to internal improvements. For my own part, I cheerfully accord to the Federal Government the power of subscribing stock, in companies incorporated by the State, for the purpose of making roads and canals; and I entertain no doubt whatever but that we can, under the Constitution, appropriate the money of our constituents directly to the construction of internal improvements, with the consent of the States through which they may pass. These powers I shall ever be willing to exercise, upon all proper occasions. But I shall never be driven to support any road, or any canal, which my judgment disapproves, by a fear of the senseless clamor which is always attempted to be raised against members upon this floor, as enemies to internal improvement, who dare to vote against any measure which the Committee on Roads and Canals think proper to bring before this House. It was my intention to discuss the power of Congress to pass the bill, and its policy, separately. Upon reflection I find these subjects are so intimately blended, they cannot be separated. I shall therefore consider them together.

"Before, however, I enter upon the subject, it will be necessary to present a short historical sketch of the Cumberland Road. It owes its origin to a compact between the State of Ohio and the United States. In 1802, Congress proposed to the convention which formed the constitution of Ohio, that they would grant to that State one section of land to each township, for the use of schools; that they would also grant to it several tracts of land on which there were salt springs; and that five per cent. of the net proceeds of the future sale of public lands within its territory should be applied to the purpose of making public roads, 'leading from the navigable waters emptying into the Atlantic to the Ohio, to the said State, and through the same.' The 83act, however, distinctly declares that such roads shall be laid out under the authority of Congress, 'with the consent of the several States through which the road shall pass.' These terms were offered by Congress, to the State of Ohio, provided she would exempt, by an irrevocable ordinance, all the land which should be sold by the United States within her territory, from every species of taxation, for the space of five years, after the day of sale. This proposition of Congress was accepted by the State of Ohio, and it thus became a compact, the terms of which could not be changed without the consent of both the contracting parties. By the terms of the compact, this five per cent. of the net proceeds of the sales of the public land was applicable to two objects; the first, the construction of roads leading from the Atlantic to the State of Ohio; and the second, the construction of roads within that State. In 1803, Congress, at the request of Ohio, apportioned this fund between these two objects. Three of the five per cent. was appropriated to the construction of roads within the State, leaving only two per cent. applicable to roads leading from the navigable waters of the Atlantic to it.

"In March, 1806, Congress determined to apply this two per cent. fund to the object for which it was destined, and passed 'an act to regulate the laying out and making of a road from Cumberland, in the State of Maryland, to the State of Ohio.' Under the provisions of this act, before the President could proceed to cut a single tree upon the route of the road, it was made necessary to obtain the consent of the States through which it passed. The Federal Government asked Maryland, Pennsylvania and Virginia for permission to make it, and each of them granted this privilege in the same manner that they would have done to a private individual, or to a corporation created by their own laws. Congress, at that day, asserted no other right than a mere power to appropriate the money of their constituents to the construction of this road, after the consent of these States should be obtained. The idea of a sovereign power in this government to make the road, and to exercise jurisdiction over it, for the purpose of keeping it in repair, does not, then, appear to have ever entered the imagination of the warmest advocate for Federal power. The federalism of that day would have shrunk with horror from such a spectre. There is a circumstance worthy of remark in the act of the Legislature of Pennsylvania, which was passed in April, 1807, authorizing the President of the United States to open this road. It grants this power upon condition that the road should pass through Uniontown and Washington, if practicable. The grant was accepted upon this condition, and the road was constructed. Its length is one hundred and thirty miles, and its construction and repairs have cost the United States one million seven hundred and sixty-six thousand one hundred and sixty-six dollars and thirty-eight cents; whilst the two per cent. fund which we had bound ourselves to apply to this purpose, amounted, on the 30th of June, 1822, the date of the last official statement within my knowledge, only to the sum of one hundred and eighty-seven thousand seven hundred and eighty-six dollars and thirty-one cents, less than one-ninth of the cost of the road. This road has cost the 84United States more than thirteen thousand five hundred dollars per mile. This extravagant expenditure shows conclusively that it is much more politic for us to enlist individual interest in the cause of Internal Improvement, by subscribing stock, than to become ourselves sole proprietors. Any government, unless under extraordinary circumstances, will pay one-third more for constructing a road or canal, than would be expended by individuals in accomplishing the same object.

"I shall now proceed to the argument. Upon a review of this brief history, what is the conclusion at which we must arrive? That this road was made by the United States, as a mere proprietor, to carry into effect a contract with the State of Ohio, and not as a sovereign. In its construction, the Federal Government proceeded as any corporation or private individual would have done. We asked the States for permission to make the road through the territories over which their sovereign authority extended. After that permission had been obtained, we appropriated the money and constructed the road. The State of Pennsylvania even annexed a condition to her grant, with which the United States complied. She also conferred upon the agents of the United States the power of taking materials for the construction and repair of this road, without the consent of the owner, making a just compensation therefor. This compensation was to be ascertained under the laws of the State, and not under those of the United States. The mode of proceeding to assess damages in such cases against the United States was precisely the same as it is against corporations, created by her own laws, for the purpose of constructing roads.

"What, then, does this precedent establish? Simply, that the United States may appropriate money for the construction of a road through the territories of a State, with its consent; and I do not entertain the least doubt but that we possess this power. What does the present bill propose? To change the character which the United States has hitherto sustained, in relation to this road, from that of a simple proprietor to a sovereign. To declare to the nation, that, although they had to ask the States of Maryland, Pennsylvania and Virginia, for permission to make the road, now, after it is completed, they will exercise jurisdiction over it, and collect tolls upon it, under the authority of their own laws, for the purpose of keeping it in repair. We will not ask the States to erect toll-gates for us. We are determined to exercise that power ourselves. The Federal Government first introduced itself into the States as a friend, by permission; it now wishes to hold possession as a sovereign, by power. This road was made in the manner that one independent sovereign would construct a road through the territories of another. Had Virginia been a party to the compact with Ohio, instead of the United States, she would have asked the permission of Maryland and Pennsylvania to construct the Cumberland Road through their territories, and it would have been granted. But what would have been our astonishment, after this permission, had Virginia attempted to assume jurisdiction over the road in Pennsylvania, to erect toll-gates upon it under the authority of her own laws, and 85to punish offenders against these laws in her own courts. Yet the two cases are nearly parallel.

The right to demand toll, and to stop and punish passengers for refusing to pay it, is emphatically a sovereign right, and has ever been so considered amongst civilized nations. The power to erect toll-gates necessarily implies, 1st, The stoppage of the passenger until he shall pay the toll; 2d, His trial and punishment, if he should, either by force or by fraud, evade, or attempt to evade, its payment; 3d, A discretionary power as to the amount of toll; 4th, The trial and punishment of persons who may wilfully injure the road, or violate the police established upon it. These powers are necessarily implied. Without the exercise of them, you could not proceed with safety to collect the toll for a single day. Other powers will soon be exercised. If you compel passengers to pay toll, the power of protecting them whilst travelling along your road is almost a necessary incident. The sovereign, who receives the toll, ought naturally to possess the power of protecting him who pays it. To vest the power of demanding toll in one sovereign, and the protection of the traveller's person in another, would be almost an absurdity. The Federal Government would probably, ere long, exercise the power of trying and punishing murders and robberies, and all other offences committed upon the road. To what jurisdiction would the trial and punishment of these offences necessarily belong? To the courts of the United States, and to them alone. In Ohio, in New York, in Virginia, and in Maryland, it has been determined that State courts, even if Congress should confer it, have no jurisdiction over any penal action, or criminal offence, against the laws of the United States. Even if these decisions were incorrect, still it has never been seriously contended that State courts were bound to take jurisdiction in such cases. It must be admitted, by all, that Congress have not the power to compel an execution of their criminal or penal laws by the courts of the States. This is sufficient for my argument. Even if the power existed, in State courts, they never ought, unless upon extraordinary occasions, to try and to punish offences committed against the United States. The peace and the harmony of the people of this country require that the powers of the two governments should never be blended. The dividing line between their separate jurisdictions should be clearly marked; otherwise dangerous collisions between them must be the inevitable consequence. In two of the States through which this road passes, it has already been determined that their courts cannot take jurisdiction over offences committed against the laws of Congress. What, then, is the inevitable consequence? All the penal enactments of this bill, or of the future bills which it will become necessary to pass to supply its defects, must be carried into execution by the Federal courts. Any citizen of the United States, charged with the most trifling offence against the police of this road, must be dragged for trial to the Federal court of that State within whose jurisdiction it is alleged to have been committed. If committed in Maryland, the trial must take place in Baltimore; if in Pennsylvania, at Clarksburg.

The distance of one hundred or two hundred miles, which he would be compelled to travel to take his trial, and the expenses which he must necessarily incur, would, in themselves, be a severe punishment for a more aggravated offence. Besides, the people of the neighborhood would be harassed in attending as witnesses at such a great distance from their places of abode. These, and many other inconveniences, which I shall not enumerate, would soon compel Congress to authorize the appointment of justices of the peace, or some other inferior tribunals, along the whole extent of the Cumberland Road. Can any man lay his hand upon his heart and say that, in his conscience, he believes the Federal Constitution ever intended to bestow such powers on Congress? The great divisions of power, distinctly marked in that instrument, are external and internal. The first are conferred upon the General Government—the last, with but few exceptions, and those distinctly defined, remain in possession of the States. It never—never was intended that the vast and mighty machinery of this Government should be introduced into the domestic, the local, the interior concerns of the States, or that it should spend its power in collecting toll at a turnpike gate. I have not been presenting possible cases to the committee. I have confined myself to what must be the necessary effects of the passage of the bill now before us. By what authority is such a tremendous power claimed? That it is not expressly given by the Constitution, is certain. If it exists at all, it must, therefore, be incidental to some express power; and in the language of the Constitution, "be necessary and proper for carrying that power into execution." From the very nature of incidental power, it cannot transcend the specific power which calls it into existence. The stream cannot flow higher than its fountain. This principle applies, with peculiar force, to the construction of the Constitution. For the purpose of carrying into effect any of its specific powers, it would be absurd to contend that you might exercise another power, greater and more dangerous than that expressly given. The means must be subordinate to the end. Were any other construction to prevail, this Government would no longer be one of limited powers.

The present case affords a striking and forcible illustration of this principle. Let it be granted that you have a right, as proprietor, by the permission of the States, to make a road through their territories, can it ever follow, as an incident to this mere power of appropriating the public money, that you may exercise jurisdiction over this very road, as a sovereign? If you could, the incident is as much greater than the principal, as sovereign is superior to individual power. It does follow that you can keep the road in repair, by appropriations, in the same manner that you have made it; but this is the utmost limit of your power. What, Sir? Exclusive jurisdiction over the road, for its preservation, and for the punishment of all offenders who travel upon it, and that as an incident to the mere power of expending your money upon its construction! The idea is absurd.

Under the power given to Congress "to establish post offices and post roads," the Federal Government possess the undoubted right of converting any road already constructed, within any State of this Union, into a post road.

Let it also be granted, for the sake of the argument, that they possess the power, independently of the will of the States, to construct as many post roads throughout the Union as they think proper, and to keep them in repair; does it follow that they can establish toll-gates upon such roads? Certainly not. What is the nature of the powder conferred upon Congress? It is a mere right to carry and to protect the mails. It is confined to a single purpose—to the transportation of the mail, and the punishment of offences which violate that right. This is the sole object of the power—the sole purpose for which it was called into existence. Over some post roads, the mail is carried once per day, and over others once per week. With what justice can it be contended that this right of passage for a single purpose—this occasional use of the roads within the different States for post roads—vests in Congress the power of closing up these roads against all the citizens of those States, at all times, until they have paid such a toll as we think proper to impose. Let me present the naked argument of gentlemen before their own eyes. Congress have the right, under the Constitution, "to establish post offices and post roads." As an incident they possess the power of constructing post roads. As another incident to this right of passage for a single purpose they possess the power to assume jurisdiction over all post roads in the different States, and prevent any person from passing over them, unless upon such terms as they may prescribe. This would, indeed, be construction construed. I would like the gentleman from Virginia (Mr. Mercer) to furnish the committee with an answer to this argument. If I were to grant to that gentleman a right of passage, for a particular purpose only, over a road which belonged to me, what would be my surprise and my indignation, were he to shut it up, by the erection of toll-gates, and prohibited me from passing unless I paid him toll.

Should Congress act upon the precedent which the passage of this bill would establish, it is impossible to foresee the dangers which must follow, to the States and to the people of this country. Upon this branch of the question, permit me to quote the language of Mr. Monroe, in his celebrated message of May, 1822, denying the constitutional power of Congress to erect toll-gates on the Cumberland Road. "If," said he, "the United States possessed the power contended for under this grant, might they not, on adopting the roads of the individual States for the carriage of the mail, as has been done, assume jurisdiction over them, and preclude a right to interfere with, or alter them? Might they not establish turnpikes, and exercise all the other acts of sovereignty above stated, over such roads, necessary to protect them from injury, and defray the expense of repairing them? Surely, if the right exists, these consequences necessarily followed, as soon as the road was established. The absurdity of such a pretension must be apparent to all who examine it. In this way, a large portion of the territory of every State might be taken from it; for there is scarcely a road in any State which will not be used for the transportation of the mail. A new field for legislation and internal government would thus be opened." Arguments of the same nature would apply with equal, if not greater force, to those roads which might be used by the United States for the transportation of military stores, or as the medium of commerce between the different States. I shall not now enlarge upon this branch of the subject, believing it, as I do, to be wholly unnecessary. There is another view of this subject, which I deem to be conclusive. The Constitution of the United States provides that "Congress shall have power to exercise exclusive legislation, in all cases whatsoever, over such district (not exceeding ten miles square) as may, by cession of particular States, and the acceptance of Congress, become the seat of the Government of the United States, and to exercise the like authority over all places purchased by the consent of the Legislature of the State in which the same shall be, for the erection of forts, magazines, arsenals, dockyards and other needful buildings." This is the only clause in the Constitution which authorizes the Federal Government to acquire jurisdiction over any portion of the territory of the States; and this power is expressly confined to such forts, magazines, arsenals, dockyards, and other needful buildings, as the States may consider necessary for the defence of the country. You will thus, Sir, perceive with what jealousy our ancestors conferred jurisdiction upon this Government—even over such places as were absolutely necessary for the exercise of the power of war. This power,—which is the power of self-defence—of self-preservation—the power given to this Government of wielding the whole physical force of the country for the preservation of its existence and its liberties—does not confer any implied jurisdiction over the smallest portion of territory. An express authority is given to acquire jurisdiction, for military and for naval purposes, and for them alone, with the consent of the States. Unless that consent has been first obtained, the vast power of war confers no incidental jurisdiction, even over the cannon in your national fortifications. How, then, can it be contended, with the least hope of success, that the same Constitution, which thus expressly limits our power of acquiring jurisdiction, to particular spots, necessary for the purpose of national defence, should, by implication, as an incident to the power to establish post offices and post roads, authorize us to assume jurisdiction over a road one hundred and thirty miles in length, and over all the other post roads in the country. If this construction be correct, all the limitations upon Federal power, contained in the Constitution, are idle and vain. There is no power which this Government shall ever wish to usurp, which cannot, by ingenuity, be found lurking in some of the express powers granted by the Constitution. In my humble judgment, the argument in favor of the constructive power to pass the sedition law is much more plausible than any that can be urged by the advocates of this bill, in favor of its passage. I beg gentlemen to reflect, before they vote in its favor.

I thank the gentleman from Ohio (Mr. Vance) for having reminded me of the resolution passed by the Legislature of Pennsylvania, at their last session, 89which authorizes the Federal Government to erect toll-gates upon this road, within that Commonwealth; to "enforce the collection of tolls, and, generally, to do and perform any and every other act and thing which may be deemed necessary, to ensure the permanent repair and preservation of the said road."

I feel the most unfeigned respect for the Legislature of my native State. Their deliberate opinion, upon any subject, will always have a powerful influence over my judgment. It is fairly entitled to as much consideration as the opinion of this or any other legislative body in the Union. This resolution, however, was adopted, as I have been informed, without much deliberation and without debate. It owes its passage to the anxious desire which that body feel to preserve the Cumberland Road from ruin. The constitutional question was not brought into discussion. Had it been fairly submitted to that Republican Legislature, I most solemnly believe they would have been the last in this Union to sanction the assumption, by this Government, of a jurisdiction so ultra-Federal in its nature, and so well calculated to destroy the rights of the States.

But this resolution can have no influence upon the present discussion. The people of the State of Pennsylvania never conferred upon their Legislature the power to cede jurisdiction over any portion of their territory to the United States, or to any other sovereign. If the Legislatures of the different States could exercise such a power, the road to consolidation would be direct. If they can cede jurisdiction to this Government over any portion of their territories, they can cede the whole, and thus altogether destroy the Federal system.

Even if the States possessed the power to cede, the United States have no power to accept such cessions. Their authority to accept cessions of jurisdiction is confined to places "for the erection of forts, magazines, arsenals, dockyards and other needful buildings." Mr. Monroe, in the message to which I have already referred, declares his opinion "that Congress do not possess this power; that the States, individually, cannot grant it; for, although they may assent to the appropriation of money, within their limits, for such purposes, they can grant no power of jurisdiction, or sovereignty, by special compacts with the United States."

I think it is thus rendered abundantly clear that, if Congress do not possess the power, under the Federal Constitution, to pass this bill, the States through which the road passes cannot confer it upon them. I feel convinced that even the gentleman who reported this bill (Mr. Mercer) will not contend that the resolution of the Legislature of Pennsylvania could bestow any jurisdiction upon the Government. I am justified in this reference, because that resolution is, in its nature, conditional, and requires that the amount of tolls collected in Pennsylvania shall be applied, exclusively, to the repair of the road within that State; and the present bill contains no provision to carry this condition into effect. The gentleman cannot, therefore, derive his authority to pass this bill from a grant the provisions of which he has disregarded.

This question has already been settled, so far as a solemn legislative precedent can settle any question. During the session of 1821–2, a bill, similar in its provisions to the one now before the committee, passed both Houses of Congress. The vote, on its passage in this House, was eighty-seven in the affirmative, and sixty-eight in the negative. Mr. Monroe, then President of the United States, returned this bill to the House of Representatives, with his objections. So powerful, and so convincing, were his arguments, that, upon its reconsideration, but sixty-eight members voted in the affirmative, whilst seventy-two voted in the negative. Thus, Sir, you perceive, that this House have already solemnly declared, in accordance with the deliberate opinion of the late President of the United States, that Congress do not possess the power to erect toll-gates upon the Cumberland Road. That distinguished individual was the last of the race of Revolutionary Presidents, and, from the soundness of his judgment and the elevated stations which he has occupied, his opinion is entitled to the utmost respect. He was an actor in many of the political scenes of that day when the Constitution was framed, and when it went into operation, under the auspices of Washington—"all which he saw, and part of which he was." He is, therefore, one of the few surviving statesmen who, from actual knowledge, can inform the present generation what were the opinions of the past. The solemnity and the ability with which he has resisted the exercise of the power of Congress to pass this bill prove, conclusively, the great importance which he attached to the subject.

During that session, I first had the honor of a seat in this House; I voted for the passage of that bill. I had not reflected upon the constitutional question, and I was an advocate of the policy of keeping the road in repair by collecting tolls from those who travelled upon it. After I read the constitutional objections of Mr. Monroe my opinion was changed, and I have ever since been endeavoring, upon all proper occasions, to atone for my vote, by advocating a cession of the road to the respective States through which it passes, that they may erect toll-gates upon it and keep it in repair.

There was a time in the history of this country—I refer to the days of the first President of the United States—when the Government was feeble, and when, in addition to its own powers, the weight of his personal character was necessary fairly to put it in motion. Jealousy of Federal power was then the order of the day. The gulf of consolidation then yawned before the imagination of many of our wisest and best patriots, ready to swallow up the rights of the States and the liberties of the people. In those days, this vast machine had scarcely got into regular motion. Its power and its patronage were then in their infancy, and there was, perhaps, more danger that the jealousy of the States should destroy efficiency of the Federal Government than that it should crush their power. Times have changed. The days of its feebleness and of childhood have passed away. It is now a giant—a Briareus—stretching forth its hundred arms, dispensing its patronage, and increasing its power over every portion of the Union. What patronage and what power have the States to oppose to this increasing influence? Glance your eye over the extent of the Union; compare State offices with those of the United States; and whether avarice or ambition be consulted, those which belong to the General Government are greatly to be preferred to the offices which the States can bestow. Jealousy of Federal power—not of a narrow and mean character, but a watchful and uncompromising jealousy—is now the dictate of the soundest patriotism. The General Government possesses the exclusive right to impose duties upon imports—by far the most productive and the most popular source of revenue. United and powerful efforts are now making to destroy the revenue which the States derive from sales at auction. This Government is now asked to interpose its power between the buyer and seller, and put down public sales of merchandise within the different States—a subject heretofore believed to be within the exclusive jurisdiction of the State sovereignties. Whilst the Federal Government has been advancing with rapid strides, the people of the States have seldom been awakened to a sense of their danger. In the late political struggle, they were aroused, and they nobly maintained their own rights. This, I trust, will always be the case hereafter. Thank Heaven! whilst the people continue true to themselves, the Constitution contains within itself those principles which must ever preserve it. From its very nature—from a difference of opinion as to the constructive powers which may be necessary and proper to carry those which are enumerated into effect—it must ever call into existence two parties, the one jealous of Federal, the other of State power; the one anxious to extend Federal influence, the other wedded to State rights; the one desirous to limit, the other to extend, the power and the patronage of the General Government. In the intermediate space there will be much debatable ground; but a general outline will still remain sufficiently distinct to mark the division between the political parties which have divided, and which will probably continue to divide, the people of this country. Jealousy of Federal power had long been slumbering. The voice of Virginia sounding the alarm has at length awakened several of her sister States; and, although they believe her to be too strict in her construction of the Constitution and her doctrines concerning State rights, yet, they are now willing to do justice to the steadiness and patriotism of her political character. She has kept alive a wholesome jealousy of Federal power. If, then, there be a party in this country friendly to the rights of the States and of the people, I call upon them to oppose the passage of this bill. Should it become a law, it will establish a precedent under the authority of which the sovereign power of this Government can be brought home into the domestic concerns of every State in the Union. We may then take under our own jurisdiction every road over which the mail is carried; every road over which our soldiers and warlike munitions may pass; and every road used for the purpose of carrying on commerce between the several States. Once establish this strained construction of the Federal Constitution, and I would ask gentlemen to point out the limit where this splendid government shall be compelled to stay its chariot wheels. Might it not then drive on to consolidation, under the sanction of the Constitution?

92Is there any necessity for venturing upon this dangerous and doubtful measure? I appeal to those gentlemen who suppose the power to be clear, what motive they can have for forcing this measure upon us, who are of a different opinion? Can it make any difference to them whether those toll-gates shall be erected under a law of the United States, or under State authority? Cannot the Legislature of Pennsylvania enact this bill into a law as well as the Congress of the United States? Nobody will doubt their right. I trust no gentleman upon this floor will question the fidelity of that State in complying with all her engagements. She has ever been true to every trust. If she should accept of the cession, as I have no doubt she would, I will pledge myself that you shall never again hear of the road, unless it be that she has kept it in good repair, and that under her care it has answered every purpose for which it was intended.

I know that some popular feeling has been excited against myself in that portion of Pennsylvania though which the road passes. I have been represented as one of its greatest enemies. I now take occasion thus publicly to deny this allegation. It is true that I cannot vote in favor of the passage of this bill, and thus, in my judgment, violate the oath which I have taken to support the Constitution of the United States. No man can expect this from me. But it is equally true that I have heretofore supported appropriations for the repair of this road; and should my amendment prevail, I shall vote in favor of the appropriation of one hundred thousand dollars for that purpose which is contained in this bill.

At a late period in the second session of this Congress, February 6, 1829, a resolution was introduced by Mr. Smyth of Virginia, proposing to amend the Constitution so as to make every President ineligible to the office a second time. Whether this was aimed at General Jackson, who had been elected President in the autumn of 1828, and was to be inaugurated in about thirty days, or whether it had no special object, it was generally regarded as a subject for the discussion of which the remaining time of this Congress was entirely insufficient. Upon a motion to postpone the resolution to the 3d of March, Mr. Buchanan said:

He should vote in favor of the postponement of this resolution until the 3d of March. He did not think that the great constitutional question which it presented ought to be decided, without more time and more reflection than it would be possible to bestow upon it at this late period of the session. We had heard the able and ingenious argument of the gentleman from Virginia (Mr. Smyth) in favor of the proposition, whilst no argument had been urged upon the other side of the question. He said that a more important question could not be presented in a republic, than a proposition to change 93the Constitution in regard to the election of the Supreme Executive Magistrate. "It is better to bear the ills we have, than fly to others that we know not of," unless the existing evils are great, and we have a moral certainty that the change will not be productive of still greater evils. The Constitution has been once changed since its adoption, and it is now generally admitted that the alteration was for the worse, and not for the better. This change grew out of the excitement of the moment. It provided against the existence of an evil which, probably, would not again have occurred for a long period of time; but in doing so, it has rendered it almost certain that the election of a President shall often devolve upon the House of Representatives. Had the Constitution remained in its original form; had each elector continued to vote for two persons, instead of one; it could rarely, if ever, have occurred that some one candidate would not have received a majority of all the electoral votes. By this change, we have thus entailed a great evil upon the country.

The example of Washington, which has been followed by Jefferson, Madison and Monroe, has forever determined that no President shall be more than once re-elected. This principle is now become as sacred as if it were written in the Constitution. I would incline to leave to the people of the United States, without incorporating it in the Constitution, to decide whether a President should serve longer than one term. The day may come, when dangers shall lower over us, and when we may have a President at the helm of State who possesses the confidence of the country, and is better able to weather the storm than any other pilot; shall we, then, under such circumstances, deprive the people of the United States of the power of obtaining his services for a second term? Shall we pass a decree, as fixed as fate, to bind the American people, and prevent them from ever re-electing such a man? I am not afraid to trust them with this power.

There is another reason why the House should not be called upon to decide this question hastily. It is a great evil to keep the public mind excited, as it would be, by the election of a new President at the end of each term of four years. Under the existing system, it is

probable that, as a general rule, a President, elected by the people, will once be re-elected, unless he shall by his conduct have deprived himself of public confidence. This will, in many instances, prevent the recurrence of a political storm more than once in eight years. These are some of the suggestions which induce me to vote for the postponement of this resolution to a day that will render it impossible for us to act upon it during the present session of Congress. We ought to have ample time to consider this subject before we act.
94

CHAPTER VI.

1829–1831.

THE FIRST ELECTION OF GENERAL JACKSON—BUCHANAN AGAIN ELECTED TO THE HOUSE OF REPRESENTATIVES—HE BECOMES CHAIRMAN OF THE JUDICIARY COMMITTEE—IMPEACHMENT OF JUDGE PECK—BUCHANAN DEFEATS A REPEAL OF THE 25TH SECTION OF THE JUDICIARY ACT—PROPOSED IN PENNSYLVANIA AS A CANDIDATE FOR THE VICE-PRESIDENCY—WISHES TO RETIRE FROM PUBLIC LIFE—FITNESS FOR GREAT SUCCESS AT THE BAR.

General Jackson was elected President of the United States in the autumn of 1828, by a majority of forty-eight electoral votes over Mr. John Quincy Adams, and was inaugurated March 4, 1829. Mr. Calhoun became Vice-President by a majority of forty-one electoral votes. Mr. Buchanan had entered into the popular canvass in favor of General Jackson with much zeal and activity. His efforts to secure for the General the popular vote of Pennsylvania, which were begun in the summer of 1827, were in danger of being embarrassed at that time by the General's misconception of the purpose of Mr. Buchanan's interview with him, which took place in 1824, while the election of a President was pending in the House of Representatives. But Mr. Buchanan conducted himself in that matter with so much discretion and forbearance that his influence with General Jackson's Pennsylvania friends was not seriously impaired. When the canvass of 1828 came on, he was in a position to be regarded as one of the most efficient political supporters of General Jackson in the State; and indeed it was mainly through his influence that the whole of her twenty-eight electoral votes was secured for the candidate whose election he desired. Yet this commanding position did not lead him to expect office of any kind in the new administration, nor does he appear to have desired any. He was 95re-elected to his old seat in Congress, and was in attendance at the opening of the first session of the 21st Congress in December, 1829. He now became Chairman of the Judiciary Committee of the House, and as such had very weighty duties to perform. One of the first of these duties, and one that he discharged with signal ability, required him to introduce and advocate a bill to amend and extend the judicial system of the United States, by including in the circuit court system the States of Louisiana, Indiana, Mississippi, Illinois, Alabama, and Missouri, which had hitherto had only district courts, and by increasing the number of judges of the Supreme Court to nine. Mr. Buchanan's speech in explanation of this measure, delivered January 14, 1830, was as important a one as has been made upon the subject. The measure which he advocated was not adopted at that time; but his speech may be resorted to at all times for its valuable discussion of a question that has not yet lost its interest,—the question of releasing the judges of the Supreme Court entirely from the performance of circuit duties. Until I read this speech, I was not aware how wisely and comprehensively Mr. Buchanan could deal with such a question. The following passages seem to me to justify a very high estimate of his powers, as they certainly contain much wisdom:

Having thus given a hasty sketch of the history of the Judiciary of the United States, and of the jurisdiction of the circuit courts which this bill proposes to extend to the six new States of the Union, I shall now proceed to present the views of the Committee on the Judiciary in relation to this important subject. In doing this, I feel that, before I can expect the passage of the bill, I must satisfy the committee, first, that such a change or modification of the present judiciary system ought to be adopted, as will place the Western States on an equal footing with the other States of the Union; and, second, that the present bill contains the best provisions which, under all the circumstances, can be devised for accomplishing this purpose.

And first, in regard to the States of Ohio, Kentucky, and Tennessee. It may be said that the existing law has already established circuit courts in these three States, and why then should they complain? In answer to this question, I ask gentlemen to look at a map of the United States, and examine the extent of this circuit. The distance which the judge is compelled to travel, by land, for the purpose of attending the different circuit courts, is, of itself, almost sufficient, in a few years, to destroy any common constitution. 96From Columbus, in Ohio, he proceeds to Frankfort, in Kentucky; from Frankfort to Nashville; and from Nashville, across the Cumberland mountain, to Knoxville. When we reflect that, in addition to his attendance of the courts in each of these States, twice in the year, he is obliged annually to attend the Supreme Court in Washington, we must all admit that his labors are very severe.

This circuit is not only too extensive, but there is a great press of judicial business in each of the States of which it is composed. In addition to the ordinary sources of litigation for the circuit courts throughout the Union, particular causes have existed for its extraordinary accumulation in each of these States. It will be recollected that, under the Constitution and laws of the United States, the circuit courts may try land causes between citizens of the same State, provided they claim under grants from different States. In Tennessee, grants under that State and the State of North Carolina, for the same land, often come into conflict in the circuit court. The interfering grants of Virginia and Kentucky are a fruitful source of business for the circuit court of Kentucky. These causes, from their very nature, are difficult and important, and must occupy much time and attention. Within the Virginia military district of Ohio, there are also many disputed land titles.

Another cause has contributed much to swell the business of the circuit court of Kentucky. The want of confidence of the citizens of other States in the judicial tribunals of that State, has greatly added to the number of suits in the circuit court. Many plaintiff's, who could, with greater expedition, have recovered their demands in the courts of the State, were compelled, by the impolitic acts of the State Legislature, to resort to the courts of the United States. Whilst these laws were enforced by the State courts, they were disregarded by those of the Union. In making these remarks, I am confident no representative from that patriotic State will mistake my meaning. I rejoice that the difficulties are now at an end, and that the people of Kentucky have discovered the ruinous policy of interposing the arm of the law to shield a debtor from the just demands of his creditor. That gallant and chivalrous people, who possess a finer soil and a finer climate than any other State of the Union, will now, I trust, improve and enjoy the bounties which nature has bestowed upon them with a lavish hand. As their experience has been severe, I trust their reformation will be complete. Still, however, many of the causes which originated in past years, are yet depending in the circuit court of that State. In 1826, when a similar bill was before this House, we had the most authentic information that there were nine hundred and fifty causes then pending in the circuit court of Kentucky, one hundred and sixty in the circuit court for the western district, and about the same number in that for the eastern district of Tennessee, and upwards of two hundred in Ohio. Upon that occasion, a memorial was presented from the bar of Nashville, signed by G. W. Campbell as chairman, and Felix Grundy, at present a Senator of the United States, as secretary. These gentlemen are both well known to this House, and to the country. That memorial declares that "the seventh circuit, consisting of Kentucky, Ohio, and Tennessee, is too large for the duties of it to be devolved on one man; and it was absolutely impossible for the judge assigned to this circuit to fulfil the letter of the law designating his duties." Such has been the delay of justice in the State of Tennessee, "that some of the important causes now pending in their circuit courts are older than the professional career of almost every man at the bar."

The number of causes depending in the seventh circuit, I am informed, has been somewhat reduced since 1826; but still the evil is great, and demands a remedy. If it were possible for one man to transact the judicial business of that circuit, I should have as much confidence that it would be accomplished by the justice of the Supreme Court to which it is assigned, as by any other judge in the Union. His ability and his perseverance are well known to the nation. The labor, however, both of body and mind, is too great for any individual.

Has not the delay of justice in this circuit almost amounted to its denial? Are the States which compose it placed upon the same footing, in this respect, with other States of the Union? Have they not a right to complain? Many evils follow in the train of tardy justice. It deranges the whole business of society. It tempts the dishonest and the needy to set up unjust and fraudulent defences against the payment of just debts, knowing that the day of trial is far distant. It thus ruins the honest creditor, by depriving him of the funds which he had a right to expect at or near the appointed time of payment; and it ultimately tends to destroy all confidence between man and man.

A greater curse can scarcely be inflicted upon the people of any State, than to have their land titles unsettled. What, then, must be the condition of Tennessee, where there are many disputed land titles, when we are informed, by undoubted authority, "that some of the important causes now pending in their circuit courts are older than the professional career of almost every man at the bar." Instead of being astonished at the complaints of the people of this circuit, I am astonished at their forbearance. A judiciary, able and willing to compel men to perform their contracts, and to decide their controversies, is one of the greatest political blessings which any people can enjoy; and it is one which the people of this country have a right to expect from their Government. The present bill proposes to accomplish this object, by creating a new circuit out of the States of Kentucky and Tennessee. This circuit will afford sufficient employment for one justice of the Supreme Court.

Without insisting further upon the propriety, nay, the necessity, of organizing the circuit courts of Ohio, Kentucky, and Tennessee, in such a manner as to enable them to transact the business of the people, I shall now proceed to consider the situation of the six new States, Louisiana, Indiana, Mississippi, Illinois, Alabama, and Missouri. Their grievances are of a different character. They do not so much complain of the delay of justice, as that Congress has so long refused to extend to them the circuit court system, as it exists in all the other States. As they successively came into the Union, they were each provided with a district court and a district judge, possessing circuit court powers. The acts which introduced them into our political family declare that they shall "be admitted into the Union on an equal footing with the original States, in all respects whatever." I do not mean to contend that by virtue of these acts we were bound immediately to extend to them the circuit court system. Such has not been the practice of Congress, in regard to other States in a similar situation. I contend, however, that these acts do impose an obligation upon us to place them "on an equal footing with the original States," in regard to the judiciary, as soon as their wants require it, and the circumstances of the country permit it to be done. That time has, in my opinion, arrived. Louisiana has now been nearly eighteen years a member of the Union, and is one of our most commercial States; and yet, until this day, she has been without a circuit court. It is more than thirteen years since Indiana was admitted; and even our youngest sister, Missouri, will soon have been nine years in the family. Why should not these six States be admitted to the same judicial privileges which all the others now enjoy? Even if there were no better reason, they have a right to demand it for the mere sake of uniformity. I admit this is an argument dictated by State pride; but is not that a noble feeling? Is it not a feeling which will ever characterize freemen? Have they not a right to say to us, if the circuit court system be good for you, it will be good for us? You have no right to exclusive privileges. If you are sovereign States, so are we. By the terms of our admission, we are perfectly your equals. We have long submitted to the want of this system, from deference to your judgment; but the day has now arrived when we demand it from you as our right. But there are several other good reasons why the system ought to be extended to these States. And, in the first place, the justices of the Supreme Court are selected from the very highest order of the profession. There is scarcely a lawyer in the United States who would not be proud of an elevation to that bench. A man ambitious of honest fame ought not to desire a more exalted theatre for the display of ability and usefulness. Besides, the salary annexed to this office is sufficient to command the best talents of the country. I ask you, sir, is it not a serious grievance for those States to be deprived of the services of such a man in their courts? I ask you whether it is equal justice, that whilst, in eighteen States of the Union, no man can be deprived of his life, his liberty, or his property, by the judgment of a circuit court, without the concurrence of two judges, and one of them a justice of the Supreme Court, in the remaining six the fate of the citizen is determined by the decision of a single district judge? Who are, generally speaking, these district judges? In asking this question, I mean to treat them with no disrespect. They receive but small salaries, and their sphere of action is confined to their own particular districts. There is nothing either in the salary or in the station which would induce a distinguished lawyer, 99unless under peculiar circumstances, to accept the appointment. And yet the judgment of this individual, in six States of the Union, is final and conclusive, in all cases of law, of equity, and of admiralty and maritime jurisdiction, wherein the amount of the controversy does not exceed two thousand dollars. Nay, the grievance is incomparably greater. His opinion in all criminal cases, no matter how aggravated may be their nature, is final and conclusive. A citizen of these States may be deprived of his life, or of his character, which ought to be dearer than life, by the sentence of a district judge; against which there is no redress, and from which there can be no appeal.

There is another point of view in which the inequality and injustice of the present system, in the new States, is very striking. In order to produce a final decision, both the judges of a circuit court must concur. If they be divided in opinion, the point of difference is certified to the Supreme Court, for their decision; and this, whether the amount in controversy be great or small. The same rule applies to criminal cases. In such a court, no man can be deprived of life, of liberty, or of property, by a criminal prosecution, without the clear opinion of the two judges that his conviction is sanctioned by the laws of the land. If the question be doubtful or important, or if it be one of the first impression, the judges, even when they do not really differ, often agree to divide, pro forma, so that the point may be solemnly argued and decided in the Supreme Court. Thus, the citizen of every State in which a circuit court exists, has a shield of protection cast over him, of which he cannot be deprived, without the deliberate opinion of two judges; whilst the district judge of the six new Western States must alone finally decide every criminal question, and every civil controversy in which the amount in dispute does not exceed two thousand dollars.

In the eastern district of Louisiana, the causes of admiralty and maritime jurisdiction decided by the district court must be numerous and important. If a circuit court were established for that State, a party who considered himself aggrieved might appeal to it from the district court in every case in which the amount in controversy exceeded fifty dollars. At present there is no appeal, unless the value of the controversy exceeds two thousand dollars; and then it must be made directly to the Supreme Court, a tribunal so far remote from the city of New Orleans, as to deter suitors from availing themselves of this privilege.

I shall not further exhaust the patience of the committee on this branch of the subject. I flatter myself that I have demonstrated the necessity for such an alteration of the existing laws as will confer upon the people of Ohio, Kentucky, and Tennessee, and of the six new Western States, the same benefits from the judiciary, as those which the people of the other States now enjoy.

The great question, then, which remains for discussion is, does the present bill present the best plan for accomplishing this purpose, which, under all circumstances, can be devised? It is incumbent upon me to sustain the affirmative 100of this proposition. There have been but two plans proposed to the Committee on the Judiciary, and but two can be proposed, with the least hope of success. The one an extension of the present system, which the bill now before the committee contemplates, and the other a resort to the system which was adopted in the days of the elder Adams, of detaching the justices of the Supreme Court from the performance of circuit duties, and appointing circuit judges to take their places. After much reflection upon this subject I do not think that the two systems can be compared, without producing a conviction in favor of that which has long been established. The system of detaching the judges of the Supreme Court from the circuits has been already tried, and it has already met the decided hostility of the people of this country. No act passed during the stormy and turbulent administration of the elder Adams, which excited more general indignation among the people. The courts which it established were then, and have been ever since, branded with the name of the "midnight judiciary." I am far from being one of those who believe the people to be infallible. They are often deceived by the arts of demagogues; but this deception endures only for a season. They are always honest, and possess much sagacity. If, therefore, they get wrong, it is almost certain they will speedily return to correct opinions. They have long since done justice to other acts of that administration, which at the time they condemned; but the feeling against the judiciary established under it remains the same. Indeed, many now condemn that system, who were formerly its advocates. In 1826, when a bill, similar in its provisions to the bill now before the committee, was under discussion in this House, a motion was made by a gentleman from Virginia [Mr. Mercer] to recommit it to the Committee on the Judiciary, with an instruction so to amend it, as to discharge the judges of the Supreme Court from attendance on the circuit courts, and to provide a uniform system for the administration of justice in the inferior courts of the United States. Although this motion was sustained with zeal and eloquence and ability by the mover, and by several other gentlemen, yet, when it came to the vote, it was placed in a lean minority, and, I believe, was negatived without a division. It is morally certain that such a bill could not now be carried. It would, therefore, have been vain and idle in the Committee on the Judiciary to have reported such a bill. If the Western States should be doomed to wait for a redress of their grievances, until public opinion shall change upon this subject, it will, probably, be a long time before they will obtain relief.

But, Sir, there are most powerful reasons for believing that public opinion upon this subject is correct. What would be the natural consequences of detaching the judges of the Supreme Court from circuit duties? It would bring them and their families from the circuits in which they now reside; and this city would become their permanent residence. They would naturally come here; because here, and nowhere else, would they then have official business to transact. What would be the probable effect of such a change of residence? The tendency of everything within the ten miles square is towards the Executive of the Union. He is here the centre of attraction. No matter what political revolutions may take place, no matter who may be up or who may be down, the proposition is equally true. Human nature is not changed under a Republican Government. We find that citizens of a republic are worshippers of power, as well as the subjects of a monarchy. Would you think it wise to bring the justices of the Supreme Court from their residence in the States, where they breathe the pure air of the country, and assemble them here within the very vortex of Executive influence? Instead of being independent judges, scattered over the surface of the Union, their feelings identified with the States of which they are citizens, is there no danger that, in the lapse of time, you would convert them into minions of the Executive? I am far, very far, from supposing that any man, who either is or who will be a justice of the Supreme Court, could be actually corrupted; but if you place them in a situation where they or their relatives would naturally become candidates for Executive patronage, you place them, in some degree, under the control of Executive influence. If there should now exist any just cause for the complaints against the Supreme Court, that in their decisions they are partial to Federal rather than to State authority (and I do not say that there is), that which at present may be but an imaginary fear might soon become a substantial reality. I would place them beyond the reach of temptation. I would suffer them to remain, as they are at present, citizens of their respective States, visiting this city annually to discharge their high duties, as members of the Supreme Court. This single view of the subject, if there were no other, ought, in my judgment, to be conclusive.

Let us now suppose, for the sake of the argument, that the withdrawal of the justices of the Supreme Court from their circuit duties, and their residence in this city, would produce no such effects, as I apprehend, upon the judges themselves; what would be the probable effect upon public opinion? It has been said, and wisely said, that the first object of every judicial tribunal ought to be to do justice; the second, to satisfy the people that justice has been done. It is of the utmost importance in this country that the judges of the Supreme Court should possess the confidence of the public. This they now do in an eminent degree. How have they acquired it? By travelling over their circuits, and personally showing themselves to the people of the country, in the able and honest discharge of their high duties, and by their extensive intercourse with the members of the profession on the circuits in each State, who, after all, are the best judges of judicial merit, and whose opinions upon this subject have a powerful influence upon the community. Elevated above the storms of faction and of party which have sometimes lowered over us, like the sun, they have pursued their steady course, unawed by threats, unseduced by flattery. They have thus acquired that public confidence which never fails to follow the performance of great and good actions, when brought home to the personal observation of the people.

Would they continue to enjoy this extensive public confidence, should they no longer be seen by the people of the States, in the discharge of their high 102and important duties, but be confined, in the exercise of them, to the gloomy and vaulted apartment which they now occupy in this Capitol? Would they not be considered as a distant and dangerous tribunal? Would the people, when excited by strong feeling, patiently submit to have the most solemn acts of their State Legislatures swept from the statute-book, by the decision of judges whom they never saw, and whom they had been taught to consider with jealousy and suspicion? At present, even in those States where their decisions have been most violently opposed, the highest respect has been felt for the judges by whom they were pronounced, because the people have had an opportunity of personally knowing that they were both great and good men. Look at the illustrious individual who is now the Chief Justice of the United States. His decisions upon constitutional questions have ever been hostile to the opinions of a vast majority of the people of his own State; and yet with what respect and veneration has he been viewed by Virginia? Is there a Virginian, whose heart does not beat with honest pride when the just fame of the Chief Justice is the subject of conversation? They consider him, as he truly is, one of the greatest and best men which this country has ever produced. Think ye that such would have been the case, had he been confined to the city of Washington, and never known to the people, except in pronouncing judgments in this Capitol, annulling their State laws, and calculated to humble their State pride? Whilst I continue to be a member of this House, I shall never incur the odium of giving a vote for any change in the judiciary system the effect of which would, in my opinion, diminish the respect in which the Supreme Court is now held by the people of this country.

The judges whom you would appoint to perform the circuit duties, if able and honest men, would soon take the place which the judges of the Supreme Court now occupy in the affections of the people; and the reversal of their judgments, when they happened to be in accordance with strong public feeling, would naturally increase the mass of discontent against the Supreme Court.

There are other reasons, equally powerful, against the withdrawal of the judges from the circuits. What effect would such a measure probably produce upon the ability of the judges themselves to perform their duties? Would it not be very unfortunate?

No judges upon earth ever had such various and important duties to perform, as the justices of the Supreme Court. In England, whence we have derived our laws, they have distinct courts of equity, courts of common law, courts of admiralty, and courts in which the civil law is administered. In each of these courts, they have distinct judges; and perfection in any of these branches is certain to be rewarded by the honors of that country. The judges of our Supreme Court, both on their circuits and in banc, are called upon to adjudicate on all these codes. But this is not all. Our Union consists of twenty-four sovereign States, in all of which there are different laws and peculiar customs. The common and equity law have thus been changed 103and inflected into a hundred different shapes, and adapted to the various wants and opinions of the different members of our confederacy. The judicial act of 1789 declares "that the laws of the several States, except where the Constitution, treaties, or statutes of the United States shall otherwise require or provide," shall be regarded as rules of decision in the courts of the United States. The justices of the Supreme Court ought, therefore, to be acquainted with the ever-varying codes of the different States.

There is still another branch of their jurisdiction, of a grand and imposing character, which places them far above the celebrated Amphictyonic council. The Constitution of the United States has made them the arbiters between conflicting sovereigns. They decide whether the sovereign power of the States has been exercised in conformity with the Constitution and laws of the United States; and, if this has not been done, they declare the laws of the State Legislatures to be void. Their decisions thus control the exercise of sovereign power. No tribunal ever existed, possessing the same, or even similar authority. Now, Sir, suppose you bring these judges to Washington, and employ them in banc but six weeks or two months in the year, is it not certain that they will gradually become less and less fit to decide upon these different codes, and that they will at length nearly lose all recollection of the peculiar local laws of the different States? Every judicial duty which each of them would then be required to perform, would be to prepare and deliver a few opinions annually in banc.

The judgment, like every other faculty of the mind, requires exercise to preserve its vigor. That judge who decides the most causes, is likely to decide them the best. He who is in the daily habit of applying general principles to the decision of cases, as they arise upon the circuits, is at the same time qualifying himself in the best manner for the duties of his station on the bench of the Supreme Court.

Is it probable that the long literary leisure of the judges in this city, during ten months of the year, would be devoted to searching the two hundred volumes of jarring decisions of State courts, or in studying the acts of twenty-four State Legislatures? The man must have a singular taste and a firm resolution who, in his closet, could travel over this barren waste. And even if he should, what would be the consequence? The truth is, such knowledge cannot be obtained; and after it has been acquired, it cannot be preserved, except by constant practice. There are subjects which, when the memory has once grasped, it retains forever. It has no such attachment for acts of Assembly, acts of Congress, and reports of adjudged cases, fixing their construction. This species of knowledge, under the present system, will always be possessed by the judges of the Supreme Court; because, in the performance of their circuit duties, they are placed in a situation in which it is daily expounded to them, and in which they are daily compelled to decide questions arising upon it. Change this system, make them exclusively judges of an appellate court, and you render it highly probable that their knowledge of the general principles of the laws of their country will become more and more faint, and that they will finally almost lose the recollection of the peculiar local systems of the different States. "Practice makes perfect," is a maxim applicable to every pursuit in life. It applies with peculiar force to that of a judge. I think I might appeal for the truth of this position to the long experience of the distinguished gentleman from New York, now by my side (Mr. Spencer). A man, by study, may become a profound lawyer in theory, but nothing except practice can make him an able judge. I call upon every member of the profession in this House to say whether he does not feel himself to be a better lawyer at the end of a long term, than at the beginning. It is the circuit employment, imposed upon the judges of England and the United States, which has rendered them what they are. In my opinion, both the usefulness and the character of the Supreme Court depend much upon its continuance.

I now approach what I know will be urged as the greatest objection to the passage of this bill—that it will extend the number of the judges of the Supreme Court to nine. If the necessities of the country required that their number should be increased to ten, I would feel no objection to such a measure. The time has not yet arrived, however, when, in my opinion, such a necessity exists. Gentlemen, in considering this subject, ought to take those extended views which belong to statesmen. When we reflect upon the vast extent of our country, and the various systems of law under which the people of the different States are governed, I cannot conceive that nine or even ten judges are too great a number to compose our appellate tribunal. That number would afford a judicial representation upon the bench of each large portion of the Union. Not, Sir, a representation of sectional feelings or of the party excitements of the day, but of that peculiar species of legal knowledge necessary to adjudicate wisely upon the laws of the different States. For example, I ask what judge now upon the bench possesses, or can possess, a practical knowledge of the laws of Louisiana? Their system is so peculiar, that it is almost impossible for a man to decide correctly upon all cases arising under it, who has never been practically acquainted with the practice of their courts. Increase the number of judges to nine, and you will then have them scattered throughout all the various portions of the Union. The streams of legal knowledge peculiar to the different States will then flow to the bench of the Supreme Court as to a great reservoir, from whence they will be distributed throughout the Union. There will then always be sufficient local information upon the bench, if I may use the expression, to detect all the ingenious fallacies of the bar, and to enable them to decide correctly upon local questions. I admit, if the judges were confined to appellate duties alone, nine or ten would probably be too great a number. Then there might be danger that some of them would become mere nonentities, contenting themselves simply with voting aye or no in the majority or minority. There would then also be danger that the Executive might select inefficient men for this high station, who were his personal favorites, expecting their incapacity to be shielded from public observation by the splendid talents of 105some of the other judges upon the bench. Under the present system we have no such danger to apprehend. Each judge must now feel his own personal responsibility. He is obliged to preside in the courts throughout his circuit, and to bring home the law and the justice of his country to his fellow-citizens in each of the districts of which it is composed. Much is expected from a judge placed in his exalted station; and he must attain to the high standard of public opinion by which he is judged, or incur the reproach of holding an office to which he is not entitled. No man in any station in this country can place himself above public opinion.

Upon the subject of judicial appointments, public opinion has always been correct. No factious demagogue, no man, merely because he has sung hosannas to the powers that be, can arrive at the bench of the Supreme Court. The Executive himself will always be constrained by the force of public sentiment, whilst the present system continues, to select judges for that court from the ablest and best men of the circuit; and such has been the course which he has hitherto almost invariably pursued. Were he to pursue any other, he would inevitably incur popular odium. Under the existing system, there can be no danger in increasing the number of the judges to nine. But take them from their circuits, destroy their feeling of personal responsibility by removing them from the independent courts over which they now preside, and make them merely an appellate tribunal, and I admit there would be danger, not only of improper appointments, but that a portion of them, in the lapse of time, might become incompetent to discharge the duties of their station.

But, Sir, have we no examples of appellate courts consisting of a greater number than either nine or ten judges, which have been approved by experience? The Senate of the State of New York has always been their court of appeals; and, notwithstanding they changed their constitution a few years ago, so much were the people attached to this court, that it remains unchanged. In England, the twelve judges, in fact, compose the court of appeals. Whenever the House of Lords sits in a judicial character, they are summoned to attend, and their opinions are decisive of almost every question. I do not pretend to speak accurately, but I doubt whether the House of Lords have decided two cases, in opposition to the opinion of the judges, for the last fifty years. In England there is also the court of exchequer chamber, consisting of the twelve judges, and sometimes of the lord chancellor also, into which such causes may be adjourned from the three superior courts, as the judges find to be difficult of decision, before any judgment is given upon them in the court in which they originated. The court of exchequer chamber is also a court of appeals, in the strictest sense of the word, in many cases which I shall not take time to enumerate.

I cannot avoid believing that the prejudice which exists in the minds of some gentlemen, against increasing the number of the judges of the Supreme Court to nine, arises from the circumstance that the appellate courts of the different States generally consist of a fewer number. But is there not a striking difference between the cases? It does not follow that because four or five may be a sufficient number in a single State where one uniform system of laws prevails, nine or ten would be too many on the bench of the Supreme Court, which administers the laws of twenty-four States, and decides questions arising under all the codes in use in the civilized world. Indeed, if four or five judges be not too many for the court of appeals in a State, it is a strong argument that nine or ten are not too great a number for the court of appeals of the Union. Upon the whole, I ask, would it be wise in this committee, disregarding the voice of experience, to destroy a system which has worked well in practice for forty years, and resort to a dangerous and untried experiment, merely from a vague apprehension that nine judges will destroy the usefulness and character of that court, which has been raised by seven to its present exalted elevation.

It will, no doubt, be objected to this bill, as it has been upon a former occasion, that the present system cannot be permanent, and that, ere long, the judges of the Supreme Courts must, from necessity, be withdrawn from their circuits. To this objection there is a conclusive answer. We know that the system is now sufficient for the wants of the country, and let posterity provide for themselves. Let us not establish courts which are unnecessary in the present day, because we believe that hereafter they may be required to do the business of the country.

But, if it were necessary, I believe it might be demonstrated that ten justices of the Supreme Court will be sufficient to do all the judicial business of the country which is required of them under the present system, until the youngest member of this House shall be sleeping with his fathers. Six judges have done all the business of the States east of the Alleghany mountains, from the adoption of the Federal Constitution up till this day; and still their duties are not laborious. If it should be deemed proper by Congress, these fifteen Eastern States might be arranged into five circuits instead of six, upon the occurrence of the next vacancy in any of them, without the least inconvenience either to the judges or to the people; and thus it would be rendered unnecessary to increase the bench of the Supreme Court beyond nine, even after the admission of Michigan and Arkansas into the Union. The business of the Federal courts, except in a few States, will probably increase but little for a long time to come. One branch of it must, before many years, be entirely lopped away. I allude to the controversies between citizens of the same State claiming lands under grants from different States. This will greatly diminish their business both in Tennessee and Kentucky. Besides, the State tribunals will generally be preferred by aliens and by citizens of other States for the mere recovery of debts, on account of their superior expedition.

I should here close my remarks, if it were not necessary to direct the attention of the committee for a few minutes to the details of the bill. And here permit me to express my regret that my friend from Kentucky (Mr. Wickliffe) has thought proper to propose an amendment to add three, instead 107of two, judges to the Supreme Court. Had a majority of the Committee on the Judiciary believed ten judges, instead of nine, to be necessary, I should have yielded my opinion, as I did upon a former occasion, and given the bill my support in the House. This I should have done to prevent division among its friends, believing it to be a mere question of time: for ten will become necessary in a few years, unless the number of the Eastern circuits should be reduced to five.

Another important matter which devolved upon Mr. Buchanan as Chairman of the Judiciary Committee, related to the impeachment of Judge James H. Peck, the United States district judge for the district of Missouri. The facts of this singular case were briefly these: Judge Peck had decided a land-cause against certain parties who were represented in his court by an attorney and counsellor named Lawless. Lawless published in a St. Louis newspaper some comments on the Judge's opinion, by no means intemperate in their character. The Judge thereupon attached Lawless for a contempt, caused him to be imprisoned twenty-four hours in the common jail, and suspended him from practice for a period of eighteen months. Upon these facts, when brought before the House of Representatives by Lawless' memorial, there could be but one action. The Judiciary Committee voted an impeachment of the Judge, and Mr. Buchanan reported their recommendation on the 23d of March, 1830. He said that the committee deemed it most fair towards the accused not to report at length their reasons for arriving at the conclusion that the Judge ought to be impeached, but that they thought it advisable to follow the precedent which had been established in the case of the impeachment of Judge Chase. A desultory discussion followed upon a motion to print the report and the documents, and upon an amendment to include the address which it seems that the Judge had been allowed to make to the committee. But before any vote was taken, the Speaker, on the 5th of April, presented a memorial from Judge Peck, praying the House to allow him to present a written exposition of the facts and law of the case, and to call witnesses to substantiate it, or else to vote the impeachment at once on "the partial evidence" which the committee had heard. In the course of these proceedings the House, if it had not been better guided, might have established 108an unfortunate precedent. While the resolution reported by the Judiciary Committee for the impeachment of the Judge was pending in Committee of the Whole, Mr. Everett moved a counter-resolution that there was not sufficient evidence of evil intent to authorize the House to impeach Judge Peck of high misdemeanors in office. This, in effect, would have converted the grand inquest into a tribunal for the determination of the whole question of guilt or innocence, upon allegations and proofs on the one side and the other. It was opposed by Mr. Storrs, Mr. Ellsworth, Mr. Wickliffe and others, and was negatived. The resolution reported by Mr. Buchanan for the impeachment of the Judge was then adopted by the Committee of the Whole, and reported to the House, after which Mr. Buchanan demanded the yeas and nays, which resulted in a vote of 123 for the impeachment and 49 against it. An article of impeachment was prepared by Mr. Buchanan, and was by order of the House presented to the Senate. The managers appointed to conduct the impeachment on the part of the House were Mr. Buchanan, Henry R. Storrs of New York, George McDuffie of South Carolina, Ambrose Spencer of New York, and Charles Wickliffe of Kentucky.

The Senate was organized as a court of impeachment on the 25th of May, 1830; but the trial was postponed to the second Monday of the next session of Congress. It began on that day, December 20, 1830. It was Mr. Buchanan's duty to close the case on behalf of the managers, in reply to Mr. Wirt and Mr. Meredith of Baltimore, the counsel for Judge Peck. Of Mr. Buchanan's speech, I have found no adequate report. It was delivered on the 28th of January, 1831. Contemporary notices of it show that it was an argument of marked ability. His positions as given in the Annals of Congress were in substance the following:

He declared that the usurpation of an authority not legally possessed by a judge, or the manifest abuse of a power really given, was a misbehavior in the sense of the Constitution for which he should be dismissed from office. He contended that the conduct of Judge Peck, in the case of Mr. Lawless, was in express violation of the Constitution and the laws of the land; that the circumstances of that case were amply sufficient to show a criminal intention on his part in the summary punishment of Mr. Lawless; that in order to prove the criminality of his intention it was not necessary to demonstrate an actually malicious intention, or a lurking revenge; that the infliction upon Mr. Lawless of a summary and cruel punishment, for having written an article decorous in its language, was itself sufficient to prove the badness of the motive; that the consequences of the Judge's actions were indicative of his intentions; that our courts had no right to punish, as for contempts, in a summary mode, libels, even in pending causes; and that if he succeeded, as he believed he should, in establishing these positions, he should consider that he had a right to demand the judgment of the court against the respondent.

He took the further position that the publication of Mr. Lawless, under the signature of "A Citizen," could not, in a trial upon an indictment for libel, be established to be libellous, according to the Constitution and laws of the land; that the paper was, on its face, perfectly harmless in itself; and that, so far as it went, it was not an unfair representation of the opinion of Judge Peck. The honorable manager critically and legally analyzed the nine last specifications in the publication, to establish these points. He then proceeded to sum up and descant upon the testimony produced in the case before the court of impeachment, in order to show the arbitrary and cruel conduct of Judge Peck; and in a peroration, marked by its ardent eloquence, he declared that if this man escaped, the declaration of a distinguished politician of this country, that the power of impeachment was but the scarecrow of the Constitution, would be fully verified; that when this trial commenced, he recoiled with horror from the idea of limiting, and rendering precarious and dependent, the tenure of the judicial office, but that the acquittal of the respondent would reconcile him to that evil, as one less than a hopeless and remediless submission to judicial usurpation and tyranny, at least so far as respected the inferior courts.

God forbid that the limitation should ever be extended to the Supreme Court. Mercy to the respondent would be cruelty to the American people.

Judge Peck was acquitted by a vote of 21 for the impeachment and 22 against it, the constitutional vote of two-thirds requisite for conviction not being obtained. It is quite apparent that no party feeling entered into the case.

[GEO. W. BUCHANAN TO JAMES BUCHANAN]
Pittsburgh, November 5, 1830.
Dear Brother:—

I had the honor to receive by last night's mail a letter from Mr. Van Buren, enclosing me a commission from the President for the district attorneyship. This day I will acknowledge its receipt. I am sincerely glad both on your account and my own that the President has appointed me. It banishes in a moment all those suspicions which some persons entertained of his coldness towards you. It should be my highest ambition to justify the appointment by a faithful discharge of official duty.

My appointment appears to be received very well in this city. It will excite some feelings of envy towards me among the young members of the bar. My path, however, is very plain. It shall not alter my conduct or manner in any respect.

I am, in haste, your grateful and affectionate brother,

Geo. W. Buchanan.

The most signal service rendered by Mr. Buchanan in the 21st Congress, as Chairman of the Judiciary Committee, was in a minority report made by him on the 24th of January, 1831, upon a proposition to repeal the twenty-fifth section of the judiciary act of 1789, which gave the Supreme Court appellate jurisdiction, by writ of error to the State courts, in cases where the Constitution, treaties, and laws of the United States are drawn in question. A resolution to inquire into the expediency of repealing this great organic law having been referred to the committee, a majority of the committee made an elaborate report in favor of the repeal, through Mr. Smith of South Carolina, accompanied by a bill to effect the repeal. Mr. Buchanan's counter-report, which had the concurrence of two other members, caused the rejection of the bill, by a vote of 138 to 51. I know of few constitutional discussions which evince a more thorough knowledge or more accurate views of the nature of our mixed system of Government than this report from the pen of Mr. Buchanan. If it be said that the argument is now familiar to us, or that it could have been drawn from various sources, let it be observed that this document shows that Mr. Buchanan was, at this comparatively early period of his life, a well-instructed constitutional jurist; and that while no one could originate at that day any novel views of this important subject, it was no small merit to be able to set forth clearly and cogently the whole substance of such a topic. I think no apology is needed for the insertion here of this valuable paper. It may be prefaced by an extract from a letter of Mr. Buchanan's youngest brother, George W. Buchanan, which shows how it was received by the public in Pennsylvania:

111Pittsburgh, February 4, 1831.

...... I have read with the highest degree of satisfaction your able report from the minority of the Judiciary Committee. That document will identify your name with the most important constitutional question which has been presented to the consideration of Congress for many years. It was looked for with much anxiety, and is now spoken of by politicians of every party as a lucid and powerful appeal to the patriotism of Congress. If the question was to be started, I am sincerely glad that it has arisen while you occupied the chair of the Judiciary Committee......

House of Representatives, January 24, 1831.

The Committee on the Judiciary, to which was referred a resolution of the House of Representatives of the 21st ultimo, instructing them "to inquire into the expediency of repealing or modifying the twenty-fifth section of an act entitled 'An act to establish the judicial courts of the United States,' passed the 24th September, 1789," having made a report, accompanied by a bill to repeal the same, the minority of that committee, differing in opinion from their associates upon this important question, deem it to be their duty to submit to the House the following report:

The Constitution of the United States has conferred upon Congress certain enumerated powers, and expressly authorizes that body "to make all laws which shall be necessary and proper for carrying these powers into execution." In the construction of this instrument, it has become an axiom, the truth of which cannot be controverted, that "the General Government, though limited as to its objects, is supreme with respect to those objects."

The Constitution has also conferred upon the President, "by and with the advice and consent of the Senate, provided two-thirds of the Senators present concur," the power to make treaties.

By the second section of the sixth article of this instrument it is declared, in emphatic language, that "this Constitution, and the laws of the United States which shall be made in pursuance thereof, and all treaties made, or which shall be made, under the authority of the United States, shall be the supreme law of the land; and the judges in every State shall be bound thereby, anything in the constitution or laws of any State to the contrary notwithstanding."

The Constitution having conferred upon Congress the power of legislation over certain objects, and upon the President and Senate the power of making treaties with foreign nations, the next question which naturally presented itself to those who framed it was, in what manner it would be most proper that the Constitution itself, and the laws and treaties made under its authority, should be carried into execution. They have decided this question in the following strong and comprehensive language: "The judicial power shall extend to all cases, in law and equity, arising under this Constitution, the laws of the United States, and treaties made, or which shall be made, under their authority." [Art. 3, Sec. 2.] This provision is the only one which could 112have been made in consistency with the character of the Government established by the Constitution. It would have been a strange anomaly had that instrument established a judiciary whose powers did not embrace all the laws and all the treaties made under its authority. The symmetry of the system would thus have been destroyed; and, in many cases, Congress would have had to depend exclusively for the execution of their own laws upon the judiciary of the States. This principle would have been at war with the spirit which pervades the whole Constitution. It was clearly the intention of its framers to create a Government which should have the power of construing and executing its own laws, without any obstruction from State authority. Accordingly, we find that the judicial power of the United States extends, in express terms, "to all cases," in law and in equity, arising under the Constitution, the laws, and the treaties of the United States. This general language comprehends precisely what it ought to comprehend.

If the judicial powers of the United States does thus extend to "all cases" arising under the Constitution, the laws, and treaties of the Union, how could this power be brought into action over such cases without a law of Congress investing the Supreme Court with the original and appellate jurisdiction embraced by the Constitution?

It was the imperious duty of Congress to make such a law, and it is equally its duty to continue it; indeed, without it, the judicial power of the United States is limited and restricted to such cases only as arise in the Federal courts, and is never brought to bear upon numerous cases, evidently within its range.

When Congress, in the year 1789, legislated upon this subject, they knew that the State courts would often be called upon, in the trial of causes, to give a construction to the Constitution, the treaties, and laws of the United States. What, then, was to be done? If the decisions of the State courts should be final, the Constitution and laws of the Union might be construed to mean one thing in one State, and another thing in another State. All uniformity in their construction would thus be destroyed. Besides, we might, if this were the case, get into serious conflicts with foreign nations, as a treaty might receive one construction in Pennsylvania, another in Virginia, and a third in New York. Some common and uniform standard of construction was absolutely necessary.

To remedy these and other inconveniences, the first Congress of the United States, composed, in a considerable proportion, of the framers of the Constitution, passed the 25th section of the judicial act of the 24th September, 1789. It is in the following words: "Sec. 25. And be it further enacted, That a final judgment or decree in any suit, in the highest court of law or equity of a State, in which a decision in the suit could be had, where is drawn in question the validity of a treaty or statute of, or an authority exercised under, the United States, and the decision is against their validity; or where is drawn in question the validity of a statute of, or an authority exercised under, any State, on the ground of their being repugnant to the Constitution, treaties, or laws of the United States, and the decision is in favor of such their validity; or where is drawn in question the construction of any clause of the Constitution, or of a treaty or statute of, or commission held under the United States, and the decision is against the title, right, privilege, or exemption, specially set up or claimed by either party under such clause of the said Constitution, treaty, statute, or commission, may be re-examined and reversed, or affirmed in the Supreme Court of the United States upon a writ of error, the citation being signed by the chief justice, or judge, or chancellor of the court rendering or passing the judgment or decree complained of, or by a justice of the Supreme Court of the United States in the same manner, and under the same regulations, and the writ shall have the same effect, as if the judgment or decree complained of had been rendered or passed in a circuit court; and the proceeding upon the reversal shall also be the same, except that the Supreme Court, instead of remanding the cause for a final decision, as before provided, may, at their discretion, if the cause shall have been once remanded before, proceed to a final decision of the same, and award execution. But no other error shall be assigned or regarded as a ground of reversal in any such case as aforesaid, than such as appears on the face of the record, and immediately respects the before-mentioned questions of validity, or construction of the said Constitution, treaties, statutes, commissions, or authorities, in dispute."

This section embraces three classes of cases. The first, those in which a State court should decide a law or treaty of the United States to be void, either because it violated the Constitution of the United States, or for any other reason. Ought there not in such cases to be an appeal to the Supreme Court of the United States? Without such an appeal, the General Government might be obliged to behold its own laws and its solemn treaties annulled by the judiciary of every State in the Union, without the power of redress.

The second class of cases is of a different character. It embraces those causes in which the validity of State laws is contested, upon the principle that they violate the Constitution, the laws, or the treaties of the United States, and have, therefore, been enacted in opposition to the authority of the "supreme law of the land." Cases of this description have been of frequent occurrence. It has often been drawn into question before the State courts, whether State laws did or did not violate the Constitution of the United States. Is it not then essential to the preservation of the General Government, that the Supreme Court of the United States should possess the power of reviewing the judgments of State courts in all cases wherein they have established the validity of a State law in opposition to the Constitution and laws of the United States?

The third class differs essentially from each of the two first. In the cases embraced by it, neither the validity of acts of Congress, nor of treaties, nor of State laws is called in question. This clause of the 25th section merely confers upon the Supreme Court the appellate jurisdiction of construing the Constitution, laws, and treaties of the United States, when their protection has been invoked by parties to suits before the State courts, and has been denied by their decision. Without the exercise of this power, in cases originating in the State courts, the Constitution, laws, and treaties of the United States would be left to be finally construed and executed by a judicial power, over which Congress has no control.

This section does not interfere, either directly or indirectly, with the independence of the State courts in finally deciding all cases arising exclusively under their own constitution and laws. It leaves them in the enjoyment of every power which they possessed before the adoption of the Federal Constitution. It merely declares that, as that Constitution established a new form of Government, and consequently gave to the State courts the power of construing, in certain cases, the Constitution, the laws, and the treaties of the United States, the Supreme Court of the United States should, to this limited extent, but not beyond it, possess the power of reviewing their judgments. The section itself declares that no other error shall be assigned or regarded as a ground of reversal, in any such case as aforesaid, than such as appears on the face of the record, and immediately respects the before-mentioned questions of validity or construction of the said Constitution, treaties, statutes, commissions, or authorities in dispute.

The minority of the committee will now proceed to advance, in a more distinct form, a few of the reasons why, in their opinion, the 25th section of this act ought not to be repealed.

And, in the first place, it ought to be the chief object of all Governments to protect individual rights. In almost every case involving a question before a State court under this section of the judiciary act, the Constitution, laws, or treaties of the United States are interposed for the protection of individuals. Does a citizen invoke the protection of an act of Congress upon a trial before a State court which decides that act to be unconstitutional and void, and renders judgment against him? This section secures his right of appeal from such a decision to the Supreme Court of the United States.

When a citizen, in a suit before a State court, contends that a State law, by which he is assailed, is a violation of the Constitution of the United States and therefore void (if his plea should be overruled), he may bring this question before the Supreme Court of the United States.

In like manner, when an individual claims any right before a State court under the Constitution or laws of the United States, and the decision is against his claim, he may appeal to the Supreme Court of the United States.

If this section were repealed, all these important individual rights would be forfeited. The history of our country abundantly proves that individual States are liable to high excitements and strong prejudices. The judges of these States would be more or less than men if they did not participate in the feelings of the community by which they are surrounded. Under the influence of these excitements, individuals, whose rights happen to clash with the prevailing feeling of the State, would have but a slender hope of obtaining justice before 115a State tribunal. There would be the power and the influence of the State sovereignty on the one side, and an individual who had made himself obnoxious to popular odium on the other. In such cases, ought the liberty or the property of a citizen, so far as he claims the same under the Constitution or laws of the United States, to be decided before a State court, without an appeal to the Supreme Court of the United States, on whom the construction of this very Constitution and these laws has been conferred, in all cases, by the Constitution?

The Supreme Court, considering the elevated character of its judges, and that they reside in parts of the Union remote from each other, can never be liable to local excitements and local prejudices. To that tribunal our citizens can appeal with safety and with confidence (as long as the 25th section of the judicial act shall remain upon the statute book) whenever they consider that their rights, under the Constitution and laws of the United States, have been violated by a State court. Besides, should this section be repealed, it would produce a denial of equal justice to parties drawing in question the Constitution, laws, or treaties of the United States. In civil actions, the plaintiff might then bring his action in a Federal or State court, as he pleased, and as he thought he should be most likely to succeed; whilst the defendant would have no option, but must abide the consequences without the power of removing the cause from a State into a Federal court, except in the single case of his being sued out of the district in which he resides; and this, although he might have a conclusive defence under the Constitution and laws of the United States.

Another reason for preserving this section is, that without it there would be no uniformity in the construction and administration of the Constitution, laws, and treaties of the United States. If the courts of twenty-four distinct, sovereign States, each possess the power, in the last resort, of deciding upon the Constitution and laws of the United States, their construction may be different in every State of the Union. That act of Congress which conforms to the Constitution of the United States, and is valid in the opinion of the supreme court of Georgia, may be a direct violation of the provisions of that instrument, and be void in the judgment of the supreme court of South Carolina. A State law in Virginia might in this manner be declared constitutional, whilst the same law, if passed by the Legislature of Pennsylvania, would be void. Nay, what would be still more absurd, a law or treaty of the United States with a foreign nation, admitted to be constitutionally made, might secure rights to the citizens of one State, which would be denied to those of another. Although the same Constitution and laws govern the Union, yet the rights acquired under them would vary with every degree of latitude. Surely the framers of the Constitution would have left their work incomplete, had they established no common tribunal to decide its own construction, and that of the laws and treaties made under its authority. They are not liable to this charge, because they have given express power to the Judiciary of the Union over "all cases, in law and equity, arising under this 116Constitution, the laws of the United States, and treaties made, or which shall be made, under their authority."

The first Congress of the United States have, to a considerable extent, carried this power into execution by the passage of the judicial act, and it contains no provision more important than the 25th section.

This section ought not to be repealed, because, in the opinion of the minority of the Committee on the Judiciary, its repeal would seriously endanger the existence of this Union. The chief evil which existed under the old confederation, and which gave birth to the present Constitution, was that the General Government could not act directly upon the people, but only by requisition upon sovereign States. The consequence was, that the States either obeyed or disobeyed these requisitions, as they thought proper. The present Constitution was intended to enable the Government of the United States to act immediately upon the people of the States, and to carry its own laws into full execution, by virtue of its own authority. If this section were repealed, the General Government would be deprived of the power, by means of its own judiciary, to give effect either to the Constitution which called it into existence, or to the laws and treaties made under its authority. It would be compelled to submit, in many important cases, to the decisions of State courts; and thus the very evil which the present Constitution was intended to prevent would be entailed upon the people. The judiciary of the States might refuse to carry into effect the laws of the United States; and without that appeal to the Supreme

Court which the 25th section authorizes, these laws would thus be entirely annulled, and could not be executed without a resort to force.

This position may be illustrated by a few striking examples. Suppose the Legislature of one of the States, believing the tariff laws to be unconstitutional, should determine that they ought not to be executed within its limits. They accordingly pass a law, imposing the severest penalties upon the collector and other custom-house officers of the United States within their territory, if they should collect the duties on the importation of foreign merchandise. The collector proceeds to discharge the duties of his office under the laws of the United States, and he is condemned and punished before a State court for violating this State law. Repeal this section, and the decision of the State court would be final and conclusive; and any State could thus nullify any act of Congress which she deemed to be unconstitutional.

The Executive of one of the States, in a message to the Legislature, has declared it to be his opinion, that the land belonging to the United States within her territory is now the property of the State, by virtue of her sovereign authority. Should the Legislature be of the same opinion, and pass a law for the punishment of the land officers of the United States who should sell any of the public lands within her limits, this transfer of property might be virtually accomplished by the repeal of the 25th section of the judicial act. Our land officers might then be severely punished, and thus prohibited by the courts of that State from performing their duty under the laws of the 117Union, without the possibility of redress in any constitutional or legal form. In this manner, the title of the United States to a vast domain, which has cost the nation many millions, and which justly belongs to the people of the several States, would be defeated or greatly impaired.

Another illustration might be introduced. Suppose the Legislature of Pennsylvania, being of opinion that the charter of the Bank of the United States is unconstitutional, were to declare it to be a nuisance, and inflict penalties upon all its officers for making discounts or receiving deposits. Should the courts of that State carry such a law into effect, without the 25th section there would be no appeal from their decision; and the Legislature and courts of a single State might thus prostrate an institution established under the Constitution and laws of the United States.

In all such cases, redress can now be peaceably obtained in the ordinary administration of justice. A writ of error issues from the Supreme Court, which finally decides the question whether the act of Congress was constitutional or not; and if they determine in the affirmative, the judgment of the State court is reversed. The laws are thus substituted instead of arms, and the States kept within their proper orbits by the judicial authority. But if no such appeal existed, then, upon the occurrence of cases of this character, the General Government would be compelled to determine whether the Union should be dissolved, or whether there should be a recurrence to force—an awful alternative, which we trust may never be presented. We will not attempt further to portray the evils which might result from the abandonment of the present judicial system. They will strike every reflecting mind.

It has of late years been contended that this section of the judicial act was unconstitutional, and that Congress do not possess the power of investing the Supreme Court with appellate jurisdiction in any case which has been finally decided in the courts of the States. It has also been contended that, even if they do possess this power, it does not extend to cases in which a State is a party. On this branch of the question, we would refer the House to the very able and conclusive argument of the Supreme Court of the United States, in the cases of Martin vs. Hunter's Lessee (1st Wheaton, 304) and Cohens vs. the State of Virginia (6 Wheaton, 264) by which the affirmative of these propositions is clearly established. It may be proper, however, that we should make a few observations upon this part of the question. Those who have argued in favor of these positions, assert that the general words of the Constitution, extending the judicial power of the Union "to all cases, in law and equity," arising under the Constitution and laws of the United States, ought, by construction, to be restricted to such cases in law and equity as may originate in the courts of the Union. They would thus establish a limitation at war with the letter, and, in our opinion, equally at war with the spirit of the instrument. Had such been the intention of the framers of the Constitution, they well knew in what language to express that intention. Had it been their purpose to restrict the meaning of the general language which they had used in the first clause of the section, they could have done 118so with much propriety in the second. This clause, after providing "that, in all cases affecting ambassadors, other public ministers, and consuls, and those in which a State shall be a party, the Supreme Court shall have original jurisdiction," proceeds to declare "that, in all the other cases before mentioned, the Supreme Court shall have appellate jurisdiction, both as to law and fact, with such exceptions, and under such regulations, as the Congress shall make." On the supposition contended for, it is wholly unaccountable that the framers of the Constitution did not limit the natural effect of the words used in the first clause, by making the second to read "that, in all the other cases before mentioned," arising in the inferior courts of the United States, "the Supreme Court shall have appellate jurisdiction." But no such restriction exists; and, from the fair import of the words used in both clauses, the Supreme Court possess the power of finally deciding "all cases, in law and equity," arising under the Constitution, the laws, and the treaties of the United States, no matter whether they may have originated in a Federal or in a State court, and no matter whether States or individuals be the parties.

But it is not our intention to enter into a protracted constitutional argument upon the present occasion, because this question has long since been put at rest, if any constitutional question can ever be considered as settled in this country. The Federalist, which is now considered a text-book in regard to the construction of the Constitution, and deservedly so, as well from the great merit of the work as the high character of its authors, is clear and explicit on this subject. After reasoning upon it at some length, the author of the 83d number of that production arrives at the following conclusion: "To confine, therefore, the general expressions which gave appellate jurisdiction to the Supreme Court to appeals from the subordinate Federal courts, instead of allowing their extension to the State courts, would be to abridge the latitude of the terms, in subversion of the intent, contrary to every sound rule of interpretation."

The Federalist, it will be recollected, was written between the formation of the Constitution and its adoption by the States. Immediately after its adoption, Congress, by passing the 25th section of the judicial act, now sought to be repealed, fully confirmed this construction. This appellate jurisdiction has ever since been exercised by the Supreme Court in a great variety of cases; and we are not aware that the constitutionality of its exercise has ever been questioned by the decision of any State court, except in a single instance, which did not occur until the year 1815. And even in that case (Hunter vs. Fairfax), the judgment of the Supreme Court was carried into effect according to the existing law, without endangering the peace of the country.

The last topic to which we would advert is, the claim which has been set up to exempt the judgments obtained by the States of this Union, before their own courts, in civil and criminal suits, prosecuted in their name, from being reviewed by the Supreme Court of the United States upon a writ of error. Much stress has been laid by those who sustain this claim, upon the general 119proposition that a sovereign independent State cannot be sued, except by its own consent. But does this proposition apply, in its extent, to the States of this Union. That is the question for discussion.

We have in this country an authority much higher than that of sovereign States. It is the authority of the sovereign people of each State. In their State conventions they ratified the Constitution of the United States; and so far as that Constitution has deprived the States of any of the attributes of sovereignty, they are bound by it, because such was the will of the people. The Constitution, thus called into existence by the will of the people of the several States, has declared itself, and the laws and treaties which should emanate from its authority, to be "the supreme law of the land;" and the judges in every State shall be bound thereby, anything in the Constitution or laws of any State to the contrary notwithstanding.

Why, then, should a State, who has obtained a judgment in her own courts against an individual, in violation of this "supreme law of the land," be protected from having her judgment reversed by the Supreme Court of the United States? Is there any reason, either in the Constitution or in natural justice, why judgments obtained by a State in her own courts should be held sacred, notwithstanding they violated the Constitution and laws of the Union, which would not apply, at least with equal force, in favor of individual plaintiffs? The Constitution subjects to the review of the Supreme Court all cases in law or equity arising under itself, or the laws of the Union. It excepts no case bearing this character. Whether the party be a State or an individual, all must alike bow to the sovereign will of the people, expressed in the Constitution of the United States.

In suits brought by a State against an individual in her own courts, there is much greater danger of oppression, considering the relative power and influence of the parties, than there would be in controversies between individuals. And are these to be the only cases selected, in which the citizen shall not be permitted to protect himself by the Constitution and laws of the Union before the Supreme Court of the United States? Is it not sufficient that, under the Constitution, the States cannot be sued as defendants, without adding to this, by a strained and unnatural construction, the additional privilege that the judgments which they may obtain as plaintiffs or prosecutors before their own courts, whether right or wrong, shall in all cases be irreversible?

We will not repeat the considerations which have been already urged to prove that, unless this provision of the Constitution applies to the States, the rights of individuals will be sacrificed, all uniformity of decision abandoned, and each one of the States will have it in her power to set the Constitution and laws of the United States at defiance.

The eleventh amendment to the Constitution of the United States interferes in no respect with the principles for which we have contended. It is in these words:

"The judicial power of the United States shall not be construed to extend to any suit, in law or equity, commenced or prosecuted against one of the 120United States by citizens of another State, or by citizens or subjects of any foreign State."

Chief Justice Marshall, in delivering the opinion of the court in the case of Cohens vs. Virginia, has given so clear, and in our opinion, so correct an exposition of the true construction of the amendment, that we shall, in conclusion, present to the House a few extracts from that opinion, instead of any argument of our own. He says that "the first impression made on the mind by this amendment is, that it was intended for those cases, and for those only, in which some demand against a State is made by an individual in the courts of the Union. If we consider the causes to which it is to be traced, we are conducted to the same conclusion. A general interest might well be felt, in leaving to a State the full power of consulting its convenience in the adjustment of its debts, or of other claims upon it; but no interest could be felt in so changing the relation between the whole and its parts, as to strip the Government of the means of protecting, by the instrumentality of its courts, the Constitution and laws from active violation. The words of the amendment appear to the court to justify and require this construction.

"To commence a suit, is to demand something by the institution of process in a court of justice; and to prosecute the suit is, according to the common acceptation of language, to continue that demand. By a suit commenced by an individual against a State, we should understand a process sued out by that individual against the State, for the purpose of establishing some claim against it by the judgment of a court; and the prosecution of that suit is its continuance. Whatever may be the stages of its progress, the actor is still the same. Suits had been commenced in the Supreme Court against some of the States before the amendment was introduced into Congress, and others might be commenced before it should be adopted by the State Legislatures, and might be depending at the time of its adoption. The object of the amendment was not only to prevent the commencement of future suits, but to arrest the prosecution of those which might be commenced when this article should form a part of the Constitution. It therefore embraces both objects; and its meaning is, that the judicial power shall not be construed to extend to any suit which may be commenced, or which, if already commenced, may be prosecuted against a State, by the citizens of another State. If a suit, brought in one court, and carried by legal process to a supervising court, be a continuation of the same suit, then this suit is not commenced nor prosecuted against a State. It is clearly, in its commencement, the suit of a State against an individual, which suit is transferred to this court, not for the purpose of asserting any claim against the State, but for the purpose of asserting a constitutional defence against a claim made by a State.

"Under the judiciary act, the effect of a writ of error is simply to bring the record into court, and submit the judgment of the inferior tribunal to re-examination. It does not, in any manner, act upon the parties; it acts only on the record. It removes the record into the supervising tribunal. Where, then, a State obtains a judgment against an individual, and the court rendering 121such judgment overrules a defence set up under the Constitution or laws of the United States, the transfer of this record into the Supreme Court for the sole purpose of inquiring whether the judgment violates the Constitution or laws of the United States can, with no propriety, we think, be denominated a suit commenced or prosecuted against the State, whose judgment is so far re-examined. Nothing is demanded from the State. No claim against it, of any description, is asserted or prosecuted. The party is not to be restored to the possession of anything. Essentially, it is an appeal on a single point; and the defendant who appeals from a judgment rendered against him, is never said to commence or prosecute a suit against the plaintiff, who has obtained the judgment. The writ of error is given rather than an appeal, because it is the more usual mode of removing suits at common law; and because, perhaps, it is more technically proper, where a single point of law, and not the whole case, is to be re-examined. But an appeal might be given, and might be so regulated as to effect every purpose of a writ of error. The mode of removal is form, not substance. Whether it be by writ of error or appeal, no claim is asserted, no demand is made by the original defendant; he only asserts the constitutional right to have his defence examined by that tribunal whose province it is to construe the Constitution and laws of the Union.

"The only part of the proceeding which is in any manner personal is the citation. And what is the citation? It is simply notice to the opposite party that the record is transferred into another court, where he may appear, or decline to appear, as his judgment or inclination may determine. As the party who has obtained a judgment is out of court, and may, therefore, not know that his cause is removed, common justice requires that notice of the fact should be given him: but this notice is not a suit, nor has it the effect of process. If the party does not choose to appear, he cannot be brought into court, nor is his failure to appear considered as a default. Judgment cannot be given against him for his non-appearance; but the judgment is to be re-examined, and reversed or affirmed, in like manner as if the party had appeared and argued his cause.

"The point of view in which this writ of error, with its citation, has been considered uniformly in the courts of the Union, has been well illustrated by a reference to the course of this court in suits instituted by the United States. The universally received opinion is, that no suit can be commenced or prosecuted against the United States; that the judiciary act does not authorize such suits; yet writs of error, accompanied with citations, have uniformly issued for the removal of judgments in favor of the United States into a superior court, where they have, like those in favor of an individual, been re-examined, and affirmed or reversed. It has never been suggested that such writ of error was a suit against the United States, and therefore not within the jurisdiction of the appellate court.

"It is, then, the opinion of the court that the defendant who removes a judgment rendered against him by a State court into this court, for the purpose of re-examining the question whether that judgment be in violation of the Constitution or laws of the United States, does not commence or prosecute a suit against the State, whatever may be its opinion, where the effect of the writ may be to restore the party to the possession of a thing which he demands."

All which is respectfully submitted.

James Buchanan, Wm. W. Ellsworth, E. D. White.

It was Mr. Buchanan's intention to retire from public life at the close of this session of Congress in March, 1831. But in the early part of February, without his previous knowledge, a movement was set on foot in Pennsylvania to bring him forward as the candidate of that State for the Vice-Presidency at the next election, on the ticket with General Jackson, whose re-election to the Presidency was already anticipated by his party. As soon as information of this purpose reached Mr. Buchanan, he did what he could to discourage it, as will appear from the following letter to one of his Pennsylvania friends and neighbors:

[JAMES BUCHANAN TO GEORGE PLITT, ESQ.]

Washington, February 18, 1831.

Dear Sir:—

I received your kind letter of the 7th instant and the Chester County Democrat of the 8th by the same mail; and I confess the information which they contained was wholly unexpected. I can say nothing upon the subject to which they refer, unless it be to express a profound and grateful sense of the kindness and partiality of those of my friends in Chester County who would elevate me to a station to which I have never aspired. I cannot flatter myself, for a single moment, that the people of the State will respond to a nomination which I feel has been dictated in a great degree by personal friendship; and I shall retire to private life, after the close of the present session, without casting one lingering look behind. As a private citizen I shall always remember with the deepest sensibility the many favors which I have received from the people of the district whom I have so long represented, perfectly convinced that they have already bestowed upon me quite as many honors as I have ever deserved.

I sent you by yesterday's mail a copy of the correspondence between the President and Vice-President. Its publication has not produced the sensation here which was expected. I think it will not injure General Jackson in the estimation of his friends in

Pennsylvania. Its effect, however, will be still more to divide the personal friends of Mr. Crawford and Mr. Calhoun.

The speech which I made upon Peck's trial will probably not appear until a full report of the case shall be published. The commendations which have been bestowed upon it, both here and elsewhere, have been of a character so far beyond its merits that I fear the public will be disappointed upon the appearance in print.

I would suggest to you the propriety of considering this letter confidential so far as it regards myself. The subject is of a nature so delicate, and anything I can say upon it is so liable to misconstruction, that I should not have answered your letter, had I not felt that you have always deserved my friendship, and that I might rely with confidence on your discretion.

From your friend,

James Buchanan.

P. S.—What is now the state of anti-masonry in your county?

The truth is that a longer continuance in public life did not accord with Mr. Buchanan's plans. His professional income had fallen to the low rate of about $2000 per annum, and he determined to restore it to what it had previously been, and to take his chances for raising it still higher.

He had many qualifications for great success at the bar: competent learning, untiring industry, a ready and pleasing address, an uncommon reasoning power, and a reputation of perfect integrity. Had he been impelled by the wants of a family to devote himself exclusively to his profession, there can be no doubt that he would have risen in it to great eminence. His talents were not of that order which would have enabled him to unite in his own person the very different functions of a statesman and a lawyer; a union which has been exhibited in a very marked manner by only one person in America, and perhaps by no one in England. But my estimate of Mr. Buchanan's abilities leads me to say, that if he had not at this period of his life been again drawn into a political career, he would have ranked among the first lawyers of his time. He must have soon encased in the forensic discussion of constitutional questions. He had very early imbibed a deep reverence for the Constitution of the United States, and his turn of mind would have adapted him to the handling of questions such as were then arising and are likely long to arise upon its interpretation. 124As he grew older and his sphere of professional employment became widened, he must have been found at the bar of the Supreme Court of the United States, if not as the peer of Webster and Pinkney, at least as the peer of many against whom those great advocates had to put forth their strength. But from such a professional career Mr. Buchanan was drawn away, not by the prospect of the Vice-Presidency, but by the unexpected offer of the mission to Russia, an account of which will be found in the next chapter.

[FROM GEORGE W. BUCHANAN.]

Pittsburgh, March 4, 1830.

Dear Brother:—

I am much pleased to observe from the U. S. Telegraph of the 25th ultimo that you have taken a manly stand on the constitutional side of the Indian question. In this pleasure there is no doubt a spice of personal vanity, as your sentiments, so far as they can be inferred from the debate, are in perfect accordance with my own. It is a question which has produced an unaccountable excitement in our city. Every word on the subject is devoured with wonderful avidity; and I can assure you that you did not put too high an estimate on public feeling when you moved for the printing of ten thousand copies of the report. As public opinion is yet unsettled, it is important that the report of the committee, if temperate and decided, should have an extensive circulation.

I have read your speech on the Judiciary with great interest and advantage. The legal gentlemen in our city have highly complimented both its style and research. The best evidence of its effect is, that all those with whom I have conversed on the subject are decidedly in favor of your bill.

Anti-masonry is still flourishing. I do not know the state of feeling in the eastern section of Pennsylvania, but I am now perfectly convinced that no western county will return a mason to the next Legislature. Strong, however, as anti-masonry is, much of its apparent strength is borrowed from extrinsic circumstances. In this city, for instance, many persons are anxious to be rid of a set of rulers who have managed with so much political dexterity as to control the destinies of this county for many years. These men happen to be masons. No other hobby could be mounted with the same prospect of success. The honest anti-masons, the old Adams men, and the disappointed office-seekers are easily induced to unite their influence against the "powers that be." The motley materials are thus thrown into one caldron and stirred up into a dangerous compound. These remarks I have made to account for the extraordinary strength of anti-masonry in this quarter......

I am obliged to you for the salutary counsel contained in your last letter. I believe that a whole volume of advice (both moral and political) is contained 125in that single direction, "Be wise as the serpent, but harmless as the dove." ...... My health is very good.

Your grateful and affectionate brother,

Geo. W. Buchanan.

It appears, however, that a meeting was held at Lancaster in March, at which he was nominated for the Vice-Presidency, with what effect may be learned from the following letters written by his brother George from Pittsburgh:

[GEORGE W. BUCHANAN TO JAMES BUCHANAN.]

Pittsburgh, March 23, 1831.

Dear Brother:—

I have just read with great pleasure the proceedings of the Lancaster meeting which nominated you for the Vice-Presidency. Whether success shall crown the exertions of your friends or not, no public man can receive so flattering and precious a testimonial as the unanimous and unsolicited voice of his neighbors and acquaintants. In this part of the State, the idea seems to take very well. Both this county and Washington will, I think, hold meetings in your favor. I saw the editor of the Manufacturer this morning and ascertained that he will be disposed to take a prominent part. The Democrat will probably not be unfavorable. The editor, however, is a very timid creature.

On Thursday last I was so unfortunate as to fall and break my arm. The pain has subsided in a great degree, and I think that my arm will be restored in a short time to its wonted strength and action. I can now attend to any business that does not require the use of both hands.

I write under a feeling of great inconvenience, and will therefore close.

Your grateful and affectionate brother,

Geo. W. Buchanan.

Pittsburgh, April 29, 1831.

Dear Brother:—

I have been absent from home in attendance upon a sale of United States property at Uniontown for a week past. I succeeded in effecting a very good disposition of the property. The Government, I have no doubt, will approve my proceedings.

I find that in every county in which I have been, your nomination for the Vice-Presidency is very popular. In Fayette and Washington there will scarcely be a division of sentiment. Still, however, it is thought proper to suspend all public proceedings in your favor till the time of holding their regular Democratic meetings in the summer. That course will also be adopted in this county. Every leading Jackson politician here, with the exception of one or two Ingham men, is favorable to your nomination. It will, however, be probably better to wait for a further expression of public opinion at the regular meetings of the party throughout the State. I observe that in the Kentucky Gazette your name is placed on the Democratic ticket, under General Jackson's.

It is believed here that the appointment of Attorney-General has been tendered to you. If so, I hope that you will accept it. It is a most honorable station, and free from that abuse which attaches to the Secretaryships. Will Van Buren be a candidate for the Vice-Presidency?

My arm is not yet so far restored as to be of any use. I trust, however, that the weakness is only of a temporary nature. My health, in other respects, is good.

I am your grateful brother,
Geo. W. Buchanan.

Mr. Buchanan returned to Lancaster after this meeting had been held. His nomination to the Vice-Presidency continued to be agitated in other parts of Pennsylvania, and in June a great meeting of the supporters of General Jackson was held at Williamsport, of which George Buchanan gives the following account:

[GEORGE W. BUCHANAN TO JAMES BUCHANAN.]
Pittsburgh, June 15, 1831.
Dear Brother:—

I arrived here on Thursday. The heat was so oppressive on horseback that I sold my horse at Bellefonte, and returned in the stage. The journey has, in a very great degree, restored my health.

The Jackson meeting at Williamsport was an exceedingly respectable one. Fifteen counties were represented. There can be no doubt that you were the Pennsylvanian to whom the resolution respecting the Vice-Presidency was intended to point. I have every reason to believe that your name would have been inserted by an almost unanimous vote, if Mr. Potter, from Centier, had not been detained at home by the illness of his wife. He would have offered a resolution nominating you; and I can say, from information of the most undoubted credit, that at least two-thirds of all the jurors would have warmly sustained it. Mr. Ward, editor of the Susquehanna Register, and Mr. Youngman, editor of the Union Times, with both of whom I became intimately acquainted, are decidedly favorable to your nomination. They are intelligent young men, and have, in a warm and flattering manner, solicited my correspondence.

In the Western country, I find that the Ingham faction is extremely weak. Out of Bradford County, and apart from their family connections, they appear to have no friends in the West. The people in our district speak very favorably of Mr. Muhlenburg as the next Governor, and, I assure you, I did nothing to discountenance that feeling. The popularity of the present Governor has been injured by the appointment of General McKean, the proposition to tax coal, and the character of certain county appointments. The resolution adopted at our meeting, and opposing General Jackson's course in the

Cabinet affair, was intended as a direct censure upon Messrs. Ingham, &c. Owing to the relation I bore to you and to General Jackson, I determined to take no active part in the meeting.

I should like very much to see you and hold a long conversation on matters and things. In July I shall endeavor to visit Franklin County, and, if you should be unable to meet me there, I will extend my journey to Lancaster.

Governor Wolf left our city this morning for Erie. He was here at the time of my arrival, and, in company with several ladies and gentleman, I escorted him to Economy. He was exceedingly well received by the people of that singular village. His plain manners and German language endeared him very much to Raff and his whole Society. The Governor treated me with great attention, and evinced a disposition to be very familiar. His daughter, however, pleased my fancy much more than the old gentleman himself. She is a very interesting lady, and has well nigh stolen my heart.

I observe that the newspapers are determined to give you some office. They now make you Minister to Russia. Is this report true? If so, it will then become your duty to consider what sort of a Secretary your brother George would make. It would be a very interesting time to visit Europe.[25]

I remain your grateful and affectionate brother,

Geo. W. Buchanan.

128

CHAPTER VII.

1831–1833.

JOHN RANDOLPH OF ROANOKE MADE MINISTER TO RUSSIA—FAILURE OF MR. RANDOLPH'S HEALTH—THE MISSION OFFERED TO MR. BUCHANAN—HIS MOTHER'S OPPOSITION TO HIS ACCEPTANCE—EMBARKS AT NEW YORK AND ARRIVES AT LIVERPOOL—LETTERS FROM ENGLAND—JOURNEY TO ST. PETERSBURG—CORRESPONDENCE WITH FRIENDS AT HOME.

After General Jackson became President in March, 1829, he determined to offer the Mission to Russia to "John Randolph of Roanoke." This offer was made in September of that year, and was then accepted; but the nomination was not submitted to the Senate until the following May. It was confirmed without opposition from any quarter.[26]

Before he sailed, Mr. Randolph had leave granted him by the President to spend the following winter in the south of Europe, if the state of his health should require it. He remained at St. Petersburg only long enough to be accredited. His constitution was too far impaired to admit of his encountering the rigors of a Russian winter. He left the affairs of the legation in the hands of Mr. Clay, the Secretary, and went to England.

In his annual message in December (1830), the President communicated to Congress the fact of Mr. Randolph's necessary absence from his post, on leave, and said that the public interests in that quarter would still be attended to by the Minister, 129through the Secretary. When the annual appropriation bill came before the House of Representatives in January (1831), a long and acrimonious discussion took place upon a motion to strike out the salary of the Minister to Russia. It was contended that the Mission was actually, if not technically, vacant; and it was charged that the appointment of Mr. Randolph, with the understanding that he might leave his post at his own discretion, was a "job." To this it was answered by the friends of the Administration that the responsibility for his appointment lay with the President and the Senate; that in the Senate the opposition entirely approved of the appointment; and that for the House to refuse to pay the salary of a Minister because he was absent from his post on leave given by the President, would be highly improper. In the course of this debate, Mr. Buchanan made a temperate and judicious speech, in which he defended the appointment. The result was that the appropriation was retained in the bill and the bill was passed.[27]

It became necessary, however, in the spring of this year, for the President to recall Mr. Randolph and to select his successor. In those days, the public men of the country did not propose themselves for such appointments. The first intimation that reached Mr. Buchanan of the President's wish to make him Minister to Russia, came to him in a letter from a confidential friend of the President.

130[MAJOR EATON TO MR. BUCHANAN.]
(Private.) Washington, May 31, 1831.
Dear Sir:—

Where are you, and what doing? I cannot tell, having heard nothing from you since the adjournment of Congress. That you are doing well, though, I have no doubt and earnestly hope.

I introduce myself to you now at the request and by the direction of the President. The Mission to St. Petersburg is expected shortly to become vacant. It will afford the President pleasure to confide this trust to you, if it shall suit your convenience to accept it. He desires me to make known his wishes to you and to solicit an answer. It is at the present an important and a highly interesting part of the world. For reasons not material now to be explained, the President desires that you will consider this communication entirely of a confidential character.

With great respect,
J. H. Eaton.

[MR. BUCHANAN TO MAJOR EATON.]
Lancaster, June 4, 1831.
Dear Sir:—

I received your letter last evening, offering me, "by the direction of the President," the Mission to St. Petersburg. I feel with the deepest sensibility this pledge of the kindness of the President, and the recollection of it shall ever be engraven on my grateful memory. My attachment for him, both personal and political, has been of the warmest character, and he has now engrafted upon that feeling a strong sense of individual gratitude.

There is but a single circumstance which induces me to doubt whether I ought to accept the Mission. I wish to be placed in no public station in which I cannot discharge my duty with usefulness to the country and honor to the administration of General Jackson. Ignorant as I now am of the French language, I doubt whether I could acquire a sufficient knowledge of it in proper time to enable me to hold that free communion with the political circles in St. Petersburg which I consider essential to the able discharge of the duties of a foreign minister. I have much business now on hand which I could not immediately leave without doing serious injury to individuals who have confided in me. Will you be so kind as to inform me at what time the President would think the public interest required me to leave the country in case I should accept the Mission?

Please to remember me to the President in the strongest terms. Accept my thanks for your uniform kindness, and present my respects to Mrs. Eaton. I remain
Sincerely your friend,
James Buchanan.

131[EATON TO BUCHANAN.]

(Private.) Washington City, June 7, 1831.
Dear Sir:—

I have just received your letter, and will show it to the President, whom I shall see during the day. The difficulty you suggest can no doubt be remedied. Mr. R. is not expected to return before July or August; it would then be too late in the season to reach St. Petersburg by water transportation. To depart in September would create the necessity of travelling over land from Hamburg or Havre. This, I am confident, the President would not ask of you. I feel satisfied that he will grant the indulgence asked and defer your departure until next spring. But I will see him, and if I be wrong in this, I will again write you to-morrow;—if no letter come, you may understand by the silence that my suggestions are approved by the President.
Very truly yours,
J. H. Eaton.
P. S. I will write to you to-morrow or the next day, at any rate.
3 o'clock. I sent your letter to the President. In answer he thus writes: "Say to Mr. Buchanan that he will not be required to go out before next winter or spring, that he may reach St. Petersburg on the breaking up of the ice—unless something more than is now expected arises, when the President will rely upon Mr. Buchanan's patriotism to proceed. He will have sufficient time to arrange his affairs."
[BUCHANAN TO EATON.]
Lancaster, June 12, 1831.
Dear Sir:—

After the receipt of your last kind letter of the 7th inst., with the extract from the President's note to you annexed, granting me all the indulgence I could have desired, I can no longer hesitate to accept the Russian Mission. I fear that the necessary arrangements, both of a professional and private character, which I must soon begin to make preparatory to leaving the country—together with the study of the French language, which I intend to commence—may disclose the fact that this Mission has been offered to me and accepted. Indeed, from the publications in the newspapers it was believed by many before I had any intimation that such an intention existed on the part of the President. Is there any reason why I should for the present defer these preparations? Please to present my grateful compliments to the President, and believe me to be
Sincerely your friend,
James Buchanan.
Hon. John H. Eaton.
132[EATON TO BUCHANAN.]
Washington, June 15, 1831.
Dear Sir:—

On receiving your letter this morning I referred it to the President, and he has returned me a hasty note, which I enclose to you. It is quite like himself, candid and frank.
With great regard, yours,
J. H. Eaton.
[EATON TO JACKSON.]
Dear Sir:—

I send you a letter to-day received from Mr. Buchanan. What shall I say to him?

Yours,
J. H. Eaton.
[JACKSON TO EATON.]
Dear Sir:—

Say to him in reply, to go on and make his preparations and let the newspapers make any comments that they may think proper, and mind them not. It is only necessary that he should not give them any information on this subject—the journals will say what they please, and be it so.
Yours,
A. J.
[LIVINGSTON TO BUCHANAN.]
(Private.) Washington, August 2, 1831.
My Dear Sir:—

Mr. Taney having given me your letter of the 26th July, with a request that I would communicate it to the President, I did so; and he has directed me to say that it was not deemed proper to make the offer of the Russian Mission public until Mr. Randolph's return should make the place vacant, and that when that event happened he would direct me to write to you.
The former communications were made to you while I was confined to my bed, and did not pass through my Department, or they would have been put in a shape that would have spared you any embarrassment on the subject.
I am, my dear Sir, with the greatest regard and esteem,
Your friend and humble servant,
Edw. Livingston.[28]
133[TANEY TO BUCHANAN.]
(Confidential.)   Washington, August 2, 1831.
My Dear Sir:—

I received your letter and immediately waited on Mr. Livingston, and placed it in his hands, requesting him to ascertain whether your appointment and acceptance might not at once be made public. Mr. Livingston informed me to-day that he had seen the President, and that the only reason for desiring that nothing should be said about it was that Mr. Randolph had not yet returned, and that he did not wish that your appointment should be formally made and publicly announced until Mr. Randolph arrived in this country. The Secretary of State will, however, write to you himself to-day. I omitted to ask him when Mr. Randolph was expected, but he will probably mention the time in his letter to you. I can readily imagine that the present state of things may be rather embarrassing to you, and hope it will not be long before an appointment which I am quite sure will give great satisfaction to our friends, can be officially made known.
Mr. Livingston intends to go to New York in the course of this week in order to have a conference with Mr. McLane and Mr. Van Buren before the latter sails for England. He will leave Washington on Thursday, unless he should learn in the mean time that Mr. McLane is on his way to this place. And as an interview with him on your affairs would, I presume, be agreeable to you, perhaps you may make it convenient to meet him in New York. Governor Cass has accepted the appointment of Secretary of War, and was to leave home on the first of this month, and expected to be here before the 15th.

Wishing you, my dear Sir, a pleasant excursion, and regretting that my engagements here will prevent me from joining you at Saratoga, I am

Most truly your friend and obedient servant,

R. B. Taney.

There was one member of Mr. Buchanan's family who was decidedly opposed to his acceptance of this mission. This was his mother, then at the age of 65. It would be interesting to know what was the special reason which led this excellent and intelligent lady to feel as she did about this appointment. Whether it was anything more than a presentiment that she should never see him again after he had crossed the ocean, or whether she thought that it would not be wise for him to venture in a new path of public life, can only be inferred from the following letter, which she wrote to him after his decision had been made:

134[MRS. BUCHANAN TO HER SON JAMES.]

October 21 [1831].

Mr Dear Son:—

With Harriet's permission, I write you a few lines in her letter. I feel deep solicitude respecting your mission to Russia, and perhaps I am too late in laying [before you] my objections, which, in my estimation, are formidable. Would it not be practicable, even now, to decline its acceptance? Your political career has been of that description which ought to gratify your ambition; and as to pecuniary matters, they are no object to you. If you can, consistently with the character of a gentleman and a man of honor, decline, how great a gratification it would be to me. May God of His infinite goodness, dispose of us in whatever way may promote His glory and secure our everlasting felicity, is the prayer of your affectionate

Mother.

P. S.—At what time do you intend paying us that visit, previous to your departure from the country which gave you birth, and I expect, to me, the last visit? Do not disappoint me, but certainly come.

There is no record of this visit, which was indeed the last, but which was undoubtedly made. One of the strongest reasons that weighed with Mr. Buchanan against his acceptance of this mission was his mother's advanced age, and the probability that he might never see her again. In the latter part of August and the early part of September, he was absent from Lancaster on a journey to the East, on account of his health. On his return, he wrote a private letter to General Jackson; part of which, however, is wanting in the copy before me:

[MR. BUCHANAN TO GENERAL JACKSON.]

Lancaster, September 10, 1831.

Dear General:—

Having had the bilious fever severely for the last three autumns, I was advised by my physicians to go to the North this summer, as the best means of preventing its recurrence. Accordingly, I have been wandering about among the New Yorkers and the Yankees for several weeks past. I reached home but last night. Whilst I was at Boston, the anti-masonic letter of Mr. Adams made its appearance. This folly, although it caps the climax, is in perfect character with the history of his conduct. It is a melancholy spectacle to see a man who has held the first office acting as he has done. It is 135now believed seriously, even by his former friends, that he is courting the anti-masonic nomination. He and Rush are a par nobile fratrum. I was happy to find everywhere that the little specks which appeared on the political horizon—about the time you changed your Cabinet—have been entirely dissipated. It could not have been otherwise. In the opinion of your friends, the present Cabinet is just such a one as it ought to be. In this State, your strength has alarmed those who evidently wished to abandon you, and they are now the loudest in your support. It not being in their power to affect you, they are pushing another purpose with all their might. They are strenuously opposed to a national convention to nominate a Vice-President; and through the inadvertence of our friends who are without suspicion, it appears to be settled that a State convention, which will meet to nominate a Governor on the 4th of March next, will also select a candidate for the Vice-Presidency. This nomination ought to be made by a Jackson convention on the 8th of January. The consequence will be that the State administration—on account of its extensive patronage and the interest felt by all the State office-holders in sending their particular friends to the convention—will probably be able to control the nomination. George M. Dallas is unquestionably the candidate of the State administration, and of all those who are the friends of Mr. Ingham and Calhoun. Now I have no wish to be a candidate for the Vice-Presidency; on the contrary, my nomination was put up without my consent, and it is my intention to decline, but I desire to do it——

[The residue of the original letter is lost.]

Although Mr. Buchanan had accepted the offer of the Russian Mission, his nomination could not be submitted to the Senate until after that body had assembled in December, 1831. It was acted upon in the Senate in the early part of January, 1832, and from the following letter from Mr. Livingston, the Secretary of State, it appears that the nomination was confirmed by an unanimous or nearly unanimous vote:

[LIVINGSTON TO BUCHANAN.]

(Private and unofficial.) Washington, Jan. 12, 1832.

My Dear Sir:—

I pray you to receive my congratulations on your appointment and the unanimity with which your nomination is understood to have been confirmed by the Senate—a favor which it is believed will not be conferred upon all of us. Allow me also to ask at what time you can arrange your affairs for a departure. Have you designated any one to serve as your Secretary of Legation? You know that your wishes will be consulted on the occasion. Should you not desire that Mr. Clay should be retained in that situation, I could mention a gentleman who would be highly useful to you. He speaks most of the modern languages, has travelled in Europe and made good use of his travels; he is now employed in my Department and I should part with him with very great regret, but being sincerely attached to him I consider his advancement, not my interest or convenience, in this application; for he, Dr. Greenhow, enjoys my fullest confidence and you will, if you take him, find him every way worthy of yours, and well calculated by his manners, deportment and knowledge of the world to aid you in the lighter but very necessary duties of your station, as well as to perform those of a more important kind with which you may entrust him.

Two or three apples of discord have, as you will perceive by the papers, been thrown in both houses—each of them sufficient to create a warfare that will last during a session.

I am, my dear Sir, with high regard,

Your most obedient servant,

Edw. Livingston.

With what feelings Mr. Buchanan left his home in Lancaster and proceeded to Washington, and thence to New York to take passage for Liverpool, may be gathered from the following portions of his diary:

March 21, 1832.

I left Lancaster in the stage early in the morning for Washington and arrived in Baltimore the same evening. Although my feelings are not very easily excited, yet my impressions on this day were solemn and sad. I was leaving a city where I had spent the best years of my life, where I had been uniformly a popular favorite, and, above all, where I had many good and true friends who had never abandoned me, under the most trying circumstances. Among these people I had acquired a competence for a man of moderate wishes, and I think I may say without vanity my professional and personal character stood very high. I was about to embark in a new pursuit, and one in which my heart never was; to leave the most free and happy country on earth for a despotism more severe than any [other] which exists in Europe. These gloomy reflections often came athwart my mind. They were succeeded, however, by a sense of reliance on that good Providence which hitherto had blessed and sustained me, and by a conviction that I was about to go upon an important mission in which I might be made the instrument in His hands of rendering important services to my country.

Sunday, April 8th.

I set sail from New York for Liverpool on board the "Silas Richards," Captain Henry Holdridge, accompanied by Lieutenant John W. Barry, of the U. S. army, as private secretary, and Edward Landrick, a mulatto servant. I suffered from sea-sickness during nearly the whole voyage. Our fellow-passengers were kind and agreeable. Dr. Hosack of New York 137gave Charles Archibald, Esq., the son of the Attorney-General of Nova Scotia, a letter of introduction to me, which he delivered on ship-board. I found him to be an amiable and intelligent young gentleman, and enjoyed much pleasure in his society. There was a Mr. Walter—an Englishman—from London, on board, a man of general information, who was always ready and always willing to defend all the institutions of his own country, whether good or bad. He would have been a very agreeable companion, had he been willing to converse instead of making speeches. Notwithstanding, he was warm-hearted and kind, and the impression he made upon me was quite favorable. In addition to these passengers, we had a Mr. Clapham from Leeds, Mr. Stuart from Pittsburg, Mr. and Mrs. McGee and Mr. Moller of New York, Mr. McBride of Dublin, Mr. Morris of Brockville, U. C., and his sister-in-law, Mrs. Morris, from —— in the same province, Mr. Osmond, a preacher of the Society of Friends, from Indiana, going to London to attend the yearly meeting, Mrs. and Miss Taylor of New York.

The captain was an excellent seaman, a gentleman in his manners, and possessed much more information than could have been expected from one in his profession who had crossed the Atlantic eighty-eight times. We saw Cape Clear, the southwestern point of Ireland on Sunday, the 22d; but were detained by head winds for several days on that coast. Several of us had determined to go on board a fishing boat and land at Cork, and proceed from thence to Dublin, but were prevented by adverse winds from approaching the shore. We arrived in Liverpool on Thursday, the 3d May, about 12 o'clock (noon), after a passage of 25 days. When the pilot came on board, he informed us that Liverpool was clear of cholera, but that it was raging both in Cork and Dublin. We took lodgings at the Adelphi Hotel. The passengers on this day gave Captain Holdridge a dinner at "The Star and Garter," at which I presided. Mr. Brown and Mr. Ogden, our consul, were present as guests.

Friday, May 4th.

Mr. Brown of Liverpool took me about in his carriage and showed me the town of Liverpool. The appearance of the people, their manners and their language are so similar to those of New York that I could scarcely realize I was in England. The brick of which the houses are built when new have a dirty yellow appearance and the coal dust soon gives them a darker hue. This imparts a gloomy appearance to the town and deprives it of that light and cheerful hue which we experience in Philadelphia and New York. It is a place of great wealth and vast commerce, although the approach to it is tedious and difficult and altogether impracticable at low tide. The Mersey is but a small river compared with those in America. Its docks are admirable and very extensive, covering a space actually under water of between eighty and ninety English acres. The cemetery is well worthy of observation. Mr. Barry and myself dined with Mr. Brown at his country house about three miles from Liverpool. It is beautifully situated, the grounds around it highly improved, and both its external and internal appearance 138prove the wealth and the taste of its opulent and hospitable owner.[29] Francis B. Ogden, Esq., the American consul, and several other gentlemen were of the party. We spent a very pleasant afternoon and evening.

Mr. Ogden has wandered much over the world. He is an agreeable and warm-hearted fellow and something, I should suppose, of what we call "a gimcrack" in America. He has given me a cipher of his own invention which he says is the best in the world—and that it may be continually changed, so that my secretary may decipher one letter and yet know nothing about any other. During our stay at Liverpool we received many attentions. We were particularly indebted to Mr. Crary and Mr. Carnes, for whom I had letters of introduction from my friend John S. Crary of New York. I could not help observing at this place what a strong impression the successful operations of our Government had produced on the minds of Englishmen. Our national character now stands high, notwithstanding the efforts which have been made to traduce it.

Saturday, 5th.

Left Liverpool on the railroad, and arrived at Manchester—a distance of thirty miles—in one hour and twenty-five minutes. There are two tunnels, one of about 2200 yards, under the city, to communicate with the vessels at the docks, the other about 200 yards, passing under a hill in the suburbs.

The following letter to his youngest brother, lately the Rector of Oxford Church, Philadelphia, gives his first impressions of England:

[MR. BUCHANAN TO HIS BROTHER EDWARD.]

London, May 12, 1832.

My Dear Brother:—

We left Liverpool on Saturday morning last and arrived in this city on Tuesday. On our way, after passing over the railroad to Manchester, we visited Birmingham, Kenilworth Castle, Warwick Castle, Stratford-upon-Avon, Blenheim and Oxford. Every portion of the country that we have seen is in the highest state of cultivation, and its appearance at this season of the year is delightful. One thing, however, which must strike every American traveller, is the mercenary spirit of all that class of people with whom he comes in contact on the road. No person performs any office for you, no matter how slight, without expecting to be paid. Indeed travelling and living here are very extravagant, and not the slightest part of the trouble and expense are the perquisites which it is expected you will give to servants of all kinds, post-boys, coachmen, etc.

I have visited the cathedrals of Oxford and Westminster Abbey—two of the finest specimens of Gothic architecture in England. I have not time to 139give you a description of either. They are gloomy, venerable piles, and give birth to many solemn associations. They recall past ages to your view, and raise the mighty dead of former generations to be your companions. As places of worship, however, they must be very damp and uncomfortable. In Ireland the people have ceased to pay tithes. They submit to have their articles seized, but the proctors can find no purchasers for such articles at any price. The consequence has been that nearly all payments have ceased. This country is at present in a very distracted state. Never since the days of Charles I. has there been such an excitement among the mass of the people. What will be the event, God only knows. The king [William IV.], who this day week was one of the most popular monarchs who ever sat upon any throne, is now detested or rather despised by the people. His refusal to create the number of peers necessary to carry the Reform Bill, and his alleged hypocrisy throughout the whole proceeding, have occasioned this change in public sentiment. I should not be astonished at a revolution; but yet I hope and trust that the people may obtain their just rights without resorting to such a dreadful alternative. The Church is not popular. Its rich livings are conferred upon the younger branches of noble houses more with a view of making a provision for their temporal wants than of providing for the spiritual welfare of the people committed to their charge. The best course is pursued in our own country, where men choose the ministry from conscientious motives, and the people provide for them voluntarily. The present system of tithes cannot continue much longer in this country without some modification, unless there should be a much stronger government than exists at present. Indeed, from everything I have seen, although this is a country of vast wealth and resources, and of very advanced civilization, I thank my God that I was born an American rather than an Englishman.

I expect, God willing, to leave this place for St. Petersburg on Friday next, the day of the sailing of the steam packet, and I hope to reach the end of my journey on or about the first of June. I am anxious once more to feel settled. From all the information I can receive the diplomatic circle of St. Petersburg is a very agreeable one, and the Emperor and Court entertain the most friendly feelings towards our country. Prince Lieven, the Russian ambassador to this country, has been very polite to me. Although I do not anticipate much happiness during my continuance abroad, yet I have no doubt, with the blessing of Providence, I shall be content. You need not expect to hear from me again until I shall reach St. Petersburg. Please to send this letter to mother, and drop a few lines to Maria. Write to me often. I feel very anxious to hear from George. I trust in Heaven that he may be restored to health. You will perceive by the papers that the cholera has almost entirely disappeared from this city; indeed, it never was very formidable here. I was at Covent Garden Theatre on Thursday evening, and saw Young's Tragedy of Revenge performed. Mr. Young, the most celebrated tragedian of England, performed the part of Zanga. It was a most masterly performance, and excited the deepest interest. Although I have always 140admired that play, I never felt all its force and beauty until that night. Give my love to mother, Jane, Harriet, George, Mr. Lane and all the family, and believe me ever to be

Your affectionate brother,

James Buchanan.

12:30, Monday, May 14th.

The Duke of Wellington is Premier; the members of his Cabinet not yet known. Mr. Buchanan went from London to Hamburg by a packet, and thence made the overland journey to St. Petersburg. I find only the following traces of his travel: Tuesday, May 22d [1832].

The appearance of Hamburg is calculated to make a favorable impression. It is situated on the northern bank of the Elbe, the river here running a little to the north of west. The old part of the town along and near to the river has a very antiquated appearance. Most of the houses are built with their ends fronting on the street, and they are composed of wooden frame-work, the interstices being filled up with brick. In this respect they resemble the ancient houses of Lancaster. Many of these houses are three stories, and some of them more in height up to the square—the gable end, and above it, contains one and two and three stories with windows on the street until it comes to a point ornamented with various figures.

The new part of the city is beautiful. In the northern part of it there is a small lake, called the "Binnen Alster," nearly square, and about a quarter of a mile on each side. Around this lake, except on the northern side, there are ranges of very fine houses built in the modern style, at a considerable distance from it, so as to leave room not only for the street, but for spacious walks shaded by trees, with benches placed at convenient distances. Still further to the north there is a larger lake communicating with the former called the "Grosse Alster." All around this lake and along the small stream which feeds it there are shaded walks, public gardens and grass plots laid out with much taste, and kept in perfect repair. The graveyard in the midst of them shows that man's long home may be made a subject of attraction for the living; and my own feelings taught me that those who are led to the place appointed for all living, from curiosity, may leave it under solemn and useful impressions.

I called this morning upon John Cuthbert, Esq., our consul, and left at the house of Mr. Gossler, a senator of Hamburg, a letter of introduction, with my card, which I had received from his brother at New York. Mr. Cuthbert called with me on Monsieur Bacheracht, the consul-general from Russia, who was sick in bed, and I left at his house the letter from Prince Lieven. We also called on Mr. Parish, but did not see him.

141This is one of the ancient free cities of Germany. It is governed by a Senate, consisting of twenty-four members, composed of lawyers and merchants, each one-half. The Senate fills up its own vacancies as they occur. It also elects four of its own members burgesses, in whom the executive authority is vested. The deliberations of the Senate are in secret. The duties on goods imported are but one-half per cent. ad valorem, and the other taxes upon the people are very light. They appear to be contented and happy, and I have yet seen but one beggar on the streets. Indeed their language and appearance strongly reminded me of Lancaster. The Senate also elects four Syndicks, but not of their own body.

According to their laws no foreigner can be a resident merchant here, unless he goes through the forms and submits to the expense and inconvenience of becoming a burgher. Mr. Cuthbert claimed for an American naturalized citizen this privilege under our treaty with Hamburg, without becoming a burgher, and after some correspondence on the subject it was granted. This is a privilege which the English have never yet obtained. I advised Mr. Cuthbert to send the correspondence to the Secretary of State.

The outlet of the lakes into the river furnishes a water-power sufficient to turn several mills, and water for a canal which is very useful in connecting the river with the upper part of the city. It is strange that not a single dock has been erected on the river by this ancient city.

The constitution of Hamburg, although far from being free in the just acceptation of the term, has secured to the citizens enviable advantages, compared with many of the other states of Germany.

We dine with Mr. Gossler to-morrow.

(Here follows a minute account of the coins in common use in Hamburg.)
May 23d.
We dined with Mr. Gossler, the son, in the country; his father, to whom we had the letter, being now in England. Our host had resided in Boston, and about three years ago married Miss Bray of that city. She is related to the Elliott family, and is a sprightly, pleasant woman, who talks very well. Besides our host and hostess, the company consisted of Mr. William Gossler, their uncle, an old bachelor; Mr. Charles H. Carnegy, a young Scotchman who came in the packet with us from London; Mr. Wainwright, from Boston, also our fellow-passenger; Mr. Barry, and myself. We spent a very agreeable afternoon and evening. We received an invitation from Mr. Richard Parish to dine with him on Sunday at his country place, which we were obliged to decline, intending to leave for Lubeck on Saturday.

Thursday, May 24th.
In the morning, we visited Altona, a Danish town in Holstein adjoining Hamburg, and below it on the river. Its appearance is similar to that of the old part of Hamburg, though it contains some fine modern houses. The 142public walks are also pleasant here. The population is said to be 25,000. In the afternoon, we ascended the steeple of St. Michael's, and had a fine view of the city. It is 480 feet in height. The church is a fine building. I observed in it an altar, at some distance from the pulpit, with an image above it of our Saviour on the cross. This in a Lutheran Church was new to me.

Before I enter upon the business of the mission, some of the private letters which Mr. Buchanan wrote to his friends at home, during the summer of 1832, will be found to contain matters of interest. Whatever other accomplishments he possessed or wanted, he certainly wrote very agreeable letters. One of the first persons to whom he wrote, after his arrival at St. Petersburg, was General Jackson.

[MR. BUCHANAN TO GENERAL JACKSON.]
St. Petersburg, June 22, 1832.
Dear General:—

You will, ere this reaches you, have heard of my arrival in this capital, through the Department of State. Certainly it is not the place I should select for my residence, though it may be justly termed a city of palaces. The climate is healthy, but very cold. Indeed it can scarcely be said that summer has yet commenced. Their winter continues about seven months. At this season there is literally no night. I feel confident I could read common print at 12 P. M. I use no candles. The Americans and English here say they suffer more from the heat than from the cold during winter. All the houses have double casements, double windows, and very thick walls, and they are heated by stoves to a high degree of temperature. The Russians still wear their cloaks in the streets. The great objection which an American must feel to a residence in this country does not arise from the climate, though that is bad enough; it is because here there is no freedom of the Press, no public opinion, and but little political conversation, and that very much guarded. In short, we live in the calm of despotism. And what makes this situation much more unpleasant to me is, that from some cause or other, I know not yet what, this mission seldom receives any letters or newspapers from the United States. I beg that you would take up this subject yourself, and then it will be attended to. But this by the way.

It must be admitted, however, if we can believe the concurrent opinion of all the foreigners resident here with whom I have conversed, that the Emperor Nicholas is one of the best of despots. As a man of excellent private character, as a husband, a father, a brother, and a friend, his life presents a fit example for all his subjects. But still he is a despot. But little occurred on my presentation to his Majesty worthy of repetition, except what is contained 143in the despatch. He told me he had one American in his service as his aide—that was Mr. Munroe; that he was not then in St. Petersburg, having gone on board one of the ships in the fleet for the purpose of making a campaign (for exercise and instruction, I presume), and that he intended to be transferred from the military to the naval service.

The empress talked very freely. She spoke on several subjects, and with great rapidity. Amongst other things she observed we were wise in America not to involve ourselves in the foolish troubles of Europe; but she added that we had troubles enough among ourselves at home, and alluded to our difficulties with some of the Southern States. I endeavored in a few words to explain this subject to her; but she still persisted in expressing the same opinion, and, of course, I would not argue the point. The truth is, that the people of Europe, and more especially those of this country, cannot be made to understand the operations of our Government. Upon hearing of any severe conflicts of opinion in the United States, they believe what they wish, that a revolution may be the consequence. God forbid that the Union should be in any danger! If unfortunate events should occur tending to destroy the influence of our example, constitutional liberty throughout the rest of the world would receive a blow from which it might never recover. In making these remarks, I do not mean to state that the Russian government are unfriendly to the people of the United States; on the contrary, I believe they prefer us decidedly either to the English or French; but yet they must attribute to our example the existence of those liberal principles in Europe which give them so much trouble. Upon the whole, my interview with the empress was quite agreeable.

There are three ambassadors at this court: Lord Heytesbury, the English; the Marshal Duke of Treviso (Mortier), the French; and Count Figlemont, the Austrian; and a number of ministers plenipotentiary of my own grade. In point of rank I am at the tail of the list, and I should be very sorry to suppose I would ever reach the head. The rule upon this subject, however, is wholly unexceptionable: the minister who has been longest here ranks the highest in his own grade. The Diplomatic Corps have received me very kindly. This I may attribute to the high character my country is everywhere acquiring. Your foreign policy has had no small influence on public opinion throughout Europe. It is supposed Marshal Mortier is not very agreeable to this government: he is the officer who blew up the Kremlin.

I have taken a comfortable and well-furnished house in a beautiful situation fronting on the Neva, to which I expect to remove next week. My family will consist of Mr. J. Randolph Clay [Secretary of the Legation], whom I have invited to live with me, Lieutenant Barry [private secretary], and myself. My expenses will be great, but I shall endeavor to keep them within my outfit and salary.

From an examination of the correspondence between Mr. Clay and the Department I fear I shall have difficulties in the settlement of my accounts. It was not possible for him with the most rigid economy to exist as chargé 144d'affaires upon his salary, had he received all to which he was entitled, and yet he has received but about $1880 per annum. So far as I can understand the subject, the difficulty has arisen solely from the circumstance that we are authorized to draw on Amsterdam, and not on London. Surely this circumstance cannot change the amount of salary to which a minister is entitled by law, nor ought Mr. Clay to receive less at a more expensive court than Mr. Vail receives in England. Mr. Livingston told me it would make no difference to me whether I drew on Amsterdam or London, and this may eventually be the case; but I am very anxious to avoid the difficulty of having a troublesome account to settle with the Department. I should esteem it, therefore, a particular favor, if it be just, that you would authorize me to draw on London. Every difficulty on this subject would be removed, if we were allowed five rubles here for a dollar, which is the manner in which our consul settles his accounts; and I should suppose, from a communication received by Mr. Clay from my friend Mr. Pleasonton, that he now believes this to be correct. Pardon me for thus troubling you with my own affairs......

[MR. BUCHANAN TO HIS BROTHER EDWARD.]
St. Petersburg, July 15–27, 1832.
My Dear Brother:—

I received yours of the 4th of June on the 19th inst. It contains melancholy information. I trust each one of us may be able to say in relation to ourselves "God's will be done!" I fear there is but little hope for poor George. May his latter end be peace! God grant that he may recover! ———'s marriage must have been a gloomy ceremony. I hope, however, that joy may succeed to gloom, and that her marriage may be happy. I fear that her husband's health is not good. I would thank you to make it a point to wish them happiness in my name. May they be united in spirit here and be heirs of glory hereafter! From some unaccountable neglect either at the Department of State or the Legation in London, I have received no newspapers from the United States since my arrival in this city except those which came in the vessels with your two letters of the 3d of May and 4th of June; and these letters are all I have received from our country except one from Mr. Reynolds of Lancaster. I have thus been entirely deprived of the pleasure of hearing anything from my relations but what you have communicated. I shall endeavor to correct this evil; but in the meantime it would be better to send letters intended for me to Mr. Crary or some other friend in New York who would enclose them to our chargé in London (Mr. Vail). I presume no ship will leave America for St. Petersburg after you shall have received this letter until early in the next spring. I hope my friends in New York will not neglect to send me newspapers by every such opportunity.

I cannot complain of my situation here, though it is not very agreeable. The press is under so strict a censorship that nothing is published except what the government pleases. Every avenue through which liberal opinions might enter this empire is carefully closed; and in fact but few even of the higher classes of society know much of our country or its institutions. An American minister, therefore, to this court enjoys but few of the advantages he would derive from the character of his country either in England or France. Notwithstanding, I have been treated very civilly, particularly by the Diplomatic Corps and the English, who are numerous here. We have an Episcopal church, of which a Mr. Law is the rector. He is said to be a good man, and is a tolerably good preacher; I have heard him twice. The service of the English Church is very long; I think the retrenchments made in it by the Church in the United States have been very judicious. There is also a Methodist church here, which I have not visited.

The higher classes among the Russians in St. Petersburg have, I fear, but little religion; and the common people are very ignorant and superstitious. Although the Greek differs from the Latin Church in regard to the use of images, yet they cross themselves here, with much apparent devotion, before consecrated pictures, which are put up everywhere throughout the city; and in passing the churches. Among this class there is no honesty; they will always cheat you if they can. To this rule I have not met with a single exception. Although I am far from believing that a Puritanical observance of Sunday is required of us, yet I confess I have been shocked with its profanation in this country. The emperor and empress, who are models of correct moral deportment in other respects, give their balls and grand fêtes on Sunday evening; and I am confident it has never entered their thoughts that in this respect they were acting incorrectly.

My domestic arrangements are very comfortable. My house is excellent and very well furnished. It has the benefit of a fine view of the Neva, and a southern exposure, which in this land of frost and snow is a great advantage. We have not yet had one day which could be called summer. The weather has been cool, and indeed the season has been more remarkable than any which the oldest inhabitants have ever experienced. In common seasons they have about six weeks of very warm weather. It is healthy and my health is good.

Mr. Clay and Mr. Barry are very agreeable young gentlemen. The latter desires to be remembered to you. The mulatto man I brought with me from the United States is a valuable servant. I know not what I should do without him.

Give my kindest love to George. I have written to him since my arrival here. Give my love to mother, Jane, Maria, Harriet and all the family. I have not yet written to Maria; I shall do so soon. Should you be in New York on the receipt of this, remember me to my friends there. Praying to God that we may meet again in health and prosperity in our native land, I remain

Your affectionate brother,

James Buchanan.

146[MR. BUCHANAN TO JOHN B. STERIGERE.]

St. Petersburg, August 2, N. S. 1832.

My Dear Sir:—

Here I am, pleasantly situated in my own house, which commands a delightful view of the Neva and all the vessels which enter this port. The city is magnificent and beautiful. The buildings, both public and private, have been constructed upon a grand scale; but the people are ignorant and barbarous. With the exception of the merchants and a few others in the commercial cities, there is no intermediate rank between the nobleman and the slave. The serfs, however, are not unkindly treated. They are attached to the soil, and in general are not bound to labor for their masters more than three days in the week. Besides they are furnished with land which they cultivate for themselves. No one can be here for a month without being fully convinced that these people are wholly unfit to take any share in the government, and it is doubtless the policy of the emperor and nobles to keep them in this state of ignorance. Throughout Germany the people have generally received the rudiments of education and are fit for free institutions; but here despotism must yet prevail for a long time. How happy ought we to be in America! Would that we knew our own happiness! Coming abroad can teach an American no other lesson but to love his country, its institutions and its laws better, much better than he did before.

The emperor and the empress in their domestic relations are worthy of all praise. In this respect their example is excellent, and I am inclined to believe it has had a favorable effect upon the conduct of their nobles. Still that is far from being of the best character.

From my own observation and experience since I left home, I do not think a wise American ought to desire a foreign mission. For my own part I should greatly prefer a seat in the Senate to any mission which the Government could confer upon me. I trust, however, that I shall be instrumental during my sojourn here in benefiting my country. If my labors in accomplishing the objects of my mission were closed I should be very desirous of returning home; but I shall remain as long as duty requires, and endeavor to be content.

There has been great neglect in the Department of State or somewhere else in forwarding my letters and newspapers. I have not yet received a single newspaper, except a few which were sent me by some friends direct from New York, and the two or three letters that have reached me refer me to the papers for political news. This being the case, I charge you by our mutual friendship to write to me often and give me all the news. Please to send your letters to Campbell P. White or some other friend in New York, not to the Department of State; and direct them to the care of Aaron Vail, Esquire, our chargé in London. Perhaps it might be better to enclose them to him. He is a very good fellow and will be attentive in forwarding them. I was much pleased with him in London.

It seems Van Buren has been nominated by the Baltimore Convention;[30] but Pennsylvania has not yet yielded her pretensions in favor of Mr. Wilkins. I fervently hope that such a course will be pursued by our State as not to endanger its vote in favor of General Jackson.

I have been well treated since my arrival by the Diplomatic Corps generally; but particularly so by Lord Heytesbury the English, and the Duke of Treviso the French ambassador, and by the Swedish and Hanoverian ministers. So far as regards my personal feelings I am very sorry that Lord H. has been replaced by Lord Durham. The latter does not promise to be so popular as the former. I have not yet learned to submit patiently to the drudgery of etiquette. It is the most formal court in Europe and one must conform to its rules. Foreign ministers must drive a carriage and four with a postilion, and have a servant behind decked out in a more queer dress than our militia generals. This servant is called a "chasseur" and has in his chapeau a plume of feathers. To this plume, as it passes, the detachment of soldiers present arms, and individual soldiers take off their hats. How absurd all this appears to a republican! It was with some degree of apprehension that I took a house on the north side of the river, although by far the best I could find; because no foreign minister had resided on this side before; but it has succeeded, and since I have set the example I have no doubt it will be followed by others, as it has many advantages over the opposite shore.

Let me hear how you are succeeding at the law. Be not discouraged. Persevere and with the blessing of Heaven your success is certain. Remember me kindly to Mr. Paulding, Mr. Patterson, and all my other friends whom you may chance to meet. If you all think as often of me as I do of you, I shall be freshly remembered.

Ever your sincere friend,
James Buchanan.

[MR. BUCHANAN TO HIS BROTHER EDWARD.]
St. Petersburg, September 1–13, 1832.
Dear Brother:—

I received your very agreeable letter of the 15th July on the 4th September. I was very anxious indeed to hear from poor George, and regret to learn that which I have for some time apprehended, that we can indulge but little hope of his final recovery. Still it is a great satisfaction to know that he does not feel alarmed at the prospect of death. I trust his philosophy may be of the genuine Christian character and that he may have disarmed death of its sting by saving faith in the Redeemer of mankind. Still hope will linger and is unwilling to abandon us when so near and dear a relative is the object.

I congratulate you upon your admission to the ministry and trust that you may be an instrument in doing much good to your fellow-men......

The last advices from America have brought us most distressing news concerning the progress of the cholera. We have heard that it was subsiding in New York, but that it was making great ravages in Philadelphia. God grant that it may not have extended into the interior of Pennsylvania. I am now very anxious for news from America and expect it by the next steamboat in a few days. There have been a few cases of cholera in St. Petersburg during the present season. As the newspapers here publish nothing upon the subject and there are no reports from the police made public there has been scarcely any alarm. Indeed I suppose that a large majority of the people know nothing of its existence. Dr. Le Fevre, the physician of the British Embassy, told me to-day that in the course of his practice, which is very extensive, he had met no case for the last two weeks. Those places in Europe which have suffered from the disease one year, generally have experienced a slight return of it the next.

I think this climate will be favorable to my health, at least in regard to the bilious complaints with which of late years I have been so much afflicted. My life glides on smoothly here. The place is becoming more agreeable to me as my acquaintance extends; yet I still feel like a stranger in a strange land. I have so far mastered the French language as to be able to read and understand it without much difficulty. It will be some time, however, before I shall speak it fluently.

The Diplomatic Corps yesterday attended a Te Deum at the Church of St. Alexander Nevsky. It was the day of that saint, who is the greatest in the Russian calendar. The service was very magnificent and imposing; though the tones of an organ would have made it grander. These are not used in the Greek churches. The emperor was there and appeared to be very devout. He often crossed himself, and in one part of the ceremony kissed the hand of the archbishop. Think of the proudest and most powerful potentate on earth still continuing to do so much reverence to the clergy! Among other miracles, this saint, it is said, rode up the Neva on a grindstone. After the service had concluded in the church, we were present at the erection of a granite column to the memory of the late Emperor Alexander—the largest and heaviest which has ever been erected, it is said, in ancient or modern times. There were 2000 men and an immense quantity of machinery employed.

I say again, rely upon the divine blessing and your own judgment in all things, and I shall be content; but let it be taken coolly and not under the influence of the idle talk of others. Settle in no place merely for the sake of a settlement. You shall not be at any loss for money. Give my love to mother and all the family, and believe me to be
Ever your affectionate brother,
James Buchanan.

149[MR. BUCHANAN TO GENERAL JACKSON.]
St. Petersburg, October 1–13, 1832.
Dear General:—

I avail myself of the present opportunity of writing to you with the more eagerness, as I know not when I shall again enjoy that pleasure. The last steamboat for the season will leave here in about a fortnight, and after that period no safe opportunity may soon offer. To put my letters in the post-office here would be most certainly to expose them to the Russian government; indeed they scarcely think it necessary to do up the seals decently of those which I receive.

Both the emperor and Count Nesselrode have returned to the capital. I may therefore expect a final answer to our propositions in a few days. I dined with the count yesterday, who treated me with marked attention. I suppose he thought it incumbent on him to do so, as it was the first time he had invited me. The dinner was given to the French ambassador, the Duke of Treviso, who leaves here to-day in the steamboat on leave of absence. Whether he will ever return is, I think, doubtful. I do not express this opinion, because I believe there is danger of immediate hostilities between the two countries; on the contrary, I am satisfied they will remain at peace whilst Louis Philippe shall continue on the throne and pursue his present course of policy. How long the present state of things may last in France is the question. I think you may rest satisfied that Russia will not go to war for the King of Holland. She will suffer France and England to carry into effect the decrees of the London conference against him. This, however, will cause much irritation here and in Prussia. Indeed, from my intercourse with the Russian nobility, I believe a war with France to preserve Belgium for the King of Holland would be highly popular. The emperor, however, has, I am almost confident, determined it shall not be for the present. This is wise, for I am persuaded that Russia has not yet sufficiently recovered from the four wars which she has sustained since the accession of the present emperor, to enable her to be as formidable and efficient as the world believes her. As long, therefore, as things remain as they are in France, there will not be war. An attempt on her part to interfere forcibly with either Germany or Poland would instantly change the aspect of affairs.

News of the death of King Ferdinand of Spain arrived here a few days ago, but has since been contradicted. In the mean time it produced a great sensation. It is considered that his death without a son must necessarily produce a civil war in that ill-fated country, and perhaps make the rest of Europe parties. His imprudent abolition of the Salique Law in favor of his daughter, it is thought, will not be submitted to by Don Carlos, in favor of whose succession the whole of the Apostolical party will be found ranged. The government here ardently desires the defeat of Don Pedro. Indeed any change in Europe in favor of liberal principles would be disagreeable to them, 150and they even occasionally publish ill-natured articles concerning the United States. This you will perceive from the last St. Petersburg Journal, a file of which I shall send by Mr. Mitchell, for whom I have obtained a courier's passport. The articles contained in newspapers here have the more meaning, as the press is under a most rigid censorship. I am well acquainted, however, with the chief censor, Count Laval, who is one of those noblemen who have been the most polite to me, and I shall take some opportunity of conversing with him on this subject.

England is, I think, fast losing her consideration on the Continent. The present ministry are not believed to possess much ability, at least for conducting foreign affairs; and they have so many embarrassing domestic questions on their hands independently of the national debt, that they cannot without the most urgent necessity involve the country in a war. They have negotiated and paid for making Belgium a virtual province of France—Greece of Russia; and, I think, they are in a fair way of losing their commercial advantages in Portugal by an affected neutrality between the hopeful brothers of the house of Braganza, for which they receive no credit, at least in this country. Although Lord Durham was treated with the most distinguished attention by the emperor, he received almost none from the nobility; and they indulge in a bitterness of remark both against him and his country which shows what are their feelings towards England. Besides, he was an eccentric nobleman, and is the subject of as many ridiculous stories as my predecessor. I am sincerely glad that he has in some degree taken the place of the latter in the gossip of this city. But this is a subject to which I would not advert in writing to any other person. They have no free press here; but they make up for the want of it in private scandal in relation to all subjects on which they can talk with safety. The present British minister, Mr. Bligh, is a plain, agreeable, and unassuming gentleman, with whom my relations are of the most friendly character.

Within the last six weeks I have had the good fortune to make the acquaintance of several noble families of the very highest rank, and I am beginning to receive many attentions from that class. Their coldness and jealousy towards strangers generally are fast disappearing in relation to myself. Some accidental circumstances which it would be useless to detail have contributed much to this result. I consider this a fortunate circumstance, as the nobility exercise great influence in this country. I think in my despatch of the 9th of August last I spoke rather too harshly of them as a class; and although, with a few exceptions, I by no means admire them, yet this shows how dangerous it is to form opinions too hastily. The influence of the example of the present emperor and empress, in the correctness of their private deportment, is doing their nobility much good.

Too much care cannot be taken in selecting a minister for this court. Indeed it would be difficult to find many suitable persons in our country for this mission. In London and in Paris, our ministers enjoy the consideration to which they are entitled from the exalted character of their country; but 151here the character of the country must depend in a considerable degree upon that of the minister. The principles of the American Government, the connection between our greatness and prosperity as a nation, and the freedom of our institutions, are a sealed book in regard to the Russians. Their own press dare publish nothing upon the subject, and all foreign papers, unless those of the most illiberal character, are prohibited. The higher classes here must in a great degree receive their information concerning our country from our minister. This sufficiently points out what ought to be his qualifications, and I regret my own deficiency in some important particulars. Great talents are by no means so requisite as an easy address, insinuating manners, and a perfect knowledge of the French language. (In the latter I have already made considerable advances.) Above all he ought to have a genuine American heart, in which I know I am not deficient, always anxious to seize every favorable opportunity, and many such occur, of making an impression in favor of his country. There is one great disadvantage, however, under which a minister here labors; and that is, the total inadequacy of the salary. These people are fond of extravagance and show, and have not the least taste for Republican simplicity and economy. In order that a minister may hold a high place in their esteem, he must be able to return their civilities. They judge much by appearances. The want of this reciprocity will be attributed to the meanness of the minister or that of his country, or both. Even the representative of his Sardinian Majesty receives $16,000 per annum. Now if I had $100,000 per annum, I would not pursue any course of conduct in this respect which I should be ashamed to exhibit to my countrymen; but surely if they were aware that their minister could not return with Republican simplicity and dignity the civilities which he cannot avoid receiving without giving offence, they would consent to an increase of salary. I think $15,000 would be sufficient for the purpose without the outfit. Perhaps it would be better to fix it at $13,000, with the expense of a furnished house. At all events, I must give some large dinners.

I make these remarks without feeling the slightest personal interest in them, because nothing short of your express commands would induce me to remain here longer than two years from the time of my arrival; and I trust something may occur to justify my return to my native land within a shorter period. I feel, however, if I had such a salary I could leave a much more favorable impression of my country behind me. By the bye, I do not know yet what I am to receive; if I should have to lose the exchange between this and Amsterdam at its present rate, my salary will but little exceed $8,000. If ever a change shall be made the salary of the minister here ought to be fixed in silver roubles.

I have lately seen much of Mr. Politica, who is still attached to the Foreign Office. His feelings towards our country appear to be very friendly. From his conversation, I have reason to anticipate a favorable issue to our negotiations; but I shall not allow myself to confide much in unofficial conversations. I have no doubt that they feel it would be their interest to 152negotiate with us; and they appreciate highly the advantages of our trade; yet they entertain such strong prejudices against commercial treaties, and there are so many wheels within wheels in the complex system of their policy that it is safest not to expect a treaty with too much confidence. I have no doubt, should they conclude one with us, England would insist upon being placed on the same footing. Besides, Count Cancrene, the Minister of Finance, is understood to be opposed to all commercial treaties. I ought to state that I believe the omission to invite Mr. Barry to the reviews was unintentional, and Count Nesselrode expressed his sorrow to Baron Krudener for the neglect before the latter left this city.

I shall soon be looking with great anxiety for news concerning our elections. I read your veto message with very great pleasure. Although rather inclined to be friendly to the re-charter of the Bank of the United States, yet I am now free to say, I should vote for no bill for that purpose liable to the objections of that which passed both Houses of Congress. I am glad to observe the spirit which seems to animate the Republican party of Pennsylvania, in relation to this subject. I entertain no apprehension concerning the result of your election; but I wish to see you come into office for a second period with that triumphant majority which you are entitled to receive, both from the wisdom and success of your foreign and domestic policy. I cannot think that the unnatural union between the Clay men and the Anti-masons will reduce your majority; as I believe the mass of both these parties is honest and cannot approve such a political partnership.

Pardon me for not taking the trouble of correcting and re-writing this long and rambling letter. I should do so did I not know it was only intended for friendly eyes. I now receive my newspapers with tolerable regularity, through the kindness of my friends in Hamburg and Lubeck. This regulation will cease at the close of the present month, when the steamboats will be discontinued. Please to present my best respects to the members of your Cabinet. I have been for some time expecting a letter from Major Barry. Remember me kindly to your family, and believe me to be, wherever my lot may be cast,

Your faithful, devoted and grateful friend,
James Buchanan.

[MR. BUCHANAN TO HIS BROTHER EDWARD.]
St. Petersburg, October 13th, 1832.
My Dear Brother:—

I received yours of the 12th August dated Union, Va., on the 2d instant. It gave me a gloomy picture of the state of poor George's health and has deprived me of the last ray of hope in relation to his recovery. Indeed whilst I am writing this I have too much cause to apprehend that your next will announce that he has bidden an eternal adieu to this vain and transitory 153world. I had conceived the highest hopes of his future eminence and usefulness. His talents were of the first order, his manners were popular and his principles were, I believe, perfectly pure. Alas! that his sun, which rose so brightly and promised such a brilliant day, should so soon be extinguished. Such seems to have been the inscrutable decree of an all-wise Providence. May our dear mother and may we all be enabled to say, "Father, Thy will be done." I feel the deepest gratitude towards Dr. Semmes for his kindness. My acquaintance with him was but slight, but I shall make it a point, should I ever have an opportunity, of manifesting to him how much I have been penetrated by his kindness. In the meantime do not fail to make my sentiments known to him. It is probable that ere long I shall address him a letter returning him my thanks. You can readily conceive what anxiety I shall feel until the arrival of your next. I trust it may have pleased Providence to enable poor George to reach Mercersburg.

My time here is gliding on not unpleasantly. When I reflect upon my past life and the many merciful dispensations of which I have been the subject, I cannot be too thankful to the Almighty. This land of despotism is not the place where an American minister ought to have expected many friends, particularly as the Russian nobility have but little disposition to cultivate the acquaintance of strangers; it has yet so happened that several of the very highest order have shown me much kindness, and I have some reason to believe I shall be a favorite. The English merchants, who are numerous, wealthy and respectable, have been very civil, and the Diplomatic Corps have paid me all the attention I could desire. Still I shall be happy when the day arrives that I can with honor leave this elevated station and return to my native land.

The ladies here, as they are almost everywhere, are the best part of society. Many of them and their children speak English very well, whose husbands cannot speak a word of that language. There is a Princess Tscherbatoff here with whom I have become very intimate. She has a charming family and they have travelled much through Europe. She is a lady of uncommon intellect, brilliant accomplishments, and yet preserves great personal attractions. I mention her name for the purpose of introducing a circumstance somewhat singular. By some means or other she got hold of the "Pilgrim's Progress," and it has evidently produced a considerable effect upon her feelings. She has read several of the old English devotional books and likes to converse upon the subject of religion. It is strange that my first and most intimate acquaintance with a Russian Princess should have been with one conversant with the writings of such men as John Bunyan and Isaac Watts. I doubt whether there is another like her in this respect throughout the Empire. She is a member of the Greek Church and attached to it; but informs me that she often goes to hear a Mr. Neal preach, who is, I believe, a kind of English Methodist. Her religion, and I sincerely believe she possesses it, does not prevent her from being very gay and entering into the fashionable amusements of her class. There is no estimating the good which an able and pious man may be instrumental in performing, not only in his own generation, but long after he has been gathered to his fathers.

The weather is now about as cold here as it is in Pennsylvania towards the close of November. We have already had a slight fall of snow and several severe frosts. In going out to dinner in the country on the last day of September, I observed a very large oats field in shock. Very little of it had been taken in. You may judge of the nature of the climate from this circumstance, though this season has been remarkably cold and damp. I can now readily believe, what I have often heard since my arrival, that I should suffer less from cold in this country than in my own. They regulate the heat of the houses by a thermometer; and their stoves are so admirably contrived that they are large and beautiful ornaments, and consume but very little wood compared with those of our own country. My health still continues to be good, thank God!

Give my kindest love to my mother—how often do I now think of her with gratitude and affection! to Jane, Maria, and Harriet, and to poor George, if he be still living. Remember me to Mr. Lane, affectionately, and to all the family.

I shall send this letter enclosed to Mr. Lane, with directions that they may read it if you should not be in Mercersburg. Remember me to Uncle John, Alexander and his lady, Mr. Reynolds and his lady, and to Mrs. Martin and Molly Talbot, and believe me to be ever Your faithful and affectionate brother,

James Buchanan.
[MR. BUCHANAN TO MRS. SLAYMAKER.]
St. Petersburg, October 31, 1832.
Dear Madam:—

I received your kind and agreeable letter of the 20th August last on the 8th instant. I scarcely know anything the perusal of which could have afforded me more pleasure. I left no friend in my native land for whose interest and welfare I have a greater solicitude than for your own. How could it be otherwise? Your conduct since the lamented death of your husband, whose memory I shall ever cherish, has been a model of propriety. The severest critic could not find fault with any part of it, unless it be that you have too much secluded yourself from society, of which you are so well calculated to be an agreeable and instructive member. I have never heretofore expressed these sentiments to you because you might have considered them the language of flattery. As they now proceed from "a stranger in a strange land," I cannot believe you will doubt their sincerity.

I fear I cannot with truth defend the chastity of the Empress Catharine. She was a disciple of the school of the French philosophers, and was therefore wholly destitute of religion—the surest safeguard of female virtue. Her natural disposition was, however, good, and where her ambition and her pleasures were not concerned she was an amiable and kind-hearted woman. The Princess Dalgorouski, one of my most intimate friends in this city (if I ought to use the term upon so short an acquaintance), is the granddaughter of the youngest brother of the Orloffs. She has several times amused me with anecdotes which she had heard from her grandfather, all tending to prove the goodness of Catharine's heart. Among other things, it was not at all uncommon for her to rise in the morning and light her own fire, rather than disturb the slumbers of any of her attendants. She took great delight not only in educating her own grandchildren, but others of the same age about the court. Her son Paul, however, was always her aversion. When he succeeded to the throne he acted like a madman, and I have often had to laugh at the pranks of his tyranny. For example, he issued an edict commanding all persons, whether male or female, either in the summer or the winter, upon his approach to alight from their carriages and stand in the street uncovered before him as he passed. Of course the latter part of the rule applied to foot passengers. An English merchant, still living in this city, attempted upon one occasion to make his escape as the Emperor approached, but he was observed by the keen eye of Paul, and was immediately sent for to the palace. His defence was that he was near-sighted; and the Emperor immediately presented him with a pair of spectacles, and commanded him never to be seen in public without having them upon his nose. The command was literally obeyed, and the merchant has ever since worn the spectacles. The anecdote is literally true.

The Emperor Alexander was a mild and amiable man; but his example, until near the close of his life, was not calculated to restrain the dissoluteness of manners which prevailed in the days of Catharine. Circumstances, too tedious to mention in the limits of a hasty letter, made him at last esteem his wife, the Empress Elizabeth, as she deserved. In the commencement of his reign, he was a libertine, but he died a fanatic. It is delightful to hear of the familiar intercourse which he held with his subjects. He visited many families in this city as a private gentleman whom etiquette prevented from appearing at court; and upon such occasions he was as free and familiar, even with the children, as though he had been of an equal rank. He died disgusted with his high station, and exclaimed to Doctor Wyley, his physician, who was remonstrating with him for not using his prescriptions, "I am sick of this world, why should I desire to live?" Such is the end of human greatness.

The present emperor is, I think, the finest looking man, take him altogether, I have ever beheld; besides he is a prince of great energy and ability. However we may detest his conduct towards the Poles, which has no doubt been exaggerated in the English and French papers, his moral conduct, as well as that of the empress, in all their domestic relations is without a blemish. Their example in this respect has already had a happy influence on the nobility of this country. On Saturday last I attended a Te Deum at court, celebrated on the occasion of the birth of a young grand duke; and the gaieties of the season are expected to commence as soon as the empress shall recover from her accouchement. She is remarkably fond of dancing, in which she excels.

My time begins to pass much more pleasantly, or to speak with greater accuracy, less unpleasantly than it did at first. To be an American minister is but a slender passport to the kind attentions of the Russian nobility. They know but little of our country, and probably desire to know still less, as they are afraid of the contamination of liberty. I have, therefore, had to make my own way in their society with but little adventitious aid, and I confess I am sometimes astonished at my own success. Among the ladies, who, in every portion of the world, are the best part of society, I have many agreeable acquaintances. A greater number of them speak the English language than of the gentlemen. Besides, since my arrival here, I have learned to read and write the French, and now begin to speak it in cases of necessity.

Besides the nobility there is an agreeable and respectable society here of wealthy English and German merchants, among whom I have spent many pleasant hours. Although they are not received at court, many members of the Diplomatic Corps eat their good dinners, and treat them as they ought to be treated, with kindness and civility. I hope to visit Moscow before my return to the United States, and that, too, under favorable circumstances.

I sincerely rejoiced to hear of the good fortune of our friends of the Wheatlands. Lydia is a good little girl and deserves to be happy. I was pleased with the anecdotes you gave me in relation to the match, and the joy which my good friend Grace displayed upon the occasion. My worst wish towards them is that they may derive all the happiness from it which they anticipate. They are an excellent family, with whom I could wish you to be more intimate. I would be better pleased with them, for their own sakes, if they were less extravagant; "but take them for all and all," I feel the warmest interest in their welfare. I regret to learn that Aunt Anne, in a state of depressed health and spirits, has felt herself under the necessity of leaving her comfortable home in Lancaster, to take charge of her son Henry's family at the iron works. It is just such conduct, however, as I should have expected from that excellent and exemplary woman; she will always sacrifice her own comfort to a sense of duty, or to the call of humanity. I shall never forget her kindness towards myself. I beg of you to present her my best love (I think I may venture to use the expression). Remember me kindly also to Anny, and to Henry, Stephen and Samuel.

I have always appreciated the friendship of your mother as it deserved, and have felt proud of her confidence. I trust that your hopes may be realized, and that it may please Providence yet to permit me to enjoy many happy hours in her society. She possesses an admirable faculty of saying much in few words, and there is a point in her character which gives a peculiar force to her expressions. I know her to be an excellent mother and an excellent friend, and I warmly reciprocate her kind feelings. Say to her that I ardently wish her many pleasant days, and that the circumstances which have heretofore occurred to vex her peace may not prevent her from enjoying an old age of comfort and happiness. Remember me also in kindness to all your sisters.

But in what terms shall I speak of Mrs. H.? None of my friends, except yourself, have mentioned her name in their letters, and I need scarcely add that I did not even indulge the hope of receiving one from herself. This I can say of her, and I now speak from actual knowledge, that her manners and her talents would grace the most powerful and splendid court in Europe. I fear, however, that such a treasure is not destined to bless my pilgrimage.

I altogether approve your conduct in taking the Judge's daughter into your family. He is a most excellent man, and will know how to appreciate your kindness. I regret to say I have received no letter from him since I left the United States. When you see him, please to present him my kindest remembrance. I heartily rejoice that you did not remove to Columbia or Marietta.

From my last information from the United States I have reason to hope that the good city of Lancaster has escaped the cholera. We have had some of it here during the summer, but not so much as to produce any serious alarm. I believe it has almost, if not altogether, disappeared. Mr. Clay, my Secretary of Legation, has been very anxious to visit home during the approaching winter, and I have given him leave to go by the last steamboat for the season, which will leave this to-morrow, Mr. Barry having agreed to officiate in his stead during his absence. He will be the bearer of despatches, and intends to visit Lancaster. I hope you will favor me with a long letter by him, and give me all the little news of the town; for you have often said I was a great gossip. I shall keep this letter open until I can ascertain whether I shall have time to write to Mr. Reynolds, so that if not I may add a postscript intended for him. The truth is that at present I am very much occupied. A tyro in diplomacy, I am compelled to encounter the most adroit and skilful politicians in the world, with no other weapons except a little practical common sense, knowledge and downright honesty. Should I fail, and I by no means despair of success, I wish to convince my government that I have done my duty. It is probable that Mr. Clay will take no private letters from me to the United States, except for my mother and yourself. I need scarcely add that I have not time to write this over, and give it such a polish as an answer to your letter deserves. When you write, which I hope will be often, please to say nothing of Russia in your letters but what may be favorable, as the post office here is not too secure. This caution, however, does not apply to that one with which I hope you will gratify me by Mr. Clay. Please to remember me kindly to the whole family at the Wheatlands, to Mr. and Mrs. Reynolds and Miss Lydia and Dr. Semple—to my old friend 158Miss Mary Carpenter, and to all others bearing that character whom you may meet.

Wishing you Heaven's best blessing, I remain,

Ever your faithful and devoted friend,

James Buchanan.

P. S. Please to remember me to Mr. Amos Slaymaker and Henry and his wife. I hope Mr. Dickenson may, ere this reaches you, be restored to his flock, and have a son and heir to bless his marriage bed.

I shall not have time to write to Mr. Reynolds. Please to deliver him the enclosed, and tell him that I have no journal later than the 10th August, although my other papers have arrived up till the middle of September. You may also say to him, but to him alone and caution him not to repeat it, that the prospects of success in my mission, after many difficulties, now begin to appear bright. I have received no letter from him lately. Mr. Clay will not leave this for a fortnight yet, and I shall send this letter by another opportunity to London.

As the reader has already learned, Mr. Buchanan had two very promising younger brothers, one of whom died five years before he went abroad, and the other was living and in apparently good health when he left the country. The elder of these two, William Speer Buchanan, died at Chambersburg in his 22d year, on the nineteenth of December, 1827, a few months after his admission to the bar. He had graduated at Princeton in 1822, and studied his profession at Chambersburg and at the law school in Litchfield, Connecticut. His father died while he was still at Princeton: and a letter from his mother to his brother James, written in 1821, which lies before me, gives indications of his early character.[31]

William Buchanan did not, like his next youngest brother, live to show what he might have become. This other, and perhaps 159more brilliant member of the family, George W. Buchanan, graduated at Dickinson college in Carlisle, in 1826, at the age of eighteen, with the highest honors of his class. Being nearly twenty years younger than James, the latter, after the death of their father, took a parental interest in promoting his prospects, and guiding his professional education, he studied law in Chambersburg and Pittsburgh, and being admitted to the bar in Pittsburgh in 1828, he began to practise there. In the autumn of 1830, as the reader has seen, he was, doubtless on his brother's request, appointed by President Jackson United States District Attorney for the Western District of Pennsylvania. Probably no man ever received a similar appointment at so early an age; he was only two and twenty; but his letters, some of which have been quoted, show great maturity of character; and as his application for the appointment must have been supported by the influence of other persons as well as by that of his brother, it is safe to assume that the office was intrusted to fit hands. He was already acquiring a lucrative private practice, when, in the summer of 1832, his health began to fail. He died in November of that year, and the following letter of Mr. Buchanan to his brother Edward relates to the sad termination of his illness:

St. Petersburg, Jan. 9th, N. S. 1832.

My Dear Brother:—

I have received your three letters of the 10th and 26th September and of the 12th November: the first on the 21st October, the second not till the 2d instant, and the last on the 28th December. You will thus perceive that the one announcing the death of poor George had a very long passage, having got out of the usual line and lain at Paris a considerable time. I had heard of this melancholy event long before its arrival. How consoling it is to reflect that he had made his peace with Heaven before he departed from earth. All men desire to die the death of the righteous; but a large portion of the human race are unwilling to lead their life. I can say sincerely for myself that I desire to be a Christian, and I think I could withdraw from the vanities and follies of the world without suffering many pangs. I have thought much upon the subject since my arrival in this strange land, and sometimes almost persuade myself that I am a Christian; but I am often haunted by the spirit of scepticism and doubt. My true feeling upon many occasions is: "Lord, I would believe; help Thou mine unbelief." Yet I am far from being an unbeliever. 160Ere this reaches you, you will probably have heard of the conclusion of the commercial treaty, which was the principal object of my mission. My success under all the circumstances seems to have been almost providential. I have had many difficulties to contend with and much serious opposition to encounter; but through the blessing of Providence I have been made the instrument of accomplishing a work in which all my predecessors had failed. I trust it will receive the approbation and promote the interests of my country.

I entertain some faint hopes that I may be permitted to leave St. Petersburg by the last steamboat of the next season; though it is probable I shall be obliged to remain another winter. Nothing, however, shall detain me longer than two years from the time of my arrival, except an urgent sense of public duty or the request of General Jackson, neither of which I anticipate. My anxiety to return home is increased by the present state of health of mother and Jane. It is not in any degree occasioned by want of kindness on the part of the people here. On the contrary, I am everywhere received in the most polite and friendly manner, and have good reason to believe I am rather a favorite, even with the emperor and empress themselves.

I shall undertake to advise you strongly not to remain in Allegheny Town. A letter which I have received from Dr. Yates confirms me in this opinion. I am glad to find this seems to be your own determination. There are but two brothers of us and you ought to use every precaution to preserve your health consistent with your duty......

My health is good, thank God, and I trust it may so continue with His blessing until we shall all once more meet again. With much love to mother and the rest of the family, I remain

Your affectionate brother,
James Buchanan.
161
CHAPTER VIII.
1832–1833.

NEGOTIATION OF TREATIES—COUNT NESSELRODE—HIS CHARACTERISTIC MANAGEMENT OF OPPOSING COLLEAGUES—THE EMPEROR NICHOLAS—HIS SUDDEN ANNOUNCEMENT OF HIS CONSENT TO A COMMERCIAL TREATY—WHY NO TREATY CONCERNING MARITIME RIGHTS WAS MADE—RUSSIAN COMPLAINTS ABOUT THE AMERICAN PRESS—BARON SACKEN'S IMPRUDENT NOTE—BUCHANAN SKILFULLY EXONERATES HIS GOVERNMENT—SENSITIVENESS OF THE EMPEROR ON THE SUBJECT OF POLAND.

The serious business of negotiation began soon after Mr. Buchanan's arrival in St. Petersburg. He was charged with the duty of proposing a commercial treaty with Russia, and also a treaty respecting maritime rights. It would be impossible to attempt to carry my readers through the maze of notes, protocols, and despatches which resulted in the successful accomplishment of the main object of this mission. A brief account of the principal persons concerned in the negotiation, and a narrative of its general course, together with a few of its most striking incidents, will perhaps be interesting.

At the head of the Russian chancery at this time was Count Nesselrode, the great minister, who, in 1814, as the plenipotentiary of the Emperor Alexander, signed the treaty between the Allied Powers and Napoleon, which wrested from the latter the empire of France and the kingdom of Italy, and confined his dominion to the island of Elba. Nesselrode, too, in the same capacity, along with Lord Castelreagh and Prince Talleyrand, concluded the second treaty of Paris between the Allied Powers and France, after the final overthrow of Napoleon at Waterloo, the treaty which restored the Bourbons to their throne. This distinguished person was the son of a nobleman of German descent, who had been in the service of the Empress Catharine II., and therefore, as well on account of the traditions of his house, 162as of his remarkable abilities and erudition, he must have been an interesting person to meet. He was, with all his practical astuteness, a man of moderate and rational views. He appears to have taken kindly to Mr. Buchanan from the

115

first; but he was not predisposed to a commercial treaty with the United States, and, indeed, he had not bestowed much attention upon the subject. It had not been his habit, or the habit of any of the Russian statesmen, during the long wars in which Russia had been engaged prior to the year 1815, to look much beyond the confines of Europe and those portions of the East which were involved in the European system. Still, however, Count Nesselrode was open to conviction upon the importance of a commercial treaty with the United States; and it will appear in the sequel that the treaty was at length carried in the cabinet, against strenuous opposition, by his very dexterous management, seconded by Mr. Buchanan's skilful course and ample knowledge of the subject.

Baron Krudener, who was at this time the Russian Minister at Washington, but who was at home on leave of absence when Mr. Buchanan came to St. Petersburg, was opposed to all commercial treaties. So was Count Cancrene, the minister of finance. He was an embodiment of the old traditionary policy of Russia, which did not favor close or special commercial alliances. From the time of the Empress Catharine, the relations between Russia and this country had always been friendly; but there had been no treaties concluded between the two countries, since the Government of this Union had taken its present form, down to the year 1824. The convention negotiated in that year by Mr. Middleton, and ratified in 1825, was quite inadequate to reach the various interests of trade that had since grown up, and was still less adapted to promote an increase of the commerce between Russia and the United States. To make a treaty which would answer these great purposes; establish the principle that would entitle either party to require an equal participation in the favors extended to other nations; provide for the residence and functions of consuls and vice-consuls; regulate the rates of duties to be levied oil the merchandise of each country by the other, so far as to prevent undue discrimination in favor of the products of other countries; 163and fix the succession of the personal estates of citizens or subjects of either country dying in the territories of the other; all this constituted a task to be committed on our side to able hands, considering the obstacles that had to be removed. Mr. Buchanan was at the age of thirty-eight, when he undertook this labor. Although he was without official experience in diplomacy, I think it evident that he had been a student of the diplomatic history of his own country and of public law to a considerable extent; and what he did not know of the trade between Russia and the United States before he left home, he made himself master of soon after he arrived at St. Petersburg. He spoke of himself in a letter quoted in the last chapter, as a tyro in diplomacy, with no weapons but a little practical common sense, knowledge, and downright honesty, with which to encounter the most adroit and skilful politicians in the world. It will be seen that he found the encounter a hard one. But his manners were conciliatory; his tact was never at fault, so far as I can discover; and it is evident that he was a favorite in all the circles of Russian society into which he entered. He found that his weapons, good sense, knowledge of his subject, and a certain honest tenacity of purpose, were sufficient for all the demands of his position. When he first reached St. Petersburg, his knowledge of the French language was quite imperfect, but he soon acquired sufficient facility in speaking it for the ordinary purposes of conversation. Count Nesselrode did not speak English well, but he could converse in that language, although he did not like to trust himself to it entirely. Mr. Buchanan's French was perhaps rather better than the count's English. They do not seem in their intercourse to have used an interpreter, but in one or the other language they got on together very well.

After Mr. Buchanan's arrival and the necessary formalities had been gone through according to the rigid etiquette of the Russian court, he wrote privately to General Jackson on the 22d of June (1832) in regard to the prospects of his mission, as follows:

[MR. BUCHANAN TO GENERAL JACKSON.]
St. Petersburg, June 22, 1832.
. . . .
I am not without hope of succeeding in the negotiation, though I can say nothing upon the subject with the least degree of certainty. I entertain this hope chiefly because I am now fully convinced it is their interest to enter into a treaty of commerce with us. In a casual conversation the other day with Baron Krudener I explained my views of the great advantages Russia derived from our commerce with St. Petersburg, and how much, in my opinion, the agriculture and the general prosperity of the colonies on the Black Sea would be promoted by encouraging American navigation in that quarter. Yesterday I had another conversation with the baron from which it was evident he had been conversing with Count Nesselrode upon the subject; and the impression which I have received from him is rather favorable. Still it is of a character so vague that I place but little reliance upon it. I shall see Count Nesselrode at one o'clock to-day, and will keep this letter open until after our interview.

3.30. I have just returned from Count Nesselrode's, and from our interview I entertain a hope, I may say a good hope, that I shall be able to conclude both treaties with this government. I am sorry I shall not have time to prepare a despatch for Mr. Livingston to be sent by Captain Ramsay. He shall hear from me, however, by the first safe opportunity. [There is one subject to which I desire briefly to direct your attention. I should write to the department about it, but my views are not yet sufficiently distinct to place them there upon record, and besides there is not now time. In case a treaty should be made with this government on the subject of maritime rights, its provisions ought to be framed with great care, because it will probably be a model for similar treaties with other nations. In looking over the project in my possession, I find one provision which it strikes me the cabinet ought to re-examine. It is the proviso to the first article. This proviso was not introduced into our earlier treaties. It first found a place in that with Spain and has since been copied into our treaties with Colombia, Central America and Brazil.

Why should this limitation exist? I shall allude to my views by presenting a supposed case, for I have not time to do more.

Suppose Great Britain, which does not recognize the principle that "free ships make free goods," and Russia to be engaged in war after the treaty, the United States being neutral.

1. Would it not be greatly for our interest (more particularly as from our character we shall generally be a neutral nation) if our ships could carry the goods of Englishmen to Russia and all over the world, without these goods being subjected to capture by the armed vessels of Russia?

2. Would not great embarrassments arise if Russian vessels of war, after ascertaining that a vessel belonged to a citizen of the United States, which is all they could do under the general principle, should then under the proviso be permitted to inquire into the ownership of the cargo, and if they suspected it belonged in whole or in part to English subjects, to seize and take it before a prize court?

3. This proviso could only have been introduced to force England into the adoption of the rule that "the flag covers the cargo;" but how can it produce that effect? It will render the property of an Englishman as insecure on board an American as a British vessel; it being equally liable to seizure in either. But let the rule be general, let our flag protect the cargo, no matter who may be the owner, and then English merchants will have the strongest inducements to employ our navigation.

4. Would not the promise make the treaty itself a felo de se, whenever Russia shall be at war with a nation which does not recognize the general rule?

5. If England should at any time be neutral and we at war, the general rule adopted between us and Russia will not prevent us from capturing our enemies' goods on board British vessels.

6. These suggestions become of much more importance when we consider that we may have similar treaties with many nations.

These crude remarks are merely intended to direct your attention to the subject. I consider it very important and should like to hear from the department in relation to it as soon as possible. We shall first take up the treaty of commerce, I presume; indeed Count Nesselrode has asked for my views in writing on that subject.

It might be of consequence to me to have a copy of our treaty with Turkey.]

In haste, I am, with the greatest respect,

Your friend,

James Buchanan.

P. S. Please remember me to the members of your cabinet and also your family.

2d P. S. Captain Ramsay, for whom I had obtained a courier's passport, will not go to-day; but I have fortunately just heard of a vessel about sailing for Boston, by which I send this.

At a little later period, Mr. Buchanan formally submitted to Count Nesselrode the propositions which he had been instructed to make as the basis of a commercial treaty, and those which related to the subject of maritime rights, or the rights of neutrals during war. Nothing definite was arrived at on either topic until the 8th-10th of October. On that day, Mr. Buchanan received a note from Count Nesselrode, requesting him to call at the Foreign Office on the succeeding Monday. What followed 166was certainly a most remarkable occurrence. The count began the conversation by asking whether the answer which he was about to make to the American propositions would be in time to reach Washington before the next meeting of Congress. Mr. Buchanan replied that it would not, but said that it might reach Washington within a fortnight after that period. The count then asked if the answer could be sent immediately. Mr. Buchanan replied that if, as he hoped, the answer should be favorable, he would take measures to send it at once. The count then stated reasons, which had led the emperor to decline the American proposition for concluding a treaty of commerce and navigation between the two countries, but made no allusion to the proposed treaty concerning maritime rights. Here there was a dilemma, for which Mr. Buchanan was not prepared by anything that had preceded; for although he was well aware of the interior opposition to a commercial treaty in the Russian cabinet, and was not very sanguine of success, he had placed his hopes on Count Nesselrode's ability and disposition to overcome that opposition. That the emperor had come to an unfavorable decision, and that Count Nesselrode had been directed to communicate it, was rather an unexpected event. Nesselrode, however, contrived to make Mr. Buchanan understand that the emperor had yielded in this matter to the opinions of Count Cancrene, the minister of finance, and of M. de Blondorff, the minister of the interior, and that the result had not been in accordance with his, Nesselrode's, judgment. Such an occurrence could hardly have taken place in an English cabinet, still less would it have been communicated to a foreign minister; but in Russia it was perhaps not uncommon for the prime minister to be overruled by his colleagues. But Count Nesselrode knew a way to get over all such difficulties; and he proceeded in a very characteristic manner to accomplish what he intended. He went over anew the whole ground, encouraging Mr. Buchanan to develop again the reasons which made a commercial treaty desirable for both countries and finally requested him to put them in the shape of a formal note. He then assumed a very confidential tone, which may be best described by Mr. Buchanan's own account, given in his despatch of October 19–21, to the secretary of state.

"Towards the conclusion of the interview he laid aside altogether, or at least appeared to do so, the wary diplomatist, and his manners became frank and candid. He made the request and repeated it, that I should submit a new proposition for the conclusion of a commercial treaty, and accompany it by an abstract of the explanations which I had just made, impressing it upon me to advert especially to the trade with the Black Sea, and the moral influence, to use his own expression, which such a treaty might have on the people of the United States. I told him I should do so with pleasure. He then requested me to send it as soon as I conveniently could and he would immediately submit it to the emperor, and give me an answer before the departure of the last steamboat, which was to leave St. Petersburg on Wednesday, the 19–21 instant. He afterwards asked me whether I intended to send the note to Washington which he had delivered to me, by the next steamboat; and from his manner it was easy to perceive that he wished I would not. I replied that I should certainly delay sending it until the last steamboat, hoping that in the meantime I might receive a better one......

Some conversation, not necessary to be repeated, was held on other subjects, and I took my leave much satisfied with the interview and arguing from it the most happy results, should Count Nesselrode possess sufficient influence to carry his own wishes into effect, against those of Count Cancrene."

In a short time after Mr. Buchanan's new communication had been sent to Count Nesselrode, a further step was taken in what might almost be called a diplomatic intrigue. Baron de Brunnow, a counsellor of state, and the confidential friend of Count Nesselrode, called upon Mr. Buchanan, and informing him that he came by the count's request, said that Mr. Buchanan's views contained in his note were perfectly satisfactory to the count, and that they were so clearly and distinctly expressed that they could not be misapprehended, and that the count would be happy to become the medium of presenting them to the emperor, and would use his influence to have them adopted. But in order that nothing might appear which would show that Count Nesselrode had requested Mr. Buchanan to submit a new proposition for a commercial treaty, the baron desired Mr. Buchanan to modify the language of his note, so that it would not appear to be written in compliance with any wish which the count had expressed. Perceiving the struggle which was about to ensue in the cabinet between Nesselrode and Cancrene, Mr. Buchanan at once agreed to change the phraseology of his note. Baron Brunnow requested that it might be done immediately, as it was Count Nesselrode's intention to have the note translated into French on that day, and to go with it to the emperor on the next morning, so that an answer might, if possible, be obtained before the departure of the next steamboat. Baron Brunnow made no secret of Count Cancrene's opposition to all commercial treaties, but said that Count Nesselrode saw no objection to such a one as Mr. Buchanan had proposed; that he had repeated Mr. Buchanan's observation that "statesmen often found it expedient to yield even to honest prejudices for the purpose of promoting the public good," and had said that he had no doubt such a treaty would produce a beneficial effect on the American trade with the Black Sea.

This mode of facilitating Count Nesselrode's movements being arranged, the conversation between Mr. Buchanan and Baron Brunnow turned upon the proposed treaty concerning maritime rights, of which an account will be given hereafter. Excepting the interchange of formal notes relating to the commercial treaty, nothing further occurred until the 31st of October, when Mr. Buchanan calling at the Foreign Office by appointment, found Count Nesselrode "in fine spirits and in the most frank and candid mood." But he said that it would be impossible to conclude the treaty before the end of a fortnight. In making the arrangements for sending to the United States the new notes which had passed, the count expressed the strongest desire that the British government should not obtain any knowledge that such a treaty was in contemplation; and for this reason he offered to send Mr. Buchanan's despatch for Washington by a Russian courier, to be delivered to Mr. Vail, the American chargé in London. Mr. Buchanan preferred another channel of communication with Mr. Vail, and through that channel his despatch was sent off on the following day. The attitude in which it left the whole affair of the commercial treaty was thus summed up by Mr. Buchanan:

"For several weeks before the receipt of Count Nesselrode's first note, I had but little expectation of concluding a commercial treaty. Mr. Kielchen, lately appointed consul at Boston by this government, informed me, some time ago, that Count Cancrene had resolved never to consent to the conclusion of such a treaty with any power whilst he continued in the ministry, 169and his influence with the emperor, particularly on commercial subjects, was universally admitted to be very great. He has the character of being an obstinate man; and I scarcely allowed myself to hope, either that he would change, or be defeated in his purpose. I feel the more happy, therefore, in being able to congratulate you upon our present favorable prospects."

Nothing was heard from Count Nesselrode for nearly a month; but on the evening of November 21st Mr. Buchanan met him at a party. The count took Mr. Buchanan aside, and told him that he believed he was now ready for him, and proposed to send him a project of a treaty of commerce which should be founded on the provisions of the American treaties with Prussia, Sweden and Austria. Long interviews and oral discussions of this project then took place at the Foreign Office between Mr. Buchanan, Count Nesselrode, Baron Brunnow and Baron Sacken. In these discussions Mr. Buchanan evinced the most thorough acquaintance with the whole subject, and gave the Russian statesmen information which was new to them and greatly surprised them. At length all the details of the treaty were settled, and by the 17th of December it was prepared for signature in duplicate, in the French and English languages. Still the treaty was not yet signed. For the purpose of expediting the matter, Mr. Buchanan made a suggestion that as the emperor's fête day, or his saint's day, was to be celebrated on the 18th December, N. S., that it should be signed on that day. Count Nesselrode was pleased with the suggestion, and said that Mr. Buchanan's wish should be gratified, if possible. Baron Sacken doubted if it would be practicable, but the count said it must be done, and that Mr. Clay, the American Secretary of Legation, could assist them in making the copies. This occurred on the 13th of December, N. S. It was not, however, until Mr. Buchanan was in the presence of the emperor, at his levée on the morning of the 18th, that he felt finally assured that the treaty would be signed, although Count Nesselrode had informed him on the 15th that he was authorized to sign it. What occurred at the emperor's levée will be best told by Mr. Buchanan himself:

On Tuesday morning, the 18th, we went to the emperor's levée; and on this occasion a singular occurrence took place in relation to the treaty.

170The strictest secrecy had been preserved throughout the negotiation. Indeed I do not believe an individual, except those immediately concerned, had the least idea that negotiations were even pending. A rumor of the refusal of this government to make the treaty had circulated two months ago, and I was then repeatedly informed in conversation, that it was in vain for any nation to attempt to conclude a treaty of commerce with the Russian government, whilst Count Cancrene continued to be minister of finance. Count Nesselrode had on one occasion intimated a desire that the British

120

government should not obtain a knowledge that negotiations were proceeding, and this was an additional reason on our part for observing the greatest caution.

It ought to be remembered, however, that this intimation was given before information had reached St. Petersburg of the conclusion of the late treaty between France and England in relation to the Belgian question. The diplomatic corps, according to the etiquette, were arranged in a line to receive the emperor and empress; and Mr. Bligh, the English minister, occupied the station immediately below myself. You may judge of my astonishment when the emperor, accosting me in French, in a tone of voice which could be heard by all around, said, "I signed the order yesterday that the treaty should be executed according to your wishes;" and then immediately turning to Mr. Bligh asked him to become the interpreter of this information. He (Mr. Bligh) is a most amiable man, and his astonishment and embarrassment were so striking that I felt for him most sincerely. This incident has already given rise to considerable speculation among the knowing ones of St. Petersburg; probably much more than it deserves.

I ought to remark that when I was presented to the emperor, I understood but little, I might almost say no, French; and there was then an interpreter present. Supposing this still to be the case, the emperor must have thought that an interpreter was necessary, and he was correct to a certain extent, for I have not yet had sufficient practice to attempt to speak French in the presence of the whole court. I trust this may not long be the case; but I still more ardently hope I may not very long continue in a situation where it will be necessary to speak that language.

There can be no doubt but that all which occurred was designed on the part of the emperor; and what must have rendered it still more embarrassing to Mr. Bligh was, that one object of Lord Durham's mission is said to have been the conclusion of a commercial treaty with Russia.

After the emperor had retired, Mr. Bligh, in manifest confusion, told me he feared he had been a very bad interpreter, and asked me what kind of a treaty we had been concluding with Russia, to which I replied it was a treaty of commerce.

Count Nesselrode was not present at the moment, and from his manner when I informed him of the incident, I believe he had not previously received any intimation of the emperor's intention to make such a disclosure.

The count and myself afterwards proceeded from the palace to the 171Foreign Office and there signed the treaty. The only persons present were Baron Brunnow and Baron Sacken. On this occasion but little worthy of repetition occurred. They all exhibited the greatest cordiality and good will, and the count emphatically declared that he believed we had that day completed a work which would result in benefits to both nations.

On taking my leave, I expressed no more than I felt, in thanking him for his kind and candid conduct throughout the whole negotiation, and he paid me some compliments in return.......

Thus, sir, you have in my different despatches a faithful history of the whole progress of the negotiation up to its termination. Independently of the positive advantages secured to our commerce by the treaty, and of the stipulation prohibiting Russia from granting favors to any other nation at our expense, there is another consideration which deserves attention. I think I cannot be mistaken in asserting that if the feelings of the Russians towards our country in the days of the Emperor Alexander were of a kindly character, which I have no reason to doubt, they have undergone some change since the accession of his present majesty. In a future despatch I may probably state my reasons for this impression. The very fact, however, of concluding the present treaty and thus distinguishing us from other commercial nations, connected with the time and manner in which his majesty thought proper to announce it, will have a powerful influence favorable to our country among the members of a court where every look and every word of the emperor is noted and observed almost as if he were a Divinity. I may say that I have already experienced a change: even Count Cancrene, in a conversation with Baron Steiglitz of this city, has expressed his assent to the treaty, observing at the same time that the United States formed an exception to his general principles on this subject. He added a compliment to myself of such a character as I know I do not deserve, and therefore I shall not repeat.[32]

In announcing to the Secretary of State (on the 20th of December, 1832, N. S.) the conclusion of the commercial treaty, Mr. Buchanan said:

"I have now the pleasure of transmitting to you a treaty of commerce and navigation, which was signed on Tuesday last, the 18th instant, between the United States and Russia, by Count Nesselrode and myself. I congratulate the President, that after many fruitless attempts have been made by our Government to conclude such a treaty, it has at last been accomplished.

"Like yourself, I confess, I did not entertain sanguine hopes of success when I left Washington. The despatch of Mr. Randolph upon this subject was indeed very discouraging. The difficulties in prospect, however, served only to inspire me with a stronger resolution to accomplish, if practicable, the wishes of the President. This I trust has been done without the slightest sacrifice, in my person, of either the dignity or the honor of the country. Should my conduct throughout this difficult, and in some respects extraordinary negotiation, receive his approbation and that of the Senate, I shall be amply compensated for my labors."

That Mr. Buchanan was not equally successful in concluding a treaty concerning maritime rights is a matter that admits of easy explanation. In the communication which was made to him by Count Nesselrode in October (1832), there was conveyed a respectful refusal to make the commercial treaty. At the interview which took place afterward between Baron Brunnow and Mr. Buchanan, at the house of the latter, after they had arranged for re-opening the negotiation concerning a commercial treaty, there was a conversation on the other subject, which was thus reported by Mr. Buchanan to the Secretary of State:

After our conversation ended on this subject,—I referred to that portion of the note of Count Nesselrode which declined our offer to conclude a treaty on maritime rights, and said that the President would probably not be prepared for this refusal. I told him that on the 28th August, 1828, N. S., a few months before the election of General Jackson, Baron Krudener had addressed a communication to the Department of State which gave a strong assurance that the emperor was willing to conclude such a treaty. That when General Jackson assumed the reins of Government in the month of March following, he had found this communication on file, and that was the principal reason why he had given Mr. Randolph instructions to conclude a treaty concerning neutral rights. I was therefore surprised no allusion whatever had been made to this important letter in the note of Count Nesselrode, and that he had passed it over as though it had never existed, whilst he referred to the note he had addressed to Mr. Middleton so long ago as the 1st of February, 1824, for the purpose of explaining the views of the imperial government at the present moment.

I then produced the communication of Baron Krudener to Mr. Brent of the 16–28th of August, 1828, and read it to Baron Brunnow. After he had perused it himself, he expressed his surprise at its contents, and said he did not believe a copy of it had been transmitted to the Foreign Office; that he could say for himself he had never seen it before. He thought the baron must have gone further than his instructions had warranted;

and that instead 173of expressing the willingness of the emperor to adopt by mutual agreement, the principles concerning neutral rights proposed by the United States, he ought merely to have expressed the concurrence of the emperor in those principles and his desire to preserve and protect them. He added that these rights were best maintained by the power of nations, and we had nobly defended them during our late war with England. I replied, that was very true, and the United States were becoming more and more powerful every year, and had less and less occasion to rely upon treaties for the maintenance of their neutral rights.

I afterwards remarked that I thought the count, from the tenor of his note, had probably overlooked one circumstance of importance in considering this subject, as he had placed the refusal chiefly on the ground that it would be useless for only two powers to conclude such a treaty between themselves. That the fact was, the United States already had treaties of a similar character with several nations, which I enumerated, and that if Russia had concluded this treaty, in case she should hereafter unfortunately be engaged in war with any of these powers, the property of her subjects would be secure from capture by their ships of war, on board of American vessels. He replied that as to Prussia, Sweden, and Holland there was little danger of any war between them and Russia; and that we had no such treaties with the maritime powers with whom Russia was likely to be engaged in hostilities.

(Evidently, as I supposed, alluding to England and France.)

In the course of the conversation, I regretted that I had never seen the note addressed by Count Nesselrode to Mr. Middleton in February, 1824, and that there was no copy of it in the archives of the legation here. He then said he would take pleasure in sending me a copy, and thought he might assure me with perfect confidence, from the feelings of Count Nesselrode towards myself, that he would be happy to send me at all times copies of any other papers I might desire from the Foreign Office.

He at first proposed to repeat this conversation to Count Nesselrode. I replied I had no objection. It was not intended by me as an attempt to renew the negotiation at the present time; but merely to make some suggestions to him in free conversation. Before he took leave, however, he said he believed that as his mission to me had been of a special character, he would report nothing to the count but what had a relation to the commercial treaty—except that I desired to have a copy of his note to Mr. Middleton; but that after the other subject was finally disposed of, he thought I ought to mention these things to Count Nesselrode myself. I told him I probably might, that what I had said to him on this subject, had been communicated in a frank and friendly spirit, and I considered it altogether unofficial. No doubt he repeated every word.

What is here related occurred in the autumn of 1832, and the subject of maritime rights was not again alluded to until 174the following spring. Writing to General Jackson a private letter on the 29th of May, 1833, Mr. Buchanan said:

I fear I shall not be able to conclude the treaty concerning maritime rights, though I shall use my best exertions. My late attempt to introduce the subject was not very successful, as you will have seen from my last despatch.

I have now, after much reflection, determined on my plan of operations. It would not be consistent with the high character of our Government, or with what I am confident would be your wishes, that I should make another direct official proposition, without a previous intimation that it would be well received; and we might thus be subjected to another direct refusal so soon after the last. It is therefore my intention to present my views of the subject in the form of an unofficial note, and to express them with as much clearness and force as I am capable [of]. I shall not in this note seek a renewal of the negotiation; though I shall leave it clearly to be inferred that such is my desire. If they should not move in the business afterwards, it would neither be proper nor dignified to press them further.

I am convinced they are endeavoring to manage England at present, and that this is an unpropitious moment to urge them to adopt principles of public law which would give offence to that nation. Besides, Russia has now a large navy, and but a small commercial marine; and it is not for such a power as she now believes herself to be, to desire to change the law of nations in such a manner as to abridge her belligerent rights. The principle "that free ships shall make free goods," will always be most popular with nations who possess a large commercial marine and a small navy, and whose policy is peaceful. But I shall do my best. I hope this question may be determined by the beginning of August, as I should then have the opportunity of seeing something more of Europe, and yet reach the United States about the end of November. By the last accounts, my mother's health was decidedly better, so that on that ground I need not so much hasten my return.

I have received many letters which give me strong assurances that I shall be elected to the Senate. I confess, however, that I feel very doubtful of success. The men in Pennsylvania, who have risen to power by the popularity of your name, while in heart they are opposed to you, will do every thing they can to prevent my election. The present governor is greatly influenced by their counsels, and his patronage is very great and very powerful. Besides, the Nullifiers and their organ, the Telegraph, will show me no quarter. Thank God! I know how to be content with a private station, and I shall leave the Legislature to do just as they please......

Our excellent consul here is in very bad health from the severity of the climate. His physician says that he must travel, and that immediately: but I entertain some doubts whether he has sufficient strength left for the purpose. It is said, however, that he was restored once before by a change of climate, when in an equally weak condition. He purposes to set off in a few weeks, 175and Mr. Clay, who will have little else to attend to, will do his business cheerfully during his absence. I sincerely wish he could obtain a situation in a milder climate. It would be a most happy circumstance for the commerce of the United States if all our consuls were like Mr. G. After sending my note to Count Nesselrode, I intend to visit Moscow for a few days, as he is to be absent himself. I beg to present my respects to your family, and to Messrs. Barry, Taney, McLane and Woodbury. The simple truth is, that the Russian government, since the intimation made by Baron Krudener just before General Jackson became President, had changed its mind in regard to the subject of maritime rights. The reason for declining to make the treaty in 1832–33, as explained by Count Pozzo di Borgo to Mr. Buchanan, in Paris, accords entirely with what Mr. Buchanan had learned at St. Petersburg.[33] The attitude of the Belgian question, and the relations of Russia towards England, precluded the acceptance of the American proposal to establish by treaty between Russia and the United States the principle that "free ships make free goods."

All of Mr. Buchanan's official duties at St. Petersburg were not, however, so entirely pleasant as the negotiation of the commercial treaty. While this negotiation was in its early stage, Baron Sacken, who had been left by Baron Krudener as Russian chargé d'affaires at Washington, made to the Secretary of State a somewhat offensive communication, complaining of certain articles in The Globe, the official paper of the American Government, concerning the conduct of Russia towards Poland. The complaint was doubtless made in ignorance of the fact that although the Globe was the official gazette of our Government, the President had no control over or responsibility for its editorial articles, or the articles which it copied from English or French journals. The freedom of the press in this country was not understood by Russian officials; and although it does not appear that Baron Sacken's act was directed from St. Petersburg, there can be no doubt that in making the complaint he did what he believed would be acceptable to his superiors at home. He, however, considerably overshot the mark, in the tone and manner of his communication to the Department of State, and it became necessary for the President to direct Mr. Buchanan to lay the matter before the Russian government. This was done by a despatch from Mr. Livingston, courteous but firm, pointing out the impossibility of exercising in this country any governmental constraint over the press, and making very clear the offensive imputation of insincerity on the part of the President contained in Baron Sacken's note. This occurrence was not known at St. Petersburg, at least it was not known to Mr. Buchanan, while the negotiation of the commercial treaty was pending. On the receipt of Mr. Livingston's despatch, which was written early in January, 1833, Mr. Buchanan had an interview with Count Nesselrode on the subject, of which he gave the following account to the Secretary of State:

February 26th, 1833.

On yesterday at 2 o'clock, P. M., I had a conference with the count. I inquired if he had yet received from Washington the answer of Mr. Livingston to Baron Sacken's note of the 14th of October last; to which he replied in the affirmative. After expressing my regret that anything unpleasant should have occurred at Washington in the intercourse between the two governments, whilst everything here had been proceeding so harmoniously, I observed:

That Baron Sacken himself, in his note to Mr. Brent, had admitted that the President, throughout the whole course of his administration, had constantly expressed a desire to be on friendly terms with Russia. But the President's feelings had not been confined to mere official declarations to the Russian government; they had been expressed, in strong terms, before the world in each of his annual messages to Congress, previous to the date of Baron Sacken's note. Besides they had been always manifested by his conduct.

The baron [I said], with a full knowledge of these facts, had addressed this note to Mr. Brent, which was not only offensive in its general tone, but more especially so in imputing a want of sincerity to the President, and in effect charging him with tacitly encouraging the abuse of the emperor by the American newspapers, whilst he was professing friendship towards the Russian government. Such a charge was well calculated to make a strong impression upon General Jackson, a man who, during his whole life, had been distinguished for sincerity and frankness. When, after Mr. Clay's departure, I had perused this note, with which his excellency had been good enough to furnish me, I was convinced the President could not pass it over in silence; and I had since been astonished not to have received, until very recently, any communication on the subject.

I had now discovered that the reason of this delay was an anxious desire on the part of the President to avoid everything unpleasant in the intercourse between the two countries; and had formed an expectation that Baron Sacken himself, after reflection, would have rendered it unnecessary to bring the subject before the imperial government. In this hope the President had been disappointed. Nearly two months had transpired before Mr. Livingston answered his note. In the meantime, a fair opportunity was afforded him to withdraw it, and a verbal intimation given that this would be more agreeable to the President than to take the only notice of it which he could take with propriety. Mr. Livingston had supposed that, under the circumstances, the baron would have felt it to be his duty to visit Washington, where, at a verbal conference, the affair might have been satisfactorily adjusted. In this opinion he found he was mistaken. At length, on the 4th December, he addressed the baron this answer, which places in a striking light the most offensive part of his note, the charge of insincerity. Even in it, however, the President's feelings of amity for Russia and respect for the emperor are reiterated.

After this answer, Mr. Livingston waited nearly another month, confident that a disavowal of any offensive intention would, at least, have been made. This not having been done, he has sent me instructions, under date of the 3d January last, to bring the subject under the notice of the imperial government; and it is for that purpose I have solicited the present interview.

The count expressed his regret that any misunderstanding should have occurred between Baron Sacken and Mr. Livingston; it was evident the former never could have intended anything offensive to the President, as he had taken the precaution of submitting his note of the 14th of October to Mr. Livingston in New York before it was transmitted to the Department, who not only made no objection to it at the time, but informed him it should be answered in a few days. The count then asked if Mr. Livingston had not communicated this circumstance to me in his despatches. I replied in the negative, and from my manner intimated some doubt as to its existence; when he took up the despatch of Baron Sacken and read to me, in French, a statement of this fact. He said, if Mr. Livingston had at that time objected to any part of the note, the baron would have immediately changed its phraseology. I replied that the President at least had certainly never seen the note previous to its receipt at the Department; and it appeared to me manifestly to contain an imputation on his sincerity, and was besides offensive in its general character. He did not attempt to justify its language, but repeated that he thought Baron Sacken never could have intended to write anything offensive to the President. If he had, it would have been done in violation of his instructions. That the feelings of the emperor as well as his own were of the most friendly nature towards the Government of the United States, and that, in particular, both the emperor and himself entertained the highest respect and esteem for the character of the President. That neither of them would ever think of sanctioning the imputation of insincerity or 178anything that was dishonorable to General Jackson, and he was very sorry Baron Sacken had written a note the effect of which was to wound his feelings.

As the count did not still seem to be altogether satisfied that the note attributed insincerity to the professions of the President, I then took it up and pointed out in as clear and striking a manner as I could, the most offensive passages which it contained. After I had done, he repeated in substance what he had said before, but without any qualification whatever, expressing both his own sorrow and that of the emperor, that Baron Sacken should have written a note calculated to wound the feelings of General Jackson, or to give him any cause of offence. He added, that the baron either already had left, or would soon leave the United States; and he had no doubt, that soon after the arrival of the treaty and of Baron Krudener at Washington, all matters would be explained to the satisfaction of the President; by whom, he trusted, this unpleasant occurrence would be entirely forgotten.

With this explanation, I expressed myself perfectly satisfied, and assured him I should have great pleasure in communicating it to the President.

He then observed that, judging from the despatch of Baron Sacken, this unfortunate business seemed to have been a succession of mistakes. That Mr. Livingston, through Mr. Kremer, had pointed out to the baron the exceptional parts of his note; but whilst he was engaged in correcting them, and before sufficient time for this purpose had been afforded, he had received Mr. Livingston's note of the 4th of December.

In the course of the interview, the count read me several detached paragraphs from Baron Sacken's despatch, and from their character I received the impression that he had become alarmed at the consequences of his own conduct, and was endeavoring to justify it in the best manner he could.

We afterwards had some conversation respecting the publications in our newspapers, in which allusion was made to the explanations I had given him on this subject in December. He stated distinctly that they were now fully aware of the difficulties which would attend any attempt to interfere with the press under our form of Government.

In obedience to your instructions, I now read to him the greater part of Despatch No. 5, and explained the nature of the only connection which our Government has with the official paper. After having done so, I asked him to consider the consequences of an unsuccessful attempt on the part of the administration at Washington to control the Globe; and told him that in that event, the editor, by publishing it to the world, would make both the emperor and the President subjects of abuse throughout the Union. The press was essentially free in our country. Even the Congress of the United States had no power to pass any law for the punishment of a libel on the President. This subject was exclusively under the jurisdiction of the several States.

That, it was true, editors were often influenced by the counsel of those whom they respected, therefore I had communicated his request to General Jackson, that he would advise the editor of the Globe to desist hereafter from offensive publications against Russia, but even this would be a delicate matter to proceed from a person holding the office of President of the United States. I then informed him that I had been much pleased, some weeks since, to observe in the St. Petersburg Journal an official contradiction of some of the acts attributed to the Russian government of Poland; that I had sent the paper which contained it to the Department of State, and had no doubt it would be extensively published in the United States. He expressed great satisfaction that I had taken the trouble, and said it would be very agreeable to them to have this contradiction circulated throughout our country.

It is scarcely worth repeating that he objected, in a good-natured manner, to the designation of Baron Sacken's note in the despatch as "a formal note," observing that a formal note always commenced with "the undersigned," and not the first person. This was intended to be an informal note, and that was the reason it had been submitted to Mr. Livingston before it was transmitted to the Department of State.

I congratulate you that this unpleasant affair has had such an auspicious termination. We shall, I think, hear no more complaints from this quarter, on the subject of publications in the American newspapers, especially if the editor of the Globe should be a little more circumspect in his course hereafter.

In regard to the subject of Polish affairs, the treatment of which by the Globe was the occasion of Baron Sacken's imprudent note, it will be seen hereafter that the emperor was peculiarly sensitive to the comments of the foreign press. Mr. Buchanan, who had the best opportunity for observation while he was in St. Petersburg, formed the opinion that the personal attacks upon the emperor, on account of the conduct of his government towards the Poles, with which the English, French, and American journals abounded, were to a certain extent unjust; that the inveterate national hatreds with which the Russian and Polish races regarded each other, were at the bottom of most of the difficulties with which the emperor had to contend; and that the fact that Russian officers were intrusted with power in Poland over a race whom they hated and by whom they were hated in turn, inevitably led to many of the cruelties and oppressions with which the world outside of Russia resounded, and which were charged upon the emperor personally, as if he had designed them. Buchanan did not palliate or excuse the conduct of the Russian government towards the Poles; nor does he seem on any occasion, when it was proper for him to refer to it, to have allowed any one to suppose that he defended it. But in writing to his own Government or to his friends at home, he 180did not hesitate to say that he thought many of the causes which produced the oppression that so roused the indignation of the world, lay deep in the national hatred between the two races, and were not to be imputed to an arbitrary and cruel temper in the emperor.

He looked upon the despotism which he saw with the calm eye of an observer who could comprehend its character and trace its operations, without doing injustice to the reigning monarch. He saw a vast nation entirely incapable of any thing like constitutional liberty, and governed by the absolute will of one man, to obey whom was at once a point of religion, loyalty and patriotism. Between the nobility and the throne, there was no middle class, capable of thinking or acting upon any political subject; and the nobility, as a rule, were capable and desirous of no other political training, ideas or aspirations than such as would fit them for the part of useful servants of an emperor whom they adored, and of a system which constituted their country the most peculiar and the least free of any in Europe. The statesmen who were formed under such a system were, as might naturally be expected, accomplished in many ways, subtle and often powerful reasoners; and they were not seldom among the ablest men of the age. When they were made to understand how completely, as Mr. Buchanan said, they and we were "political antipodes," they found no difficulty in yielding to the necessity of respecting a state of things in America which was so unlike any thing that they knew at home. At first, Count Nesselrode could not understand how a government could have an official organ, and yet disclaim responsibility to a foreign power for what that organ said in its editorial columns. But when it was explained to him that the American Government did disclaim that responsibility, and was obliged to do so by the nature of its political institutions, he did not make it his business to argue the point, but gracefully accepted the explanation and put an end to the whole of the misunderstanding.

It must be confessed, however, that while Mr. Buchanan fully and firmly carried out his instructions and procured all the admission that his own Government desired, in regard to Baron Sacken's note, it was a pretty fine distinction that his Government 181had to draw. It was perfectly true that the Globe was the official gazette of the American Government, and yet that its editorial columns could not be legally controlled by the President. Still it might be a question whether an American administration should have had an official organ, with which it was connected on such terms that the editor or conductor was just as independent of its influence or its power, as if he published a newspaper that was not connected in any way with the Government. Both at home and abroad, the editorial columns of the Globe were liable to be regarded as speaking the sentiments of the administration; and when it became necessary to disclaim that they did so, the explanation, although made upon undeniable facts, was an awkward one to make. Mr. Buchanan certainly felt it to be so, for in writing to the Secretary of State, after he had obtained from Count Nesselrode all the disavowal that was desired, he said:

I have time but for few remarks upon this strange interview.

It serves to show how indispensable it is that our minister to this country should be kept advised of every proceeding in the United States which may affect the relations between the two nations. He has indeed a most difficult part to perform. He must be cautious in the extreme, and is under the habitual necessity of concealing his real sentiments. It is utterly impossible for these people to realize the state of affairs in the United States. We are political antipodes, and hence the great difficulty of maintaining those friendly relations which are so important to the interests of our country. I know not when the despatch was received containing a copy of Baron Sacken's note to Mr. Brent, or what influence it might have had upon the negotiation had it reached him [Nesselrode] at an earlier period. Of this, however, I feel confident, that, if a copy of this note had been transmitted [to me] immediately after its receipt, this unpleasant interview might have been avoided altogether....

I would suggest the policy of advising the editor of the Globe to abstain at least from severe editorial paragraphs respecting the emperor of Russia. Neither the cause of Poland nor of human liberty could suffer by his silence in a country where there are so many faithful sentinels, and I should, by all means, advise the publication of a strong editorial paragraph in the Globe, expressing a proper sense of the good feelings of the emperor of Russia, evinced towards the United States in making us an exception to his general policy by concluding the commercial treaty. If this should be done, and more particularly if the President should, even in the slightest manner, allude to the circumstance in his inaugural address, it would be very grateful personally to the feelings of the emperor.

182I have felt it my duty to take measures, though they may be expensive to the Government, of having the semi-weekly Globe transmitted to me through the post-office from London. Will you be particular in giving directions that it shall be regularly forwarded from New York by every packet. It is true it will be read at the post-office here; but should it contain anything offensive, I shall know it almost as soon as this government and before the Russian minister at Washington can have an opportunity of transmitting any inflammatory commentaries. I assure you, I feel the delicacy of my position; but knowing your distinguished abilities and long experience, if I could but only attract your special regard to this mission, I think, between us, we might, in perfect consistency with the high and independent character of our own country, keep his imperial majesty in a state of better feeling towards us than almost any other nation. We have much to gain by such a course and nothing to lose.

I requested Mr. Vail, some time ago, to send me the semi-weekly Globe by mail from London. Although this may be expensive to the Government, it cannot be avoided, and it is absolutely necessary that I should receive it. It would seem, however, that the department has ceased forwarding them to London. Will you be kind enough to give directions that they shall be sent, in a separate parcel, by every Liverpool packet from New York.

183

CHAPTER IX.

1832–1833.

GENERAL JACKSON'S SECOND ELECTION—GRAVE PUBLIC EVENTS AT HOME REFLECTED IN MR. BUCHANAN'S LETTERS FROM HIS FRIENDS—FEELINGS OF GENERAL JACKSON TOWARDS THE "NULLIFIERS"—MOVEMENTS IN PENNSYLVANIA FOR ELECTING MR. BUCHANAN TO THE SENATE OF THE UNITED STATES—HE MAKES A JOURNEY TO MOSCOW—RETURN TO ST. PETERSBURG—DEATH OF HIS MOTHER—SINGULAR INTERVIEW WITH THE EMPEROR NICHOLAS AT HIS AUDIENCE OF LEAVE.

Mr. Buchanan, as the reader has seen, went abroad in the spring of 1832. Events of great consequence occurred at home during his absence. The great debate in the Senate on nullification, between Mr. Webster and Col. Hayne, which took place in 1830, had not been followed in South Carolina by any surrender of the doctrine maintained by the

Nullifiers. In November, 1832, the people of South Carolina, assembled in convention, adopted their celebrated ordinance which declared the existing tariff law of the United States null and void within her limits, as an unconstitutional exercise of power. General Jackson who had been re-elected President in the same month, defeating Mr. Clay and all the other candidates by a very large majority of the electoral votes, issued his proclamation against the Nullifiers on the 10th of December.[34] Then followed the introduction of the "Force Bill" into the Senate in January, 1833; a measure designed to secure the collection of the revenue against the obstruction of the State laws of South Carolina; Mr. Webster's support of this measure of the administration; and the consequent expectation of a political union between him and General Jackson. This union, however, was prevented by an irreconcilable difference between Mr. Webster and General Jackson and his friends on the subject of the currency 184and the Bank of the United States. In 1832 the President had vetoed a bill to continue the Bank in existence. Early in June the President left Washington on a tour to the Eastern States, and while in Boston, during the month of June, he determined to remove the public deposits from the Bank of the United States, and to place them in certain selected State banks. These events and the excitements attending them are touched upon in the private letters which Mr. Buchanan received from his friends, not the least interesting of which was one from General Jackson, expressing his feelings in regard to his proclamation in a very characteristic manner. From one of these letters, too, we may gather that steps were already taking to elect Mr. Buchanan to the Senate of the United States.

[FROM A FRIEND IN WASHINGTON.]

Washington City, August 1, 1832.

Dear Sir:—

Of course you receive regular files of American papers, and I shall therefore not be able to give you much news of a public or political nature.

Thinking, however, you may overlook some things of importance, I shall confine myself to them. The tariff bill, having passed in a modified form (reducing the duties on protected, and taking them off nearly altogether on unprotected articles, to the wants of the Government), it was supposed the excitement in the South would be allayed, if not entirely subdued; but this, I am sorry to say, has not been the case in South Carolina. Messrs. Hayne, Miller, McDuffie, etc., have published an address to the people of South Carolina, in which they state, that the protective system has now become the settled policy of the country, and advise an open resistance to the act. Their legislature will, I have no doubt, recommend the same course, and before another year, I am firmly of the opinion, rebellion will be the order of the day, accompanied with all its horrors. The moment that a drop of blood is shed by the South, in resisting the laws, there will be a general rising of the people, and where is the hand that will be able to stop the fearful wrath of the sovereign people? Duff Green, in his paper of yesterday, said: "That he will write as long as writing will be of any effect; when that ceases, he will adopt the sword. If South Carolina is to be sacrificed, the tyrant will be met on the banks of the Potomac, and many, very many, are the sons of her sister States who will rally beneath her standard. We say to her gallant sons, go on! Yours is the cause of liberty, and the eyes of all her votaries are upon you!"

When language like this is held by the leader of the party, at the seat of 185Government of the Union, under the immediate eyes of the heads of the nation, and suffered to pass unpunished, it is indeed time for the people seriously to think of a civil war. The leaders in this affair will have much to answer for, and be assured they will be held accountable.

The bank bill has passed, by a small majority, in both Houses of Congress, and the President (true to his principles) has returned it (without his signature) with his objections. There appeared to be great excitement at the time, but it was only occasioned by the brawling of the opposition. A large meeting was got up in Philadelphia, at which a few Jackson men of no note attended, but all would not do. The next week, the Jackson men met to express their opinions, and they resolved unanimously to support "Andrew Jackson, bank or no bank, veto or no veto." At this meeting there were between ten and fifteen thousand people, citizens of the city and county, the largest meeting, I am told, that ever assembled in Philadelphia within the recollection of the oldest inhabitants.

[GENERAL JACKSON TO MR. BUCHANAN.]

(Private.) Washington, March 21, 1833.

Dear Sir:—

Your letter by Mr. Clay was handed me on his arrival. The fact of there being no means of conveyance, my not having ascertained Mr. Clay's determination in regard to his return to you, and the immense and heavy pressure of public business have caused me to delay my reply. Nullification, the corrupting influence of the Bank, the union of Calhoun and Clay, supported by the corrupt and wicked of all parties, engaged all my attention. The liberty of the people requires that wicked projects, and evil combinations against the Government should be exposed and counteracted.

I met nullification at its threshhold. My proclamation was well timed, as it at once opened the eyes of the people to the wicked designs of the Nullifiers, whose real motives had too long remained concealed. The public ceased to be deluded by the promise of securing by nullification "a peaceful and constitutional modification of the tariff."

They investigated the subject, and saw that, although the tariff was made the ostensible object, a separation of the confederacy was the real purpose of its originators and supporters.

The expression of public opinion elicited by the proclamation, from Maine to Louisiana, has so firmly repudiated the absurd doctrine of nullification and secession, that it is not probable that we shall be troubled with them again shortly.

The advices of to-day inform us that South Carolina has repealed her ordinance and all the laws based upon it.[35] Thus die nullification and secession, 186but leave behind the remembrance of their authors and abettors, which holds them up to scorn and indignation, and will transmit them to posterity as traitors to the best of governments.

The treaty is as good a one as we could expect or desire, and if you can close the other as satisfactorily, it will be a happy result, and place you in the highest rank of our able and fortunate diplomatists.

Mr. Clay has conversed with me freely, and has determined, under all the circumstances, to return to you.

If Mr. Clay had not taken this determination, be well assured that your request in respect to his successor would have received my most anxious attention. You should have had one in whom you could with safety confide. I had thought of Mr. Vail, now at London, who has signified his inclination to remain abroad, as secretary of legation, when relieved by a minister.

Mr. Clay can be left as chargé-d'affaires when your duty to your aged mother may make it necessary for you to return to her and your country.

Knowing, as I do, that you will not leave your post until you bring to a close the negotiation now under discussion, I have said to the Secretary of State to grant you permission to return whenever you may ask it. But should an emergency arise which will render it inconvenient, if not impossible, for you to write and receive an answer from the state department before, from the feeble health of your mother, it may be necessary for you to return, you will consider yourself as being hereby authorized to leave the court of Russia, and return, leaving Mr. Clay in charge of our affairs there.

I must refer you to Mr. Clay, and the newspapers, which I have requested the Secretary of State to send you, for the news and politics of the day. I must, however, add, that in the late election, good old Democratic Pennsylvania has greatly increased my debt of gratitude to her, which I can only attempt to discharge by renewed and increasing vigilance and exertions in so administering the Government as to perpetuate the prosperity and happiness of the whole people.

Accept of my best wishes for your health and happiness, and for your safe return to your country and friends. Give my kind respects to Mr. Barry, and believe me to be sincerely Your friend,

Andrew Jackson.

[MR. BUCHANAN TO GENERAL JACKSON.]

St. Petersburg, May 22, 1833

Dear General:—

I had the pleasure of receiving, by Mr. Clay, your kind letter of the 21st March. And here allow me to tender you my grateful thanks for the permission which you have granted me to return home. Indeed, I, for some time, had scarcely indulged the hope that I should be allowed to leave St. Petersburg before the next spring; this permission, therefore, was a most 187agreeable surprise, and adds another to the many obligations I owe to your kindness. I hope I may yet have an opportunity of displaying my gratitude by my actions. Although I shall leave St. Petersburg with pleasure, yet I shall always gratefully remember the kindness with which I have been treated here. My great objection to the country is the extreme jealousy and suspicion of the government. A public minister, in order successfully to discharge his duties and avoid giving offense, must conceal the most ennobling sentiments of his soul. We are continually surrounded by spies, both of high and low degree in life. You can scarcely hire a servant who is not a secret agent of the police.

There is one mitigating circumstance in Russian despotism. In other portions of Europe we behold nations prepared and anxious for the enjoyment of liberty, yet compelled to groan beneath the yoke. No such spectacle is presented in this country. The most ardent Republican, after having resided here for one year, would be clearly convinced that the mass of this people, composed as it is of ignorant and superstitious barbarians, who are also slaves, is not fit for political freedom. Besides, they are perfectly contented. The emperor seems to me to be the very beau ideal of a sovereign for Russia, and in my opinion, notwithstanding his conduct towards Poland, he is an abler and a better man than any of those by whom he is surrounded. I flatter myself that a favorable change has been effected in his feelings towards the United States since my arrival. Indeed, at the first I was treated with great neglect, as Mr. Clay had always been. I was glad he returned. It would be difficult to find a more agreeable Secretary of Legation. I also entertain a very high opinion of Mr. Vail.

I sincerely rejoice that our domestic differences seem almost to have ended. Independently of their fatal influence at home, they had greatly injured the character of the country abroad. The advocates of despotism throughout Europe beheld our dissensions with delight; whilst the friends of freedom sickened at the spectacle. God grant that the restless spirits which have kindled the flame in South Carolina may neither be willing nor able to promote disunion by rendering the Southern States generally disaffected towards the best of governments.

Whilst these dissensions are ever to be deplored in themselves, they have been most propitious for your fame. We generally find but few extracts from American papers in the European journals; but whilst the South Carolina question was pending, your proclamation, as well as every material fact necessary to elucidate its history, was published on this side of the Atlantic. I have a hundred times heard, with pride and pleasure, the warmest commendations of your conduct, and have not met with a single dissenting voice. I was the other day obliged to laugh heartily at the sentiment of a Russian nobleman, which he considered the highest commendation. He said it was a pity that such a man as you had not been king of England instead of William the Fourth, for then Ireland would have been kept in good order and O'Connell would long since have been punished as he deserved.

188I might have told him you were not the stuff of which kings are made, and if you had possessed the power Ireland would have had her grievances removed and received justice, and that then there might have been no occasion for severity......

James Buchanan.

[FROM S. PLEASONTON.]

Washington, April 2d, 1833.

Dear Sir:—

I take the opportunity afforded by the return of Mr. Clay to St. Petersburg to write to you, in the certainty that the letter will be safely delivered.

The compromising tariff act passed at the last session has been accepted pretty generally at the South, and has been received at the North much better than I expected, so that the alarm and anxiety which existed on the subject have been removed.

Much clamor, however, is yet kept up at the South, including Virginia, on the subject of the President's 10th December proclamation, and what is called the enforcing bill. The proclamation in my opinion contains the true Union doctrine, and does General Jackson great honor; and the enforcing bill was absolutely called for by the attitude which South Carolina had assumed. The State rights gentlemen, however, in the South, are for denying all right to the Union, as if the two governments were not formed by the same people and for their benefit. Absurd as these State rights doctrines are when carried fully out, I fear they will be pushed to an open rebellion by the Southern States before many years shall elapse.

I was in hopes that when Mr. Livingston went to France, as he will do probably in June next, that you would have been called to the Department of State, but it seems a different arrangement is to be made. Mr. McLane is to go to the Department of State, and it is said a gentleman from Pennsylvania, who has never been spoken of for the Treasury, is to be appointed to that department. As Dallas and Wilkins have been much talked of for this department, I am somewhat in hopes that the person referred to may be yourself. Be that as it may, I feel pretty confident that you will be elected to the Senate of the United States at the next meeting of the legislature, if you should be at home in season. They have made two or three trials to elect a senator during the session without effect, and from all I can learn the legislature will adjourn without making an election, so that the election will lie over until the next session.

Mrs. Pleasonton is now pretty well, though she has had several severe attacks in the course of the winter. Mathilda, with her husband, left us yesterday morning for Philadelphia. She had been ill for nearly two months, and was not able to leave us until yesterday. Augustus is exceedingly studious and is getting a good share of professional business. I have great hopes of him. Laura is still in Philadelphia, but will complete her education in the month of May. Mrs. P. intended to have written to you but she has not had it in her power, having been much engaged for Mathilda. I send you by Mr. Clay, copies, or rather duplicates, of two letters written to you some time ago about your accounts.

Mr. Clay can inform you of many particulars which will interest you, but I presume will say nothing of his friend [John] Randolph, who is now decidedly and zealously in the opposition. He was here lately and behaved in the most eccentric manner.

As you may not have seen all the documents communicated to Congress by the President in relation to South Carolina, I have determined to burthen Mr. Clay with them. They are accordingly enclosed.

With great regard, I remain, dear sir, your friend and obedient servant,
S. Pleasonton.

[MR. BUCHANAN TO JOHN B. STERIGERE.]
St. Petersburg, May 19, 1833.
My Dear Sir:—

I think you are mistaken in supposing I should have been elected to the Senate had I been at home. The opposition against me from many causes would have been too strong. Indeed, I have an impression that my public career is drawing near its close, and I can assure you this feeling does not cost me a single pang. All I feel concerned about is to know what I shall employ myself about after my return. To recommence the practice of the law in Lancaster would not be very agreeable. If my attachments for that place as well as my native State were not so strong, I should have no difficulty in arriving at a conclusion. I would at once go either to New York or Baltimore; and even if I should ever desire to rise to political distinction, I believe I could do it sooner in the latter place than in any part of Pennsylvania. What do you think of this project? Say nothing about it. I have not written a word on the subject to any other person. I see the appointment of Judge Sutherland announced some weeks ago. Judging from the feelings displayed in the election of printers to Congress, I should not have been astonished at his election as Speaker by the next House of Representatives.

The winter here has been very long, but I have not at all suffered from the cold. The great thickness of the walls of the houses, their double windows and doors, and their stoves built of tile, render their houses much more comfortable in very cold weather than our own. They are always heated according to a thermometer, and preserved at an equal temperature. Indeed, I have suffered more from the heat than the cold during the winter. But its length has been intolerable. The Neva was frozen for nearly six months. It broke up on the 25th ultimo; but still, until within a few days, there is a little ice occasionally running which comes from the Lake Ladoga.

On the 9th instant the navigation opened at Cronstadt. Four noble American ships led the way, and with a fine breeze and under full sail they passed through the ice and made an opening for the vessels of other nations. The character of our masters of vessels and supercargoes stands much higher here than that of the same class belonging to any other nation. They have much more intelligence. This Court requires a man of peculiar talent. There are but few of our countrymen fit to be sent here as minister. Here the character of the country depends much upon that of the minister. The sources of information respecting our republican institutions which are open throughout the rest of Europe are closed in this country. A favorable impression must be made upon the nobility by personal intercourse, and in order that this may be done it is absolutely necessary that the minister should occasionally entertain them and mix freely in their society. Such is the difference between Russian and American society, I am satisfied that Levett Harris would be a more useful minister here than Daniel Webster. I make this remark on the presumption that for years to come we shall have no serious business to transact.

After looking about me here, I was much at a loss to know what course to pursue. Without ruin to my private fortune I could not entertain as others did. Not to entertain at all I might almost as well not have been here except for the treaty. After some time I determined that I would give them good dinners in a plain republican style, for their splendid entertainments, and the plan has succeeded. I have never even put livery on a domestic in my house;—a remarkable circumstance in this country.

I think I may say, I am a favorite here, and especially with the emperor and empress. They have always treated me during the past winter in such a manner as even to excite observation. I am really astonished at my own success in this respect, for in sober truth, I say that, in my own opinion, I possess but few of the requisites of being successful in St. Petersburg society. I trust and hope that I may be permitted to return to my beloved native land this fall; and if Providence should continue to bless my endeavors, I think the character of the United States will stand upon a fairer footing with his Imperial Majesty than it has ever done since his accession to the throne.

May 22d.

Mr. Randolph Clay returned here on the 19th, bringing me a great number of letters from my friends and the President's permission to return home this fall. God willing! I shall be with you about the end of November. These letters hold out flattering prospects of my election to the Senate at the next session.

I confess I consider this event very doubtful, and shall take care not to set my heart upon it.

Mr. Barry leaves me to-day for London, and I have no time to add anything more. Please to write soon, and believe me ever to be your sincere friend,

James Buchanan.

P. S.—Remember me to Paulding, Patterson, Kittera and my other friends. I wrote once to the latter, but have never received an answer from him.

191[FROM LOUIS McLANE.]

(Unofficial.)   Washington, June 20, 1832.

My Dear Sir:—

It affords me sincere pleasure to devote a portion of my early labors in this Department[36] to you, whom I have known so long, and esteemed so highly. In one form or other you will hereafter receive more frequent communications from me, for I have already made a regulation by which a semi-monthly communication will be kept up from the Department with our principal ministers abroad. This is not only due to their character, but necessary to keep them informed of our principal domestic and foreign relations. This regulation will be independent of such special communications as the particular state of the missions respectively may [render] necessary.

You have no friend in this country who participated more sincerely than I in the success of your negotiation, and if the President needed anything to strengthen his friendship for you, or his confidence in your zeal and ability, your labors on that occasion would have afforded it. He has probably told you so himself, as I understood from him that he intended to write you.

...... The President is on a tour through the northern and eastern cities. He will go to Portland and thence up the lakes, through New York to Ohio and Pennsylvania, and expects to return here about the middle of July. I accompanied him as far as New York, and thence returned to my post. His health and spirits, notwithstanding the great fatigue to which he was perpetually exposed, had considerably improved, and I now have great hopes that he will derive advantage from his journey. His journey to New York was quite a triumphal procession, and his reception everywhere indescribably gratifying and imposing. The enthusiasm and cordial out-pouring of the kindest feelings of the heart, with which he was everywhere greeted, could not be exceeded, and the committees from the East, who met him in New York, assured us that a similar reception awaited his further progress. In Boston, both parties were emulating each other's exertions, and Webster, it was understood, had cut short his tour in the West, in order to receive him. This would be a sharp alliance, and yet it is altogether probable. On the part of Webster's friends, it is ardently desired and incessantly urged; on his own part he affects to consider the President's hostility to the bank as the only barrier. But I consider this only the last qualm of a frail lady, who notwithstanding, finally falls into the arms of the seducer. In the Senate, Webster's accession may be important, in the country its effect will be at least doubtful; especially with the democracy of New England. If, however, the President can identify the power of his name and character and hold upon the affections of the people with any individual, all opposition, however combined, must be hopeless. It is evident to me that no man ever lived, who exerted the same influence over the great body of the people as General Jackson; and if he devote the remainder of his term to tranquilize the public mind, he will go into retirement with greater fame than any other man in our history. The bank is the only disturbing question, and that he might overthrow, after all its iniquities, without a jar, unless by premature changing the [deposits], he should seriously derange the business and currency of the country. He is strongly disposed to take that step, both from his own hostility to the institution, and from the importunate [advice] of many of his friends. It would, in my opinion, be injudicious and prejudicial to the community; but the probability is it will be done either before or immediately after the commencement of the next session of Congress.

The affairs in the South are once more tranquil, and nullification may be said to be extinct. There are men in that quarter, however, who seriously meditate further difficulties, and there is just reason to apprehend that these will not be satisfied short of a Southern convention, leading to a Southern confederacy.

The elements of popular excitement only are wanting to make their purpose discernible to all, and the grave question has been revived for this purpose. So far it has not been successful, though it is evidently making some impression in one or two of the States south of the Potomac, and you know better than I can tell you, that the spirit of revolution is progressive, though it may be slow.

On all other points, our affairs at home are prosperous, and the prospect gratifying; and the new lines of party will not be very distinctly defined until toward the close of the next session of Congress.

I saw, while in Philadelphia with the President, many of your friends, who affectionately inquired after you, and you may be satisfied that your absence from the country has not served to weaken their attachment.

Now, my dear sir, I have taken up already too much of your time with this uninteresting letter, and I will therefore relieve you from a greater part of it. I will only add the wish of Mrs. McL—— to be brought to your remembrance, and the assurance of the continued respect and regard with which I am unaffectedly your friend and servant,

Louis McLane.

The principal object of the mission being accomplished, Mr. Buchanan began his journey to Moscow early in June, and was absent from St. Petersburg about a month. In making selections from his journals and letters relating to this tour, as well as those which he kept on his travels homeward after he finally left Russia, I shall omit descriptions of places and countries that are now familiar to multitudes of Americans, and shall quote only those which are of interest because they give 193accounts of persons or things as they impressed him at the time, and which are out of the beaten path of guide books as they then were or have since become, or which relate to the public affairs of that period.

Tuesday at 8 P. M., June 4, 1833.

Left St. Petersburg and arrived at Novogorod about 12 midi on Wednesday. Visited the church of St. Sophia, said to be founded by Wladimir in 1040. His tomb, at which they say miracles are wrought, is in it. The paintings are numerous and barbarous. The interior has a rude magnificence. Went into the sanctum sanctorum, where women are never admitted. There they consecrate the Eucharist in the Greek Church, out of the view of the people; unlike the Latin in this respect. The priest afterwards carries it out on his head, to be adored by the people.

The sides of the western door are lined with bronze, from which jutted out in bronze a number of strange and barbarous figures not unlike those of Mexico. They must have been Christian and even Russian in their origin, as one of them represented an Archimandrite in full dress. The inscriptions were Sclavonian. Our guide said they were conquered from the Swedes by St. Wladimir. The church is west of the river. It and several other buildings are surrounded by a brick wall, with turrets, etc., etc., about twenty-five feet high and eighteen thick and nearly a mile in circumference, a ditch beneath.

There are also the remains of another rampart and ditch, a considerable distance from the former. The church of St. Sophia is surrounded by a dome and four cupolas of the character peculiar to Russia.

The former is gilt and the others plated with silver, so they say. The celebrated monastery of St. Anthony we did not visit. There is scarcely any appearance of ancient ruins to indicate the former greatness of Novogorod. This arises from the nature of the materials of which it was built.

On Wednesday night we stayed at Zaitsova, an excellent inn.

The public houses are generally bad, beyond what an American can have any idea of; nevertheless, a few on this road were good. This inn is maintained in a degree by the emperor.

The peasants are jolly, good-natured fellows, who drive furiously and seem happy. They are all rogues, nevertheless. In appearance and conduct they are very unlike those of Petersburg.

Saturday, June 8.

We arrived in Moscow at 10 o'clock A. M. The road is the best over which I have ever travelled. It is macadamized in the most perfect manner, and the traveller pays no toll. About 175 versts, or five posts, are yet unfinished between Chotilova and Tiver. This fraction is the old road and partly composed of sand, partly of the trunks of trees laid across, and partly of large stones, and in some places it is very bad. The posting is eight cents 194per verst for four horses and ten cents for the post adjoining St. Petersburg and Moscow.

The horses, though mean in their appearance, travel with great speed. They uniformly place the four abreast when travelling by post in Russia. The post-boys always cross themselves devoutly before ascending their seats; though they, in common with all the other Russian mousiques whom I have ever met, will cheat you if they can.

At every post station we found a number of these—with their long beards and their tanned sheepskins—ready to grease the carriage or perform any other menial service. At night they lie down on the road and around the post-houses, and sleep on the ground. Indeed Russians of the highest class appear to know little of the comforts of a good bed. The country presents a forlorn aspect for 150 versts from St. Petersburg. It is both poor and flat, and the villages have a wretched appearance. They all consist of log huts with their gables towards the street. As you approach Waldi, the country becomes somewhat better and more undulating, and more attention seems to have been paid to its cultivation. It afterwards resumes its level appearance as you advance to Moscow, but still it is much better in every respect than near St. Petersburg. With a single exception we did not observe a nobleman's seat along the whole route, and this one had a mean appearance. Nothing affords variety to the dull and monotonous scenery except the churches, which present the only interesting objects in the landscape.

Tiver is the principal town of the government of that name. It was finally conquered in 1483. The city is handsome and has the appearance of prosperity. It is situated on both sides of the Volga. When I approached this river, I could not resist the feeling of how strange it was that I should be on its banks.

Sunday afternoon, 9th.

We went to the promenade, at three versts from the city, on the Petersburg road.

Monday morning, 10th.

We visited Madame S—— and had some conversation with her which would have been agreeable but for the constant interruption of a parrot which screeched as if it had been hired for the occasion. She had accompanied Mr. Wells of Philadelphia last year to the monastery of the Trinity. Her son is to go with us to the Kremlin to-morrow.

The appearance of Moscow must have greatly improved since its conflagration in 1812. It has lost, however, in a great degree, that romantic and Asiatic appearance which it formerly presented. The cumbrous and rude magnificence of palaces irregularly scattered among Tartar huts, has given place to airy and regular streets in all directions. It appears to be in a prosperous condition. That which chiefly distinguishes it from other cities is the immense number of churches. Their cupolas, of all colors and of all forms, rising above the summits of the houses and glittering in the sun, are very 195striking and imposing objects. In this respect no city in the world, except Constantinople, can be compared with it. In the evening we visited the Russian Theatre. Both the infernal regions and the Elysian fields were well represented on the stage.

Tuesday.

It rained all day. Dined with Madame Novaselsoff. She is one of the three daughters of —— —— Orloff, the youngest brother of the three who left no son—immensely rich—had one son, an only child, who was killed in a duel some nine years ago. Aide-de-camp of Emperor—Ischermoff was his antagonist. Both fell. His mother lives upon his memory. She says she is now building two churches, one on the spot where he expired and the other on her estate——a monument. She has established schools, one on the Lancasterian plan, among her peasants. I told her she ought to live for her peasants and consider them her children. Her example also might produce great effect. She said she had no object to live for, and when it was the will of God, she would go cheerfully; that her affections were fixed on another world. She had a full length likeness of her son in her parlor, and different other portraits of him scattered about; his drawings, etc., etc.

Wednesday morning.

We visited the Foundling Hospital, or the Imperial House of Education, as it is called. We had a letter for Dr. Alfonskoi, the chief medical officer attached to the institution, and he, together with Baron Stackelberg, the superintendent, conducted us through the apartments. This hospital is the glory of Moscow and is the most extensive establishment of the kind in the world. It is perfectly well conducted in all its departments.

The object of the institution is twofold. The first is limited to the preservation of the lives of the foundlings and rearing them as peasants of the crown, and the second extends to their education and their freedom. The number of infants of the first description amounted to 6500 the last year. Each of these requires a separate nurse, and from the peculiar state of society in Russia, these are provided without the least difficulty. The peasant women throughout the province of Moscow (and others are excluded) come daily in considerable numbers to offer their services as nurses. Each one receives a foundling and after remaining with it a few weeks in the hospital, she and the child are sent to the village to which she belongs. For the maintenance of this child, until it attains the age of twelve years, she receives five roubles per month, or sixty per annum. Three thousand foundlings had been received during the present year. The boys and girls thus raised are sent upon the lands of the crown and become peasants. The former are not exempted from serving in the army.

It was quite a novel spectacle for me to pass through the long ranges of women, with infants in their arms, or in the cradle. Everything was clean and in good order; though the women were anything but good-looking.

I believe most of the children received are legitimate, of poor parents. It 196is called the Imperial House of Education, not a foundling hospital, and the former name is more applicable to it than the latter.

They borrow at 4 and lend at 5; not 5 and 6, as the Guide says.

Baron Stackelberg told Mr. G. that the institution had 7,000,000 roubles clear after all expenses at the end of each year—sed quere.

The second class are very different from the first. They consist of those foundlings for whom 150 roubles are advanced at the time they enter the establishment. But as the institution can accommodate a greater number than are sent to it upon these terms, the deficiency is supplied by selections made sometimes from children of the first class, but most generally from those of poor parents of Moscow. These all continue in the institution until they receive their education. They are free when they depart from it and are not liable to be drafted as soldiers. A sufficiently accurate account of these is to be found in the Guide. There are at present 550 boys and as many girls of this description.

We dined with Dr. Alfonskoi. His wife is a communicative, agreeable woman who expresses her opinion freely upon all subjects. Whilst at table I received the impression from her conversation that she took me for an Englishman, notwithstanding I had been introduced to her as the American minister. I did not consider this remarkable, from the ignorance which prevails throughout this country concerning the United States. On the evening of this day I had a still more decided example. Mr. G. and myself went to pay a visit to "The Prince Ouroussoff, master of the court of his I. M., and senator." Whilst I was conversing with the daughter, the princess asked Mr. G. if the United States still belonged to England. He replied that they were independent and constituted a separate government. She said this must have been since 1812, and when he informed her that their independence had been recognized by England since 1783, she was much astonished. Among other things she wished to know whether they spoke the English language in America.

We visited the Souchareva Bashnia. This is a lofty and extensive building on an elevated position, in the second story of which is the reservoir to supply the city with water. This is brought eighteen versts. The top of the edifice affords a fine view of the city.
All the buildings of this establishment escaped the conflagration of 1812. They contain at present a population of more than 5,000, and have a distinct police.
Thursday Morning.
Before breakfast I visited the mineral-water establishment. It is situated near the Moscow, about four versts above the Kremlin. There you find waters of twenty-four different kinds prepared in imitation of those which are most celebrated throughout Europe. I took a glass of Carlsbad, the taste of which reminded me of that of Saratoga. Indeed the whole scene resembled that exhibited there. There were a great number of ladies and gentlemen 197walking in the promenades, drinking and talking; but the ladies of Saratoga were not there. The water is drawn by cocks from different vessels prepared for containing it, and placed contiguous to each other in a row.
This establishment has been recently made by a joint stock company. The emperor has subscribed a number of shares. In St. Petersburg they are about to get up a similar establishment. There were to be six hundred shares at five hundred roubles each; but three times that amount was subscribed at once. Dr. Myer, whom I met there to-day, is now here as agent from St. Petersburg to gain information, and observe the operation of the establishment at Moscow.
We ascended the belfry of Ivan Vélikoi (Jean le Grand). It receives its name from the Church of St. John, which it surmounts. From there we had another fine view of the city. There are thirty-one bells in the belfry. All in the Kremlin are collected in it.—Vide the Guide.
From thence we proceeded to the treasury of the Kremlin and examined its contents. It is fully described in the Guide, with the exception of some things which have been added since its publication.
These are chiefly the trophies of the conquest of poor unhappy Poland. They are the two thrones—the sceptre, the globe, and the sword of the emperor of Russia as king of Poland, which have been brought from Warsaw.
The portraits of all the kings of Poland are now hung up in their order in this Russian arsenal where the treasure is kept. We saw there also the flags which had been presented to the Polish army by the Emperor Alexander, and also the original constitution of Poland on the floor at his feet. It was placed there by the express command of his present majesty.
The glorious standard of Poland which waved triumphantly over many a well fought field, but which the most exalted courage and self-devotion could no longer maintain against brutal and barbarian force, is there exhibited. The white eagle has been obliged to cower beneath the double-headed monster of Russia. May it again soar! though to all human appearance it has sunk forever.
The head of John Sobieski is one of the most noble and commanding I have ever beheld. The famous standard which he took from the Turks at Vienna when Poland saved Europe from the sway of the Infidel, is now in the same hall with the portrait of the hero and the king who commanded her army on that celebrated day. We afterwards visited the ancient and the modern palaces. The contrast between the two exhibits the change between ancient and modern times in striking colors. In one of the rooms of the latter, among other ancient portraits, we saw one of the Princess Sophia. She was an extraordinary woman, and must have had a very fine face. I have an interest in this woman, and am willing to disbelieve the crime which Peter the Great attributed to her, of

an intention to assassinate him. How must her proud and ambitious spirit have been chafed by being confined to a monastery after having reigned with so much distinction. Accompanied 198by Mr. Thal, we rode out of the Barrier de Drogomirov, two or three versts on the road to Smolensko, to the summit of the last of three hills which rise gradually above each other, from whence we had a fine view of the city. It was from this quarter that the French entered. Bonaparte slept the first night at Petrovski, a place near the St. Petersburg road, about three versts from the city.

Friday Morning, June 2–14th.

I went with Mr. Gretsch, the editor of the Bee at St. Petersburg, to see the famous monastery of Novo Devitcher where we saw the tomb of the Princess Sophia, who took the veil under the name of Suzanna, and was buried in 1704. For the rest, see the Guide, 183, 184. Mr. G. and myself visited and went through the mosque. In this country, all churches must be open. Unfortunately we arrived a little too late for the service.

John the Third, in 1473, married the Princess Sophia, the daughter of Thomas Paléologus Porphyrogénétus, who was the brother of Constantine Paléologus, who died in 1453, whilst seeing his capital fall under the dominion of the Turks. By his unison with the last descendant of the Paléologus, John the Third considered himself as the heir of their crown, and after his marriage he substituted the eagle with two heads for the cavalier which was then the arms of the grand principality, and it was then that he took the title of Tsar.

Saturday.

This Mr. Gretsch is the editor of the Northern Bee of St. Petersburg, the principal Russian journal. He is also on a visit here for the first time. He came up to me the other day at the Treasury and introduced himself, since when he has been uncommonly kind. He appears to be, for I know not what he is, a frank, open-hearted, talkative, well-informed person, but something of a bore. He laughingly styled the sultan this morning "our Governor General of Turkey." I am persuaded this is now the feeling in Russia. They believe themselves to be already the virtual masters of Constantinople.

Mr. G. and myself afterwards went to the Mountain of Sparrows. It is on the southwest of the city opposite or nearly so the monastery of Novo Devitcher. From thence you have the best view of Moscow, and it is truly a beautiful and magnificent spectacle. It was here that they commenced the foundation of the cathedral of St. Sauveur, in consequence of a vow of the Emperor Alexander during the French war; but it has been discontinued, and will be erected in another part of the city. The place was found to be too extensive and too expensive, though the vow was to build the greatest and most magnificent church in Russia.

We next visited the garden of Niéschouchin, from whence also we had another fine view of the city. We there saw a theatre sub Jove.

The opinion of Dr. Alfonskoi on the cholera is that it arises in all cases from a defect of heat in the system, and his universal remedy, after he came to understand the disease, was the hot, very hot bath. He is fully convinced 199it was not contagious. It seized on those whose digestive powers had been enfeebled by drunkenness or high living. I told him of Dr. Stevens' saline treatment, and he said, from the development of heat, [which] the salt produced in the system, it might have been a good remedy. The cholera, Dr. A. thinks, came from the earth, is connected with gravity. The grip is its opposite and is connected with electricity. This last the best evidence that the cholera has finally disappeared. The stomach the root, as of a tree, etc.

Sunday, 16th June.

I went to the English chapel, and heard an excellent, animated, evangelical discourse, from the Rev. Matthew Camidge, the pastor. His text was 2 Peter 3d chapter, from —— to ——. It was on the subject of the long suffering of God with sinners, and the repentance to which this should naturally lead, etc., etc. The judgment-day will come by surprise as many temporal judgments do after long suffering.

There is to be a theatrical entertainment this evening in the open air, at the garden of Nieschouchin, and afterwards a party at Madame Paschkoff's. My old Presbyterian notions will prevent me from attending either. After church I paid some visits to the Skariatines, etc.

The English chapel was consumed in the conflagration of 1812, and has been rebuilt but a few years since. It contains no organ. They sing well. The pastor receives about £200, the half of which comes from England. I was struck with the solemnity of this little congregation in a strange land. May God be with them! It was the most impressive sermon I have heard since I left America.

Monday, 5–17th June.

We visited, in company with Mr. Gretsch, and particularly examined the interior of the cathedrals of the Annunciation, of the Assumption, and of St. Michael the Archangel. They are sufficiently described in the Guide. We also visited the ancient palace of the Patriarchs, and saw everything that was contained therein. The apartments of his holiness were very small and simple, though the state rooms must have been considered magnificent in Russia a century and a half ago. We there saw the apparatus for making the holy oil, which is distributed throughout Russia. It is only prepared once in three years. How wise it was in Peter the Great to abolish the Patriarchate! Few men would have had the courage to make the attempt. From the ignorance of the Russians and their proneness to superstition, he must have continued to be as he formerly was, the rival of the czars themselves.

From thence we went to the Alexander Institution, so called after his majesty. Whilst the cholera raged in Moscow, many of the children of poor noble families were deprived of their parents, and thus became destitute orphans. To relieve their wants and furnish them with an education, this institution was first established by the present emperor. Being pleased with 200its operation, he has made it permanent. The orphan children of poor nobles from any part of the empire are now received there, and all their expenses defrayed. The emperor purchased for the purposes of this institution the house and grounds of a nobleman, Count Rasoumoffsky, for which he gave 1,200,000 roubles B. A. The extent of these private establishments of the Russian nobility may be judged of, from the circumstances that this house and the adjacent buildings appertaining to it now, accommodate 250 boys and as many girls, with all the necessary professors and domestics.

Here the former are taught the Russian, French, German and Latin languages; geometry, geography, drawing, dancing, etc., etc., and the latter are instructed in all these branches, except Latin and geometry, and in the other accomplishments which more particularly belong to females. There are three classes of each.

We heard the first class of the young ladies examined in French and geography, and then specimens of their drawing, embroidery and other needle-work were exhibited to us. They acquitted themselves very creditably. They also played for us on the piano. As a compliment to myself, they were examined on the geography of the United States. What struck me with great force, was that the little girls in the second and third classes recited pieces from the French and German, as well as the Russian, with apparent facility, and so far as I could judge, with a perfect accent.

They certainly have the most wonderful talent for acquiring languages of any people in the world.

We afterwards went through the apartments of the boys and heard them examined. One of the boys was asked who was the greatest man that America had produced, and he promptly answered Washington. The thrill of delight which I experienced at the moment, I shall not undertake to describe. He hesitated in his answer to the second question, who was the next, as probably many Americans would; and was then asked who was the celebrated ambassador of the United States at Paris, to which he replied Franklin. He first said Ptolemy Philadelphus, but corrected himself immediately.

The most imposing spectacle I witnessed here was all the girls collected at dinner. They were all dressed alike, in green frocks and white aprons, which came over their arms. When we entered, they were all ranged at their different places and were standing up. Those who were distinguished, were placed at two small tables in the centre. Previous to taking their seats, they sang a hymn in Russian as a blessing. Their performance was excellent. Here the goodness and piety of the female heart shone out in a striking manner. The little girls exhibited the warmest and most lively devotion, and frequently crossed themselves with all that sincerity and ardor of manner which can never be counterfeited at their age. The dinner was very good. One circumstance is worthy of remark. Mr. Gretsch made a little address in Russian to one of the female classes, which Mr. Guerreiro understood. 201He informed them that I was the minister of the United States, a great and powerful republic. That the people there were well educated and well informed; but that every person had to labor. That their Government was a good one; but no paternal emperor existed there, who would become the father of orphans and educate them at his own expense. He concluded by impressing upon their minds how grateful they ought to be to the emperor, and how much a monarchical government ought, on this account, to be preferred to a republic.

The emperor is very fond of this institution, of which he is the founder. Indeed, in different forms and in different manners nearly all the children of the Russian nobility of both sexes are educated in imperial institutions, and in some degree at the expense of the government. We visited the garden where there was a considerable number of very little boys and girls too young for any of the classes. It is the emperor's delight, they say, to go among them and play with them, to he down upon the ground and let them cover him, and to toss them about in all directions. From all I have heard, a great fondness for children is one of the traits of the emperor's character. He is quick and warm in his feelings, and at the moment of irritation would be severe: but his passion soon subsides, and the empress receives great credit for correcting this fault in his temper. I am more and more convinced every day that he could have pursued no other course with safety towards the Poles than that which he did. The bitterness against them is extreme, and there is scarcely a monument of antiquities in the Kremlin which does not relate to battles lost and won between the two nations. Their mutual enmity is truly hereditary. The emperor advances two hundred thousand roubles per annum to this institution, and has lately given it a million of roubles, which is to accumulate for the purpose of forming a capital for its support. The foundation of a new and extensive building has already been laid for the better accommodation of the pupils.

The chamberlain, Tchenchine, is the principal director, and Mr. Davydoff the chief professor, with both of whom I was much pleased, as well as with Madame Tchenchine, the wife of the former.

From thence, accompanied by Messrs. Tchenchine and Davydoff, we visited the Armenian institution, founded in 1806 by the Messieurs Lazareff, wealthy Armenian noblemen, for the benefit chiefly of native Armenians, wheresoever they may be scattered. The memoir presented to me by Mr. D. will sufficiently explain the object of it. There you saw in the form and in the face of the pupils the Asiatic traits. One of them, a native of Calcutta, spoke English to me. There are several private institutions for the education of youth at Moscow, founded by private munificence, and whether ostentation may have been the moving cause or not, still they are very valuable to the community. We partook here of an elegant déjeuner-à-fourchette. There are now forty-five scholars gratis and twenty-five who pay fifty roubles per month, in the institution, so says Mr. Davydoff. We dined to-day with the governor-general, Prince Galitzine, and a select party. He is a dignified gentleman of the old school, with great simplicity of manners, and is revered by the people high and low of the city and province of Moscow. He speaks English tolerably well, and we had much conversation concerning the United States. He commanded the cavalry at the battle of Borodino, and represented it, as it has been always represented, as a most murderous battle on both sides.

We spent the evening at Prince Ourousoff's. I had almost forgot to mention that in our visits to the cathedrals and the patriarchal palace we were accompanied by Mr. Polevoy, the editor of the Moscow Telegraph, at Moscow, who is engaged in writing a history of Russia, and by another savant, Professor John Snéquireff.

The former gave me several exemplaries of Russian antiquities as a souvenir.

Tuesday Morning.

Mr. Gretsch, Mr. Guerreiro and myself set out for the Trostza monastery, a place famous in Russian history. It is sixty-two versts north of Moscow. We left by the barrier of Trostza. We found the road covered with numerous parties of pilgrims on foot, going to pay their devotions at the shrine of St. Sierge, the founder. The women were, I think, nearly ten to one for the men. In ancient times the sovereigns of Russia used to go on foot from Moscow to worship at this shrine; the pious Catharine was, I believe, the last who performed this pilgrimage in this manner.

The villages and churches along the road are nearly all celebrated in Russian history. At about seven versts from the principal convent there is a monastery for nuns dependent upon it. We found the church at this monastery crowded with pilgrims, crossing themselves; many were on their knees before the pictures, and the most devout touched the floor with their foreheads. There is nothing in the Greek liturgy which sanctions the worship of these pictures. Indeed, images are excluded. It was, however, impossible to resist the belief that these poor creatures considered them something more than mere pictures.

When we arrived at Trostza we found that the governor-general had sent an officer to show me all the antiquities and curiosities of the place; and had not Mr. Guerreiro told them in my absence that he knew it would be disagreeable to me, I should have been received by a military guard. I thus avoided what to me would have been unpleasant.

We were first presented to the Reverend Father Antoine, the archimandrite or abbot of the monastery. In my life I have never beheld a more heavenly expression of countenance. It spoke that he was at peace with heaven and with his fellow-men, and possessed a heart overflowing with Christian benevolence and charity. He spoke no French nor English, and my conversation with him was through Mr. Gretsch as interpreter. He is very intelligent and perfectly modest and unassuming in his manners. In his appearance he is not more than thirty-five. His long beard was of a most beautiful chestnut color, and made his appearance venerable notwithstanding his comparative youth. I shall never forget the impression which this man made upon me.

He showed us all the antiquities himself; and first we made a circuit on the ancient wall. It is a mile round and at least twenty-two feet thick, and its great glory is that the Poles have never been able to pass it. This he communicated to us with evident satisfaction. It was in ancient times the strongest fortification in Russia, and was perfectly impregnable before the use of artillery. An imperial palace formerly existed within it, not a trace of which now remains.

St. Sierge was a pious and patriotic hermit who, in the reign of Dimitri Danshoy, retired to this spot, which was then a wilderness. Some well authenticated facts exist which may well inspire a superstitious people with great veneration for this spot. Among others of a recent date, when the plague raged in Moscow during the days of the Empress Catharine, notwithstanding the gates of the monastery were always open to the crowds of pilgrims who then frequented the shrine, no case of plague occurred within the walls. The same may be observed in regard to the recent cholera.

After the circuit of the walls, we passed through the different churches. That where the reliques of St. Sierge are deposited was much crowded. His shrine is very rich. The church was crowded with pilgrims.

The interior of these churches resembles the others we had seen. The iconostase is the covering ascending from the floor to the summit, which conceals from public view the place where the sacrament is consecrated. Upon it are uniformly painted, in several rows, holy pictures of the Virgin and of the saints. In the ancient churches these are sufficiently rude and barbarous, but richly ornamented.

In passing from one church to another we saw a square brick wall covered with boards, but without any inscription, which contains the remains of Boris Goudounoff and his family. The bodies of the father and the son were taken by the fury of the people from the cathedral of St. Michael, where they were deposited with those of the other czars, and were afterwards brought to Trostza. They were formerly within the walls of a church; but, it needing repairs, in the time of the madman Paul, he ordered the walls which extended over these remains to be taken down, and the limits of this church to be restricted so as to leave them without a covering. Whilst the good archimandrite was relating this circumstance, he was evidently much affected by the barbarity of the action. This was done because Paul believed Goudounoff to be a usurper.

He has been charged with the crime of having caused the murder of the true Dimitri, the last branch of the family of Rurick. But this is a most obscure period of Russian history, and their great historian, Karamsin, leaves the question in doubt. In all other respects he was an excellent sovereign, and Peter the Great always spoke of him in terms of the highest respect.

We afterwards visited the sacristy and there saw a great many splendid sacred robes and vessels. All the sovereigns in succession of the house of 204Romanoff have presented their gifts, with the exception of Peter the Great, and there are several prior to that period. The specimens of embroidery wrought by the Empresses Elizabeth, Anne and Catharine the Second are very rich and magnificent. Peter the Great deprived this monastery of all its disposable wealth for which he gave them receipts, and Catharine took their lands and their peasants from them. But Peter built a church there, at least so the archimandrite said, and pointed it out to us.

The greatest curiosity in the sacristy is the miraculous crystal, or white stone, in the body of which is clearly defined and represented in black a monk in his black robes kneeling before a crucifix. It requires no effort of the imagination to present this spectacle to the eye. It is clearly and distinctly defined. I examined this stone with great care, and certainly but with little faith, and yet I am under the impression that the likeness of the monk and

the crucifix are contained in the very body of the crystal itself, and are not artificial......
Nature, amid the infinite variety of her productions, has given birth to this curious piece of workmanship. The Father Antoine, in a solemn and impressive manner, presented each of us with a consecrated picture of St. Sierge.

The Father Antoine then accompanied us to that portion of the buildings destined for the students of divinity, of which there are 100 at Trostza, and the same number of monks. There we were presented to the archimandrites; Polycarpe, rector of the ecclesiastical academy, a fat and jolly-looking monk, who laced his tea strong with cherry brandy and took his wine kindly; to Peter, ancient archimandrite of the Russian mission at Peking, who has a long white beard and venerable appearance, and read Chinese aloud for our amusement; to Neophyte, formerly substitute of Peter at Peking; and to the monk Tsidore, librarian of the ecclesiastical academy. Their wine and their tea were both excellent, and we spent an hour or two very pleasantly with them. There is a room in these apartments, the ceiling of which contains paintings of the different exploits of Peter the Great; a tribute of his daughter, the Empress Elizabeth. Upon taking leave, Polycarpe presented me several treatises in Russ as a keepsake. Upon taking leave of Antoine, I submitted to be kissed by him according to the Russian fashion, first on the right cheek, then on the left, and then on the mouth. This was my first regular experiment of the kind.
Wednesday.
We dined at Mr. Cavenaugh's with a party of English. Among others I met Mr. Camidge there. His appearance, manners and conversation in private society did not answer the expectations I had formed of him from his preaching.
Thursday.
On the 20th of June we left Moscow at eight in the evening, and arrived at St. Petersburg on Monday, the 24th, at 2 P. M., having slept two nights on the road. At Vouischnije Volotschok we saw the sluice connecting the Tivortza with the Atsta. It can only be used by vessels going towards St. Petersburg.
205The following letter to one of his Pennsylvania friends was written immediately after his return to St. Petersburg.
[MR. BUCHANAN TO G. LEIPER, ESQ.]
St. Petersburg, July 3, 1833.
My Good Friend:—

It was with no ordinary pleasure that I received a letter by Mr. Clay with your well-known superscription. You make a strong mark, and your writing would be known among a thousand. I now have the joyful anticipation of being ere long once more among you. A land reposing under the calm of despotism is not the country for me. An American of proper feelings who visits any portion of Europe, must thank his God that his lot has been cast in the United States. For my own part, I feel that I am a much greater Republican than ever.

I hope with the blessing of Heaven to be able to leave St. Petersburg in perfect consistency with the interests of my country some time during the next month. I shall then spend a few weeks in seeing other parts of Europe, and embark for home the last of October or beginning of November.

I have recently returned from a short excursion to Moscow; the city which rolled back the tide of victory upon Napoleon. St. Petersburg is a cosmopolite city; but at Moscow you see Russia. It is a most picturesque and beautiful city. Its numerous churches surmounted by cupolas of every form and of every color give it a romantic and an Asiatic appearance. Many of these are gilt, and when the rays of the sun are reflected from them, the eye is dazzled with the richness and splendor of the spectacle. From Moscow I made a pilgrimage to the shrine of St. Sierge, a distance of forty miles. Going and returning I suppose we saw ten thousand pilgrims upon the way. They were chiefly of the fair sex, and nearly all on foot. This shrine is at the Monastery of the Trinity, a place famous in Russian history, having been at the same time a convent, a palace, and a fortification. Here the family of the czars have often taken refuge. In passing round on the top of the walls with the abbot (which is more than a mile in circumference), he told me in a tone of triumph and national antipathy that these walls had never been taken by the Poles; on taking leave he presented me with a consecrated picture of St. Sierge, and from him I submitted to the operation of being kissed, first on the right cheek, then on the left, and finally plump on the mouth. This is the general custom of the country; but it was my first experiment of the kind. The pious Catharine, although she seized the peasants and the broad acres of this monastery, made a pilgrimage on foot from Moscow to the shrine of St. Sierge. But enough of this bagatelle.

On Saturday last, the 29th ultimo, we had news from New York via London up till the 1st, a wonderfully short passage. We then heard of the death of Randolph, and of the appointment of Mr. Duane as Secretary of the Treasury. I have no doubt the latter will make a good officer, and he shows 206great courage in undertaking the Treasury at the present moment. My best wishes attend him.

I think it more than probable that my political life is drawing to a close, and I confess I look upon the prospect without regret. Office is not necessary for my happiness. I can enjoy myself with the blessing of God, under my own vine and my own fig tree. Whoever embarks on the stormy ocean of politics must calculate to make a shipwreck of contentment and tranquility. I have served the old hero faithfully and zealously, and he has done more for me than I could have expected. But I hope ere long to talk over my travels and my ups and downs along with Edwards and yourself and a few other friends in the good old county of Delaware. By the bye, I have a crow to pick with Edwards. I wrote to him and he has never answered my letter.

I am obliged to write at full gallop. Safe opportunities are so rare, and when they occur, so much of my time is taken up in writing despatches, that I have but little left for my private friends.

Remember me kindly to Edwards and his charming wife, to Dick, the doctor, your brothers, Kane, Lescine, Judge Engle, and my other friends. Please to present my most respectful compliments to Mrs. Leiper, and believe me, in whatever land my lot may be cast, to be always your friend,

James Buchanan.

The following brief account of one of the national fêtes is recorded soon after his return to St. Petersburg:

The Fete at Peterhoff, Saturday, July 1–13, 1833.

The English palace was provided for the reception of the Diplomatic Corps, where we lived with Count Daschkaw, the grand master of ceremonies, Count Matuscervie, and some masters of the court. Everything was provided for us in handsome style, for which, according to custom, I paid the court servants two hundred roubles at my departure.

In the morning we went to visit the gardens upon singular vehicles on four wheels and drawn by two splendid horses. I can describe it no better than by imagining a double sofa with a single back, on which ten of us could sit back to back comfortably, five on each side. The foot-board was within about a foot of the ground.

The water-works are the chief object of attraction. The water is conveyed in a canal for the distance of about thirty versts to the palace of Peterhoff, which is situate at the summit and on the brink of the second bank of the Gulf of Finland. From it there is a steep descent of about thirty feet to the extensive plain on the southern shore of the Gulf, which is covered by the immense garden. It is this descent which has enabled them to present so many varieties of water-works. In the gardens above, on a level with the palace (the English garden), the water is tastefully distributed into several lakes, etc.

The water falls in several broad sheets over different steps immediately in front of the palace. One range of these is gilt, and in a clear day must present a splendid spectacle. They place candles under the shutes of the water and thus have an illumination under the water, which did not, however, produce the effect I expected.

There are many long walks in the gardens, I should say more than a verst in length, at the intersection of which are little lakes, and in the centre of them jet d'eaus.

On the sides of these walks, and all around the little lakes, were frame-works to a considerable elevation, destined for the candles.

We rode all through these different walks. In front of one of the lakes stands the little palace of Marly, built by Peter the Great. Everything is preserved there just as he left it; and it was curious to observe the progress of luxury in comparing his clothing and accommodations with those of the imperial family in the present day. There is a carp which has been in the lake for a century, with a collar round its neck. It, with others, comes to the edge of the water at the sound of a bell, every morning, to receive its breakfast.

We went over to the ball about eight in the evening, where the emperor and empress and the rest of us polonaised, and all things were conducted as on the 1st January, only the crowd was not so great. After supper, about half-past eleven, the emperor, empress, Prince Albert of Prussia, and other members of the I. F., mounted one of these vehicles. They were followed in others by the members of the court of D. C., and thus we slowly promenaded through all these walks, the sides of which were covered by immense crowds of spectators. The effect of the illumination was brilliant. The Grand Duke Michel was on horseback, and great precautions were evidently taken, on account of the Polish conspiracy.

About half-past one we ended. The distance to Peterhoff 26 versts. Mr. Lander and Captain Ranlett, Americans, were there in the ball room, in dominos, etc., etc.

[TO THE HON. E. LIVINGSTON, SECRETARY OF STATE.]
American Legation,
St. Petersburg, July 3, 1833, N. S.

}
Sir:—

On the 28th ultimo I had an interview with Count Nesselrode on the subject of the application which I made on the 5–17 May, in behalf of Messrs. Shaw & Co., of Boston. The question has not yet been decided.

After the conversation upon this subject, the count informed me that Baron Krudener, in his last despatch, had acknowledged the receipt of the emperor's ratification of the treaty, and on the first instant I received a note from him communicating the intelligence that the ratifications had been exchanged at Washington on the 11th of May. At this interview I had hoped he would say something concerning the proposed treaty on neutral rights, and gave the conversation such a turn as would naturally lead to the subject.

I enquired when the emperor would leave St. Petersburg. He answered that his majesty would not set out upon his journey into the interior until after the commencement of

August. I then replied that before his departure, I should solicit my audience of leave, as I intended to return to the United States during the approaching autumn.

He expressed his regret at my determination and their satisfaction with my conduct as a minister; but made no allusion whatever, either to the treaty or to my note of the 18–30 of May. I felt that it would not be becoming for me again to press this subject upon his attention, and thus we parted.

Perhaps it might have been better under the circumstances not to have attempted a renewal of the negotiation at the present moment.

This government has, for some time, been in possession of secret information which has given them much concern.

The impression is that it was first communicated to the emperor by Louis Philippe. A number of Poles at Paris, driven to desperation by their sufferings, have solemnly sworn before God, and pledged themselves to each other, to assassinate the emperor, at any personal peril.

The first intimation which the public had of the existence of the conspiracy was the publication on the 8–20 June, in the St. Petersburg Journal, of an address presented to the emperor at Helsingfors, during his late visit to Finland; the subject was again referred to in the succeeding number of the 15–27 of the same month. I herewith transmit you both these numbers.

From the desperation of the Poles, and their determined character, this information has excited considerable alarm in St. Petersburg. The people here, whilst they admire and respect the emperor as the author of their security and prosperity, look with fearful apprehension to the future, in the event of his assassination.

The heir apparent is yet a minor, and although he possesses a most amiable disposition, it is believed he is deficient both in talent and strength of character. The Grand Duke Michel, who would become regent, is as universally disliked as the emperor is esteemed. Indeed, in such an event, many of the foreigners in St. Petersburg, knowing the deadly hostility felt against them by the lower orders of Russians, would entertain serious apprehensions for their lives and their property. Such is the miserable condition of despotism; and such is the feeling here, at the very moment when this government, more by its superior policy than its power, has acquired a commanding influence throughout Europe.

Still greater precautions now exist than did formerly, in regard to the admission of strangers into the country. The emperor no longer appears in the streets like a private citizen. It is said that he is always surrounded by guards. But from what I have heard, he rather submits to these regulations 209of his ministers than approves of them himself. He is a bold and fearless man, and manifests no apprehension whatever. If the Poles have determined to play the part of Scaevola, he at least will not enact that of Porsenna.

Three of the conspirators have been seized in Russia. After all I cannot feel that there is much danger. I send you the Journal of yesterday, containing our latest news from Constantinople.

This despatch will be carried to London by Mr. Gibson, our consul. He has been ill for some time, and his disease is, I fear, now approaching its crisis. He is very feeble, has a bad cough, and throws up much blood. His physician informed him that his only hope was to leave St. Petersburg, and that immediately. Mr. Clay will perform his duties during his absence, and we are both happy to render all the services in our power to so worthy a man and so good an officer.

After having written the foregoing, I had the pleasure of receiving your Despatch No. 11, dated on the 30th April. It has been long on the passage. By the Hamburg Reporter received on the 29th ultimo, we had New York dates, via London, up till the first of that month.

On the 19th of July, Mr. Buchanan received the melancholy news that his mother had died in the previous May.

[TO REV. EDWARD Y. BUCHANAN.]
St. Petersburg, July 20, 1833.
My Dear Brother:—

I received your kind letters, of the 7th and 17th May, on yesterday afternoon; the latter communicating the melancholy intelligence of mother's death.[37] The news was a severe and unexpected blow. I had hoped, by the blessing of God, to see her once more on this side of eternity. Indeed, this desire was one of the chief reasons which made me so reluctant to spend another winter in Russia.

210But it has been the will of the Almighty to take her to Himself, and we must bow in humble reverence. I received at the same time a letter from Mr. Henry, which gave me the consolatory assurance that she had died the death of a Christian, and that her latter end was peace.

It is my present intention to leave St. Petersburg on the 7th August, and I feel almost confident, with the blessing of Heaven, that I shall be able with propriety, to bring all the business of my mission to a close before that day.

My present purpose is to go by the steamboat to Lubeck, and thence by Hamburg, Amsterdam, the Hague, and Brussels to Paris, where I shall probably spend a fortnight. I shall then proceed to London, Edinburgh, Glasgow, Belfast and Dublin, from which city I intend to cross over to Liverpool, and sail for New York by the packet of the 24th October. It is my intention, if possible, to see Romilton and Derry. I hope to reach the United States in the beginning of December.

I have recently returned from a very agreeable excursion to Moscow; but I must defer a description of this city, the ancient capital of the czars, until we meet again. Whilst there, I visited the celebrated monastery of Iwitza, at the distance of forty miles. In the estimation of the Russians, it is a very holy place. It was anciently a strong fortress, which contained a palace as well as a convent, and is much connected with the history of Russia. The sovereigns formerly made pilgrimages on foot from Moscow to the shrine of St. Sierge, at this monastery. The Empress Catharine the Second, was the last who performed this act of devotion. Going and returning there, I am confident we met at the least 10,000 pilgrims on foot. They appeared to be of a low order of people, and the great majority were females.

I have but little time before the departure of the boat, and must close. Remember me affectionately to my sister, I don't know her Christian name, to the Doctor and Maria. I am glad to hear that the latter are so comfortably situated, and hope you may all live together in Christian peace and in prosperity. Remember me kindly to Judge and Mrs. Shippen, Mr. and Mrs. Barlow, and believe me to be ever your affectionate brother, James Buchanan.

P. S.—I wrote to our dear mother on the 3d instant.

[TO THE SECRETARY OF STATE.]
Legation of the United States,
St. Petersburg, July 31, N. S. 1833.
On Friday last, the 28th instant, I had an interview with Count Nesselrode, for the purpose of making the necessary arrangements previous to my departure from this country.

After the usual salutations, he introduced the subject of the commercial treaty, which is one of his favorite topics. The opposition made to it in the imperial council, and the difficulties which he there encountered and overcame, seem to have inspired him with a feeling of paternity towards this treaty. After some general conversation, relating chiefly to its favorable reception in the United States, I changed the subject, and remarked, that in our last interview I had entirely forgotten to mention that his explanation in regard to Baron Sacken's note was entirely satisfactory to the President. It might be proper to observe, however, that Mr. Livingston differed materially from the baron in relation to some of the facts attending this unpleasant transaction, and it had, at first, been my intention to bring these points of difference specially under the notice of his excellency; but after reflection, I had determined that it was best upon the whole not to revive the subject. He immediately replied it was wholly unnecessary; he wished the whole subject to be buried in oblivion and there remain as if it had never existed. He expressed his pleasure in the strongest terms that the President was satisfied with the explanation, and then laughingly observed that Baron Sacken and Mr. Livingston were now both hors du combat: the one was no longer chargé nor the other Secretary of State. I felt the less inclined to enter into any detail upon this subject, as Mr. Livingston admits that Baron Sacken did show him the offensive note at New York, and that he did not make any objections to its style, though he is convinced this took place after the note had been sent to Mr. Brent and not before, as the baron had informed Count Nesselrode. When I returned home, I discovered that the count, before our interview, must have had in his possession a copy of Mr. Livingston's Despatch No. 11, giving his own explanation of the whole transaction. During my absence, the post-office had sent me the duplicate of that despatch which, like all the communications I have ever received through the same channel, had been evidently opened. How it got there, I know not, because it had been forwarded to this city by the ship Birmingham from New York via Charleston.

After this subject was disposed of, I told the count that as all our official intercourse had been of the most frank and friendly character, I felt it to be my duty to explain to him the reasons which would induce me to leave Russia sooner than I had at first intended. A short time before the departure of Mr. Clay with the treaty last winter, I had received information of my brother's death and of the declining health of my mother and eldest sister. These circumstances had naturally produced a desire to return home, and had besides imposed upon me new and urgent duties towards my family. In a private letter which I addressed to the President by Mr. Clay, I suggested that these considerations might induce me to ask for permission to leave St. Petersburg sooner than I had intended; and upon his return in May last, I had received my letter of recall with the discretionary power of presenting it when I might think proper. The recent melancholy intelligence of my mother's death had increased my anxiety, and made the reasons for my departure still more urgent.

He expressed his sorrow that I had been so unfortunate as to have lost my mother and my brother since my arrival in St. Petersburg, and his regret that these circumstances should have rendered my departure necessary.

I told him I had not in the beginning intended to remain longer than two years,—I was no diplomat, and had never any desire to pursue this career. That I should now return to private life; but in whatever circumstances I might hereafter be placed, it would always afford me great pleasure to exert any humble influence I might possess in cementing the bonds of friendship which now so happily united the two countries.

He complimented me by saying, I had shown myself to be both an able and a successful diplomat, and he could assure me I had contributed much, since my arrival in this country, to promote kindly feelings between the two governments. He hoped I would carry with me agreeable souvenirs of my residence in St. Petersburg, and that my influence at home might be used in perpetuating the good understanding which now so happily existed.

I had taken with me a copy of my letter of recall and of the concluding paragraph of Despatch No. 9, and upon presenting them, I read the latter to the count, containing an assurance of the high consideration with which the personal character of the emperor had inspired the President, and of the wishes he formed for his happiness and the prosperity of his empire. To this I added that such an assurance, proceeding from the source it did, was in itself the strongest evidence of its own sincerity......

James Buchanan.

All things being arranged for his departure, Mr. Buchanan had his audience of leave of the emperor on the 5th of August, of which he gave a striking account to the Secretary of State in the following despatch written two days afterward:

[TO THE HON. LOUIS McLANE, SECRETARY OF STATE.]

St. Petersburg, August 7, 1833, N. S.

Sir:—

On Monday last, the 5th instant, I had my audience of leave of the emperor, at the Palace of Peterhoff, twenty-six versts distant from this city. The conduct and conversation of his majesty throughout the interview were highly gratifying to myself; because they convinced me that I had conciliated his favorable opinion. This ought to be, next to the honest and independent discharge of his duty, the first object of a minister to Russia. Without it, he can never effectually serve his country.

Towards the conclusion of this interview, you will perceive that the emperor appeared to lay aside his official dignity and conversed frankly and with great feeling upon subjects which I could never have imagined he would introduce.

When I first entered he said: "What is the reason you are going to leave us? I am very sorry for it. You have given us great satisfaction whilst you have been amongst us." After explaining to him the reason for my departure, he expressed his sympathy for me on account of the recent loss of my mother, and made some inquiries in relation to my family which I need not repeat. I then observed that, at the first, I had not intended to remain longer than two years. I was no diplomat, having never been engaged in that service before, and it was probable I should never again represent my country abroad. He said he liked me the better for it. He was no diplomat himself; his policy was always frank and open, and those who believed otherwise had greatly mistaken his character.

I then presented to him my letter of recall, and told him I had been instructed to assure him on this occasion of the continued desire felt by the President to foster the good understanding which now so happily subsisted between the two nations; and to express the high consideration with which his majesty's personal character had inspired the President, and the wishes which he cherished for his happiness and the prosperity of his empire.

He said it was very gratifying to his feelings to receive such an assurance from General Jackson. He had shown himself to be a man both of integrity and firmness, and he valued his good opinion very highly. He felt a great respect for the people of the United States. They were a true and loyal people, and he should always endeavor to promote the most friendly relations with our country.

I then added, to that of General Jackson, my own humble testimonial of regard for his personal character, and the gratitude which I felt for his uniform kindness towards myself upon all occasions when I had the honor of meeting him. He replied that he felt much indebted to me for my good opinion, and trusted I should never have occasion to change it. He hoped I would remember him with kindness when I returned to my own country. He entertained a high personal regard for myself; and it was a source of peculiar pleasure to him, that it had fallen to my lot to conclude the commercial treaty between the two countries. He was glad this treaty had given satisfaction in the United States, and he believed it would serve to strengthen the attachment between two nations who ought always to be friends.

I observed it was one of the most agreeable occurrences of my life, to have been instrumental in concluding this treaty. I had no doubt it would be mutually beneficial to both countries. That wherever I was and whatever might be my lot, I should never cease to cherish the most ardent wishes for his happiness, and to use my humble influence in cementing the friendship between the two nations. This had been my constant object throughout the period of my mission. He said I had been eminently successful, and again assured me that my conduct had given him great satisfaction.

He then alluded, with considerable feeling, to the late debate in the House of Commons concerning Polish affairs; he observed that he was the representative of a great and powerful nation. This station imposed upon him many and arduous duties. He had acted in his public character, and upon views of public policy. But instead of considering the subject in this light, they seemed to have been instigated by a desire to abuse him personally. 214He could appeal to God and his own conscience for the purity and correctness of his conduct; and whilst that was the case, he should have peace within his own bosom, and would not regard the opinion of the world. This was a delicate subject. I replied that I had read the debate with considerable surprise. The distance at which my rank placed me from his majesty had enabled me to know but comparatively little of his personal character from my own observation; but judging from that knowledge, as well as from the information I had been able to collect, since my arrival in St. Petersburg, I entertained not a doubt he had been treated with great injustice. Indeed, it was impossible for any person who knew him, to believe that the representation made in that debate could be true.

And here permit me to declare that this is my honest conviction. I yield to no man in abhorrence for the different partitions of Poland, and in a desire to see the independence of that brave and gallant people re-established; but truth compels me to say that the cruelties of the Imperial Government towards them have been greatly exaggerated. It is even notorious here that in several instances the sons of Polish patriots who died fighting for national independence are receiving their education at the expense of the emperor, and are treated by him with distinguished kindness. The exaggerated impressions which have been spread throughout the world upon this subject arise, in a great degree, from the want of anything like a free press in Russia. From this cause, the representations of the injured party pass every where current, almost without contradiction. Still, it cannot be denied that whenever Russian officers are entrusted with power over Poles, it will most probably be abused. This arises from the ancient and malignant personal hatred existing between the two races.

The emperor afterwards observed that the English nation had, in his opinion, been acting very unwisely. They had got tired of a constitution under which they had risen to a high degree of greatness, and which had secured them many blessings, and he feared they were now about to prostrate their most valuable institutions. He then asked me what route I intended to take on my return home. I told him I should pass through Hamburg, Amsterdam, the Hague and Brussels to Paris, where I expected to spend a few weeks.

From thence I should pass over to London, and finally embark from Liverpool for the United States. I said I had no particular desire to visit Paris; on the contrary, I should rather spend what time I had to spare in seeing a part of England, Scotland and Ireland; but it would be considered strange for an American to return from Europe without seeing Paris, the centre of so many attractions. This gave him occasion to speak of France. He said I was quite right in my intention to visit Paris. The French were a singular people. They were so fickle in their character, and had such a restless desire to disturb the peace of the world that they were always dangerous. They had tried every form of government and could not rest satisfied with any.

French emissaries were now endeavoring every where to excite disturbances and destroy the peace all over Europe.

215I observed we had always pursued a different course in America. We were no propagandists. Perfectly satisfied with our institutions, we left to every other nation the task of managing their own concerns in their own manner. This had been the uniform policy of our Government since its origin.

He replied that he knew the character of our nation well, and repeated they were a true and loyal people: He had the greatest confidence in them. His own policy was the same as ours. He was no propagandist himself. All he desired was peace. He never interfered with the concerns of other nations when it could possibly be avoided. He desired peace above all things for Russia. But he said it seemed as if there were at present an evil spirit abroad throughout the world. He appeared to be particularly the object of its malevolence. (Evidently alluding to the Polish conspiracy.) He was in the hands of the Almighty, and would endeavor to do his duty fearlessly and honestly in the station where Providence had placed him, and in humble submission would leave the event to His will. Here he was evidently affected.

He then bade me adieu, and embraced and saluted me according to the Russian custom, a ceremony for which I was wholly unprepared, and which I could not have anticipated. Whilst we were taking leave, he told me to tell General Jackson to send him another minister exactly like myself. He wished for no better.

Upon leaving his presence I was sensibly impressed with the vanity of human greatness. The circumstances brought forcibly to memory the closing scene of the life of the Emperor Alexander. Throughout his last illness he refused to take medicine, and thus suffered his disease, which was not at the first considered dangerous, to become mortal. When Sir James Wylie, his physician, told him that unless he would submit to medical treatment his disease must prove fatal, the Emperor Alexander regarded him earnestly, and exclaimed in the most solemn manner, "and why should I desire to live?" He continued to reject all remedies, and his death was the consequence. On the truth of this anecdote you may rely. There was no foundation for the report that he had been poisoned.

At the first, I had determined to suppress such parts of this conversation as were evidently confidential, together with the kind things which the emperor said to me personally; but I afterwards concluded that it was my duty under my instructions to report the whole. This is done, under a full conviction that it will never meet the public eye.

I had on the same day my audience of leave of the empress, who was very gracious, but what passed upon this occasion is not properly the subject for a despatch.

I took leave of Count Nesselrode this morning, and presented Mr. Clay as chargé-d'affaires. Time presses, and I shall leave him in his first despatch to give you a particular account of this interview. It was entirely satisfactory.

Thus has my mission terminated; and I cannot be mistaken when I say that these people now evince a much better feeling both towards our Government and the head of it than they did on my arrival. I have taken great pains, upon all proper occasions, to make the character and conduct of General Jackson known. Nothing more was necessary to make the man who enjoys the highest rank in our country stand also the first in their esteem.

I have not seen or heard anything of Baron Sacken since his arrival in this city.

Within the past few days it has been known here that the emperor had refused to receive Sir Stratford Canning as ambassador from England. As his reasons were altogether personal, this refusal can produce no serious difficulty between the two nations. The Russians say that Sir Stratford, when here before, evinced a captious and jealous disposition, which rendered him very disagreeable.

I expect to reach the United States about the last of November or beginning of December.

Yours very respectfully,
James Buchanan.

CHAPTER X.

1833.

DEPARTURE FROM ST. PETERSBURG—JOURNEY TO PARIS—PRINCESS LIEVEN—POZZO DI BORGO—DUC DE BROGLIE—GENERAL LAFAYETTE—LOUIS PHILIPPE—ARRIVAL IN LONDON—DINNER AT PRINCE LIEVEN'S AND LORD PALMERSTON'S—PRINCE TALLEYRAND.

Mr. Buchanan commenced his homeward journey on the 8th of August (1833). Omitting what merely relates to places and things now well known to all travelers, I select the following passages from his diary:

Thursday, August 8, 1833.

I left St. Petersburg. Mr. Bligh, Mr. Gevers and Mr. Clay accompanied me as far as Cronstadt. At 6 o'clock in the afternoon we passed the guard ship and arrived at Travemunde, on Tuesday, the 13th, between 12 and 1 o'clock in the day, after a rough and stormy passage. The boat (Alexandra) has not sufficient steam power for her tonnage, having only 140 horse-power for more than 700 tons, and the consequence is that she can make but little way against a head wind. The price of the passage is 250 roubles ($50), the consequence of an indiscreet monopoly which has been granted by the emperor.

We had on board the Princess Lieven and her two youngest sons, the Princes George and Arthur, called after the late king[38] and the Duke of Wellington—the one about thirteen, the other nine—fine boys. Count Matuscervie was also on board, bound for Aberdeenshire on a hunting expedition. He is excessively fond of horse-racing, hunting and all field sports, and seems to take much greater delight in talking of these subjects, than those of a serious nature. The princess has in a great degree lost that beauty which captivated the king and the Duke of W. Her nose is now sharp and her face somewhat red; but her manners and conversation are very fine. I consider her superior to Matuscervie as a diplomatist.[39] I endeavored to cultivate her good graces, not by assiduous attentions, which are often annoying, but by kind and respectful conduct towards her whenever the opportunity occurred unsought. I succeeded. She is a woman and possesses all the superstitious feelings in regard to omens which distinguish the Russians. The count and myself made a bet on the length of the voyage, and drank the wine before its termination. This gave her much uneasiness, and the wind became more

violent immediately after. The count wrote a complimentary certificate in the captain's [log] book, and it was signed before the close of the voyage. Immediately after we had quite a storm, which continued the whole night. I should have been alarmed myself, but thanks to the Yankee captain with whom I crossed the Atlantic, who would carry sail in a hurricane. Captain Dietz, of the boat, a round-faced and pleasant Dutchman, and a naturalized citizen of the United States, attributed our bad voyage entirely to the circumstance of having a parson aboard (The Rev. Mr. Kneill). He swore he could show all his [log] books and prove that, since he commanded a vessel, he had never made a single prosperous voyage with a clergyman on board. This was added to the stock of the princess's superstition, and I found her uneasy at the idea of having him on board, on their passage from Hamburg to London. I told her I considered it almost a moral phenomenon to see such a woman believing in these presages. She said she had not un esprit fort. She could not help it. She said Lady Holland was as bad as herself in this respect. It was she [Lady Holland] who had first informed her that it was bad luck to set out on a journey on Friday. The princess did not believe it; but she had once tried it; her carriage was broken, and she injured, so as not to be entirely recovered for a year.
Lord Wellington, she said, never thought himself wrong. He was always right, in his opinion. He had committed three great blunders whilst he was minister.
The first was in sending Prince Polignac to govern France. The duke had told her that this prince was the greatest man in France. Politeness alone had prevented her from laughing in his face. He was mediocre parmi les mediocres; besides, he was obstinate to the very last degree. The second was on the Catholic emancipation question; and the third in refusing all reform after having himself opened the door for it.
Lord Lowther had called to see her in Hamburg, and informed her that there would have been, a few days ago, a new ministry in England, but for the timidity of Sir Robert Peel. I told her I thought this was prudence in Sir Robert. The Tories could not now govern England. She concurred in opinion with me; said the duke was now near seventy, and could not afford to wait, but that was not the case with Sir Robert. We talked of the Polish question, etc., etc...... Met Mr. Wheaton, his wife and daughter in Hamburg.[40]
219Tuesday, at 12 o'clock (day).
We left Cologne and arrived in Aix-la-Chapelle, a distance of nine and a quarter German miles, through Bergheim and Juliers. The latter strongly fortified.
The king of Prussia seems to be determined to strengthen himself in this country. Judging from what I have observed myself and heard from others, he cannot rely upon the affections of the people. Indeed, they talk very freely. They all refer to the days of Napoleon; and compare their situation then with what it is at present. The old maitre d'hotel at Bergheim, who has kept a public house for fifty years, and who seems to be a sensible and honest-hearted old man, told me that the taxes were not half so heavy under Napoleon as they were at present. That he was the greatest man there had ever been in the world, and they loved the French much better than the Prussians. Other travelers, who understand German, have told me that at the public tables they talk of a revolution as certain; without pretending to conjecture when it will take place.
But the king of Prussia is a wise man. He has been taught in the school of misfortune, and has been greatly benefited by the lessons of that stern mistress. There is great freedom of speech allowed throughout the Prussian dominions, and in those east of the Rhine the king is popular, notwithstanding the violation of his promise to give them a constitution. This arises from a general conviction of his wisdom and justice, and particularly from the equal conduct he has pursued towards all classes of his subjects. The people are pleased

with him, because his conduct towards the nobles has given them no cause of jealousy. He is a democratic despot, and this is perhaps the true policy of all despots.

In the Rhenish provinces, it is difficult for the people to rebel, in the midst of strong and almost impregnable fortifications and of troops faithful and well disciplined.

Saturday night, August 31, (1833).

Arrived in Paris, and went to lodgings provided for me by Mr. Harris,[41] in the Rue de Paix.

Sunday.

I walked to the Place Vendome, and saw the triumphal column. The statue of Napoleon was again placed upon its summit during the anniversary of what are called here the glorious days of the revolution of July (1830). I also visited the garden of the Tuileries, the Champs Elysées, and the Place of Louis XVI, between the two. Here this unfortunate monarch was executed.

A column is to be erected in the centre, exactly resembling Cleopatra's Needle. There is a model of it now standing. Dined with Mr. Harris—a man sufficiently civil and ceremonious, but a mannerist...... He has been so long in Europe as to have lost much of his American feelings, if he ever possessed them in a strong degree. Not unskilful as a diplomatist. He is remembered kindly in Russia, whilst such men as Bayard and Pinkney are forgotten. He seems to have done his duty in relation to the confirmation of the French treaty by the chambers.

Monday.

Called on the Duke of Treviso (Mortier) and General Lafayette; found them both in the country; took a drive with Mr. Harris into the Bois de Boulogne. He is exceedingly anxious to be appointed minister to Russia. I also visited Notre Dame.

Tuesday.

Visited the Louvre. Whilst there, met very unexpectedly Walter Patterson, Esq., of the State of New York, and Mr. Stevenson and Mr. Burns, of the same State.

Afterwards called with Mr. Harris on Count Pozzo di Borgo;[42] had an interesting conversation with him. He thinks the French selfish, that their courage proceeds from vanity, and that they are wholly unfit for the enjoyment of constitutional liberty. He says they will fight well, when seen, but are incapable of sustaining disasters. He has done everything he could to preserve peace; but if war must come, he thinks the French mistaken as to its result. If one were to judge merely from the striking superiority of the Russian over the French troops in appearance, this conclusion would seem very natural.

Saturday, Sunday and Monday.

So unwell that I could not go out. Mr. Harris made a dinner party of Americans for me on Saturday, which, much to my regret, I could not attend. General Lafayette called and sat nearly an hour with me before he went to this dinner; but I was in great pain the whole time.

Judging from what I have heard from the General, Major Poussin and others, I have no doubt the Republican party are making rapid advances in France. This is not confined to the lower orders, but extends to the highest circles. From all I can observe and learn, they are wholly unprepared for republican institutions. They want political virtue as much as any people. They are very selfish, destitute in a great degree of religion, and are always discontented with the present because they hope something from change. Political virtue, with the exception of Lafayette and a few others, don't exist among them.

The policy of the latter [Lafayette] is that France shall now school herself preparatory to republican institutions, for fifteen or twenty years. But I think he is afraid the change will take place sooner. He has lost much of his popularity in France, because they believe him to be an imbecile, and because he will not lead the Republican party to immediate action. He has lost all confidence in Louis Philippe, who, in my opinion, is as desirous of being a Legitimate as the Emperor Alexander.

In case of general republican commotions in France, a continental war becomes inevitable. The three great powers of Europe are preparing for it, and if one were to judge from the appearance of the Russian and Prussian soldiers compared with the French, he would be tempted to doubt the result. There is an energy in liberty, however, and there will probably be such an aid to its cause among the oppressed of Germany, Poland and other nations, that we may cherish the hope that France will not be overrun. I do not consider the French either safe or good apostles of liberty. I sincerely hope I am mistaken. Everything here is now Bonaparte; and at present they appear to live upon the memory of their greatness under him.

I ought always to remember with gratitude the kindness of Mr. Emlen, Doctor Fisher and Mr. Patterson[43] during my three days' sickness. Hope to be out to-morrow again.

Thursday, 12th.

Thank God! a fine day. Visited the Duc de Broglie, in company with Mr. Harris. Conversation concerning the omission of the French Chamber to ratify the treaty.

I told him that, however the government here might be able to satisfy that at Washington, and understand each other on the subject, their explanations could not reach the people of the United States. I had no doubt the transaction would give rise to much unpleasant feeling among our people, and might lead to an unhappy state of feeling between the two countries. That I should not be astonished if this were to manifest itself on the meeting of Congress. He said that he was very sorry, Mr. Harris could appreciate his exertions; he was happy to say that the feeling in favor of the treaty was growing; the advantages of the commerce were becoming more manifest, and he had no doubt that one of the first acts which the Chamber would perform after its meeting, would be to ratify it. He hoped it would come so soon that Congress would receive the news before there was any expression of feeling. [He] Criminated Mr. Dupin in relation to it—said he only called for the papers because he knew that all the reports of previous commissions had been against the treaty. He said, although not a member of the administration which made it, he approved it and would now make such a treaty.[44]

September 13th.

I dined to-day with Count Pozzo di Borgo. Before dinner he took Mr. Harris and myself into a room apart from the rest of the company, and told me he wished to communicate to me, so that I might inform the President, on my return, what was the true condition of Europe at the present moment. He said there did not exist at the present any immediate apprehension of war; though from the state of things there was no telling at what time war might take place.

Everything was unsettled in France; they were a turbulent and restless people, and busily employed with their propaganda. They were wholly unfit for liberal institutions; and, in fact, these were not what they wanted. They wished again for the glory of the times of Bonaparte. He could himself, in a month, raise an insurrection in France; but what the allied powers wanted was peace, and peace they would maintain so long as they could consistently with propriety. That this they did not wish from fear of the result. Far from it. They, to wit, Russia, Prussia and Austria, were indissolubly united, and war with one would be war with all.

Those three powers, with the German Confederation, could, in three months, bring an army of 600,000 men into the field, 500,000 infantry and 100,000 cavalry, and have an army of reserve of the same number. The French journals were continually attacking them without cause, for interfering with foreign states, but I understood him to say that Austria would interfere in Piedmont, and if the French should attempt to prevent it, the allies would make common cause against them. They disliked and distrusted France very much; England not so much. If the latter would act a prudent and proper part, she might have great influence on the affairs of Europe; but the English ministry were fools. They were encouraging France, and yet it was almost certain they would not fire a gun in defence of the latter. England depended upon her commerce, and she could not afford to lose that of the whole continent of Europe, which she would do in the event of war. She had acted very foolishly in giving Belgium to France.

What he wished me especially to tell the President was that he hoped the United States in the event of a war would cause their neutrality to be respected, and would not suffer the existence of illegal blockades. That in the event of war, England would have every interest to cripple American commerce; for, in that event, the commerce of the world would fall into the hands of Americans. That the English must even use their vessels to carry articles essentially necessary to them from the north of Europe.

223I promised I would communicate all he had said to the President, and observed that when we were comparatively feeble, we had gone to war for the purpose of maintaining our neutral rights upon the ocean; and that at this time of day, when we were much more powerful, neither the President nor people of the United States would suffer them to be violated with impunity. Our policy was peaceful; we never interfered with the political concerns of other nations. The strictest neutrality we should observe both from principle and from policy. This had been the course of our Government ever since the celebrated proclamation of neutrality of General Washington, which I explained to him. I was not now afraid that England would, as she had done before, attempt to violate the neutral rights of a nation which in six months could put to sea fifty ships of the line and heavy frigates. He expressed some admiration and astonishment at this statement, which was confirmed by Mr. Harris, and observed he could not believe that they would.

The conversation then turned upon the French treaty. He said he had been speaking several times to Broglie, as he called him, upon the subject. He had done what he could for us. Broglie was well disposed, and he thought with the assistance of Lafayette and his friends, it would be ratified very early in the next session. I told him I had understood that Mr. Dupin, the President of the Chamber, was rather opposed to us. He said that Dupin was an unprincipled man, I think he said a rascal, very selfish, and fond of money. He was now receiving a pension of 200 or 300 pounds. I did not understand exactly from whom. After we went to table, we had much conversation in nearly the same strain. He told me he wished I could be present at two or three sittings of the Chamber. They were like cats, all in a passion, and all making a noise, and afterwards laughing; wholly unfit for liberty. They wanted such a man as Bonaparte and glory again, not liberty.

Before we went to table I asked him what he thought of Louis Philippe, and whether the allied sovereigns had confidence in his character. He answered equivocally. Said Louis Philippe might be well disposed; but he might be controlled by the factions, and made to do what he did not approve. His government wanted strength.

At table, in speaking of the emperor [Nicholas], I said I had taken occasion, since my arrival in France, to speak of the personal character of the emperor to some persons, as I thought it deserved. He replied as if I had mentioned the name of Lafayette, which I did not, and asked what Lafayette had thought of that. I said that General Lafayette was aware of the good personal character of the emperor, and that of the empress, and the happy influence of their example on the Russian nobility, and had freely admitted it. He said that the general had lost his influence with Louis Philippe, and in a great degree in

France. I observed that whatever opinion others might express concerning him, I considered it the duty of every American to speak with gratitude of him. Mr. Harris here shook his head at me, but I continued to talk about him, and the donation we had made him. The count said it 224was all spent, and I replied I was very sorry for it. Various subjects were talked over, and the count took leave of me in the kindest and most affectionate manner. He was glad to have an opportunity of communicating this information to a gentleman of my character, who had been sent on a special mission to Russia, and acquitted himself in such a manner as I had done. General Jackson might probably have never heard of him; but he had often [heard] of the general, and respected his character very highly. I told him his name was known throughout the political world. General Jackson would be proud of his good opinion, which I should not fail to communicate.

I forgot to mention that, at the proper place, I introduced the subject of the treaty concerning maritime rights, and said one object of my mission was to make a treaty which should assert these rights as between the two nations. He replied that he presumed it had been explained to me that the reason why Russia did not accede to this treaty at the present moment was the delicate relations between them and England. Such a treaty at this time would set England in a flame. Russia was but a second-rate naval power. She agreed, however, entirely with the principles concerning maritime rights maintained by us, and at the proper time would assert them in the same manner as if she had entered into the treaty. In the course of the conversation, he observed that the influence of Russia was firmly established in Constantinople. Yes, I observed, she had been acting whilst the other powers were talking. I asked the true character of the sultan, and he spoke of him as rather a wavering and weak man, etc.

Mr. Buchanan, after visiting the interesting old city of Rouen, embarked at Havre for Southampton, and arrived at Thompson's Hotel in Cavendish Square, London, on the 18th of September. A dinner at Prince Lieven's and another at Lord Palmerston's are the only things worthy of note that I find in his journal kept during this visit.

Monday, September 23.

Dined at Prince Lieven's.

The company were the Prince and Princess, Prince Talleyrand and the Duchess de Dino[45], Prince Esterhazy, Baron Wessenberg, Lord Palmerston, Baron Bülow, Mr. Dedal, Mr. Vail, the Earl and Countess of Sefton, Mr. Lomonosoff and myself—fourteen. The whole London conference there. A dinner given to Prince Talleyrand, who left London the next day for Paris.

They were all very civil and kind to me, particularly Princess Lieven, Lord Palmerston and Prince Esterhazy. After dinner, I was introduced to Prince Talleyrand by Lord Palmerston, at the solicitation of the latter. He at once 225asked me, in French, if I could speak French. I told him not well, but I could understand it. He then asked some questions about America, and inquired particularly for the family of General Hamilton, and about the descendants of General Schuyler. He said that when he was minister for Foreign Affairs, Colonel Burr came to Paris and sent his card to him. He returned the card, with a message that he had the portrait of General Hamilton hanging up in his parlor.

They told me, before I made his acquaintance, that though eighty-three, by his own acknowledgment, his mind was as active as ever. This I doubt. He has the appearance of a very old man, though not very thin, like the French. At dinner he spoke very little, though he ate with a good appetite. They say he eats but one meal a day. After dinner he was a little more sprightly. He accepted an invitation to dine again with the Prince and Princess on the 8th December, at half-past seven, with pleasantry. Baron Bülow told me the next day that his ability and skill in the conference were wonderful. He would lie down and say nothing whilst all the rest were talking, but when they got tired and into confusion, he would come out with great power, and restore all things to their proper order.

Lord Palmerston did not arrive at the dinner till after we had sat down, about eight o'clock. They say he is never punctual. He is an agreeable and open-hearted man to appearance. I had much conversation with him on three occasions, particularly after his own dinner, and he must be a great hypocrite if not in favor of promoting the most friendly relations between England and the United States. Prince Esterhazy on this day expressed his admiration of the President, and his warm friendship towards the American people, and said this was the feeling of Prince Metternich. He had recommended to the emperor to open diplomatic relations with us, which the latter had acceded to, and a minister would soon be sent. He spoke of his own country, Hungary, with great devotion, and said he never would have been a diplomat but for the friendship of the late king (George IV.). He pressed me several times to give Americans letters of introduction to him.

Tuesday, 24.

Dined at Lord Palmerston's.

Lord Palmerston's dinner consisted of his Lordship, Princes Esterhazy and Lieven, Barons Bülow, Wessenberg and Ompteda, Mr. Backhouse, Mr. Vail, Mr. Bacourt, Sir George Shea, Mr. Sullivan, Mr. Sullivan, Jr. and myself.

I sat next Baron Bülow at table. He talked freely of the conduct of the King of Holland. Blamed his obstinacy and perverseness. Said he might yet bring ruin on his own head. The Dutch were an excellent people. He had deceived them, induced them to believe that all he wanted was the separation of Holland from Belgium upon fair terms, when he was only keeping the question open in the hope that he might get Belgium under his dominion again, which the Dutch did not wish. When they discovered they had been deceived, he did not know what might be the consequence. He said he could not anticipate when the conference would end. The King of Holland 226could have got better terms formerly than it was possible for him now. He told me significantly that the King of Prussia would not meet the emperors of Russia and Austria in conference. The whole conversation coming from the Prussian minister to the conference astonished me.

Mr. Bates[46] told me the English were fifty years behind the Americans in commercial enterprise and shipbuilding. He was examined before a committee of the House of Commons. When questioned upon this subject, he said he had been kindly received and treated in England, and did not like to answer the question and have his answers published. They then told him to give his opinion, and it should not be taken down. He told them the reason of the superiority was in the character of masters and sailors. They were educated, had a sense of character and responsibility, entirely different from the same classes in England. Masters were respectable men, and sailors were now shipped from a reading-room in Boston.

He expressed his opinion to me that the Americans would, before long, carry on the chief trade between England and China. Everything favored them. The destruction of the East India Company's charter and of the West India merchants, etc.

[He speaks of] The astonishment of the shipbuilder, when he gave the dimensions of a vessel to him, and his astonishment afterwards at being shown the American vessel which was his model, etc.

227

CHAPTER XI.

1833–1836.

MR. BUCHANAN RETURNS HOME—GREETING FROM GENERAL JACKSON—ELECTED TO THE SENATE OF THE UNITED STATES—STATE OF PARTIES—THE GREAT WHIG LEADERS IN THE SENATE—PERIL OF A WAR WITH FRANCE.

Mr. Buchanan was greeted on his arrival at his home in Lancaster by the following letter from General Jackson:

[GENERAL JACKSON TO MR. BUCHANAN.]
Washington, Nov. 18, 1833.
My Dear Sir:—

I have received your note by Mr. John Van Buren, and am delighted to hear that you have reached your country in good health, after so long an absence in her service. I anticipate much pleasure from the personal interview, which you have promised me I shall have in the course of this week, but do not desire to hasten you more than your convenience, or the wishes of your friends will permit. I leave until then all else that I would say, except my congratulation on your safe arrival, which I beg you to accept with my best wishes for your health and happiness.

Very sincerely and respectfully,
Andrew Jackson.

The winter of 1833–34 appears to have been passed in private occupations which have left no traces. But in the latter part of the summer of 1834, Mr. Buchanan was appointed one of the commissioners on the part of the State of Pennsylvania, to arrange with commissioners of the State of New Jersey, concerning the use of the waters of the Delaware. It was not entirely convenient for him to accept this appointment; but as it was to be a public service without any pecuniary compensation, he felt that he had no alternative. How long he was occupied about it, I have not discovered. In the following December, the election of a Senator of the United States, to 228succeed Mr. Wilkins, who had been appointed minister to Russia, was to be made by the Legislature of Pennsylvania. Mr. Buchanan was chosen on the 6th of December (1834), upon the fourth balloting; his principal competitors being Joel B. Sutherland, James Clarke, and Amos Ellmaker. He was of course elected by the Democratic members of the Legislature, and as a supporter of the administration of President Jackson.[47]

The correspondence which took place between him and those who elected him, is of interest now, chiefly because it discloses that he held to what has been called the doctrine of instruction; that is to say, the right of a State Legislature to direct the vote of a Senator of the State in Congress, and the duty of the Senator to obey the direction.

[TO THE HON. JAMES BUCHANAN.]
Harrisburg, Dec. 8, 1834.
Dear Sir:—

Ere this reaches you, doubtless you will have been notified of your election to the Senate of the United States, by the Legislative body of this State to which we have the honor to belong. And it is with unfeigned gratification that we individually can claim a participation in the confidence which has on this occasion been reposed in your talents and integrity. Nor is that gratification by any means lessened, from the consideration that you are the personal as well as the political friend of both our State and National Executives, who have done so much within their respective spheres to exalt the character and promote the interests of our State and Nation. And above all, who, in their official relations, so nobly stood forth in the rescue of our common country from the grasp of a corrupt moneyed monopoly, as reckless as it was aristocratical, and as merciless as it was powerful. And it is with no less pride than pleasure that we shall look to you, in your new and high relations, as the champion of the measures projected by our venerable President, Andrew Jackson, and seconded by our worthy Executive, George Wolf.

Respectfully your friends and obedient servants,
(Signed by)   Jacob Kern,
and Seventy other Members.

The following communication, in reply, was laid before the members, at a meeting held in the Capitol on the 7th instant, by Col. Jacob Kern, Speaker of the Senate:

229[TO JACOB KERN, ESQ., AND OTHERS, MEMBERS OF THE LEGISLATURE OF PENNSYLVANIA.]

Washington, Dec. 22, 1834.

Gentlemen:—

I want language to express my feelings on the perusal of your kind letter, which was delivered to me at the moment I was about to leave Harrisburg. Elevated by your free and unsolicited suffrages to the only public station I desire to occupy, it shall be my constant endeavor to justify, by my conduct, the generous confidence which you have thus reposed. The interest and the honor of Pennsylvania, so far as you have committed them to my hands, shall never be wilfully abandoned or betrayed.

Although you have not asked me for any pledge or promise relating to my course in the Senate, yet I am sensible that many of you desire I should express my opinion publicly in regard to the right of legislative instruction. I shall do so with the utmost frankness. On this question I have not, and never have had, any serious difficulties. The right results from the very nature of our institutions. The will of the people, when fully and fairly expressed, ought to be obeyed by all their political agents. This is the very nature and essence of a representative democracy.

Without entering into an argument upon the general question, which would be altogether misplaced upon the present occasion, it may not be improper to observe that the principle applies with redoubled force to Senators in Congress. They represent the sovereign States, who are the parties to that constitutional compact which called the federal union into existence. In the Senate, these States are represented as distinct communities, each entitled to the same number of votes, without regard to their population. In that body they are all equal, as they were before the adoption of the federal constitution. Here, emphatically, if any where, the voice of the States ought to be heard, and ought to be obeyed. Shall it then be said that a Senator possesses the constitutional right to violate the express instructions of the sovereign State which he represents, and wield the power and the vote which have been conferred upon him for the benefit of his constituents in a manner which they have solemnly declared to be ruinous to their dearest interests, or dangerous to their liberties! The bare statement of the proposition carries conviction to my mind. All, or nearly all the State Legislatures, have long been in the practice of instructing their Senators, and this affords the strongest evidence of the principle upon which the custom is founded.

It has been objected, that the right of instruction may destroy the tenure of the Senatorial office, and render it subject to all the political fluctuations in the several States. But the Senator is only bound to obey: he is not called upon to resign. And although there may be circumstances in which a man of honor might feel himself constrained to retire from the public service rather than give the vote of his State against his own convictions, yet these cases must, from their nature, be of rare occurrence.

Besides, this objection implies an entire want of confidence in the State legislatures. It supposes that they may become the instruments of faction for the purpose of harassing Senators, and compelling them to resign. In fact, it results in the principle that the people are incapable of managing their own concerns, and are, therefore, under the necessity of conferring an irresponsible political power upon one of their own number, to save them from themselves. From the nature of our institutions, we must repose such a degree of confidence in the State legislatures as to presume that they will not abuse the power with which they have been intrusted.

If it should ever clearly appear, in any case, that the immediate representatives of the people have not obeyed their will in voting instructions, this might present an exception to the general rule. Such an occurrence, however, though possible, is highly improbable. It is not to be presumed that State legislatures will exercise this important power, unless upon grave and solemn occasions, after mature deliberation and a thorough knowledge of the public will.

I have thus expressed my opinion freely upon this important question, though I am well aware it differs from that of some of the ablest and best men of our country.[48]

In relation to the course which I intend to pursue in the Senate, I shall say but little. My conduct must speak for itself. I feel sensible that in point of ability I shall disappoint the partial expectations of my friends. To become distinguished in that body, the ablest in the world in proportion to its numbers, requires a stretch of intellect and a range of political knowledge and experience, which I do not pretend to possess. Whilst, therefore, I cannot become "the champion of the measures projected by our venerable President," I shall, both from principle and inclination, give them an honest and consistent support.

Before concluding this letter, permit me to state my entire concurrence in the sentiments you have expressed concerning "our worthy executive, George Wolf." In the darkest hour of pressure and of panic during the last winter, when the internal improvements of the State were, to all appearance, about to be arrested, he stood unmoved, and met the storm in a manner which proved him to be the able, faithful, and fearless representative of Pennsylvania Democracy. His message contributed much to dispel the gloom which, for a time, seemed to have settled on our country. It was the bright dawn of that glorious day of prosperity which we have since enjoyed.

With sentiments of the most profound gratitude and respect, I remain

Your obedient servant,

James Buchanan.

As I am now to trace a long senatorial career, which began at a period when the Senate of the United States contained men of the very highest ability and renown, it is proper to give a brief account of the state of parties and the questions of the time, and to fix Mr. Buchanan's position among the statesmen whom he had to meet. When he took his seat in the Senate, on the 15th of December, 1834, General Jackson was in his second term of office, which began on the 4th of March, 1833. He had received a very large majority of the electoral votes—seventy-four more than were necessary to a choice. Mr. Van Buren had become Vice-President by a majority of electoral votes less than General Jackson's, by the number of thirty. He was, of course, in the chair of the Senate. In Congress and throughout the country, the supporters of the administration had become known as the Democratic party, the old term of "Republicans," and the more recent one of "Jackson men," being generally dropped.[49] The opposition had become classified and consolidated under the name of the Whig party, a term substituted for that of "National

Republicans." Their leader and candidate in the presidential election of 1832 was Mr. Clay.[50] There was a third party, known as the "Anti-Masons," who gave the seven electoral votes of Vermont to Mr. Wirt, as their candidate for the Presidency, and to Amos Ellmaker of Pennsylvania as their candidate for the Vice-Presidency. Notwithstanding General Jackson's great popularity and influence throughout the country, a large majority of the Senate were opposed to his administration and his measures. This opposition became concentrated and intensified by the President's removal of the public deposits from the Bank of the United States, into certain selected State banks. A resolution, strongly 232condemning this act, had been carried in the Senate, by twenty-eight yeas against eighteen nays, on the 28th of March, 1834, nine months before Mr. Buchanan entered the Senate. This vote may therefore be regarded as a general index of the relative strength of parties in that body when Mr. Buchanan became a member of it. How this great opposition majority became so changed three years afterward, that the friends of General Jackson were able to expunge this resolution from the records of the Senate, will appear hereafter. The leading Senators of the opposition at the commencement of the session, in December, 1834, and distinctly classified as Whigs, were Mr. Clay, Mr. Webster, Mr. Clayton of Delaware, Mr. Ewing of Ohio, and Mr. Frelinghuysen and Mr. Southard of New Jersey.

The most important Democratic or administration Senators were, Messrs. Wright of New York, Benton of Missouri, and Mr. King of Alabama. Calhoun stood apart from both the political parties. He had been chosen Vice-President in 1828 by the same party which then elected General Jackson for the first time, and he then had the same electoral votes, with the exception of seven of the votes of Georgia. He was consequently in the Chair of the Senate in 1830, when the great debate took place between Mr. Webster and Colonel Hayne on the subject of nullification. In 1833, when the South Carolina doctrine of nullification culminated in a threatened resistance to collection of the Federal revenue within her borders, and made it necessary for General Jackson to issue his celebrated proclamation, Mr. Calhoun was elected as a senator in Congress from South Carolina, and he determined to resign the Vice-Presidency. In December, 1832, he took his seat in the Senate. The breach between him and the President, which was caused by the attitude of the latter towards the "Nullifiers," was understood to be widened by the probability that Mr. Van Buren would be the Democratic candidate for the Presidency, to succeed General Jackson in 1837, and by the well-known wish of the latter that Mr. Van Buren should become his successor. The breach between Mr. Calhoun and the President became still farther widened, when the State of South Carolina adopted her famous ordinance for preventing the collection of the Federal revenue within her limits. From General Jackson's known firmness of character 233and tendency to severe measures, Mr. Calhoun found himself in some personal danger. Then followed Mr. Clay's interposition, by means of his compromise tariff, which was designed to ward off an actual collision between the federal executive and the nullifying leaders of South Carolina. Mr. Calhoun was thus saved from personal humiliation, and perhaps from some personal peril. But no real reconciliation took place between him and General Jackson, and he remained in an isolated position in the Senate, a great and powerful debater, vindicating with singular ability, when a proper occasion offered, his peculiar views of the nature of the Constitution, always discharging his duties as a senator with entire purity, but never acting upon any measure as a member of either of the political parties into which the Senate was divided.

Taking the entire composition of the Senate at that period, with the opposing forces of the Democratic and the Whig parties, and with Mr. Calhoun's intermediate position, there has never been a period in the history of that body, when there was more real power of debate displayed, or when public measures were more thoroughly considered. If Mr. Clay, Mr. Calhoun and Mr. Webster towered above the other senators, there were not wanting men who may be said to have approached them in ability; and if Mr. Clay and Mr. Webster, on the Whig side, sometimes appeared to give to the opposition a preponderating intellectual force, it was not always a supremacy that could be said to be undisputed by their Democratic opponents, although they did for a long time control the action of the Senate. The country looked on upon these great senatorial contests with predilections which varied, of course, with the political feelings and associations of men; but the President, his measures and his policy, notwithstanding the power of the Senatorial opposition, continued to grow in the popular favor, and to receive constant proofs of the popular support. To some of the principal questions of the time I now turn. The first in which Mr. Buchanan took part, soon after he entered the Senate, related to the conduct of France.

In 1831 a convention was concluded between the United States and the government of King Louis Philippe, by which 234the latter bound itself to pay to the United States twenty-five millions of francs, for the liquidation of certain claims of American citizens against France, and to be distributed to the claimants by the American Government, as it should determine. The Government of the United States, on its part, engaged to pay to the French government one million five hundred thousand francs, to liquidate the claims, urged by the French government for its citizens, on the United States, and to be distributed by the French government, as it should determine. Each party bound itself to pay its stipulated sum in six annual instalments: those payable by the United States to be deducted from the larger sums payable by France. The first French instalment, $4,166,666.66, became due at the expiration of one year next following the exchange of ratifications. The exchange of ratifications took place February 2d, 1832, and consequently the first French instalment became due on the 3d of February, 1833. A bill of exchange was drawn by the Secretary of the Treasury on the French Minister of Finance, for the amount of the instalment, and sold to the Bank of the United States. Payment was refused at the French Treasury when the bill was presented, for the reason that the Legislative Chambers had made no appropriation to meet the instalment. We have seen that when Mr. Buchanan was in Paris, in the summer of 1833 he held conversations on this matter with the Duc de Broglie and Count Pozzo di Borgo; from which it appears that moderate and rational persons in France then believed that the Chambers would at the next session make the necessary appropriation. In December, 1833, President Jackson, in his annual message to Congress, adverted to this subject, and said that he had despatched an envoy to the French government to attend to it, and that he had received from that government assurances that at the next meeting of the Chambers it would be brought forward and satisfactorily disposed of. He added that if he should be disappointed in this hope, the subject would be again brought before Congress, "in such manner as the occasion might require." The opposition in France regarded this as a menace. The subject was brought before the Chambers several times, but in April, 1834, the appropriation 235necessary to carry the treaty into effect was refused. The king's government then sent a national vessel to this country, bearing the king's assurance that the Chambers should be called together, after the election of new members, as soon as the charter would permit, and that the influence of the executive should be exerted to procure the necessary appropriation, in time to be communicated to the President before the assembling of Congress in December, 1834. The Chambers met on the 31st of July, but this matter was not acted upon, and they were prorogued to the 29th of December.

New assurances were given by the French government that at the ensuing session the appropriation should be pressed. In his annual message of December, 1834, the President made severe comments on the course of all branches of the French government, and recommended a law authorizing reprisals on French property, in case the appropriation should not be made at the ensuing session of the Chambers. This was the attitude of the matter when Mr. Buchanan entered the Senate.[51]

The Senate's Committee on Foreign Affairs, at the head of which was Mr. Clay, had made a report against the adoption of the President's recommendation. On the 14th of January, (1835) on a resolution introduced by Mr. Cuthbert of Georgia, Mr. Buchanan took occasion to say:

236In Senate, January 14, 1835.

France had, before the close of the last session of Congress, declared that it was the unanimous determination of the king's government to appear before the new legislature with its treaty and its bill in hand, and that its intention was to do all that the charter allowed to hasten, as much as possible, the period of the new presentation of the rejected law. The President rested satisfied with this assurance, and, on the faith of it, did not present the subject to Congress. How has France redeemed this pledge? Has that government hastened, as much as possible, the presentation of the rejected law? At the first meeting of the new legislature the law was not presented; and in the face of this engagement, the Chambers were prorogued, not to meet in the autumn, but on the 29th of December, the very latest day which custom had sanctioned. If this assurance had any meaning at all, it was that the Chambers should be convened at least in sufficient time to communicate to the President information that they had assembled, before the meeting of Congress. The President, at the date of the message, was not aware that the Chambers would assemble on the first of the month. No such information had been communicated to him. It now appears that they did assemble on that day. And the only reason that he should vote for the resolution was, that he was willing to wait until the result of their deliberations could be known.

What effect this circumstance might have had on the President's mind, had he known of its existence, he was not prepared to say. He had no information to give on that subject. There is a point, sir, said Mr. Buchanan, in the intercourse between nations, at which diplomacy must end, and a nation must either consent to abandon her rights, or assert them by force. After having negotiated for a quarter of a century to obtain a treaty to redress the wrongs of our injured citizens, and after the French Chamber has once deliberately rejected that treaty, will not this point have been reached, should the Chamber again refuse to make the appropriation? If this be so, is it not right, is it not fair, to present the alternative to France? Would she not have just cause to complain if we should not adopt this very course? To inform her frankly and freely that we have arrived at this point, I am solemnly convinced, is the best diplomacy to which we can resort to obtain redress for the wrongs of the injured claimants. France will then have the alternative fairly presented; and it will be for her to decide whether she will involve herself in war with her ancient ally, rather than pay those claims which the Executive branch of her Government have determined to be just by a solemn treaty. Such an attitude on the part of America will do more for the execution of the treaty than any temporizing measures of policy which we can adopt. I never was more clearly impressed with the truth of any proposition.

France, from the language of the President, will have no right to consider this a menace. It is no more than to say, diplomacy has ended, and the treaty must be executed, or we shall, however reluctantly, be compelled to 237take redress into our own hands. France is a brave and a chivalrous nation; her whole history proves that she is not to be intimidated, even by Europe in arms; but she is wise as well as warlike. To inform her that our rights must be asserted, is to place her in the serious and solemn position of deciding whether she will resist the payment of a just debt by force. Whenever she is convinced that this result is inevitable, the money will be paid; and although I hope I may be mistaken, I believe there will be no payment until she knows we shall assume this attitude. France has never appeared to regard the question in this serious light.

It has been asked what the American Congress would do placed in similar circumstances. Would they appropriate money with a menace impending over their heads? I answer, no, never. But I should never consider it a menace, if, after refusing to vote an appropriation to carry a treaty into effect, a foreign government in the spirit of candor, in language mild and courteous, such as that used by the President, were to inform us they could not abandon their rights, and, however painful it may be, they should be compelled, by a sense of duty, to assert them by force.

After some further discussion, the resolution was so modified as to declare that it was at that time inexpedient to adopt any legislative measure in regard to the state of affairs between the United States and France. In this form the resolution was unanimously adopted.

The President's message was received in Paris in the early part of January (1835). It was resented as a threat. The French minister at Washington was recalled, and on the 13th of January, the day before the vote in the Senate, Mr. Livingston, the minister of the United States at Paris, was informed that his passports were at his service. But a bill was introduced by the ministry in the Chambers, to make the necessary appropriation. It was passed in the latter part of April, but with an amendment making the payment conditional upon an apology from President Jackson for the language of his message of the previous December. There was little likelihood that any such apology would be made for language addressed by the President to the people of the United States through their representatives in Congress. On the contrary, in the early part of the next session (January, 1836) the world was somewhat startled by a recommendation made to Congress by the President, of partial non-intercourse with France.[52] On the 18th of January, 238on a motion by Mr. Clay to refer this recommendation to the Committee on Foreign Affairs,

Mr. Buchanan said that he had been so much gratified with the message which had just been read, that he could not, and he thought he ought not, at this the very first moment, to refrain from expressing his entire approbation of its general tone and spirit. He had watched with intense anxiety the progress of our unfortunate controversy with France. He had hoped, sincerely hoped, that the explanations which had been made by Mr. Livingston, and officially approved by the President of the United States, would have proved satisfactory to the French government. In this he had found his hopes to be vain. After this effort had failed, he felt a degree of confidence, almost amounting to moral assurance, that the last message to Congress would have been hailed by France, as it was by the American people, as the olive branch which would have restored amity and good understanding between us and our ancient ally. Even in this, he feared, he was again doomed to be disappointed. The government of France, unless they change their determination, will not consider this message as sufficient. We have the terms clearly prescribed by the Duke de Broglie, upon which, and upon which alone, the French government will consent to comply with the treaty, and to pay the five millions of dollars to our injured fellow-citizens. Speculation is now at an end. The clouds and darkness which have hung over this question have vanished. It is now made clear as a sunbeam.

The money will not be paid, says the organ of the French government, unless the Government of the United States shall address its claim officially in writing to France, accompanied by what appeared to him, and he believed would appear to the whole American people, without distinction of party, to be a degrading apology. The striking peculiarity of the case, the one which he would undertake to say distinguished it from any other case which had arisen in modern times, in the intercourse between independent nations, was, that the very terms of this apology were dictated to the American Government by the French Secretary of Foreign Affairs. One of these terms was, that it had never entered into the intention (pensée), the thought of this Government, to call in question the good faith of the government of France.

But the French Government proceed still further. Upon the refusal to make this apology, which they ought to have known would never be made—could never be made—they are not content to leave question where it then was. They have given us notice in advance that they will consider our refusal to 239make this degrading apology an evidence that the misunderstanding did not proceed on our part from mere error and mistake.

In addition to all this, the last note of the Duke de Broglie to Mr. Barton declares that the Government of the United States knows that henceforward the execution of the treaty must depend upon itself. They thus leave us to decide whether we shall make the apology in the prescribed terms, or abandon our claim to the fulfillment of the treaty.

He would not allow himself to express the feelings which were excited in his mind upon hearing these letters of the Duke de Broglie read. Most sincerely, most ardently, did he hope that the French government, when this message reached them, if not before, might reconsider their determination, and that all our difficulties might yet pass away. But their language is now clear, specific, incapable of ambiguity or doubt. It would, then, become our duty calmly, but firmly, to take such a stand as the interests and the honor of the country may require.

Mr. B. had already said much more than he intended when he rose. He would, however, make another remark before he took his seat. He felt a proper degree of confidence, he might add a great degree of confidence, in the President of the United States. He knew him to be honest and firm, and faithful to his country; prompt to resent its injuries and avenge its wrongs. He confessed he had anticipated a message of a stronger character. He had supposed that a general non-intercourse with France would, at least, have been recommended. But the recommendation was confined to the mere refusal to admit French ships or French productions to enter our ports. It left France free to receive her supplies of cotton from the United States, without which the manufacturers of that country could not exist. This was wise, it was prudent; it left to France to judge for herself if this unnatural contest must still continue, whether she would close her ports against our vessels and our productions.

In the spring of 1832 (Mr. B. did not recollect precisely the time) Congress passed an act to carry into effect our part of the treaty. Under this treaty, the wines of France had ever since been admitted into the United States upon the favorable terms therein stipulated. Her silks were imported free of duty, in contradistinction to those which came from beyond the Cape of Good Hope. She had for years been enjoying these privileges. Nothing milder, then, could possibly be recommended than to withdraw these advantages from her, and to exclude her vessels and her productions from our ports.

Mr. Buchanan said that when he made the observations which had called forth the remarks of the Senator from South Carolina, (Mr. Calhoun) he had believed the message to be the harbinger of peace, and not of war. This was still his opinion. In this respect he differed entirely from the gentleman. Under this impression, he had then risen merely to remark that, considering the provocation which we had received, the tone, the spirit, and the recommendations themselves, of the message, were mild and prudent, and were well 240calculated to make an impression upon France, and to render her sensible of her injustice.

It had been far from his intention to excite a general debate on the French question, and he would not be drawn into it now by the remarks of the Senator from South Carolina. He must, however, be permitted to say, he was sorry, very sorry, that the gentleman had proclaimed that, if war should come, we are the authors of that war, and it would be the fault, not of the French, but of the American Government. Such a declaration, proceeding from such a source, from a voice so powerful and so potent, would be heard on the other side of the Atlantic, and there might produce a most injurious effect. He was happy to say that this sentiment was directly at war with the opinion of our Committee on Foreign Relations, who, in their report of the last session, had expressed the decided opinion that the American Government, should it become necessary, must insist upon the execution of the treaty. It was at war with the unanimous resolution of the House of Representatives of the same session, declaring that the treaty must be maintained. He believed it was equally at war with the feelings and opinions of the American people. Whilst he expressed his hope and his belief that this message would prove to be the olive branch of peace, still there was so much uncertainty in the event, that it now became our imperative duty to prepare for the worst. Shall we (said Mr. B.) whilst a powerful fleet is riding along our southern coast, in a menacing attitude, sit here and withhold from the President the means which are necessary to place our country in a state of defence? He trusted this would never, never be the case.

The messages and documents were then read, and referred to the Committee on Foreign Relations, as moved by Mr. Clay.

On the last night of the session, which terminated on the 3d-4th of March, 1835, an amendment made in the House of Representatives, to the Fortification bill, was before the Senate. It proposed:

"That the sum of three millions of dollars be and the same is hereby appropriated, out of any money in the treasury not otherwise appropriated, to be expended, in whole or in part, under the direction of the President of the United States, for the military and naval service, including fortifications and ordnance and increase of the navy: Provided such expenditures shall be rendered necessary for the defence of the country, prior to the next meeting of Congress."

The motive of this amendment was to enable the President to put the country into a more efficient state of defence, in view of the danger of a war with France. It was opposed by Mr. Webster and Mr. Clay as an unconstitutional mode of action, 241and also because the state of the French question did not require such action. Mr. Buchanan (on the 3d of March, 1835,) vindicated the amendment in the following manner:

Mr. Buchanan said he was astonished at the remarks which had been made by gentlemen on the subject of this appropriation. The most fearful apprehensions had been expressed, the destruction of our liberties had been predicted, if we should grant to the President three millions of dollars to defend the country, in case it should become necessary to expend it for that purpose, before the next meeting of Congress. For his part, he could realize no such dangers.

Gentlemen have said, and said truly, that the Constitution of the United States has conferred upon Congress, and Congress alone, the power of declaring war. When they go further, and state that this appropriation will enable the executive to make war upon

France, without the consent of Congress, they are, in my humble judgment, entirely mistaken.

Sir, said Mr. B., what is the true nature, and what are the legitimate objects of this appropriation? Do we not know that, although the President cannot make offensive war against France, France may make war upon us; and that we may thus be involved in hostilities in spite of ourselves, before the next meeting of Congress? If the Chamber of Deputies should determine to violate the treaty, and to fix an enduring stigma upon the public faith of the French nation, is it certain that France may not proceed a step further, and strike the first blow? Mr. Livingston himself, in the correspondence which had been communicated to us by the President, has expressed serious apprehensions that this may be the result. France may consider war, eventually, to be inevitable; she may, and I trust does, believe that we have determined not to submit patiently to her violation of a solemn treaty and thus abandon the just claims of our injured citizens; and taking advantage of our unprepared condition, she may commence hostilities herself. The first blow is often half the battle between nations as well as individuals. Have we any security that such will not be her conduct? Have we any reason to believe she will wait until we are ready? Her past history forbids us to indulge too securely in any such belief. If she should adopt this course, in what a fearful condition shall we place the country, if we adjourn without making this appropriation! The Senate will observe that not a dollar of this money can be drawn from the Treasury, unless it shall become necessary for the defence of the country, prior to the next meeting of Congress.

Another circumstance which renders this appropriation indispensable is, that Congress cannot possibly be convened by the President much before their usual time of meeting. There are, I believe, nine States in this Union, who have not yet elected their representatives to the next Congress. Some of these elections will take place in April, and others not till August, and even October. We have now arrived almost at the last hour of our political existence; and shall we leave the country wholly defenceless until the meeting of the next Congress? Gentlemen have warned us of the fearful responsibility which we should incur in making this appropriation. Sir, said Mr. B., I warn them that the responsibility will be still more dreadful, should we refuse it. In that event, what will be our condition should we be attacked by France? Our sea-coast, from Georgia to Maine, will be exposed to the incursions of the enemy; our cities may be plundered and burned; the national character may be disgraced; and all this whilst we have an overflowing Treasury. When I view the consequences which may possibly flow from our refusal to make this grant, I repeat that the responsibility of withholding it may become truly dreadful. No portion of it shall rest upon my shoulders.

Our constitutional right to appropriate this money is unquestionable. Whilst I express this opinion, I am sorry that the present appropriation is not more specific in its objects. Appropriation bills ought to be passed in such a manner as to leave as little to executive discretion as possible. The purposes for which the money is to be applied ought to be clearly and distinctly stated. If there were time to do it, the bill might be improved in this respect. But, sir, this is an extraordinary crisis, and demands prompt action. We must now take it as it is, or not take it at all. There is no time left to make the changes which might be desired.

Gentlemen have contended that, under this appropriation, the President would be authorized to increase the army, and appoint as many new officers to command it as he thought proper. But this is not the case. He could not, under any just construction of this bill, raise a single new company, or appoint a single officer, not authorized by existing laws. No such power is conferred upon him by its terms. It will authorize him to expend three millions of the public money, should the contingency happen which it contemplates, for putting the vessels of war now in ordinary in a condition for actual service, and for completing those the building of which has already been authorized by Congress. The money may also be applied to the completion and repair of our fortifications, and in placing them in a state of security and defence against any attack. Should it become necessary to call out the militia under existing laws, to garrison these fortifications, or defend our coast, this money may also be expended for that purpose. There is nothing in the language of the appropriation to justify the construction that the President might raise new armies, and create new officers to command them.

It is my own impression that there will be no necessity for expending any portion of this money. If there should be, however: and it is the part of wisdom to provide against such a contingency; let the responsibility rest upon those who refuse the appropriation. The country will be left defenceless, and the very knowledge of this circumstance may invite an attack.

The entire Fortification Bill failed to be passed at this session, in consequence of the disagreement between the two houses in 243regard to this three million appropriation. At the next session, which began in December, 1835, Colonel Benton of Missouri introduced in the Senate certain resolutions for setting apart so much of the surplus revenue as might be necessary for the defence and permanent security of the country. On the 1st and 2d of February, 1836, Mr. Buchanan addressed the Senate on these resolutions as follows:

Mr. President: I am much better pleased with the first resolution offered by the Senator from Missouri (Mr. Benton) since he has modified it upon the suggestion of the Senator from Tennessee (Mr. Grundy). When individuals have more money than they know how to expend, they often squander it foolishly. The remark applies, perhaps, with still greater force to nations. When our Treasury is overflowing, Congress, who are but mere trustees for the people, ought to be especially on their guard against wasteful expenditures of the public money. The surplus can be applied to some good and useful purpose. I am willing to grant all that may be necessary for the public defence but no more. I am therefore pleased that the resolution has assumed its present form.

The true question involved in this discussion is, on whom ought the responsibility to rest for having adjourned on the 3d of March last without providing for the defence of the country. There can be no doubt a fearful responsibility rests somewhere. For my own part, I should have been willing to leave the decision of this question to our constituents. I am a man of peace; and dislike the crimination and recrimination which this discussion must necessarily produce. But it is vain to regret what cannot now be avoided. The friends of the administration have been attacked; and we must now defend ourselves. I deem it necessary, therefore, to state the reasons why I voted, on the 3d of March last, in favor of the appropriation of three millions for the defence of the country, and why I glory in that vote.

The language used by Senators in reference to this appropriation has been very strong. It has been denounced as a violation of the Constitution. It has been declared to be such a measure as would not have received the support of the minority, had they believed it could prevail, and they would be held responsible for it. It has been stigmatized as most unusual—most astonishing—most surprising. And finally, to cap the climax, it has been proclaimed that the passage of such an appropriation would be virtually to create a dictator, and to surrender the power of the purse and the sword into the hands of the President.

I voted for that appropriation under the highest convictions of public duty, and I now intend to defend my vote against all these charges.

In examining the circumstances which not only justified this appropriation, but rendered it absolutely necessary, I am forced into the discussion of the French question. We have been told, that if we should go to war with France, we are the authors of that war. The Senator from New Jersey (Mr. Southard), has declared that it will be produced by the boastful vanity of one man, the petulance of another, and the fitful violence of a third. It would not be difficult to conjecture who are the individuals to whom the Senator alludes. He has also informed us, that in the event of such a war, the guilt which must rest somewhere will be tremendous.

Now, sir, I shall undertake to prove, that scarcely an example exists in history of a powerful and independent nation having suffered such wrongs and indignities as we have done from France, with so much patience and forbearance. If France should now resort to arms,—if our defenceless seacoast should be plundered,—if the blood of our citizens should be shed,—the responsibility of the Senate, to use the language of the gentleman, will be tremendous. I shall not follow the example of the Senator, and say, their guilt,—because that would be to attribute to them an evil intention, which I believe did not exist. In discussing this subject, I shall first present to the view of the Senate the precise attitude of the two nations towards each other, when the appropriation of three millions was refused, and then examine the reasons which have been urged to justify this refusal. After having done so, I shall exhibit our relations with France as they exist at the present moment, for the purpose of proving that we ought now to adopt the resolutions of the gentleman from Missouri, and grant all necessary appropriations for the defence of the country.

In discussing this subject, it is not my intention to follow the fortification bill either into the chamber of the committee of conference, or into the hall of the House of Representatives. It is not my purpose to explain the confusion which then existed, and which always must exist after midnight, on the last evening of the session. I shall contend that the Senate ought to have voted the three millions; that the fortification bill ought to have passed the Senate with this amendment; and that, therefore, the Senate is responsible not only for the loss of this appropriation, but for that of the entire bill.

What then was the attitude in which we stood towards France at the moment when the Senate rejected this appropriation for the defence of the country? What, at that moment, was known, or ought to have been known, in regard to this question by every Senator on this floor?

The justice of our claims upon France are now admitted by all mankind. Our generosity was equal to their justice. When she was crushed in the dust by Europe in arms—when her cities were garrisoned by a foreign foe—when her independence was trampled under foot, we refused to urge our claims. This was due to our ancient ally. It was due to our grateful remembrance of the days of other years. The testimony of Lafayette conclusively establishes this fact. In the Chamber of Deputies, on 13th June, 1833, he declared that we had refused to unite with the enemies of France in urging our claims in 1814 and 1815; and that, if we had done so, these claims would then have been settled. This circumstance will constitute one of the brightest pages of our history.

Was the sum secured to our injured fellow-citizens by the treaty of the 4th July, 1831, more than they had a right to demand? Let the report of our Committee on Foreign Relations, at the last session, answer this question. They concur entirely with the President, in the statement he had made in his message, that it was absolutely certain the indemnity fell far short of the actual amount of our just claims, independently of damages and interest for the detention; and that it was well known at the time that in this respect, the settlement involved a sacrifice. But there is now no longer room for any conjecture or doubt upon this subject. The commissioners under the treaty have closed their labors. From the very nature of their constitution, it became the interest of every claimant to reduce the other claims as much as possible, so that his own dividend might thus be increased. After a laborious and patient investigation, the claims which have been allowed by the commissioners amount to $9,352,193.47. Each claimant will receive but little more than half his principal, at the end of a quarter of a century, after losing all the interest. Why then has this treaty remained without execution on the part of France, until this day? Our Committee on Foreign Relations, at the last session, declared their conviction that the King of France "had invariably, on all suitable occasions, manifested an anxious desire, faithfully and honestly, to fulfil the engagements contracted under his authority and in his name." They say, that "the opposition to the execution of the treaty, and the payment of our just claims, does not proceed from the king's government, but from a majority in the Chamber of Deputies."

Now, sir, it is my purpose to contest this opinion, and to show, as I think I can conclusively, that it is not a just inference from the facts.

And here, to prevent all possible misconstruction, either on this side, or on the other side of the Atlantic, if by any accident my humble remarks should ever travel to such a distance, permit me to say that I am solely responsible for them myself. These opinions were in a degree formed while I was in a foreign land, and were there freely expressed upon all suitable occasions. I was then beyond the sphere of party influence and felt only as an American citizen.

Is it not then manifest, to use the language of Mr. Livingston in his note to the Count de Rigny of the 3d August, 1834, that the French government have never appreciated the importance of the subject at its just value? There are two modes in which the king could have manifested this anxious desire faithfully to fulfil the treaty. These are, by words and by actions. When a man's words and his actions correspond, you have the highest evidence of his sincerity. Even then he may be a hypocrite in the eyes of that Being before whom the fountains of human action are unveiled. But when a man's words and his actions are at variance,—when he promises and does not perform or even attempt to perform,—when "he speaks the word of 246promise to the ear and breaks it to the hope,"—the whole world will at once pronounce him insincere. If this be true in the transactions of common life, with how much more force does it apply to the intercourse between diplomatists? The deceitfulness of diplomacy has become almost a proverb. In Europe the talent of over-reaching gives a minister the glory of diplomatic skill. The French school has been distinguished in this art. To prove it, I need only mention the name of Talleyrand. The American school teaches far different lessons. On this our success has, in a great degree, depended. The skillful diplomatists of Europe are foiled by the downright honesty and directness of purpose which have characterized all our negotiations.

Even the established forms of diplomacy contain much unmeaning language, which is perfectly understood by everybody, and deceives nobody. If ministers have avowed their sincerity, and their ardent desire to execute the treaty; to deny them, on our part, would be insulting, and might lead to the most unpleasant consequences. In forming an estimate of their intentions, therefore, every wise man will regard their actions, rather than their words. By their deeds they shall be known. Let us then test the French government by this touchstone of truth.

The ratifications of the treaty of the 4th July, 1831, were exchanged at Washington, on the 2d February, 1832. When this treaty arrived in Paris, the French Chambers were in session, and they continued in session for several weeks. They did not adjourn, until the

19th of April. No time more propitious for presenting this treaty to the Chambers, could have been selected, than that very moment. Europe then was, as I believe it still is, one vast magazine of gunpowder. It was generally believed, that the Polish revolution was the spark which would produce the explosion. There was imminent danger of a continental war, in which France, to preserve her existence, would have to put forth all her energies. Russia, Prussia, and Austria, were armed and ready for the battle. It was then the clear policy of France to be at a good understanding with the United States. If it had been the ardent desire of the king's government, to carry into effect the stipulations of the treaty, they would have presented it to the Chambers before their adjournment. This would undoubtedly have been the course pursued by any President of the United States, under similar circumstances. But the treaty was not presented.

I freely admit, that this omission, standing by itself, might be explained by the near approach of the adjournment, at the time the treaty arrived from Washington. It is one important link, however, in the chain of circumstances, which cannot be omitted.

The Government of the United States proceeded immediately to execute their part of the treaty. By the act of the 13th July, 1832, the duties on French wines were reduced according to its terms, to take effect from the day of the exchange of ratifications. At the same session, the Congress of the United States, impelled no doubt by their kindly feelings towards France, which had been roused into action by what they believed to be a final and equitable settlement of all our disputes, voluntarily reduced the duty upon silks coming from this side of the Cape of Good Hope to five per cent., whilst those beyond were fixed at ten per cent. And at the next session, on the 2d of March, 1833, this duty of five per cent. was taken off altogether; and ever since, French silks have been admitted into our country free of duty. There is now, in fact, a discriminating duty of ten per cent. in their favor, over silks from beyond the Cape of Good Hope.

What has France gained by these measures, in duties on her wines and her silks, which she would otherwise have been bound to pay? I have called upon the Secretary of the Treasury, for the purpose of ascertaining the amount. I now hold in my hand a tabular statement, prepared at my request, which shows, that had the duties remained what they were at the date of the ratification of the treaty, these articles, since that time, would have paid into the Treasury on the 30th September, 1834, the sum of $3,061,525. Judging from the large importations which have since been made, I feel no hesitation in declaring it as my opinion that, at the present moment, these duties would amount to more than the whole indemnity which France has engaged to pay to our fellow-citizens. Before the conclusion of the ten years mentioned in the treaty, she will have been freed from the payment of duties to an amount considerably above twelve millions of dollars.

By the same act of the 13th July, 1832, a board of commissioners was established to receive, examine, and decide the claims of our citizens under the treaty, who were to meet on the first day of the following August. This act also directed the Secretary of the Treasury to cause the several instalments, with the interest thereon, payable to the United States in virtue of the convention, to be received from the French government and transferred to the United States in such manner as he may deem best. In this respect the provisions of the act corresponded with the terms of the treaty, which prescribe that the money shall be paid into the hands of such person or persons as shall be authorized to receive it by the Government of the United States.

Were the French government immediately informed of all these proceedings? Who can doubt it? Certainly no one at all acquainted with the vigilance and zeal of their diplomatic agents.

The 19th of November, 1832, the day for the meeting of the Chambers, at length arrived.—Every American was anxious to know what the king would say in his speech concerning the treaty. No one could doubt but that he would strongly recommend to the Chambers to make the appropriation of twenty-five millions of francs, the first instalment of which would become due on the 2d of February following. All, however, which the speech contains in relation to the treaty is comprised in the following sentences: "I have also ordered my minister to communicate to you the treaty concluded on the 4th July, 1831, between my government and that of the United States of America. This arrangement puts an end to the reciprocal claims of the two countries." Now, sir, I am well aware of the brevity and non-committal character of kings' speeches in Europe. I know the necessity which exists there for circumspection and caution. But making every fair allowance for these considerations, I may at least say, that the speech does not manifest an anxious desire to carry the treaty into effect. What might the king have said; what ought he have said; what would he have said had he felt this anxious desire? It might all have been embraced in a single additional sentence, such as the following: "The Congress of the United States have already provided for the admission of French wines into their ports upon the terms of this treaty, and have voluntarily reduced their duties upon French silks, I must, therefore, request you to grant me the means of discharging the first instalment which will become due, under this treaty, on the 2d day of February next." The king did not even ask the Chambers for the money necessary to redeem the faith of France. In this respect the debt due to the United States is placed in striking contrast to the Greek loan.—Immediately after the two sentences of the speech, which I have already quoted, the king proceeds: "You will likewise be called to examine the treaty by which Prince Otho of Bavaria is called to the throne of Greece. I shall have to request from you the means of guaranteeing, in union with my allies, a loan which is indispensable for the establishment of the new State founded by our cares and concurrence."

The establishment of the new State founded by our cares and concurrence! Russia, sir, has made greater advances by her skill in diplomacy than by her vast physical power. Unless I am much mistaken, the creation of this new State, with Prince Otho as its king, will accomplish the very object which it was the interest and purpose of France to defeat. It will, in the end, virtually convert Greece into a Russian province. I could say much more on the subject, but I forbear. My present purpose is merely to present in a striking view, the difference between the king's language in relation to our treaty, and that treaty which placed the son of the king of Bavaria on the throne of Greece.

Time passed away, and the 2d February, 1833, the day when the first instalment under the treaty became due, arrived. It was to be paid "into the hands of such person or persons as shall be authorized by the Government of the United States to receive it." The money on that day ought to have been ready at Paris. But strange, but most wonderful as it may appear, although the Chambers had been in session from the 19th of November until the 2d of February, the king's government had never even presented the treaty to the Chambers,—had never even asked them for a grant of the money necessary to fulfil its engagements. Well might Mr. Livingston say, that they had never properly appreciated the importance of the subject.

The Government of the United States, knowing that the king in his speech had promised to present the treaty to the Chambers, and knowing that they had been in session since November, might have taken means to demand the first instalment at Paris on the 2d day of February. Strictly speaking, it was their duty to do so, acting as trustees for the claimants. But they did not draw a bill of exchange at Washington for the first instalment, until five days after it had become due at Paris. This bill was not presented to the

French government for payment until the 23d of March, 1833. Even at that day the French ministry had not presented either the treaty, or a bill to carry it into effect, to the Chambers. The faith of France was thus violated by the neglect of the king's government, long before any bill was presented. They, and not the Chambers, are responsible for this violation. It was even impossible for the Chambers to prevent it. Had this treaty and bill been laid before them in time to have enabled them to redeem the faith of France, the loyalty of the French character would never have permitted them to be guilty of a positive violation of national honor. The faith of the nation was forfeited before they were called upon to act. The responsibility was voluntarily assumed by the king's ministers. The Chambers are clear of it. Besides, the ministry were all powerful with the Chambers during that session. They carried everything they urged. Even the bill providing the means of guaranteeing the Greek loan became a law. Can it then for a single moment be believed that if a bill to carry into effect our treaty—a treaty securing such important advantages to France—had been presented at an early period of the session, and had been pressed by the ministry, that they would have failed in the attempt? At all events, it was their imperative duty to pursue this course. The aspect of the political horizon in Europe was still lowering. There was still imminent danger of a general war. France was still in a position to make her dread any serious misunderstanding with the United States.

After all this, on the 26th March, the Duke de Broglie, in a note to Mr. Niles, our chargé d'affaires at Paris, stated that it was "a source of regret, and, indeed, of astonishment, that the Government of the United States did not think proper to have an understanding with that of France, before taking this step." What step? The demand of an honest debt, almost two months after it had been due, under a solemn treaty. Indeed, the duke, judging from the tone of his note, appears almost to have considered the demand an insult. To make a positive engagement to pay a fixed sum on a particular day, and when that sum is demanded nearly two months after, to express astonishment to the creditor, would, in private life, be considered trifling and evasive.

The excuse made by the French ministry for their conduct is altogether vain. Had they dreaded the vote of the Chambers—had they been afraid to appear before them with their treaty and their bill, they would, and they ought to have communicated their apprehensions to this Government, and asked it to suspend the demand of the money. But they had never whispered such a suspicion, after the exchange of their ratifications of the treaty; and the first intimation of it on this side of the Atlantic, was accompanied by the astounding fact that the French government had dishonored our bill. It is true, that before the treaty was signed, they had expressed some apprehensions to Mr. Rives on this subject. These, it would seem, from their subsequent conduct, were merely diplomatic, and intended to produce delay; because, from the date of the treaty, on the 4th July, 1831, until after our bill of exchange was dishonored in March, 1833, no intimation of danger from that quarter was ever suggested. These circumstances made a great noise throughout Europe, and soon became the subject of general remark.

On the 6th of April, 1833, a year and more than two months after the exchange of the ratifications at Washington, the treaty and bill were first presented to the French Chambers. The session closed on the 25th of April, without any further action on the subject. No attempt was made by the ministry to press it; and as the session would terminate so soon, perhaps no attempt ought to have been made. But, as a new session was to commence the day after the termination of the old, and to continue two months, a favorable opportunity was thus presented to urge the passage of the law upon the Chambers. Was this done? No, sir. The ministry still continued to pursue the same course. They suffered the remainder of the month of April to pass, the month of May to pass, and not until the eleventh of June, only fifteen days before the close of the session, did they again present the bill to carry into effect the treaty. It was referred to a committee, of which Mr. Benjamin Delessert was the chairman. On the 18th of June, he made a report. This report contains a severe reprimand of the French government for not having presented the bill at an earlier period of the session; and expresses the hope that the treaty may be communicated at the opening of the next session. If we are to judge of the opinion of the Chamber from the tone and character of this report, instead of being hostile to the execution of the treaty, had it been presented to them in proper time, they felt every disposition to regard it in a favorable light. I shall read the whole report—it is very short, and is as follows:

"Gentlemen: The committee charged by you, to examine the bill relative to the treaty, concluded on the 4th of July, 1831, between France and the United States, has demanded a number of documents and reports, which must be examined, in order to obtain a complete knowledge of so important a transaction.

"The committee was soon convinced that a conscientious examination of these papers would require much time; and that, at so advanced a period of the session, its labors would have no definitive result. It regrets that, from motives which the government only can explain, the bill was not presented earlier to the Chamber for discussion. It regrets this so much the more as it is convinced of the importance of the treaty, which essentially interests our maritime commerce, our agriculture, and our manufactures.

"Several chambers of commerce, particularly those of Paris and Lyons, have manifested an ardent desire that the business should be speedily terminated.

"The committee would be satisfied if, after a deeper study of the question, it could enlighten the Chamber with regard to the justice of the claims alleged by each of the parties to the treaty, and which form the basis of it; 251but as time does not allow a definitive report to be made on the subject, it considers itself as the organ of the Chamber, in expressing the wish that this treaty be communicated, at the opening of the next session; and that its result may be such as to strengthen the bonds of friendship, which must ever exist between two nations so long united by common interest and sympathy."

After a careful review of this whole transaction, I am convinced that the government of France never would have pursued such a course towards us, had they entertained a just sense of our power, and our willingness to exert it in behalf of our injured fellow-citizens. Had Russia or Austria been her creditors, instead of ourselves, the debt would have been paid when it became due; or, at the least, the ministers of the king would have exerted themselves, in a far different manner, to obtain the necessary appropriation from the Chambers. I am again constrained, however reluctantly, to adopt the opinion which I had formed at the moment. Our fierce political strife in this country is not understood in Europe; and least of all, perhaps, in France. During the autumn of 1832, and the session of 1832–3, it was believed abroad that we were on the very eve of a revolution; that our glorious Union was at the point of dissolution. I speak, sir, from actual knowledge. Whilst the advocates of despotism were looking forward, with eager hope, to see the last free republic blotted out from the face of nations, the friends of freedom throughout the world were disheartened, and dreaded the result of our experiment. The storm did rage in this country with the utmost violence. It is no wonder that those friends of liberty, on the other side of the Atlantic, who did not know how to appreciate the recuperative energies of a free and enlightened people, governed by Federal and State institutions of their own choice, should have been alarmed for the safety of the Republic. For myself I can say that I never felt any serious apprehension; yet the thrill of delight with which I received the news of the passage of the famous compromise law of March, 1833, can never be effaced from my memory. I did not then stop to inquire into the nature of its provisions. It was enough for me to know that the Republic was safe, not only in my own opinion, but in the opinion of the world.

Suppose, sir, that the President of the United States, under similar circumstances, had withheld a treaty from Congress requiring an appropriation, for fourteen months after it had been duly ratified, and had thus forfeited the national faith to a foreign government, what would have been the consequence? Sir, he ought to have been, he would have been impeached. No circumstances could ever have justified such conduct in the eyes of the American Congress or the American people.

After all the provocation which the President had received, as the representative of his country, what was his conduct? It might have been supposed that this violent man, as the Senator from New Jersey (Mr. Southard) has designated him, would at once have recommended decisive measures. Judging from his energy,—from his well-known devotion to the interests of 252his country,—and above all, from his famous declaration to ask nothing from foreign nations but what was right, and to submit to nothing wrong, I should have expected from him an indignant message at the commencement of the next session of Congress. Instead of that, the message of December, 1833, in relation to French affairs, is of the mildest character. It breathes a spirit of confident hope that our ancient ally would do us justice during the next session of the Chambers. His exposition of the subject is concluded by the following declaration:

"As this subject involves important interests, and has attracted a considerable share of the public attention, I have deemed it proper to make this explicit statement of its actual condition; and should I be disappointed in the hope now entertained, the subject will be again brought to the notice of Congress in such a manner as the occasion may require."

And thus ends the first act of this astonishing historical drama. Throughout the whole of it, beginning, middle and end, the French government, and not the French Chambers, were exclusively to blame.

We have now arrived at the mission of Mr. Livingston. He reached Paris in September, 1833. The Duc de Broglie assured him "that the king's government would willingly and without hesitation promise to direct the deliberations of the Chambers to the projet de loi relative to the execution of the convention of July 4, 1831, on the day after the Chamber is constituted, and to employ every means to secure the happy conclusion of an affair, the final determination of which the United States cannot desire more ardently than ourselves." After this assurance, and after all that had passed, it was confidently expected that the king would, in strong terms, have recommended the adoption of the appropriation by the Chambers. In this we were again doomed to disappointment. In his opening speech he made no direct allusion to the subject. He simply says, that, "the financial laws, and those required for the execution of treaties, will be presented to you." The bill was presented, and debated, and finally rejected by the Chamber of Deputies on the 1st day of April, 1834, by a vote of 176 to 168. It is not my present purpose to dwell upon the causes of this rejection. No doubt the principal one was that the French ministers were surrounded near the conclusion of the debate, and were unable at the moment to show that the captures at St. Sebastians were not included in our treaty with Spain. I am sorry they were not better prepared upon this point; but I attribute to them no blame on that account.

It has been urged over and over again, both on this floor and elsewhere, that the rejection of the treaty was occasioned by the publication in this country of Mr. Rives's letter to Mr. Livingston of the 8th of July, 1831. Is this the fact? If it be so it ought to be known to the world. If it be not, both the character of this Government and of Mr. Rives should be rescued from the imputation. What is the opinion expressed in this letter? Is it that the American claimants would obtain, under the treaty, more than the amount of their just claims? No such thing. Is it that they would obtain the 253amount of their just claims with interest? Not even this. The negotiator merely expresses the opinion that they would receive every cent of the principal. He does not allege that they would receive one cent of interest for a delay of nearly a quarter of a century. This opinion is evidently founded upon that expressed by Mr. Gallatin in a despatch dated on the 14th January, 1822, cited by Mr. Rives, in which the former expresses his belief that five millions of dollars would satisfy all our just claims. It ought to be observed that the sum stipulated to be paid by the treaty is only 25,000,000 of francs, or about $4,700,000; and that more than nine years had elapsed between the date of Mr. Gallatin's despatch and the signing of the treaty. These facts all appear on the face of the letter, with the additional fact that the statements of the claimants, which have from time to time been presented to Congress, carry the amount of the claims much higher. These statements, however, Mr. Rives did not believe were a safe guide.

This is the amount of the letter, when fairly analyzed, which, it is alleged, destroyed the treaty before the French Chambers. If a copy of it had been placed in the hands of every Deputy, it could not possibly have produced any such effect.

That it did not occasion the rejection of the treaty is absolutely certain. I have examined the whole debate for the purpose of discovering any allusion to this letter; but I have examined it in vain. Not the slightest trace of the letter can be detected in any of the numerous speeches delivered on that occasion. The topics of opposition were various, and several of them of a strange character; but the letter is not even once alluded to throughout the whole debate. If its existence were known at the time in the French Chamber, this letter, written by a minister to his own government, expressing a favorable opinion of the result of his own negotiations, was a document of a character so natural, so much to be expected, that not one Deputy in opposition to the treaty believed it to be of sufficient importance even to merit a passing notice. Still, I have often thought it strange it had never been mentioned in the debate. The mystery is now resolved. The truth is, this letter, which is alleged to have produced such fatal effects, was entirely unknown to the members of the French Chamber when they rejected the treaty. This fact is well established by a letter from Mr. Jay, the chairman of the committee appointed by the Chamber of Deputies to investigate our claims, addressed to Mr. Gibbes, and dated at Paris on the 24th January, 1835. I shall read it.

(Extract of a letter from Mr. Jay to Mr. Gibbes, dated 24th January, 1835.)—"It is asserted in the American prints that the rejection of the American treaty by the Chamber of Deputies, at their last session, was chiefly owing to the publication of a letter from Mr. Rives to his own Government. This is an error, which justice to that distinguished statesman, and a sense of his unremitting exertions to promote the interests of his Government while here, induce me formally to contradict. No such evidence appears in the debates; and in none of my conversations with the members have I heard his letter 254alleged as the motive for disputing the amount due. I much question, indeed, if any other Deputy than myself ever read the letter alluded to."

We have now arrived at that point of time when a majority of the French Chambers arrayed themselves against the treaty. This decision was made on the 1st April, 1834. Some apprehensions then prevailed among the king and his ministers. The business was now becoming serious. New assurances had now become necessary to prevent the President from presenting the whole transaction to Congress, which they knew would still be in session, when the information of the rejection would reach the United States. In his annual message, at the commencement of the session, it will be recollected, he had declared that should he be disappointed in the hope then entertained, he would again bring the subject before Congress, in such a manner as the occasion might require. They knew that he was a man who performed his promises, and a great effort was to be made to induce him to change his purpose.

Accordingly a French brig of war, the Cuirassier, is fitted out with despatches to Mr. Serrurier. They reached him on the 3d June. On the 4th, he has an interview with Mr. McLane, and makes explanations which the latter very properly requests may be reduced to writing. In compliance with this request, the French minister, on the 5th, addresses a note to Mr. McLane. After expressing the regrets of the French government at the rejection of the bill, he uses the following language: "The king's government, sir, after this rejection, the object of so much painful disappointment to both governments, has deliberated, and its unanimous determination has been to make an appeal from the first vote of the present Chamber to the next Chamber, and to appear before the next legislature with its treaty and its bill in hand.

"It flatters itself that the light already thrown upon this serious question, during these first debates, and the expression of the public wishes becoming each day more clear and distinct, and, finally, a more mature examination, will have, in the mean time, modified the minds of persons, and that its own conviction will become the conviction of the Chambers. The king's government, sir, will make every loyal and constitutional effort to that effect, and will do all that its persevering persuasion of the justice and of the mutual advantages of the treaty authorizes you to expect from it. Its intention, moreover, is to do all that our constitution allows, to hasten, as much as possible, the period of the new presentation of the rejected law.

"Such, sir, are the sentiments, such the intentions of his majesty's government. I think I may rely that, on its part, the Government of the Republic will avoid, with foreseeing solicitude, in this transitory state of things, all that might become a fresh cause of irritation between the two countries, compromit the treaty, and raise up an obstacle perhaps insurmountable, to the views of reconciliation and harmony which animate the king's council."

Now, sir, examine this letter, even without any reference to the answer of Mr. McLane, and can there be a doubt as to its true construction? It was not merely the disposition, but "it was the intention of the king's government to do all that their constitution allows; to hasten, as much as possible, 255the period of the new presentation of the rejected law." The President knew that under the constitution of France the king could at any time convoke the Chambers upon three weeks' notice. It was in his power, therefore, to present this law to the Chambers whenever he thought proper. The promise was to hasten this presentation as much as possible. Without any thing further the President had a right confidently to expect that the Chambers would be convoked in season to enable him to present their decision to the Congress of the United States in his next annual message. The assurance was made on the 5th June, and Congress did not assemble until the beginning of December. But the letter of Mr. McLane, of the 27th June, removes all possible doubt from this subject. He informs Mr. Serrurier that "the President is still unable to understand the causes which led to the result of the proceeding in the Chamber, especially when he recollected the assurances which had so often been made by the king and his ministers, of their earnest desire to carry the convention into effect, and the support which the Chamber had afforded in all the other measures proposed by the king." And again:

"The assurances which M. Serrurier's letter contains, of the adherence of the king's government to the treaty, of its unanimous determination to appeal from the decision of the present to the new Chamber, and its conviction that the public wish, and a mature examination of the subject, will lead to a favorable result, and its intention to make every constitutional effort to that effect, and finally, its intention to do all that the constitution allows to hasten the presentation of the new law, have been fully considered by the President.

"Though fully sensible of the high responsibility which he owes to the American people, in a matter touching so nearly the national honor, the President, still trusting to the good faith and justice of France, willing to manifest a spirit of forbearance so long as it may be consistent with the rights and dignity of his country, and truly desiring to preserve those relations of friendship, which, commencing in our struggle for independence, form the true policy of both nations, and sincerely respecting the king's wishes, will rely upon the assurances which M. Serrurier has been instructed to offer, and will therefore await with confidence the promised appeal to the new Chamber.

"The President, in desiring the undersigned to request that his sentiments on this subject may be made known to his majesty's government, has instructed him also to state his expectation that the king, seeing the great interests now involved in the subject, and the deep solicitude felt by the people of the United States respecting it, will enable him, when presenting the subject to Congress, as his duty will require him to do at the opening of their next session, to announce at that time the result of that appeal, and of his majesty's efforts for its success."

Had this letter of Mr. McLane placed a different construction upon the engagement of the French government from that which Mr. Serrurier intended to communicate, it was his duty to make the necessary explanations 256without delay. He, in that case, would have done so instantly. It was a subject of too much importance to suffer any misapprehension to exist concerning it for a single moment.

Notwithstanding all which had passed, the President, on the faith of these assurances of the French government, suffered Congress to adjourn without presenting the subject to their view. This rash, this violent man, instigated by his own good feelings towards our ancient ally, and by his love of peace, determines that he would try them once more, that he once more would extend the olive branch before presenting to Congress and the nation a history of our wrongs. I confess I do not approve of this policy. I think the time had then arrived to manifest to France some sensibility on our part on account of her delay in executing the treaty. I believe that such a course would have been dictated by sound policy.

What were the consequences of this new manifestation of the kindly feelings of the President towards France? Was it properly appreciated by the French government? Was it received in the liberal and friendly spirit from which it had proceeded? Let the sequel answer these questions. I shall read you Mr. Livingston's opinion on the subject. In a letter to Mr. Forsyth, under date of the 22d November, 1834, he thus expresses himself: "I do not hope for any decision on our affairs before the middle of January. One motive for delay is an expectation that the message of the President may arrive before the discussion, and that it may contain something to show a strong national feeling on the subject. This is not mere conjecture: I know the fact; and I repeat now, from a full knowledge of the case, what I have more than once stated in my former despatches as my firm persuasion, that the moderate tone taken by our Government, when the rejection was first known, was attributed by some to indifference, or to a conviction on the part of the President that he would not be supported in any strong measure by the people, and by others to a consciousness that the convention had given us more than we were entitled to ask."

I shall now proceed to show in what manner the French government performed the engagement which had been made by their representative in Washington to hasten the presentation of the rejected law as much as possible.

The Chambers met on the 31st July, and the king made them a speech. This speech contains no allusion to the subject of the treaty except the following: "The laws necessary for carrying treaties into effect, and those still required for the accomplishment of the promises of the Chamber, will be presented to you in the course of this session." The rejected bill was not presented. After a session of two weeks, the Chambers were prorogued on the 16th August until the 29th December,—a day, almost a month after the next meeting of Congress.

I admit that strong reasons existed for dispensing with that part of the obligation which required the French government to present the bill at this short session. No good reason has ever been alleged to excuse them for proroguing the Chambers until so late a day as the 29th of December. They might have met, and they ought to have met, at an early period of the autumn. They have heretofore met, on different occasions, for the despatch of business, in every month of the year. It was in vain that Mr. Livingston urged the necessity of an earlier meeting on the Count de Rigny. It was in vain that he appealed to the positive engagement of the French government made by Mr. Serrurier. It was in vain that he declared to him, "that the President could not, at the opening of the next session of Congress, avoid laying before that body a statement of the then position of affairs on this interesting subject, nor, under any circumstances, permit that session to end, as it must, on the third of March, without recommending such measures as he may deem that justice and the honor of the country may require." All his remonstrances were disregarded. Instead of hastening the presentation of the rejected law as much as possible, they refused to assemble the Chambers in time even to present the bill before the meeting of Congress. Their meeting was so long delayed, as to render it almost impossible that their determination should be known in this country before the close of the session, notwithstanding the President had agreed not to present the subject to Congress at the previous session, under a firm conviction that he would receive this determination in time to lay it before them at the commencement of their next session. Is there a Senator in this hall, who can believe for a moment, that if the President had been informed the rejected bill would not be laid before the Chambers until the 29th December, he would have refrained from communicating to Congress, at their previous session, the state of the controversy between the two countries? Upon this construction, the engagement of the French government was mere words, without the slightest meaning; and the national vessel which brought it in such solemn form, might much better have remained at home. What was the apology—what was the pretext under which the king's government refused to assemble the Chambers at an earlier period? It was, that Mr. Serrurier had made no engagement to that effect, and that the intention which he had expressed in behalf of his government to do all that the constitution allows, to hasten, as much as possible, the period of the new presentation of the rejected law, meant no more than that this was their disposition. The word "intention" is thus changed into "disposition" by the Count de Rigny, and the whole engagement which was presented to the President in such an imposing form, was thus converted into a mere unmeaning profession of their desire to hasten this presentation as much as possible.

Sir, at the commencement of the session of Congress, it became the duty of the President to speak, and what could any American expect that he would say? The treaty had been violated in the first instance, by the ministers of the French king, in neglecting to lay it before the Chambers until after the first instalment was due. It was then twice submitted, at so late a period of the session, that it was impossible for the Chambers to examine and decide the question before their adjournment. On the last of these occasions, the chairman of the committee, to which the subject was referred, had reported a severe reprimand against the government, for not having sooner presented the bill, and expressed a hope that it might be presented at an early period of the next session. It was then rejected by the Chamber of Deputies; and when the French government had solemnly engaged to hasten the presentation of the rejected law, as soon as their constitution would permit, they prorogue the Chambers to the latest period which custom sanctions, in the very face of the remonstrances of the minister of the United States. I ask again, sir, before such an array of circumstances, what could any man, what could any American expect the President would say in his message? The cup of forbearance had been drained by him to the very dregs. It was then his duty to speak so as to be heard and to be regarded on the other side of the Atlantic. If the same spirit which dictated the message, or anything like it, had been manifested by Congress, the money, in my opinion, would ere this have been paid.

The question was then reduced to a single point. We demanded the execution of a solemn treaty; it had been refused. France had promised again to bring the question before the Chambers as soon as possible. The Chambers were prorogued until the latest day. The President had every reason to believe that France was trifling with us, and that the treaty would again be rejected. Is there a Senator, within the sound of my voice, who, if France had finally determined not to pay the money, would have tamely submitted to this violation of national faith? Not one!

The late war with Great Britain elevated us in the estimation of the whole world. In every portion of Europe, we have reason to be proud that we are American citizens. We have paid dearly for the exalted character we now enjoy among the nations, and we ought to preserve it and transmit it unimpaired to future generations. To them it will be a most precious inheritance.

If, after having compelled the weaker nations of the world to pay us indemnities for captures made from our citizens, we should cower before the power of France, and abandon our rights against her, when they had been secured by a solemn treaty, we should be regarded as a mere Hector among the nations. The same course which you have pursued towards the weak, you must pursue towards the powerful. If you do not, your name will become a by-word and a proverb.

But under all the provocations which the country had received, what is the character of that message? Let it be scanned with eagle eyes, and there is nothing in its language at which the most fastidious critic can take offence. It contains an enumeration of our wrongs in mild and dignified language, and a contingent recommendation of reprisals, in case the indemnity should again be rejected by the Chambers. But in this, and in all other respects, it defers entirely to the judgment of Congress. Every idea of an intended menace is excluded by the President's express declaration. He says: "Such a measure ought not to be considered by France as a menace. Her pride and power are too well known to expect any thing from her fears, and preclude the necessity of the declaration, that nothing partaking of the character of intimidation is intended by us."

I ask again, is it not forbearing in its language? Is there a single statement in it not founded upon truth? Does it even state the whole truth against France? Are there not strong points omitted? All these questions must be answered in the affirmative. On this subject we have strong evidence from the Duke de Broglie himself. In his famous letter to

Mr. Pageot of June 17th, 1835,—the arrow of the Parthian as he flew,—this fact is admitted. He says:

"If we examine in detail the message of the President of the United States, (I mean that part of it which concerns the relations between the United States and France,) it will possibly be found, that passing successively from phrase to phrase, none will be met that cannot bear an interpretation more or less plausible, nor of which, strictly speaking, it cannot be said that it is a simple exposé of such a fact, true in itself, or the assertion of such or such a right which no one contests, or the performance of such or such an obligation imposed on the President by the very nature of his functions. There will certainly be found several in which the idea of impeaching the good faith of the French government, or of acting upon it through menace or intimidation, is more or less disavowed."

It was the whole message, and not any of the detached parts, at which the French government chose to take offence.

It is not my present purpose to discuss the propriety of the recommendation of reprisals, or whether that was the best mode of redress which could have been suggested. Some decided recommendation, however, was required from the executive, both by public opinion and by the wrongs which we had so long patiently endured.

Who can suppose that the executive intended to menace France, or to obtain from her fears what would be denied by her sense of justice? The President, in this very message, expressly disclaims such an idea. Her history places her far above any such imputation. The wonder is, how she could have ever supposed the President, against his own solemn declaration, intended to do her any such injustice. She ought to have considered it as it was, a mere executive recommendation to Congress, not intended for her at all—not to operate upon her fears, but upon their deliberations in deciding whether any and what measures should be adopted to secure the execution of the treaty. But on this subject I shall say more hereafter.

We have now arrived at the special message of the President to Congress of the 26th February last; a document which has a most important bearing on the appropriation of the three millions which was rejected by the Senate. I have given this historical sketch of our controversy with France, for the purpose of bringing Senators to the very point of time, and to the precise condition of this question, when the Senate negatived that appropriation.

What had Congress done in relation to the French question when this message was presented to us? Nothing, sir, nothing. The Senate had unanimously passed a resolution on the 15th January, that it was inexpedient, at present, to adopt any legislative measure, in regard to the state of affairs between the United States and France. This unanimity was obtained by two considerations. The one was, that the French Chambers had been convened, though not for the purpose of acting upon our treaty, on the first, instead of the twenty-ninth of December, a fact unknown to the President at the date of his message. The other, that this circumstance afforded a reasonable ground of hope, that we might learn their final determination before the close of our session on the 3d March. But whatever may have been the causes, the Senate had determined that, for the present, nothing should be done.

In the House of Representatives, at the date of the special message, on the 26th February, no measure whatever had been adopted. The President had just cause to believe that the sentiments contained in his message to Congress, at the commencement of their session, were not in unison with the feelings of either branch of the legislature. He therefore determined to lay all the information in his possession before Congress, and leave it for them to decide whether any or what measures should be adopted for the defence of the country. I shall read this message. It is as follows:

"I transmit to Congress a report from the Secretary of State, with copies of all the letters received from Mr. Livingston since the message to the House of Representatives of the 6th instant, of the instructions given to that minister, and of all the late correspondence with the French government in Paris, or in Washington, except a note of Mr. Serrurier, which, for the reasons stated in the report, is not now communicated.

"It will be seen that I have deemed it my duty to instruct Mr. Livingston to quit France with his legation, and return to the United States, if an appropriation for the fulfilment of the convention shall be refused by the Chambers.

"The subject being now, in all its present aspects, before Congress, whose right it is to decide what measures are to be pursued on that event, I deem it unnecessary to make further recommendation, being confident that, on their part, every thing will be done to maintain the rights and honor of the country which the occasion requires."

The President leaves the whole question to Congress. What was the information then communicated? That a very high state of excitement existed against us in France. That the French minister had been recalled from this country; an act which is generally the immediate precursor of hostilities between nations. Besides, Mr. Livingston, who was a competent judge and on the spot, with the best means of knowledge, informed his Government that he would not be surprised, should the law be rejected, if they anticipated our reprisals, by the seizure of our vessels in port, or the attack of our ships in the Mediterranean, by a superior force. Such were his apprehensions, upon this subject, that he felt it to be his duty, without delay, to inform Commodore Patterson of the state of things, so that he might be upon his guard.

Ought these apprehensions of Mr. Livingston to have been disregarded? Let the history of that gallant people answer this question. How often has the injustice of their cause been concealed from their own view by the dazzling brilliancy of some grand and striking exploit? Glory is their passion, and their great emperor, who knew them best, often acted upon this principle. To anticipate their enemy, and commence the war with some bold stroke, would be in perfect accordance with their character.

Every Senator, when he voted upon the appropriation, must have known, or at least might have known, all the information which was contained in the documents accompanying the President's message.

It has been objected, that if the President desired this appropriation of three millions, he ought to have recommended it in his message. I protest against this principle. He acted wisely, discreetly, and with a becoming respect for Congress, to leave the whole question to their decision. This was especially proper, as we had not thought proper to adopt any measure in relation to the subject.

Suppose the President had, in his special message, recommended this appropriation, what would have been said, and justly said, upon the subject? Denunciations the most eloquent would have resounded against him throughout the whole country, from Georgia to Maine. It would have everywhere been proclaimed as an act of executive dictation. In our then existing relations with France, it would have been said, and said with much force, that such a recommendation from the executive might have had a tendency to exasperate her people, and produce war. Besides, I shall never consent to adopt the principle that we ought to take no measures to defend the country, without the recommendation of the executive. This would be to submit to that very dictation, against which, on other occasions, gentlemen themselves have so loudly protested. No, sir, I shall always assert the perfect right of Congress to act upon such subjects, independently of any executive recommendation.

This special message was referred to the Committee on Foreign Relations, in the House of Representatives, on the 26th February. On the next day they reported three resolutions, one of which was, "that contingent preparation ought to be made, to meet any emergency growing out of our relations with France." The session was rapidly drawing to a close. But a few days of it then remained. It would have been vain to act upon this resolution. It was a mere abstraction. Had it been adopted, it could have produced no effect; the money was wanted to place the country in a state of defence, and not a mere opinion that it ought to be granted. The chairman of the Committee on Foreign Relations, therefore, on the 28th February, had this resolution laid upon the table, and gave notice that he would move an amendment to the fortification bill, appropriating three millions of dollars, one million to the army, and two millions to the navy, to provide for the contingent defence of the country.

262It has been urged, that because the President, in his last annual message, has said that this contingent appropriation was inserted according to his views, that some blame attaches to him from the mode of its introduction. Without pretending to know the fact, I will venture the assertion, that he never requested any member, either of this or the other branch of the legislature, to make such a motion. He had taken his stand—he had left the whole subject to Congress. From this he never departed. If the chairman of any committee, or any other member of the Senate or the House, called upon him to know his views upon the subject, he no doubt communicated them freely and frankly. This is his nature. Surely no blame can attach to him for having expressed his opinion upon this subject to any member who might ask it. It has been the uniform course pursued on such occasions.

On the 2d of March, the House of Representatives, by a unanimous vote, resolved that, in their opinion, the treaty with France, of the 4th July, 1831, should be maintained, and its execution insisted on. This was no party vote. It was dictated by a common American feeling, which rose superior to party. After this solemn declaration of the House, made in the face of the world, how could it be supposed they would adjourn, without endeavoring to place the country in an attitude of defence? What, sir! The representatives of the people, with an overflowing treasury, to leave the country naked and exposed to hostile invasion, and to make no provision for our navy, after having declared unanimously that the treaty should be maintained! Who could have supposed it?

On the 3d of March, upon the motion of the chairman of the Committee on Foreign Relations (Mr. Cambreleng) and in pursuance of the notice which he had given on the 28th of February, this appropriation of three millions was annexed as an amendment to the fortification bill. The vote upon the question was 109 in the affirmative, and 77 in the negative. This vote, although not unanimous, like the former, was no party vote. The bill, thus amended, was brought to the Senate. Now, sir, let me ask, if this appropriation had proceeded from the House alone, without any message or any suggestion from the executive, would this not have been a legitimate source? Ought such an appropriation to be opposed in the Senate, because it had not received executive sanction? Have the Representatives of the people no right to originate a bill for the defence and security of their constituents and their country, without first consulting the will of the President? For one, I shall never submit to any such a slavish principle. It would make the Executive every thing, and Congress nothing.

Had the indemnity been absolutely rejected by the Chambers, the two nations would have been placed in a state of defiance towards each other. In such a condition it was the right—nay, more, it was the imperative duty of the House of Representatives to make contingent preparation for the worst. The urgency of the case was still more striking, because in ten or eleven of the States Representatives could not be elected until months after the adjournment, 263and, therefore, Congress could not have been assembled to meet any emergency which might occur.

But, sir, does it require a recommendation of the Executive, or a vote of the House of Representatives, to originate such an appropriation? Any individual Senator or member of the House may do it with the strictest propriety. Did the Senator from Delaware (Mr. Clayton) ask the approbation of the President, before he made the motion at the last session, which does him so much honor, to increase the appropriation for fortifications half a million? How did the amendments proposed by the Senator from Massachusetts (Mr. Webster) to the fortification bill of the last session originate? I presume from the Committee of Finance, of which he was the chairman. No doubt he conferred with the head of the proper Executive Department, according to the custom in such cases; but still these appropriations of more than four hundred thousand dollars had their origin in that committee. It was a proper, a legitimate source. Is then the ancient practice to be changed, and must it become a standing rule that we are to appropriate no money without the orders or the expressed wish of the Executive? I trust not.

The form of this appropriation has been objected to. I shall read it.

"And be it further enacted, That the sum of three millions of dollars be, and the same is hereby, appropriated out of any money in the Treasury not otherwise appropriated, to be expended, in whole or in part, under the direction of the President of the United States, for the military and naval service, including fortifications and ordnance, and increase of the navy; Provided, such expenditures shall be rendered necessary, for the defence of the country, prior to the next meeting of Congress."

It has been urged that to grant money in such general terms would have been a violation of the Constitution. I do not understand that the Senator from Massachusetts (Mr. Webster), at the present session, has distinctly placed it upon this ground. Other Senators have done so in the strongest terms. Is there any thing in the Constitution which touches the question? It simply declares that "no money shall be drawn from the Treasury, but in consequence of appropriations made by law." Whether these appropriations shall be general or specific, is left entirely, as it ought to have been, to the discretion of Congress. I admit that, ex vi termini, an appropriation of money must have a reference to some object. But whether you refer to a class, or to an individual, to the genus or to the species, your appropriation is equally constitutional. The degree of specification necessary to make the law valid never can become a constitutional question. The terms of the instrument are as broad and as general as the English language can make them. In this particular, as in almost every other, the framers of the Constitution have manifested their wisdom and their foresight. Cases may occur and have occurred in the history of this Government, demanding the strictest secrecy; cases in which to specify, would be to defeat the very object of the appropriation. A remarkable example of this kind occurs in the administration of Mr. Jefferson, to which I shall presently advert.

264There are other cases in which from the very nature of things you cannot specify the objects of an appropriation without the gift of prophecy. I take the present to be a clear case of this description. The appropriation was contingent; it was to be for the defence of the country. How then could it have been specific? How could you foresee when, or where, or how the attack of France would be made? Without this foreknowledge, you could not designate when, or where, or how it would become necessary to use the money. This must depend upon France, not upon ourselves. She might be disposed to confine the contest merely to a naval war. In that event it would become necessary to apply the whole sum to secure us against naval attacks. She might threaten to invade Louisiana or any other portion of the Union. The money would then be required to call out the militia, and to march them and the regular army to that point. Every thing must depend upon the movements of the enemy. It might become necessary, in order most effectually to resist the contemplated attack, to construct steam frigates or steam batteries, or it might be deemed more proper to increase your ordinary navy and complete and arm your fortifications. In a country where Congress cannot be always in session, you must in times of danger, grant some discretionary powers to the Executive. This should always be avoided when it is possible, consistently with the safety of the country. But it was wise, it was prudent in the framers of the Constitution, in order to meet such cases, to declare in general terms that "no money shall be drawn from the Treasury, but in consequence of appropriations made by law." Not specific appropriations. The terms are general and unrestricted. If the amendment had appropriated one million to fortifications, the second million to the increase of the navy, and the third to the purchase of ordnance and arms, it might have been found that a great deal too much had been appropriated to one object, and a great deal too little to another.

As a matter of expediency, as a means of limiting the discretion of executive officers, I am decidedly friendly to specific appropriations, whenever they can be made. I so declared in the debate at the last session. I then expressed a wish that this appropriation had been more specific; but upon reflection, I do not see how it could have been made much more so, unless we had possessed the gift of prophecy. But the Constitution has nothing to do with the question.

After all, I attached more value to specific appropriations before I had examined this subject, than I do at the present moment. Still I admit their importance. The clause which immediately follows in the Constitution, is the true touchstone of responsibility. Although the appropriation may be general; yet "a regular statement and account of the receipts and expenditures of all public money shall be published from time to time." No matter in what language public money may be granted to the Executive, in its expenditure, he is but the mere trustee of the American people, and he must produce to them his vouchers for every cent entrusted to his care. This constitutional provision holds him to a strict responsibility, to a responsibility 265much more severe than if Congress had been required in all cases to make specific appropriations.

How Senators can create a dictator, and give him unlimited power over the purse and the sword out of such an appropriation, I am at a loss to conceive. It is a flight of imagination beyond my reach. What, sir, to appropriate three millions for the military and naval defence of the country in case it should become necessary during the recess of Congress, and at its next meeting to compel the President to account for the whole sum he may have expended; is this to create a dictator? Is this to surrender our liberties into the hands of one man? And yet gentlemen have contended for this proposition.

What has been the practice of the Government in regard to this subject? During the period of our first two Presidents, appropriations were made in the most general terms. No one then imagined that this was a violation of the Constitution. When Mr. Jefferson came into power, this practice was changed. In his message to Congress, of December 8th, 1801, he says: "In our care too of the public contributions entrusted to our discretion, it would be prudent to multiply barriers against their dissipation, by appropriating specific sums to every specific purpose susceptible of definition." Susceptible of definition. Here is the rule, and here is the exception. He treats the subject not as a constitutional question, but as one of mere expediency. In little more than two short years after this recommendation, Mr. Jefferson found it was necessary to obtain an appropriation from Congress in the most general terms. To have made it specific, would necessarily have defeated its very object. Secrecy was necessary to success. Accordingly on the 26th February, 1803, Congress made the most extraordinary appropriation in our annals. They granted to the President the sum of two millions of dollars, "for the purpose of defraying any extraordinary expenses which may be incurred in the intercourse between the United States and foreign nations." Here, sir, was a grant almost without any limit. It was co-extensive with the whole world. Every nation on the face of the earth was within the sphere of its operation. The President might have used this money to subsidize foreign nations to destroy our liberties. That he was utterly incapable of such conduct it is scarcely necessary to observe. I do not know that I should have voted for such an unlimited grant. Still, however, there was a responsibility to be found in his obligation under the Constitution to account for its expenditure. Mr. Jefferson never used any part of this appropriation. It had been intended for the purchase of the sovereignty of New Orleans and of other possessions in that quarter; but our treaty with France of the 30th April, 1803, by which Louisiana was ceded to us, rendered it unnecessary for him to draw any part of this money from the Treasury, under the act of Congress, by which it had been granted.

Before the close of Mr. Jefferson's second term, it was found that specific appropriations in the extent to which they had been carried, had become inconvenient. Congress often granted too much for one object, and too little 266for another. This must necessarily be the case, because we cannot say beforehand precisely how much shall be required for any one purpose. On the 3d of March, 1809, an act was passed, which was approved by Mr. Jefferson, containing the following provision:

"Provided, nevertheless, That, during the recess of Congress, the President of the United States may, and he is hereby authorized, on the application of the Secretary of the proper department, and not otherwise, to direct, if in his opinion necessary for the public service, that a portion of the moneys appropriated for a particular branch of expenditure in that department, be applied to another branch of expenditure in the same department; in which case, a special account of the moneys thus transferred, and of their application, shall be laid before Congress during the first week of their next ensuing session."

Is this act constitutional? If it be so, there is an end of the question. Has its constitutionality ever been doubted? It authorizes the President to take the money appropriated by Congress for one special object and apply it to another. The money destined for any one purpose by an appropriation bill, may be diverted from that purpose by the President, and be applied to any other purpose entirely different, with no limitation whatever upon his discretion, except that money to be expended by one of the Departments, either of War, or of the Navy, or of the Treasury, could not be transferred to another Department.

It is not my intention to cite all the precedents bearing upon this question. I shall merely advert to one other. On the 10th of March, 1812, Congress appropriated five hundred thousand dollars "for the purpose of fortifying and defending the maritime frontier of the United States." This was in anticipation of the late war with Great Britain, and is as general in its terms, and leaves as much to executive discretion, as the proposed appropriation of three millions.

I trust, then, that I have established the positions that this appropriation originated from a legitimate source—was necessary for the defence and honor of the country, and violated no provision of the constitution. If so, it ought to have received the approbation of the Senate.

When the fortification bill came back to the Senate, with this appropriation attached to it by the House, the Senator from Massachusetts (Mr. Webster), instantly moved that it should be rejected. I feel no disposition to make any harsh observations in relation to that gentleman. I think, however, that his remark, that if the enemy had been thundering at the gates of the capitol, he would have moved to reject the appropriation, was a most unfortunate one for himself. I consider it nothing more than a bold figure of speech. I feel the most perfect confidence that the gentleman is now willing to vote all the money which may be necessary for the defence of the country.

Of the gentleman's sincerity in opposing this appropriation, I did not then, nor do I now entertain a doubt. He was ardent and impassioned in his manner, and was evidently in a state of highly excited feeling. Probably strong political prejudices may have influenced his judgment without his 267knowledge. He thought that a high constitutional question was involved in the amendment, and acted accordingly.

When the bill returned again to the Senate, after we had rejected, and the House had insisted upon their amendment, the Senator immediately moved that we should adhere to our rejection. I well recollect, sir, that you (Mr. King, of Alabama, was in the chair), remarked at the time, that this was a harsh motion, and should it prevail, would be well calculated to exasperate the feelings of the House, and to defeat the bill. You then observed that the proper motion would be to insist upon our rejection, and ask a conference; and that the motion to adhere ought not to be resorted to until all gentler measures had failed.

The Senator now claims the merit, and is anxious to sustain the responsibility, of having moved to reject this appropriation. He also asks, in mercy, that when the expunging process shall commence, his vote, upon this occasion, may be spared from its operation. For the sake of my country, and in undisguised sincerity of purpose, I declare, for the sake of the gentleman, I am rejoiced that the responsibility which he covets will, probably, not be so dreadful as we had just reason to apprehend. Had France attacked us, or should she yet attack us, in our present defenceless condition; should our cities be exposed to pillage, or the blood of our citizens be shed, either upon the land or the ocean; should our national character be dishonored, tremendous, indeed, would be the responsibility of the gentleman. In that event, he need not beseech us to spare his vote from the process of expunging. You might as well attempt to expunge a sunbeam. That vote will live for ever in the memory of the American people.

It was the vote of the Senate which gave the mortal blow to the fortification bill. Had they passed this appropriation of three millions, that bill would now have been a law. Where it died, it is scarcely necessary to inquire. It was in mortal agony when the consultation of six political doctors was held upon it at midnight, in our conference chamber, and it probably breathed its last, on its way from that chamber to the House of Representatives, for want of a quorum in that body.

Its fate, in one respect, I hope may yet be of service to the country. It ought to admonish us, if possible, to do all our legislative business before midnight on the last day of the session. I never shall forget the night I sat side by side, in the House of Representatives, with the Senator from Massachusetts (Mr. Webster), until the morning had nearly dawned. The most important bills were continually returning from the Senate with amendments. It would have been in the power of any one member remaining in the House to have defeated any measure by merely asking for a division. This would have shown that no quorum was present. The members who still remained were worn down and exhausted, and were thus rendered incapable of attending to their duties. It was legislation without deliberation. I trust that this evil may be now corrected. Should it not,

I do not know that, at the conclusion 268of a Congress, my conscience would be so tender as to prevent me from voting, as I have done heretofore, after midnight on the third of March.

I have one other point to discuss. I shall now proceed to present to the Senate the state of our relations with France, at the present moment, for the purpose of proving that we ought to adopt the resolutions of the Senator from Missouri (Mr. Benton), and grant all appropriations necessary for the defence of the country. For this purpose, we must again return to Paris. The President's annual message of December, 1834, arrived in that city on the 8th of January—a day propitious in our annals. The attack upon the British troops on the night of the 23d of December did not surprise them more than this message did the French ministers. After the most patient endurance of wrongs for so many years, they seemed to be astounded that the President should have asserted our rights in such a bold and manly manner. That message, sir, will produce the payment of the indemnity. What effect had it upon the character of our country abroad? Let Mr. Livingston answer this question. In writing to the Secretary of State, on the 11th January, 1835, he says: "It has certainly raised us in the estimation of other powers, if I may judge from the demeanor of their representatives here; and my opinion is, that as soon as the first excitement subsides, it will operate favorably on the councils of France." There was not an American in Paris, on that day, who, upon the perusal of this message, did not feel the flush of honest pride of country mantling in his countenance.

On the 22d of November previous, Mr. Livingston was convinced that the king was sincere in his intention of urging the execution of the treaty, and then had no doubt of the sincerity of his cabinet. The Chambers assembled on the 1st of December; and after an arduous struggle for two days against the opposition, victory perched upon the banner of the ministers. They were thus securely seated in their places. On the 6th of December Mr. Livingston again writes, that "The conversations I have had with the king and all the ministers convince me that now they are perfectly in earnest, and united on the question of the treaty, and that it will be urged with zeal and ability." In a few short days, however, a change came over their spirit. On the 22d December Mr. Livingston uses the following language in writing to the Department of State: "My last despatch (6th December) was written immediately after the vote of the Chamber of Deputies had, as it was thought, secured a majority to the administration; and it naturally excited hopes which that supposition was calculated to inspire. I soon found, however, both from the tone of the administration press and from the language of the king and all the ministers with whom I conferred on the subject, that they were not willing to put their popularity to the test on our question; it will not be made one on the determination of which the ministers are willing to risk their portfolios. The very next day, after the debate, the ministerial gazette (Des Debats) declared that, satisfied with the approbation the Chamber had given to their system, it was at perfect liberty to exercise its discretion as to particular measures which do not form an essential part of that system; and 269the communications I subsequently had with the king and the ministers confirmed me in the opinion that the law for executing our convention was to be considered as one of those free questions. I combated this opinion, and asked whether the faithful observance of treaties was not an essential part of their system; and, if so, whether it did not come within their rule."

The observance of treaties was not an essential part of their system! Victorious and securely fixed, the ministers would not risk their places in attempting to obtain from the Chambers the appropriation required to carry our treaty into execution. It would not be made a cabinet question. It was evident they had determined to pursue the same course of delay and procrastination which they had previously pursued. But the message arrived, and it roused them from their apathy. All doubts which had existed upon the subject of making the payment of our indemnity a cabinet question at once vanished. We have never heard of any such since; and it was not until some months after that the French ministers thought of annexing any condition to this payment.

On the 13th of January, Mr. Livingston had a conference with the Count de Rigny. He then explained to him the nature of a message from our President to Congress. He compared it to a family council under the French law, and showed that it was a mere communication from one branch of our Government to another, with which a foreign nation had no right to interfere, and at which they ought not to take offence. They parted on friendly terms, and again met on the same terms in the evening, at the Austrian Ambassador's. Mr. Livingston was, therefore, much astonished when, about ten o'clock at night of the same day, he received a note from the count, informing him that Mr. Serrurier, the French minister at Washington, had been recalled, and that his passports were at his service. This seems to have been a sudden determination of the French cabinet.

Now, sir, upon the presumption that France had been insulted by the message, this was the proper mode of resenting the insult. Promptly to suspend all diplomatic intercourse with the nation who had menaced her or questioned her honor, was a mode of redress worthy of her high and chivalrous character. The next impulse of wounded pride would be promptly to pay the debt which she owed, and release herself from every pecuniary obligation to the nation which had done her this wrong. These were the first determinations of the king's ministers.

France has since been placed before the world, by her rulers, in the most false position ever occupied by a brave and gallant nation. She believes herself to be insulted, and what is the consequence? She refuses to pay a debt now admitted to be just by all the branches of her government. Her wounded feelings are estimated by dollars and cents, and she withholds twenty-five millions of francs, due to a foreign nation, to soothe her injured pride. How are the mighty fallen! Truly it may be said, the days of chivalry are gone. Have the pride and the genius of Napoleon left no traces of themselves under the constitutional monarchy? In private life, if you are insulted by an individual to whom you are indebted, what is the first impulse 270of a man of honor? To owe no pecuniary obligation to the man who has wounded your feelings—to pay him the debt instantly, and to demand reparation for the insult, or at the least, to hold no friendly communication with him afterwards.

This course the king's ministers had, at first, determined to pursue. The reason why they abandoned it, I shall endeavor to explain hereafter.

Mr. Livingston, in his letter to Mr. Forsyth of the 14th January, 1835, says: "The law, it is said, will be presented to-day, and I have very little doubt that it will pass. The ministerial phalanx, reinforced by those of the opposition (and they are not a few), who will not take the responsibility of involving the country in the difficulties which they now see must ensue, will be sufficient to carry the vote."

Did Mr. Livingston intend to say France would be terrified into this measure? By no means. But, in the intercourse between independent States, there is a point at which diplomacy must end, and when a nation must either abandon her rights, or determine to assert them by the sword, or by such strong and decided measures as may eventually lead to hostilities. When this point is reached, it becomes a serious and alarming crisis for those to whom, on earth, the destiny of nations is entrusted. When the one alternative is war, either immediate or prospective, with all the miseries which follow in its train, and the other the payment of a just debt to an ancient ally and firm friend, who could doubt what must be the decision? Such was the position in which France stood toward the United States. Not only justice, but policy required the payment of the debt. In the event of war, or, of a non-intercourse between the two nations, her wine-growers, her producers and manufacturers of silk, and all her other manufacturing interests, especially those of her southern provinces, would be vitally injured. The payment of five millions of dollars would be but a drop in the ocean, compared with the extent of their sufferings. In France, they then believed that the time for diplomacy—the time for procrastination had ended. The President's message had opened their eyes to the importance of the subject. It was under this impression that Mr. Livingston predicted that the bill would pass the Chambers. That it would have done so without any condition, had Congress responded to the President's message, I do not say, by authorizing reprisals, but by manifesting a decided resolution to insist upon the execution of the treaty, will, I think, appear abundantly evident hereafter.

The French ministry having manifested their sensibility to the supposed insult, by recalling Mr. Serrurier, proceeded immediately to present the bill for the execution of the treaty to the Chambers. In presenting it on the 15th January, Mr. Humann, the minister of finance, addressed the Chamber. His speech contains the views then entertained by the French cabinet. I shall read an extract from it. He says:

"General Jackson has been in error respecting the extent of the faculties conferred upon us, by the constitution of the State; but if he has been mistaken as to the laws of our country, we will not fall into the same error with 271regard to the institutions of the United States. Now, the spirit and letter of those institutions authorize us to regard the document above named [the message], as the expression of an opinion merely personal, so long as that opinion has not received the sanction of the other two branches of the American Government. The message is a Government act, which is still incomplete, and should not lead to any of these determinations, which France is in the habit of taking in reply to a threat or insult."

The French ministry, at that time, considered the President's message, merely his personal act, until it should receive the sanction of Congress. They, then, had not dreamt of requiring an explanation of it, as the only condition on which they would pay the money. This was an after thought. The bill presented by Mr. Humann merely prescribed that the payment should not be made, "until it shall have been ascertained that the Government of the United States has done nothing to injure the interests of France." This bill was immediately referred to a committee, of which Mr. Dumon was the chairman. On the 28th of March, he reported it to the Chamber, with a provision, that the money should not be paid, if the Government of the United States shall have done anything "contrary to the dignities and the interests of France." Still we hear nothing of an explanation of the message being made a condition of the payment of the money. The clauses in the bill to which I have adverted were evidently inserted to meet the contingency of reprisals having been sanctioned by Congress.

The debate upon the bill in the Chamber of Deputies commenced on the 9th of April and terminated on the 18th. On that day General Valazé proposed his amendment declaring that "the payments in execution of the present law cannot be made until the French government shall have received satisfactory explanations with regard to the message of the President of the United States, dated the 2d December, 1834."

The Duke de Broglie, the minister of foreign affairs, accepted this amendment. I shall read his remarks on this occasion. He says: "The intention of the government has always been conformable with the desire expressed by the author of the amendment which is now before the Chambers (great agitation), the government has always meant that diplomatic relations should not be renewed with the Government of the United States until it had received satisfactory explanations. The government, therefore, does not repulse the amendment itself." After this, on the same day, the bill passed the Chamber by a vote of 289 to 137.

Well might the Chamber be agitated at such an annunciation from the minister of foreign affairs. Why this sudden change in the policy of the French government? The answer is plain. Congress had adjourned on the 4th of March, without manifesting by their actions any disposition to make the fulfilment of the treaty a serious question. Whilst our Treasury was overflowing, they had refused to make any provision for the defence of the country. They had left the whole coast of the United States from Maine to Georgia in a defenceless condition. The effect upon the French Chamber 272and the French people was such as might have been anticipated. To prove this, I shall read an extract from a speech delivered by Mr. Bignon, one of the Deputies, on the 10th April. I select this from many others, because it contains nothing which can be offensive to any Senator. It will be recollected that Mr. Bignon is the gentleman who had been more instrumental in defeating the bill at the previous session than any other member.

"President Jackson's message has astonished them (the Americans) as well as us; they have seen themselves thrown by it into a very hazardous situation. What have they done? They are too circumspect and clear-headed to express, by an official determination, their disapproval of an act which, in reality, has not received their assent. Some of them, for instance Mr. Adams, in the House of Representatives, may indeed, from a politic patriotism, have even eulogized the President's energy, and obtained from the Chamber the expression that the treaty of 1831 must be complied with; but at a preceding sitting the same member took pains to declare that he was not the defender of a system of war; he proclaimed aloud that the resolution adopted by the Senate was an expedient suggested by prudence, and he thought the House of Representatives should pursue the same course. Gentlemen, the American legislature had to resort to expedients to get out of the embarrassing dilemma in which the President's message had placed them; and they acted wisely."

From the conduct of Congress, the French Chambers were under the impression that the people of the United States would not adopt any energetic measures to compel the fulfilment of the treaty. They had no idea that the nation would sustain the President in his efforts. They had reason to believe that he was almost left alone. They appear ever since to have acted under this delusion. According to the impression of Mr. Bignon, the nation was astounded at President Jackson's message. This is the true reason why the ministry accepted the amendment requiring President Jackson to make an explanation. The best mode of obtaining justice from the powerful as well as from the weak—the best mode of elevating this nation to the lofty position she is destined to occupy among the nations of the earth—the best mode of preventing war and preserving peace, is to stand up firmly for our rights. The assertion of these rights, not by threats, but boldly, manfully, and frankly, is the surest method of obtaining justice and respect from other nations.

At so early a day as the 29th of January, Mr. Livingston had addressed a note to the Duke de Broglie, distinctly disavowing any intention on the part of the President, by his message, to intimidate France, or to charge the French government with bad faith. On the 25th of April, in another letter to the duke, he communicated to him the President's official approbation of his former note. In this last letter, he reiterates his explanations, and assures the duke that, whilst the President intended to use no menace, nor to charge any breach of faith against the king's government, he never could and never would make any explanation of his message on the demand of a foreign government. This letter would, of itself, be sufficient to give its author a high rank not only among the diplomatists, but the statesmen of his country. The sentiments it contains were unanimously approved by the American people. Although it was received by the duke before the bill had been acted upon by the Chamber of Peers, it produced no effect upon the French ministry. The bill was finally passed and obtained the sanction of the king in a form requiring the President to explain his message before the money could be paid. This state of fact distinctly raises the important question, whether a President of the United States can be questioned by a foreign government for anything contained in a message to Congress. The principle that he cannot, has already been firmly established by the practice of our Government. Even in our intercourse with France, in former times, the question has been settled. This principle results from the very nature of our institutions. It must ever be maintained inviolate. Reverse it, and you destroy the independent existence of this Republic, so far as its intercourse with foreign nations is concerned.

The Constitution requires that the President of the United States "shall, from time to time, give to the Congress information of the state of the Union, and recommend to their consideration such measures as he shall judge necessary and expedient." This information is intended not only for the use of Congress, but of the people. They are the source of all power, and from their impulse all legitimate legislation must proceed. Both Congress and the people must be informed of the state of our foreign relations by the executive. If the President cannot speak freely to them upon this subject; if he cannot give them all the information which may be necessary to enable them to act, except under the penalty of offending a foreign government, the Constitution of the United States, to this extent, becomes a dead letter. The maintenance of this principle is an indispensable condition of our existence, under the present form of Government.

If we are engaged in any controversy with a foreign nation, it is not only the right, but it is the imperative duty, of the President to communicate the facts to Congress, however much they may operate against that nation. Can we then, for a single moment, permit a foreign government to demand an apology from the President for performing one of his highest duties to the people of the United States?

Let us put an extreme case. Suppose the President, after giving a history of our wrongs to Congress, recommends not merely a resort to reprisals, but to war, against another nation. Shall this nation, which has inflicted upon us injury, be permitted to change her position, to cancel all our claims for justice, and to insist that we have become the aggressors, because a resort to arms has been recommended? I feel the most perfect confidence that not a single Senator will ever consent to yield this position to France or to any other nation. I need not labor this question. The subject has been placed in the clearest and strongest light by Mr. Livingston, in his letter to the Duke de Broglie of the 25th of April. If any possible exemption to the rule could be tolerated, surely this would not present the case. The Duke de Broglie himself, in his letter to Mr. Pageot, is constrained to admit that there is not a single offensive sentence respecting France in the message; but yet he complains of the general effect of the whole.

With a full knowledge, then, that the President could not, would not, dare not explain his message, on the demand of any foreign government, the Duke de Broglie addresses his famous letter to the chargé d'affaires at Washington. It bears date at Paris on the 17th June, 1835. Before I proceed to make any remarks upon this letter, I wish to bring its character distinctly into view of the Senate. It commences by declaring, in opposition to the principle that the President of the United States cannot be called upon by a foreign government to make explanations of a message to Congress, that, "by virtue of a clause inserted in the article first, by the Chamber of Deputies, the French government must defer making the payments agreed upon, until that of the United States shall have explained the true meaning and real purport of divers passages inserted by the President of the Union in his message at the opening of the last session of Congress, and at which all France, at the first aspect, was justly offended."

It proceeds still further, and announces that, "the government, having discovered nothing in that clause at variance with its own sentiments, or the course it had intended to pursue, the project of law thus amended on the 18th April, by the Chamber of Deputies, was carried on the 27th, to the Chamber of Peers."

The duke, after having thus distinctly stated that an explanation of the message was required as a condition of the payment of the money, and after presenting a historical sketch of the controversy, then controverts, at considerable length, the position which had been maintained by Mr. Livingston, that the President could not be questioned by a foreign government for anything contained in a message to Congress. He afterwards asserts, in the broadest terms, that the explanations which had been voluntarily made by Mr. Livingston, and sanctioned by the President, were not sufficient.

In suggesting what would satisfy France, he says, "we do not here contend about this or that phrase, this or that allegation, this or that expression; we contend about the intention itself, which has dictated that part of the message." And again, speaking of Mr. Livingston's letters of the 29th January and 25th April, he adds:

"You will easily conceive, sir, and the Cabinet of Washington will, we think, understand it also, that such phrases incidentally inserted in documents, the purport and tenor of which are purely polemical, surrounded, in some measure, by details of a controversy, which is besides not always free from bitterness, cannot dispel sufficiently the impression produced by the perusal of the message, nor strike the mind as would the same idea expressed in terms single, positive, direct, and unaccompanied by any recrimination concerning facts or incidents no longer of any importance. Such is the motive which, among many others, has placed the French government in the impossibility of acceding to the wish expressed by Mr. Livingston, towards the conclusion of his note of the 29th of April, by declaring (to the Chamber of Peers probably) that previous explanations given by the minister of the United States, and subsequently approved by the President, had satisfied it."

After having thus announced the kind of explanation which would be expected, he states, that the French government "in pausing then for the present, and waiting for the fulfilment of those engagements to be claimed, (the engagements of the treaty) and expecting those to be claimed in terms consistent with the regard due to it, it is not afraid of being accused, nor France, which it represents, of being accused of appreciating national honor by any number of millions, which it could withhold as a compensation for any injury offered to it." The letter concludes by authorizing Mr. Pageot to read it to Mr. Forsyth, and if he be desirous, to let him take a copy of it.

It is impossible to peruse this letter, able and ingenious as it is, without at once perceiving that it asks what the President can never grant, without violating the principle that France has no right to demand an explanation of his message.

On the 11th of September, Mr. Pageot, the French chargé d'affaires, called at the Department of State and read this despatch to Mr. Forsyth. The latter did not think proper to ask a copy of it; and for this he has been loudly condemned. In my judgment, his conduct was perfectly correct.

No objection can be made to this indirect mode of communication with the Government of the United States adopted by the duke. It is sanctioned by diplomatic usage. The rules, however, which govern it, are clearly deducible from its very nature. It is a mere diplomatic feeler thrown out to ascertain the views of another government. The duke himself justly observes that its object is "to avoid the irritation which might involuntarily rise from an exchange of contradictory notes in a direct controversy."

Had Mr. Forsyth asked and received a copy of this despatch, he must have given it an answer. Respect for the source from which it proceeded would have demanded this at his hands. If this answer could have been nothing but a direct refusal to comply with the suggestions of the French government, then he was correct in not requesting leave to take a copy of it. Why was this the case? Because it would have added to the difficulties of the question, already sufficiently numerous, and would have involved him in a direct controversy, which it is the very object of this mode of communication to prevent. This is the reason why it was left by the despatch itself, within his own option whether to request a copy or not; and his refusal to make this request ought to have given no offence to the French government.

Now, sir, what answer could he have given to this communication, but a direct refusal? Had not the duke been fully apprised before he wrote this despatch, that it could receive no other answer? It required explanations as a condition of the payment of the money, which he had been informed the President could never make. On this ground, then, and for the very purpose of avoiding controversy, the conduct of Mr. Forsyth is correct. But there is another reason to justify his conduct, which, I think, must carry conviction to every mind. The President proposed, in his annual message, voluntarily to declare, that he had never intended to menace France, or to impeach the faith of the French government. This he has since done in the strongest terms. As offence was taken by the French government at the language of a former message, it was believed that such a declaration in a subsequent message would be, as it ought to be, entirely satisfactory to France. Had Mr. Forsyth taken a copy of this despatch, and placed it among the archives of the Government, how could the President have made, consistently with his principles, the disclaimer which he has done? A demand for an explanation would thus have been interposed by a foreign government, which would have compelled him to remain silent. The refusal of Mr. Forsyth to ask a copy of the despatch, left the controversy in its old condition; and, so far as our government was concerned, left this letter from the Duke de Broglie to Mr. Pageot as if it never had been written. The President, therefore, remained at perfect liberty to say what he thought proper in his message.

If this letter had proposed any reasonable terms of reconciling our difficulties with France—if it had laid any foundation on which a rational hope might have rested that it would become the means of producing a result so desirable, it would have been the duty of Mr. Forsyth to request a copy. Upon much reflection, however, I must declare that I cannot imagine what good could have resulted from it in any contingency; and it might have done much evil. Had it prevented the President from speaking as he has done in his last message, concerning France, it might have involved the country in a much more serious misunderstanding with that power than existed at the present moment.

I should be glad to say no more of this despatch, if I could do so consistently with a sense of duty. Mr. Pageot did not rest satisfied with Mr. Forsyth's omission to request a copy of it, as he ought to have done. He deemed it proper to attempt to force that upon him which the despatch itself had left entirely to his own discretion. Accordingly, on the 1st of December last, he enclosed him a copy. On the third, Mr. Forsyth returned it with a polite refusal. On the fifth, Mr. Pageot again addressed Mr. Forsyth, and avowed that his intention in communicating the document, "was to make known the real disposition of my government to the President of the United States, and through him to Congress and the American people." Thus it is manifest that his purpose was to make the President the instrument by which he might appeal to the American people against the American Government. After he had failed in this effort, what is his next resort? He publishes this despatch to the people of the United States through the medium of our public journals. I now hold in my hand the number of the Courier des Etats Unis of the 20th of January, a journal published in New York, which contains the original despatch in the French language. In a subsequent number of the same journal, of the 24th January, there is an editorial article on the subject of the President's special message to Congress, and of this despatch, of a part of which I shall give my own translation. It is as follows:

"Our last number contained the despatch of M. the Duke de Broglie to the chargé d'affaires of France at Washington, concerning which the Senate had demanded such explanations as were in the power of the executive. On the same day, the late message of the President of the United States, which had been expected with so much impatience and anxiety, arrived at New York. To this document are annexed many letters of the Duke de Broglie, of Mr. Forsyth, and of Mr. Pageot, which will be read with great interest. We give a simple analysis of the least important, and an exact copy of those which have been written originally in French."

"The public attention was first occupied with the letter of the Minister of Foreign Affairs, which was known here some hours before the message of the President of the United States; and if some journals of the Government have found this publication unseasonable, made by the legation of France according to the orders which it had received, nobody, at least, has been able to deny the talent, the moderation, and the force of reasoning which have presided at its preparation."

By whom was the legation of France ordered to publish this despatch? Who alone had the power of issuing such an order? The French government. Against this positive language, I can still scarcely believe that the Duke de Broglie has given an order so highly reprehensible.

The publication of this despatch was an outrage upon all diplomatic usage. It ought to have been intended as the harbinger of peace, and not of renewed controversy. From its very nature it was secret and confidential. If not received, it ought to have been as if it never had existed. Upon any other principle, it would aggravate the controversy which such communications are always intended to prevent. It has now been diverted from its natural purpose by the French legation, and has been made the subject of an appeal by France to the American people against their own Government. It has thus greatly increased the difficulties between the two countries. It has proclaimed to the world that France requires from the President of the United States, an apology of his message as an indispensable condition of the execution of our treaty. It has, therefore, rendered it much more difficult for her to retract.

The true meaning of this despatch is now rendered manifest to the most sceptical. The Duke de Broglie, in his interview with Mr. Barton, on the 12th October last, has placed his own construction upon it. The apology which he then required from the President contains his own commentary upon this despatch. I need not read the history of that interview to the Senate, to prove that I am correct in this assertion. It must be fresh in the recollection of every Senator.

Considered as an appeal to the American people against their own Government, the publication of this despatch deserves still more serious consideration. Foreign influence, in all ages, has been the bane of republics. It has destroyed nearly all of them which have ever existed. We ought to resist its approaches on every occasion. In the very infancy of our existence as a nation, a similar attempt was made by France. It was then repulsed as became a nation of freemen. The present attempt will have the same effect on the American people. It will render them still more firm and still more united in the cause of their country.

Of Mr. Barton's recall, I need say but little. It was the direct consequence of the refusal of France to execute the treaty, without an apology from the President of his message. Diplomatic relations between the two countries had been first interrupted by France. On this subject, hear what the Count de Rigny said in his exposé read to the Chamber of Peers, on the 27th April last, on presenting the bill for the execution of our treaty. I give my own translation:

"You know the measure which the government of the king adopted at the very instant when the message, presented by the President of the Union, at the opening of the last Congress, arrived in Europe. You know that since that time, a similar measure had been adopted by President Jackson himself. The two ministers, accredited near the two governments, are reciprocally recalled; the effect of this double recall is at this moment, if not to interrupt, in all respects, the diplomatic communications between the two States, at least to interrupt them in what regards the treaty of the 4th July. If these relations ought to be renewed, and we doubt not that they ought, it is not for us hereafter to take the initiative."

On the 5th of June, the President had officially sanctioned the explanations which had been made to the French government by Mr. Livingston, in his letter of the 25th of April, as he had previously sanctioned those which had been made by the same gentleman, in his note of the 29th of January. These were considered by the President, amply sufficient to satisfy the susceptible feelings of France. In order to give them full time to produce their effect, and to afford the French ministry an ample opportunity for reflection, he delayed sending any orders to demand the money secured by the treaty until the middle of December. On the 14th of that month, Mr. Barton was instructed to call upon the Duke de Broglie, and request to be informed what were the intentions of the French government, in relation to the payment of the money secured by the treaty. He expected these instructions on the 20th of October. The special message has communicated to us the result. "We will pay the money," says the Duke de Broglie, "when the Government of the United States is ready on its part, to declare to us, by addressing its claim to us officially in writing, that it regrets the misunderstanding which has arisen between the two countries; that this misunderstanding is founded on a mistake; that it never entered into its intention to call in question the good faith of the French government, nor to take a menacing attitude towards France;" and he adds, "if the Government of the United States does not give this assurance, we shall be obliged to think that this misunderstanding is not the result of an error."

Is there any American so utterly lost to those generous feelings which love of country should inspire, as to purchase five millions with the loss of national honor? Who, for these or any number of millions, would see the venerable man, now at the head of our Government, bowing at the footstool of the throne of Louis Philippe, and like a child, prepared to say its lesson, repeating this degrading apology? First, perish the five millions,—perish a thousand times the amount. The man whose bosom has been so often bared in the defence of his country will never submit to such degrading terms. His motto has always been, death before dishonor.

Why, then, it may be asked, have I expressed a hope, a belief, that this unfortunate controversy will be amicably terminated when the two nations are now directly at issue? I will tell you why. This has been called a mere question of etiquette; and such it is, so far as

France is concerned. She has already received every explanation which the most jealous susceptibility ought to demand. These have been voluntarily tendered to her.

Since the date of the Duke de Broglie's letter to Mr. Pageot of the 17th June, we have received from the President of the United States his general message at the commencement of the session, and his special message on French affairs. Both these documents disclaim, in the strongest terms, any intention to menace France, or to impute bad faith to the French government by the message of December, 1834. Viewing the subject in this light; considering that at the interview with Mr. Barton, the duke could not have anticipated what would be the tone of these documents, I now entertain a strong hope that the French government have already reconsidered their determination. If a mediation has been proposed and accepted, I cannot entertain a doubt as to what will be the opinion of the mediator. He ought to say to France, you have already received all the explanations, and these have been voluntarily accorded, which the United States can make without national degradation. With these you ought to be satisfied. With you, it is a mere question of etiquette. All the disclaimers which you ought to desire have already been made by the President of the United States. The only question with you now is not one of substance, but merely whether these explanations are in proper form. But in regard to the United States, the question is far different. What is with you mere etiquette, is a question of life and death to them. Let the President of the United States make the apology which you have dictated,—let him once admit the right of a foreign government to question his messages to Congress, and to demand explanations of any language at which they may choose to take offence, and their independent existence as a Government, to that extent, is virtually destroyed.

We must remember that France may yield with honor; we never can, without disgrace. Will she yield? That is the question. I confess I should have entertained a stronger belief that she would, had she not published the duke's letter to Mr. Pageot as an appeal to the American people. She must still believe that the people of this country are divided in opinion in regard to the firm maintenance of their rights. In this she will find herself entirely mistaken. But should Congress, at the present session, refuse to sustain the President by adopting measures of defence; should the precedent of the last session be followed for the present year, then I shall entertain the most gloomy forebodings. The Father of his country has informed us that the best mode of preserving peace is to be prepared for war. I firmly believe, therefore, that a unanimous vote of the Senate in favor of the resolutions now before them, to follow to Europe the acceptance of the mediation, would, almost to a certainty, render it successful. It would be an act of the soundest policy as well as of the highest patriotism. It would prove, not that we intend to menace France, because such an attempt would be ridiculous; but that the American people are unanimous in the assertion of their rights, and have resolved to prepare for the worst. A French fleet is now hovering upon our coasts; and shall we sit still, with an overflowing Treasury, and leave our country defenceless? This will never be said with truth of the American Congress.

If war should come, which God forbid,—if France should still persist in her effort to degrade the American people in the person of their Chief Magistrate,—we may appeal to Heaven for the justice of our cause, and look forward with confidence to victory from that Being in whose hands is the destiny of nations.

Previous to the delivery of this speech, the President had, on the 15th of January, recommended to Congress a partial non-intercourse with France. But in a short time the government of Great Britain made an offer of mediation, which was accepted, and the whole difficulty with France was amicably adjusted.

CHAPTER XII.
1835–1837.

REMOVAL OF EXECUTIVE OFFICERS—BENTON'S "EXPUNGING" RESOLUTION.

Among the exciting topics of this period, there was no ground on which the Whigs attacked the administration of General Jackson with greater severity than that which related to his removal of executive officers. In the remarkable protest, which he sent to the Senate in 1834, against the censure which that body had passed upon his executive acts, and especially his removal of one Secretary of the Treasury who would not, and the appointment of another who would, remove the public deposits from the Bank of the United States, he had claimed a general executive power of supervision and control over all executive officers. He had made many other removals from office, which were complained of as dictated by purely political motives; and in the session of 1834–5, a bill was introduced into the Senate, one of the objects of which was to require the President, when making a nomination to fill a vacancy occasioned by the removal of any officer, to state the fact of such removal, and to render reasons for it. On this bill, Mr. Buchanan, on the 17th of February, 1835, made the following speech, which is of value now, because it relates to a topic that has not yet ceased to be a matter of controversy:

Mr. President: It is with extreme diffidence and reluctance that I rise to address you on the present occasion. It was my intention to suffer this bill to pass, contenting myself with a simple vote in the negative. This course I should have pursued, had the constitutional question been fully discussed by any gentleman on our side of the Senate. As this has not been done, I feel it to be a duty which I owe to those who sent me here, as well as to myself, to express my opinion on the subject, and the reasons on which that opinion is founded.

The present bill presents a most important question concerning our fundamental institutions. It attacks a construction of the Constitution of the United States which has been considered settled for almost half a century. Has the President, under the Constitution, the power of removing executive officers? If any question can ever be put at rest in this country, this, emphatically, ought to be considered that one. It was solemnly settled in 1789 by the first Congress of the United States. Of whom was that Congress composed? Of the men who had sustained the toils and dangers of the revolutionary war—of the men who sat in the convention which framed the Constitution, and who passed from that convention into the first Congress. These men, who laid the foundations of our Republic broad and deep, most solemnly and deliberately decided, that to the President, and to him alone, belonged the power of removal. This was not at a moment when the country was convulsed by party spirit. Very far from it. The Fathers of the Republic were then occupied in putting the Government in motion, and in establishing such principles as might preserve the liberties and promote the best interests of the American people for ages. In what condition are we, at the present moment, to rejudge the judgment of those men and reverse their solemn decision? Is not party spirit raging throughout the land? Are there not high party feelings in this body? Are we in a condition calmly and deliberately, without prejudice and without passion, to review and to condemn their judgment?

Why, sir, even if there were no authority in the Constitution for the power of removal, the decision of this body, at this time, would have but little influence among the people. They would compare the calmness—the self-possession—the freedom from political excitement of the sages who established the precedent, with the party violence and the high political feeling of the Senate at the present day; and the weight of authority would be all against us.

The debate in the first Congress was very long and very able. Every argument which patriotism and ingenuity could suggest was exhausted. The question was at length decided in the House of Representatives on the 22d June, 1789. On the yeas and nays, thirty voted in affirmance of the President's power of removal, and eighteen against it;—a large majority, considering the comparatively small number of which the House was then composed.

The question arose on the bill to establish the Department of Foreign Affairs. It contained a clause declaring the Secretary of State "to be removable from office by the President of the United States." From this clause it might have been inferred that the power of removal was intended to be conferred upon the President by Congress, and not acknowledged to exist in him under the Constitution. To remove every difficulty,—to place doubt at defiance in all future time, the words "to be removable from office by the President of the United States" were stricken from the bill, and this right was expressly acknowledged to exist independently of all legislation. By the second section of the bill, which became a law on the 27th July, 1789, 283it is declared that "the Chief Clerk in the Department of Foreign Affairs, whenever the principal officer shall be removed from office by the President of the United States, or in any other case of vacancy, shall, during such vacancy, have the charge and custody of all records, books, and papers, appertaining to the said Department." Here then is a clear, strong, distinct recognition by the House of Representatives of the President's power of removal, not by virtue of law, but under the Constitution. This phraseology was carefully adopted for the purpose of putting this very question at rest forever, so far as Congress could effect this purpose.

The bill, having passed the House of Representatives, was sent to the Senate for their concurrence. The power of removal was there solemnly considered. This was the very body which, according to the doctrine of gentlemen, has a right to control this power; and yet they affirmed the principle that it was vested in the President, and in him alone. It is true that the question was determined by the casting vote of Mr. Adams,—then the Vice-President: but the act was approved by General Washington, and the power has ever since been exercised without dispute by him and his successors in office, until after the election of the present President. Washington, the elder Adams, Jefferson, Madison, Monroe, and the younger Adams removed whom they pleased from office; but after the accession of Jackson, the existence of this power is denied. We are now required to believe that all which former Presidents have done was wrong;—that the first Congress were entirely mistaken in their construction of the Constitution:—and that the President does not possess the power of removal except with the concurrence of the Senate.

If ever a question has occurred in the history of any country which ought to be considered settled, this is that one. A solemn decision at first, adopted in practice afterwards by all branches of the Government, for five and forty years, makes the precedent one of almost irresistible force.

What then have we a right to expect on our side of the House from the opposition? Not merely that they shall prove it to be a doubtful question, but they shall present a case so clear as to render it manifest that all which has been done has been without authority, and all the removals which have ever been made, have been in violation of the Constitution. The burden rests entirely upon the gentlemen, and a ponderous load they have to sustain.

But, sir, if the question were entirely new, if it never had been decided either by precedent or by practice, I think it may be made abundantly clear, that the strength of the argument is greatly on the side of those who maintain the power.

What is the nature of the Constitution of the United States? The powers which it devolves upon the Government, are divided into three distinct classes, the Legislative, the Executive, and the Judicial. To preserve the liberties of any country, it is necessary that these three branches of the government should be kept distinct and separate as far as possible. When they are all united in the same person—this is the very definition of despotism. As you approximate to this state of things, in the same proportion you advance towards arbitrary power. These are axioms which cannot—which will not be denied.

Doubtless for wise purposes, the framers of our Constitution have in a very few excepted cases, blended these powers together. The executive, by his veto, has a control over our legislation. The Senate, although a branch of the legislature, exercises judicial power in cases of impeachment. The President nominates, "and by and with the advice and consent of the Senate," appoints all officers, except those of an inferior nature, the appointment of which may be vested by Congress "in the President alone, in the courts of law, or in the heads of departments."

Now, sir, my position is, that when the Constitution of the United States, in a special case, has conferred upon the Senate, which is essentially a branch of the legislature, a participation in executive power, you cannot by construction extend this power beyond the plain terms of the grant. It is an exception from the general rule pervading the whole instrument. Appointment to office is in the strictest sense an executive power. But it is expressly declared that the assent of the Senate shall be necessary to the exercise of this power on the part of the President. The grant to the Senate is special. In this particular case, it is an abstraction from the general executive powers granted under the Constitution to the President. According to the maxim of the common law, expressio unius est exclusio alterius—it follows conclusively that what has not been given is withheld, and remains in that branch of the Government which is the appropriate depository of executive power. The exception proves the rule. And the grant of executive power to the Senate is confined to appointments to office, and to them alone. This necessarily excludes other executive powers. It cannot, therefore, be contended with any force, as the gentleman from Massachusetts (Mr. Webster) has contended, that because the consent of the Senate is made necessary by the Constitution to appointments of officers,—that, therefore, by implication, it is necessary for their removal. Besides, these two things are very distinct in their nature, as I shall hereafter have occasion to demonstrate.

But to proceed with the argument. I shall contend that the sole power of removing executive officers is vested in the President by the Constitution. First, from a correct construction of the instrument itself; and second, even if that were doubtful, from the great danger resulting to the public interest from any other construction.

The Constitution declares in express language that "the executive power shall be vested in a President of the United States." Under these general terms, I shall, once for all, disclaim the idea of attempting to derive any portion of the power of the Chief Magistrate from any other fountain than the Constitution itself. I therefore entirely repel the imputation, so far as I am concerned, which would invest him with executive powers derived from the prerogatives of the kings or emperors of the old world. Such arguments are entirely out of the question.

285The Constitution also declares that "he shall take care that the laws be faithfully executed." These two clauses of the Constitution confer the executive power on the President, and define his duties. Is, then, the removal from office an executive power? If it be so, there is an end of the question; because the Constitution nowhere declares that the Senate, or any other human tribunal, shall participate in the exercise of this power. It will not be contended but that the power of removal exists, and must exist, somewhere. Where else can it exist but in the executive, on whom the Constitution imposes the obligation of taking care that the laws shall be faithfully executed? It will not be pretended that the power of removal is either of a legislative or judicial character. From its very nature, it belongs to the executive. In case he discovers that an officer is violating his trust—that instead of executing the laws, his conduct is in direct opposition to their requisition, is it not, strictly speaking, an executive power to arrest him in his career, by removing him from office? How could the President execute the trust confided to him, if he were destitute of this authority? If he possessed it not, he would be compelled to witness the executive officers violating the laws of Congress without the power of preventing it.

On this subject, it is impossible for me to advance anything new. It was exhausted by Mr. Madison, in the debate of 1789, in the House of Representatives. I am confident the Senate will indulge me whilst I read two extracts from his speeches on that occasion, delivered on the 16th and 17th June, 1789. The first was delivered on the 16th June, 1789, and is as follows:

"By a strict examination of the Constitution, on what appears to be its true principles, and considering the great departments of the Government in the relation they have to each other, I have my doubts whether we are not absolutely tied down to the construction declared in the bill. In the first section of the first article, it is said that all legislative powers herein granted shall be vested in a Congress of the United States. In the second article, it is affirmed that the executive power shall be vested in a President of the United States of America. In the third article, it is declared that the judicial power of the United States shall be vested in one Supreme Court; and in such inferior courts as Congress may, from time to time, ordain and establish.

"I suppose it will be readily admitted, that so far as the Constitution has separated the powers of these great departments, it would be improper to combine them together; and so far as it has left any particular department in the entire possession of the powers incident to that department, I conceive we ought not to qualify them further than they are qualified by the Constitution. The legislative powers are vested in Congress, and are to be exercised by them uncontrolled by any other department, except the Constitution has qualified it otherwise. The Constitution has qualified the legislative power, by authorizing the President to object to any act it may pass, requiring, in this case, two-thirds of both Houses to concur in making a law; but still the absolute legislative power is vested in the Congress with this qualification alone.

286"The Constitution affirms, that the executive power shall be vested in the President. Are there exceptions to this proposition? Yes, there are. The Constitution says, that in appointing to office, the Senate shall be associated with the President, unless in case of inferior officers, when the law shall otherwise direct. Have we a right to extend this exception? I believe not. If the Constitution had invested all executive power in the President, I venture to assert that the Legislature has no right to diminish or modify his executive authority."

Again:

"The doctrine, however, which seems to stand most in opposition to the principles I contend for, is, that the power to annul an appointment is, in the nature of things, incidental to the power which makes the appointment. I agree that if nothing more was said in the Constitution than that the President, by and with the advice and consent of the Senate, should appoint to office, there would be great force in saying that the power of removal resulted by a natural implication from the power of appointing. But there is another part of the Constitution, no less explicit than the one on which the gentleman's doctrine is founded; it is that part which declares that the executive power shall be vested in a President of the United States.

"The association of the Senate with the President in exercising that particular function, is an exception to this general rule, and exceptions to general rules, I conceive, are ever to be taken strictly. But there is another part of the Constitution which inclines, in my judgment, to favor the construction I put upon it; the President is required to take care that the laws be faithfully executed. If the duty to see the laws faithfully executed be required at the hands of the Executive Magistrate, it would seem that it was generally intended he should have that species of power which is necessary to accomplish that end. Now, if the officer, when once appointed, is not to depend upon the President for his official existence, but upon a distinct body, (for where there are two negatives required, either can prevent the removal,) I confess I do not see how the President can take care that the laws be faithfully executed. It is true, by a circuitous operation, he may obtain an impeachment, and even without this it is possible he may obtain the concurrence of the Senate for the purpose of displacing an officer; but would this give that species of control to the Executive Magistrate which seems to be required by the Constitution? I own, if my opinion was not contrary to that entertained by what I suppose to be the minority on this question, I should be doubtful of being mistaken, when I discovered how inconsistent that construction would make the Constitution with itself. I can hardly bring myself to imagine the wisdom of the convention who framed the Constitution contemplated such incongruity."

But, sir, if doubts could arise on the language of the Constitution itself, then it would become proper, for the purpose of ascertaining the true meaning of the instrument, to resort to arguments ab inconvenienti. The framers of the Constitution never intended it to mean what would defeat the very purposes which it was intended to accomplish. I think I can prove that to deprive the President of the power of removal would be fatal to the best interests of the country.

And first, the Senate cannot always be in session. I thank Heaven for that. We must separate and attend to our ordinary business. It is necessary for a healthy political constitution that we should breathe the fresh and pure air of the country. The political excitement would rise too high if it were not cooled off in this manner. The American people never will consent, and never ought to consent, that our sessions shall become perpetual. The framers of the Constitution never intended that this should be the case. But once establish the principle that the Senate must consent to removals, as well as to appointments, and this consequence is inevitable.

A foreign minister in a remote part of the world is pursuing a course, dangerous to the best interests, and ruinous to the character of the country. He is disgracing us abroad, and endangering the public peace. He has been intrusted with an important negotiation, and is betraying his trust. He has become corrupt, or is entirely incompetent. This information arrives at Washington, three or four days after the adjournment of Congress on the 3d of March. What is to be done? Is the President to be entirely powerless until the succeeding December, when the Senate may meet again? Shall he be obliged to wait until the mischief is entirely consummated—until the country is ruined—before he can recall the corrupt or wicked minister? Or will any gentleman contend that upon every occasion, when a removal from office becomes necessary, he shall call the Senators from their homes throughout this widely extended republic? And yet, this is the inevitable consequence of the position contended for by gentlemen. Could the framers of the Constitution ever have intended such an absurdity? This argument was also adverted to by Mr. Madison.

But again, there are great numbers of disbursing officers scattered over the Union. Information is received during the recess of the Senate, that one of them in Arkansas or at the Rocky Mountains, has been guilty of peculation, and is wasting the public money. Must the President fold his arms, and suffer him to proceed in his fraudulent course, until the next meeting of the Senate? The truth is, that the President cannot execute the laws of the Union, without this power of removal.

But cases still stronger may be presented. The heads of departments are the confidential advisers of the President. It is chiefly through their agency that he must conduct the great operations of Government. Without a direct control over them, it would be impossible for him to take care that the laws shall be faithfully executed. Suppose that one of them, during the recess of the Senate, violates his instructions, refuses to hold any intercourse with the President, and pursues a career which he believes to be in opposition to the Constitution, the laws and the best interests of the country. Shall the executive arm be paralyzed; and in such a case, must he patiently submit to all these evils until the Senate can be convened? In time of war, the country 288might be ruined by a corrupt Secretary of War, before the Senate could be assembled.

It is not my intention, on this occasion, to discuss the question of the removal of the deposits from the Bank of the United States. I merely wish to present it as a forcible illustration of my argument. Suppose the late Secretary of the Treasury had determined to remove the deposits, and the President had believed this measure would be as ruinous to the country as the friends of the bank apprehended. If the Secretary, notwithstanding the remonstrances of the President, had proceeded to issue the order for their removal, what should we have heard from those who were the loudest in their denunciations against the Executive, if he had said, my arms are tied, I have no power to arrest the act—the deposits must be removed, because I cannot remove my Secretary? Here the evil would have been done before the Senate could possibly have been assembled. I am indebted to the speech of the Senator from South Carolina (Mr. Calhoun), at the last session, for this illustration. The truth is, view the subject in any light you may, the power of removal is in its nature inseparable from the executive power.

I have been presenting the inconveniences which would arise, during the recess of the Senate, from the want of this power in the executive. But suppose the Senate to be always in session, would this remove every difficulty? By no means. Confer upon the Senate the power of rejecting removals, and you make the executive, in the language of the debate of 1789, a double-headed monster. That power on whom is devolved the execution of your laws, must be able to remove a corrupt or an incompetent agent from office, or he cannot perform his duties. The Senate may, without inconvenience, and with very great advantage to the country, participate in appointments; but when the man is once in office, the President must necessarily possess the power of turning him out in case he does not perform his duties. This power ought not to depend upon the will of the Senate; for that body have nothing to do with the execution of the laws.

If the power contended for were vested in the Senate, what would be the consequences? Still more dangerous, if possible, than any which I have yet depicted. The cases in which removals are necessary, must rapidly increase with the number of our officers and our rapidly extending population. If the President must assign reasons to the Senate for his removals, according to the provisions of this bill, or if the Senate must participate in these removals, as well as in appointments, it necessarily follows, that these reasons must be investigated. Witnesses must be examined to ascertain the truth or falsehood of the charges made against the officer sought to be removed. The case must be tried judicially. Time must be consumed to the prejudice of our other duties. The legislative functions of the Senate must thus become impaired, and feelings excited between co-ordinate branches of the Government calculated to produce a most injurious effect upon the country. In this state of things, the case might readily occur which was anticipated by Mr. Madison in 1789. A majority of the Senate might even keep one of the heads of department in office against the will of the President. Whether they would have done so or not last winter, in the case of the Secretary of the Treasury, I shall not pretend to determine.

If this power were conferred upon the Senate, it would interfere with our judicial functions to a dangerous and alarming extent. The removal of a high officer of the Government is recommended by the President to the Senate, because of official misconduct. The charges are tried before the Senate. From the very nature of the question it must become in fact a judicial investigation. The Senate determine either that he shall remain in his office or that he shall be removed. In either case, the House of Representatives, possessing the sole power of impeachment under the Constitution, determine to exercise it against this officer. But the Senate have, by their previous proceedings, utterly disqualified themselves from giving to the accused an impartial trial. They have already decided upon his guilt or his innocence. Instead of proceeding to the trial, unbiased by favor or by prejudice, their minds are inflamed, their judgments are biased, and they come to the investigation with the feelings of partisans, rather than those of judges. The House of Representatives would have a just right to complain loudly against the exercise of this power by the Senate. We should thus disqualify ourselves from judging impartially in cases between the people of the United States and the high officers of the Government.

I think I have successfully established the position that no two things can in their nature be more distinct than the power of appointment and that of removal. If this be the case, then what becomes of the argument of the gentleman from Massachusetts (Mr. Webster)? It rested entirely upon the principle, that these two powers were so identical in their nature, that because the Senate, under the Constitution, have the express power of advising and consenting to appointments, that, therefore, by implication, they must possess the power of advising and consenting to removals. The inference is without foundation.

The truth is, that the more we discuss this question, we shall have the greater reason to admire the wisdom of the Constitution, and of those enlightened and patriotic men who placed that construction upon it in the beginning, which I shall venture to predict never will be disturbed by the American people. The Senate, from the nature of the body, are fully competent to assist the President in appointments. It would change their character altogether, and paralyze the executive arm of the Government, if they were to usurp the power of interfering in removals from office. Let the Constitution and the construction of it by its founders, in this particular, be perpetual!

It has been objected that the President, by this construction, is too far removed from responsibility in the exercise of this power. But he is responsible to the American people, whose servant he is, in this as in all other cases. Unless you palsy the executive arm, and render it powerless to do good, lest it may do evil, you cannot support the doctrine which has been urged. You must vest some discretion; you must repose some confidence in the executive, 290or the wheels of Government must stand still. Should he abuse his power, he is liable to the censure of public opinion; and, in flagrant cases, he may be impeached. It was contended in the first Congress, and the same argument has been urged upon the present occasion, that the power of removal was not recognized by the Constitution—that it was a case omitted, and that, therefore, by implication, it belongs to Congress. This argument was fully met and successfully refuted in 1789. If this principle were established, the executive power would have no necessary control over executive officers. Congress might confer the power of removal upon the Senate alone, or upon the House of Representatives alone, or upon both conjointly, without any participation of the President. This Government—the admiration of the world, would present the solecism of an executive without any control over executive agents, except what might be granted to him by the legislature. We are not placed in this unfortunate predicament. The President, under the Constitution, has the power of removal. It is a constitutional power, not to be controlled by the legislature. It is a power equally sovereign in its nature with that of legislation itself. He is a co-ordinate branch of the Government, and has the same right to exercise his discretion in removals from office, that Congress possess in regard to the enactment of laws.

This brings me to consider the constitutionality of the third section of the bill now depending before us. It provides "that in all nominations made by the President to the Senate, to fill vacancies occasioned by removal from office, the fact of the removal shall be stated to the Senate at the time that the nomination is made, with a statement of the reasons for such removal."

Whence do we derive our authority to demand his reasons? If the Constitution has conferred upon him the power of removal, as I think I have clearly shown, is it not absolute in its nature and entirely free from the control of Congress? Is he not as independent in the exercise of this power as Congress in the exercise of any power conferred upon them by the Constitution? Would he not have the same authority to demand from us our reasons for rejecting a nomination, as we possess to call upon him for his reasons for making a removal? Might he not say, I am answerable to the American people, and to them alone, for the exercise of this power, in the same manner that the Senate is for the exercise of any power conferred upon them by the Constitution? With all the deference which I feel for the opinions of the Senator from Tennessee (Mr. White), I think he has arrived at the conclusion that the third section of this bill is constitutional, by blending things together which are in their nature entirely distinct. He asks, is it not in the power of Congress to create the office, to define its duties, and to change and vary these duties at pleasure? Granted. May they not, if they believe the office unnecessary, repeal the law, and must not the officer fall with it? Granted. These are legislative powers, clearly conferred upon Congress by the Constitution. It is then asked, may Congress not prescribe it as the duty of these officers to 291give reasons for their conduct? Certainly they may. And why? Because they are the creatures of Congress—they are called into existence by Congress—and they will cease to exist at the pleasure of Congress. Is this the condition of the executive, who is a co-ordinate branch of the Government, and who is answerable for his conduct, not to Congress, but to the people of the United States. What right have we to demand reasons from the servant of another as to how he performs his duties? To his own master, which, in this particular, is the American people, and to them alone, he is responsible. If Congress can command him to give reasons to the Senate for his removals, the Senate may judge of the validity of these reasons, and condemn them if they think proper. The executive of the country is thus rendered subordinate to the Senate;—a position in which the Constitution of the country never intended to place him. In my opinion, this bill as strongly negatives the constitutional power of the President to remove from office, without the concurrence of the Senate, as if it were so declared in express language. For this reason I shall vote against it.

In the next session, which commenced in December, 1836, Mr. Buchanan delivered a speech which may perhaps be regarded as the ablest of his efforts in the Senate. It related to a topic that had long been attended with intense political excitement. President Jackson's removal of the public deposits from the Bank of the United States furnished to the Whig opponents of his administration a means of attack, of which they were not slow to avail themselves. The powerful opposition, which at the time of that occurrence controlled the proceedings of the Senate, was led by Mr. Clay, who was the defeated Whig candidate for the Presidency at the election of 1832. Swaying his party in the Senate with an imperious will, and enforcing his determinations by a fascinating eloquence, Mr. Clay, on the 28th of March, 1834, carried a resolution, which was inscribed on the journal of the Senate in the following words: "That the President, in the late executive proceedings, in relation to the public revenue, has assumed upon himself authority and power not conferred by the Constitution and laws, but in derogation of both." On the 3d of March, 1835, a resolution introduced by Col. Benton, of Missouri, ordering Mr. Clay's resolution to be "expunged" from the journal, came up for consideration. The word "expunged" was stricken out by a vote in which the mover and other friends of the administration concurred, so that some other less objectionable 292phrase might be substituted. But as soon as this word was stricken out, Mr. Webster moved to lay the resolution on the table, giving notice that he would not withdraw his motion "for friend or foe." The motion was not debatable, and as the Whigs still had a majority, it was carried by a party vote. The Democratic Senators then determined that the word "expunged" should never be again surrendered. At the next session they had a majority; and Col. Benton's resolution then came up, in a form which directed that Mr. Clay's resolution of 1834 be expunged from the journal of the Senate, by drawing black lines around it, and writing across its face the words, "Expunged by order of the Senate, this —— day of —— in the year of our Lord 1837." It was upon this proposal, in reply to an impassioned speech by Mr. Clay, that Mr. Buchanan, on the 16th of January, 1837, addressed the Senate.

There is one praise to be accorded to this speech, which, considering the party character of the struggle, is not a small one. Mr. Buchanan separated what was personal and partisan in this controversy from the serious questions involved; and covering the whole field of argument upon the really important topics in a temperate and courteous but firm discussion, he placed his side of the debate upon its true merits. He began by contending that the censure, which the Senate had in 1834 passed upon the President, was unjust, because he had violated no law in ordering the Secretary of the Treasury to remove the public deposits from the Bank. He then argued that the Senate had committed an infraction of the Constitution, by recording upon its journal an accusation that the President had been guilty of an offence for which he might be impeached, and for which it would be the duty of the Senate to try him on articles of impeachment, if the House of Representatives should ever proceed against him in that manner. In thus prejudging the case, by a resolution of mere naked censure, adopted in its legislative capacity, the Senate had rendered itself incompetent to perform its high judicial function. He concluded his argument by a very ingenious and elaborate criticism of the word "expunge," arguing that there was a real and solid distinction between a physical obliteration of a record, making it impossible thereafter to be read, and such an annulment of its legal existence 293as was now proposed, and which, by leaving it in a condition to be read, would nevertheless deprive it of all force. It must be confessed that this was a very finely drawn distinction; but it was supported by no inconsiderable acuteness and force, and with great fairness of reasoning. Col. Benton's resolution was adopted by a party vote, and was immediately carried out.[53]

The following is a full report of Mr. Buchanan's speech in support of the Expunging Resolution:

Mr. President:—After the able and eloquent display of the Senator from Kentucky, (Mr. Clay) who has just resumed his seat, after having so long enchained the attention of his audience, it might be the dictate of prudence for me to remain silent. But I feel too deeply my responsibility as an American Senator, not to make the attempt to place before the Senate and the country the reasons which, in my opinion, will justify the vote which I intend to give this day.

A more grave and solemn question has rarely, if ever, been submitted to the Senate of the United States, than the one now under discussion. This Senate is now called upon to review its own decision, to rejudge its own justice, and to annihilate its own sentence, pronounced against the co-ordinate executive branch of this Government. On the 28th of March, 1834, the American Senate, in the face of the American people, in the face of the whole world, by a solemn resolution, pronounced the President of the United States to be a violator of the Constitution of his country—of that Constitution which he had solemnly sworn "to preserve, protect, and defend." Whether we consider the exalted character of the tribunal which pronounced this condemnation, or the illustrious object against which it was directed, we ought to feel deeply impressed with the high and lasting importance of the present proceeding. It is in fact, if not in form, the trial of the Senate, for having unjustly and unconstitutionally tried and condemned the President; and their accusers are the American people. In this cause I am one of the judges. In some respects, it is a painful position for me to occupy. It is vain, however, to express unavailing regrets. I must, and shall, firmly and sternly, do my duty; although in the performance of it I may wound the 294feelings of gentlemen whom I respect and esteem. I shall proceed no farther than the occasion demands, and will, therefore, justify.

Who was the President of the United States, against whom this sentence has been pronounced? Andrew Jackson—a name which every American mother, after the party strife which agitates us for the present moment shall have passed away, will, during all the generations which this Republic is destined to endure, teach her infant to lisp with that of the venerated name of Washington. The one was the founder, the other the preserver, of the liberties of his country.

If President Jackson has been guilty of violating the Constitution of the United States, let impartial justice take its course. I admit that it is no justification for such a crime, that his long life has been more distinguished by acts of disinterested patriotism than that of any American citizen now living. It is no justification that the honesty of his heart and the purity of his intentions have become proverbial, even amongst his political enemies. It is no justification that in the hour of danger, and in the day of battle, he has been his country's shield. If he has been guilty, let his name be "damned to everlasting fame," with those of Cæsar and of Napoleon.

If, on the other hand, he is pure and immaculate from the charge, let us be swift to do him justice, and to blot out the foul stigma which the Senate has placed upon his character. If we are not, he may go down to the grave in doubt as to what may be the final judgment of his country. In any event, he must soon retire to the shades of private life. Shall we, then, suffer his official term to expire, without first doing him justice? It may be said of me, as it has already been said of other Senators, that I am one of the gross adulators of the President. But, sir, I have never said thus much of him whilst he was in the meridian of his power. Now that his political sun is nearly set, I feel myself at liberty to pour forth my grateful feelings, as an American citizen, to a man who has done so much for his country. I have never, for myself, either directly or indirectly, solicited office at his hands; and my character must greatly change, if I should ever do so from any of his successors. If I should bestow upon him the meed of my poor praise, it springs from an impulse far different from that which has been attributed to the majority on this floor. I speak as an independent freeman and American Senator; and I feel proud now to have the opportunity of raising my voice in his defence.

On the 28th day of March, 1834, the Senate of the United States resolved, "that the President, in the late executive proceedings, in relation to the public revenue, has assumed upon himself authority and power not conferred by the Constitution and laws, but in derogation of both."

In discussing this subject, I shall undertake to prove, first, that this resolution is unjust; secondly, that it is unconstitutional; and in the last place, that it ought to be expunged from our journals, in the manner proposed by the Senator from Missouri (Mr. Benton). First, then, it is unjust. On this branch of the subject I had intended to confine myself to a bare expression of my own decided opinion. This point has been so often and so ably discussed, that it is impossible for me to cast any new light upon it. But as it is my intention to follow the footsteps of the Senator from Kentucky (Mr. Clay) wherever they may lead, I must again tread the ground which has been so often trodden. As the Senator, however, has confined himself to a mere passing reference to the topics which this head presents, I shall, in this particular, follow his example.

Although the resolution condemning the President is vague and general in its terms, yet we all know that it was founded upon his removal of the public deposits from the Bank of the United States. The Senator from Kentucky has contended that this act was a violation of law. And why? Because, says he, it is well known that the public money was secure in that institution; and by its charter the public deposits could not be removed from it, unless under a just apprehension that they were in danger. Now, sir, I admit that if the President had no right to remove these deposits, except for the sole reason that their safety was in danger, the Senator has established his position. But what is the fact? Was the Government thus restricted by the terms of the bank charter? I answer, no. Such a limitation is nowhere to be found in it. Let me read the sixteenth section, which is the only one relating to the subject. It enacts, "that the deposits of the money of the United States, in places in which the said bank and branches thereof may be established, shall be made in said bank or branches thereof, unless the Secretary of the Treasury shall at any other time otherwise order and direct; in which case the Secretary of the Treasury shall immediately lay before Congress, if in session, and, if not, immediately after the commencement of the next session, the reasons of such order or direction."

Is not the authority thus conferred upon the Secretary of the Treasury as broad and as ample as the English language will admit? Where is the limitation, where the restriction? One might have supposed from the argument of the Senator from Kentucky, that the charter restricted the Secretary of the Treasury from removing the deposits, unless he believed them to be insecure in the Bank of the United States; but the language of the law itself completely refutes his argument. They were to remain in the Bank of the United States, "unless the Secretary of the Treasury shall at any time otherwise order and direct." The sole limitation upon the discretion of that officer was his immediate and direct responsibility to Congress. To us he was bound to render his reasons for removing the deposits. We, and we alone, are constituted the judges as to the sufficiency of these reasons.

It would be an easy task to prove that the authors of the bank charter acted wisely in not limiting the discretion of the Secretary of the Treasury over the deposits to the single case of their apprehended insecurity. We may imagine many other reasons which would have rendered their removal both wise and expedient. But I forbear; especially as the case now before the Senate presents as striking an illustration of this proposition as I could possibly imagine. Upon what principle, then, do I justify the removal of the deposits? The Bank of the United States had determined to apply for a recharter at the session of Congress immediately preceding the last Presidential election. Preparatory to this application, and whilst it was pending, in the short space of sixteen months, it had increased its loans more than twenty-eight million dollars. They rose from forty-two millions to seventy millions between the last of December, 1830, and the first of May, 1832. Whilst this boasted regulator of the currency was thus expanding its discounts, all the local banks followed the example. The impulse of self-interest urged them to pursue this course. A delusive prosperity was thus spread over the land. Money everywhere became plenty. The bank was regarded as the beneficent parent, who was pouring her money out into the laps of her children. She thought herself wise and provident in thus rendering herself popular. The recharter passed both Houses of Congress by triumphant majorities. But then came "the frost, the killing frost." It was not so easy to propitiate "the Old Roman." Although he well knew the power and influence which the bank could exert against him at the then approaching Presidential election, he cast such considerations to the winds. He vetoed the bill, and in the most solemn manner placed himself for trial upon this question before the American people.

From that moment the faith of many of his former friends began to grow cold. The bank openly took the field against his re-election. It expended large sums in subsidizing editors, and in circulating pamphlets, and papers, and speeches, throughout the Union, calculated to inflame the public mind against the President. I merely glance at these things.

Let us pause for a single moment to consider the consequences of such conduct. What right had the bank, as a corporation, to enter the arena of politics for the purpose of defending itself, and attacking the President? Whilst I freely admit that each individual stockholder possessed the same rights, in this respect, as every other American citizen, I pray you to consider what a dangerous precedent the bank has thus established. Our banks now number nearly a thousand, and our other chartered institutions are almost innumerable. If all these corporations are to be justified in using their corporate funds for the purpose of influencing elections; of elevating their political friends, and crushing their political foes, our condition is truly deplorable. We shall thus introduce into the State a new, a dangerous, and an alarming power, the effects of which no man can anticipate. Watchful jealousy is the price which a free people must ever pay for their liberties; and this jealousy should be Argus-eyed in watching the political movements of corporations. After the bank had been defeated in the Presidential election, it adopted a new course of policy. What it had been unable to accomplish by making money plenty, it determined it would wrest from the sufferings of the people by making money scarce. Pressure and panic then became its weapons; and with these it was determined, if possible, to extort a recharter from the American people. It commenced this warfare upon the interests of the country about the first of August, 1833. In two short months it decreased its loans more than four millions of dollars, whilst the deposits of the Government with it had increased, during the same period, two millions and a quarter. I speak in round numbers.

It was then in the act of reducing its discounts at the rate of two millions of dollars per month.

The State banks had expanded their loans with the former expansion of the Bank of the United States. It now became necessary to contract them. The severest pressure began to be felt everywhere. Had the Bank of the United States been permitted a short time longer to proceed in this course, fortified as it was with the millions of the Government which it held on deposit, a scene of almost universal bankruptcy and insolvency must have been presented in our commercial cities. It thus became absolutely necessary for the President either to deprive the bank of the public deposits, as the only means of protecting the State banks, and through them the people, from these impending evils, or calmly to look on and see it spreading ruin throughout the land. It was necessary for him to adopt this policy for the purpose of preventing a universal derangement of the currency, a general sacrifice of property, and, as an inevitable consequence, the recharter of this institution. By the removal of the deposits, he struck a blow against the bank from which it has never since recovered. This was the club of Hercules with which he slew the hydra. This was the master-stroke by which he prostrated what a large majority of the American people believe to have been a corrupt and a corrupting institution. For this he is not only justified, but deserves the eternal gratitude of his country. For this the Senate have condemned him; but the people of the United States have hailed him as a deliverer.

It has been said by the Senator from Kentucky, that the President, by removing the deposits from the Bank of the United States, united in his own hands the power of the purse of the nation with that of the sword. I think it is not difficult to answer this argument. What was to become of the public money, in case it had been removed from the Bank of the United States, under its charter, for the cause which the Senator himself deems justifiable? Why, sir, it would then have been immediately remitted to the guardianship of those laws under which it had been protected before the Bank of the United States was called into existence. Such was the present case. In regard to this point, no matter whether the cause of removal were sufficient or not, the moment the deposits were actually removed they became subject to the pre-existing laws, and not to the arbitrary will of the President.

The Senator from Kentucky has contended that the President violated the Constitution and the laws, by dismissing Mr. Duane from office because he would not remove the deposits, and by appointing Mr. Taney to accomplish this purpose. I shall not discuss at any length the power of removal. It is now too late in the day to question it. That the executive possesses this power was decided by the first Congress. It has often since been discussed and decided in the same manner, and it has been exercised by every President of the United States. The President is bound by the Constitution to 298"take care that the laws be faithfully executed." If he cannot remove his executive officers, it is impossible that he can perform this duty. Every inferior officer might set up for himself; might violate the laws of the country, and put him at defiance, whilst he would remain perfectly powerless. He could not arrest their career. A foreign minister might be betraying and disgracing the nation abroad, without any power to recall him until the next meeting of the Senate. This construction of the Constitution involves so many dangers and so many absurdities, that it could not be maintained for a moment, even if there had not been a constant practice against it of almost half a century.

But it is contended by the Senator that the Secretary of the Treasury is a sort of independent power in the State, and is released from the control of the executive. And why? Simply because he is directed by law to make his annual report to Congress and not to the President. If this position be correct, then it necessarily follows that the executive is released from the obligation of taking care that the numerous and important acts of Congress regulating the fiscal concerns of the country shall be faithfully executed. The Secretary of the Treasury is thus made independent of his control. What would be the position of this officer under such a construction of the Constitution and laws, it would be very difficult to decide. And this wonderful transformation of his character has arisen from the mere circumstance that Congress have by law directed him to make an annual report to them! No, sir; the executive is responsible to Congress for the faithful execution of all the laws; and if the present or any other President should prove faithless to his high trust, the present Senate, notwithstanding all which has been said, would be as ready as their predecessors to inflict condign punishment upon him, in the mode pointed out by the Constitution.

I have now arrived at the great question of the constitutional power of the Senate to adopt the resolution of March, 1834. It is my firm conviction that the Senate possesses no such power; and it is now my purpose to establish this position. The decision on this point must depend upon a true answer to the question: Does this resolution contain any impeachable charge against the President? If it does, I trust I shall demonstrate that the Senate violated its constitutional duty in proceeding to condemn him in this manner. I shall again read the resolution:

"Resolved, That the President, in the late executive proceedings in relation to the public revenue, has assumed upon himself authority and power not conferred by the Constitution and laws, but in derogation of both."

This language is brief and comprehensive. It comes at once to the point. It bears a striking impress of the character of the Senator from Kentucky. Does it charge an impeachable offence against the President?

The fourth section of the second article of the Constitution declares that the "President, Vice-President, and all civil officers of the United States shall be removed from office on impeachment for, and conviction of, treason, bribery, or other high crimes and misdemeanors."

It has been contended that this condemnatory resolution contains no impeachable offence, because it charges no criminal intention against the President; and I admit that it does not attribute to him any corrupt motive in express words. Is this sufficient to convince the judgment of any impartial man that none was intended? Let us, for a few moments, examine this proposition. If it be well founded, the Senate may for ever hereafter usurp the power of trying, condemning, and destroying any officer of the Government, without affording him the slightest opportunity of being heard in his defence. They may abuse their power, and prostrate any object of their vengeance. It seems we have now made the discovery, that the Senate are authorized to exert this tremendous power—that they may thus assume to themselves the office both of accuser and of judge, provided the indictment contains no express allegation of a criminal intention. The President, or any officer of the Government, may be denounced by the Senate as a violator of the Constitution of his country,—as derelict in the performance of his public duties, provided there is no express imputation of an improper motive. The characters of men whose reputation is dearer to them than their lives may thus be destroyed. They may be held up to public execration by the omission of a few formal words. The condemnation of the Senate carries with it such a moral power, that perhaps there is no man in the United States, except Andrew Jackson, who could have resisted its force. No, sir; such an argument can never command conviction. That which we have no power to do directly, we can never accomplish by indirect means. We cannot by resolution convict a man of an impeachable offence, merely because we may omit the formal words of an impeachment. We must regard the substance of things, and not the mere form.

But again. Although a criminal intention be not charged, in so many words, by this resolution, yet its language, even without the attendant circumstances, clearly conveys this meaning. The President is charged with having "assumed upon himself authority and power not conferred by the Constitution and laws, but in derogation of both." "Assumed upon himself." What is the plain palpable meaning of this phrase connected with what precedes and follows? Is it not "to arrogate," "to claim or seize unjustly." These are two of the first meanings of the word assume, according to the lexicographers. To assume upon one's self is a mode of expression which is rarely taken in a good sense. As it is used here, I ask if any man of plain common understanding, after reading this resolution, would ever arrive at the conclusion that any Senator voted for it under the impression that the President was innocent of any improper intention, and that he violated the Constitution from mere mistake and from pure motives? The common sense of mankind revolts at the idea. How can it be contended, for a single moment, that you can denounce the President as a man who had "assumed upon himself" the power of violating the laws and the Constitution of his country, and in the same breath declare that you had not the least intention to criminate him, and that your language was altogether inoffensive. The two propositions are manifestly inconsistent.

300But I go one step further. If we were sitting as a court of impeachment, and the bare proposition were established to our satisfaction that the President had, in violation of the Constitution and the laws, withdrawn the public revenue of the country from the depository to whose charge Congress had committed it, and assumed the control over it himself, we would be bound to convict him of a high official misdemeanor. Under such circumstances, we should be bound to infer a criminal intention from this illegal and unconstitutional act. Criminal justice could never be administered,—society could not exist, if the tribunals of the country should not attribute evil motives to illegal and unconstitutional conduct. Omniscience alone can examine the heart. When poor frail man is placed in the judgment-seat, he must infer the intentions of the accused from his actions. That "the tree is known by its fruits" is an axiom which we have derived from the fountain of all truth. Does a poor, naked, hungry wretch, at this inclement season of the year, take from my pocket a single dollar; the law infers a criminal intent, and he must be convicted and punished as a thief, though he may have been actuated by no other motive than that of saving his wife and his children from starvation. And shall a different rule be applied to the President of the United States? Shall it be said of a man elevated to the highest station on earth, for his wisdom, his integrity, and his virtues, with all his constitutional advisers around him, when he violates the Constitution of his country and usurps the control over its entire revenue, that he may successfully defend himself by declaring he had done this deed without any criminal intention? No, sir; in such a case, above all others, the criminal intention must be inferred from the unconstitutional exercise of high and dangerous powers. The safety of the Republic demands that the President of the United States should never shield himself behind such flimsy pretexts. This resolution, therefore, although it may not have assumed the form of an article of impeachment, possesses all the substance.

It was my fate some years ago to have assisted as a manager, in behalf of the House of Representatives, in the trial of an impeachment before this body. It then became my duty to examine all the precedents in such cases which had occurred under our Government, since the adoption of the Federal Constitution. On that occasion, I found one which has a strong bearing upon this question. I refer to the case of Judge Pickering. He was tried and condemned by the Senate upon all the four articles exhibited against him; although the first three contained no other charge than that of making decisions contrary to law, in a cause involving a mere question of property, and then refusing to grant the party injured an appeal from his decision, to which he was entitled. From the clear violation of law in this case, the Senate must have inferred an impure and improper motive.

If any thing further were wanting to prove that the resolution of the Senate contained a criminal and impeachable charge against the President, it might be demonstrated from all the circumstances attending the transaction. Whilst this resolution was in progress through the Senate, the Bank of the United States was employed in producing panic and pressure throughout the land. Much actual suffering was experienced by the people; and where that did not exist, they dreaded unknown and awful calamities. Confidence between man and man was at an end. There was a fearful pause in the business of the country. We were then engaged in the most violent party conflict recorded in our annals. To use the language of the Senator from Kentucky, we were in the midst of a revolution. On the one side it was contended that the power over the purse of the nation had been usurped by the President; that in his own person he had united this power with that of the sword, and that the liberties of the people were gone, unless he could be arrested in his mad career. On the other hand, the friends of the President maintained that the removal of the deposits from the Bank of the United States was an act of stern justice to the people; that it was strictly legal and constitutional; that he was impelled to it by the highest and purest principles of patriotism; and that it was the only means of prostrating an institution which threatened the destruction of our dearest rights and liberties. During this terrific conflict public indignation was aroused to such a degree, that the President received a great number of anonymous letters, threatening him with assassination unless he should restore the deposits.

It was during the pendency of this conflict throughout the country, that the Senator from Kentucky thought proper, on the 26th December, 1833, to present his condemnatory resolution to the Senate. And here, sir, permit me to say that I do not believe there was any corrupt connection between any Senator upon this floor and the Bank of the United States. But it was at this inauspicious moment that the resolution was introduced. How was it supported by the Senator from Kentucky? He told us that a revolution had already commenced. He told us that by the 3d of March, 1837, if the progress of innovation should continue, there would be scarcely a vestige remaining of the Government and policy as they had existed prior to the 3d March, 1829. That in a term of years a little more than that which was required to establish our liberties, the Government would be transformed into an elective monarchy—the worst of all forms of government. He compared the measure adopted by General Jackson with the conduct of the usurping Cæsar, who, after he had overrun Italy in sixty days, and conquered the liberties of his native country, terrified the Tribune Metellus, who guarded the treasury of the Roman people, and seized it by open force. He declared that the President had proclaimed an open, palpable, and daring usurpation. He concluded by asserting that the premonitory symptoms of despotism were upon us; and if Congress did not apply an instantaneous and effective remedy, the fatal collapse would soon come on, and we should die—ignobly die! base, mean, and abject slaves, the scorn and contempt of mankind, unpitied, unwept, and unmourned. What a spectacle was then presented in this Chamber! We are told, in the reports of the day, that, when he took his seat, there was repeated and loud applause in the galleries. This, it will be remembered, was the introductory speech of the Senator. In my opinion, it was one of the ablest and most eloquent of all his able and eloquent speeches. He was then riding upon the whirlwind and directing the storm. At the time I read it, for I was not then in the Senate, it reminded me of the able, the vindictive, and the eloquent appeal of Mr. Burke before the House of Lords, on the impeachment of Warren Hastings, in which he denounced that governor-general as the ravager and oppressor of India, and the scourge of the millions who had been placed under his authority.

And yet, we are now told that this resolution did not intend to impute any criminal motive to the President. That he was a good old man, though not a good constitutional lawyer: and that he knew better how to wield the sword than to construe the Constitution. [Mr. Clay here rose to explain. He said, "I never have said and never will say, that personally I acquitted the President of any improper intention. I lament that I cannot say it. But what I did say, was that the act of the Senate of 1834 is free from the imputation of any criminal motives."]

Sir, said Mr. B., this avowal is in character with the frank and manly nature of the Senator from Kentucky. It is no more than what I expected from him. The imputation of any improper motive to the President has been again and again disclaimed by other Senators upon this floor. The Senator from Kentucky has now boldly come out in his true colors, and avows the principles which he held at the time. He acknowledges that he did not acquit the President from improper intentions, when charging him with a violation of the Constitution of his country.

This trial of the President before the Senate, continued for three months. During this whole period, instead of the evidence which a judicial tribunal ought to receive, exciting memorials, signed by vast numbers of the people, and well calculated to inflame the passions of his judges, were daily pouring in upon the Senate. He was denounced upon this floor by every odious epithet which belongs to tyrants. Finally, the obnoxious resolution was adopted by the vote of the Senate, on the 28th day of March, 1834. After the exposition which I have made, can any impartial mind doubt but that this resolution intended to charge against the President a wilful and daring violation of the Constitution and the laws? I think not.

The Senator from Kentucky has argued, with his usual power, that the functions of the Senate, acting in a legislative capacity, are not to be restricted, because it is possible that the same question, in another form, may come before us judicially. I concur in the truth and justice of this position. We must perform our legislative duties; and if, in the investigation of facts, having legislation distinctly in view, we should incidentally be led to the investigation of criminal charges, it is a necessity imposed upon us by our condition, from which we cannot escape. It results from the varying nature of our duties, and not from our own will. I admit that it would be difficult to mark the precise line which separates our legislative from our judicial functions. I shall not attempt it. In many cases, from necessity, they are in some degree intermingled. The present resolution, however, stands far in advance of this 303line. It is placed in bold relief, and is clear of all such difficulties. It is a mere naked resolution of censure. It refers solely to the past conduct of the President, and condemns it in the strongest terms, without even proposing any act of legislation by which the evil may be remedied hereafter. It was judgment upon the past alone; not prevention for the future. Nay, more: the resolution is so vague and general in its terms that it is impossible to ascertain from its face the cause of the President's condemnation. The Senate have resolved that the executive "has assumed upon himself authority and power not conferred by the Constitution and laws, but in derogation of both." What is the specification under this charge? Why, that he has acted thus, "in the late executive proceedings in relation to the public revenue?" What executive proceedings? The resolution leaves us entirely in the dark upon this subject. How could any legislation spring from such a resolution? It is impossible. None such was ever attempted.

If the resolution had preserved its original phraseology—if it had condemned the President for dismissing one Secretary of the Treasury because he would not remove the deposits, and for appointing his successor to effect this purpose, the Senator might then have contended that the evil was distinctly pointed out; and, although no legislation was proposed, the remedy might be applied hereafter. But he has deprived himself even of this feeble argument. He has left us upon an ocean of uncertainty, without chart or compass. "The late executive proceedings in relation to the revenue," is a phrase of the most general and indefinite character. Every Senator who voted in favor of this resolution may have acted upon different principles. To procure its passage, nothing more was necessary than that a majority should unite in the conclusion that the President had violated the Constitution and the laws in some one or other of his numerous acts in relation to the public revenue. The views of Senators constituting the majority may have varied from each other to any conceivable extent; and yet they may have united in the final vote. That this was the fact to a considerable extent, I have always understood. It is utterly impossible, either that such a proceeding could ever have been intended to become the basis of legislation, or that legislative action could have ever sprung from such a source.

I flatter myself, then, I have succeeded in proving that this resolution charged the President with a high official misdemeanor, wholly disconnected from legislation, which, if true, ought to have subjected him to impeachment.

This brings me directly to the question, had the Senate any power, under the Constitution, to adopt such a resolution? In other words, can the Senate condemn a public officer by a simple resolution, for an offence which would subject him to an impeachment? To state the proposition, is to answer this question in the negative. Dreadful would be the consequences if we possess and should exercise such a power.

This body is invested with high and responsible powers of a legislative, an executive, and a judicial character. No person can enter it until he has attained a mature age. Our term of service is longer than that of any other elective functionary. If Senators will have it so, it is the most aristocratic branch of our Government. For what purpose did the framers of the Constitution confer upon it these varied and important powers, and this long tenure of office? The answer is plain. It was placed in this secure and elevated position that it might be above the storms of faction which so often inflame the passions of men. It never was intended to be an arena for political gladiators. Until the second session of the third Congress, the Senate always sat with closed doors, except in the single instance when the eligibility of Mr. Gallatin to a seat in the body was the subject of discussion. Of this particular practice, however, I cannot approve. I merely state it, to show the intention of those who formed the Constitution. I was informed by one of the most eminent statesmen and Senators which this country has ever produced, now no more (the late Mr. King), that for some years after the Federal Government commenced its operation, the debates of the Senate resembled conversations rather than speeches, and that it originated but few legislative measures. Senators were then critics rather than authors in legislation. Whether its gain in eloquence, since it has become a popular assembly, and since the sound of thundering applause has been heard in our galleries at the denunciation of the President, has been an equivalent for its loss in true dignity, may well be doubted. To give this body its just influence with the people, it ought to preserve itself as free as possible from angry political discussions. In the performance of our executive duties, in the ratification of treaties, and in the confirmation of nominations, the Constitution has connected us with the executive. The efficient and successful administration of the Government therefore requires that we should move on together in as much harmony as may be consistent with the independent exercise of our respective functions.

But above all, we should be the most cautious in guarding our judicial character from suspicion. We constitute the high court of impeachment of this nation, before which every officer of the Government may be arraigned. To this tribunal is committed the character of men whose character is far dearer to them than their lives. We should be the rock standing in the midst of the ocean, for the purpose of affording a shelter to the faithful officer from unjust persecution, against which the billows might dash themselves in vain. Whilst we are a terror to evil doers, we should be a praise to those who do well. We should never voluntarily perform any act which might prejudice our judgment, or render us suspected as a judicial tribunal. More especially, when the President of the United States is arraigned at the bar of public opinion for offences which might subject him to an impeachment, we should remain not only chaste but unsuspected. Better, infinitely better, would it be for us not to manifest our feeling, even in a case in which we were morally certain the House of Representatives would not prefer before us articles of impeachment, than to reach the object of our disapprobation by a usurpation of their rights. It is true that when the Senate passed the resolution condemning the President, a majority in the House were of a different 305opinion. But the next elections might have changed that majority into a minority. The House might then have voted articles of impeachment against the President. Under such circumstances, I pray you to consider in what a condition the Senate would have been placed. They had already prejudged the case. They had already convicted the President, and denounced him to the world as a violator of the Constitution. In criminal prosecutions, even against the greatest malefactor, if a juror has prejudged the cause, he cannot enter the jury box. The Senate had rendered itself wholly incompetent in this case to perform its highest judicial functions. The trial of the President, had articles of impeachment been preferred against him, would have been but a solemn mockery of justice.

The Constitution of the United States has carefully provided against such an enormous evil, by declaring that "the House of Representatives shall have the sole power of impeachment," and "the Senate shall have the sole power to try all impeachments." Until the accused is brought before us by the House, it is a manifest violation of our solemn duty to condemn him by a resolution.

If a court of criminal jurisdiction, without any indictment having been found by a grand jury, without having given the defendant notice to appear, without having afforded him an opportunity of cross-examining the witnesses against him, and making his defence, should resolve that he was guilty of a high crime, and place this conviction upon their records, all mankind would exclaim against the injustice and unconstitutionality of the act. Wherein consists the difference between this case and the condemnation of the President? In nothing, except that such a conviction by the Senate, on account of its exalted character, would fall with tenfold force upon its object. I have often been astonished, notwithstanding the extended and well deserved popularity of General Jackson, that the moral influence of this condemnation by the Senate had not crushed him. With what tremendous effect might this assumed power of the Senate be used to blast the reputation of any man who might fall under its displeasure! The precedent is extremely dangerous; and the American people have wisely determined to blot it out forever.

It is painful to reflect what might have been the condition of the country, if at the inauspicious moment of the passage of the resolution against the President, its interests and its honor had rendered it necessary to engage in a foreign war. The fearful consequences of such a condition, at such a moment, must strike every mind. Would the Senate then have confided to the President the necessary power to defend the country? Where could the sinews of war have been found? In what condition was this body, at that moment, to act upon an important treaty negotiated by the President, or upon any of his nominations? But I forbear to enlarge upon this topic.

I have now arrived at the last point in this discussion. Do the Senate possess the power, under the Constitution, of expunging the resolution of March, 1834, from their journals, in the manner proposed by the Senator from Missouri? (Mr. Benton.) I cheerfully admit we must show that this is not contrary to the Constitution; for we can never redress one violation of that instrument by committing another. Before I proceed to this branch of the subject, I shall put myself right, by a brief historical reminiscence. I entered the Senate in December, 1834, fresh from the ranks of the people, without the slightest feeling of hostility against any Senator on this floor. I then thought that the resolution of the Senator from Missouri was too severe in proposing to expunge. Although I was anxious to record, in strong terms, my entire disapprobation of the resolution of March, 1834, yet I was willing to accomplish this object without doing more violence to the feelings of my associates on this floor, than was absolutely necessary to justify the President. Actuated by these friendly motives, I exerted all my little influence with the Senator from Missouri, to induce him to abandon the word expunge, and substitute some others in its place. I knew that this word was exceedingly obnoxious to the Senators who had voted for the former resolution. Other friends of his also exerted their influence; and at length his kindly feelings prevailed, and he consented to abandon that word, although it was peculiarly dear to him. I speak from my own knowledge. "All which I saw and part of which I was."

The resolution of the Senator from Missouri came before the Senate on the 3d of March, 1835. Under it the resolution of March, 1834, was "ordered to be expunged from the journal," for reasons appearing on its face, which I need not enumerate. The Senator from Tennessee (Mr. White) moved to amend the resolution of the Senator from Missouri, by striking out the order to expunge, with the reasons for it, and inserting in their stead the words, "rescinded, reversed, repealed, and declared to be null and void." Some difference of opinion then arose among the friends of the Administration as to the words which should be substituted in place of the order to expunge. For the purpose of leaving this question perfectly open, you, sir, (Mr. King, of Alabama, was in the chair,) then moved to amend the original motion of Mr. Benton, by striking out the words, "ordered to be expunged from the journal of the Senate." This motion prevailed, on the ayes and noes, by a vote of 39 to 7; and amongst the ayes, the name of the Senator from Missouri is recorded. The resolution was thus left a blank, in its most essential features, ready to be filled up as the Senate might direct. The era of good feeling, in regard to this subject had commenced. It was nipped in the bud, however, by the Senator from Massachusetts (Mr. Webster). Whilst the resolution was still in blank, he rose in his place, and proclaimed the triumph of the Constitution, by the vote to strike out the word expunge, and then moved to lay the resolution on the table, declaring that he would neither withdraw his motion for friend nor foe. This motion precluded all amendment and all debate. It prevailed by a party vote; and thus we were left with our resolution a blank. Such was the manner in which the Senators in opposition received our advances of courtesy and kindness, in the moment of their strength and our weakness. Had the Senator from Massachusetts suffered us to proceed but for five minutes, we should have filled up the blank in the resolution. It would then have assumed a distinct form, and they would never afterwards have heard of the word expunge. We should have been content with the words "rescinded, reversed, repealed, and declared to be null and void." But the conduct of the Senator from Massachusetts on that occasion, and that of the party with which he acted, roused the indignation of every friend of the Administration on this floor. We then determined that the word expunge should never again be surrendered.

The Senator from Kentucky has introduced a precedent from the proceedings of the House of Representatives of Pennsylvania, for the purpose of proving that we have no right to adopt this resolution. To this I can have no possible objection. But I can tell the Senator, if I were convinced that I had voted wrong, when comparatively a boy, more than twenty years ago, the fear of being termed inconsistent would not now deter me from voting right upon the same question. I do not, however, repent of my vote upon that occasion. I would now vote in the same manner, under similar circumstances. I should not vote to expunge, under any circumstances, any proceeding from the journals by obliterating the record. If I do not prove before I take my seat, that the case in the Legislature of Pennsylvania was essentially different from that now before the Senate, I shall agree to be proclaimed inconsistent and time-serving.

It was my settled conviction at the commencement of the last session of Congress, that the Senate had no power to obliterate their journal. This was shaken, but not removed, by the argument of the Senator from Louisiana, (Mr. Porter), who confessedly made the ablest speech on the other side of the question. The Constitution declares that "each House shall keep a journal of its proceedings, and from time to time publish the same, excepting such parts as may in their judgment require secrecy." What was the position which that Senator then attempted to maintain? In order to prove that we had no power to obliterate or destroy our journals, he thought it necessary to contend that the word "keep" as used in the Constitution, means both to record and to preserve. This appeared to me to be a mere begging of the question.

I shall attempt no definition of the word "keep." At least since the days of Plato, we know that definitions have been dangerous. Yet I think that the meaning of this word, as applied to the subject matter, is so plain that he who runs may read. If I direct my agent to keep a journal of his proceedings, and publish the same, my palpable meaning is, that he shall write these proceedings down, from day to day, and publish what he has written for general information. After he has obeyed my commands, after he has kept his journal, and published it to the world, he has executed the essential part of the trust confided to him. What becomes of this original manuscript journal afterwards, is a matter of total indifference. So in regard to the manuscript journals of either House of Congress: after more than a thousand copies have been printed, and published, and distributed over the Union, it is a matter of not the least importance what disposition may be made of them. 308They have answered their purpose, and, in any practical view, become useless. If they were burnt, or otherwise destroyed, it would not be an event of the slightest public consequence. Such indifference has prevailed upon this subject, that these journals have been considered, in the House of Representatives, as so much waste paper, and, during a period of thirty-four years after the organization of the Government, they were actually destroyed. From this circumstance, no public or private inconvenience has been or ever can be sustained; because our printed journals are received in evidence in all courts of justice in the same manner as if the originals were produced.

The Senator from Louisiana has discovered that to "keep" means both "to record" and "to preserve." But can you give this, or any other word in the English language, two distinct and independent meanings at the same time, as applied to the same subject? I think not. From the imperfection of human language, from the impossibility of having appropriate words to express every idea, the same word, as applied to different subjects, has a variety of significations. As applied to any one subject, it cannot, at the same time, convey two distinct meanings. In the Constitution it must mean either "to write down," or "to preserve." It cannot have both significations. Let Senators, then, take their choice. If it signifies "to write down," as it unquestionably does, what becomes of the constitutional injunction to preserve? The truth is, that the Constitution has not provided what shall be done with the manuscript journal, after it has served the purposes for which it was called into existence. When it has been published to the people of the United States, for whose use it was ordered to be kept; after it has thus been perpetuated, and they have been furnished with the means of judging of the public conduct of their public servants, it ceases to be an object of the least importance. Whether it be thrown into the garret of the Capitol with other useless lumber, or be destroyed, is a matter of no public interest. It has probably never once been referred to in the history of our Government. If it should ever be determined to be a violation of the Constitution to obliterate or destroy this manuscript journal, it must be upon different principles from those which have been urged in this debate. My own impression is, that as the framers of the Constitution have directed us to keep a journal, a constructive duty may be implied from this command, which would forbid us to obliterate or destroy it. Under this impression, I should vote, as I did twenty years ago, in the Legislature of Pennsylvania, against any proposition actually to expunge any part of the journal. But waiving this unprofitable discussion, let us proceed to the real point in controversy.

Is any such proceeding as that of actually expunging the journal, proposed by the resolution of the Senator from Missouri? I answer, no such thing. If the Constitution had, in express terms, directed us to record and to preserve a journal of our proceedings, there is nothing in the resolution now before us which would be inconsistent with such a provision.

Is the drawing of a black line around the resolution of the Senate, of March, 3091834, to obliterate or deface it? On the contrary, is it not to render it more conspicuous,—to place it in bold relief,—to give it a prominence in the public view, beyond any other proceeding of this body, in past, and I trust, in all future time. If the argument of Senators were, not that we have no power to obliterate; but that the Senate possessed no power to render one portion of the journal more conspicuous than another, it would have had much greater force. Why, sir, by means of this very proceeding, that portion of our journal upon which it operates will be rescued from a slumber which would otherwise have been eternal, and, fac-similes of the original resolution, without a word or a letter defaced, will be circulated over the whole Union.

But, sir, this resolution also directs that across the face of the condemnatory resolution there shall be written by the Secretary, "Expunged by the order of the Senate this —— day of ——, in the year of our Lord 1837."

Will this obliterate any part of the original resolution? If it does, the duty of the Secretary will be performed in a very bungling manner. No such thing is intended. It would be easy to remove every scruple from every mind upon this subject, by amending the resolution of the Senator from Missouri, so as to direct the Secretary to perform his duty in such a manner as not to obliterate any part of the condemnatory resolution. Such a direction, however, appears to me to be wholly unnecessary. The nature of the whole proceeding is very plain. We now adopt a resolution, expressing our strong reprobation of the original resolution; and for this purpose we use the word "expunged," as the strongest term which we can apply. We then direct our Secretary to draw black lines around it, and place such a reference to our proceedings of this day upon its face, that in all time to come, whoever may inspect this portion of our journal, will be pointed at once to the record of its condemnation. What lawyer has not observed upon the margin of the judgment docket, if the original judgment has been removed to a superior court, and there reversed, a minute of such reversal? In our editions of the statutes, have we not all noted the repeal of any of them, which may have taken place at a subsequent period? Who ever heard, in the one case or the other, that this was obliterating or destroying the record, or the book? So in this case, we make a mere reference to our future proceeding upon the face of the resolution, instead of the margin. Suppose we should only repeal the obnoxious resolution, and direct such a reference to be made upon its face? Would any Senator contend that this would be an obliteration of the journal?

But it has been contended that the word expunge is not the appropriate word; and we have wrested it from its true signification, in applying it to the present case. Even if this allegation were correct, the answer would be at hand. You might then convict us of bad taste, but not of a violation of the Constitution. On the face of the resolution we have stated distinctly what we mean. We have directed the Secretary in what manner he shall understand it, and we have excluded the idea that it is our intention to obliterate or to destroy the journal.

310But I shall contend that the word expunge is the appropriate word, and that there is not another in the English language so precisely adapted to convey our meaning. I shall show, from the highest literary and parliamentary authorities, that the word has acquired a signification entirely distinct from that of actual obliteration. Let me proceed immediately to this task. After citing my authorities, I shall proceed with the argument. First, then, for those of a literary character. I read from Crabbe's Synonymes, page 140; and every Senator will admit that this is a work of established reputation. In speaking of the use of the word expunge, the author says: "When the contents of a book are in part rejected, they are aptly described as being expunged; in this manner the free-thinking sects expunge everything from the Bible which does not suit their purpose, or they expunge from their creed what does not humor their passions." The idea that an actual obliteration was intended in these cases would be manifestly absurd. In the same page there is a quotation from Mr. Burke to illustrate the meaning of this word. "I believe," says he, "that any person who was of age to take a part in public concerns forty years ago (if the intermediate space were expunged from his memory), could hardly credit his senses when he should hear that an army of two hundred thousand men was kept up in this island." I shall now cite Mr. Jefferson as a literary authority. He has often been referred to on this floor as a standard in politics. For this high authority, I am indebted to my friend from Louisiana (Mr. Nicholas). In the original draft of the declaration of independence, he uses the word expunge in the following manner: "Such has been the patient sufferance of these colonies; and such is now the necessity which constrains them to expunge their former systems of government." Although the word alter was substituted for expunge, I presume upon the ground that this was too strong a term, yet the change does not detract from the literary authority of the precedent.—Jefferson's Correspondence, &c., 1st volume, page 17.

I presume that I have shown that the word expunge has acquired a distinct metaphorical meaning in our literature, which excludes the idea of actual obliteration. If I should proceed one step further, and prove that in legislative proceedings it has acquired the very same signification, I shall then have fully established my position. For this purpose I cite, first, "the Secret Proceedings and Debates of the Federal Convention." In page 118, we find the following entries: "On motion to expunge the clause of the qualification as to age, it was carried—ten States against one." Again: "On the clause respecting the ineligibility to any other office, it was moved that the words 'by any particular State,' be expunged—four States for, five against, and two divided." So page 119: "The last blank was filled up with one year, and carried—eight ayes, two noes, one divided."

"Mr. Pinckney moved to expunge the clause—agreed to, nem. con." Again: "Mr. Butler moved to expunge the clause of the stipends—lost, seven against, three for, one divided." Again, in page 157: "Mr. Pinckney moved that that part of the clause which disqualifies a person from holding an office in 311the State be expunged, because the first and best characters in a State may thereby be deprived of a seat in the national council."

"Question put to strike out the words moved for and carried—eight ayes, three noes."

It will thus be perceived that in the proceedings of the very convention which formed the Constitution under which we are now governed, the word expunge was often used in its figurative sense. It will certainly not be asserted, or even intimated, by any Senator here, that when these motions to expunge prevailed, the words of the original draft of the Constitution were actually obliterated or defaced. The meaning is palpable. These provisions were merely rejected; not actually blotted out.

But I shall now produce a precedent precisely in point. It presents itself in the proceedings of the Senate of Massachusetts, and refers to the famous resolution of that body adopted on the 15th day of June, 1813, in relation to the capture of the British vessel Peacock; denouncing the late war, and declaring that it was not becoming in a moral and religious people, to express any approbation of military or naval exploits which were not immediately connected with the defence of our seacoast. Massachusetts adopted the following resolution:

"Resolved That the aforesaid resolve of the fifteenth day of June, A. D. 1813, and the preamble thereof, be, and the same are hereby, expunged from the journals of the Senate."

It is self-evident that, in this case, not the least intention existed of defacing the old manuscript journal. The word "expunge" was used in its figurative signification, just as it is in the case before us, to express the strongest reprobation of the former proceeding. That proceeding was to be expunged solely by force of the subsequent resolution, and not by any actual obliteration. There never was any actual obliteration of the journal.

Judging, then, from the highest English authorities, from the works of celebrated authors and statesmen, and from the proceedings of legislative bodies, is it not evident that the word expunge has acquired a distinct meaning, altogether inconsistent with any actual obliteration?

All that we have heard about defacing and destroying the journal are mere phantoms, which have been conjured up to terrify the timid. We intend no such thing. We only mean, most strongly, to express our conviction that the condemnatory resolution ought never to have found a place on the journal. If more authorities were wanting, I might refer to the Legislature of Virginia. The present expunging resolution is in exact conformity with their instructions to their Senators. As a matter of taste, I cannot say that I much admire their plan, though I entertain no doubt but that it is perfectly constitutional. That State is highly literary; and I think I have established that their Legislature, when they used the word expunge, without intending thereby to effect an actual obliteration of the journal, justly appreciated the meaning of the language which they employed.

The word expunge is, in my opinion, the only one which we could have 312used, clearly and forcibly to accomplish our purpose. Even if it had not been sanctioned by practice as a parliamentary word, we ought ourselves to have first established the precedent. It suits the case precisely. If you rescind, reverse, or repeal a resolution; you thereby admit that it once had some constitutional or legal authority. If you declare it to have been null and void from the beginning; this is but the expression of your own opinion that such was the fact. This word expunge acts upon the resolution itself. It at once goes to its origin, and destroys its legal existence as if it had never been. It does not merely kill, but it annihilates. Parliamentary practice has changed the meaning of several other words from their primitive signification, in a similar manner with that of the word expunge. The original signification of the word rescind is "to cut off." Usage has made it mean, in reference to a law or resolution, to abrogate or repeal it. We every day hear motions "to strike out." What is the literal meaning of this expression? The question may be best answered by asking another. If I were to request you to strike out a line from your letter, and you were willing to comply with my request, what would be your conduct? You would run your pen through it immediately. You would literally strike it out. Yet what use do we make of this phrase every day in our legislative proceedings? If I make a motion to strike out a section from a bill and it prevails, the Secretary encloses the printed copy of it in black lines, and makes a note on the margin that it has been stricken out. The original he never touches. Why then should not the word expunge, without obliterating the proceeding to which it is directed, signify to destroy as if it never had existed?

After all that has been said, I think I need scarcely again recur to the Pennsylvania precedent. It is evident from the whole of that proceeding that an actual expunging of the journal was intended, if it had not already been executed. I have no recollection whatever of the circumstances, but I am under a perfect conviction, from the face of the journal, that such was the nature of the case. I should vote now as I did then, after a period of more than twenty years. Both my vote, and the motion which I subsequently made upon that occasion, evidently proceeded upon this principle. The question arose in this manner, as it appears from the journal. On the 10th of February, 1816, "The Speaker informed the House that a constitutional question being involved in a decision by him yesterday, on a motion to expunge certain proceedings from the journal, he was desirous of having the opinion of the House on that decision," viz: "that a majority can expunge from the journal proceedings in which the yeas and nays have not been called." Now, as no trace whatever appears upon the journal of the preceding day of the motion to which the Speaker refers, it is highly probable, nay, it is almost certain, that the proceedings had been actually expunged before he asked the advice of the House.

No man feels with more sensibility, the necessity which compels him to perform an unkind act towards his brother Senators than myself; but we have 313now arrived at that point when imperious duty demands that we should either adopt this expunging resolution or abandon it forever. Already much precious time has been employed in its discussion. The moment has arrived when we must act. Senators in the opposition console themselves with the belief that posterity will do them justice, should it be denied to them by the present generation. They place their own names in the one scale and ours in the other, and flatter themselves with the hope that before that tribunal at least, their weight will preponderate. For my own part, I am willing to abide the issue. I am willing to be judged for the vote which I shall give to-day, not only by the present, but by future generations, should my obscure name ever be mentioned in after times. After the passions and prejudices of the present moment shall have subsided, and the impartial historian shall come to record the proceedings of this day, he will say that the distinguished men who passed the resolution condemning the President were urged on to the act by a desire to occupy the high places in the Government. That an ambition noble in itself, but not wisely regulated, had obscured their judgment, and impelled them to the adoption of a measure unjust, illegal, and unconstitutional. That in order to vindicate both the Constitution and the President, we were justified in passing this expunging resolution, and thus stamping the former proceeding with our strongest disapprobation.

I rejoice in the belief that this promises to be one of the last highly exciting questions of the present day. During the period of General Jackson's civil administration, what has he not done for the American people? During this period he has had more difficult and dangerous questions to settle, both at home and abroad,—questions which aroused more intensely the passions of men,—than any of his predecessors. They are now all happily ended, except the one which we shall this day bring to a close,

"And all the clouds that lowered upon our house
In the deep bosom of the ocean buried."

The country now enjoys abundant prosperity at home, whilst it is respected and admired by foreign nations. Although the waves may yet be in some agitation from the effect of the storms through which we have passed, yet I think I can perceive the rainbow of peace extending itself across the firmament of Heaven.

Should the next administration pursue the same course of policy with the present—should it dispense equal justice to all portions and all interests of the Union, without sacrificing any—should it be conducted with prudence and with firmness, and I doubt not but that this will be the case—we shall hereafter enjoy comparative peace and quiet in our day. This will be the precious fruit of the energy, the toils, and the wisdom of the pilot who has conducted us in safety through the storms of his tempestuous administration.

I am now prepared for the question. I shall vote for this resolution; but not cheerfully. I regret the necessity which exists for passing it; but I believe that imperious duty demands its adoption. If I know my own heart, 314I can truly say that I am not actuated by any desire to obtain a miserable, petty, personal triumph, either for myself, or for the President of the United States, over my associates upon this floor.

I am now ready to record my vote, and thus, in the opprobrious language of Senators in the opposition, to become one of the executioners of the condemnatory resolution.

315

CHAPTER XIII.

1836.

FIRST INTRODUCTION OF THE SUBJECT OF SLAVERY IN THE SENATE, DURING THE ADMINISTRATION OF JACKSON—PETITIONS FOR ITS ABOLITION IN THE DISTRICT OF COLUMBIA—THE RIGHT OF PETITION VINDICATED BY BUCHANAN—INCENDIARY PUBLICATIONS—ADMISSION OF MICHIGAN INTO THE UNION—STATUARY FOR THE CAPITOL—AFFAIRS OF TEXAS.

In the latter part of the second administration of General Jackson, the subject of slavery began to be pressed upon the attention of Congress by petitions for its abolition in the District of Columbia.

In a future chapter will be traced the origin and progress of the anti-slavery agitation in the Northern States. At present, it is only needful for me to describe Mr. Buchanan's course as a Senator, on the different aspects of this subject which arose during the second administration of General Jackson. On the 7th of January, 1836, two petitions were presented in the Senate, signed by citizens of Ohio, praying for the abolition of slavery in the District of Columbia. Mr. Calhoun demanded that they should be read, and, after the reading, he objected to their being received. Mr. Buchanan made the following remarks in replying to Mr. Calhoun:

Mr. Buchanan said that, for two or three weeks past, there had been in his possession a memorial from the Cain Quarterly Meeting of the religious Society of Friends, in the State of Pennsylvania, requesting Congress to abolish slavery and the slave trade within the District of Columbia. This memorial was not a printed form—its language was not that in established use for such documents. It did not proceed from those desperate fanatics who have been endeavoring to disturb the security and peace of society in the Southern States, by the distribution of incendiary pamphlets and papers. Far different is the truth. It emanates from a society of Christians, whose object had always been to promote peace and good-will among men, and who have been the efficient and persevering friends of humanity in every clime. To 316their untiring efforts, more than to those of any other denomination of Christians, we owe the progress which has been made in abolishing the African slave trade throughout the world. This memorial was their testimony against the existence of slavery. This testimony they had borne for more than a century. Of the purity of their motives, there could not be a question.

He had omitted to present this memorial at an earlier day, because he had thought that, on its presentation at the proper time, much good might be done. He had believed that, by private consultations, some resolution might be devised upon this exciting subject which would obtain the unanimous vote of the Senate. If there was one man in that body not willing to adopt a proper measure to calm the troubled spirit of the South, he did not know him. This, in his judgment, would be the best mode of accomplishing the object which we all desire to accomplish. The proper course to attain this result was, in his opinion, to refer the subject, either to a select committee, or to the Committee for the District of Columbia. They would examine it in all its bearings, they would ascertain the views and feelings of individual Senators, and he had no doubt they would be able to recommend some measure to the Senate on which they could all unite. This would have a most happy effect upon the country. He had intended, upon presenting the memorial which he had in charge, to have suggested this mode of proceeding. He regretted, therefore, he had not known that his friend from Ohio (Mr. Morris) was in possession of memorials having a similar object in view. If he had been informed of it, he should have endeavored to persuade him to wait until Monday next, when he (Mr. B.) would have been prepared to pursue the course he had indicated. But the question has now been forced upon us. No (said Mr. B.), it has not been forced upon me, because I am glad to have a suitable occasion of expressing my opinions upon the subject.

The memorial which I have in my possession is entitled to the utmost respect, from the character of the memorialists. As I entirely dissent from the opinion which they express, that we ought to abolish slavery in the District of Columbia, I feel it to be due to them, to myself, and to the Senate, respectfully, but firmly, to state the reasons why I cannot advocate their views or acquiesce in their conclusions.

If any one principle of constitutional law can, at this day, be considered as settled, it is, that Congress have no right, no power, over the question of slavery within those States where it exists. The property of the master in his slave existed in full force before the Federal Constitution was adopted. It was a subject which then belonged, as it still belongs, to the exclusive jurisdiction of the several States. These States, by the adoption of the Constitution, never yielded to the General Government any right to interfere with the question. It remains where it was previous to the establishment of our confederacy.

The Constitution has, in the clearest terms, recognized the right of property in slaves. It prohibits any State into which a slave may have fled from passing any law to discharge him from slavery, and declares that he shall be 317delivered up by the authorities of such State to his master. Nay, more, it makes the existence of slavery the foundation of political power, by giving to those States within which it exists representatives in Congress, not only in proportion to the whole number of free persons, but also in proportion to three-fifths of the number of slaves.

An occasion very fortunately arose in the first Congress to settle this question forever. The Society for the abolition of Slavery in Pennsylvania brought it before that Congress by a memorial which was presented on the 11th day of February, 1790. After the subject had been discussed for several days, and after solemn deliberation, the House of Representatives, in Committee of the Whole, on the 23d day of March, 1790, resolved "That Congress have no authority to interfere in the emancipation of slaves, or in the treatment of them within any of the States; it remaining with the several States alone to provide any regulations therein, which humanity and true policy may require."

I have thought it would be proper to present this decision, which was made almost half a century ago, distinctly to the view of the American people. The language of the resolution is clear, precise, and definite. It leaves the question where the Constitution left it, and where, so far as I am concerned, it ever shall remain. The Constitution of the United States never would have been called into existence,—instead of the innumerable blessings which have flowed from our happy Union, we should have had anarchy, jealousy, and civil war among the sister Republics of which our confederacy is composed, had not the free States abandoned all control over this question. For one, whatever may be my opinions upon the abstract question of slavery, (and I am free to confess they are those of the people of Pennsylvania,) I shall never attempt to violate this fundamental compact. The Union will be dissolved, and incalculable evils will arise from its ashes, the moment any such attempt is seriously made by the free States in Congress.

What, then, are the circumstances under which these memorials are now presented? A number of fanatics, led on by foreign incendiaries, have been scattering "arrows, firebrands, and death" throughout the Southern States. The natural tendency of their publications is to produce dissatisfaction and revolt among the slaves, and to incite their wild passions to vengeance. All history, as well as the present condition of the slaves, proves that there can be no danger of the final result of a servile war. But, in the mean time, what dreadful scenes may be enacted before such an insurrection, which would spare neither age nor sex, could be suppressed! What agony of mind must be suffered, especially by the gentler sex, in consequence of these publications! Many a mother clasps her infant to her bosom when she retires to rest, under dreadful apprehensions that she may be aroused from her slumbers by the savage yells of the slaves by whom she is surrounded. These are the works of the abolitionists. That their motives may be honest I do not doubt, but their zeal is without knowledge. The history of the human race 318presents numerous examples of ignorant enthusiasts, the purity of whose intentions cannot be doubted, who have spread devastation and bloodshed over the face of the earth.

These fanatics, instead of benefiting the slaves who are the objects of their regard, have inflicted serious injury upon them. Self-preservation is the first law of nature. The masters, for the sake of their wives and children, for the sake of all that is near and dear to them on earth, must tighten the reins of authority over their slaves. They must thus counteract the efforts of the abolitionists. The slaves are denied many indulgences which their masters would otherwise cheerfully grant. They must be kept in such a state of bondage as effectually to prevent their rising. These are the injurious effects produced by the abolitionists upon the slave himself. Whilst, on the one hand, they render his condition miserable, by presenting to his mind vague notions of freedom never to be realized, on the other, they make it doubly miserable, by compelling the master to be severe, in order to prevent any attempts at insurrection. They thus render it impossible for the master to treat his slave according to the dictates of his heart and his feelings. Besides, do not the abolitionists perceive that the spirit which is thus roused must protract to an indefinite period the emancipation of the slave? The necessary effect of their efforts is to render desperate those to whom the power of emancipation really belongs. I believe most conscientiously, in whatever light this subject can be viewed, that the best interests of the slave require that the question should be left, where the Constitution has left it, to the slaveholding States themselves, without foreign interference.

This being a true statement of the case, as applied to the States where slavery exists, what is now asked by these memorialists? That in this District of ten miles square—a District carved out of two slaveholding States, and surrounded by them on all sides—slavery shall be abolished. What would be the effects of granting their request? You would thus erect a citadel in the very heart of these States, upon a territory which they have ceded to you for a far different purpose, from which abolitionists and incendiaries could securely attack the peace and safety of their citizens. You establish a spot within the slaveholding States which would be a city of refuge for run-away slaves. You create by law a central point from which trains of gunpowder may be securely laid, extending into the surrounding States, which may, at any moment, produce a fearful and destructive explosion. By passing such a law, you introduce the enemy into the very bosom of these two States, and afford him every opportunity to produce a servile insurrection. Is there any reasonable man who can for one moment suppose that Virginia and Maryland would have ceded the District of Columbia to the United States, if they had entertained the slightest idea that Congress would ever use it for any such purpose? They ceded it for your use, for your convenience, and not for their own destruction. When slavery ceases to exist, under the laws of Virginia and Maryland, then, and not till then, ought it to be abolished in the District of Columbia.

319(Mr. B. said that, notwithstanding these were his opinions, he could not vote for the motion of the Senator from South Carolina (Mr. Calhoun) not to receive these memorials. He would not at present proceed to state his reasons, still hoping the Senate could yet agree upon some course which would prove satisfactory to all. With this view, he moved that the whole subject be postponed until Monday next.)

When the following Monday came (January 11th, 1836), Mr. Buchanan said:

He was now about to present the memorial of the Caln Quarterly Meeting of the Religious Society of Friends in Pennsylvania, requesting Congress to abolish slavery and the slave trade in the District of Columbia. On this subject he had expressed his opinions to the Senate on Thursday last, and he had no disposition to repeat them at present. He would say, however, that on a review of these opinions, he was perfectly satisfied with them. All he should now say was, that the memorial which he was about to present was perfectly respectful in its language. Indeed, it could not possibly be otherwise, considering the respectable source from which it emanated.

It would become his duty to make some motion in regard to this memorial. On Thursday last, he had suggested that in his judgment the best course to pursue was to refer these memorials to a selected committee, or to the committee for the District of Columbia. He still thought so; but he now found that insurmountable obstacles presented themselves to such a reference.

In presenting this memorial and in exerting himself so far as in him lay, to secure for it that respectful reception by the Senate which it deserved, he should do his duty to the memorialists. After it should receive this reception, he should have a duty to perform to himself and to his country. He was clearly of opinion, for the reasons he had stated on Thursday last, that Congress ought not at this time to abolish slavery in the District of Columbia, and that it was our duty promptly to place this exciting question at rest. He should, therefore, move that the memorial be read, and that the prayer of the memorialists be rejected.

At a subsequent day (January 19th), the pending question was, on the reception of the Memorial of the Pennsylvania Quakers, or Friends; and on this question Mr. Buchanan said:

It was not now his intention to repeat anything he had said on a former occasion in regard to the abolition of slavery in this District. The remarks which he had then made, after much reflection, still met his entire approbation. He would not now have alluded to them were it not for the misapprehension which still appeared to prevail upon this floor in regard to the state of Northern feeling on this subject.

Those remarks had, he believed, been more extensively circulated throughout Pennsylvania than any which he had ever made upon any occasion. If they had been censured anywhere in that State, by any party, the fact was unknown to him. On the contrary, he had strong reasons to believe they had been received with general approbation.

He was not in the habit of using private letters to sustain any position which he might take upon this floor or elsewhere. He would say, however, that since he had presented the memorial now the subject of consideration before the Senate, he had received another memorial of a similar character from the city of Philadelphia. This memorial had been transmitted to him by two gentlemen whose name and character would be the strongest guaranty for the truth of their assertions, did he feel himself at liberty to make them known to the Senate. He would not even have alluded to their letter, but that it related to a public subject in which the country was deeply interested, and accompanied the memorial which they had requested him to present to the Senate. The following is an extract from this letter:

"Although we have not the pleasure of thy acquaintance, permit us on this occasion to express our satisfaction with thy remarks in the Senate some weeks since, in which the opinion was forcibly sustained that no sensible man at the North would advocate the right of Congress to interfere with the subject of slavery in the slave States themselves. We are fully persuaded this is the fact in our neighborhood.

"In a pretty extensive acquaintance with the friends of abolition in this city, we unhesitatingly declare that we have never heard such an opinion advocated, and we defy our opponents to point out a man that has ever circulated any publication calculated to produce discord in the Southern States.

"But whilst we fully recognize this view, we are aware that the Constitution guaranties to us the right of memorializing Congress on any subject connected with the welfare of the District of Columbia, and we intend ever to exercise it in the spirit of charity and good-feeling."

Mr. B. believed this statement to be true. Although all the people of Pennsylvania were opposed to slavery in the abstract, yet they would not sanction any attempts to excite the slaves of the Southern States to insurrection and bloodshed. Whilst they knew their own rights, and would maintain them, they never would invade the rights of others which had been secured by the Federal Constitution. He was proud to say this had always been the character and the conduct of the State which he had in part the honor to represent in her relations with her sister States.

He felt himself justified in declaring that Pennsylvania was perfectly sound upon this question. Abolitionists there may be in Pennsylvania, but it had never been his fate to meet a single one. If we have a man amongst us who desires, by the circulation of incendiary publications and pictures throughout the slaveholding States, to produce a servile insurrection, and thus to abolish slavery, he knew him not. In the language of the letter he had just read, whatever might be the case further north, he might defy any gentleman to point out a man in Pennsylvania who has ever circulated any publication calculated to produce discord in the Southern States.

321He had heard within the last few days that emissaries were now traveling throughout Pennsylvania for the purpose of propagating the doctrine of immediate abolition. He thought he might venture to predict that they would fail in their attempts.

Although he did not mean at present to discuss the general question, yet the Senator from South Carolina (Mr. Preston) must permit him to say that, in his remarks of yesterday, he had done much to dignify the cause of abolition, and to give its supporters a character which they did not deserve.

Mr. B. was not so well able to judge what effect those remarks might produce on the South; but he protested against the accuracy of the statements which that gentleman had made in regard to the condition of Northern feeling on this subject. His information had been incorrect. If the gloomy coloring of the picture which he had presented could be considered any thing but a fancy sketch, the South might believe that the time had arrived when it would be their duty to decide whether it was not necessary to dissolve this Union, for the protection of their rights. Mr. B. thought far otherwise. This crisis had not arrived, and, he trusted, never would arrive. The force of public opinion will prostrate this fanatical and dangerous spirit. He must say, however, that the enemies of the cause of abolition at the North had a right to expect that gentlemen from the South would not adopt a course which might tend to increase our difficulties. They ought to permit us to judge for ourselves in this matter, and to throw no obstacles in our way which the nature of the subject does not necessarily present.

Let it be once understood that the sacred right of petition and the cause of the abolitionists must rise or must fall together, and the consequences may be fatal. I would, therefore, warn Southern gentlemen to reflect seriously in what situation they place their friends in the North, by insisting that this petition shall not be received.

We have just as little right to interfere with slavery in the South, as we have to touch the right of petition. Whence is this right derived? Can a republican government exist without it? Man might as well attempt to exist without breathing the vital air. No government possessing any of the elements of liberty has ever existed, or can ever exist, unless its citizens or subjects enjoy this right. From the very structure of your Government, from the very establishment of a Senate and House of Representatives, the right of petition naturally and necessarily resulted. A representative republic, established by the people, without the people having the right to make their wants and their wishes known to their servants, would be the most palpable absurdity. This right, even if it were not expressly sanctioned by the Constitution, would result from its very nature. It could not be controlled by any action of Congress, or either branch of it. If the Constitution had been silent upon the subject, the only consequence would be, that it would stand in the very front rank of those rights of the people which are expressly guarantied to them by the ninth article of the amendments to that instrument, inserted from abundant but necessary caution. I shall read this 322article. It declares that "the enumeration in the Constitution of certain rights shall not be construed to deny or disparage others retained by the people." It would, without any express provision, have stood in the same rank with the liberty of speech and of the press, and have been entirely beyond the control of the Government. It is a right which could not have been infringed without extinguishing the vital spirit of our institutions. If any had been so bold as to attempt to violate it, it would have been a conclusive argument to say to them that the Constitution has given you no power over the right of petition, and you dare not touch it.

The Senator from South Carolina (Mr. Calhoun) has justly denominated the amendments to the Constitution as our Bill of Rights. The jealousy which the States entertained of federal power brought these amendments into existence. They supposed that, in future times, Congress might desire to extend the powers of this Government, and usurp the rights which were not granted them by the people of the States. From a provident caution, they have, in express terms, denied to Congress every sort of control over religion; over the freedom of speech and of the press; and over the right of petition. The first article of the amendments declares that "Congress shall make no law respecting an establishment of religion, or prohibiting the free exercise thereof; or abridging the freedom of speech or of the press; or the right of the people peaceably to assemble, and to petition the Government for a redress of grievances."

Now, sir, what is the first position taken by the Senator from South Carolina against receiving this memorial? I desire to quote him with perfect accuracy. He says that the Constitution prohibits Congress from passing any law to abridge the right of petition; that, to refuse to receive this petition, would not be to pass any such law, and that therefore, the Constitution would not be violated by such a refusal.

Does not the Senator perceive that, if this doctrine can be maintained, the right of petition is gone forever? It is a mere empty name. The Senate would possess the power of controlling it at their will and pleasure. No matter what may be the prayer of any petition; no matter how just may be the grievances of the people demanding redress, we may refuse to hear their complaints, and inform them that this is one of our prerogatives; because, to refuse to receive their petition is not the passage of a law abridging their right to petition. How can the gentleman escape from this consequence? Is the Senate to be the arbiter? Are we to decide what the people may petition for, and what they shall not bring before us? Is the servant to dictate to the master? Such a construction can never be the true one.

The most striking feature of this argument is, that the very article of the Constitution which was intended to guard the right of petition with the most jealous care is thus perverted from its original intention, and made the instrument of destroying this very right. What we cannot do by law, what is beyond the power of both Houses of Congress and the President, according to the gentleman's argument, the Senate can of itself accomplish. The 323Senate alone, if his argument be correct, may abridge the right of petition, acting in its separate capacity, though it could not, as one branch of the Legislature, consent to any law which would confer upon itself this power.

What is the true history and character of this article of the Constitution? In the thirteenth year of the reign of that "royal scoundrel" Charles the Second, as the Senator from Virginia (Mr. Leigh) has justly denominated him, an act of Parliament was passed, abridging the right of petition. It declared that "no petition to the king or either House of Parliament, for any alteration in Church or State, shall be signed by above twenty persons, unless the matter thereof be approved by three justices of the peace, or the major part of the grand jury in the county; and in London by the lord mayor, aldermen, and common council; nor shall any petition be presented by more than ten persons at a time." Each Senator will readily perceive that the right of petition was thus laid almost entirely prostrate at the feet of the sovereign. The justices of the peace, and the sheriffs who selected the grand juries, were his creatures, appointed and removed at his pleasure. Out of the city of London, without their consent, no petition for an alteration in Church or State could be signed by more than twenty individuals. At the revolution of 1688, the Bill of Rights guaranteed to English subjects the right of petitioning the king, but the courts of justice decided that it did not repeal the statute of the second Charles. This statute still remained in force at the adoption of the federal Constitution. Such was the state of the law in that country, from which we have derived most of our institutions, when this amendment to the Constitution was adopted.

Although the Constitution, as it came from the hands of its framers, gave to Congress no power to touch the right of petition, yet some of the States to whom it was submitted for ratification, apprehending the time might arrive when Congress would be disposed to act like the British Parliament, expressly withdrew the subject from our control. Not satisfied with the fact that no power over it had been granted by the Constitution, they determined to prohibit us in express terms from ever exercising such a power. This is the true history of the first article of our Bill of Rights.

Let me put another case to the Senator from South Carolina. Some years since, as a manager on the part of the House of Representatives, I had the honor to appear before this body, then sitting as a high court of impeachment. In that case, the accused, when sitting as a district judge of the United States, had brought an attorney of his court before him by an attachment for contempt, and without any trial by jury had convicted him of a libel, and sentenced him to imprisonment. The judge was acquitted; and at the moment I thought this decision had placed the freedom of the press in danger. If the sedition law were clearly unconstitutional, and nobody now doubts it; if Congress could not confer upon the courts of the United States, by express enactment, any question over the power of libel, I thought it monstrous that a judge, without the intervention of a jury, under highly excited feelings, should be permitted to try and to punish libels committed against himself 324according to his will and pleasure. My apprehensions were of but short duration. A few days after the acquittal of this judge, the Senate, without one dissenting voice, passed a bill, not to create a new law, but declaratory of what the old law, or rather what the Constitution was, under which no federal judge will ever again dare to punish a libel as a contempt. The constitutional provision in favor of the liberty of the press was thus redeemed from judicial construction.

Now, sir, we must all admit that libels of the grossest character are daily published against the Senate and its individual members. Suppose an attempt should be made to bring one of these libelers before us, and to punish him for a contempt, would the gentleman from South Carolina contend that we might do so without violating the Constitution, and that we might convict him and sentence him to imprisonment, because such a conviction and sentence would not be the passage of a law abridging the freedom of the press? The gentleman's excited feelings upon the subject of abolition have led his judgment astray. No construction can be correct which would lead to such palpable absurdities.

The very language of this amendment itself contains the strongest recognition of the right of petition. In the clearest terms, it presupposes its existence. How can you abridge a right which has no previous existence? On this question I deem the argument of my friend from Georgia (Mr. King) conclusive. The amendment assumes that the people have the right to petition for the redress of grievances, and places it beyond the power of Congress to touch this sacred right. The truth is, that the authors of the amendment believed this to be a Government of such tremendous power that it was necessary, in express terms, to withdraw from its grasp their most essential rights. The right of every citizen to worship his God according to the dictates of his own conscience; his right freely to speak, and freely to print and publish his thoughts to the world; and his right to petition the Government for a redress of grievances, are placed entirely beyond the control of the Congress of the United States, or either of its branches. There may they ever remain! These fundamental principles of liberty are companions. They rest upon the same foundation. They must stand or must fall together. They will be maintained so long as American liberty shall endure.

The next argument advanced by the gentleman is, that we are not bound to receive this petition, because to grant its prayer would be unconstitutional? In this argument I shall not touch the question, whether Congress possess the power to abolish slavery in the District of Columbia or not. Suppose they do not, can the gentleman maintain the position, that we are authorized by the Constitution to refuse to receive a petition from the people, because we may deem the object of it unconstitutional? Whence is any such restriction of the right of petition derived? Who gave it to us? Is it to be found in the Constitution? The people are not constitutional lawyers; but they feel oppression, and know when they are aggrieved. They present their complaints to us in the form of a petition. I ask, by what authority can we refuse to receive it? They have a right to spread their wishes and their wants before us, and to ask for redress. We are bound respectfully to consider their request; and the best answer which we can give them is, that they have not conferred upon us the power, under the Constitution of the United States, to grant them the relief which they desire. On any other principle we may first decide that we have no power over a particular subject, and then refuse to hear the petitions of the people in relation to it. We would thus place the constitutional right of our constituents to petition at the mercy of our own discretion.

Again, sir, we possess the power of originating amendments to the Constitution. Although, therefore, we may not be able to grant the petitioners relief, such a petition may induce us to exercise this power, and to ask for a new grant of authority from the States.

The gentleman's third proposition was, that we are not bound to receive this petition, because it is no grievance to the citizens of any of the States, that slavery exists in this District. But who are to be the judges, in the first instance, whether the people are aggrieved or not? Is it those who suffer, or fancy they suffer, or the Senate? If we are to decide when they ought to feel aggrieved, and when they ought to be satisfied, if the tribunal to whom their petitions are addressed may refuse to receive them, because, in their opinion, there was no just cause of complaint, the right of petition is destroyed. It would be but a poor answer to their petitions to tell them they ought not to have felt aggrieved, that they are mistaken, and that, therefore, their complaints would not be received by their servants.

I may be asked, is there no case in which I would be willing to refuse to receive a petition? I answer that it must be a very strong one indeed to justify such a refusal. There is one exception, however, which results from the very nature of the right itself. Neither the body addressed nor any of its members must be insulted, under the pretext of exercising this right. It must not be perverted from its purpose, and be made the instrument of degrading the body to which the petition is addressed. Such a petition would be in fraud of the right itself, and the necessary power of self-protection and self-preservation inherent in every legislative body confers upon it the authority of defending itself against direct insults presented in this or any other form. Beyond this exception I would not go; and it is solely for the purpose of self-protection, in my opinion, that the rules of the Senate enable any of its members to raise the question, whether a petition shall be received or not. If the rule has any other object in view, it is a violation of the Constitution.

I would confine this exception within the narrowest limits. The acts of the body addressed may be freely canvassed by the people, and they may be shown to be unjust or unconstitutional. These may be the very reasons why the petition is presented. "To speak his mind is every freeman's right." They may and they ought to express themselves with that manly independence which belongs to American citizens. To exclude their petition, it must appear palpable that an insult to the body was intended, and not a redress of grievances.

Extreme cases have been put by the Senator from South Carolina. Ridiculous or extravagant petitions may be presented; though I should think that scarcely a sane man could be found in this country who would ask Congress to abolish slavery in the State of Georgia. In such a case I would receive the petition, and consign it at once to that merited contempt which it would deserve. The Constitution secures the right of being heard by petition to every citizen; and I would not abridge it because he happened to be a fool. The proposition is almost too plain for argument, that if the people have a constitutional right to petition, a corresponding duty is imposed upon us to receive their petitions. From the very nature of things, rights and duties are reciprocal. The human mind cannot conceive of the one without the other. They are relative terms. If the people have a right to command, it is the duty of their servants to obey. If I have a right to a sum of money, it is the duty of my debtor to pay it to me. If the people have a right to petition their representatives, it is our duty to receive their petition.

This question was solemnly determined by the Senate more than thirty years ago. Neither before nor since that time, so far as I can learn, has the general right of petition ever been called in question, until the motion now under consideration was made by the Senator from South Carolina. Of course I do not speak of cases embraced within the exception which I have just stated. No Senator has ever contended that this is one of them. To prove my position, I shall read an extract from our journals. On Monday, the 21st January, 1805, "Mr. Logan presented a petition signed Thomas Morris, Clerk, in behalf of the meeting of the representatives of the people called Quakers, in Pennsylvania, New Jersey, etc., stating that the petitioners, from a sense of religious duty, had again come forward to plead the cause of their oppressed and degraded fellow-men of the African race; and, on the question, "Shall this petition be received?" it passed in the affirmative; yeas, 19; nays, 9.

"The yeas and nays being required by one-fifth of the Senators present, those who voted in the affirmative are—Messrs. Adams, Mass., Bayard, Del., Brown, Ky., Condict, N. J., Franklin, N. C., Hillhouse, Conn., Howland, R. I., Logan, Penn., Maclay, Penn., Mitchell, N. Y., Alcott, N. H., Pickering, Mass., Plumer, N. H., Smith, Ohio, Smith, Vt., Stone, N. C., Sumpter, S. C., White, Del., Worthington, Ohio.

"And those who voted in the negative are—Anderson, Tenn., Baldwin, Ga., Bradley, Vt., Cocke, Tenn., Jackson, Ga., Moore, Va., Smith, Md., Smith, N. Y., and Wright, Md.

"So the petition was read."

The Senate will perceive that I have added to the names of the members of the Senate that of the States which they each represented. The Senator from South Carolina will see that, among those who, upon this occasion, sustained the right of petition, there is found the name of General Sumpter, his distinguished predecessor. I wish him also to observe that but seven Senators from slaveholding States voted against receiving the petition; although it was of a character well calculated to excite their hostile and jealous feelings.

236

The present, sir, is a real controversy between liberty and power. In my humble judgment, it is far the most important question which has been before the Senate since I have had the honor of occupying a seat in this body. It is a contest between those, however unintentionally, who desire to abridge the right of the people, in asking their servants for a redress of grievances, and those who desire to leave it, as the Constitution left it, free as the air. Petitions ought ever to find their way into the Senate without impediment; and I trust that the decision upon this question will result in the establishment of one of the dearest rights which a free people can enjoy.

Now, sir, why should the Senator from South Carolina urge the motion which he has made? I wish I could persuade him to withdraw it. We of the North honestly believe, and I feel confident he will not doubt our sincerity, that we cannot vote for his motion without violating our duty to God and to the country—without disregarding the oath which we have sworn, to support the Constitution. This is not the condition of those who advocate his motion. It is not pretended that the Constitution imposes any obligation upon them to vote for this motion. With them it is a question of mere expediency; with us, one of constitutional duty. I ask gentlemen of the South, for their own sake, as well as for that of their friends in the North, to vote against this motion. It will place us all in a false position, where neither their sentiments nor ours will be properly understood.

The people of the North are justly jealous of their rights and liberties. Among these, they hold the right of petition to be one of the most sacred character. I would say to the gentlemen of the South, why then will you array yourselves, without any necessity, against this right? You believe that we are much divided on the question of abolition; why, then, will you introduce another element of discord amongst us, which may do your cause much harm, and which cannot possibly do it any good? When you possess an impregnable fortress, if you will defend it, why take shelter in an outwork, where defeat is certain? Why select the very weakest position, one on which you will yourselves present a divided front to the enemy, when it is in your power to choose one on which you and we can all unite? You will thus afford an opportunity to the abolitionists at the North to form a false issue with your friends. You place us in such a condition that we cannot defend you, without infringing the sacred right of petition. Do you not perceive that the question of abolition may thus be indissolubly connected, in public estimation, with a cause which we can never abandon. If the abolitionists themselves had been consulted, I will venture to assert, they ought to have advised the very course which has been adopted by their greatest enemies.

The vote upon this unfortunate motion may do almost equal harm in the South. It may produce an impression there, that we who will vote against 328the motion are not friendly to the protection of their constitutional rights. It may arouse jealousy and suspicion, where none ought to exist; and may thus magnify a danger which has already been greatly exaggerated. In defending any great cause, it is always disastrous to take a position which cannot be maintained. Your forces thus become scattered and inefficient, and the enemy may obtain possession of the citadel whilst you are vainly attempting to defend an outpost. I am sorry, indeed, that this motion has been made.

I shall now proceed to defend my own motion from the attacks which have been made upon it. It has been equally opposed by both extremes. I have not found, upon the present occasion, the maxim to be true, that "in medio tutissimus ibis." The Senator from Louisiana (Mr. Porter), and the Senator from Massachusetts (Mr. Webster), seem both to believe that little, if any, difference exists between the refusal to receive a petition, and the rejection of its prayer after it has been received. Indeed, the gentleman from Louisiana, whom I am happy to call my friend, says he can see no difference at all between these motions. At the moment I heard this remark, I was inclined to believe that it proceeded from that confusion of ideas which sometimes exists in the clearest heads of the country from which he derives his origin, and from which I am myself proud to be descended. What, sir, no difference between refusing to receive a request at all, and actually receiving it and considering it respectfully, and afterwards deciding, without delay, that it is not in your power to grant it! There is no man in the country, acquainted with the meaning of the plainest words in the English language, who will not recognize the distinction in a moment.

If a constituent of that gentleman should present to him a written request, and he should tell him to go about his business, and take his paper with him, that he would not have any thing to do with him or it: this would be to refuse to receive the petition.

On the other hand, if the gentleman should receive this written request of his constituent, read it over carefully and respectfully, and file it away among his papers, but, finding it was of an unreasonable or dangerous character, he should inform him, without taking further time to reflect upon it, that the case was a plain one, and that he could not, consistently with what he believed to be his duty, grant the request: this would be to reject the prayer of the petition.

There is as much difference between the two cases, as there would be between kicking a man down stairs who attempted to enter your house, and receiving him politely, examining his request, and then refusing to comply with it.

It has been suggested that the most proper course would be to refer this petition to a committee. What possible good can result from referring it? Is there a Senator on this floor who has not long since determined whether he will vote to abolish slavery in this District or not? Does any gentleman require the report of a committee, in order to enable him to decide this question? Not one.

329By granting the prayer of this memorial, as I observed on a former occasion, you would establish a magazine of gunpowder here, from which trains might be laid into the surrounding States, which would produce fearful explosions. In the very heart of the slave-holding States themselves you would erect an impregnable citadel from whence the abolitionists might securely spread throughout these States, by circulating their incendiary pamphlets and pictures, the seeds of disunion, insurrection, and servile war. You would thus take advantage of Virginia and Maryland in ceding to you this District, without expressly forbidding Congress to abolish slavery here whilst it exists within their limits. No man can, for one moment, suppose that they would have made this cession upon any other terms, had they imagined that a necessity could ever exist for such a restriction. Whatever may be my opinion of the power of Congress, under the Constitution, to interfere with this question, about which at present I say nothing, I shall as steadily and as sternly oppose its exercise as if I believed no such power to exist.

In making the motion now before the Senate, I intended to adopt as strong a measure as I could, consistently with the right of petition and a proper respect for the petitioners. I am the last man in the world who would, intentionally, treat these respectable constituents of my own with disrespect. I know them well, and prize them highly. On a former occasion I did ample justice to their character. I deny that they are abolitionists. I cannot, however, conceive how any person could have supposed that it was disrespectful to them to refuse to grant their prayer in the first instance, and not disrespectful to refuse to grant it after their memorial had been referred to a committee. In the first case their memorial will be received by the Senate, and will be filed among the records of the country. That it has already been the subject of sufficient deliberation and debate; that it has already occupied a due portion of the time of the Senate, cannot be doubted or denied. Every one acquainted with the proceedings of courts of justice must know that often, very often, when petitions are presented to them, the request is refused without any delay. This is always done in a plain case by a competent judge. And yet who ever heard that this was treating the petitioner with disrespect? In order to be respectful to these memorialists, must we go through the unmeaning form, in this case, of referring the memorial to a committee, and pretending to deliberate when we are now all fully prepared to decide?

I repeat, too, that I intended to make as strong a motion in this case as the circumstances would justify. It is necessary that we should use every constitutional effort to suppress the agitation which now disturbs the land. This is necessary, as much for the happiness and future prospects of the slave as for the security of the master. Before this storm began to rage, the laws in regard to slaves had been greatly ameliorated by the slave-holding States; they enjoyed many privileges which were unknown in former times. In some of the slave States prospective and gradual emancipation was publicly and seriously discussed. But now, thanks to the abolitionists, the slaves have been deprived of these privileges, and whilst the integrity of the Union is endangered, their prospect of final emancipation is delayed to an indefinite period. To leave this question where the Constitution has left it, to the slave-holding States themselves, is equally dictated by a humane regard for the slave as well as for their masters.

There are other objections to the reference of this memorial to a committee, which must, I think, be conclusive. I ask the Senate, after witnessing the debate upon the present question, to what conclusion could this committee arrive? If they attempted to assert any principle beyond the naked proposition before us, that the prayer of the memorialists ought not to be granted, we would be cast into a labyrinth of difficulties. It would be confusion worse confounded. If we wish to obtain a strong vote, and thus at the same time tranquilize the South and the North upon this exciting topic, the reference of it to a committee would be the most unfortunate course which we could adopt. Senators are divided into four classes on this question. The first believe that to abolish slavery in this District would be a violation of the Constitution of the United States. Should the committee recommend any proposition of a less decided character, these Senators would feel it to be their duty to attempt to amend it, by asserting this principle; and thus we should excite another dangerous and unprofitable debate. The second class, although they may not believe that the subject is constitutionally beyond the control of Congress, yet they think that the acts of cession from Maryland and Virginia to the United States forbid us to act upon the subject. These gentlemen would insist upon the affirmance of this proposition. The third class would not go as far as either of the former. They do not believe that the subject is placed beyond the power of Congress, either by the Constitution or by the compacts of cession, yet they are as firmly opposed to granting the prayer of the petition, whilst slavery continues to exist in Maryland and Virginia, as if they held both these opinions. They know that these States never would have ceded this territory of ten miles square to the United States upon any other condition, if it had entered into their conception that Congress would make an attempt, sooner or later, to convert it into a free district. Besides, they are convinced that to exercise this power, at an earlier period, would seriously endanger not only the peace and harmony of the Union, but its very existence. This class of Senators, whilst they entertain these opinions, which ought to be entirely satisfactory to the South, could never consent to vote for a resolution declaring that to act upon the subject would be a violation of the Constitution or of the compacts. The fourth class, and probably not the least numerous, are opposed to the agitation of the question, under existing circumstances, and will vote against the abolition of slavery in this District at the present moment, but would be unwilling to give any vote which might pledge them for the future. Here are the elements of discord. Although we can all, or nearly all, agree in the general result, yet we should differ essentially in the means of arriving at it. The politic and the wise course, then, is to adopt my motion that the prayer 331of the memorialists ought to be rejected. Each gentleman will arrive at this conclusion in his own way. Although we may thus travel different roads, we will all reach the same point. Should the committee go one step further than report this very proposition, we should at once be separated into four divisions; and the result must be that the whole subject would finally be laid upon the table, and thus the abolitionists would obtain a victory over the friends of the Union both to the North and to the South. Before I made the motion now before the Senate, I deliberately and anxiously considered all these embarrassing difficulties. At the first, I was under the impression that the reference of this subject to a committee would be the wisest course. In view of all the difficulties, however, I changed my opinion: and I am now willing, most cheerfully, to assume all the responsibility which may rest upon me for having made this motion.

I might have moved to lay the memorial upon the table; but I did not believe that this would be doing that justice to the South which she has a right to demand at our hands. She is entitled to the strongest vote, upon the strongest proposition, which gentlemen can give, without violating their principles.

I have but a few more words to say. As events have deprived me of the occupation assigned to me by the Senator from North Carolina (Mr. Mangum), I feel myself at liberty to invade the province allotted by the same gentleman to the Senator from New York (Mr. Wright), and to defend a distinguished member of the Albany Regency. In this I am a mere volunteer. I choose thus to act because Governor Marcy has expressed my opinions better than I could do myself.

And here, permit me to say that, in my judgment, Southern gentlemen who are not satisfied with his last message, so far as it relates to the abolitionists, are very unreasonable. With the general tone and spirit of that message no one has found any fault; no one can justly find any fault. In point of fact, it is not even liable to the solitary objection which has been urged against it, that he did not recommend to the legislature the passage of a law for the purpose of punishing those abolitionists who, in that State, should attempt to excite insurrection and sedition in the slaveholding States, by the circulation of inflammatory publications and pictures. It is true that he does not advise the immediate passage of such a law, but this was because he thought public opinion would be sufficient to put them down. He, however, looks to it as eventually proper, in case, contrary to his opinion, such a measure should become necessary to arrest the evil. He expressly asserts, and clearly proves, that the legislature possesses the power to pass such a law. This is the scope and spirit of his message.

Ought he to have recommended the immediate passage of such a law? I think not. The history of mankind, in all ages, demonstrates that the surest mode of giving importance to any sect, whether in politics or religion, is to subject its members to persecution. It has become a proverb, that "the blood of the martyrs is the seed of the church." By persecution, religious 332sects, maintaining doctrines the most absurd and the most extravagant—doctrines directly at war with the pure faith and principles announced to the world by the Divine Author of our religion, have been magnified into importance. I do not believe there is any State in this Union (unless the information which we have received from the Senators from Vermont might make that State an exception), where penal laws of the character proposed would not advance, instead of destroying the cause of the abolitionists. I feel confident such would be the event in Pennsylvania. Severe legislation, unless there is a manifest necessity for it, is always prejudicial. This question may be safely left to public opinion, which, in our age, and in our country, like a mighty torrent, sweeps away error. The people, although they may sometimes be misled in the beginning, always judge correctly in the end. Let severe penal laws on this subject be enacted in any State—let a few honest but misguided enthusiasts be prosecuted under them—let them be tried and punished in the face of the country, and you will thus excite the sympathies of the people, and create a hundred abolitionists where one only now exists. Southern gentlemen have no right to doubt our sincerity on this subject, and they ought to permit us to judge for ourselves as to the best mode of allaying the excitement which they believe exists among ourselves.

If the spirit of abolition had become so extensive and so formidable as some gentlemen suppose, we might justly be alarmed for the existence of this Union. Comparatively speaking, I believe it to be weak and powerless, though it is noisy. Without excitement got up here or elsewhere, which may continue its existence for some time longer, it will pass away in a short period, like the other excitements which have disturbed the public mind, and are now almost forgotten.

On the 9th of March (1836) the following proceedings took place:

The Senate proceeded to consider the petition of the Society of Friends in Philadelphia, on the subject of the abolition of slavery in the District of Columbia.

The question being on the motion "that the petition be not received"—Mr. Calhoun addressed the Senate in reply to what had fallen from other Senators on the subject.

Mr. Clay made a few remarks in explanation, called for by some part of the remarks of the Senator from South Carolina.

The question was then taken on the motion of Mr. Calhoun, "Shall the petition be received?" and decided as follows:

Yeas,—Messrs. Benton, Brown, Buchanan, Clay, Clayton, Crittenden, Davis, Ewing of Ill., Ewing of Ohio, Goldsborough, Grundy, Hendricks, Hill, Hubbard, Kent, King of Ala., King of Ga., Knight, Linn, McKean, Morris, Naudain, Niles, Prentiss, Robbins, Robinson, Ruggles, Shepley, Southard, Swift, Tallmadge, Tipton, Tomlinson, Wall, Webster, Wright.—36.

333Nays.—Messrs. Black, Calhoun, Cuthbert, Leigh, Moore, Nicholas, Preston, Porter, Walker, White.—10.

The question being next on the motion of Mr. Buchanan, to reject the prayer of the petition,

Mr. Clay made some remarks on the motion, and concluded by moving to amend it by adding to it:—

For the Senate, without now affirming or denying the constitutional power of Congress to grant the prayer of the petition, believes, even supposing the power uncontested, which it is not, that the exercise of it would be inexpedient;

1st. Because the people of the District of Columbia have not themselves petitioned for the abolition of slavery within the District.

2d. Because the States of Virginia and Maryland would be injuriously affected by such a measure, whilst the institution of slavery continues to subsist within their respective jurisdictions, and neither of these States would probably have ceded to the United States the territory now forming the District if it had anticipated the adoption of any such measure without clearly and expressly guarding against it. And,

3d. Because the injury which would be inflicted by exciting alarm and apprehension in the States tolerating slavery, and by disturbing the harmony between them and the other members of the Confederacy, would far exceed any practical benefit which could possibly flow from the abolition of slavery within the District.

Mr. Porter wished more time to reflect, and moved to lay the motion on the table, but withdrew it at the instance of Mr. Buchanan.

Mr. Buchanan said that some remarks, both of the Senator from South Carolina (Mr. Calhoun), and of the Senator from Kentucky (Mr. Clay), compelled him to make a few observations in his own defence.

Sir, said Mr. B., I rejoice at the result of the vote which has this day been recorded. It will forever secure to the citizens of this country, the sacred right of petition. The question has now been finally settled by a decisive vote of the Senate. The memorial which I presented from a portion of the highly respectable Society of Friends, has been received by a triumphant majority. Another happy consequence of this vote is, that abolition is forever separated from the right of petition. The abolitionists will now never be able to connect their cause with the violation of a right so justly dear to the people. They must now stand alone. This is the very position in which every friend of the Union, both to the North and the South, ought to desire to see them placed.

From the remarks which have just been made by the Senators from South Carolina and Kentucky, it might almost be supposed that my motion to reject the prayer of the memorialists, was trifling with the right of petition, which, in the course of debate, I have defended with all my power. Is there the slightest foundation for such an imputation? The memorial has been received by the Senate, and has been read. If this 334body are in doubt whether they will grant its prayer—if they wish further information upon this subject than what they already possess, then they ought to refer it. On the other hand, if every Senator has already determined how he will vote upon the question, why send the memorial to a committee? It presents but one simple question for our decision. It asks us to abolish slavery in the District of Columbia. My motion proposes that this prayer shall be rejected. Now, is it not self-evident to every Senator upon this floor, that any committee which can be formed out of this body, will arrive at the same conclusion? Why, then, refer this memorial to obtain a report, when we already know what that report will be? Why keep the question open for further agitation and debate? Should it be referred to a committee, upon their report, we shall have the same ground to travel over again which we have been treading for so long a time. I have yet to learn that when a petition is presented to any tribunal, in a case so clear as not to require deliberation, that it is either disrespectful to the petitioners, or that it infringes the right of petition, to decide against its prayer without delay.

But in this case, powerful reasons exist why the memorial ought not to be referred. Although we all agree that slavery ought not to be abolished in the District of Columbia, yet we arrive at this conclusion by different courses of reasoning. Before I presented this memorial, I endeavored to ascertain from Senators whether it would be possible to obtain a strong vote in favor of any proposition more specific in its terms than that now before the Senate. I found this would be impossible. I then made the motion to reject the prayer of the memorial, after much deliberation.

I found the Senate divided upon this subject into four sections. One portion was opposed to the prayer of the memorial, because, in their opinion, it would be unconstitutional to grant it; another, because it would violate our compacts of cession with Virginia and Maryland; a third, because it would be inexpedient and unjust to abolish slavery in this District, whilst it exists in the surrounding States; and a fourth, who were unwilling to go even to this extent, but who equally condemned its abolition at the present moment. Here were the elements of discord. Whilst all, or nearly all, are harmonious in their conclusion that the prayer of the petition ought not to be granted, their premises are far different. My object was to get the strongest vote, for the purpose of calming the agitation, both to the

South and to the North. In order to accomplish this purpose, my motion must be one on which the largest majority could agree, and on which each member might vote for his own peculiar reasons. I ask what motion could I have made, so well calculated to attain the end, as the one now before the Senate?

The amendment which has just been proposed by the Senator from Kentucky will, I fear, prove to be the apple of discord in this body. It is too strong a measure for one portion of the Senate, whilst it is too weak for another. Those who believe that we have no power under the Constitution to abolish slavery in this District, will not vote for the amendment, because it does recognize this principle; whilst such gentlemen as deem it inexpedient at the 335present time to act upon the subject, but who do not wish to commit themselves for the future, will be equally opposed to the reasons which this amendment assigns. For my own part, individually, I should not object to the amendment. I could most cheerfully vote for all the principles which it contains. If I believed it would unite in its favor as large a majority of the Senate as the motion which I have made, unaccompanied by these reasons, it should have my support. But this, I am convinced, will not be the case; and my purpose is to obtain the largest vote possible, because this will have the strongest influence upon public opinion. It would most effectually check the agitation upon this subject.

Sir, said Mr. B., this question of domestic slavery is the weak point in our institutions. Tariffs may be raised almost to prohibition, and then they may be reduced so as to yield no adequate protection to the manufacturer; our Union is sufficiently strong to endure the shock. Fierce political storms may arise—the moral elements of the country may be convulsed by the struggles of ambitious men for the highest honors of the Government—the sunshine does not more certainly succeed the storm, than that all will again be peace. Touch this question of slavery seriously—let it once be made manifest to the people of the South that they cannot live with us, except in a state of continual apprehension and alarm for their wives and their children, for all that is near and dear to them upon the earth,—and the Union is from that moment dissolved. It does not then become a question of expediency, but of self-preservation. It is a question brought home to the fireside, to the domestic circle of every white man in the Southern States. This day, this dark and gloomy day for the Republic, will, I most devoutly trust and believe, never arrive. Although, in Pennsylvania, we are all opposed to slavery in the abstract, yet we will never violate the constitutional compact which we have made with our sister States. Their rights will be held sacred by us. Under the Constitution it is their own question; and there let it remain.

Mr. Preston said there may be other reasons; he had some which were stronger than those assigned, and he should vote against these, which contained a negative pregnant, looking to a state of things when Congress could act on the subject.

Mr. Porter said one of his reasons for wishing to lay on the table the amendment was, that he might examine and ascertain if such reasons as would be satisfactory to him, so as to command his vote, could be assigned. He renewed his motion, and again withdrew it; when

Mr. Clay stated that he had no objection to let the amendment lie for further examination. After a few words from Mr. Cuthbert, on motion of Mr. Morris, the Senate adjourned.

On the 11th of March, the following proceedings occurred:

Mr. Leigh rose, and said that, in pursuance of the promise which he yesterday made to the Senate to move to resume the consideration of the abolition 336petition at the earliest moment that he should have decided what course his duty required him to pursue in regard to the amendment which he yesterday offered to the motion for rejection, now moved that the Senate take up that subject.

The motion having been agreed to, Mr. Leigh withdrew the amendment offered by him yesterday; and the question recurred on Mr. Buchanan's motion that the prayer of the petition be rejected.

[The following is a copy of the petition:

To the Senate and House of Representatives of the United States:

The memorial of Caln Quarterly Meeting of the Religious Society of Friends, commonly called Quakers, respectfully represents: That, having long felt deep sympathy with that portion of the inhabitants of these United States which is held in bondage, and having no doubt that the happiness and interests, moral and pecuniary, of both master and slave, and our whole community, would be greatly promoted if the inestimable right to liberty was extended equally to all, we contemplate with extreme regret that the District of Columbia, over which you possess entire control, is acknowledged to be one of the greatest marts for the traffic in the persons of human beings in the known world, notwithstanding the principles of the Constitution declare that all men have an unalienable right to the blessing of liberty.

We therefore earnestly desire that you will enact such laws as will secure the right of freedom to every human being residing within the constitutional jurisdiction of Congress, and prohibit every species of traffic in the persons of men, which is as inconsistent in principle, and inhuman in practice, as the foreign slave trade.

Signed by direction, and on behalf of the aforesaid quarterly meeting, held in Lancaster county, Pennsylvania, the 19th of 11 mo., 1835.

Lindley Coats,

Esther Hayes,

Clerks.]

The yeas and nays were ordered on the question of rejection.

Mr. McKean moved to amend the motion by striking out all after the word "that"— (namely, the words "the prayer of the petition to be rejected,") and inserting "it is inexpedient at this time to legislate on the subject of slavery in the District of Columbia." On this question the yeas and nays were ordered, on his motion.

The question being taken, it was decided as follows:

Yeas—Messrs. Hendricks, McKean—2.

Nays—Messrs. Benton, Black, Brown, Buchanan, Clay, Crittenden, Cuthbert, Davis, Ewing of Illinois, Ewing of Ohio, Goldsborough, Grundy, Hill, Hubbard, King of Alabama, King of Georgia, Knight, Leigh, Linn, Nicholas, Niles, Porter, Prentiss, Preston, Robbins, Robinson, Ruggles, Shepley, Swift, Tallmadge, Tipton, Tomlinson, Walker, Wall, Webster, White, Wright—37.

Mr. McKean moved to amend the motion by inserting between the first 337word "that" and the words "the prayer of the petition be rejected," the words "inexpedient to legislate on the subject of slavery in the District of Columbia, and that."

On this question he called for the yeas and nays, which were ordered.

The question was then taken, and decided as follows:

Yeas—Messrs. Ewing of Ohio, Hendricks, McKean—3.

Nays—Messrs. Benton, Black, Brown, Buchanan, Clay, Crittenden, Cuthbert, Davis, Ewing of Illinois, Goldsborough, Grundy, Hill, Hubbard, King of Alabama, King of Georgia, Knight, Leigh, Linn, Moore, Niles, Nicholas, Preston, Porter, Robbins, Robinson, Ruggles, Shepley, Swift, Tallmadge, Tipton, Tomlinson, Walker, Wall, Webster, White, Wright—36.

The question being on the original motion of Mr. Buchanan, "that the prayer of the petition be rejected"—

Mr. McKean said that, in offering the amendments which he had proposed, he had discharged his conscience of an imperative duty. It had pleased the Senate to reject these amendments, and, as he was thus deprived of the power of making the motion more palatable, all that he could now do was to vote for the proposition of his colleague.

Same day, after debate.—The question was then taken on the motion to reject the prayer of the petition, and decided as follows:

Yeas—Messrs. Benton, Black, Brown, Buchanan, Clay, Crittenden, Cuthbert, Ewing of Illinois, Ewing of Ohio, Goldsborough, Grundy, Hill, Hubbard, King of Alabama, King of Georgia, Leigh, Linn, McKean, Moore, Nicholas, Niles, Porter, Preston, Robbins, Robinson, Ruggles, Shepley, Tallmadge, Tipton, Tomlinson, Walker, Wall, White, Wright—34.

Nays—Messrs. Davis, Hendricks, Knight, Prentiss, Swift, Webster—6.

So the prayer of the petition was rejected.

On the 25th of April, Mr. Buchanan presented a petition from the Society of Friends, in Philadelphia, on which he said:

He rose to present the memorial of the Yearly Meeting of the religious Society of Friends, which had been recently held in the city of Philadelphia, remonstrating against the admission of Arkansas into the Union, whilst a provision remained in her constitution which admits of and may perpetuate slavery. This Yearly Meeting embraced within its jurisdiction the greater part of Pennsylvania and New Jersey, the whole of the State of Delaware, and the Eastern Shore of Maryland. The language of this memorial was perfectly respectful. Indeed, it could not be otherwise, considering the source from which it emanated. It breathed throughout the pure and Christian spirit which had always animated the Society of Friends; and although he did not concur with them in opinion, their memorial was entitled to be received with great respect.

When the highly respectable committee,[54] which had charge of this memorial, 338called upon him this morning, and requested him to present it to the Senate, he had felt it to be his duty to inform them in what relation he stood to the question. He stated to them that he had been requested by the delegate from Arkansas to take charge of the application of that Territory to be admitted into the Union, and that he had cheerfully taken upon himself the performance of this duty. He also read to them the 8th section of the act of Congress of 6th March, 1820, containing the famous Missouri compromise; and informed them that the whole Territory of Arkansas was south of the parallel of 36 degrees and a half of north latitude; and that he regarded this compromise, considering the exciting and alarming circumstances under which it was made, and the dangers to the existence of the Union which it had removed, to be almost as sacred as a constitutional provision. That there might be no mistake on the subject, he had also informed them that in presenting their memorial he should feel it to be his duty to state these facts to the Senate. With this course on his part they were satisfied, and still continued their request that he might present the memorial. He now did so with great pleasure. He hoped it might be received by the Senate with all the respect it so highly deserved. He asked that it might be read; and as the question of the admission of Arkansas was no longer before us, he moved that it might be laid upon the table. The memorial was accordingly read, and was ordered to be laid upon the table.

The next time that the subject of slavery came before the Senate was in June, 1836. It then arose upon a bill which had been proposed in conformity with a special recommendation by President Jackson, in his annual message of December, 1835, to restrain the use of the mails for the circulation of incendiary publications. The bill contained the following provisions:

Be it enacted, &c., That it shall not be lawful for any deputy postmaster, in any State, Territory, or District of the United States, knowingly to deliver to any person whatever, any pamphlet, newspaper, handbill, or other printed paper or pictorial representation touching the subject of slavery, where, by the laws of the said State, Territory, or District, their circulation is prohibited; and any deputy postmaster who shall be guilty thereof, shall be forthwith removed from office.

Sec. 2. And be it further enacted, That nothing in the acts of Congress to establish and regulate the Post Office Department, shall be construed to protect any deputy postmaster, mail carrier, or other officer or agent of said department, who shall knowingly circulate in any State, Territory, or District, as aforesaid, any such pamphlet, newspaper, handbill, or other printed paper or pictorial representation, forbidden by the laws of such State, Territory, or District.

Sec. 3. And be it further enacted by the authority aforesaid, That the deputy postmasters of the offices where the pamphlets, newspapers, handbills, or other printed papers or pictorial representations aforesaid, may arrive for delivery, shall, under the instructions of the Postmaster General, from time to time give notice of the same, so that they may be withdrawn, by the person who deposited them originally to be mailed, and if the same shall not be withdrawn in one month thereafter, shall be burnt or otherwise destroyed. This bill, on the 2d of June, 1836, was ordered to be engrossed and read a third time, by the casting vote of Mr. Van Buren, the Vice-President. On the 8th of June the following debate and proceedings took place:

Mr. Webster addressed the Senate at length in opposition to the bill, commencing his argument against what he contended was its vagueness and obscurity in not sufficiently defining what were the publications, the circulation of which it intended to prohibit. The bill provided that it should not be lawful for any deputy postmaster, in any State, Territory, or District of the United States, knowingly to deliver to any person whatever, any pamphlet, newspaper, handbill, or other printed matter or pictorial representation, touching the subject of slavery, where by the laws of said State, District, or Territory, their circulation was prohibited. Under this provision Mr. W. contended that it was impossible to say what publications might not be prohibited from circulation. No matter what was the publication, whether for or against slavery—if it touched the subject in any shape or form, it would fall under the prohibition. Even the Constitution of the United States might be prohibited; and the person who was clothed with the power to judge in this delicate matter was one of the deputy postmasters who, notwithstanding the difficulties with which he was encompassed in coming to a correct decision must decide correctly, under pain of being removed from office. It would be necessary, also, he said, for the deputy postmasters referred to in this bill to make themselves acquainted with all the various laws passed by the States, touching this subject of slavery, and to decide them, no matter how variant they might be with each other. Mr. W. also contended that the bill conflicted with that provision in the Constitution which prohibited Congress from passing any law to abridge the freedom of speech or of the press. What was the liberty of the press? he asked. It was the liberty of printing as well as the liberty of publishing, in all the ordinary modes of publication; and was not the circulation of the papers through the mails an ordinary mode of publication? He was afraid that they were in some danger of taking a step in this matter, that they might hereafter have cause to regret, by its being contended that whatever in this bill applies to publications touching slavery, applies to other publications that the States might think proper to prohibit; and Congress might, under this example, be called upon to pass laws to suppress the circulation of political, religious, or any other description of publications, which produced excitement in the States. Was this bill in accordance with the general force and temper of the Constitution and its amendments? It was not in accordance with that provision of the instrument, under which the freedom of speech and of the press was secured. Whatever laws the State Legislatures might pass on the subject, Congress was restrained from legislating in any manner whatever, with regard to the press. It would be admitted, that if a newspaper came directed to him, he had a property in it; and how could any man, then, take that property and burn it without due form of law? and he did not know how this newspaper could be pronounced an unlawful publication and having no property in it, without a legal trial.

Mr. W. argued against the right to examine into the nature of publications sent to the post-office, and said that the right of an individual in his papers, was secured to him in every free country in the world. In England, it was expressly provided that the papers of the subject shall be free from all unreasonable searches and seizures—language, he said, to be found in our Constitution. This principle established in England, so essential to liberty, had been followed out in France, where the right of printing and publishing was secured in the fullest extent; the individual publishing being amenable to the laws for what he published; and every man printed and published what he pleased, at his peril. Mr. W. went on at some length to show that the bill was contrary to that provision of the Constitution, which prohibits Congress to pass any law abridging the freedom of speech or of the press.

Mr. Buchanan said, that as he had voted for the engrossment of this bill, and should vote for its final passage, he felt himself bound to defend and justify his vote against the argument of the Senator from Massachusetts (Mr. Webster). In doing so, he would imitate that Senator, if in no other respect, at least in being brief.

It is indispensable to the clear and distinct understanding of any argument, to know precisely what is the question under discussion. Without this knowledge, we cannot tell whether in any or what degree the argument is applicable to the subject. What, then, is the naked question now under discussion, stripped of all the mist which has been cast around it? This bill embraced but a single principle, though this principle was carried out through three sections. It provides that deputy postmasters, within the limits of such slaveholding States as have found it necessary for their own safety to pass laws making it penal to circulate inflammatory publications and pictorial representations calculated to excite the slaves to insurrection, shall not be protected by the laws of the United States, in violating these State laws. Postmasters within these States who shall knowingly distribute such publications are liable to be removed from office. The bill also provides that the post-office laws of the United States shall not protect postmasters, mail carriers, or other officers or agents of the department who shall knowingly circulate such incendiary publications, from the penalties denounced against this offence under the laws of the States. This is the spirit and principle of the bill. It does no more than to withdraw the protection of the laws of the United States, establishing the Post Office Department, from postmasters and other agents of this Government who shall wilfully transgress State laws deemed absolutely necessary to secure the States, within which they exist, from servile insurrection.

This bill did not affect, in the slightest degree, any of the non-slaveholding States. Neither did it apply to any of the slaveholding States, except those within which the danger of insurrection had become so imminent as to compel them to pass laws of the character referred to in the bill.

Of the policy and justice of passing such a bill he could not doubt, provided we possess the power. No person would contend that this Government ought to become the instrument of exciting insurrection within any of the States, unless we were constrained to pursue this course by an overruling constitutional necessity. The question then is, does any such necessity exist? Are we bound by the Constitution of the United States, through our post-offices, to circulate publications among the slaves, the direct tendency of which is to excite their passions and rouse them to insurrection? Have we no power to stay our hand in any case? Even if a portion of this Union were in a state of open rebellion against the United States, must we aid and assist the rebels by communicating to them, through our Post Office Department, such publications and information as may encourage and promote their designs against the very existence of the confederacy itself? If the Constitution of the United States has placed us in this deplorable condition, we must yield to its mandates, no matter what may be the consequences.

Mr. B. did not believe that the Constitution placed us in any such position. Our power over the mails was as broad and general as any words in the English language could confer. The Constitution declares that "Congress shall have power to establish post-offices and post roads." This is the only provision which it contains touching the subject. After the establishment of these post-offices and post roads, who shall decide upon the purposes for which they shall be used? He answered, Congress, and Congress alone. There was no limitation, no restriction, whatever, upon our discretion contained in the bond. We have the power to decide what shall and what shall not be carried in the mail, and what shall be the rate of postage. He freely admitted that, unless in extreme cases, where the safety of the Republic was involved, we should never exercise this power of discrimination between what papers should and should not be circulated through the mail. The Constitution, however, has conferred upon us this general power, probably for the very purpose of meeting these extreme cases; and it is one which, from its delicate nature, we shall not be likely to abuse.

He differed entirely from the opinion of the Senator from South Carolina (Mr. Calhoun), as to the source whence the power was derived to pass this bill. No action of the State Legislatures could either confer it or take it away. It was perfect and complete in itself under the Federal Constitution, or it had no existence. With that Senator he entirely concurred in opinion, that the sedition law was clearly unconstitutional. Congress have no power to abridge the freedom of the press, or to pass any law to prevent or to punish any publication whatever. He understood the freedom of the press to mean precisely what the Senator from Massachusetts had stated. But does it follow, as the gentleman contends, that because we have no power over the press, that therefore we are bound to carry and distribute anything and everything which may proceed from it, even if it should be calculated to stir up insurrection or to destroy the Government? So far as this Government is concerned, every person may print, and publish, and circulate whatever he pleases; but are we, therefore, compelled to become his agents, and to circulate for him everything he may choose to publish? This is the question. Any gentleman upon this floor may write what he thinks proper against my character; but because he can exercise this liberty, am I therefore bound to carry and to circulate what he has written? So any individual within the broad limits of this Union, without previous restraint and without danger of punishment from the Federal Government, may publish what is calculated to aid and assist the enemies of the country in open war; but does it follow, as a necessary consequence, that this very Government is bound to carry and circulate such publications through its mails? A more perfect non sequitur never had been presented to his mind. It was one thing not to restrain or punish publications; it was another and an entirely

different thing to carry and circulate them after they have been published. The one is merely passive; the other is active. It was one thing to leave our citizens entirely free to print and publish and circulate what they pleased; and it was another thing to call upon us to aid in their circulation. From the prohibition to make any law "abridging the freedom of speech or of the press," it could never be inferred that we must provide by law for the circulation through the post-office of everything which the press might publish. And yet this is the argument both of the Senator from Massachusetts and the Senator from South Carolina. If this argument were well founded, it was very clear to his mind, that no State law could confer upon Congress any power to pass this bill. We derived our powers from the Federal Constitution, and from that alone. If, under its provisions, we have had no authority to pass the bill, we could derive no such authority from the laws of the States. Why, then, did Mr. B. vote for a bill to prevent the circulation of publications prohibited by State laws? Not because we derived any power from these laws; but, under the circumstances, they contained the best rule to guide us in deciding what publications were dangerous. The States were the best judges of what was necessary for their own safety and protection; and they would not call for the passage of this bill, unless they were firmly convinced that the situation in which they were placed imperiously demanded it. They were willing to submit to a great evil in depriving themselves of information which might be valuable to them, in order to avoid the still greater evil that would result from the circulation of these publications and pictorial representations among their slaves. Such a law would not be permitted to exist after the necessity for it had ended. He was therefore willing, upon this occasion, to refer to the laws of the States, not for the purpose of conferring any power on Congress, but merely for a description of the publications which it should be unlawful for our deputy-postmasters within these States to circulate. This bill was in strict conformity with the recommendations contained in the President's message on this subject, which had, he believed, found favor everywhere. The principles of this message, which had been pronounced unconstitutional by the Senator from South Carolina (Mr. Calhoun), had, he believed, been highly commended in a resolution passed by the legislature of that State. He would read an extract from the President's message:
"In connection with these provisions in relation to the Post Office Department, I must also invite your attention to the painful excitement produced in the South, by attempts to circulate through the mails inflammatory appeals addressed to the passions of the slaves, in prints, and in various sorts of publications, calculated to stimulate them to insurrection, and to produce all the horrors of a servile war.
"There is, doubtless, no respectable portion of our countrymen who can be so far misled as to feel any other sentiment than that of indignant regret at conduct so destructive of the harmony and peace of the country, and so repugnant to the principles of our national compact, and to the dictates of humanity and religion. Our happiness and prosperity essentially depend upon peace within our borders—and peace depends upon the maintenance, in good faith, of those compromises of the Constitution upon which the Union is founded. It is fortunate for the country that the good sense, the generous feeling, and the deep-rooted attachment of the people of the non-slaveholding States to the Union, and to their fellow-citizens of the same blood in the South, have given so strong and impressive a tone to the sentiments entertained against the proceedings of the misguided persons who have engaged in these unconstitutional and wicked attempts, and especially against the emissaries from foreign parts who have dared to interfere in this matter, as to authorize the hope, that those attempts will no longer be persisted in. But if these expressions of the public will shall not be sufficient to effect so desirable a result, not a doubt can be entertained that the non-slaveholding States, so far from

countenancing the slightest interference with the constitutional rights of the South, will be prompt to exercise their authority in suppressing, so far as in them lies, whatever is calculated to produce this evil.

"In leaving the care of other branches of this interesting subject to the State authorities, to whom they properly belong, it is nevertheless proper for Congress to take such measures as will prevent the Post Office Department, which was designed to foster an amicable intercourse and correspondence between all the members of the confederacy, from being used as an instrument of an opposite character. The General Government, to which the great trust is confided, of preserving inviolate the relations created among the States by the Constitution, is especially bound to avoid in its own action, anything that may disturb them. I would, therefore, call the special attention of Congress to the subject, and respectfully suggest the propriety of passing such 344a law as will prohibit, under severe penalties, the circulation in the Southern States, through the mail, of incendiary publications intended to instigate the slaves to insurrection."

In reply to Mr. Webster, Mr. B. said, that he did not think there was any vagueness in that part of the bill on which the gentleman had commented, except what arose from the nature of the subject. It is vague, says the gentleman, because it contains no description of the publications, the circulation of which it intends to prohibit, except the words "touching the subject of slavery." On this foundation he had erected a considerable portion of his argument. Mr. B. acknowledged that if the bill contained no other description than this, it would be impossible to carry it into execution. But this was not the fact. The subsequent language restricted this vague description; because it confined the operation of the bill to such publications only, "touching the subject of slavery," as were prohibited from circulation by the laws of the respective States.

We have, said Mr. B., wisely and properly referred, for the description of the offence, to the laws of the different States which will be embraced by the bill. It was just—it was politic—it was treating those States with a proper degree of respect, to make our law conform with their laws, and thus to take care that no conflict should arise between our deputy postmasters and their State authorities. Could the gentleman from Massachusetts himself make the bill more explicit? He could not do it, consistently with the principles upon which it was founded, without incorporating into its provisions all the laws of all the States who had thought proper to pass laws upon this subject. Our deputy postmasters were resident citizens of those States. They were bound to know the State laws under which they lived, and all that this bill requires is, that they shall not violate them.

The Senator from Massachusetts has contended that any newspaper which had been sent to an individual by mail, and was deposited in a post-office, was his property; and we had, therefore, no right to say it should not be delivered. But this was begging the question. It was taking that for granted which remained to be proved. If Congress, as he (Mr. B.) had contended, possessed the incontestable power of declaring what should and what should not be circulated through the mails, no man could have the right to demand from any post-office that which the law had declared should not thus be circulated. If we can, without violating the Constitution, say that these inflammatory publications tending to excite servile war shall not be distributed by our postmasters among the individuals to whom they are directed, no question of property could then arise. No man can have a property in that which is a violation of the law. It then becomes a question, not of property, but of public safety. Admit the gentleman's premises, that we have no right to pass any law upon this subject, and he can establish his position that a property exists in those publications whilst in the post-offices. Without this admission, his argument entirely fails.

He felt as reluctant as any man could feel, to vote for any law interfering with the circulation through the mails of any publication whatever, no matter what might be its character. But if the slaves within any Southern State were in rebellion, or if a palpable or well-founded danger of such a rebellion existed, with his present convictions, should he refuse to prevent the circulation of publications tending to encourage or excite insurrection, he would consider himself an accomplice in their guilt. He entertained no doubt whatever of the power of Congress to pass this bill, or of the propriety of exercising that power. He would not have voted for the bill which had been reported by the Senator from South Carolina, (Mr. Calhoun) because he thought it a measure far beyond what was required by the necessity of the case. This bill, whilst it was sufficiently strong to correct the evil, would be confined in its operation to those States within which the danger existed.

Mr. Davis (of Massachusetts) stated at length his objections to the passage of the bill. Senators assumed that there were no difficulties in the way, because the post-office power gave to Congress the right to decide what should be carried in the mails. On a former occasion he had said all that was proper in regard to this matter. He then drew the attention of the Senate to the constitutional question involved, and demonstrated, as he thought, that there was no authority in the Constitution to pass this bill, or anything like it. The language of the Constitution was very simple: it only said that Congress should have the power to establish post-offices and post roads. Now what was a post-office, in the meaning of the Constitution? To understand this, it would be necessary to ascertain what was the meaning held at the time the Constitution was adopted. You had a post-office at the time the Constitution was made, and a press also; and the provision in the Constitution was made in reference to both these known things. The object in establishing the post-office, then, was to send abroad intelligence throughout the country; and it was intended for the transmission of newspapers, pamphlets, judicial and legislative proceedings, and all matters emanating from the press, relating to politics, literature, and science, and for the transmission of private letters. It would be, therefore, in his opinion, in conflict with the provision of the Constitution, giving Congress the power to establish the post-office, as well as an abridgment of the freedom of the press, to carry into effect the provisions of the bill.

The Senator from Pennsylvania reiterated the argument used the other day by his friend from Georgia, that you have no right to diffuse publications through the agency of the post-office, for the purpose of exciting a servile war. Now let me tell the gentleman, (said Mr. D.) that this is an old argument against the liberty of the press, and that it has been used whenever it was thought necessary to establish a censorship over it. The public morals were said to be in danger; it was necessary to prevent licentiousness, tumult, and sedition; and the public good required that the licentiousness of the press should be restrained. All these were the plausible pretences under which the freedom of the press had been violated in all ages. Now they knew that the press was at all times corrupt; but when they came to decide the question whether the tares should be rooted up, and the wheat along with it, those who had decided in favor of liberty, had always decided that it was better to put up with a lesser evil than to draw down upon themselves one of such fearful magnitude, as must result from the destruction of the press. Mr. D. contended that the power to be given to the deputy postmasters to decide what should, and what should not be distributed from the post-office, gave them a dangerous discretion over a very delicate matter, and that the power was one highly susceptible of abuse, and always liable to misconstruction.

Mr. Grundy (of Tennessee) observed that this bill was intended simply to prevent any officer of the Government, who should violate the laws of the States in which he resided, from sheltering himself under the post-office law. As the bill now stood, the objections with regard to abridging the freedom of the press had no application whatever. There was no provision in the bill interfering with the printing or publishing of any matter whatever, nor was it even pretended that Congress possessed the power of doing so. It was not even said that certain publications, no matter how incendiary in their character, should not be deposited in the post-office, and transmitted through the mails. Therefore all the objections that he had heard to the bill fell to the ground. In this bill, the Government simply said to the individuals in its employ, "We will not help you to do an act in violation of the laws of the State in which you live." That was the ground on which the bill was framed, and it could not be pretended that this was an abridgment of the liberty of the press. It was only the Government declining to assist an individual in the violation of the law, and that was the whole bill. The Government, under the Constitution, had an entire control of the Post-Office Department. It had the power to regulate what matters should be carried through the mails, and what should not. We say to everybody that to these slaveholding States you may transmit through the mails what you please, but if you transmit to one of our officers what is prohibited by the laws of the State in which he resides, we shall say to that officer, you shall not put on the mantle of the Government to assist you in the violation of that law; you shall be subject to the penalties of the State laws, besides removal from office. In fact there was not the slightest pretext for saying that this bill violates in the remotest degree the freedom of the press. Nothing should be carried in the mails but what was proper for transmission through them; but if there was anything sent through them tending to excite insurrection and bloodshed, how could there be an objection to the passage of a law, saying that it should not be delivered out of the post-office?

The gentleman from Massachusetts objected to the vagueness of the bill in saying what shall not be distributed from the post-offices. How could the matter, he asked, be made more specific? When the publication arrived at the post-office where it was prohibited, and was about to be handed out, the State law would be consulted, and by it, it would be decided whether it was in violation of the State law or not, and it could thus be determined whether it was proper for delivery. He should not say anything as to the report—he 347did not concur in it farther than that this was a great evil, and should be corrected in the mildest way that it could be done. This bill did not affect any individual but those of the post-offices of the States where laws have been passed prohibiting publications and pictorial representations, calculated to excite insurrection among the slaves. He was opposed to the original bill, because it interfered with what publications should be deposited in, as well as delivered from, the post-offices. But it was only at the delivery office where this bill would operate, and the postmaster at such office would be operated on by the laws of the State in which it is situated. If this bill was not passed, nothing could be done, and the post-office would be made (for there were persons wicked enough to do it) the medium through which to send fire-brands throughout the country.

Mr. Clay said that he considered this bill totally unnecessary and uncalled for by public sentiment; and in this he differed with the Senator from Pennsylvania (Mr. Buchanan); for he believed that the President's message on the subject had met with general disapprobation; that it was unconstitutional; and if not so, that it contained a principle of a most dangerous and alarming character. When he saw that the exercise of the most extraordinary and dangerous power had been assumed by the head of the post-office, and that it had been sustained by this message, he turned his attention to the subject and inquired whether it was necessary that the General Government should, under any circumstances, exercise such a power, and whether it possessed it; and after much reflection, he had come to the conclusion, that they could not pass any law interfering with the subject in any shape or form whatever.

The evil complained of was the circulation of papers having a certain tendency. The papers, unless circulated, did no harm, and while in the post-office or in the mail—it was a circulation solely which constituted the evil. It was the taking them out of the mail, and the use that was to be made of them, that constituted the mischief.—Then it was perfectly competent to the State authorities to apply the remedy. The instant that a prohibited paper was handed out, whether to a citizen or sojourner, he was subject to the laws which might compel him either to surrender them or burn them. He considered the bill not only unnecessary, but as a law of a dangerous, if not a doubtful authority.

It was objected that it was vague and indefinite in its character; and how is that objection got over? The bill provided that it shall not be lawful for any deputy postmaster, in any State, Territory, or District of the United States, knowingly to deliver to any person whatever, any pamphlet, newspaper, handbill, or other printed paper or pictorial representation, touching the subject of slavery, where, by the laws of said State, Territory, or District, their circulation is prohibited. Now, what could be more vague and indefinite than this description? Now, could it be decided by this description, what publications should be withheld from distribution? The gentleman from Pennsylvania said that the laws of the States would supply the omission. He thought the Senator was premature in saying that there would be a precision 348in State laws, before he showed it by producing the law. He had seen no such law, and he did not know whether the description in the bill was applicable or not. There was another objection to this part of the bill: it applied not only to the present laws of the States, but to any future laws they might pass.

Mr. C. denied that the bill applied to the slaveholding States only, and went on to argue that it could be applied to all the States, and to any publication touching the subject of slavery whatever, whether for or against it, if such publication was only prohibited by the laws of such State. Thus, for instance, a non-slaveholding State might prohibit publications in defence of the institution of slavery, and this bill would apply to it as well as to the laws of the slaveholding States; but the law would be inoperative: it declared that the deputy postmaster should not be amenable, unless he knowingly shall deliver, etc. Why, the postmaster might plead ignorance, and of course the law would be inoperative. But he wanted to know whence Congress derived the power to pass this law. It was said that it was to carry into effect the laws of the States. Where did they get such authority? He thought that their only authority to pass laws was in pursuance of the Constitution; but to pass laws to carry into effect the laws of the States, was a most prolific authority, and there was no knowing where it was to stop: it would make the legislation of Congress dependent upon the legislation of twenty-four different sovereignties. He thought the bill was of a most dangerous tendency. The Senator from Pennsylvania asked if the post-office power did not give them the right to regulate what should be carried in the mails. Why, there was no such power as that claimed in the bill; and if they passed such a law, it would be exercising a most dangerous power. Why, if such doctrine prevailed, the Government might designate the persons, or parties, or classes who should have the benefit of the mails, excluding all others.

It was too often in the condemnation of a particular evil that they were urged on to measures of a dangerous tendency. All must agree as to the dangerous consequences of persons residing out of certain States transmitting to them incendiary publications, calculating to promote civil war and bloodshed. All must see the evil, and a great evil it was, and he hoped that a stop would be put to it; but Congress had no power to pass beyond the Constitution for the purpose of correcting it. The States alone had the power, and their power was ample for the purpose. He hoped never to see the time when the General Government should undertake to correct the evil by such measures as the one before them. If (said Mr. C.) you can pass this law to prohibit the delivery through the post-office of publications touching the subject of slavery, might they not also pass laws to prohibit any citizen of New York or Massachusetts from publishing and transmitting through the mails touching that subject? If you may touch the subject of slavery at all, why not go to the root of the evil? Suppose one of the Southern States were to pass a law of this kind, would you not be called upon by all the arguments now used in favor of this bill, to carry such laws into effect? Mr. C. concluded by saying that the bill was calculated to destroy all the landmarks of the Constitution, establish a precedent for dangerous legislation, and to lead to incalculable mischief. There was no necessity for so dangerous an assumption of authority, the State laws being perfectly competent to correct the evil complained of. He must say, that from the first to the last he was opposed to the measure.

Mr. Calhoun could not concur with the views taken by the Senators from Massachusetts and Kentucky, that this bill would comprehend in its provisions all publications touching the subject of slavery. In order to bring any publications within the provision of the bill, two qualifications were necessary. The first was, that it must relate to the subject of slavery; and the next was, that it must be prohibited by the laws of the States to which it is transmitted. He thought that this was the view that would be taken of it by the courts. The object of this bill was to make it the duty of the postmasters in the States to conform to the laws of such States, and not to deliver out papers in violation of their laws. The simple question was, had this Government the power to say to its officers, you shall not violate the laws of the States in which you reside? Could it go further, and make it their duty to co-operate with the States in carrying their laws into effect? This was the simple question. Now could any man doubt that Congress possessed the power to pass both measures, so that their officers might not come in conflict with the State laws? Indeed, he looked upon measures of this kind to prevent conflicts between the General and State Governments, which were likely to ensue, as essentially necessary, for it was evident that when such conflicts took place, the State must have the ascendancy. Mr. C. then briefly recapitulated the principles on which this bill was founded, and contended that it was in aid of laws passed by the States, as far as Congress had the power constitutionally to go, and assumed no power to prohibit or interfere with the publication or circulation of any paper whatever; it only declared, that the officers of the Government should not make their official stations a shield for violating the State laws. Was there any one there who would say, that the States had not the power to pass laws prohibiting, and making penal, the circulation of papers calculated to excite insurrection among their slaves? It being admitted that they could, could not Congress order its officers to abstain from the violation of these laws? We do not (said Mr. C.) pass a law to abridge the freedom of the press, or to prohibit the publication and circulation of any paper whatever—this has been done by the States already. The inhibition of the Constitution was on Congress, and not on the States, who possessed full power to pass any laws they thought proper. They knew that there were several precedents to sanction this bill. Congress had passed laws to abstain from the violation of the health laws of the States. Could any one say that the Constitution gave to Congress the power to pass quarantine laws? He had not adverted to the message of the President on this subject, because he believed that the President acted from the best motives, and that that part of the message 350was drawn up without sufficient reflection. He denied, however, that this message was in conformity with the Constitution. It would be directly abridging the liberty of the press for Congress to pass such laws as the President recommended. One part of the message he would refer to, which was in these words:

"I would, therefore, call the special attention of Congress to the subject, and respectfully suggest the propriety of passing such a law as will prohibit, under severe penalties, the circulation in the Southern States, through the mail, of incendiary publications, intended to instigate the slaves to insurrection." This was clearly unconstitutional, for it not only recommended the prohibition of publications and circulation of incendiary papers (abridging the freedom of the press), but it recommended also the infliction of severe penalties, which powers were expressly prohibited by the Constitution. On no other principle could this ever be defended, than that it was simply abstaining from a violation of the laws of the States.

The Senator from Kentucky contended that this bill was useless, and he (Mr. C.) agreed that it was so in one sense, and that was, with or without this bill, the Southern States would execute their own laws against the circulation of such papers. It was a case of life and death with them; and did anybody suppose that they would permit so many magazines in their bosoms, to blow them to destruction, as these post-offices must be, if these incendiary publications continued to be circulated through them? While the Southern States contained so many postmasters opposed to their institutions, as it was in his own State, where almost every postmaster was opposed to it, it was absolutely necessary for them to take effectual measures for their own security. It was the assertion of the principle, that the States had a right to protect themselves, which made the bill valuable in his eye; it prevented the conflict which would be likely to take place between the General and State Governments, unless some measure of the kind should be adopted. The States had a right to go to the extent of this bill, and they would be wanting to themselves and to posterity, if they omitted to do it. It was on the doctrine of State rights and State intervention, that he supported this bill, and on no other grounds.

The Senator from Massachusetts objected to the returning of these papers, whose delivery was prohibited. He regretted this as much as the Senator did, but his objection was, that it did not go far enough; he thought that these papers should be delivered to the prosecuting officers of the States, to enable them to ferret out the designs of the incendiaries.

Mr. Webster remarked, that in general, it might be safely said, that when different gentlemen supported a measure admitted to be of a novel character, and placed their defence of it on different and inconsistent grounds, a very simple person might believe, in such case, that there were no very strong grounds for adopting the measure. The Senator from Pennsylvania and the Senator from South Carolina not only placed their defence of their bill on opposite grounds, but each opposed the principles on which the other founded 351his support of it. Where the object to be gained was apparently good, and the case urgent, as it was represented to be, how could limitations of power stand against powerful opponents, which have always been urging to despotism? Now, against the objects of this bill, he had not a word to say; but with constitutional lawyers, there was a great difference between the object and the means to carry it into effect. It was not the object to be gained, but the means to attain it, which they should look to, for though the object might be good, the means might not be so. His objections went to the means and not to the object; and he did not yield the argument because the object was a good one, and the case was urgent. It was better to limit the power, and run the risk of injury from the want of it, than to give a power which might be exercised in a dangerous manner. The Senator from Pennsylvania said that this bill was calling on Congress to do nothing but to abstain from violating the laws of the States. It was one thing, said the Senator, for Congress to abstain from giving these incendiary papers circulation, and another to pass laws saying that they shall not be published. But if Congress had no mail through which these papers could be transmitted, what did the gentleman mean by Congress abstaining from giving them circulation? It meant that Congress should interfere and should create an especial exception as to what should be transmitted by their ordinary channel of intelligence, and that that exception should be caused by the character of the writing or publication. He contended that Congress had not the power, drawn from the character of the paper, to decide whether it should be carried in the mail or not, for such decision would be a direct abridgment of the freedom of the press. He confessed that he was shocked at the doctrine. He looked back to the alien and sedition laws which were so universally condemned throughout the country, and what was their object? Certainly to prohibit publications of a dangerous tendency. Mr. W. here quoted the sedition law, to show the objects it intended to effect. But the deputy postmasters (Mr. W. said) must look into the newspaper mail to see if there were any publications in it touching the subject of slavery calculated to excite insurrections among the slaves.

Now, said Mr. W., the country would have been rent into atoms if the sedition law, instead of saying that papers should not be published in such and such a way, had declared that the deputy postmasters should have the power to search the mails to see if they contained any publications calculated to "bring the Government into disrepute, promote insurrection, and lead to foreign war," the evils the sedition law intended to guard against. All the papers described in the law of '99 were unlawful by the laws of any of the States, and yet that law which had created so much excitement and met with such general reprobation, contained nothing like the power claimed by this bill. Any law distinguishing what shall or shall not go into the mails, founded on the sentiments of the paper, and making the deputy postmaster the judge, he should say, was expressly unconstitutional, if not recommended by gentlemen of such high authority. This bill (said Mr. W.) went beyond the recommendation of the President, for his recommendation was, that the person who circulated the papers described by him should be punished by severe penalties. Now, this was the old law of liberty—there was not a word of previous restraint in it as imposed by this bill. Mr. W. then went into an argument to show the vagueness of the bill in describing the paper, the delivery of which was prohibited. Under it, it was impossible to determine what publications should be prohibited; abolition pamphlets were to be stopped at the South, and anti-abolition papers were to be stopped at the North. In reply to Mr. Buchanan, he said that he did not assume that these prohibited publications either were or were not property. All he said was, that they ought not to make the deputy postmasters the judge, and take away the property without the authority of law. What he had to say was, that it was a question of property or no property, and that they could not make the deputy postmaster the judge of the fact, as he could not be a judge of property known to the Constitution and the law.

Mr. Buchanan said he had not anticipated, when he first addressed the Senate upon this subject, that he should have occasion to make any further remarks, but the Senator from Massachusetts had replied to his argument, in such a special manner, that he felt himself constrained to reply to some of his remarks. Now, permit me to say (continued Mr. B.) that he has not at all met the point of my argument. He has invested this subject with an air of greater importance and responsibility than it deserves: he has played around it with all his powers, but without touching the real question involved in the discussion. Congress has no power (says the gentleman) to pass any law abridging the freedom of speech or of the press. Granted. He most freely admitted that Congress had no power to touch the press at all. We can pass no law whatever either to prevent or to punish any publication, under any circumstances whatever. The sedition law violated this principle. It punished libels against the Federal Government and its officers; and having met with general reprobation, it was repealed, or permitted to expire by its own limitation, he did not recollect which.

Mr. B. said he admitted these premises of the gentleman in their broadest extent; but did they justify his conclusions? In order to maintain his argument, he must prove that the Constitution, in declaring that Congress shall not pass any law abridging the freedom of the press, has thereby, and from the force of these terms alone, commanded us to circulate and distribute, through our post-offices, everything which the press may publish, no matter whether it shall promote insurrection and civil war or not. This is the proposition which he must establish. All the gentleman's remarks in favor of the liberty of the press met his cordial approbation; but they did not apply to the constitutional question then under discussion. He had argued this question precisely as if, in addition to the words already in the Constitution, that "Congress shall make no law abridging the freedom of speech or of the press," there had been inserted, "or to prevent the circulation of any production of 353the press through the post-offices." But these words were not in the instrument; and the only question was, whether the one prohibition could be inferred from the other. Mr. B. said he was in favor of a plain and literal construction of the Constitution. He took it for his guide; and he could never consent to interpolate what its framers never intended should be there. They have conferred upon Congress, in express terms, a general discretion in regard to the Post Office Department; and the question then was, shall we exercise it in the manner proposed by this bill, for the purpose of preventing servile war, bloodshed and disunion?

How had the gentleman from Massachusetts met his argument? He says that the principles upon which the Senator from South Carolina (Mr. Calhoun) and himself had sustained this bill, were at variance with each other; and that this of itself was sufficient to cast doubt over the measure. But was it the first time the gentleman had known correct conclusions to be drawn from varying or even unfounded premises? The bill itself ought not to be condemned for the arguments of its friends. He would remind the gentleman of the advice given by a distinguished English judge, to a young friend about to occupy a judicial station in the West Indies, which was, never to give reasons for his judgments, where it could be avoided; because his natural sense and perception of justice would almost always enable him to decide correctly, though he might, and probably often would, assign insufficient reasons for his decisions. This bill ought to be judged by its own provisions, and ought not to be condemned for the reasons in support of it which had been advanced either by the Senator from South Carolina or himself.

The Senator from Massachusetts had argued as though he (Mr. B.) had said, that as the end proposed by this measure was good, he should vote for it, notwithstanding the means might be unconstitutional.

[Here Mr. Webster explained, and said he had not imputed to Mr. B. such an argument.]

Mr. B. proceeded. The Senator did not mean this imputation; but his argument seemed to imply as much. However necessary he might believe this bill to be, if he did not find a clear warrant for its passage in the Constitution, it should never have his support. He never could believe that this Government, having exclusive control over the Post-Office

Department in all its various relations, was yet so impotent to prevent evil, that it must, under the fundamental law which called it into existence, whether it would or not, distribute publications tending directly to promote servile insurrection, and to produce its own destruction.

The Senator from South Carolina (Mr. Calhoun) had misapprehended him in one particular. He (Mr. B.) had disclaimed all authority to pass this bill derived from State laws, or from any other source than the Constitution of the United States. He had not said he would vote for a similar bill in all cases where the State Legislatures might think proper to pass laws to prohibit the circulation of any publication whatever. He considered the passage of such laws merely as evidence of the necessity for legislation by Congress; 354but he was very far from adopting the principle that it should be conclusive evidence in all cases. Congress must judge for itself under all the circumstances of each particular case.

In reply to the Senator from Massachusetts, Mr. B. said that this bill would not be a penal law. Everything like a penalty had been stricken from its provisions, unless the removal of a deputy postmaster from office by the Postmaster General might be viewed in that light. By it we merely directed our agent not to violate State laws by distributing publications calculated to excite insurrection. He would not have occasion to study all the laws of all the States on the subject of slavery, as the Senator from Massachusetts had alleged. All that would be required of him was to know the laws of the State of which he was a citizen, and to take care not to violate them.

The gentleman had said that he (Mr. B.) had mistaken the recommendation contained in the President's message. Now he undertook to assert that this bill was in conformity with the recommendation of the President, and carried it out in all essential particulars.

[Here Mr. B. again read the last paragraph of the message which he had read before.]

Now, sir, (said Mr. B.) does not the President expressly assert that Congress has authority to regulate what shall be distributed through the post-offices, and does he not "suggest the propriety of passing such a law as will prohibit, under severe penalties, the circulation in the Southern States, through the mail, of incendiary publications, intended to instigate the slaves to insurrection?" Except that this bill contained no severe penalties, it was framed both in its spirit and in its letter according to the suggestion of the President. What other bill could we pass of a milder character than the one now before us, to prevent the circulation of these incendiary publications? Let the President's recommendation be entitled to what weight it might, this bill was in exact accordance with it.

The Senator from Massachusetts had contended that this bill conferred upon deputy postmasters the power of depriving individuals of their property in newspapers and other publications, in violation of that clause in the Constitution, which declares that no person shall be deprived of his property without due process of law. By this bill we had not attempted to shield any postmaster from legal responsibility for his conduct. We could not do so, if we would. We had merely prescribed for him, as we had done for our other agents, the line of his duty. We did not attempt to protect him from the suit of any person who might consider himself aggrieved. If any individual to whom a publication was directed, and who had demanded it from the postmaster and had been refused, should believe our law to be unconstitutional, he might bring this question before the judiciary, and try it, like any other question. All our officers and agents are liable to be sued, and if the law under which they acted should prove to be unconstitutional, it would afford them no protection. On the present occasion we proposed to proceed in the spirit of the common law principle, that any individual may abate a nuisance; though 355he thereby rendered himself responsible, in case it should appear afterwards that the thing abated was not a nuisance. So here, the postmaster refusing to deliver a newspaper under our law, would be responsible in damages to the party aggrieved, in case it should appear that the law under which he had acted was unconstitutional.

As to the necessity for passing this bill, he should say but a few words. It was very easy for gentlemen to say that necessity was the plea of tyrants. He admitted it had been so, and would be so in all time to come. But after all, if we possessed the power to legislate in this case, from our situation we were compelled to judge whether it was necessary to call it into efficient action or not. This duty devolved upon us. We could not avoid deciding this question. Was it not, then, within our knowledge that the slaveholding States had been attempted to be flooded with pamphlets and pictorial representations calculated to excite servile insurrection? Had we not seen upon this floor many of these pictorial representations, whose direct effect would be to excite the wild and brutal passions of the slaves to cut the throats of their masters? Within the last few months, had there not been blood shed? and had there not been several attempted insurrections in some of the Southern States? These facts were incontestable. Believing and knowing all this to be true, he said the case of necessity, in his judgment, was fully established, and he should vote for the passage of the bill.

Mr. Cuthbert (of Georgia) was not desirous to throw himself into the current of this debate at this time. The position which he held—the infrequency of his occupying that floor, and the indisposition under which he labored, authorized him to expect the attention of the Senate for a short time, when he should be better able to address them than he then was. He therefore hoped the Senate would indulge him in an opportunity of being heard on the subject, by postponing it, to be taken up within a very short period. It appeared to him that the Senator from Pennsylvania had said precisely what should have been said in support of this bill. It appeared to him that that Senator had given an unanswerable reply to the Senator from Massachusetts on points on which he principally relied for his opposition to the measure before them. What is the state of the case (said Mr. C.)? The deputy postmaster in one of the States holds in his hand an incendiary publication, intended to carry blood and desolation through the land. Is he bound in duty to hold it from circulation? If he gives it to another, the evil intended by that publication will ensue; but then your officer, contends the Senator from Massachusetts, is bound to deliver it, because you have no power to pass a law abridging the freedom of the press. According to this doctrine, that which an individual cannot do, your officer is bound to do. It appeared to him that the obvious necessity of this law was to prevent the post-office agents from committing a criminal offence against the laws of the States, and then shielding themselves under the post-office law. But the Senator from Massachusetts had not met this point, but had rather evaded and played around it. This was a question which should not be discussed with the chicanery of a pettifogging lawyer, 356but should be considered with those enlarged ideas and noble sentiments which belong to the statesman. They should argue it as became enlightened patriots, anxious to promote harmony and good feeling through our common country, and to preserve all its parts from the dangers of insurrection.

He denied that property could be affected by this law, as contended by the Senator from Massachusetts. There could be no property in these incendiary publications. The postmaster holds in his hand that which, by the laws of the States, is in the condition of stolen property, and he is bound to give it back. He holds in his hand what, by his own judgment, he considers not to be property—which his own judgment condemns, and he is therefore bound to resign it. The Senator from Massachusetts said, rightly, that the person to whom this publication is directed may come forward and demand it, under the provision of this law. Now, if the Senator thought there was anything wanting in this provision of the bill, why did he not propose an amendment? If he did propose any, he (Mr. C.) had not heard it. The property is not to be destroyed; it must be returned to him who sent it.

In another point of view (Mr. C. said), the postmaster must judge whether these papers are legal or not. He holds in his hand papers which the laws of his State have said shall not be circulated, under a penalty. Is he not to decide whether he shall incur that penalty or not? How stood the argument of the Senator from Massachusetts? He requires that the officer shall violate the laws of his State, or that the General Government shall protect him in it. With regard to the members that compose the Senate, every gentleman was conscious in his own breast of a strong desire to prevent the evils of a servile war in the Southern States. Of this he was confident. But with regard to the Senator from Massachusetts, he should be guilty of a want of candor if he allowed him that clearness of judgment which belonged to the statesman; he should be wanting in that sincerity of heart on which he had ever prided himself, if he declared his conviction that the honorable Senator had treated this subject with the liberal and impartial spirit it deserved. The gentleman's course had uniformly been opposed to all those measures which tended to quiet the country, and heal those sectional dissensions which disturb the Union.

When a large and overwhelming vote was taken in the Senate, on the motion of the Senator from Pennsylvania, believed by all to be so necessary to settle a question, threatening the most fearful consequences, it was held to be highly desirable that there should be an unanimous vote. Yet, on an occasion when the Senator could well have shown a desire to harmonize and conciliate, his vote was found in the negative. Again, the Senator from Massachusetts had put forth a paper calculated to excite great distrust in the body of the people affected by it. He alluded to the resolutions adopted at a meeting held in Boston on the subject of slavery, of which the gentleman was said to be the author, in which it was declared that Congress had the power to regulate the transfer of slaves from one State to another. Mr. C. said that he had addressed the Senate but seldom, and as he wished to be heard on this subject more at large, when his health was better and under more favorable circumstances, he hoped the Senate would indulge him by a postponement.

Mr. Webster said that he had heard the remarks of the Senator from Georgia (Mr. Cuthbert) with attention and with respect; and considering his speech of a personal character, it became him to notice it; but as the gentleman proposed to discuss this subject more at large when his health was better, and, as he said, under circumstances less tending to irritation, he should postpone his reply till then. He should hear the gentleman with pleasure, and he looked forward to it with much solicitude, and should endeavor to reply to him according to his best abilities. Mr. W. then entered into a lengthy reply to the remarks of Mr. Buchanan, in the course of which he contended that the law was unnecessary, because the States had at present the power to punish the deputy postmasters who should circulate incendiary publications in violation of their laws.

Mr. Buchanan did not rise again to argue the question. He did not feel any petty desire to have the last word. He should now merely remark that the Senator from Massachusetts, in his last observations, had done nothing more than again to restate his proposition, without offering any new argument in its support. He reminded him of another powerful man, in the ancient time, who was condemned to roll a large stone to the top of a mountain, which was always falling back upon him, and which he never could accomplish. The gentleman's position was one which even his great powers did not enable him to maintain.

Mr. B. should not again have risen but for the purpose of making a single remark. The Senator from Massachusetts had just expressed the opinion that deputy postmasters could be punished, under State authority, for circulating inflammatory pamphlets and papers in violation of State laws. If this be true, then all the power over the post-office which we confer by this bill already exists in the States. The effect of it, then, will be nothing more than to express our assent to the exercise of a power over deputy postmasters by the States, which the gentleman admits to exist already. Upon this principle there can be no objection to the adoption of the present measure.

Mr. Cuthbert only rose to repeat the request that the Senate would, by the postponement of the subject to a short day, allow him an opportunity of being heard on it when his health was better.

Mr. C. then moved to lay the bill on the table; which motion was lost.

The bill was then rejected by the following vote:

Yeas—Messrs. Black, Brown, Buchanan, Calhoun, Cuthbert, Grundy, King of Alabama, King of Georgia, Mangum, Moore, Nicholas, Porter, Preston, Rives, Robinson, Tallmadge, Walker, White and Wright—19.

Nays—Messrs. Benton, Clay, Crittenden, Davis, Ewing of Illinois, Ewing of Ohio, Goldsborough, Hendricks, Hubbard, Kent, Knight, Leigh, McKean, Morris, Naudain, Niles, Prentiss, Ruggles, Shepley, Southard, Swift, Tipton, Tomlinson, Wall, and Webster—25.

358During this session of Congress (1836), Michigan sought admission into the Union. The following speech was made by Mr. Buchanan on the first of April, in reply to some of the arguments against the admission of that State:

Mr. President: Nothing was more remote from my intention, when I closed my remarks on Wednesday last, than again to address you on the subject of the admission of Michigan into the Union; but my argument on that occasion has been so strongly assailed by the Senator from New Jersey (Mr. Southard), and other gentlemen, that I feel myself almost constrained to reply. Even under this strong necessity, I would not now trespass upon your time, if I believed I should thus provoke a protracted debate, and thereby prevent the decision of the question before we adjourn this afternoon.

I shall undertake to demonstrate, notwithstanding all that has been said, that under the ordinance of 1787, aliens who were residents of the Northwestern Territory, had a clear right to exercise the elective franchise.

The territory ceded by Virginia to the United States was sufficiently extensive for an immense empire. The parties to this compact of cession contemplated that it would form five sovereign States of this Union. At that early period we had just emerged from our revolutionary struggle, and none of the jealousy was then felt against foreigners, and particularly against Irish foreigners, which now appears to haunt some gentlemen. There had then been no attempts made to get up a native American party in this country. The blood of the gallant Irish had flowed freely upon every battle-field in defence of the liberties which we now enjoy. Besides, the Senate will well recollect that the ordinance was passed before the adoption of our present Constitution, and whilst the power of naturalization remained with the several States. In some, and perhaps in all of them, it required so short a residence, and so little trouble, to be changed from an alien to a citizen, that the process could be performed without the least difficulty. I repeat that no jealousy whatever then existed against foreigners.

What, at that early period, was the condition of the vast Territory, part of which has been formed into the State of Michigan? It was a wilderness and a frontier. The wise men of the old Congress who framed this ordinance desired to promote its population, and to render it a barrier against foreign invasion. They were willing that all persons, whether citizens of any of the States, or foreigners, who should establish a fixed residence in the Territory, and become the owners of a freehold, might not only enjoy the privilege of voting, but that of holding offices. In regard to the construction of the ordinance itself, I shall not follow in detail the argument of the Senator from New Jersey. Indeed, I do not consider it a question for construction. The language is so plain, that he who runs may read. No ingenuity can cast the slightest shade of doubt over it.

The ordinance declares that "so soon as there shall be five thousand free male inhabitants of full age, in the district, upon giving proof thereof to the 359governor, they shall receive authority, with time and place, to elect representatives from their counties or townships, to represent them in the general assembly; provided that, for every five hundred free male inhabitants, there shall be one representative, and so on, progressively, with the number of free male inhabitants, shall the right of representation increase, until the number of representatives shall amount to twenty-five; after which the number and proportion of representatives shall be regulated by the legislature; provided, that no person be eligible or qualified to act as a representative, unless he shall have been a citizen of one of the United States three years, and be a resident in the district, or unless he shall have resided in the district three years; and in either case, shall likewise hold in his own right, in fee simple, two hundred acres of land within the same; provided also, that a freehold of fifty acres of land in the district, having been a citizen of one of the States, and being resident in the district, or the like freehold and two years residence in the district, shall be necessary to qualify a man as an elector of a representative."

Now, sir, I have said that this language is too plain for construction. When had the people of this Territory the right to elect representatives? Was it when there were five thousand free male citizens within its borders? By no means; but as soon as there were that number of free male inhabitants, whether citizens or not. Who were entitled to vote at these elections? They, referring directly and immediately to the five thousand free male inhabitants of full age.

The subsequent portion of the clause which I have just read, makes this question, if possible, still plainer. It divides those capable of being elected representatives, as well as the electors, into two distinct classes, conferring advantages, in both cases, upon those inhabitants who had been citizens of one of the States for a period of three years. If a candidate for the House of Representatives had been "a citizen of one of the United States three years," he was eligible, although he might not have been a resident of the Territory for more than a single day. Nothing more, in this case, is required than that he should be a resident. No period of residence was necessary. If the candidate, on the other hand, belonged to the second class—if he had been a naturalized citizen of one of the States for less than three years, or if he still continued to be an alien, in order to render him eligible as a representative, he must "have resided in the district three years." In short, if he had been a citizen for three years, it was no matter how brief his residence might have been; but if "a free male inhabitant" of any other description, a residence of three years was indispensable. A similar distinction prevails in regard to the electors. "A citizen of any of the States, if a resident of the district but for a single day, had a right to exercise the elective franchise. If, on the other hand, he were not a citizen, "two years residence in the district" was required.

The property qualification was the same both for citizens and for other residents.

[Mr. Buchanan here read other portions of the ordinance to prove that its framers were careful in their use of terms, and always distinguished with great precision, between the use of the words "free male inhabitants," and "citizens of one of the United States," etc. He also referred, as a further proof of his position, to the language of that portion of the ordinance which provides for the election of the legislative council.]

Now, sir, said Mr. B., have I not clearly established the position, that, under this ordinance, aliens were entitled to elect and to be elected, provided they had resided a sufficient time in the territory, and were possessed of the necessary freehold qualification? If I can comprehend the meaning of the plainest English words, neither doubt nor difficulty can longer rest upon this question.

But it has been urged that in order to become a freeholder, a person must first have been a citizen of one of the States. In reply, I might content myself by saying that this is begging the question. It is assuming the very proposition to be proved. But I shall give this objection two answers. In the first place, although I have become somewhat rusty in my legal knowledge, yet I feel perfectly safe in asserting, that, under the strict principles of the common law of England, an alien may purchase real estate, may hold real estate, may transmit real estate to his heirs, or devise it by his will. His title is good against all mankind, except the crown; and can only be divested by what in technical language is termed "an office found" in favor of the king. Admitting that the Government in this country possessed the same right, they have, in the most solemn terms, abandoned it, by holding out inducements, under the ordinance, to foreigners, to become the proprietors of real estate within the Northwestern Territory.

An answer still more conclusive may be given to this objection. The old Congress which framed the ordinance had the unquestionable power to enable aliens to purchase and hold real estate. It was their policy to promote the settlement of this Territory; and for this purpose they have plainly declared, by the ordinance, that aliens, or in other words, that any free male inhabitant, might hold real estate. Even at this day aliens, without any restriction, purchase lands from the United States. To lure them to make purchases, as we have done, and then to attempt to forfeit their estates, would be a violation of every principle of justice and public faith.

The Congress of the United States have repeatedly, in relation to Ohio, Indiana, and Illinois, placed the same construction on this ordinance which I have done. I shall not exhaust either myself, or the Senate, by referring to more than one or two of these instances. In April, 1802, when Congress passed the act authorizing the people of Ohio to form a constitution and State government, it became necessary to prescribe the qualifications of the electors of delegates to the convention. They performed this duty in the fourth section of that act. It declares as follows: "That all male citizens of the United States who shall have arrived at full age, and resided within the said Territory at least one year previous to the day of election, and shall have paid a territorial or county tax, and all persons having, in other respects, the legal qualifications to vote for representatives in the general assembly of the territory, be, and they are hereby, authorized to choose representatives to form a convention."

Who were these persons having, in other respects, the legal qualifications to vote for Territorial representatives? Let the ordinance itself answer this question. They were free male persons, not citizens of the United States, who held a freehold in fifty acres of land within the Territory, and had resided there for two years. Congress, actuated by the more liberal and enlightened spirit of the age, in the year 1802, dispensed with the freehold qualification in regard to citizens of the United States. They suffered it to remain, however, in relation to those persons within the Territory who were not citizens: but who possessed the legal qualifications, in other respects, to vote for Territorial representatives. I shall merely refer to another instance in the case of Illinois. On the 20th May, 1812, Congress passed an act to extend the right of suffrage in that Territory. Under this act, no freehold was necessary, in any case, to the exercise of the elective franchise. The spirit of the age had corrected this error in politics. I am glad of it. Our own experience has taught us that the citizen, in humble circumstances, who pays his personal tax, feels as deep an interest in the welfare of the country, and would make as many sacrifices to promote its prosperity and glory, as the man who has an income of thousands from his real estate. Wealth has never been, and never can be, a true standard of patriotism. By the first section of this act, Congress declared that "each and every free white male person, who shall have attained the age of twenty-one years, and who shall have paid a county or Territorial tax, and who shall have resided one year in said Territory previous to any general election, and be, at the time of such election, a resident thereof, shall be entitled to vote for members of the legislative council and house of representatives for the said Territory." You perceive, sir, that Congress, by this act, no longer retained the distinction which they had established in regard to Ohio, between citizens of the United States and persons in other respects entitled to vote for members of the Territorial legislature. They are all blended together into the same mass, and the elective franchise is conferred upon them all, under the denomination of free white male persons, who have paid taxes and resided one year in the Territory. The phrase citizens of the United States does not once occur in the act. In the second and third sections these free white male persons are denominated citizens of the Territory, not citizens of the United States. Under the ordinance of 1787, they were, in fact, constituted citizens of the Territory; and this phraseology is, therefore, perfectly correct.

The Senator from New Jersey (Mr. Southard) has undertaken the Herculean task of proving that neither the ordinance nor the act of 1802, in relation to Ohio, nor the act to which I have just referred, nor the other similar acts conferred upon any persons not citizens of the United States the right of voting. How far he has been successful, I shall leave for the Senate to judge.

362These portions of the ordinance to which I have heretofore referred were subject to the control of Congress. They have been modified and changed in several instances, some of which have been referred to and commented upon in this debate. But I now come to speak of one of those articles of the ordinance, essential to the correct decision of this question, which is placed beyond the power of Congress. To use its own emphatic language, they "shall be considered as articles of compact between the original States and the people and States in the said Territory, and forever remain unalterable, unless by common consent." This solemn agreement has been confirmed by the Constitution of the United States. No person either denies or doubts the sacred character and the binding force of this contract. The fifth of these articles of this ordinance declares as follows: "And whenever any of the said States shall have sixty thousand free inhabitants therein, such State shall be admitted by its delegates into the Congress of the United States, on an equal footing with the original States, in all respects whatever; and shall be at liberty to form a permanent constitution and State government; provided the constitution and government so to be formed shall be republican, and in conformity to the principles contained in these articles; and, so far as it can be consistent with the general interest of the confederacy, such admission shall be allowed at an earlier period, and when there may be a less number of free inhabitants in the State than sixty thousand."

Now, sir, under this provision, these sixty thousand free inhabitants had a right to frame a constitution whenever they pleased. They had a right to determine which of them should be electors of delegates to their own convention for that purpose, and which of them should not. It rested solely within their own discretion, whether the elective franchise should be confined to the citizens of the United States, or be extended to other inhabitants of the Territory. It was the right and the duty of Congress first to determine the boundaries of the States to be formed within the limits of the Northwestern Territory. Had this duty been performed, the free inhabitants of Michigan, after they amounted to sixty thousand, would have become a distinct political community under the ordinance. They would have possessed the sovereign right to form a constitution; and if the constitution were republican, and in conformity to the ordinance, they might have demanded admission, by their delegates, into the Congress of the United States. They could not have been refused without a direct violation of the solemnly pledged faith of the nation. If Congress had objected that persons, not citizens of the United States, had been permitted to vote at the election for delegates, they might have triumphantly presented this ordinance, and declared that the question was settled by its terms and its spirit; that the time had arrived when they were entitled to shake off their Territorial dependence, and assume an equal rank with the other States of the Union. Throughout the ordinance there is a marked distinction between "free inhabitants" and "citizens of the United States."

It is true that Congress have never yet determined the boundaries of the State of Michigan; but their omission to do so could not affect, in any degree, 363the right of the free male inhabitants to vote for delegates to the convention which framed their constitution. As soon as Michigan shall have been admitted into the Union, the boundaries of Wisconsin will then be irrevocably determined. It will be the last of the five States into which the Northwestern Territory can be divided under the terms of the ordinance. When that Territory shall contain sixty thousand free inhabitants, they will have an absolute right to demand admission, as a State, into the Union, and we cannot refuse to admit them without violating the public faith. Still, I should not advise them to frame a constitution without a previous act of Congress.

The precedent in the case of Tennessee, on which I commented when I addressed the Senate on Wednesday last, has completely silenced all opposition in regard to the necessity of a previous act of Congress to enable the people of Michigan to form a State constitution. It now seems to be conceded, that our subsequent approbation is equivalent to our previous action. This can no longer be doubted. We have the unquestionable power of waiving any irregularities in the method of framing the constitution, had any such existed. It is wiser, I admit, for Congress, in the first instance, to pass such an act; but, after they had refused to do so, from year to year, the people of Michigan had no other alternative but either to take the matter into their own hands, or abandon the hope of admission into the Union, within any reasonable time.

But I am not done with this Tennessee precedent.

It will be recollected that when North Carolina ceded to the United States the territory which now composes the State of Tennessee, it was specially stipulated that the inhabitants within the same should "enjoy all the privileges, benefits and advantages," set forth in the ordinance for the government of the Northwestern Territory. This provision makes the case of Tennessee one precisely in point with the present. I would ask, then, who voted at the election for delegates to frame the constitution of Tennessee? Let the proclamation of Governor Blount, issued in obedience to an act of the Territorial legislature, answer this question. He declares "that all free males (not free male citizens,) twenty-one years of age and upwards," shall be entitled to vote. Under this proclamation every free male inhabitant of the Territory had a right to vote, no matter how short a time his inhabitancy may have continued. In this respect it differs from the Territorial law of Michigan, which requires a previous residence of three months.

With a full knowledge of these facts, General Washington, in his message to Congress of the 8th of April, 1796, on the subject of the admission of Tennessee into the Union, declares that "among the privileges, benefits and advantages thus secured to the inhabitants of the Territory south of the river Ohio, appear to be the right of forming a permanent constitution and state of government, and of admission as a State by its delegates into the Congress of the United States, on an equal footing with the original States in all respects whatever, when it should have therein sixty thousand free inhabitants; provided the constitution and government so to be formed should be republican, and in conformity to the principles contained in the articles of the said ordinance."

The State of Tennessee was accordingly admitted. At this early day, when the ordinance was better understood than it can be at present, no objection was made from any quarter, so far as I can learn, that delegates to the convention which formed the constitution of that State, were voted for by inhabitants who were not citizens of the United States. Certain it is, that no such question was raised by General Washington. Even Mr. King, whose report was decidedly adverse to the admission of this State, never, in the most distant manner, adverts to this objection which has now been so strongly urged by Senators.

I stated when I last addressed the Senate, as a proposition clearly established, that under the ordinance, the States formed out of the Northwestern Territory had a right to confer the elective franchise upon the inhabitants resident within them at the time of the adoption of their constitutions, whether they were citizens or not. I then also asserted, that the States of Ohio and Illinois had not only exercised this power to the extent which Michigan had done, but had gone much further. They had not, like Michigan, confined the elective franchise to inhabitants actually resident within their respective States, at the time of the adoption of their constitutions; but had made a general provision by which all such inhabitants, though not citizens, would be entitled to vote in all future time. These positions, which I thought impregnable, have been violently assailed; and it has been contended that, under the provisions of these constitutions, no persons, except citizens of the United States, are entitled to vote. This renders it necessary that I should again turn to these constitutions. The first section of the fourth article of the constitution of Ohio declares, that "in all elections, all white male inhabitants, above the age of twenty-one years, having resided in the State one year next preceding the election, and who have paid, or are charged with, a State or county tax, shall enjoy the right of an elector; but no person shall be entitled to vote, except in the county or district in which he shall actually reside at the time of the election." The fifth section of the same article varies the expression, and confers the right of voting "on white male persons," who are compelled to labor on the roads. These "white male inhabitants," or "white male persons," are not required to be citizens of the United States. The terms are as general as they can be. They embrace all persons, whether citizens of the United States or not, who have resided within the State for one year, and are in other respects qualified. Besides, it would be easy to show, by adverting to other parts of this constitution, that the framers of it, in several cases, when they intended to confine its benefits to citizens of the United States, have so declared in express terms. We have heard it stated that by a judicial decision, the right to vote has been restricted to citizens of the United States. This decision has not been produced. I should be very much pleased to see it. I am aware that judicial construction can work wonders; but if any court has decided that "all white male inhabitants," or "white male persons," are restricted in their meaning to white male citizens of the United States, it is a stretch of judicial construction which surpasses anything of which I could have conceived.

The constitution of Illinois is still more general in its provisions. It declares that "in all elections, all white male inhabitants, above the age of twenty-one years, having resided in the State six months, next preceding the election, shall enjoy the right of an elector; but no person shall be entitled to vote except in the county or district in which he shall actually reside at the time of the election." We have been informed by the Senators from Illinois, that the practice of that State has always conformed to the plain meaning of the constitution. At this day, any alien, who has resided within that State for six months, is in the full enjoyment of the elective franchise. Indeed, this privilege has induced aliens to settle in that State in preference to others where they cannot vote until after they have become citizens of the United States.

Now, sir, I wish to be fairly understood upon this question. As a general principle, I do not think that any State of this Union ought to permit any person to exercise the right of an elector who is not either a native or a naturalized citizen of the United States. There may have been, and I think there was, a propriety in conferring the elective franchise upon the inhabitants of the Territory, actually resident therein, although not citizens, who had a right under the ordinance to participate in the formation of the constitution. Beyond this, the power, even under the ordinance, is extremely doubtful. Michigan has wisely confined herself within these limits. She has not followed the example of Ohio and Illinois. These States have been admitted into the Union, notwithstanding the extravagant provisions in their constitutions in favor of foreigners. Would it not then be extremely ungracious to exclude Michigan, when no foreigner can ever hereafter enjoy the right of voting, except such as were resident within the limits of the State at the time of the formation of her constitution?

According to the census, it would appear that not more than from five to six hundred aliens could have been in that situation. At the present time it is probable that many of these have become naturalized citizens. The evil, if it be one, is very small. Within a short period it will entirely disappear. Would it be wise, would it be politic, would it be statesman-like, to annul all that has been done by the convention of Michigan, merely for this reason? Ought we, on this account, to defer the final settlement of the disputed boundary between Ohio and Michigan, and thus again give rise to anarchy and confusion, and perhaps to the shedding of blood? Do you feel confident, that the people of Michigan, after you have violated their rights, by refusing to admit them into the Union at this time, would ever act under your law authorizing them to form a new constitution? We must all desire to see this unfortunate boundary question settled; and the passage of this bill presents the best, if not the only means, of accomplishing a result so desirable. Have the people of Michigan, or any portion of them, ever complained of this part of their constitution? I would ask, by what authority have the Senators from Ohio and New Jersey (Messrs. Ewing and Southard) raised this objection, whilst the people themselves are content? Even if they did commit an error in this respect, we ought to treat them as children, and not as enemies. It is the part of greatness and magnanimity to pass over unimportant errors of judgment committed by those who are, in some degree, dependent upon us. It would, indeed, be a severe measure of justice, for the Congress of the United States, after having admitted Ohio and Illinois into the Union, to close the door of admission against Michigan. This, in truth, would be straining at a gnat, and swallowing a camel.

Suppose you deprive the people of Michigan of a territory to which they all believe, however erroneously, they have a right, and transfer it to Ohio, and then drive them from your door and refuse to admit them into the Union; can any Senator here view the probable consequences with composure? They are a high-spirited and manly people. You cannot blame them for that. They are bone of your bone, and flesh of your flesh. They have been taught, by your example, to resist what they believe to be oppression. Will they patiently submit to your decree? Will they tamely surrender up to Ohio that territory of which they have been in possession for thirty years? Their past history proves conclusively that they will maintain what they believe to be their rights, to the death. You may have civil war as the direct consequence of your vote this day. Should the amendment of the Senator from Ohio (Mr. Ewing) prevail, whilst it will leave unsettled the question of boundary so important to his own State, it may, and probably will produce, scenes of bloodshed and civil war along the boundary line. I have expressed the opinion, that Congress possess the power of annexing the territory in dispute to the State of Ohio, and that it is expedient to exercise it. The only mode of extorting a reluctant consent from the people of Michigan to this disposition, is to make it a condition of their admission, under their present constitution, into the Union. The bill proposes to do so, and, in my humble judgment, Ohio is deeply interested in its passage.

I shall now, following the example of my friend from New York (Mr. Wright), proceed to make some suggestions upon another point. They are intended merely as suggestions, for I can say with truth I have formed no decided opinion upon the subject. A friend called to see me last evening, and attempted to maintain the proposition that the several States, under the Constitution of the United States, and independent of the ordinance applicable to the Northwestern Territory, had the power of conferring the right to vote upon foreigners resident within their territories. This opinion was at war with all my former impressions. He requested me to do as he had done, and to read over the Constitution of the United States carefully, with a view to this question. I have complied with his request, and shall now throw out a few suggestions upon this subject, merely to elicit the opinion of others.

The older I grow, the more I am inclined to be what is called "a State rights man." The peace and security of this Union depend upon giving to the Constitution a literal and fair construction, such as would be placed upon it by a plain, intelligent man, and not by ingenious constructions, to increase the powers of this Government, and thereby diminish those of the States. The rights of the States, reserved to them by that instrument, ought ever to be held sacred. If then the Constitution leaves to them to decide according to their own discretion, unrestricted and unlimited, who shall be electors, it follows as a necessary consequence that they may, if they think proper, confer upon resident aliens the right of voting.

It has been supposed, and is perhaps generally believed, that this power has been abridged by that clause in the Constitution which declares, that "the citizens of each State shall be entitled to all privileges and immunities of citizens of the several States." Does then a State, by conferring upon a person, not a citizen of the United States, the privilege of voting, necessarily constitute him a citizen of such State? Is the elective franchise so essentially connected with the citizenship, that the one cannot exist without the other? This is the question. If it be so, no State can exercise this power; because, no State, by bestowing upon an alien the privilege of voting, can make him a citizen of that State, and thereby confer upon him "the privileges and immunities of citizens of the several States."

Citizens are either natives of the country, or they are naturalized. To Congress exclusively belongs the power of naturalization; and I freely admit, that no foreigner can become a citizen of the United States, but by complying with the provisions of the acts of Congress upon this subject. But still we are brought back to the question, may not a State bestow upon a resident alien the right to vote, within its limits, as a personal privilege, without conferring upon him the other privileges of citizenship, or ever intending to render it obligatory upon the other States to receive him as a citizen? Might not Virginia refuse to a foreigner who had voted in Illinois, without having been naturalized, "the privileges and immunities" of one of her citizens, without any violation of the Constitution of the United States? Would such an alien have any pretext for claiming, under the Constitution of the United States, the right to vote within a State where citizens of the United States alone are voters?

It is certain that the Constitution of the United States, in the broadest terms, leaves to the States the qualifications of their own electors, or rather it does not restrict them in any manner upon this question. The second section of the first article provides "that the House of Representatives shall be composed of members chosen every second year by the people of the several States, and the electors in each State shall have the qualifications requisite for electors of the most numerous branch of the State Legislature." By the first section of the second article, "each State shall appoint, in such manner as the Legislature thereof may direct, a number of electors equal to the whole number of Senators and Representatives to which the State may be entitled in the Congress." Both these provisions seem to recognize in the States the most absolute discretion in deciding who shall be qualified electors. There is no declaration or intimation throughout the whole instrument that these electors shall be citizens 368of the United States. Are the States not left to exercise this discretion in the same sovereign manner they did before they became parties to the Federal Constitution? There is at least strong plausibility in the argument, especially when we consider that the framers of the Constitution in order more effectually to guard the reserved rights of the States, inserted a provision, "that the powers not delegated to the United States by the Constitution, nor prohibited by it to the States, are reserved to the States respectively, or to the people."

Without any stretch of imagination, we might conceive a case in which this question would shake our Union to the very centre. Suppose that the decision of the next Presidential election should depend upon the vote of Illinois; and it could be made to appear, that the aliens who voted under the Constitution in that State, had turned the scale in favor of the successful candidate. What would then be the consequence? Have we a right to rejudge her justice? to interfere with her sovereign rights? to declare that her Legislature could not appoint electors of President and Vice President in such manner as they thought proper, and to annul the election?

It is curious to remark, that except in a few instances, the Constitution of the United States has not prescribed that the officers elected or appointed under its authority, shall be citizens; and we all know in practice, that the Senate have been constantly in the habit of confirming the nominations of foreigners as consuls of the United States. They have repeatedly done so, I believe, in regard to other officers.

I repeat that, on this question, I have formed no fixed opinion one way or the other. On the other points of the case, I entertain the clearest conviction, that Michigan is entitled to admission into the Union.

I have thus completed all I intend to say upon this subject. I have been most reluctantly drawn a second time into this debate. I had the admission of Arkansas specially entrusted to my care. Few, if any, of the objections urged against Michigan, are applicable to

Arkansas; but I could not conceal from myself the fact, that the admission of the one depended upon that of the other; and I am equally anxious to receive both the sisters. The people of Texas were at this time engaged in their revolutionary effort to make themselves independent of Mexico. It was deemed necessary to authorize the President of the United States to accept the services of volunteers for the defence of the frontiers. On a bill introduced for this purpose, and which had passed the House of Representatives, Mr. Buchanan, on the 4th of May, said:

He had no doubt but that the Government of the United States, in regard to Mexico, had pursued, and would pursue, the course which had been sanctioned by all its experience in relation to questions of this kind. One principle had been established in the political history of the country; had grown with its growth, and strengthened with its strength; and without knowing what the President had done or would do in this matter, he had no doubt but he would strictly adhere to that established principle in our institutions, never to interfere with the internal policy or domestic concerns of foreign nations. The famous proclamation of neutrality of General Washington first asserted that principle, and to it our Government had always adhered. We consider, said Mr. B., all nations "enemies in war, and in peace, friends."

In regard to Mexico, he considered Santa Anna as an usurper. The federal constitution, established for the Republic of Mexico, and which Texas, as a part of that Republic, had sworn to support, had been trampled on by him, and Texas, in his eyes, and in the eyes of all mankind, was justified in rebelling against him. Whether the Texans acted consistently with a true policy at the time, in declaring their independence, he should not discuss, nor should he decide; but as a man and an American, he should be rejoiced to see them successful in maintaining their liberties, and he trusted in God they would be so. He would, however, leave them to rely on their own bravery, with every hope and prayer that the God of battles would shield them with his protection.

If Santa Anna excited the Indians within our territory to deeds of massacre and blood; if he should excite a spirit among them which he cannot restrain; and if, in consequence, the blood of our women and children on the frontier shall flow, he undoubtedly ought to be held responsible. Mr. B. saw a strong necessity for sending a force to the frontiers, not only to restrain the natural disposition of the Indians to deeds of violence, but because they could place no confidence in a man who had so little command of his temper, who had shown so cruel and sanguinary a disposition as Santa Anna had. He was for having a force speedily sent to that frontier, and a force of mounted men or dragoons, as suggested by the Senator from Missouri (Mr. Linn), but he was against interfering in the war now raging in Texas, unless an attack should be made on us.

If it were left for him to decide to which bill a preference should be given by the Senate, he would first take up the bill providing for this additional force for the protection of the frontiers; but he had been instructed by an authority which he was bound to respect and obey, and he must, therefore, vote to take up the land bill. He should vote with the warmest friends of that bill in its favor till it was either carried through or defeated. To-day or to-morrow, the land bill would be finally disposed of; it now stood in the way of everything else; and he would then be for proceeding with the appropriation bills as rapidly as possible. He should have said nothing about instructions, had not this question of preference been brought up. After the decision of the land bill, he should give his hearty support to carry through the bills necessary for the defence of the country, with as much expedition as possible.

In Senate, Monday, May 9, 1836.

Mr. Preston presented the petition of a number of the citizens of Philadelphia, on the subject of the affairs of Texas; and praying Congress to acknowledge the independence of that country.

Mr. Buchanan said he had received several memorials from the city of Philadelphia, of the same character as those which had been presented by the Senator from South Carolina (Mr. Preston). He had intended to present them this morning to the Senate, but was prevented from doing so at the proper time by an accidental circumstance. It was also his intention to have accompanied their presentation by some remarks. These he thought best to offer now, rather than to wait until to-morrow morning, and then become instrumental in getting up another debate.

These memorials asked Congress "to recognize the independence of Texas, and at such time, and in such manner, as may be deemed proper, interpose to terminate the conflict which now rages in that country."

In some remarks, which he had submitted to the Senate a few days since, and which, like all other proceedings in this body, had been much misrepresented abroad, he had indulged the feelings of a man and an American citizen. What he then uttered were the sentiments of his own heart, in relation to the existing trouble in Texas. But when he was called on as a Senator to recognize the independence of that country, he thought it prudent to refer back to the conduct of our ancestors, when placed in similar circumstances, and to derive lessons of wisdom from their example. If there was any one principle of our public policy which had been well settled—one which had been acted upon by every administration, and which had met the approbation not only of this country, but of every civilized government with which we have intercourse, it was that we should never interfere in the domestic concerns of other nations. Recognizing in the people of every nation the absolute right to adopt such forms of government as they thought proper, we had always preserved the strictest neutrality between the parties, in every country, whilst engaged in civil war. We had left all nations perfectly free, so far as we were concerned, to establish, to maintain, or to change their forms of government, according to their own sovereign will and pleasure. It would indeed be surprising, and more than that, it would be unnatural, if the sympathies of the American people should not be deeply, earnestly enlisted in favor of those who drew the sword for liberty throughout the world, no matter where it was raised to strike. Beyond this we had never proceeded.

The peaceful influence of our example upon other nations was much greater—the cause of free government was thus more efficiently promoted than if we should waste the blood and treasure of the people of the United States in foreign wars, waged even to maintain the sacred cause of liberty. The world must be persuaded, it could not be conquered. Besides, said Mr. B., we can never, with any proper regard for the welfare of our constituents, 371devote their energies and their resources to the cause of planting and sustaining free institutions among the people of other nations.

Acting upon these principles, we had always recognized existing governments de facto, whether they were constitutional or despotic. We had the same amicable relations with despotisms as with free governments; because we had no right to quarrel with people of any nation on account of the form of government which they might think proper to adopt or to sanction. It was their affair, not ours. We would not tolerate such interference from abroad; and we ought to demean ourselves towards foreign nations as we should require them to act towards ourselves.

A very striking illustration of this principle had been presented, during the present administration, in the case of Portugal. We recognized Don Miguel's government, because he was de facto in possession of the throne, apparently with the consent of the Portuguese people. In this respect, Mr. B. believed, we stood alone, or nearly alone, among the nations of the earth. When he was expelled from that country, and the present queen seemed to be firmly seated upon the throne, we had no difficulty, pursuing our established policy, in recognizing her government.

A still more striking case, and one to the very point in question, had occurred during Mr. Monroe's administration. The Spanish provinces, throughout the whole continent of America, had raised the standard of rebellion against the king of Spain. They were struggling for liberty against oppression. The feelings of the American people were devotedly enlisted in their favor. Our ardent wishes and our prayers for their success, continued throughout the whole long and bloody conflict. But we took no other part in their cause; and we rendered them no assistance, except the strong moral influence exerted over the world by our well-known feelings and opinions in their favor. When, said Mr. B., did we recognize their independence? Not till after they had achieved it by their arms; not until the contest was over, and victory had perched upon their banners; not until the good fight had been fought and won. We then led the van in acknowledging their independence. But until they were independent in fact, we resisted every effort and every eloquent appeal which was made in their behalf, to induce us to depart from the settled policy of the country. When the fact of their actual independence was established; then, and not till then, did we acknowledge it.

He would rejoice should similar success attend the arms of the Texans. He trusted they would yet conquer their independence against the myrmidons of Santa Anna. In that event, there was no man in the country who would vote more cheerfully to recognize it than himself. Until that time should arrive, he must continue to act upon the firmly established principle which had been our guide for nearly half a century.

Mr. B. believed that no President of the United States had ever been more strongly convinced of the necessity of maintaining this principle inviolate than General Jackson. His whole conduct towards foreign governments had made this manifest. Whilst, said Mr. B., he requires justice from all, he treats all with justice. In his annual message, at the commencement of the present session, he informed Congress that instructions had been given to the district attorneys of the United States, to prosecute all persons who might attempt to violate our neutrality in the civil war between Mexico and Texas. He also stated that he had apprised the government of Mexico that we should require the integrity of our territory to be scrupulously respected by both parties. He thus declared to the world, not only that we had determined to be neutral between the parties, but that our neutrality must be respected by both. This afforded abundant evidence of his disposition neither to interfere with the internal concerns of other nations, nor to submit to any violation of the law of nations by them. Mr. B. entertained not a doubt that the line of conduct which he had marked out for himself, in the beginning, he would pursue until the end, so far as the executive Government was concerned.

It was obviously necessary to concentrate a strong military force on the confines of Texas, not only to enforce our neutrality, but to protect the lives and property of our fellow-citizens. This had been done; but the commanding general had been strictly prohibited from acting, except on the defensive.

Such a force was absolutely necessary to preserve inviolate our treaty with Mexico. Under it, we were bound to maintain peace among the Indian nations along the frontier of the two countries, and to restrain the Indians within our territory by force, if that should become necessary, from making war upon Mexico. This obligation was reciprocal and bound both parties. If the Indians from Texas should be let slip upon our frontier; if they, or Santa Anna, or any other power should attempt to invade our territory, then every American would say, repel force by force, and return blow for blow. Our cause and our quarrel would be just.

But, said Mr. B., let us not, by departing from our settled policy, give rise to the suspicion that we have got up this war for the purpose of wresting Texas from those to whom, under the faith of treaties, it justly belongs. Since the treaty with Spain of 1819, there could no longer be any doubt, but that this province was a part of Mexico. He was sorry for it; but such was the undeniable fact. Let us then follow the course which we had pursued, under similar circumstances, in all other cases.

Mr. B. said his blood boiled whilst contemplating the cruelties and the barbarities which were said to have been committed by the Mexicans in this contest. The heart sickened and revolted at such a spectacle. But, as an American Senator, he could give the Texans nothing except his prayers and his good wishes.

In Senate, Friday, May 20, 1836.

Mr. Calhoun, from the Committee of Conference appointed on the part of the Senate, to confer with a committee of the House on the disagreeing votes of the two Houses as to the Senate's amendment to the bill authorizing the President to accept the services of ten thousand volunteers for the defence of the western frontiers, reported that the committees of the two Houses had 373had a meeting, but that they had not been able to effect the objects for which they were appointed, having sat the whole day without coming to any agreement whatever.

Mr. King of Alabama (from the same committee) observed that it was true that they had come to no agreement on the point at issue between the two Houses, inasmuch as some gentlemen seemed to think that they had the whole bill under consideration, and that they had the power to modify it at pleasure. He hoped that when the Senate again appointed a committee of conference, they would appoint gentlemen who would be willing to confine their deliberations to the subject of disagreement, and not think themselves authorized to take the range of the whole bill.

Mr. Calhoun replied that the committee did confine themselves to the subject of disagreement, until finding that there was no possibility of coming to an agreement on that point, they entered into a more enlarged discussion, for the purpose of ascertaining whether the bill could not be so framed as to meet the concurrence of both Houses. His understanding was, that when a committee of conference came to a proposition that could not be agreed on, the whole subject was open to them.

Mr. King recollected exactly the state of the case. The proposition last made was, that they should extend the term of service of the militia force of the United States for a year, instead of its being a volunteer militia force. This was the last subject of conference; and after talking until half-past five o'clock, the committee found that they could come to no agreement whatever.

Mr. Buchanan said that he had been a member of the Committee of Conference; and if a second committee should now be appointed, he hoped he would be excused from serving upon it. He did not believe that the appointment of the same committee by the Senate and the House could result in any practical good. They had been busily engaged in the Conference Chamber until a late hour yesterday, and when they had separated, they were further, if possible, from agreeing, than when they had first met.

For his own part, he could not feel the force of the constitutional objections which had been made by the Senator from South Carolina (Mr. Calhoun). It was true that the amendment which had been proposed by the Senate to the bill of the House was somewhat vague and ambiguous in its terms. He had thought, at one time, during the conference, that we should have agreed upon an amendment to the Senate's amendment, which would have made the bill much more explicit, and would have removed all the constitutional objections of the gentlemen. When it came to the final vote, he found that he had been mistaken.

The amendment proposed in the Committee of Conference provided that none of the officers should be appointed by the President, until the volunteers were actually mustered into the service of the United States. Until that moment, the companies which might be formed would thus be considered as mere voluntary associations, under no pledge whatever, except that of honor, to enter the service of their country. When once, however, this pledge was redeemed—when they were mustered into the service—they became a portion of the army of the United States for the period of six or twelve months; and then there could not possibly be a constitutional objection to the appointment of their officers by the President. Congress possessed the power to raise armies in any manner they thought proper. Whether they obtained soldiers by individual enlistments, or whether the patriotic young men of the country chose to associate together as volunteers, and come in masses, we had an equal right to receive them. The one mode of obtaining soldiers was just as constitutional as the other.

The amendment which had been proposed, whilst it practically insured to the companies the selection of their own company officers, did not interfere with the constitutional powers of the President. The volunteers themselves were to designate such officers, and if the President approved of such designations, these officers would be appointed. This would be the best and strongest recommendation which could be presented to him; and, no doubt, he would always obey the wishes of the companies, unless in cases where powerful and satisfactory reasons existed to render it improper.

Until these volunteers should actually enter the service, they would continue to be militia men of the States, and liable to perform militia duty in the States. Their character would not be changed. They would not constitute a dormant standing army in the States, with officers appointed by the President, as had been urged, but would be mere associations, bound together by no law but that of honor. Such men would always be ready to obey the call of their country in case of necessity.

The Senator from South Carolina (Mr. Calhoun) did argue that it would be a violation of the Constitution for the President to appoint these officers without the previous advice and consent of the Senate. Whatever doubt might have rested upon this point at the organization of our Government, this power had been exercised, over and over again, ever since the adoption of the Constitution, under all administrations. The precedents were numerous. One act had been read which passed during the late war, conferring upon the President, in express terms, the power of appointing all the officers of the military force to be raised under its provisions, but requiring him to submit these appointments to the Senate for their approbation at the next session. The very same thing was proposed to be done by this act, in regard to all the officers above the rank of captain.

He was afraid to trust his memory in attempting to state the proceedings of the Committee of Conference. So much had been said, that he could not, if he would, undertake to report it all. We did not confine ourselves to the point of disagreement between the two Houses; but almost every question relating to the military defence of the country had been ably and eloquently discussed. He had derived much information on this subject from the members of that committee.

There was one fact which he would mention, and which demanded the serious consideration of the country at the present crisis. A gallant and distinguished officer, who was a member of the committee, (Gen. Ripley) had stated, that, according to his recollection, the history of our Indian wars did not present a single case in which a volunteer force had been beaten by the Indians. Our disasters in this kind of warfare had always been suffered by the regular troops. Our recent experience was certainly in accordance with this statement. This important fact, however, established the necessity of raising volunteer corps, in some form or other, composed of the brave and hardy youth, accustomed to the modes of Indian warfare, and who were able and willing to fight the Indians, man to man, according to their own custom. Such men would best protect our citizens from the ravages of the Indians, and would soon put an end to the Creek war. He had said more than he intended, as his chief object in rising had been to request that he might not be appointed a member of the new Committee of Conference.

Mr. Buchanan could not now but hope, after having heard the observations of the Senator from South Carolina (Mr. Calhoun), that a Committee of Conference might yet agree upon some compromise which would be acceptable to both Houses. He now believed, from what he had just heard from several members of the other House, that another committee ought to be appointed.

The Senator from South Carolina had not, he believed, denied any of the positions which he had stated. They did not materially differ as to their constitutional views on this subject. His (Mr. B.'s) positions were these: that any number of individuals within the States might associate together, either in companies, battalions, or divisions, for the purpose of entering the army of the United States, for six or for twelve months, upon any contingency which might render their services necessary; that these associations would be voluntary and not compulsory; and would be held together by no tie but that sense of honor which binds a man to enter the service of his country, after he has declared, in the presence of the world, that such was his determination; and that these volunteers, after having arrived at the place of rendezvous, and after having been mustered into service, but not before, became a part of the regular army of the United States; and the President could then, by and with the advice and consent of the Senate, appoint their officers. At one period of the conference, he had believed that the committee would arrive at these conclusions.

One of the objections of the Senator from South Carolina was, that the appointment of the captains of companies and other inferior officers ought, like that of the superior officers, to be submitted to the Senate. Mr. B. had been perfectly willing and was still willing to adopt this modification. He could not, however, agree, nor did he understand the gentleman now to insist upon it, that these offices could not be filled without the previous advice of the Senate. Such a provision would render the law perfectly nugatory. We might not, and probably would not, be in session when these appointments must be made. The same necessity which the gentleman alleges to have existed during the late war, for authorizing the President to make appointments, during the recess of the Senate, will exist in regard to the appointments to be made under this act.—Besides, whatever might be our opinion in regard to the power of the President, if the question were now, for the first time, submitted to us, Congress have so often authorized him to make appointments, during the recess, to be submitted to the Senate at its next session, that this constitutional question must be considered as settled.

As to the act of 1812, which had just been cited by the other Senator from South Carolina (Mr. Preston), he thought it went too far. He would not say that it was unconstitutional, because he had not examined the subject sufficiently to express a positive opinion. This he would say, however, that it did authorize the existence of a dormant military force within the several States, commanded by officers appointed by the President of the United States, and liable to be called into service at any moment he might think proper.

The individuals composing this force were exempted from militia duty within the States. Upon the principles contained in this act, the militia of the several States might be subverted, and a national militia, under the command of national officers, might be substituted in its stead. This would certainly be at war with the spirit of the Constitution, which reserves to the States respectively the appointment of the officers of the militia, and the authority of training them according to the discipline prescribed by Congress. The militia emphatically belongs to the States, and not to the General Government; and it might be very dangerous for the States to surrender their control over this force into the hands of Congress.

Under the act cited by the gentleman, a portion of the militia was taken from the control of the States, and relieved from the performance of militia duty, whilst they remained in the heart of the country, mixed up with the other citizens. This did seem to him to interfere with the power of the States over their militia, contrary to the provisions of the Constitution. But these objections did not apply to the bill before them, nor to the amendment he had suggested. They had drawn a broad line of separation between the force to be raised and the militia of the States. What they proposed was, that these volunteers should associate themselves together for the purpose of offering their services to their country, and that when they arrived at their places of rendezvous, they should enrol themselves, and be mustered into service as a part of the regular army; but until then, that they should remain as they were, citizens of the several States, liable to the performance of the militia duty of the States. With these views, he was confident that a new Committee of Conference might come to such an agreement as would be acceptable to both Houses, and he therefore hoped that one would be appointed. He was almost ashamed to say that he had never acquainted himself sufficiently with the rules which governed the proceedings of a Committee of Conference. His common sense, however, had taught him that it was the duty of such a committee to confine itself to the point of disagreement between the two Houses; but he had been informed by gentlemen of great 377experience that the whole subject of the bill was open to them. Acting upon this principle, they had got into a general discussion as to the relative value of volunteer and regular as well as common militia forces. He believed now that a Committee of Conference might do some good, and that by steering clear of the constitutional scruples of gentlemen, they might agree on some amendments that would render the bill acceptable to both Houses, and thus enable them speedily to adopt a measure so urgently demanded for the protection of the suffering inhabitants of the frontiers.

Mr. B. said, as he should not be a member of the new Committee of Conference, he would read the amendment which had been so much discussed in the old committee: "Be it enacted, That the said volunteers shall form themselves into companies, and designate their company officers, who, if he approve of such designations, shall be commissioned by the President, after they shall have been mustered into service; and that the President be, and hereby is, authorized to organize the volunteers so mustered into service, as aforesaid, into battalions, squadrons, regiments, brigades and divisions, as soon as the number of volunteers shall render such organization, in his judgment, expedient, and shall then appoint the necessary officers, which appointment shall be submitted to the Senate at its next session."
378
CHAPTER XIV.
1837–1840.

BILL TO PREVENT THE INTERFERENCE OF FEDERAL OFFICERS WITH ELECTIONS—DEVOTION OF THE FOLLOWERS OF JACKSON—THE WHIG PARTY LESS COMPACT IN CONSEQUENCE OF THE RIVALRY BETWEEN MR. CLAY AND MR. WEBSTER—RETROSPECTIVE REVIEW OF THE BANK QUESTION—THE SPECIE CIRCULAR—GREAT FINANCIAL DISASTERS.

Toward the close of General Jackson's administration a bill was pending in the Senate to prevent the interference of certain federal officers with elections; a subject which has not yet lost its interest. On this bill, on the 14th of February, 1839, Mr. Buchanan made the following speech:

Mr. President: The question raised for discussion by the bill now before the Senate, is very simple in its character. This bill proposes to punish, by a fine of five hundred dollars—the one moiety payable to the informer, and the other to the United States—and by a perpetual disability to hold office under the United States, any officer of this Government, below the rank of a district attorney, who "shall, by word, message, or writing, or in any other manner whatsoever, endeavor to persuade any elector to give, or dissuade any elector from giving, his vote for the choice of any person to be elector of President and Vice President of the United States," or to be a Senator or Representative in Congress, or to be a governor or lieutenant-governor, or senator or representative, within any State of the Union, "or for the choice of any person to serve in any public office established by the law of any of the States." The officers of the United States against whom the penalties of this bill are denounced, consist of marshals and their deputies, postmasters and their deputies, receivers and registers of land offices, and their deputies and clerks; surveyors general of the public lands, and their deputies and assistants; collectors, surveyors, naval officers, weighers, gaugers, appraisers, or other officers or persons concerned or employed in the charging, collecting, levying or managing the customs, or any branch thereof; and engineers, officers, or agents, employed or concerned in the execution or superintendence of any of the public works. The Senator from Kentucky (Mr. Crittenden), before he commenced his remarks, moved to amend the bill by striking from it the pecuniary penalty 379and perpetual disability against these officers, and substituting, in their stead, the penalty of a removal from office by the President, upon the production of evidence satisfactory to him that any of them had been guilty of the offence.

Now, for myself (said Mr. B.), I shall not vote for this amendment. I will not take advantage of the amiable weakness of my friend from Kentucky, in yielding to the solicitation of others that which his own judgment approved. I will more especially not give such a vote, because the proposed amendment makes no change in the principle of the bill. There is a beautiful harmony and consistency in its provisions as it came fresh from its author which ought to be preserved. I shall not assist in marring any of its fair proportions. Let it remain in its perfect original form, and let its friends upon this floor come up to the baptismal font, and act as its sponsors; and let its avowed principles be recognized as the established doctrines of the political church to which they are all devoted. No, sir, no; if a village postmaster should dare to exercise the freedom of speech, guarantied to him by an antiquated instrument, called the Constitution of the United States, and have the audacity "to endeavor to persuade any elector" to vote for Martin Van Buren, or what would be a much more aggravated offence, dissuade any good Whig from voting for the other distinguished Senator from Kentucky, (Mr. Clay), a mere forfeiture of his office would bear no just proportion to the enormity of the crime. Let such a daring criminal be fined five hundred dollars; let him be disqualified forever from holding any office under the Government; and let him be pointed at as a man of blasted reputation all the days of his life. With honest Dogberry, in the play of "Much ado about Nothing," I pronounce the offence to be "flat burglary as ever was committed."

There is another reason why I shall vote against the amendment. An issue has been fairly made between the Senator from Kentucky and my friend from New Jersey, (Mr. Wall), who, from what we have heard in the course of this debate, has but a few shattered planks left on which he can escape from a total shipwreck of his fair fame. In mercy to him I would not remove any of them. Let him have a chance for his life. He has dared to make a report against the bill in its original form, as it was referred to the committee of which he is the chairman; and for this cause has encountered all the withering denunciations of the Senators from Kentucky and Virginia, (Messrs. Crittenden and Rives). In justice to him, the aspect of the question should not now be changed. Let us, then, have the bill, the whole bill, and nothing but the bill, against which his report was directed.

It would seem almost unnecessary to discuss the question whether this bill be constitutional or not; as the Senator from Kentucky, throughout the whole course of his argument, never once attempted to point to any clause of the Constitution on which it could be supported. It is true that he did cite some precedents in our legislation, which he supposes have a bearing on the subject; but which, I shall undertake to prove, hereafter, are wholly inapplicable. 380The Senator from Virginia (Mr. Rives) has gone further into the argument, and has attempted to prove that this bill is constitutional. At the proper time, I shall endeavor to furnish the proper answer to his remarks. By-the-by, this Constitution is a terrible bugbear. Whilst a member of the other House, I once heard an old gentleman exclaim, when it was cited against one of his favorite measures, "what a vast deal of good it prevents us from doing!" After this bill shall have passed, it will be a bugbear no longer, so far as the freedom of speech or the press is concerned. It will not then alarm even political children.

The gentlemen have a precedent for their bill. Yes, sir, they have a precedent in the sedition law; but it does not go far enough for their purpose. That law, which is the only true precedent on which this bill can be founded, and on which alone it can be sustained, permitted every man to write and to publish what he pleased concerning public men and public measures, and only held him responsible in case his charges should prove to be false. But this bill is a gag law. It goes to the fountain at once, and prohibits the officer not only from writing, but from speaking anything good, bad, or indifferent, whether true or false, on any subject whatever which may affect any pending election from that of a President down to a constable. It has a much broader sweep than the sedition law, which did not interfere with the liberty of speech, however much it may have abridged the freedom of the press. Indeed, among the more enlightened despotisms of Europe, I know not one which prohibits the freedom of speech on all public subjects; it is only in free and enlightened America that we propose actually to insert the gag. The sedition law was bad enough, God knows; but it extended only to the use of the pen, not to that of the tongue. There is, therefore, no parallel between the two cases.

Had it not been for the existence of the sedition law, I should have supposed it to be impossible that there could have been two opinions in regard to the utter unconstitutionality of this bill. The Constitution, in language so plain as to leave no room for misconstruction, declares that "Congress shall make no law abridging the freedom of speech or of the press." The rule is universal. There is no exception. This bill proposes not only to abridge, but utterly to destroy the freedom of speech, and of the press; to interdict their use altogether to the enumerated officers, on all questions touching the election of any officer of the Federal or State Government. A plain man would naturally suppose that, barely to state the contradiction between the Constitution and this bill was to decide the question. Not so. An ingenious and astute lawyer, in favor of a liberal construction of that instrument, can, by inference and ingenuity, confer powers upon Congress in direct violation both of its letter and its spirit, and of which its framers never once dreamed. Such was the power to pass the sedition law. That law engrafted one limitation upon the freedom of the press. It, in effect, changed the meaning of the general terms "Congress shall make no law abridging the freedom of speech or of the press," and excepted from their operation any law which 381might be passed to punish libels against the President, the Government, or either House of Congress. The present bill, in principle at least, proceeds much further. It excepts from the general prohibition of the Constitution the power of punishing all persons holding offices under the Government of the United States who shall dare either to speak or to write at all on questions which may affect the result of any election. This interpolation must be inserted, before gentlemen can show any power to pass the present bill. They cannot advance one step in their argument without it. This Constitution can never be construed according to the meaning of its framers but by men of plain, well-informed, and practical judgment. Common sense is its best expounder. Ingenious men, disposed to raise one implication upon another in favor of Federal power, and to make each previous precedent the foundation on which to proceed another step in the march toward consolidation, may soon make it mean anything or nothing. The liberties of this country can only be preserved by a strict construction of the enumerated powers granted by the States to Congress.

Before I proceed further in my argument against the constitutionality of this bill, it will be proper that I should develop some of its latent beauties. I desire to delineate a little more precisely its character—to present some of its striking features, and to show what it is in principle, and what it will prove to be in practice.

There are twenty-six sovereign States in this Confederacy, united by a Federal compact, called the Constitution of the United States. Each individual elector in this country sustains two distinct characters. He is a citizen of some one of the States, and he is also a citizen of the United States. Now, what does this bill propose? In the older States of this Confederacy, all the Federal officers which we have in the interior are postmasters. It is true that at our ports of entry there are custom-house officers; but in Pennsylvania, for example, from the Schuylkill to the Ohio and to Lake Erie, our people scarcely feel their connection with the General Government except through the medium of the Post Office Department. These postmasters are very numerous. They are planted in every village and at every cross road. They are agents for disseminating information throughout the country. I might probably say that in nine instances out of ten the office is scarcely worth holding on account of its pecuniary emoluments. In most cases, the postmaster accepts it for the accommodation of his neighbors.

Now this postmaster is generally a man of property and of character, having a deep stake in the community and in the faithful administration and execution of the laws. Two candidates are presented to the people for office; say that of a justice of the peace. If one of these village postmasters should, in the exercise of his unquestionable rights as a citizen of Pennsylvania, advise his neighbor to vote for one of these candidates, and against the other, this bill dooms him to a fine of five hundred dollars, and to a perpetual disqualification from ever holding any office under the Government of the United States. No matter whether the merits which he may have ascribed to one 382of the candidates be true as holy writ, and the delinquencies which he may have charged against the other may be susceptible of the clearest proof, this will not arrest the vengeance of the bill. He is doomed to remain mute, although his dearest interests may be involved, or incur its penalties. A gag is to be put into his mouth, and he is to be punished if he dare to express a preference for one candidate over the other. And let me tell the gentleman, these postmasters hold all sorts of political opinions. In my own State a considerable proportion of their number are Whigs and Antimasons, opposed to the present Administration. I might cite other examples to depict the enormity of this bill, but I consider it wholly unnecessary. I might ascend from the justice of the peace or the constable, through all the gradations of elective office, State and Federal, to the President of the United States, and show, that at each ascending grade, the violation of the rights of the citizen becomes more and more outrageous. I might enumerate the weighers and the gaugers, and the other proscribed classes of inferior office holders, and paint the mad and wanton injustice which this bill would inflict upon them. But enough.

The man who would accept office upon such terms, must forfeit all self-respect, and would become at once a fit tool for corruption and for despotism. He must be degraded in his own eyes, and degraded in the eyes of his fellow-citizens below the rank of a freeman. If you desire to depreciate the Government itself under which we live, you cannot do it more effectually than by placing such a stigma on its officers.

Why, sir, you could not, by any possibility, carry such a law into execution. If it should pass to-morrow, it would fall a dead letter upon your statute book. I would not advocate a forcible resistance to any law, and do not believe that such was the intention of my friend from New Jersey (Mr. Wall), when he spoke of resistance; but does not the Senator from Virginia know that laws may be passed of a character so odious, that nobody could be found to carry them into execution? Such are all laws which are entirely opposed to the spirit of the age, and the united and overwhelming current of public opinion. I firmly believe this to be the character of the present bill.

But suppose me to be mistaken in this opinion, and that the law could be carried into execution, what would be the consequences? The doomed officer, the postmaster, the weigher or the gauger, is placed in the midst of a thinking, acting, busy population. Everything around him is proceeding with the impetuosity of steam. Public opinion is marching onward with giant strides. The officer is talked at and talked to, daily and hourly, by the surrounding multitude, whilst the law compels him to close his lips in silence. Under such circumstances, it would be impossible for human nature long to refrain. What then? If he utters a syllable on any of the exciting political topics of the day, and these are all involved in the perpetual canvass which is proceeding for offices, high and low, he is at once seized upon by some harpy of an informer. This bill offers a most tempting bribe to such eavesdroppers. 383It would soon call into existence such a race, to dog and surround each officer, and to catch up every incautious word which might be construed into an endeavor to persuade or to dissuade an elector. Each individual in society is stimulated by this bill to become a common informer, by the tempting offer of a bribe of two hundred and fifty dollars in each particular case. The proscribed officer thus becomes his prey, and, in most cases, will be glad to compromise with him for the payment of a great part, or the whole, of the penalty of five hundred dollars, in order to avoid the stigma of perpetual disability to hold any office under this Government.

There is another remark which I desire to make on this branch of the subject. Whenever you attempt to violate the plain letter and spirit of the Constitution, a thousand evils, of which you have never dreamed, present themselves in the perspective. This law can alone be executed by the courts of the United States. Where are they situated? In the large States, such as Pennsylvania or Virginia, they are held at great distances from each other. A postmaster in either of these States, the income of whose office does not exceed fifty dollars per annum, may be dragged from home, a distance of one hundred and fifty or two hundred miles, to stand his trial under this bill before a federal court. The expense would be enormous, whilst he is obliged to appear before a tribunal far from the place where his character, and that of his prosecutor, are known and appreciated. Under such circumstances, he would almost be certain to become the victim of the common informer, under this most unjust and unconstitutional law. He would either be convicted, or compelled to buy his peace at almost any price.

In conferring the powers enumerated in the Constitution on the Federal Government, the States expressly reserved to themselves respectively, or to their people, all the powers not delegated by it to the United States, or prohibited by it to the States. Now, I would ask the Senator from Kentucky when, or where, or how has the State of Pennsylvania surrendered to Congress the right of depriving any of her citizens, who may accept office under the General Government, of the freedom of speech or of the press? Where is it declared by the Constitution, either in express terms, or from what clause can it fairly be inferred, that Congress may make a forfeiture of the dearest of all political rights, an indispensable condition of office? Each one of the people of Pennsylvania, under her constitution and laws, is secured in the inalienable right of speaking his thoughts. The State, as well as each individual citizen, has the deepest interest in the preservation of this right. I ask the gentleman to lay his finger on the clause of the Constitution by which it has been surrendered. Where is it declared, or from what can it be inferred, that because the States have yielded to the Federal Government their citizens to execute public trusts under the General Government, that, therefore, they have yielded the rights of those citizens to express their opinions freely concerning public men and public measures? The proposition appears to me to be full of absurdity. In regard to the qualifications of electors, the States have granted no power whatever to the United States. This subject they 384have expressly reserved from federal control. The legislatures of the States, and they alone, under the Constitution, possess the power of prescribing the qualifications of the electors of members of the House of Representatives in Congress. They have reserved the same power to themselves in regard to voters for the choice of electors of President and Vice President. What, then, does this bill attempt? To separate two things which reason and the Almighty himself have united beyond all power of separation. You might as well attempt, by arbitrary laws, to separate human life from the power of breathing the vital air, as to detach the elective franchise from freedom of thought, of speech, and of the press. In this atmosphere alone can it live, and move, and have its being. To speak his thoughts is every free elector's inalienable right. Freedom of speech and of the press are both the sword and shield of our Republican institutions. To declare that when the citizens of a State accept office from the General Government, they thereby forfeit this right to express an opinion in relation to the public concerns of their own State and of the nation, is palpable tyranny. In the language referred to in the report, "it puts bridles into their mouths and saddles upon their backs," and degrades them from the rank of a reasoning animal. The English precedent of the Senator was wiser, much wiser, in depriving these officers of the right of suffrage altogether. It does not attempt to separate by the power of man two things which Heaven itself has indissolubly united.

If, therefore, the Constitution contained no express provision whatever prohibiting Congress from passing any law abridging the freedom of speech or of the press, I think I have shown conclusively that the power to pass this bill could not be inferred from any of its express grants of power. But the Constitution is not silent on the subject. Before its adoption by the States, it was dreaded by the jealous patriots of the day, that the Federal Government might usurp the liberties of the people by attacking the liberty of speech and of the press. They, therefore, insisted upon the insertion of an express provision, as an amendment, which, in all time to come, would prevent Congress from interfering with these inestimable rights. The amendment to which I have often referred was adopted, and these rights were expressly excepted from the powers of the Federal Government. And yet, in the very face of this express negative of federal power, we find the Senator from Kentucky coming forward with his bill declaring direct war against any exercise of the freedom of speech and of the press by those citizens of the States who happen to be office holders under the General Government.

But, says the Senator from Virginia, Congress possess, and have exercised, the unquestionable power of creating offices under the Constitution; and they may, therefore, annex to the holding of those offices such a condition as that prescribed by the bill, or rather the amendment of the Senator from Kentucky. Now, sir, what is this but to say that Congress may declare that any citizen of Pennsylvania, who accepts a federal office, shall take it upon condition that it shall be forfeited the moment he exercises the dearest political right guarantied to him and every other citizen, by the Constitution of the United States? Can Congress impose any such condition upon an office? If they can, they can repeal the most solemn provision of the Constitution, and render it a dead letter in regard to every person in the employment of the General Government. All mankind may then speak and publish what they please, except those individuals who have been selected, I hope, generally, for their integrity and ability, to execute the important public trusts of the country.

The Senator from Kentucky has adduced several precedents to prove that similar powers have been already exercised by Congress in other cases. Let us examine them for a moment. Congress, says he, has declared that an Indian agent who shall himself trade with the Indians, shall be punished for this act. But why? It is because this agent is vested with the power of granting to our citizens licenses to trade with the Indians, and thus to take care that they shall not be imposed upon and cheated. To allow him, therefore, to trade with them himself, would be to make him a judge in his own cause, and to withdraw from them that protection which the law intended. Besides, Congress have received from the States, by the Constitution, the power to regulate commerce with the Indian tribes. The whole subject is thus placed under their control. What, then, is this precedent worth? Is not the trading of an Indian agent with the Indians an express and palpable violation of a duty necessarily involved in his office? Can any thing be clearer than the power and the duty of Congress to punish him for this offence? But what interference can there be between the performance of the duties required by law from a postmaster, or from any other of the proscribed officers, and his expression of an opinion to his neighbor, either for or against any candidate for public office? If the postmaster, for example, performs his whole official duty, if he receives and delivers the letters entrusted to his care, and regularly settles his accounts with the department, what human power can arbitrarily place a gag in his mouth, and declare that he shall be punished for exercising the freedom of speech and of the press, upon the pretext that the exercise of these rights of a freeman are inconsistent with the duties of his office? You might just as well punish him or deprive him of his office for speaking or writing on natural philosophy, or mathematics, or any other scientific subject. You would have the same power to violate that clause in the Constitution conferring upon every man the free exercise of religion, and punish him for expressing his opinion on religious subjects, for attending prayer meetings or bible societies, or for endeavoring to persuade or dissuade any member of the religious society to which he belongs in relation to the choice of its pastor. The principle is precisely the same in both cases. Your power hath this extent, no more. You can punish the officer for neglecting or for violating the duties which appropriately belong to his office. You can not repeal the Constitution by declaring it to be an official duty that he shall abandon the constitutional right of speaking his thoughts upon any subject whatsoever, whether religious, scientific, or political. In other words, you have no right to declare that he shall become a slave when he becomes an officer.

386A similar answer, if it were necessary, might be given to the Senator's other precedents. Officers of the customs are prohibited from owning any vessel or cargo under a pecuniary penalty. And why? Because they themselves are to direct and superintend the entry of vessels and cargoes belonging to other persons and the collection of duties; and to allow them to transact this business for themselves, would be to make them judges in their own cause. It would be an evident violation of the duty naturally attached to their office. But will any one contend that their constitutional freedom of speech, in regard to candidates for office, is incompatible with the proper entry or unloading of vessels engaged either in foreign commerce or the coasting trade?

So the register of a land office is prohibited from entering lands in his own name, or, in other words, from selling lands to himself.

Such are the precedents which the Senator has cited to justify himself in depriving the officers embraced by his bill of the right of freedom of speech and of the press.

But I do not mean even to rest the constitutional question here. From the very nature of the Constitution itself, two great political parties must ever exist in this country. You may call them by what names you will, their principles must ever continue to be the same. The one, dreading federal power, will ever be friendly to a strict construction of the powers delegated to the Federal Government and to State rights. The other equally dreading federal weakness, will ever advocate such a liberal construction of the Constitution as will confer upon the General Government as much power as possible, consistently with a free interpretation of the terms of the instrument. The one party is alarmed at the danger of consolidation; the other at that of disunion. In the days of the elder Adams the party friendly to a liberal construction of the Constitution got into power. And what did they do? Among other things, in the very face of that clause of the Constitution which prohibited Congress from passing any law abridging the freedom of speech or of the press, they passed the sedition law. What were its provisions? It punished false, scandalous, and malicious libels against the Government of the United States, either House of Congress, or the President, by a fine not exceeding two thousand dollars and imprisonment not exceeding two years.

At the present day, it would be useless to waste the time of the Senate in proving that this law was a violation of the Constitution. It is now admitted that Congress, in passing it, had transcended their powers. If any principle has been established beyond a doubt by the almost unanimous opinion of the people of the United States, it is, that the sedition law was unconstitutional. Such is the strong and universal feeling against it, that if it could now be revived, the authors would probably meet a similar fate with those deluded and desperate men in France who have themselves lately fallen victims upon the same altar on which they had determined to sacrifice the liberty of the press.

The popular odium which followed this law was not so much excited by its 387particular provisions, as by the fact, that any law upon the subject was a violation of the Constitution, and would establish a precedent for giving such a construction to it as would swallow up the rights of the States and of their people in the gulf of federal power. The Constitution had declared that "Congress shall pass no law abridging the freedom of speech or of the press." Its framers well knew that, under the laws of each of the States composing this Union, libels were punishable. They, therefore, left the character of all officers created under the Constitution and laws of the United States to be protected by the laws of the several States. They were afraid to give this Government any authority over the subject of libels, lest its colossal power might be wielded against the liberty of the press. Congress were, therefore, prohibited from passing any law upon the subject, whether good or bad. It was not merely because the law was unjust in itself, though it was bad enough, Heaven knows, that the indignant Republicans of that day rose against it; but it was because it violated the Constitution. It expired by its own limitation in March, 1801; but not until it had utterly prostrated the political party which gave it birth.

Now, sir, I shall say a few words concerning the Virginia and Kentucky resolutions of 1798; although the Senator from Virginia may consider it sacrilege in me to discuss this subject. I have at all times, ever since I read and understood these resolutions, held to the political doctrines which they inculcate; and I can assure the Senator I have studied them with care. I will read a few extracts from the Virginia resolutions:

The General Assembly, in the third resolution, "doth explicitly and peremptorily declare, that it views the powers of the Federal Government, as resulting from the compact, to which the States are parties, as limited by the plain sense and intention of the instrument constituting that compact—and as no further valid than they are authorized by the grants enumerated in that compact;" and in the fourth resolution, they express their deep regret, "that a spirit has, in sundry instances, been manifested by the Federal Government, to enlarge its powers by forced constructions of the constitutional charter which defines them." In regard to the sedition law, they declare that its passage was the exercise of "a power not delegated by the Constitution; but, on the contrary, expressly and positively forbidden by one of the amendments thereto; a power, which, more than any other, ought to produce universal alarm; because it is levelled against that right of freely examining public characters and measures, and of free communication among the people thereon, which has ever been justly deemed the only effectual guardian of every other right."

Now, sir, what is the essence, what is the root of all these resolutions? It consists of one plain, clear, fundamental principle, from which all others proceed as branches. It is this, that patriotism—that the permanence of our institutions—that all the principles of correct construction require, that the Federal Government shall be limited to the express powers granted to it by the States, and that no implied powers shall ever be exercised, except such as 388are evidently and plainly necessary to carry the express powers into effect. This is the foundation, the corner stone, the vital principle of all the Virginia and Kentucky resolutions. It was because the sedition law violated this principle, that the Republican statesmen of Virginia and Kentucky opposed it with such a determined spirit. It was, as Mr. Madison says in his report, because such a loose construction of the Constitution as would bring this law within its pale, would lay the foundation from which the friends of a strong central government might proceed to rob the States and the people of their liberties, and establish a consolidated government. It was the first stride towards a limited monarchy.

The Federalists of that day honestly believed that the Government should be strengthened at the centre, and that the pulsations of the heart were not powerful enough to extend a wholesome circulation to the extremities. They, therefore, used every effort to enlarge the powers of the Federal Government by construction. This was the touchstone which then divided parties, and which will continue to divide them until, which God forbid, the Government shall cease to exist.

Now, sir, if I have correctly stated the principle which runs through all the Virginia and Kentucky resolutions, I would ask whether the bill now before the Senate is not a more palpable violation of this principle than the sedition law. I shall now proceed to establish this position.

In the first place, then, the sedition law did not interfere with the freedom of speech. The citizen might speak what he thought and say what he pleased without subjecting himself to its penalties. Under the despotisms of Europe there is a strict censorship over the press. Everything written for publication must undergo the supervision and correction of a Government censor before it can be published. In the most despotic countries, however, some indulgence is granted to the liberty of speech on political questions. The bill establishes more than a universal censorship over the freedom of speech. It compels the officer to be silent altogether on political questions. He dare not utter a word without incurring its penalties. In this country, every public question connects itself with our elections. If there be two candidates for any State Legislature, and the election should turn upon internal improvements, or the division of a county, the officer is as much exposed to the universal sweep of this bill, in case he utters a word in favor of the one or against the other, as though it were the Presidential election. He is equally doomed to silence in the one case as in the other. Such tyranny is unknown to the sedition law.

Whilst I was abroad some years ago, I heard an anecdote highly creditable to the King of Prussia, who, although a despot, is, by his subjects, called a Democratic King. The revolutionary war of Poland against Russia was then raging, and the Polish subjects of the Prussian king were highly excited in favor of their brethren under the dominion of Russia. They talked very freely in favor of taking part in the contest; of casting off the Prussian yoke, and uniting with their brethren in re-establishing the independence of Poland. 389The counsellors of the king advised him to prohibit and to punish this freedom of speech. He answered that he would do no such thing; that he would suffer them to express their opinions, and that there was less danger that they would rise against his government than if they remained silent. This was the remark of a liberal and a wise man, who had been instructed in the school of adversity.

But, in this favored land of liberty, in the nineteenth century, we are about to deny to our citizens the privilege of speaking their thoughts. This is the first attempt which I have ever known or read of, either in England or in this country, to punish the expression of opinions relative to candidates for office as a crime. If ever this was done in England, even in the reigns of the Tudors or the Stuarts, it must have been a Star Chamber offence. In the more enlightened despotisms of Europe, they will learn, with astonishment, that a bill has been introduced into the Senate of the United States, proposing to punish a postmaster for expressing his opinion in favor of a candidate for office, as if this were an enormous crime, with a fine of five hundred dollars, and a perpetual disability to hold any other office under the Government. Even under the common law of England, oral slander is not punishable as a crime. The party injured by it is left to his private remedy. In the second place, the sedition law, although it did abridge, did not, like this bill, totally destroy the freedom of the press. The sedition law deprived no man of the right or the power, in the first instance, to write and publish to the world any strictures upon the Government which he might think proper. To be sure, if in exercising this privilege he violated the truth, he was made responsible to its penalties. This bill reaches the very fountains of thought. Its object is to prevent its victims from speaking or writing at all. No matter how innocent, or praiseworthy, or true, may be the conversation or the publication, still if it can be construed into an endeavor to persuade any elector to give his vote for a particular candidate, he is doomed to a fine of five hundred dollars, and a perpetual disability to hold office.

Again: under the sedition law, the accused was permitted to protect himself against its penalties, by giving the truth of his charge in evidence. Any individual who had accused the President of the United States of being a bad and dangerous man, who was aiming a blow at the liberties of his country, and desired to usurp the powers of the Government by a latitudinarian construction of the Constitution, was protected by this law from all responsibility, provided he could prove the truth of these allegations to the satisfaction of a court and jury of his countrymen. Not so the present bill. If a postmaster, or a land officer, or a weigher, or a gauger, should endeavor to dissuade any elector from voting for a particular candidate, and should say that this candidate has been guilty of a crime, and therefore his election would be dangerous to the country, and is brought before a court and jury for trial under this bill, he must be convicted, although he may be able to prove the truth of his charge by evidence as clear as a sunbeam. The old English maxim, "the greater the truth the greater the libel," is again revived, with some show of reason; because the language of truth would be more powerful in persuading or dissuading an elector than that of falsehood. Although every member of the court and the jury might personally know that what the accused had uttered was the truth, yet, under the provisions of this bill, they would be bound to convict and sentence him to suffer its penalties.

I think I have thus established my position that this bill is worse, and more glaringly unconstitutional, than the sedition law.

I now approach the argument of the Senator from Virginia in favor of the constitutionality of this bill. The old argument in favor of the sedition law, as stated by Mr. Madison in his report, was that the general phrases in the preamble and one clause of the Constitution were sufficiently powerful to extend the limited grants of power contained in the body of the instrument, and to confer upon Congress the authority to enact any law they might think proper for the common defence and the general welfare. This doctrine has long since been exploded, and was not adverted to by the Senator from Virginia. We are informed by the same authority, that another argument used, was, that all the State Legislatures had passed laws for the punishment of libels; and that, therefore, the same power belonged to the Government of the United States. A similar argument could not be urged by the Senator in support of this bill; because no State Legislature ever has, and I will venture to say no State Legislature ever will pass such a bill as that now before the Senate. To what argument then did the Senator resort? I shall endeavor to state it fairly. He asks if a judge were to use the freedom of speech or of the press, in canvassing the merits of a cause before the people, which it would become his duty afterwards to decide, would it be an abridgment of this freedom to punish him for such conduct? I answer, certainly not. But does not the gentleman perceive that the offence in this case is substantive and independent, and amounts to a total violation of his official duty, for which he ought to be impeached? The language, oral or printed, which he has used, is the mere agent which he has employed in the commission of the offence. This argument is a begging of the question; for it assumes that, under the Constitution, Congress possess the power to punish one citizen for persuading another, by fair argument, to give his vote for or against any candidate for office. This is the very principle to be established. Again he asks, suppose one of the officers embraced by the bill were to use the freedom of speech or of the press, in saying to an elector, if you will give your vote for such a candidate, I will procure you an office, would not such an officer be punishable? I answer, certainly he would under the State laws; because this would be an attempt to procure a vote by corrupt and improper means. It is a distinct offence, the punishment of which in no manner interferes with the liberty of speech or the press when exercised to accomplish constitutional purposes. A similar answer might be given to his interrogatory in regard to giving a challenge, by word or by writing, to fight a duel. The last question, which capped the climax of his argument, was, if a man be guilty of a false and malicious libel against an innocent person, may you not punish him, under the Constitution, without invading the freedom of speech or of the press—because it is not the words he may use which you punish, but the falsehood of the charge, the evil intention, and the injury inflicted? I ask the Senator if this argument is not a justification of the sedition law to the fullest extent? I have taken down the Senator's words, and cannot be mistaken in their meaning. What did the sedition law declare? That the authors of "false, scandalous and malicious" libels, with the evil intentions enumerated in the act, should incur its penalties. It was not the mere words published that were punished, but it was their falsehood, their malice, and their evil intentions. The constitutionality of the sedition law is, therefore, embraced not only within the spirit, but within the very words, of the Senator's argument. Has he not, however unconsciously, defended the sedition law? This argument, to my knowledge, never occurred to those who passed that law; but it is one which, if well founded, would give us the power to-morrow to pass another sedition law.

Do not Senators perceive that the passage of this bill would utterly disfranchise a large and respectable class of our people? Under it, what would be the condition of all the editors of your political journals, whose business and whose duty it is to enlighten public opinion in regard to the merits or demerits of candidates for office? Pass this law, and you declare that no editor of a public paper, of either party, is capable or worthy of holding any of the proscribed offices. He must at once either abandon his paper, and with it the means of supporting himself and his family, or he must surrender any little office which he may hold under the Government.

And yet this bill is supported by my friend from Virginia, who, to use his own language, "has been imbued with the principles of Democracy, and a regard for State rights, from his earliest youth." If such a charge should ever be made against him hereafter, his speech and his vote in favor of this bill, will acquit him before any court in Christendom, where the truth may be given in evidence. I yet trust that he may never vote for its passage. Every measure of this kind betrays a want of confidence in the intelligence and patriotism of the American people. It is founded on a distrust of their judgment and integrity. Do you suppose that when a man is appointed a collector or a postmaster, he acquires any more influence over the people than he had before? No, sir! On the contrary, his influence is often diminished, instead of being increased. The people of this country are abundantly capable of judging whether he is more influenced by love of country or love of office. If they should determine that his motives are purely mercenary for supporting a political party, this will destroy his influence. If he be a noisy, violent, and meddling politician, he will do the administration under which he has been appointed, much more harm than good. Let me assure gentlemen that the people are able to take care of themselves. They do not require the interposition of Congress to prevent them from being deceived and led astray by the influence of office holders. Whilst this is my fixed opinion, I think the number of federal officers ought to be strictly limited to the actual necessities of the Government. Pursue this course, and, my life for it, all the land officers, and postmasters, and weighers, and gaugers, which you shall send abroad over the country, can never influence the people to betray their own cause. For my own part, I entertain the most perfect confidence in their intelligence as well as integrity.

That office holders possess comparatively but little influence over the people, will conclusively appear from the brief history of the last two years, the period during which this dreaded man, Mr. Van Buren, has been in office. What has all this alarming influence of the office holders effected at the only points where they are to be found in any considerable number? In the city of Philadelphia, notwithstanding all the influence of the custom-house, the post-office, and the mint, the majority at the last election against the administration was tremendous, being, I believe, upwards of four thousand. The Prætorian guards, as they have been called, performed but little service on that day in that city. On the other hand, look at the interior of Pennsylvania. There the governor, whose patronage within the limits of the State was as great, under the old Constitution, as that of the King of England, had filled every office with enemies of the present administration. Of this I do not complain; for, whether right or wrong, it has been the long established practice of both parties. It is true that many of the postmasters were friendly to the administration; but it is equally certain, that a large proportion of them warmly espoused the cause of the opposition. What was the result? Those wielding the vast patronage were entirely routed, notwithstanding the exertions of the office holders. Gentlemen may quiet their alarms, and be assured that the people cannot be persuaded to abandon their principles by the influence of men in office.

Again: let us look at the State of New York for another example. There the Albany regency were seated in power. The Democratic party was well drilled. All the office holders of the State and of the city were friendly to the administration. Besides, in my opinion, they fought in the righteous cause; and this same abused Albany regency who were their leaders, was composed of as able and as honest men as were ever at the head of any State government. What was the result there? With all this official power and patronage, both of the State and Federal Governments, we were beaten, horse, foot and dragoons. There is not the least necessity for passing an unconstitutional law, to save the people from the influence of the office holders.

Have we not been beaten in all the large cities of the Union, where only there are federal officers in any considerable number? What has been our fate in New York, Philadelphia, Boston, Baltimore, and New Orleans? We have been vanquished in all of them. The hobgoblins and chimeras dire respecting the influence of office holders, which terrify gentlemen, exist only in their own imagination. The people of this country are not the tame and servile creatures who can be seduced from their purpose by the persuasion of the office holders. It is true that in 1828 I did say that the office holders 393were the enlisted soldiers of that administration by which they were sustained. This was too strong an expression. But admit them to be enlisted soldiers; and whilst I do not deny them some influence, there is no danger to be apprehended from it, as long as there is virtue and intelligence among our people.

And here I hope the Senator from Kentucky will pardon me for suggesting to him an amendment to his bill. He has, I think, made one or two mistakes in the classification of his officers; though, in the general, it is sufficiently perfect. The principle would seem to have been to separate what may be called the aristocracy of office holders from the plebeians. Those of the elevated class are still permitted to enjoy the freedom of speech and of the press, whilst the hard-working operatives among them are denied this privilege. The heads of departments and bureaus, the officers of the army and navy, the superintendents and officers of our mints, and our district attorneys are not affected by this bill. These gentlemen are privileged by their elevation. They are too high to be reached by its provisions. Who, then, ought to care whether weighers and gaugers, and village postmasters, and hard-handed draymen, and such inferior people shall be permitted to express their thoughts on public affairs? I would suggest, however, that the collectors of our principal seaports, the marshals of our extensive judicial districts, and the post-masters in our principal cities receive compensation sufficient to enable them to figure in "good society." They ought to rank with the district attorneys, and should be elevated from the plebeian to the patrician rank of office holders. They ought to be allowed the freedom of speech and of the press. As to the subordinate officers, they are not worth the trouble of a thought.

To be sure there is one palpable absurdity on the face of the bill. Its avowed purpose is to prevent office holders from exercising an influence in elections. Why, then, except from its operation all those office holders, who, from their station in society, can exercise the most extensive influence, and confine its provisions to the humbler, but not less meritorious class, whose opinions can have but a limited influence over their fellow-men? The district attorney, for example, is excepted—the very man of all others, who, from his position and talents, has the best opportunity of exerting an extensive influence. He may ride over his district, and make political speeches to secure the election of his favorite candidate. He is too high a mark for the gentleman's bill. But if the subordinates of the custom-house, or the petty postmaster at the cross-roads with an income of fifty dollars per annum, shall dare, even in private conversation, to persuade an elector to vote for or against any candidate, he is to be punished by a fine of five hundred dollars, and a perpetual disability to hold any office under the Government. Was there ever a bill more unequal or more unjust?

Now, sir, I might here, with great propriety, and very much to the relief both of my audience and myself, leave this subject; but there are still some other observations which I conceive it to be my duty to add to what I have already said. Most of them will be elicited by the very strong remarks of my friend from Virginia; for I trust that I may still be permitted to call him by that name.

He and I entered the House of Representatives almost together. I believe he came into it but two years after myself. We soon formed a mutual friendship, which has ever since, I may say, on my part, with great sincerity, continued to exist. We fought shoulder to shoulder, and his great powers were united with my feeble efforts in prostrating the administration of the younger Adams. General Jackson came into power; and during the whole period of that administration he was the steady, unwavering supporter of all its leading measures, except the Specie Circular and his advocacy of the currency bill; and, on that bill, I stood by him, in opposition to the administration. Whilst this man of destiny was in power—this mail of the lion heart, whose will the Whigs declared was law, and whose roaring terrified all the other beasts of the forest, and subdued them into silence—where was then the Senator from Virginia? He was our chosen champion in the fight. Whilst General Jackson was exerting all this tremendous influence, and marshalling all his trained bands of office holders to do his bidding, according to the language of the opposition, these denunciations had no terror for the Senator from Virginia. Never in my life did I perform a duty of friendship with greater ardor than when, on one occasion, I came to his rescue from an unjust attack made against him by the Whigs in relation to a part of his conduct whilst minister in France. After holding out so long together, ought he not, at least, to have parted from us in peace, and bade us a kind adieu? In abandoning our camp, why did he shoot Parthian arrows behind him? In taking leave of us, I hope not forever, is it not too hard for us to hear ourselves denounced by the gentleman in the language which he has used? "He is amazed and bewildered with the scenes passing before him. Whither, he asks, will the mad dominion of party carry us? His mind is filled with despondency as to the fate of his country. Shall we emulate the servility of the senate and people of Rome? You already have your Prætorian bands in this city." I might quote from his speech other phrases of a similar character; but these are sufficient. I do not believe that any of these expressions were aimed at me personally; yet they strike me with the mass of my political friends, and I feel bound to give them a passing notice.

And why, let me ask the Senator, why did he not sooner make the discovery of the appalling danger of executive influence? Is there more to be dreaded from that cause, under the present administration, than under that which is past? Is Martin Van Buren more formidable than General Jackson was? Let his favorite author, De Tocqueville, answer this question. He says, "the power of General Jackson perpetually increases, but that of the President declines; in his hands the Federal Government is strong, but it will pass enfeebled into the hands of his successor." Do not all now know this to be the truth? Has not the Government passed enfeebled into the hands of his successor? We see it, and feel it, and know it, from every thing which is passing around us. The civilian has succeeded the conqueror; and, I must be permitted to say, has exercised his high powers with great moderation and purity of purpose. In what manner has he ever abused his patronage? In this particular, of what can the gentleman complain?

In February, 1828, I did say that the office holders were the enlisted soldiers of the administration. But did I then propose to gag them? Did I propose to deprive them of the freedom of speech and of the press? No, sir, no! Notwithstanding the number of them scattered over the country, I was not afraid of their influence. On the contrary, I commended the administration for adhering to its friends. I then used the following language:

"In my humble judgment, the present administration could not have proceeded a single year, with the least hope of re-election, but for their patronage. This patronage may have been used unwisely, as my friend from Kentucky [Mr. Letcher] (and I am still proud to call him my friend, notwithstanding our political opposition) has insinuated. I have never blamed them, I shall never blame them, for adhering to their friends. Be true to your friends and they will be true to you, is the dictate both of justice and of sound policy. I shall never participate in abusing the administration for remembering their friends. If you go too much abroad with this patronage, for the purpose of making new friends, you will offend your old ones, and make but very insincere converts."

What was my opinion in 1828, when I was in the opposition, is still my opinion in 1839, when I am in the majority. I say now, that the administration which goes abroad with its patronage to make converts of its enemies, at the expense of its friends, acts both with ingratitude and injustice. Such an administration deserves to be prostrated. Although neither from principle nor from feeling am I a root and branch man, yet, in this respect, I adopt the opinion of General Washington, the first, the greatest, the wisest, and the best of our Presidents. I prefer him either to General Jackson or to the great apostle of American liberty. This opinion, however, may proceed from the relics of old Federalism. On this subject General Washington says: "I shall not, whilst I have the honor to administer the Government, bring a man into any office of consequence, knowingly, whose political tenets are adverse to the measures which the General Government is pursuing; for this, in my opinion, would be a sort of political suicide. That it would embarrass its movements is certain."

Now, sir, if any freak of destiny should ever place me in one of these executive departments, and I feel very certain that it never will, I shall tell you the course I would pursue. I should not become an inquisitor of the political opinions of the subordinate office holders, who are receiving salaries of some eight hundred or a thousand dollars a year. For the higher and more responsible offices, however, I would select able, faithful, and well-tried political friends who felt a deep and devoted interest in the success of my measures. And this not for the purpose of concealment, for no public officer ought to be afraid of the scrutiny of the world; but that they might cheerfully co-operate with me in promoting what I believed to be the public interest. I would have no person around me, either to hold back in the traces, or to thwart and defeat my purposes. With General Washington I believe that any other course "would be a sort of political suicide."

In executing the duties of a public office, I should act upon the same principles that would govern my conduct in regard to a private trust. If the Senator from Virginia were to constitute me his attorney, to transact any important business, I should never employ assistants whom I believed to be openly and avowedly hostile to his interests.

But says the Senator, you already have your Prætorian bands in this city. He doubtless alludes to the officeholders in the different departments of the Government; and, I ask, is Mr. Van Buren's influence over them greatly to be dreaded? If, sir, the President relies upon such troops he will most certainly be defeated. These Prætorian bands are, to a great extent, on the side of the Senator from Kentucky and his political friends. I would now do them great injustice if I were to call them the enlisted soldiers of the administration. Whilst General Jackson was here they did keep tolerably quiet, but now I understand that many of these heads of bureaus and clerks use the freedom of speech and of the press without reserve against the measures of his successor. Of course I speak from common report. God forbid that I should become an inquisitor as to any man's politics. It is generally understood that about one-half of them are open enemies of the present administration. I have some acquaintance with a few of those who are called its friends; and among this few I know several, who, although they declare they are in favor of the re-election of Mr. Van Buren, yet they are decidedly opposed to all his prominent measures. Surrounded by such Prætorian bands, what has this tyrant done? Nothing, literally nothing. I believe he is the very last man in the country who can justly be charged with using his official patronage to control the freedom of elections. His forbearance towards his political enemies in office will unquestionably injure him to some extent, and especially in those States where, under the common party law, no person dreams of being permitted to hold office from his political enemies. His liberality in this respect has been condemned by many of his friends, whilst he is accused by his enemies of using his official patronage for corrupt political purposes. This is a hard fate. The Senator must, therefore, pardon me, after having his own high authority in favor of General Jackson's administration, if, under that of his successor, I cannot now see the dangers of executive patronage in a formidable light.

There was one charge made by the Senator from Virginia against the present administration, which I should have been the first man to sustain, had I believed it to be well founded. Had the President evinced a determination, in the face of all his principles and professions, to form a permanent connection in violation of law, between the Government and the Bank of the United States, or any other State bank, he should, in this particular, have encountered my unqualified opposition. In such an event, I should have been willing to serve under the command of the Senator against the administration; and 397hundreds and thousands of the unbought and incorruptible Democracy would have rallied to our standard. I am convinced, however, from the reports of the Secretaries of the Treasury and of War, and from the other lights which have been shed upon the subject, that "their poverty and not their will consented" to the partial and limited connection which resulted from the sale of the bond to the Bank of the United States. Such seems to have been the general opinion on this floor, because no Senator came to the aid of the gentleman from Virginia in sustaining this charge. "Where was Roderick then?" Why did not the Senator from Kentucky come to the rescue and sustain his friend from Virginia in the accusation against the administration of having again connected itself with the Bank of the United States?

The Senator from Virginia has informed us, that in his State, a law exists, prohibiting any man who holds office under the Federal Government from holding, at the same time, a State office. This law prevents the same individual from serving two masters. A similar law, I believe, exists in every State of this Union. If there is not, there ought to be. The Federal and State Governments ought to be kept as distinct and independent of each other as possible. The General Government ought never to be permitted to insinuate itself into the concerns of the States, by using their officers as its officers. These incompatible laws proceed from a wise and wholesome jealousy of federal power, and a proper regard for State rights. I heartily approve them. Then, sir, if there be danger in trusting a postmaster of the General Government with the commission of a magistrate under State authority, how infinitely more dangerous would it be to suffer the administration to connect itself with all the State banks of the country? What immense influence over the people of the States could the Federal Government thus acquire! Suffer it to deposit the public money at pleasure with these banks, and permit them to loan it out for their own benefit, and you establish a vast federal influence, not over weighers and gaugers and postmasters, but over the presidents, and directors, and cashiers, and debtors, and creditors of these institutions. You bind them to you by the strongest of all ties, that of self-interest; and they are men who, from their position, cannot fail to exercise an extensive influence over the people of the States. I am a State rights man, and am therefore opposed to any connection between this Government and the State banks; and last of all to such a connection with the Bank of the United States, which is the most powerful of them all. This is one of the chief reasons why I am in favor of an independent Treasury. And yet, friendly to State rights as the Senator professes to be, he complains of the President for opposing such a connection with the State banks, and thereby voluntarily depriving himself of the power and influence which must ever result from such an union.

There are other reasons why I am friendly to an independent Treasury; but this is not the proper occasion to discuss them. I shall merely advert to one which, in my opinion, renders an immediate separation from the banks indispensable to the public interest. The importation of foreign goods into New York, since the commencement of the present year, very far exceeds, according to our information, the corresponding importations during the year 1836, although they were greater in that year than they had ever been since the origin of our Government. This must at once create a large debt against us in England. Meanwhile, what is our condition at home? New York has established what is called a free banking law, under whose provisions more than fifty banks had been established in the beginning of January last, and I know not how many since, with permission to increase their capital to four hundred and eighty-seven millions of dollars. These banks do not even profess to proceed upon the ancient, safe and well established principle of making the specie in their vaults bear some just and reasonable proportion to their circulation and deposits. Another and a novel principle is adopted. State loans and mortgages upon real estate are made to take the place of gold and silver; and an amount of bank notes may be issued equal to the amount of these securities deposited with the comptroller. There is no restriction whatever imposed on these banks in regard to specie, except that they are required to hold eleven pence in the dollar, not of their circulation and deposits united, but of their circulation alone. Well may that able officer have declared, in his report to the legislature, that "it is now evident that the point of danger is not an exclusive metallic currency, but an exclusive paper currency, so redundant and universal as to excite apprehensions for its stability." The amount of paper issues of these banks, and the amount of bank credits, must rapidly expand the paper circulation, and again produce extravagant speculation. The example of New York will have a powerful influence on the other States of the Union. Already has Georgia established a free banking law; and a bill for the same purpose is now before the legislature of Pennsylvania. If the signs of the times do not deceive me, we shall have another explosion sooner, much sooner than I had anticipated. The Senator from Massachusetts (Mr. Webster) nods his assent. [Here Mr. Webster said, "I think so also."] This paper bubble must, from its nature, go on rapidly expanding, until it reaches the bursting point. The recent suspension of specie payments by the Branch Bank of Mobile, in the State of my friend from Alabama, (Mr. King), may be the remote and distant thunder premonitory of the approaching storm. This is all foreign, however, to the subject before the Senate. I desire now to declare solemnly in advance, that if this explosion should come, and the money of the people in the Treasury should again be converted into irredeemable bank paper and bank credits, the administration will be guiltless of the deed. We have tried, but tried in vain, to establish an independent Treasury, where this money would be safe, in the custody of officers responsible to the people.

There is one incident in relation to the Bank of the United States which my friend from Virginia may be curious to know. Under the Pennsylvania charter it was prohibited from issuing notes under ten dollars. I had fondly hoped that this example might be gradually followed by our legislature in regard to the other banks, until the time should arrive when our whole circulation under ten dollars should consist of gold and silver. The free banking law of New York has enabled the bank to nullify this restriction. Under this law it has established a bank in the city of New York, the capital of which may be increased to $50,000,000, and has transferred to the comptroller of that State Michigan State loan to the amount of $200,000. And what notes, Mr. President, do you suppose it has taken in lieu of this amount of loan? Not an assortment of different denominations, as the other banks have done, but forty thousand five dollar notes. These five dollar notes will be paid out and circulated by the bank at Philadelphia; and thus the wise ten dollar restriction contained in its Pennsylvania charter is completely annulled.

If, therefore, I could believe for a moment that this Government intended to form a permanent connection with the Bank of the United States, and again make it the general depository and fiscal agent of the Treasury, even if no other principle were involved than that of the enormous increase of executive patronage which must necessarily follow, I should at once stand with my friend from Virginia in opposition to the administration. But I would not go over with him to the enemy's camp. I have somewhere read a eulogy on the wisdom of the Catholic church, for tolerating much freedom of opinion in non-essentials among its members. A pious, an enthusiastic, and an ardent spirit, which, if it belonged to any Protestant church, might produce a schism, is permitted to establish a new order, and thus to benefit, instead of injuring, the ancient establishment. I might point to a St. Dominick and a Loyola for examples. Now, sir, I admit that the Whig party is very Catholic in this respect. It tolerates great difference of opinion. Its unity almost consists in diversity. In that party we recognize "the Democratic Antimasonic" branch. Yes, sir, this is the approved name. I need not mention the names of its two distinguished leaders. The peculiar tenet of this respectable portion of the universal political Whig church is a horrible dread of the murderers of Morgan, whose ghost, like that of Hamlet's father, walks abroad, and revisits the pale glimpses of the moon, seeking vengeance on his murderers. I wish they could be found, and punished as they deserve. Though not abolitionists in the mass, they do not absolutely reject, though they may receive with an awkward grace, the overtures and aid of the abolitionists. In my portion of the country, at least, the abolitionists are either incorporated with this branch of the party, or hang upon its outskirts. The Senator from Virginia and myself could not, I think, go over to this section of the party, nor would we be received by it into full communion. The Senator from Kentucky (Mr. Clay) will, I think, find to his cost that he has done himself great injury with this branch of the opposition, by the manly and patriotic sentiments which he expressed a few days ago on the subject of abolition.

Then comes the Whig party proper, in which the Senator from Kentucky stands preeminent. I need not detail its principles. Now, I humbly apprehend, that even if the President of the United States should determine to ally himself with the bank, and force us to abandon him on that account, neither the Senator from Virginia nor myself could find refuge in the bosom of this party. We have both sinned against it beyond forgiveness. We were both in favor of the removal of the deposits—an offence which, with them, like original sin, "brought death into the world, and all our woe." For this, no penitence can atone.

Again: we both voted for the expunging resolution, which, in their opinion, was an act of base subserviency and man worship, and, withal, a palpable violation of the Constitution. So dreadful was this offence, that my friend from Delaware [Mr. Bayard] will never get over it. He has solemnly pledged himself to cry aloud and spare not, until this foul blot shall be removed from the journals of the Senate. I should be glad to know why he has not yet introduced his annual resolution to efface this unsightly stain from the record of our proceedings.

In short, we should be compelled to form a separate branch of the Whig party. We should be the deposit-removing, expunging, force bill, anti-bank Jackson Whigs. We should carry with us enough of locofocoism and other combustible materials to blow them all up. They had better have a care of us.

I hope the Senator may yet remain with us, and be persuaded that his old friends upon this floor do not resemble either the servile band in the Roman Senate under the first Cæsar, or that which afterwards degraded themselves so low as to make the favorite horse of one of his successors high priest and consul. He can never be fully received into the communion of the faithful Whigs. Although the fathers of the church here may grant him absolution, yet the rank and file of the party throughout the country will never ratify the deed.

I was pleased to hear the Senator from Virginia, on yesterday, make the explanation which he did to the Senator from North Carolina, [Mr. Strange] in regard to what he had said in favor of the British government. I cheerfully take the explanation. I did suppose he had pronounced a high-wrought eulogy upon that government; but it would not be fair to hold him, or any other Senator, to the exact meaning of words uttered in the heat and ardor of debate.

I agree with him that we are indebted for several of our most valuable institutions to our British ancestors. We have derived from them the principles of liberty established and consecrated by magna charta, the trial by jury, the petition of right, the habeus corpus act, and the revolution of 1688. And yet, notwithstanding all this, I should be very unwilling to make the British government a model for our legislation in Republican America. Look at its effects in practice. Is it a government which sheds its benign influence, like the dews of Heaven, upon all its subjects? Or is it not a government where the rights of the many are sacrificed to promote the interest of the few? The landed aristocracy have controlled the election of a majority of the members of the House of Commons; and they, themselves, compose the House of Lords. The main scope and principal object of their legislation was to promote the great landed interest, that of the large manufacturers, and of the fund holders of a national debt, amounting to more than seven hundred and fifty millions sterling. In order to accomplish these purposes, it became necessary to oppress the poor. Where is the country beneath the sun in which pauperism prevails to such a fearful extent? Is it not known to the whole world that the wages both of agricultural and manufacturing labor are reduced to the very lowest point necessary to sustain human existence? Look at Ireland,—the fairest land I have ever seen. Her laboring population is confined to the potatoe. Rarely, indeed, do they enjoy either the wheat or the beef which their country produces in such plentiful abundance. It is chiefly sent abroad for foreign consumption.

The people of England are now struggling to make their institutions more free; and I trust in God they may succeed; yet their whole system is artificial, and without breaking it down altogether, I do not perceive how the condition of the mass of the people can be much ameliorated. In the present state of the world, no friend of the human race ought probably to desire its immediate destruction. We ought to regard it rather as a beacon to warn us than as a model for our imitation. We ought never, like England, to raise up by legislation any great interests or monopolies to oppress the people, which we cannot put down without crushing the Government itself. Such is now the condition of that country. I am no admirer of the British constitution, either in church or state, as it at present exists. I desire not a splendid government for this country.

The Senator from Virginia has quoted with approbation, and sustained by argument, a sentiment from De Tocqueville to which I can never subscribe. It is this: That there is greater danger, under a Government like ours, that the Chief Magistrate may abuse his power, than under a limited monarchy; because, being elected by the people, and their sympathies being strongly enlisted in his favor, he may go on to usurp the liberties of the country with their approbation.

[Here Mr. Rives rose and explained.]

Mr. Buchanan. From the gentleman's explaination, I find that I did not misquote either his proposition or his argument. I am sorry he speaks under the dominion of so much feeling. I have none at all on the present occasion. I shall proceed, and, at the proper time, and, I trust, in the proper manner, give my answer to this proposition.

The Senator has introduced De Tocqueville as authority on this question; and, in order to give greater weight and lustre to this authority, has pronounced him superior to Montesquieu. Montesquieu was a profound thinker, and almost every sentence of his is an apothegm of wisdom. He has stood, and ever will stand, the test of time. I cannot compare De Tocqueville with Montesquieu. I think he himself would blush at such a comparison.

I may truly say that I have never met any Frenchman or Englishman who could understand the complicated relations existing between our Federal and State Governments. In this respect, De Tocqueville has not succeeded much 402better than the rest. I am disposed to quarrel with him for one thing, and that is, that he is opposed to the doctrines of the Virginia and Kentucky resolutions. He is one of those old Federalists, in the true acceptation of that term, who believe that the powers of the General Government are not sufficiently strong to protect it from the encroachment of the States. Hence one great object of his book is to prove that this Government is becoming weaker and weaker, whilst that of the States is growing stronger and stronger; and although he does not think the time near, yet the final catastrophe must be, that it will be dissolved by its own weakness, and the people at length, tired of the perpetual struggles of liberty, will finally seek repose in the arms of despotism. This result, in his opinion, is not to be brought about by the strength, but by the weakness, of the Federal Government. I might adduce many quotations to this effect from his book, but I shall trouble the Senate with but a few. He says, in summing up a long chapter on this subject, "I am strangely mistaken if the Federal Government of the United States be not constantly losing strength, retiring gradually from public affairs, and narrowing its circle of action more and more. It is naturally feeble, but it now abandons even its pretensions to strength. On the other hand, I thought that I remarked a more lively sense of independence, and a more decided attachment to provincial government, in the States. The Union is to subsist, but to subsist as a shadow; it is to be strong in certain cases, and weak in all others; in time of warfare it is to be able to concentrate all the forces of the nation, and all the resources of the country in its hands; and in time of peace its existence is to be scarcely perceptible, as if this alternate debility and vigor were natural or possible."

"I do not foresee anything for the present which may be able to check this general impulse of public opinion; the causes in which it originated do not cease to operate with the same effect. The change will therefore go on, and it may be predicted that, unless some extraordinary event occurs, the Government of the Union will grow weaker and weaker every day." Again: "So far is the Federal Government from acquiring strength and from threatening the sovereignty of the States, as it grows older, that I maintain it to be growing weaker and weaker, and that the sovereignty of the Union alone is in danger." And again: "It may, however, be foreseen even now, that when the Americans lose their Republican institutions, they will speedily arrive at a despotic government, without a long interval of limited monarchy."

Speaking of the power of the President, he says: "Hitherto no citizen has shown any disposition to expose his honor and his life, in order to become the President of the United States, because the power of that office is temporary, limited and subordinate. The prize of fortune must be great to encourage adventurers in so desperate a game. No candidate has as yet been able to arouse the dangerous enthusiasm or the passionate sympathies of the people in his favor, for the very simple reason, that when he is at the head of the Government he has but little power, but little wealth, and but little glory to share amongst his friends; and his influence in the State is too small for the 403success or the ruin of a faction to depend upon the elevation of an individual to power."

Now, if this greater than Montesquieu is to be believed, and his authority is to be relied on by the Senator from Virginia, whence his terror and alarm lest the power of the President might be strengthened by the influence of the lower class of federal office holders at elections? Why should they be deprived of the freedom of speech and of the press, upon the principle that the power of Mr. Van Buren is dangerous to the liberties of his country? The gentleman's lauded authority is entirely against his own position. Now, for my own part, I differ altogether from De Tocqueville. Although I do not believe that the power and patronage of the President can with any, even the least, justice be compared with that of the King of England, yet from the very nature of things, from the rapid increase of our population, from the number of new States, from our growing revenue and expenditures, from the additional number of officers necessary to conduct the affairs of the Government, and from many other causes which I might enumerate, I am convinced that the Federal Executive is becoming stronger and stronger. Rest assured he is not that feeble thing which De Tocqueville represents him to be. Federal power ought always to be watched with vigilant jealousy, not with unjust suspicion. It ought never to be extended by the creation of new offices, except they are absolutely necessary for the transaction of the public business.

The Whigs will be astonished to learn that, in the opinion of this author, General Jackson has greatly contributed, not to strengthen, but to weaken federal power. "Far from wishing to extend it," says he; "the President belongs to the party which is desirous of limiting that power to the bare and precise letter of the Constitution, and which never puts a construction upon that act favorable to the Government of the Union; far from standing forth as the champion of centralization, General Jackson is the agent of all the jealousies of the States; and he was placed in the lofty situation he occupies by the passions of the people which are most opposed to the central Government." He states the means adopted by this illustrious man for destroying his own power. They are: 1. Putting down internal improvements. 2. Abandoning the Indians to the legislative tyranny of the States. 3. Destroying the Bank of the United States. 4. Yielding up the tariff as a sacrifice to appease South Carolina. In this list, he mentions the abandonment by Congress of the proceeds of the sales of the public land to the new States to satisfy their importunity. These States will be astonished to learn that Mr. Clay's land bill, to which they were so violently opposed, gave them the greatest part of the revenue derived from this source; and my friend from Missouri [Mr. Benton] will doubtless be much disappointed to hear that President Jackson had completely adopted the principles of this bill. De Tocqueville has communicated this information to us, and he is high authority. Hear him: "Congress," says he, "has gone on to sell, for the profit of the nation at large, the uncultivated lands which those new States contained. But the latter at length asserted that, as they were now fully constituted, they ought 404to enjoy the exclusive right of converting the produce of these sales to their own use. As their remonstrances became more and more threatening, Congress thought fit to deprive the Union of a portion of the privileges which it had hitherto enjoyed; and, at the end of 1832, it passed a law by which the greatest part of the revenue derived from the sale of lands was made over to the new western republics, although the lands themselves were not ceded to them." And, in a note to this passage, the author says: "It is true that the President refused his assent to this law; but he completely adopted it in principle. See message of 8th December, 1833."

Here, sir, is a fair sample of the information which passes current in Europe in regard to us and our institutions, and this proceeds from the modern Montesquieu! Had he been a genuine Montesquieu, I think he would have said, General Jackson has strengthened the Federal Government by arresting it in its career of usurpation, and bringing it back to its ancient constitutional course. Thus all danger of collision, or even of jealousy, between it and the States has been avoided; and within its appropriate sphere, every clog has been removed from its vigorous action. It has thus become more powerful. Love of the Union is a sentiment deeply seated in the heart of every American. It grows with his growth, and strengthens with his strength; and never was it stronger than at the present moment. One great cause of this is, that General Jackson has denied himself every power not clearly granted by the Constitution; whilst he has, with a firmness and energy peculiar to himself, exerted all those which have been clearly conferred upon the General Government. But enough of this.

Now, sir, I cannot agree with the Senator from Virginia, according to the explanation which he has given, that there is greater danger of usurpation by an elective President, than by a limited hereditary monarch. His was an argument to prove that, in this respect, a limited monarchy has the advantage over our Republican form of Government. If this be true, then our Government, in one particular at least, is worse than that of England. Now, sir, upon what argument does the gentleman predicate this conclusion? Does he not perceive that it is upon an entire want of confidence in the people of the United States? He fears their feelings may become so enlisted in favor of some popular Chief Magistrate who has been elected by their suffrages—their passions may become so excited—that he may ride upon their backs into despotic power. Now, I do not believe any such thing. I feel the utmost confidence in the people. As long as they remain intelligent and virtuous, they will both be able and willing to defend their own cause, and protect their own liberties from the assaults of an usurper, whether they be open or disguised. Their passions will never drive them to commit suicide upon themselves. It is true the people may go wrong upon some questions. In my opinion, they have recently gone wrong in some of the States; but I rely upon their sober second thought to correct the evil. On a question, however, between liberty and slavery, until they are fit to be slaves, there can be no danger.

The Senator has expressed the opinion, with great confidence, that ours is a far stronger Executive Government than that of England; and has sustained this opinion by an enumeration of office holders, and an argument to which I shall not specially refer. Let any man institute a comparison between the two, and he will find that this is but the creation of a brilliant imagination. I got a friend in the library last evening to collect some statistical information for me on this subject. Even now, in the time of peace, the British army exceeds 101,000 men, including officers; and their vessels of war in commission are one hundred and ninety-one. How will our army of 12,000 men, and our navy consisting of twenty-six vessels in commission, compare with this array of force, and this source of patronage? The officers of the British army and navy, appointed by the crown, hold seats in Parliament, and engage actively in the business of electioneering. No law prohibits them from exerting their influence at elections; and the bill of the Senator from Kentucky, in this respect, bears a close resemblance to the act of Parliament. No jealousy is manifested in either towards the higher officers. It is only those of the humble class who are deprived of their rights.

On the 5th January, 1836, the public debt of Great Britain and Ireland amounted to £760,294,554 7s. 2-¾d. sterling, say, in round numbers, to thirty-six hundred millions of dollars. The interest of every man who owns any portion of this vast national debt is involved in and identified with the power of the British government. It is by the exertion of this power alone, that the annual interest upon his money can be collected from the people. In order to pay this interest and sustain the government, there was collected from the British people, in the form of customs and internal taxes, during the year ending on the 5th January, 1836, the sum of £52,589,992 4s. 6¼d. sterling; say, in round numbers, two hundred and fifty-two millions of dollars. What a vast field for patronage is here presented! How does our revenue, of some twenty or twenty-five millions of dollars, compare with this aggregate? Then there is the patronage attached to the East and West Indies, to the Canadas, and to British possessions scattered all over the earth. The government of England is a consolidated government. It is not like ours, composed of sovereign States, all whose domestic officers are appointed by State authority. The king is the exclusive fountain of office and of honors and of nobility throughout his vast dominions. What is the fact in regard to the General Government? With the exception of post officers, its patronage is almost exclusively confined to the appointment of custom-house officers along our maritime frontier, and land officers near our western limits. Throughout the vast intermediate space, a man may grow old without ever seeing a federal civil officer, unless it be a postmaster. I adduce these facts for the purpose, not of proving that we ought not to exercise a wholesome jealousy towards the Federal Government, but for that of showing how unjust it is to compare the power and patronage of the President of the United States with that of the king of England. You might as well compare the twinkling of the most distant star in the firmament of heaven with the blaze of the meridian sun. May this ever continue to be the case!

I will tell the Senator from Kentucky how far I am willing to proceed with him in punishing public officers. If a postmaster will abuse his franking privilege, as I know to my sorrow has been done in some instances, by converting it into the means of flooding the surrounding country, with base libels in the form of electioneering pamphlets and handbills, let such an officer be instantly dismissed and punished. If any district attorney should either favor or oppress debtors to Government, for the purpose of promoting the interest of his party, he ought to share a similar fate. So if a collector will grant privileges in the execution of his office to one importer, which he denies to another, in order to subserve the views of his party, he ought to be dismissed from office and punished for his offence. I would not tolerate any such official misconduct. But whilst a man faithfully and impartially discharges all the duties of his office, let him not be punished for expressing his opinion in regard to the merits or demerits of any candidate. Above all, let us not violate the Constitution, in order to punish an officer.

The Senator from Virginia has of late appealed to us often to rise above mere party, and to go for our country. Such appeals are not calculated to produce any deep impression on my mind; because, in supporting my party, I honestly believe I am, in the best manner, promoting the interest of my country. I am, but I trust not servilely, a party man. I support the present President, not because I think him the wisest or best man alive, but because he is the faithful and able representative of my principles. As long as he shall continue to maintain these principles, he shall receive my cordial support; but not one moment longer. I do not oppose my friends on this side of the House because I entertain unkind feelings towards them personally. On the contrary, I esteem and respect many of them highly. It is against the political principles of which they are the exponents, that I make war.

I support the President, because he is in favor of a strict and limited construction of the Constitution, according to the true spirit of the Virginia and Kentucky resolutions. I firmly believe that if this Government is to remain powerful and permanent, it can only be by never assuming doubtful powers, which must necessarily bring it into collision with the States. It is not difficult to foresee what would be the termination of such a career of usurpation on the rights of the States.

I oppose the Whig party, because, according to their reading of the Constitution, Congress possess, and they think ought to exercise, powers which would endanger the rights of the States and the liberties of the people. Such a free construction of the Constitution as can derive from the simple power "to lay and collect taxes," that of creating a National Bank, appears to me to be fraught with imminent danger to the country. I am opposed to the party so liberal in their construction of the Constitution, as to infer the existence of a power in the Federal Government to create and circulate a paper currency for the whole Union, from the clause which merely authorizes Congress "to 407regulate commerce with foreign nations and among the several States, and with the Indian tribes." Such constructions would establish precedents which might call into existence other alien and sedition laws; and it is such a construction which has given birth to the bill now before the Senate, denying the freedom of speech and of the press to a respectable portion of our citizens.

Should the time ever arrive when these principles shall be carried into practice, and when the Federal Government shall control the whole paper system of the country, either by the agency of a National Bank, or an immediate issue of its own paper, our liberties will then be in the greatest danger. In addition to the constitutional patronage of the President, confer upon him the influence which would result from the establishment of a National Bank, and you may make him too powerful for the people. Such a bank, spreading its branches into every State, controlling all the State institutions, and able to destroy any of them at pleasure, would be a fearful engine of executive power. It would indissolubly connect the money power with the power of the Federal Government; and such an union might, I fear, prove irresistible. The people of the States might still continue to exercise the right of suffrage; all the forms of the Constitution might be preserved, and they might delude themselves with the idea that they were yet free, whilst the moneyed influence had insinuated itself into the very vitals of the State, and was covertly controlling every election.

The personal attachment which bound to General Jackson the most distinguished men of his own party was compounded of something better than a sordid love of office. To them he was always "the old hero." He was their political chief, and to follow him was of the essence of patriotism. They might sometimes doubt the wisdom of his measures; but they surrendered their own judgments to his, not, as their political adversaries charged, from a slavish fear, but because they regarded him as a great man, honestly and resolutely bent on serving his country. They knew, as well as his opponents, that he had an imperious will. But they knew him better than opponents who never approached him, who held themselves aloof from all contact with his mind, and who formed their ideas of his character from the stories that told how illiterate he was; how he never wrote his State papers; how ignorant he was of constitutional law; how he gave way to his passions, and swore "by the Eternal." In nothing was the devotion of the leading men of his party to Jackson more fervid, more constant, and more true to their sense of public duty than it was in his warfare against the bank. In the whole of that 408conflict, in its progress and in its close, a band of men, who numbered among them the strongest intellects of the party, stood by him without the smallest sign of flinching. Some defections there were, but the seceders were not persons of much importance. The great body of his strongest supporters shared in his triumphs over the bank, and to the end of their lives it was to them a victory over a monster, as worthy of everlasting commemoration as the victory of St. Michael over the dragon.

In the opposite party convictions were not less strong, and in that party were some of the foremost minds of the age. As a parliamentary leader, Mr. Clay has been equalled by no man in our political history. With a personal fascination and a persuasive eloquence, he united a temper as dictatorial as Jackson's; and if he had ever become President, he would, probably, have been as tyrannical as he was accustomed to say and as many believed that Jackson was. The massive logic of Webster; his profound knowledge of our constitutional system and of political history; his full equipment in the accomplishments of a statesman; his careful and comprehensive study of every public question on which he had to act; his vast reputation and his majestic presence made him a far more formidable adversary of the administration than Mr. Clay ever was. Clay had never rendered a service comparable to Webster's defence of the Constitution against the Nullifiers and his patriotic support of General Jackson's measures in assertion of its authority. In all the political tactics of Mr. Clay—even in his "compromise tariff," by which he saved Mr. Calhoun and his followers from a great personal humiliation, and from a serious peril which they brought upon themselves—the public suspected, or believed that there might be reason to suspect, some personal motive. Webster, although as anxious to be President as Clay, although, like his great rival, ambitious in that lofty sense of ambition which consists in the desire to render eminent services to one's country in the highest attainable position, had more than once in the course of his public life given proof that he could rise above party or personal objects, and could support the measures of an administration when he approved of them, and yet refrain from going over to a party against whose course 409in other respects he was bound by his convictions to exert his utmost resistance.

Around each of these two prominent leaders of the Whig party was gathered a body of able men, who were so far united as the bond of thinking alike concerning the Republic can unite a political party, but who, in consequence of the rivalry between their respective chiefs, were never held together so compactly as their opponents, the followers of Jackson. Perhaps Mr. Clay was more fortunate in securing and holding the personal attachment of a larger number of political friends than Mr. Webster. Twice was Clay made the candidate of his party; twice was he magnanimously and vigorously supported by Webster's powerful aid; and twice he was defeated, the first time by Jackson, in 1832, and the second time by Polk, in 1844. In the interim between these two elections, namely, in 1836 and 1840, the Whig party, mainly in consequence of the unreconciled claims of its two greatest statesmen, resorted to a candidate who was personally and politically insignificant, but whom they succeeded in electing in 1840 through the circumstances of the time. But at the period of General Jackson's second Presidency, the great Whig opposition was firmly united against all his measures respecting the bank and the currency. It was a period when the leading men on all sides were governed by convictions to a very remarkable degree, notwithstanding the influence which the love of office or the desire for it exerted throughout the inferior ranks of politicians in both parties; and among the Whigs the opinion which held the financial measures of General Jackson to be most injurious to the country, was not less strong and sincere than was the belief of his supporters, that the destruction of the bank was necessary to the public welfare.

After Mr. Buchanan entered the Senate, he became conspicuous among the defenders of Jackson's financial measures. History, however fairly written, must leave it an undecided question, whether the evils and sufferings produced by Jackson's hostility to the bank were, in the long run, compensated by its destruction, and by the establishment of the doctrine that such an institution must not be allowed to exist. To one generation at least they were not compensated. It was impossible that the 410connection between the Government and the bank should be severed, as it was severed by Jackson, and be followed by the measures to which he resorted, without causing a wide-spread financial disaster, the bankruptcy and ruin of thousands, and inextricable embarrassment to the Government itself. But it is sufficient for the present purpose to describe the situation in which Jackson left the affairs of the country to his successor, and the troubles through which Mr. Van Buren and his political friends had to grope their way towards a definite solution of the true relation between the Government of the United States and the currency. A short retrospect into the history of the bank will develop the principal grounds of General Jackson's hostility to it.

There would seem to have been no reason, a priori, why the United States, if regarded simply as a nation, should not have a National Bank, to perform the same kind of functions that have been performed by similar institutions in other countries. In the luminous report made by Alexander Hamilton in December, 1790, on a National Bank, he set forth, with his accustomed ability, the advantage of having one fiscal corporation, which could act as the depositary of the public funds, transfer them from place to place as they are wanted at far distant points, enable the Government to borrow money, and furnish, under proper safeguards, a paper circulation of equally recognized value and security throughout the Union, thus increasing the amount of money available for the uses of legitimate business, and the means of effecting exchanges.[55] That the Bank of the United States, chartered by Congress in 1816, had down to the year 1833 well fulfilled these functions, there 411could be little doubt. But under the Constitution of the United States, which had established a government of enumerated and limited powers, there had always been a question whether Congress possessed authority to create such a fiscal corporation.

This question involved the fundamental rule of interpretation that ought to be applied to the powers of the Constitution:—a rule on which statesmen had differed from the day of its inauguration, and which came to be the most important dividing line between political parties, as soon as parties were formed. The chief canon of interpretation that was acted upon by those who shaped the measures of Washington's administration, and to which the sanction of his great name was given by his signature of the first charter of a national bank, was that the express and enumerated powers of the Constitution were described in general terms, for the accomplishment of certain great objects of national concern; and that whatever particular powers are necessary as means to the full execution of the general powers described in the instrument, are to be rightfully regarded as having been granted to Congress, because they were included by an implication, without which the principal powers would be nugatory. This, it was contended, would have been a necessary and logical deduction, even if the Constitution itself had not contained a clause defining the scope of the legislative power of Congress, applicable to all the general powers enumerated in the previous recitals. But with this clause, granting to Congress authority "to make all laws which shall be necessary and proper for carrying into execution the foregoing powers, and all other powers vested by this Constitution in the Government of the United States, or in any Department or officer thereof," it was claimed that Congress had ample scope for a choice of means in the execution of every enumerated power granted by the Constitution. Hence arose the doctrine of what have been called "implied powers," namely, those powers of government which result by implication from the grant of authority over certain subjects, and which, from the nature of political sovereignty, may be employed in the accomplishment of any object over which that sovereignty extends. It was not denied that the means resorted to in the exercise of an implied power must have a relation, as a means, to one or more of the 412express powers of the Constitution as its end. By the "strict constructionists," however, it was claimed, first, that the doctrine of implied powers was too broad to be allowed to a government of a special and limited character; secondly, that the Constitution itself did not grant an unlimited choice of means or instruments for the execution of its enumerated powers, but confined the choice to such as are "necessary and proper," terms that imported a restriction to those means which are indispensable in fact to the attainment of the end. In reply, it was contended by the advocates of the doctrine of implied powers that the terms "necessary and proper" did not import that the particular means employed should be so indispensable to the execution of some granted authority that the authority could not be exercised without resorting to that means; but that any means could be resorted to, which, in the exercise of a sound legislative discretion, might be found to be appropriate, convenient and conducive to the end. Such, it was argued, was the relation between a bank and certain of the express powers of the Constitution.

Satisfied by the powerful intellect and luminous pen of Hamilton that this was a correct construction of the Constitution, Washington, on the 25th of February, 1791, approved the bill which chartered the first Bank of the United States. The paper drawn up by Mr. Jefferson, on the same occasion, controverted the doctrine of implied powers with singular acuteness, and embodied those stricter principles of constitutional interpretation for which the party that he afterwards founded, and that which claimed to be its political successors, have generally contended.[56]

The charter of the first Bank of the United States expired in the year 1811, and those who had originally opposed it then defeated a bill for its renewal. In 1814–15, during the administration of Mr. Madison, while we were engaged in the war with England, it was supposed that the exigencies of the country required a national bank. A bill to create one was passed by the two houses, in January, 1815, but it was "vetoed" by Mr. Madison, and was not passed over his veto. His objections 413related to the details of the charter. As to the constitutional power to create a national bank, he considered that the repeated acts of all branches of the Government and a concurrence of the general will of the nation, had settled the question, although his personal opinion was adverse to the power. But in 1816, a new charter, which incorporated the last Bank of the United States, was passed by both houses and received the signature of Mr. Madison. This charter was limited to twenty years, and was consequently to expire in 1836.[57] In 1819 the question of its constitutional validity came before the Supreme Court of the United States, and the great mind of Chief Justice Marshall formulated in a judicial decision the doctrine of implied powers, and the bank was declared to be an instrument to which Congress could legitimately resort for the execution of certain of the powers enumerated in the Constitution.[58]

When President Jackson, in 1832, vetoed a bill for renewing the charter of the bank, it might, perhaps, have been wiser for him to have acquiesced, as Mr. Madison did, in the weight of authority and precedent on the question of constitutional power, especially since that weight had been greatly augmented by the decision of the Supreme Court. It was doubtless then, as it always must be, a delicate question whether a President is officially bound, in approving laws, by the opinion of the Judicial Department that such laws are constitutional. General Jackson considered that in his legislative capacity he was not so bound, but that while it was his duty to give due consideration to the reasoning on which the judicial decision rested, it was equally his duty to exercise his own judgment, upon a question of constitutional power, when asked to approve of a law. All his personal convictions, and the convictions of his official advisers, were adverse to the construction on which the constitutional validity of the bank charter depended; and perhaps he and they, believing that the bank, with a large capital and with certain practical powers over the whole paper circulation of the country, had entered the political field in hostility to his administration, did not choose to forego the use of any 414weapon that could be wielded against it. Aside from his personal interests as a candidate for re-election, it is but justice to believe that he honestly regarded the bank as a dangerous institution, and that he discerned, or thought he discerned, that the constitutional objection was the strongest club with which the Hydra could be assailed. In choosing this weapon, however, as his principal reliance, he enabled his opponents to represent him as a man who chose to set up his own arbitrary will against the judgment of two Congresses, two Presidents of great authority, the Supreme Court of the United States and the general acquiescence of the nation for a period of twenty years, on a question of constitutional construction. Had he placed his veto upon the renewal of its charter on grounds of expediency alone, the bank might have been compelled to wind up its concerns in a manner that would have produced less mischievous consequences to the country than those which ensued.

His next step, the removal from the bank of the public deposits, in the summer of 1833, followed by his selection of certain State banks as the keepers of the public money, and, to a certain extent, as the fiscal agents of the Government, led to a singular train of evils. Doubtless an institution, whose legal existence was to expire in three years, and which could not obtain from Congress a prolongation of its charter without using its power as a moneyed corporation to affect the politics of the country, had by this time become an unfit custodian of the public funds. Still, there was no sufficient warrant of law for placing the public funds in the custody of State banks, at the time when they were so transferred, nor had any system been matured by the executive for the consideration of Congress, which might furnish a substitute for that which had been in operation so long. The selection of certain State banks as the depositaries of the public money, was a tentative experiment, through which the country had to pass, with various disasters, before any safe and efficient substitute could be found.

The immediate effect of the withdrawal of the Government funds from the Bank of the United States, was a diminution of its loans and a consequent contraction of the currency. The immediate effect of placing those funds in a few selected State banks, was a wild speculation by their managers and other favored individuals, leading to their ruin. The assembling of Congress in December, 1833, was followed by Mr. Clay's attack upon the President, and a session through which the Senate was constantly engaged in the discussion of questions growing out of the situation in which the Government, the country, the Bank of the United States and the State banks had been placed by the executive. At length the Whigs forced from the friends of the administration a disclosure of the President's purpose to keep the public moneys in the State banks, to collect the public revenues through their agency, not to have any present legislation on the subject, and not to allow another national bank of any kind to be created. The adoption of Mr. Clay's resolutions censuring the President was followed, on the 17th of April, 1834, by the President's Protest, a document of singular ability and dignity, setting forth his views of the executive authority over all public officers, including the Secretary of the Treasury, in relation to the custody of the public funds. The Whig majority of the Senate recorded their rejection of these doctrines; but as the administration held a majority in the House of Representatives, the session terminated without any legislation to control in any way the financial experiment which the President had determined should be tried.

In the session which began in December, 1834, when Mr. Buchanan entered the Senate, the Whig majority was still unchanged, but it was destined to be overthrown by the effect of General Jackson's constantly increasing popularity and influence, which his conduct of the foreign relations of the country greatly tended to strengthen, while in domestic affairs a majority of the people, although beginning to suffer from his measures, still approved of his course in regard to the national bank. Nothing was done, however, at this session, to develope a more definite relation of the Government to the currency; it was a session in which both parties were much occupied with the selection of candidates for the Presidency. The result was, that with the aid of General Jackson's powerful influence, Mr. Van Buren became the Democratic candidate. In the autumn of 1836, he was elected by a majority of forty-six electoral votes, against General Harrison, the candidate of the Whigs.[59]

The last of the executive measures of General Jackson, in relation to the finances and monetary affairs of the country, was the so-called "Specie Circular," issued by the Secretary of the Treasury on the 11th of July, 1836. It directed that after a certain period, nothing but gold and silver should be received at the land offices in payment for the public lands. The purpose of this measure was to prevent payment for the public lands in the depreciated paper of the State banks. But in the actual condition of things, its effect was to draw the specie of the country into the vaults of the deposit banks, through the land offices; and as there was then no efficient means by which the Government could transfer its funds from place to place, as they were wanted, by any paper representative of money of equal credit through the Union, specie had to be moved to and fro in masses. The State banks which were not depositaries of the Government funds were thus weakened by the want of specie; they had to curtail their loans, and a great scarcity of money ensued in many quarters. Before Congress assembled in December the internal exchanges of the country were entirely deranged, and a general suspension of specie payments by the banks was not unlikely to take place in the not distant future.

It is not improbable that at this juncture the disasters which ensued in the next year might have been averted, if the political opponents of the administration on the one hand and its friends on the other could, by mutual concessions, have found a common ground of action. To remove the obnoxious Specie 417Circular was evidently necessary. A bill was passed for this purpose by the two houses, before the end of the session, but at so late a period that the President did not return it, and it failed to become a law. The two opposing parties might have agreed on some provision for the necessities of the Government and the wants of the people,—some mode of providing a regulator of the paper currency,—but for two great obstacles which kept them apart, the one of which was to a great extent the consequence of the other. In the large commercial cities, the principal merchants and bankers were still in favor of the establishment of a national bank, as the true remedy for existing disorders, and thence these classes almost universally acted with the Whigs. General Jackson had resolutely determined that no such institution should ever again be allowed to exist. Although, by the first use which he made of banking corporations in the fiscal concerns of the Government, he seemed to admit the power of the Government to create such corporations, his hostility to a national bank led him and his political friends to seek for the means of divorcing the fiscal concerns of the Government from all connection with banks of any kind, and to deny that the Government of the United States had any duty to perform towards the paper currency, or to provide any currency but gold and silver. Had not the question of a national bank, in consequence of the attitude of so many of the Whigs, entered largely into the issues of the approaching Presidential election, it is not improbable that the two parties, in the session of 1836-7, might have discovered and carried out some means of averting the catastrophe which followed the election. But the result was that General Jackson turned over the Government to his successor on the 4th of March, 1837, without anything having been done for the remedy of existing disorders, and with an imperative necessity for an extra session of Congress. It was summoned by Mr. Van Buren for the 4th of September, 1837. Before that day arrived, every bank in the country had ceased to pay specie.

418

CHAPTER XV.

1837—1841.

MR. VAN BUREN'S PRESIDENCY—THE FINANCIAL TROUBLES ACCUMULATING—REMEDY OF THE INDEPENDENT TREASURY—BUCHANAN ON THE CAUSES OF SPECIE SUSPENSION, AND THE PENNSYLVANIA BANK OF THE UNITED STATES—GREAT POLITICAL REVOLUTION OF 1840—BUCHANAN DECLINES A SEAT IN MR. VAN BUREN'S CABINET.

In the condition of things existing when the extra session of Congress, summoned by Mr. Van Buren, commenced (September, 1837), the immediate relief of the Government was the first necessity. The temporary expedient contemplated by the new administration, for this purpose, was to issue Treasury notes, to be used in paying the public creditors. For the permanent management of the public finances, it was proposed to make no further use of banks, but that the revenues of the Government should be deposited with certain officers of the Treasury, and be paid out to the public creditors on Treasury orders. This was the scheme which became afterwards expanded into the "Sub-Treasury." It was examined and opposed by Mr. Webster, in an elaborate speech, delivered on the 28th of

September, and on the 29th he was followed by Mr. Buchanan, in an equally extended and forcible discussion of the causes of the present distress, and the remedy that should be applied. These two speeches may be said to have exhausted the two sides of the main controversy between the opposite parties, in regard to the duty of the General Government to regulate the paper currency of the country, which then consisted of the notes of about eight hundred State banks. Such a discussion of course involved the disputed topics of those clauses of the Constitution from which the Whigs derived the power and deduced the duty of a general supervision over the paper circulation. Of Mr. Buchanan's reasoning on these subjects, 419it may be said with justice that, entering into direct controversy with Mr. Webster, he combated that eminent person's constitutional views with singular ability, and energetically defended what was derisively called "the new experiment," and was considered by the party of the administration as a divorce of the Government from all connection with banks. In conclusion he said:

Mr. Van Buren is not only correct in his statements of facts, but by his message he has for ever put to flight the charge of non-committalism—of want of decision and energy. He has assumed an attitude of moral grandeur before the American people, and has shown himself worthy to succeed General Jackson. He has elevated himself much in my own esteem. He has proved equal to the trying occasion. Even his political enemies, who cannot approve the doctrines of the message, admire its decided tone, and the ability with which it sustains what has been called the new experiment. And why should the sound of new experiments in Government grate so harshly upon the ears of the Senator from Massachusetts? Was not our Government itself, at its origin, a new and glorious experiment? Is it not now upon its trial? If it should continue to work as it has heretofore done, it will at least secure liberty to the human race, and rescue the rights of man, in every clime, from the grasp of tyrants. Still, it is, as yet, but an experiment. For its future success, it must depend upon the patriotism and the wisdom of the American people, and the Government of their choice. I sincerely believe that the establishment of the agencies which the bill proposes, will exert a most happy influence upon the success of our grand experiment, and that it will contribute, in no small degree, to the prosperous working of our institutions generally. The message will constitute the touchstone of political parties in this country for years to come; and I shall always be found ready to do battle in support of its doctrines, because their direct tendency is to keep the Federal Government within its proper limits, and to maintain the reserved rights of the States. To take care of our own money, through the agency of our own officers, without the employment of any banks, whether State or National, will, in my opinion, greatly contribute to these happy results, and in sustaining this policy, I feel confident I am advocating the true interest and the dearest rights of the people.

This allusion to the decision and energy which Mr. Van Buren had displayed in his message at the opening of the extra session, and which had raised him in Mr. Buchanan's esteem, implies that Mr. Buchanan had previously doubted about the course of the new President. The following letters from General Jackson show that he did not share those doubts.

420[GENERAL JACKSON TO MR. BUCHANAN.]

Hermitage, August 24, 1837.

My Dear Sir:-

Your much-esteemed favor of date July 28th last, has been too long neglected by me. It reached me in due course of mail and I intended replying to it immediately, but checkered health and a crowd of company interposed and prevented me that pleasure until now.

For your kind wishes, I tender you my sincere thanks—as to my fame, I rest it with my fellow-citizens—in their hands it is safe—posterity will do me justice.

The vile slanders that are heaped upon me by the calumniators of the day pass unheeded by me, and I trust will fall harmless at my feet.

What pleasure it affords to learn from you that the Keystone State of the Union are firmly united in the great Republican cause which now agitates the whole Union. This will give impulse throughout the Union to the Democratic cause, and the conflict now raging between the aristocracy of the few, aided by the banks and the paper-money credit system, against the democracy of numbers, will give a glorious triumph to Republican principles throughout our Union, and good old Republican Pennsylvania will be again hailed, as she deserves, the Keystone to our Republican arch and preserver of our glorious Union. I feel proud of her attitude, and my fervent prayers are that nothing may again occur to separate the Republican ranks, so as to give to the opposition or shinplaster party the ascendency. I feel to that State a debt of gratitude which I will cherish to my grave, and I shall ever delight in her prosperity.

I have no fears of the firmness of Mr. Van Buren; his message you will find, or my disappointment will be great, will meet the views and wishes of the great Democratic family of Pennsylvania; at present a temporizing policy would destroy him; I never knew it fail in destroying all who have adopted it. My motto is, to take principle for my guide to the public good. I have full confidence that Mr. Van Buren will adopt the same rule for his guide and all will be safe.

I have always opposed a union between Church and State. From the late combined treachery of the banks, in suspending specie payments in open violation of their charters and every honest and moral principle, and for the corrupt objects they must, from their acts, have had in view, I now think a union between banks and the Government is as dangerous as a union with the Church, and what condition would we now be in if engaged in a war with England? I trust Congress will keep this in view, and never permit the revenue of our country to be deposited with any but their own agents; it is collected by the agents of the Government, and why can it not be as safely kept and disbursed by her own agents under proper rules and restrictions by law? I can see none, nor can it add one grain of power to the executive branch more than it possesses at present; the agent can have as secure a 421deposit as any bank, and always at command by the Government to meet the appropriations by law; the revenue reduced to the wants of the Government never can be hoarded up, for as it comes in to-day, it will be disbursed to-morrow; and if all cash, no credits, will be more in favor of our home industry than all tariffs. This I hope will be recommended by the President and adopted by Congress, and then I will hail our Republic safe, and our Republican institutions permanent.

You will please pardon these hasty and crude hints. My family join me in kind salutations, and believe me your friend,

Andrew Jackson.

P. S.—Please let me occasionally hear from you.   A. J.

[JACKSON TO BUCHANAN.]

(Private.) Hermitage, December 26, 1837.

My Dear Sir:—

I have to offer you an apology for my neglect of not acknowledging sooner your kind and interesting letter of the 26th of October last, accompanied with yours and Mr. Wright's speeches on the subject of the divorce bill or sub-treasury system.

I have read these speeches with great attention and much pleasure; they give conclusive evidence of thorough knowledge of our Republican system and constitutional law, and must remain a lasting monument of the talents that made them, and they will become the text-book of the Republicans for all time to come. I regret very much that these speeches have not been more generally circulated through the South and West; they would have produced much good by enlightening the public mind.

I never for one moment distrusted the firmness of Mr. Van Buren, and I rejoice to see this confidence confirmed by his undeviating course. I have no fears of the Republic. The political tornado that has lately spread over the State of New York must have a vivifying effect upon the Republican cause. It will open the eyes of the people to the apostacy of the Conservatives, and prevent them from having the power to deceive hereafter, and will unite the Republicans from Maine to New Orleans.[60]

It has (with the exultations of the Whigs here and Mr. Bell's speech at Fanueil Hall) had a healing effect in Tennessee. The deluded White men are just awakening from their delusion, and now say, although they supported White, they can neither go for Webster nor Clay; that they have always been Republicans. The election of Mr. Foster instead of Bell to the Senate shows that Bell's popularity with the legislature is gone; and I am informed that the majority of the legislature regret the premature election of the Senator. I have no doubt but our next legislature will reverse the election of Senator, upon constitutional grounds; that there was no vacancy to fill, and none that could happen within the time for which the present legislature was elected to serve.

I hope the whole of the Republicans in Congress will rally with energy and firmness, and pass the divorce or sub-treasury bill into a law; there is no doubt of the fact that in the Senate the Republicans have a vast superiority in the argument; would to God we had equal talent in the House of Representatives. The great body of the people will support this measure, and the Conservatives will have to return to the Republican fold, or join the opposition; if they join the opposition, they then become harmless, and can no longer delude the people by their hypocrisy and apostacy. I am informed by a gentleman from Western Virginia, that Mr. Rives has, by his attitude, lost his political standing there, and Mr. Ritchie has lost his. I sincerely regret the attitude these two gentlemen have placed themselves in; common sense plainly proves that if the revenue is again placed in irresponsible State banks, after their late treachery and faithlessness to the Government, it will inevitably lead at last to the incorporation of a national bank. Can any patriot again place our revenue, on which depends our independence and safety in time of war, in the keeping of State or any other banks, over whom the Government have no control, and when the revenue might be most wanted to provide for defence, the banks might suspend, and compel the Government to make a dishonorable peace? I answer, no true patriot can advocate such a system, whatever might be his professions.

I am proud to see that the Keystone State is preparing for the struggle next October. I hope nothing may occur in the least to divide the Republican party; the opposition and some professed friends, but real apostates and hirelings of banks, will endeavor to divide the party, but I hope and trust union and harmony will prevail.

My health is improved, but my vision has failed me much; I hope it may improve. I write with great difficulty. My whole household joins me in kind regards and good wishes for your happiness. I will be happy to hear from you the prospects of the divorce passing in the Court House.

Your friend sincerely,
Andrew Jackson.
P.S.—We all present you with the joys of the season.

The bill to authorize the issue of treasury notes was passed at the extra session of Congress in 1836. The bill to establish the sub-treasury was passed in the Senate but failed in the House. The Bank of the United States, unable to obtain from Congress a prolongation of its charter, had procured a charter of incorporation from the Legislature of Pennsylvania. This new corporation became the assignee of the assets of the old one. It was now, therefore, in a singular and unprecedented 423attitude. As a Pennsylvania corporation, it had power to issue its own notes. As a trustee for winding up the affairs of the old corporation, it had in its possession the notes of the old bank. It re-issued these notes, without any authority to do so, used them in the Southern States, in exchange for the depreciated local currency, with which it bought cotton for exportation, or to pay its debts abroad, or purchased specie to replenish its vaults at home. It had thus created an obstacle to the resumption of specie payments. On the 23d of April, 1838, Mr. Buchanan made a very able speech in the Senate, in support of a bill to prevent the Pennsylvania Bank from re-issuing and circulating the notes of the old bank, giving the causes which produced the suspension of specie payments, and those which might affect a resumption. Mr. Buchanan said there was but one consideration which could induce him, at the present moment, to take any part in the discussion of the bill now before the Senate. He felt it to be his duty to defend the legislature of the State which he had, in part, the honor to represent, from the charge which had been made against them by the Senator from New Jersey [Mr. Wall] and other Senators, and by many of the public presses throughout the country, that, in rechartering the Bank of the United States, they had conferred upon it the powers of a great trading company. This charge was wholly unfounded in point of fact. The charter had not constituted it a trading company; and he felt himself bound to make the most solemn and public denial of that charge. If this bank had become the great cotton merchant which was represented, and he did not doubt the fact, it had acted in express violation of its charter. He therefore rose, not to criminate, but to defend the legislature of his native State.

The Democratic party of Pennsylvania had been, unfortunately, divided in 1835; and the consequence was the recharter of the Bank of the United States. Of the wisdom or policy of this measure (said Mr. B.) the Senate of the United States are not constituted the judges. I shall never discuss that question here. This is not the proper forum. I shall leave it to the sovereign people of the State. To them, and to them alone, are their representatives directly responsible for this recharter of the bank. As a citizen of the State, I have on all suitable occasions, both in public and in private, expressed my opinion boldly and freely upon the subject. In a letter from this city, dated on the 30th June, 1836, which was published throughout the State, I have presented my views in detail upon this question; and I feel no disposition to retract or recant a single sentiment which I then expressed. On the contrary, experience has only served to confirm my first convictions. My task is now much more agreeable. It is that of defending the very 424legislature who renewed the charter of the bank, from the charge which has been made and reïterated over and over again, here and throughout the country, of having created a vast corporation, with power to deal in cotton, or any other article of merchandise. A mere reference to the charter, will, of itself, establish my position. It leaves no room for argument or doubt. The rule of common reason, as well as of common law, is, that a corporation can exercise no power, except what has been expressly granted by its charter. The exercise of any other power is a mere naked usurpation. On the present occasion, however, I need not resort to this rule. The charter not only confers no such power of trading, but it contains an express prohibition against it. It was approved by the Governor on the 18th day of February, 1836, and the fifth fundamental article contains the following provision: "The said corporation shall not, directly or indirectly, deal or trade in any thing except bills of exchange, gold and silver bullion, or in the sale of goods really and truly pledged for money lent and not redeemed in due time, or goods which shall be the proceeds of its lands." In this particular, it is but a mere transcript from the charter granted to the late bank by Congress on the 10th of April, 1816, which was itself copied from the charter of the first Bank of the United States, established in the year 1791. I have not recently had an opportunity of examining the charter of the Bank of England, but I believe it contains a similar provision. The Senate will, therefore, at once perceive there is as little foundation for charging the legislature of Pennsylvania with conferring upon the existing bank the enormous powers of a great trading company, as there would have been for making a similar charge against the first or the last Congress which chartered a Bank of the United States. It is true that the bank, under its existing charter, can deal much more extensively in stocks than it could have done formerly; but this power does not touch the present question.

The bank, by becoming a merchant and dealing in cotton, has clearly violated its charter, and that, too, in a most essential particular. Either the legislature or the Governor may direct a scire facias to issue against it for this cause; and, if the fact be found by a jury, the Supreme Court of the State can exercise no discretion on the subject, but must, under the express terms of the act creating it, adjudge its charter to be forfeited and annulled. Whether the legislature or the Governor shall pursue this course, is for them, not for me, to decide. This bank has already so completely entwined itself around our system of internal improvements and common school education, that it doubtless believes it may violate its charter with impunity. Be this as it may, the sin of speculating in cotton lies at the door of the bank, and not at that of the legislature.

Heaven knows the legislature have been sufficiently liberal in conferring powers upon this institution; but I doubt whether a single member of that body would have voted to create a trading company, with a capital of $35,000,000, in union with banking privileges. Let us pause and reflect for a moment upon the nature and consequences of these combined powers. A bank of discount and circulation, with such an enormous capital, and a trading company united! By expanding or contracting its discounts and circulation, as a bank, it can render money plenty or money scarce, at its pleasure. It can thus raise or depress the price of cotton, or any other article, and make the market to suit its speculating purposes. The more derangement that exists in the domestic exchanges of the country, the larger will be its profits. The period of a suspension of specie payments is its best harvest, during which it can amass millions. It is clearly the interest of this bank, whatever may be its inclination, that specie payments should continue suspended, and the domestic exchanges should continue deranged as long as possible. The ruin of the country thus becomes its most abundant source of profit. Accordingly, what do we find to have been its course of policy? I have heard it described by several gentlemen from the South and Southwest, some of whom are members of this body. It has gone into that region of the Union with these resurrection notes of the old bank, the reissue of which this bill proposes to prohibit; and, in some States, it has exchanged them, the one-half for the depreciated local currency, and the other half for specie. With this local currency it has purchased cotton, and sent it to England for the purpose of paying its debts there, whilst with the specie it has replenished its vaults at home. In other States it has exchanged these dead notes of the old bank for the notes of the local banks, receiving a large premium on the transaction, and with the latter has purchased cotton on speculation. A general resumption of specie payments would at once put an end to this profitable traffic. It has, then, first violated the charter from Congress by reissuing the notes of the old bank, and then violating the charter from Pennsylvania by speculating in cotton. During the suspension of specie payments, these notes have been the only universal paper circulation throughout the country; and thus, by reissuing them, in defiance of the law, the present bank has been enabled to accumulate extravagant profits.

This charge against the bank of speculating in cotton has never, to my knowledge, been contradicted. We have heard it from the other side of the Atlantic, as well as from the South and Southwest. The Whig press of our country has commended, nay, almost glorified the bank for going into the cotton market, when that article was depressed, and making large purchases, and its friends in England have echoed these notes of praise. Its example has produced a new era in banking. We find that the Southern and Southwestern banks have also become cotton merchants; and, from present appearances, the trade in this great staple of our country is no longer to be conducted by private merchants, but by banking corporations.

Under this system, what will be the fate of your private merchants? This practice must be arrested, or they must all be ruined. The one or the other alternative is inevitable. What private individual can enter the cotton market in competition with the banks of the country? Individual enterprise can accomplish nothing in such a struggle. It would be the spear hurled by the feeble hand of the aged Priam, which scarce reached the buckler of the son of Achilles. The Bank of the United States which, according to the testimony of its president, might have destroyed, by an exertion of its power, almost every bank in the country, could, with much greater ease, destroy any private merchant who might dare to interfere with its speculations. Such a contest would be that of Hercules contending against an infant. It can acquire a monopoly against individual merchants in any branch of mercantile business in which it may engage; and, after having prostrated all competition, it can then regulate the price of any article of commerce according to its pleasure. I do not say that such is either its wish or its intention; but I mean thus to illustrate the vast and dangerous power which it may exercise as a merchant. The East India company monopolized the trade of Asia, but it possessed no banking powers. It could not, therefore, by curtailing or expanding its issues, make money scarce or make money plenty at pleasure, and thereby raise or depress the price of the articles in which it traded. In this respect its power as a merchant was inferior to that now exercised by the Bank of the United States.

How vain, then, I might almost say how ridiculous, is it for people of the South to make the attempt to establish merchants in the southern seaports for the purpose of conducting a direct trade with Europe in cotton and other articles of their production, in opposition to the Bank of the United States and their own local banks. This effort must fail, or the banks must cease to be merchants. I am glad to learn that, at the late Southern convention, this alarming usurpation by the banks of the appropriate business of the merchant has been viewed in its proper light. The time, I trust, is not far distant when they will be confined, by public opinion, to their appropriate sphere. What a fatal error it is for any free people, tempted by present and partial gain, to encourage and foster such institutions in a course which must, if pursued, inevitably crush the merchants of the country who conduct its foreign trade! As a class, these merchants are highly meritorious, and entitled to our support and protection against a power which, if suffered to be exerted, must inevitably destroy them.

Philadelphia is a city devoted to the interests of the bank; but even in that city, if it should undertake to speculate in flour, in coal, or in any other article which is poured into her market from the rich abundance of the State, such conduct would not be submitted to for a moment. The legislature of the State would at once interpose to protect our merchants.

Such an attempt would at once break the spell of bank influence. And yet it possesses no more power to deal in southern cotton than it does in Pennsylvania flour. It will remain a banker at home; whilst its mercantile speculations will be confined to the southern and southwestern provinces of its empire.

The reason will now, I think, appear manifest why the Parliament of Great Britain, the Congress of the United States, and the Legislature of Pennsylvania, have so strictly prohibited their banking institutions from dealing in any thing except bills of exchange and gold and silver bullion. If the Bank of England should dare to invade the province of the merchants and manufacturers of that country in a similar manner, the attempt would instantly be put down. Every man acquainted with the history and character of the people of England, knows that such would be the inevitable consequence. And yet this violation of law, on the part of the Bank of the United States, has been lauded in our free Republic.

As I am upon the floor, I shall proceed briefly to discuss the merits of the bill now before the Senate. It proposes to inflict a fine not exceeding ten thousand dollars, or imprisonment not less than one nor more than five years, or both such fine and imprisonment, at the discretion of the court, upon those who shall be convicted under its provisions. Against whom does it denounce these penalties? Against directors, officers, trustees, or agents of any corporation created by Congress, who, after its term of existence is ended, shall reissue the dead notes of the defunct corporation, and push them into the circulation of the country, in violation of its original charter. The bill embraces no person, acts upon no person, interferes with no person, except those whose duty it is, under the charter of the old bank, to redeem and cancel the old notes as they are presented for payment, and who, in violation of this duty, send them again into circulation.

This bill inflicts severe penalties, and, before we pass it, we ought to be entirely satisfied, first, that the guilt of the individuals who shall violate its provisions is sufficiently aggravated to justify the punishment; second, that the law will be politic in itself; and, third, that we possess the constitutional power to enact it.

First, then, as to the nature and aggravation of the offence. The charter of the late Bank of the United States expired, by its own limitation, on the 3d of March, 1836. After that day, it could issue no notes, discount no new paper, and exercise none of the usual functions of a bank. For two years thereafter, until the 3d of March, 1838, it was merely permitted to use its corporate name and capacity "for the purpose of suits for the final settlement and liquidation of the affairs and accounts of the corporation, and for the sale and disposition of their estate, real, personal, and mixed; but not for any other purpose, or in any other manner, whatsoever." Congress had granted the bank no power to make a voluntary assignment of its property to any corporation or any individual. On the contrary, the plain meaning of the charter was, that all the affairs of the institution should be wound up by its own president and directors. It received no authority to delegate this important trust to others; and yet what has it done? On the 2d day of March, 1836, one day before the charter had expired, this very president and these directors assigned all the property and effects of the old corporation to the Pennsylvania Bank of the United States. On this same day, this latter bank accepted the assignment, and agreed to "pay, satisfy and discharge all debts, contracts, and engagements, owing, entered into, or made by this [the old] bank, as the same shall become due and payable, and fulfil and execute all trusts and obligations whatsoever arising from its transactions, or from any of them, so that every creditor or rightful claimant shall be fully satisfied." By its own agreement, it has thus expressly created itself a trustee of the old bank. But this was not necessary to confer

312

upon it that character. By the bare act of accepting the assignment, it became responsible, under the laws of the land, for the performance of all the duties and trusts required by the old charter. Under the circumstances, it cannot make the slightest pretence of want of notice.

Having assumed this responsibility, the duty of the new bank was so plain that it could not have been mistaken. It had a double character to sustain. Under the charter from Pennsylvania, it became a new banking corporation; whilst, under the assignment from the old bank, it became a trustee to wind up the concerns of that institution. These two characters were in their nature separate and distinct, and never ought to have been blended. For each of these purposes it ought to have kept a separate set of books. Above all, as the privilege of circulating bank notes, and thus creating a paper currency, is that function of a bank which most deeply and vitally affects the community, the new bank ought to have canceled or destroyed all the notes of the old bank which it found in its possession on the 4th of March, 1836, and ought to have redeemed the remainder, at its counter, as they were demanded by the holders, and then destroyed them. This obligation no Senator has attempted to doubt, or to deny. But what was the course of the bank? It has grossly violated both the old and the new charter. It at once declared independence of both, and appropriated to itself all the notes of the old bank, not only those which were then still in circulation, but those which had been redeemed before it accepted the assignment, and were then lying dead in its vaults. I have now before me the first monthly statement which was ever made by the bank to the auditor general of Pennsylvania. It is dated on the 2d of April, 1836, and signed J. Cowperthwaite, acting cashier. In this statement the bank charges itself with "notes issued," $36,620,420.16; whilst in its cash account, along with its specie and the notes of State banks, it credits itself with "notes of the Bank of the United States and offices," on hand, $16,794,713.71. It thus seized these dead notes to the amount of $16,794,713.71, and transferred them into cash; whilst the difference between those on hand and those issued, equal to $19,854,706.45, was the circulation which the new bank boasted it had inherited from the old. It thus, in an instant, appropriated to itself, and adopted as its own circulation, all the notes and all the illegal branch drafts of the old bank which were then in existence. Its boldness was equal to its utter disregard of law. In this first return, it not only proclaimed to the legislature and people of Pennsylvania that it had disregarded its trust as assignee of the old bank, by seizing upon the whole of the old circulation and converting it to its own use, but that it had violated one of the fundamental provisions of its new charter.

In Pennsylvania we have, for many years past, deemed it wise to increase the specie basis of our paper circulation. We know that, under the universal law of currency, small notes and gold and silver coin of the same denomination cannot circulate together. The one will expel the other. Accordingly, 429it is now long since we prohibited our banks from issuing notes of a less denomination than five dollars. The legislature which rechartered the Bank of the United States, deemed it wise to proceed one step further in regard to this mammoth institution; and in that opinion I entirely concur. Accordingly, by the sixth fundamental article of its charter, they declare that "the notes and bills which shall be issued by order of said corporation, or under its authority, shall be binding upon it; and those made payable to order shall be assignable by endorsement, but none shall be issued of a denomination less than ten dollars."

Now, it is well known to every Senator within the sound of my voice, that a large proportion of these resurrection notes, as they have been aptly called, which have been issued and reissued by order of the new bank, are of the denomination of five dollars. Here, then, is a plain, palpable violation, not only of the spirit, but of the very letter of its charter. The Senate will perceive that the bank, as if to meet the very case, is not merely prohibited from issuing its own notes, signed by its own president and cashier, of a denomination less than ten dollars, but this prohibition is extended to the notes or bills which shall be issued by its order, or under its authority. If I should even be mistaken in this construction of the law, and I believe I am not, it would only follow that its conduct has not amounted to a legal forfeiture of its charter. In both cases the violation of the spirit of its charter, and the contravention of the wise policy of the legislature, are equally glaring. So entirely did the bank make these dead notes its own peculiar circulation, that until July last, in its monthly returns to the Auditor General of Pennsylvania, the new and the old notes are blended together, without any distinction. In that return we were, for the first time, officially informed that the bank had ever issued any notes of its own.

And here an incident occurs to me which will be an additional proof how lawless is this bank, whenever obedience to its charter interferes in the least degree with its policy. By the tenth fundamental article of that charter, it is required to "make to the Auditor General monthly returns of its condition, showing the details of its operations according to the forms of the returns the Bank of the United States now makes to the Secretary of the Treasury of the United States, or according to such form as may be established by law." From no idle curiosity, but from a desire to ascertain, as far as possible, the condition of the banks of the country, and the amount of their circulation, I requested the Auditor General, during the late special session of Congress in September, to send me the return of the bank for that month. In answer, he informed me, under date of the 22d of September, that the bank had not made any return to his office since the 15th of the preceding May. Thus, from the date of the suspension of specie payments until some time after the 22d of September last, how long I do not know, a period during which the public mind was most anxious on the subject, the bank put this provision of its charter at defiance. Whether it thus omitted its duty because at the date of the suspension of specie payments it had less than a million and a half of 430specie in its vaults, I shall not pretend to determine. If this were the reason, I have no doubt that it sent to the Auditor General all the intermediate monthly returns on the 2d of October, 1837, because at that period it had increased its gold and silver to more than three millions of dollars.

In order to illustrate the enormity of the offence now proposed to be punished, Senators have instituted several comparisons. No case which they have imagined equals the offence as it actually exists. Would it not, says one gentleman, be a flagrant breach of trust for an executor, entrusted with the settlement of his testator's estate, to reissue, and again put in circulation for his own benefit, the bills of exchange or promissory notes which he had found among the papers of the deceased, and which had been paid and extinguished in his lifetime? I answer, that it would. But, in that case, the imposition upon the community would necessarily be limited, whilst the means of detection would be ample. The same may be observed in regard to the case of the trustee, which has been suggested. What comparison do these cases bear to that of the conduct of the bank? The amount of its reissues of these dead notes of its testator is many millions. Their circulation is coextensive with the Union, and there is no possible means of detection. No man who receives this paper can tell whether it belongs to that class which the new bank originally found dead in its vaults, or to that which it has since redeemed and reissued, in violation of law; or to that which has remained circulating lawfully in the community, and has never been redeemed since the old charter expired. There is no earmark upon these notes. It is impossible to distinguish those which have been illegally reissued from the remainder.

I can imagine but one case which would present any thing like a parallel to the conduct of the bank. In October last, we authorized the issue of $10,000,000 of Treasury notes, and directed that when they were received in payment of the public dues, they should not be reissued, but be canceled. Now, suppose the Secretary of the Treasury had happened to be the president of a bank in this District, and, in that character, had reissued these dead treasury notes, which he ought to have canceled, and again put them into circulation, in violation of the law, then a case would exist which might be compared with that now before the Senate. If such a case should ever occur, would not the Secretary at once be impeached; and is there a Senator upon this floor, who would not pronounce him guilty? The pecuniary injury to the United States might be greater in the supposed than in the actual case; but the degree of moral guilt would be the same.

Whether it be politic to pass this law is a more doubtful question. Judging from past experience, the bank may openly violate its provisions with impunity. It can easily evade them by sending packages of these old notes to the South and Southwest, by its agents, there to be reissued by banks or individuals in its confidence. There is one fact, however, from which I am encouraged to hope that this law may prove effectual. No man on this floor has attempted to justify, or even to palliate, the conduct of the bank. Its best friends have not dared to utter a single word in its defence against this charge. The moral influence of their silence, and the open condemnation of its conduct by some of them, may induce the bank to obey the law.

I now approach the question—do Congress possess the power under the Constitution to pass this bill? In other words, have we power to restrain the trustees of our own bank from reissuing the old notes of that institution which have already been redeemed and ought to be destroyed? Can there be a doubt of the existence of this power? The bare statement of the question seems to me sufficient to remove every difficulty. It is almost too plain for argument. I should be glad if any gentleman would even prove this power to be doubtful. In that event I should refrain from its exercise. I am a State rights man, and in favor of a strict construction of the Constitution. The older I grow, and the more experience I acquire, the more deeply rooted does this doctrine become in my mind. I consider a strict construction of the Constitution necessary not only to the harmony which ought to exist between the Federal and State Governments, but to the perpetuation of the Union. I shall exercise no power which I do not consider clear. I call upon gentlemen, therefore, to break their determined silence upon this subject, and convince me even that the existence of the power is doubtful. If they do, I pledge myself to vote against the passage of the bill.

If this power could only be maintained by some of the arguments advanced by the friends of the bill, in the early part of this discussion, it never should receive my vote. Principles were then avowed scarcely less dangerous and unsound than the principle on which the Senator from Vermont (Mr. Prentiss) insists that the friends of the bill must claim this power. He contends that it does not exist at all, unless it be under that construction of the Constitution advocated by his friend from Massachusetts (Mr. Webster), which would give to Congress power over the whole paper currency of the country under the coining and commercial powers of the Constitution. The Senator from Connecticut (Mr. Niles) was the first in this debate who presented in bold relief the principle on which this bill can securely rest.

Neither shall I dodge this question, as some Senators have done, by taking shelter under the pretext that it is a question for the judiciary to decide, whether the general language of the bill be applicable to the officers of the Bank of the United States under the Pennsylvania charter. We all know that it was intended to embrace them. Indeed, it was their conduct, and that alone, which called this bill into existence. It is true that the provisions of the bill extend to all corporations created by Congress; but it is equally certain, that had it not been intended to apply to the Bank of the United States, it would have been confined in express terms to the District of Columbia, where alone corporations now exist under the authority of Congress. Away with all such subterfuges! I will have none of them.

Suppose, sir, that at any time within the period of two years thus allowed by the charter to the president and directors of the bank to wind up its affairs, these officers, created under your own authority, had attempted to throw thirty millions of dollars of their dead paper again into circulation, would you have had no power to pass a law to prevent and to punish such an atrocious fraud? Would you have been compelled to look on and patiently submit to such a violation of the charter which you had granted? Have you created an institution, and expressly limited its term of existence, which you cannot destroy after that term has expired? This would indeed be a political Hydra which must exist forever, without any Hercules to destroy it. If you possess no power to restrain the circulation of the notes of the old bank, they may continue to circulate forever in defiance of the power which called them into existence. You have created that which you have no power to destroy, although the law which gave it birth limited the term of its existence. Will any Senator contend that during these two years allowed by the charter for winding up the concerns of the bank, we possessed no power to restrain its president and directors from reissuing these old notes? There is no man on this floor bold enough to advance such a doctrine. This point being conceded, the power to pass the present bill follows as a necessary consequence.

If the president and directors of the old bank could not evade our authority, the next question is, whether, by assigning the property of the corporation to a trustee the day before the charter expired, and delivering up to him the old notes which ought to have been canceled, they were able to cut this trustee loose from the obligations which had been imposed upon them by the charter, and from the authority of Congress. Vain and impotent, indeed, would this Government be, if its authority could be set at nought by such a shallow contrivance. No, sir, the fountain cannot ascend beyond its source. The assignee in such a case is not released from any obligation which the assignor assumed by accepting the original charter. In regard to Congress, the trustee stands in the same situation with the president and directors of the old bank. We have the same power to compel him to wind up the concerns of the bank, according to the charter, that we might have exercised against those from whom he accepted the assignment. The question is too plain for argument.

The present case is still stronger than the one which I have presented. It is an assignment by the old Bank of the United States, not to strangers, not to third persons, but to themselves, in the new character conferred upon them by the legislature of Pennsylvania. This new charter expressly incorporates all the stockholders of the old bank, except the United States, so that the individuals composing both corporations were identical. For the purpose of effecting this transfer from themselves to themselves, they got up the machinery of one president and one board of directors for the old bank, and another president and another board of directors for the new bank. What kind of answer, then, would it be to Congress for them to say: True, we accepted a charter under your authority, by which we were bound to reissue none of our old notes after the 3d March, 1836, but we have since assumed a new character; and under our old character, we have transferred the bank which you created, to ourselves in our new character; and we have thus released ourselves from all our old obligations, and you have no constitutional power to enforce them against us? No sir, no sir; we have the power, and it is our duty, to compel the president and directors of the bank, which we established, or their assignees, to close its concerns; and this power will continue until the duty shall be finally accomplished. The one power is a necessary implication from the other. If this duty has not been performed within the two years which we have allowed for its fulfilment, our power depends not upon any such limitation, but upon the fact whether the concerns of the bank have been actually closed. If this were not the case, then all the affairs of the bank left unfinished at the end of these two years would be outlawed. This limitation was intended not to abridge the power of Congress, but to hasten the action of the president and directors in winding up the concerns of the bank. At this very session, and since the two years have expired, Congress has passed an act, without a shadow of opposition from any quarter, giving the president and directors of the old bank authority to prosecute and defend existing suits. I should be glad to see any Senator rise in his place, and make even a plausible argument in opposition to these plain and almost self-evident positions.

In this brief argument, I have not attempted to derive any power from the fact that the United States were proprietors of one-fifth of the stock of the old bank, and that they might be rendered responsible, either legally or equitably, for the eventual redemption of these dead notes. I disclaim any such source of power. To be a proprietor is one thing, and to be a sovereign is another. The mere fact that we owned stock can confer no power upon us, which we would not have possessed, had we never been interested to the amount of a dollar. We should have the same power to wind up a bank emanating from our sovereign authority in the one case as in the other. We possess the same power to close the concerns of all the banks in the District of Columbia after their charters shall have expired, although we are not proprietors of any of their stock, which we have to wind up the Bank of the United States, in which we were so deeply interested.

I need scarcely observe that I do not contend for any power to punish citizens of the United States, or even the officers of banking institutions, except such of them only as the trustees of the bank created by ourselves, for issuing these dead notes. We intend to punish the trustees under our own law, and them alone, for the violation of that law. These notes may circulate from hand to hand without rendering those who receive or those who pay them obnoxious to any punishment. Even if we possessed the power, it would be highly unjust to attempt its exercise. As I observed before, these notes have no earmarks, and no man can tell whether any one of them has been illegally reissued by the bank since the 3d March, 1836, or whether it was issued before that date, and has continued legally to circulate in the community ever since.

I repeat, I should be glad to see any Senator, and especially any one who believes that Congress possesses the constitutional power to charter a Bank of the United States, rise in his place, and make even a plausible argument in 434opposition to the plain and almost self-evident positions which I have taken in support of the power to pass this bill. Those Senators who doubt or deny our power to create such a bank are placed in a different situation, because their vote in favor of this bill might at first view seem, by implication, to concede that power. This objection does not appear to me to be sound. That question cannot be fairly raised by this bill. Whether the charter of the late bank was constitutional is no longer a fair subject of consideration. It was adopted by Congress, approved by the President, and afterwards pronounced to be constitutional by the highest judicial tribunal of the land. It thus received every sanction necessary to make it binding on the people of the United States. The question was thus settled beyond the control of any individual, and it was the duty of every good citizen to submit. Under every government there must be a time when such controversies shall cease; and you might now as well attempt to exclude Louisiana from the Union, because you may believe her admission was unconstitutional, as to act upon the principle, in the present case, that Congress had no power to charter the late bank. No man on this floor had ever avowed that he would vote to repeal the charter of the late bank, during the twenty years of its existence, because he might have thought it was originally unconstitutional. During this period all were obliged to submit. Under such circumstances, it would be carrying constitutional scruples very far, indeed, for any gentleman to contend that, although the bank has existed under the sanction of a law which we were all bound to obey, we cannot now execute that law and close its concerns, because as individuals we may have deemed it to be originally unconstitutional. If it had been so, the obligation upon us would only be the stronger to wind it up finally, and thus terminate its existence.

I most cheerfully admit that if an attempt should ever be made to charter another bank, the question of constitutional power would then again be referred to each individual member of Congress, to be decided according to the dictates of his own judgment and his own conscience.

Before I take my seat, I intend to make some remarks on the causes of the suspension of specie payments by the banks of the country, and the causes equally powerful which must, and that ere long, compel a resumption.

The late manifesto issued by the present Bank of the United States displays, upon its face, that it has inherited from the old bank an unconquerable disposition to interfere in the politics of the country. This has been its curse, its original sin, to which it owes all its calamities and all its misfortunes. It has not yet learned wisdom from its severe experience. Would that it might, and confine itself to its appropriate sphere! As a citizen of Pennsylvania, I most ardently and devoutly express this wish. It has now set itself up, as the primary power, against the resumption of specie payments, and has attempted to enlist in the same cause all the other banks of the country. Its language to them is, that "the Bank of the United States makes common cause with the other banks." And again: "They (the banks) are now safe and strong, 435and they should not venture beyond their entrenchments, while the enemy is in the plain before them." "The American banks should do, in short, what the American army did at New Orleans, stand fast behind their cotton bales, until the enemy has left the country."

Thus whilst every eye and every heart was directed to the banks, expecting anxiously from them a speedy resumption of specie payments, this grand regulator of the currency has proclaimed to the country that all its vast power will be exerted to prevent the accomplishment of our wishes.

The bank does not even attempt to conceal the fact that, in pursuing this course, it has been actuated by political hostility against the present administration. It has been boldly avowed that "if the banks resume, and are able, by sacrificing the community, to continue for a few months, it will be conclusively employed at the next elections to show that the schemes of the executive are not as destructive as they will prove hereafter." In plain language, the banks must not resume before the next elections; they must not open their vaults, pay their honest debts, and thus redeem the country from the curse of an irredeemable paper currency; because, if they should, this may operate in favor of the present administration, and place its opponents in a minority. And such is the conduct of the bank whilst it vaunts its own ability to resume immediately.

The bank proceeds still further, and complains that "bank notes are proscribed not merely from the land offices, but from all payments of every description to the Government." I would ask, has any Senator upon this floor, has any statesman of any party in the country, ever raised his voice in favor of the receipt by the Government of irredeemable bank paper? I beg their pardon; two Senators have proposed such a measure, [Messrs. Preston and Clay]; but I will do them the justice to say, that although I considered their proposition most unwise and impolitic, and resisted it as such at the time, yet they intended by this means to enable the banks the sooner to resume specie payments.

Mr. Preston. It was exclusively limited to that consideration.

Mr. Buchanan. Although the proposition was limited to the first of August, the Senators themselves upon reflection, thought it so improper that they abandoned it, and we have heard nothing of it since.

What would have been the condition of the country, at the present moment, had we received irredeemable bank notes in payments of the public dues? The banks, by our conduct, would have been encouraged to increase their discounts and expand their issues, and we should have gone from bad to worse, until, at this moment, we should have had no prospect of the resumption of specie payments. Mr. Cheves has informed us that if the Government had not stood firm in 1819 against the receipt of irredeemable notes, the banks would at that period have suspended. Much more necessary is it that we should now maintain the same ground, in order to secure a resumption. Had we pursued any other course, it is true we should have but one currency for the Government and the people; but it would have been currency 436of irredeemable bank rags, without the hope of a better. And yet the Bank of the United States complains that the Government does not receive such paper. In order to have done so, we must have repealed the existing laws upon the subject; and who has ventured to propose any such measure?

The Bank of the United States has succeeded, at the late bank convention in New York, in keeping its forces behind their cotton bales. The banks of only two States in the Union have voted against the resolution to suspend the resumption of specie payments until the first day of January next. These were New York and Mississippi; and whether the latter voted thus because their banks are ready now to resume, or desired to postpone resumption until a still more distant day, I shall not pretend to determine. After this display of power, no one will question the ability of the bank to keep its forces behind their entrenchments, unless they should be driven into the plain by the resistless power of public opinion.

Several weeks ago I attempted to imitate the illustrious examples which had been set before me on this floor, and became a political prophet. I then predicted that, before the close of the present year, commerce and manufactures would revive and flourish, and the country would be restored to its former prosperity. The signs of the times have already confirmed the truth of this prophecy. Encouraged by past experience, I shall venture to make another prediction: There is not a sound and solvent bank in any of the Atlantic States of this Union, including the Bank of the United States, which will not have resumed specie payments long before the first of January. All the opposition of the banks themselves cannot prevent this result. In the very nature of things it must come to pass. The power of public opinion is yet still greater in this country than that of the banks. The Bank of the United States will not be able to keep its forces behind their cotton bags until so late a period.

It is now too late in the day for us any longer to doubt what was the cause of the suspension of specie payments. That question has been settled on the other side as well as on this side of the Atlantic. Abundance of light has been shed upon this subject, and no two sound-judging men, at all acquainted with the facts, can arrive at different conclusions. It has already become history. And yet the bank, in its manifesto, has not once alluded to this cause. What was it? In the perpetual fluctuations which must ever be produced by our present banking system, unless it should be regulated by State legislation, of which I now almost despair, it was expanded in the commencement of the year 1837 almost to the point of explosion. The bubble is created, it expands, and reflects the most brilliant colors. Its admirers gaze upon it with hope and ecstasy, when, suddenly, it bursts, and leaves them in ruin and despair. Such has been the history of the past, and such will be that of the future. This expansion had produced, as it must ever produce, enormous speculation and over-trading. The commercial debt which we then owed to England for foreign merchandise was immense. We must have suffered the fatal collapse sooner or later, but a circumstance then occurred in England which at once produced the explosion. It was the spark applied to the magazine of gunpowder.

A similar state of expansion then existed in England. They were threatened with similar evils from extravagant bank credits, and their inevitable consequence—enormous speculation and over-trading. The Bank of England had in vain attempted to control the joint-stock banks, and confine them within reasonable limits. She at last became alarmed for her own safety. In the beginning of 1837 her stock of specie was reduced to about four millions of pounds sterling, or one-sixth of her circulation and deposits. This was not more than one-half of the proportion which, it is believed, she ought to have in order to render her secure. The state of the foreign exchanges was gradually withdrawing the remaining bullion from her vaults. At this crisis, under the influence of a panic, she withdrew her credits from the American houses in England, and ruined them. The price of cotton, in consequence, suddenly fell from nineteen and twenty cents to seven and eight cents per pound; and thus, according to the best and most discreet estimate which I have seen, we lost at least thirty million of dollars. The sum was thus, as it were in a single moment, abstracted from our means of paying the immense commercial balance against us. At the close of this disastrous operation, that balance was estimated at forty millions of dollars. What was the immediate consequence? A drain of specie then commenced from our banks for exportation, in order to pay this debt, and they were thus compelled to suspend or be ruined. Another circumstance existed to increase our embarrassments. Our merchants had drawn heavy bills upon England, predicated upon the cotton which they had shipped there, expecting to receive the old prices. In consequence of the sudden fall of prices, these bills were dishonored, and came back protested. Thus many of our largest mercantile houses were ruined.

The catastrophe proceeded from the same causes, and was similar in both countries, except that in England the banks were not compelled to suspend specie payments. The revenue of both has been insufficient to meet the current expenses of the Government, and each will be obliged to borrow nearly the same sum to supply the deficiency.

This is now history, which can neither be changed nor perverted. On both sides of the Atlantic all men of business and practical statesmen have come to the same conclusion. Away, then, with your Specie Circular, your mismanagement of the deposits, and your clamor raised by the executive against bank notes, as the causes of the suspension of specie payments. The bank calculates too much upon the political credulity of the people, when, at this late day, after the subject is perfectly understood, it attempts to palm off upon them such exploded reasons for the suspension. A convulsion which has shaken the commercial world to its centre, and has extended over three-quarters of the globe, could never spring from such trivial causes.

If the executive has been carrying on a war against the credit system of the country, and in favor of an exclusive metallic currency for the people of the United States, I am ignorant of the fact. I have never even suspected it. I believe this is a mere phantom which has been conjured up to alarm the fears of the timid. If the President ever should wage any such war, I shall not fight under his banner. The only pretext upon which this charge has been founded is, that he and his political friends desire to separate the business of the Treasury from that of the banks, not to render them hostile to each other. Until that propitious day shall arrive, we shall be forever agitated by the connection of the currency with our miserable party politics. Political panics, political pressures, charges against the Government for exercising an improper influence over the banks, and charges against the banks for interfering with the politics of the country; all, all which have kept us in a state of constant agitation for the last seven years will continue to exist, and will be brought into action upon every successive election for President and Vice President. We shall thus continue in a state of perpetual commotion; and the great interests of the country will be sacrificed. Let the Treasury and the banks part in peace, and whilst they are mutually independent, let them wage no war against each other; and I solemnly believe it would be the greatest blessing which could be conferred upon both parties. To this extent, I should go with the President if I had the power; but when I determine to obey instructions, I shall do it honestly and fairly. I shall, therefore, say no more on this subject.

It is true that at the special session I did endeavor to prove that the present banking system, under its existing regulations, was one of the very worst which the art of man could devise. Under it, ruinous expansions and revulsions must continue to succeed each other at stated periods, and many of the best and most enterprising men of the country must become its victims. I then expressed a hope, not unmingled with fear, that the State legislatures at their next session might impose wholesome restrictions upon their banking institutions—restrictions which would prove equally advantageous to the banks and the people. These legislatures have all now risen without prescribing any such regulations, and we are destined again and again to pass through the same vicissitudes which we have so often already witnessed.

The Whigs have always been exceedingly unlucky in regard to the time of these periodical revulsions, occasioned by excessive banking. They have either come too soon or too late to answer their political purposes. Had the suspension of specie payments occurred one year sooner than it did, the hero of Tippecanoe might have been the successor of the hero of New Orleans. But the revulsion came again at the wrong time; and long before the Presidential election of 1840, the country will again be prosperous. The effects of the suspension will have passed away, like the baseless fabric of a vision, without leaving a trace behind. Our late experience has been so severe, that the next bank explosion may possibly be postponed until the year 1844. Whom it may then benefit I know not, nor do I much care. One thing is certain, that these revulsions can never do anything but injury to the party in power. It is the nature of man to accuse the Government, or anything else, except his own misconduct, for his misfortunes.

439I now approach a much more agreeable part of my subject; and that is, to prove that the banks must and will speedily resume specie payments. I shall attempt to establish that now is the very time, the accepted time, the best time, and, within the period of a few months, the only time, when they can resume, without the least embarrassment. Some of the causes which will speedily effect this happy result, I shall enumerate.

In the first place, I shall do the banks of the country generally the justice to say, that since the suspension of specie payments they have curtailed their circulation and their loans to a great extent, and have done everything they reasonably could to atone for their past extravagance. The banks of Pennsylvania, including that of the United States, during a period of ten months, commencing in January, and ending in November, 1837, had reduced their circulation from twenty-five millions and a quarter to almost seventeen millions, and their discounts from eighty-six millions and a half to nearly seventy-one millions, whilst, during the same period, they had increased their specie from five millions and three-quarters to upwards of seven millions. From all I can learn, they have been since progressing at nearly the same rate, though I have not seen their official returns. The banks of other States have been generally pursuing the same course. The consequence is, that the confidence of the country in their banking institutions has been, in a great degree, restored. I feel convinced that if they should resume specie payments to-morrow, in the interior of Pennsylvania, at least, there would be no run upon them, except for as much silver change as might be required to supply the place of the miserable trash now in circulation under the denomination of shinplasters. Besides they would soon receive on deposit a greater amount from those who have been hoarding specie, under the belief that it would be safer at home than in the banks, and in the hope that they might hereafter use it to great advantage. No foreign demand now exists to drain the banks of their specie; on the contrary, the reflux tide has set in strongly, and is now wafting immense sums of gold and silver to our shores.

But, sir, another powerful cause of resumption exists. Our exports of cotton have, many months ago, paid our foreign commercial debt. Whilst that has been extinguished, the disastrous condition of our currency has reduced almost to nothing the orders of our merchants for foreign goods. Our imports are of small comparative value. In the mean time, our cotton crop of 1837 has been regularly and steadily seeking its accustomed markets in England and France. We have sold much, and bought little, and the balance in our favor is nearly all returning in specie. From the last English accounts which I have seen, the exports of specie from that country to this were still on the increase; and now, by almost every vessel from abroad which reaches our shores, we are receiving gold and silver. Specie, by the latest advices, was the most profitable means of remittance from England to the United States, yielding a profit of four per cent. When Congress met in September last, the rate of exchange against us on England was upwards of twenty per cent. It is now reduced to six per cent., which is three or 440four per cent. below the specie par. A great revolution in so short a period! It proves how vast are the resources of our country.

This great revolution has been effected by means of our cotton. The English manufacturers must have this article, or be ruined. This necessity has reversed the ordinary laws of trade, and the foreign market for it has remained firm and steady, although we bring home scarcely any equivalent, except in specie.

If a large portion of our cotton crop still remains unsold, so much the better. The golden tide will continue so much the longer to flow into our country. It is the policy of our banks to take it at the flood, and go on to fortune. If the banks do but seize the present golden opportunity, they will have completely fortified themselves before a reverse can come. This state of things cannot always continue. A reaction must occur. If the banks wait for the ebbing tide, and postpone a resumption until our merchants shall make heavy purchases abroad, and specie shall begin to be exported, they will then encounter difficulties which they need not now dread. I again repeat that this moment is the accepted time for the banks to resume.

But it is not only the ordinary laws of trade which are now bringing vast amounts of specie to our country. Two other causes are operating powerfully to produce this result. The conduct of the Bank of England, in arresting its credits to the American houses, which was the immediate cause of the suspension of specie payments, has been loudly condemned by men of all parties there. This measure has done that country nearly as much injury as it has done this, because England must always suffer from every derangement in our currency. The Bank is now conscious of this truth, and is retracing her steps. She has increased her stock of bullion between February, 1837, and March, 1838, from £4,032,090 to upwards of ten millions sterling. She is now strong, and it is her interest, as well as that of the people of England, that she should use this strength in assisting us to resume specie payments. Accordingly, she has, through the agency of one of our most intelligent and enterprising citizens, made an arrangement to furnish the banks of New York one million sterling in specie, to aid them in resuming payments in gold and silver. This million is now arriving, by instalments, in the United States. In resuming at the present moment, our banks have everything to hope, and nothing to fear, from England.

Again: The spirit of internal improvement is abroad throughout our land. States and private companies have loans to make for the purpose of erecting their public works. Money is now plenty in England, and is everywhere seeking an investment. The derangement in the business of that country has thrown capital out of employment. The rate of interest has been reduced to three and three and a half per cent. Their capitalists are anxious to make secure investments in loans to our different State governments, and incorporated companies, at a higher rate of interest than they can obtain at home. These loans are now being disposed of in England to a very large amount; and the greater proportion of their proceeds must return in specie to this country. Everything is propitious to an immediate resumption by our banks.

Will the Bank of the United States resume? I confess I do not doubt the fact. She has made a false movement, and it is the great prerogative of strength to acknowledge and retrieve an error. Her late manifesto against the resumption of specie payments has not found a single advocate on this floor. It has struck dumb all her friends. But yesterday she might have stood against the world. To-day there is none so poor as to do her reverence. Even those who must politically suffer by the resumption, because "it will be conclusively employed at the next elections, to show that the schemes of the executive are not so destructive as they will prove hereafter," have not dared to break a lance in her defence. This was not wont to be the case in days of yore, for hitherto her champions have been always ready to do battle in her cause. Notwithstanding all which has been said upon the subject, I am not one of those who believe that the Bank of the United States is not able to resume. Although the statement of her condition, as recently published, is not very flattering, yet her resources are vast. She is able if she were willing. Of this I cannot entertain a doubt.

Again: Will not the bank take compassion on the good city of Philadelphia, which has ever been devoted to its interest? Boston has been called the Athens of America; New York, the great Commercial Emporium; and Baltimore, the Monumental City; whilst Philadelphia has been distinguished by the name of the City of the Bank or marble palace; and well have her citizens earned this distinction by their loyalty. Will the bank now consent to see her commerce and trade languish, and her star wane before that of New York, rather than retrace its steps and resume specie payments? No, never. Forbid it, gratitude!

That this must be the effect, who can doubt? Merchants who come from a distance to purchase goods with money in hand will go where they can buy the cheapest; and goods at a specie standard must always be cheaper than in a depreciated currency. Those who have produce to sell, especially if the sale is to be made upon credit, will select that market where they will receive its price in a sound currency. Already the prospect of resumption in New York has made Philadelphia bank notes worth less by five per cent. than those of that city. What will this difference become when the one city shall have resumed, and the circulation of the other shall be irredeemable paper? Who that has money to remit or deposit will send it to Philadelphia, to be returned in notes depreciated to an extent which cannot be foreseen, when they can send it to New York with a perfect confidence that it will be returned to them according to the specie standard? Under such a state of things, the trade of New York must increase and flourish at the expense of that of Philadelphia. I have not time, at present, to enter into further particulars on this branch of the subject. The people of Pennsylvania have submitted patiently to the suspension of specie payments by their banks. They have bowed to the necessity which existed, and have treated them with kindness and generosity. The Bank of the United States has proclaimed its ability to resume, and our other banks are in the same situation. The necessity for a further suspension no longer exists. Pay your honest debts when you are able, is a maxim dear to the people of Pennsylvania. This duty has now become a question of morality, far transcending any question of policy. If these privileged corporations now any longer refuse to pay their honest debts, either for the sake of their own advantage, or from a desire to elevate one political party and depress another, the indignation of honest men, of all parties, will be roused against them. There will be a burst of popular feeling from our mountains and our valleys, which they will be compelled to respect. Thank God! public opinion in the interior of Pennsylvania is yet stronger than the money power. Our people will never submit to the degradation that their banks shall furnish them no currency but that of irredeemable paper; whilst, throughout the State of New York, the banks shall have resumed specie payments. Nothing could be more wounding to my own pride, as a Pennsylvanian.

If our banks should hold out, under the command of their great leader, until the first day of January next, many of them will never be able to resume. The public confidence, which their conduct since the suspension has hitherto inspired, will long ere that distant day cease to exist. No run would now be made on them in case they resume; but if they are forced into the measure by public opinion, after resisting as long as they can, the days of many of them will then be numbered. Honesty, duty, policy, all conspire to dictate to them a speedy resumption.

In conclusion, permit me to remark, that the people of the United States have abundant cause for the deepest gratitude towards that great and glorious man now in retirement for preventing the recharter of the Bank of the United States. He is emphatically the man of the age, and has left a deeper and more enduring impress upon it than any individual of our country. Still, in regard to the bank, he performed but half his work. For its completion we are indebted to the president of the bank. Had the bank confined itself, after it accepted the charter from Pennsylvania, to its mere banking and financial operations—had it exerted its power to regulate the domestic exchanges of the country—and, above all, had it taken the lead in the resumption of specie payments, a new bank, Phœnix-like, might have arisen from the ashes of the old. That danger, from present appearances, has now passed away. The open defiance of Congress by the bank—the laws of the country over and over again violated—its repeated attempts to interfere in the party politics of the day—all, all have taught the people the danger of such a vast moneyed corporation. Mr. Biddle has finished the work which General Jackson only commenced.

Not one particle of personal hostility towards that gentleman has been mingled in my discussion of the question. On the contrary, as a private gentleman, I respect him; and my personal intercourse with him, though not frequent, has been of the most agreeable character. I am always ready to do justice to his great and varied talents. I have spoken of the public conduct of the bank over which he presides with the freedom and boldness which I shall always exercise in the performance of my public duties. It is the president of the bank, not the man, that I have assailed. It is the nature of the institution over which he presides that has made him what he is. Like all other men, he must yield to his destiny. The possession of such vast and unlimited power, continued for a long period of years, would have turned the head of almost any other man, and have driven him to as great excesses.

In vain you may talk to me about paper restrictions in the charter of a bank of sufficient magnitude to be able to crush the other banks of the country. When did a vast moneyed monopoly ever regard the law, if any great interest of its own stood in the way? It will then violate its charter, and its own power will secure it impunity. It well knows that in its destruction the ruin of hundreds and thousands would be involved, and therefore it can do almost what it pleases. The history of the bank for several years past has been one continued history of violated laws, and of attempts to interfere in the politics of the country. Create another bank, and place any other man at its head, and the result will be the same. Such an institution will always hereafter prove too strong for the Government; because we cannot again expect to see, at least in our day, another Andrew Jackson in the Presidential chair. On the other hand, should such a bank, wielding the moneyed power of the country, form an alliance with the political power, and that is the natural position of the parties, their combined influence would govern the Union, and liberty might become an empty name.

Mr. Buchanan's Reply to Mr. Clay, on the same day.

Mr. Buchanan said he had never enjoyed many triumphs, and therefore he prized the more highly the one which he had won this day. He had forced the honorable Senator from Kentucky [Mr. Clay] to break that determined silence which had hitherto sealed his lips on the subject of this bill. Thus, said Mr. B., I have adorned my brow with a solitary sprig of laurel. Not one word was he to utter upon the present occasion. This he had announced publicly.

[Here Mr. Clay dissented.]

Mr. Buchanan. I thought he had announced the other day his determination not to debate the question, and stated this as the reason why he propounded to the Senator from New Jersey [Mr. Wall] the question whether, in his opinion, John Brockenbrough and Albert Gallatin could be constitutionally punished by Congress for re-issuing the old notes of the Bank of the United States.

[Mr. Clay again explained.]

Well, said Mr. Buchanan, the Senator did intend to address the Senate on this subject, and the only sprig of laurel which I ever expected to win from him has already withered. Yet still there was an evident reluctance on his 444part, which all must have observed, to enter into this contest. The Senator from Vermont [Mr. Prentiss] had made an able constitutional argument in opposition to the bill. With the exception of that gentleman, and the Senator from South Carolina (Mr. Preston), a profound silence had reigned on this (the Whig) side of the house. The question had been propounded by the Vice President, and the vote was about to be taken, when I rose and addressed the Senate. Immediately after I had taken my seat, the Senator from Kentucky sprang to his feet, and made one of his best speeches, for it belongs to the character of his mind to make the ablest efforts with the least preparation. I will venture to say he had not intended to make that speech when he entered the Senate chamber this morning.

[Mr. Clay admitted this to be the fact.]

Then, said Mr. Buchanan, I have succeeded, and my sprig of laurel is again green.

The gentleman says I may hang Nick Biddle, if I please; but I please to do no such thing. I would be sorry to subject him even to the punishment of imprisonment denounced by this bill; and if he should ever be convicted under its provisions, I hope the court may content itself with the infliction of a mere pecuniary fine. Hang Nick Biddle, indeed! I wish to keep him for the service of the Whig party, should they ever come into power.

The Senator from South Carolina [Mr. Preston] had said, at the extra session, that Mr. Biddle, if appointed Secretary of the Treasury, would, in thirty or sixty days, I forget which, heal all the disorders in the currency, and remove all the financial embarrassments of the Government. His appointment would prove a sovereign panacea for all existing evils. Now I go for this administration both from principle and inclination, and shall support the re-election of the present President; but if I were a Whig, the Senator from Kentucky would be my first choice. I should, therefore, be very sorry to deprive him of the services of Mr. Biddle, who will make, in the opinion of the Senator's friend from South Carolina, the very best Secretary of the Treasury in the whole country.

The Senator from Kentucky asks me why I do not defend Mr. Biddle, a distinguished citizen of my own State. My answer is at hand. I cannot defend his conduct as president of the bank, because I believe it to be wholly indefensible; and he has been attacked in no other character. I should have been proud and happy to undertake this task, could I have performed it consistently with my conscience. But why does the Senator propound such a question to me? I confidently expected Mr. Biddle would have been defended by a much more eloquent tongue. I defend him! when the eloquent gentlemen all around me are his own peculiar friends; and yet, strange to tell, not one of them has attempted to justify his conduct. "But yesterday he might have stood against the world." "He has fallen, fallen from his high estate." Whence this ominous silence? I wished to hear him defended, if it could be done, by gentlemen of his own political party, who have never hitherto shrunk from such a responsibility.

The Senator asserts that the Bank of the United States is no longer in existence. But are not the president, directors, and officers, the same that they were under the old charter? Has it not branch banks in at least two States—Louisiana and Georgia—and branch agencies scattered over the rest of the Union? And to render its continued existence still more palpable, has it not seized all the notes of the old bank, good, bad, and indifferent, and converted them to its own use? Why, sir, according to its very last return, it has but little more than three hundred thousand dollars of new notes in circulation, whilst the circulation of its old notes exceeds six millions. Is it not still diffusing its blessings and its benefits everywhere, in the opinion of its friends and admirers? Why has it not, then, proved to be the grand regulator of the currency, and prevented a suspension of specie payments? If that were impossible, why is it not, at least, the first among the banks to urge their resumption? Had it acted thus, it is possible it might have obtained another charter from Congress. But when we find not only that it could not save itself from the general crash, but that it is now the great leader in opposing a resumption of specie payments, we must lose our confidence in its power as a grand regulator.

But this bank, says the Senator, is a mere domestic institution of Pennsylvania. With one of its arms stretched across the Atlantic, for the purpose of loaning money, buying bills, and regulating exchanges there, whilst, with the other, it conducts immense banking and trading operations here, co-extensive with the Union, how can it be called a mere domestic institution of a single State? Nay, more: it seems, by its last manifesto, to have taken "the great commercial and pecuniary interests" of the Union into its keeping, both at home and abroad. Sir, a single State cannot furnish employment for its immense capital. It would starve within such narrow limits. It is no more a State institution now than it was under the old charter, except that its existence as the same identical corporation has been continued by an act of the legislature of Pennsylvania, instead of an act of Congress; and that, too, with much greater powers than it formerly possessed. It never ventured to plant itself in England under the old charter. No, sir, let not gentlemen delude themselves. The old Bank of the United States still lives, and moves, and has its being, without even having changed its name.

The Senator from Kentucky asks, why pass this bill? He says it is wholly unnecessary; and whilst he admits that the present bank had no legal power to reissue these old notes, he thinks it ought not to be prevented from acting thus, because these notes furnish the best and only universal currency in the Union. The Senator reminds me of the ancient heretics which existed in the Church, mentioned and condemned by the Apostle Paul. Their doctrine was, that it was lawful to do evil that good might come. It seems we are now to have a similar sect of political heretics, whose doctrine is, violate the law, if you can thereby furnish a good currency for the people. But there was not the least necessity for any such violation. As the old notes came in, the bank might have supplied their place by circulating its own new notes. They are a better currency in every respect; because the present bank is under a legal obligation to redeem them on demand. Not so in regard to the old notes. Their immediate redemption depends upon the honor of the bank, and nothing more. I have no doubt Mr. Biddle intends to redeem them, but he may be succeeded by another and a different man. Besides, the bank may, in the course of time, become insolvent; and in that event the payment of its own notes and debts must be preferred to that of these resurrection notes. It is certain that no direct remedy can be had upon them against the present bank.

The Senator denounces the present bill not only as unconstitutional, but as the most enormous stretch of power he has ever known to be attempted. I am glad to find that the Senator has become the advocate of a strict construction of the Constitution, and an enemy to the exercise of doubtful powers. In this particular we agree. And I am much pleased to learn from himself that he does not concur with the Senator from Massachusetts [Mr. Webster] in deriving power over the paper currency of the country from the clauses in the Constitution authorizing Congress to coin money and regulate commerce. By abandoning this latitudinarian construction, however, he virtually surrenders up the power to create a national bank. The Senator shakes his head, but I shall endeavor to prove that this is the dilemma in which he has placed himself. On what ground did the Supreme Court decide the bank to be constitutional? It was because Congress, possessing the express power to levy and collect taxes for the purpose of paying the debts of the United States, might create a bank by implication, if they believed it to be a necessary agent in the execution of this taxing power. Now will any man, at this day, pretend that the taxes of the Government cannot be collected, and its debts paid, without the agency of such a bank? I think not. It must have been for the purpose of extricating himself from this dilemma, and finding a power somewhere else to establish a bank, that the Senator from Massachusetts asserted a general power in Congress to create and regulate the paper currency of the country, and derived it from the coining and commercial clauses in the Constitution. I should be pleased always to agree with the Senator from Kentucky, and I am glad that we unite in denying the power claimed by the Senator from Massachusetts.

In regard to the power to pass this bill, I shall state the proposition of the Senator from Kentucky as fairly as I can. He says that the Bank of the United States is a corporation created by a sovereign State, and that this bill, intended to operate upon such a corporation, is wholly unconstitutional and subversive of State rights. Now, sir, if the bill were intended to act upon the bank, as a Pennsylvania corporation, I should abandon the argument. The president and directors of this bank sustain two characters, totally separate and distinct from each other. They are officers of the Pennsylvania Bank; and in that character they are beyond our control. But they have voluntarily assumed another character, by becoming assignees and trustees of the old bank chartered by Congress, for the purpose of winding up its concerns; and it is in this character, and this alone, that we have any jurisdiction over them. We do not attempt to interfere with the bank as a corporation of the State of Pennsylvania. No, sir; we only undertake to operate upon it as the assignee of our old bank. The gentleman asked if the old bank had assigned its property to individual trustees, could we pass any law to compel these trustees to wind up its concerns? Most certainly we could; because, no matter into whose hands the duty of winding up our bank may have passed, we should possess the power to compel a performance of that duty. This power of Congress can never be evaded or destroyed by any transfer to trustees made by officers created by our own law, whether the transfer be legal or illegal. Our power attaches to such trustees, and will continue until they shall have closed the concerns of the bank.

The gentleman says that the power to create a bank is one implication, and that to wind it up is a second implication, and to pass this bill would be piling implication upon implication, like Pelion upon Ossa, which cannot be done under the Constitution. Now, sir, to what absurdities does not this argument lead? By implication you can create a bank for a limited period, which you cannot destroy after that period has expired. Your creature, the term of whose existence you have foreordained, becomes eternal in defiance of your power. And this because you cannot add implication to implication. The gentleman asks where do you find this winding up power in the Constitution? I answer, wherever he finds the creating power. The one necessarily results from the other. If not, when you call a bank into existence, its charter, although limited to a few years, becomes in fact perpetual. You cannot create that which you cannot destroy, after it has lived its appointed time.

As to Mr. Gallatin and Mr. Brockenbrough—nobody pretends you can touch them or their banks by your law. The bill is confined to your own agents, acting under your own law, and therefore subject to your own jurisdiction. These agents are as much yours for the purpose proposed by the bill, as the president and directors of the old bank would have been. There is a perfect privity, as the lawyers would say, between the two; nay, there is a perfect identity. It is no argument to say that the old bank is dead; but even this is not the fact. We have extended its existence at the present session, without a dissenting voice, in either House, for the purpose of prosecuting and defending its suits, and it has always continued to elect a president and board of directors.

The Senator has asked, if the Bank of England or any of the banks in Canada had ceased to exist, and their agents in this country should reissue their old notes, whether we would claim the power of punishing them for that cause. This question, in my opinion, presents the only instance of haste and want of sufficient reflection in the gentleman's speech. There is no analogy between the two cases. Congress never created the Bank of England, nor any bank in Canada, and therefore Congress can never claim any power to close their concerns. We assert no power except over our own bank and its trustees. We cannot interfere with the banks of the several States, much less with those of a foreign country. The Senator thinks he has caught me in a palpable inconsistency. He says I first condemned the expansion of the banks in this country, and afterwards condemned the contraction of the Bank of England. I might have done so, in the special case of the refusal of that bank to extend its accustomed credits to the American houses, without any inconsistency; but I expressed no opinion of my own upon the subject. In stating the causes which produced the suspension of specie payments in the United States, I said that this act of the Bank of England had been condemned in that country both by their statesmen and men of business. I passed no censure whatever on the conduct of that bank, and the gentleman, therefore, need not have reminded me that it would but little regard my censure. I am content to confine my humble exertions to our own institutions at home, leaving to other gentlemen the glory of having South America on one side of the Atlantic and Greece on the other, shouting hosannas in their praise.

The gentleman asks, with a triumphant air, where are England and France at the present moment? Are they not prosperous, whilst we are embarrassed? In regard to England, I answer that money there is plenty and cheap; and this simply because business has been paralyzed by the great convulsion under which we have both suffered; and it is the capital which has been thrown out of active employment, from this very cause, which is now seeking investment at a low rate of interest. The commerce and trade of England have fallen off to such an extent that Parliament has been obliged to borrow two millions sterling to meet the current expenses of the Government. In this particular they are placed in a similar situation with ourselves. And yet after all the light which has been shed upon this subject, the gentleman still attributes that convulsion which has shaken the commercial world to its centre, to the removal of the deposits, the Specie Circular, and General Jackson.

I have but lately turned prophet; and there has been such poor success in that line on this side of the House, that I have almost determined to abandon the trade forever. In one respect I resemble the false prophets of old, because they prophesied nothing but good. This may probably result from my sanguine temperament, and my desire to look upon the bright side of human affairs. In my prophetic vision I have therefore never, like the gentleman, denounced war, pestilence, and famine against the country.

The gentleman strongly condemns the members of the present cabinet. I am willing to accord to the President the privilege of selecting his own agents and advisers, without any interference on my part. When he, or they, shall recommend measures of which I disapprove, I shall exercise my right of opposing them as an independent Senator. I do not believe that any evidence can be produced that the President and his cabinet are opposed to the credit system of the country. If this should ever appear, it will then be time enough for me to denounce such a policy. My instructions have prevented me from expressing my views at length upon this subject. They contain nothing, however, which forbid me from saying, nay I am only expressing their sentiment when I assert, that a separation of the business of the Government from that of the banks would be one of the greatest blessings which could be conferred on the country. In releasing the banks from the Government, and the Government from the banks, the interests of both parties would be promoted, mutual jealousies and recriminations would be ended, and the currency and business of the country would cease to be involved in the perpetual struggles which exist for political power.

I might say much more in reply to the gentleman, but I forbear.

Through the session of 1839–40 the financial policy of Mr. Van Buren continued to be the same. Still the plan of the "Independent Treasury," as it was called, continued to occupy the attention of the Senate, and still Mr. Buchanan was among the ablest and steadiest of its supporters. On the 12th of January, 1840, and again at the same session, on the 3d of March, he took a leading part in the discussion of these subjects. These seven years of political warfare on the relations of the General Government to the currency, commencing in 1833 and extending into the year 1840, were a period of unexampled commercial distress; and when the two parties arrayed their forces and named their candidates for the next election of a President, the Democrats, although in possession of official power, were in a position in which the prevailing public and private embarrassments could be charged by their adversaries as the direct consequence of their measures. A great political revolution was at hand. That victorious party which claimed to have been founded by Jefferson, which nearly thirty years before its present precarious situation had carried Madison through a war with England, which had by its forbearance made for Monroe "the era of good feeling," which had beaten the administration of the second Adams into the dust, which had twice elected Jackson and would have elected him a third time but for a sacred tradition of the Republic, which had enabled Jackson to name his successor, which filled the important offices and wielded the whole patronage of the Government, was now to be swept out of power by a popular tempest, such as the country had never known in a time of peace. It was broken in New York, it was broken in Pennsylvania, it was broken in 450many other States which for twelve years had been among its strongholds.

The summer and autumn of 1840 saw a popular excitement, in which there was much that history might condemn, but which the sober wisdom of history can both account for as natural, and regard as not unwholesome. There had come to be a feeling that the public men who had so long been entrusted with the Government of the country, and been sustained with so large a share of the popular confidence, who had been the peculiar friends of the people, whose party designation implied a democracy of a purer type, and a wider regard for the welfare of the masses, had grown indifferent to the general suffering. At first, the course of General Jackson towards the Bank of the United States, his vast popularity and the influence which it gave him, enabled him and his followers to maintain their power. Hardly had there ever been a popular confidence greater than that which was reposed in Jackson, through the whole of his conflict with a moneyed institution, which a great majority of the people of the United States regarded, with him, as a dangerous instrument. But when year after year passed away and nothing was done for the relief of the prevailing embarrassment, when thousands had become bankrupt, when labor was unemployed or was remunerated in a depreciated and discredited currency, when the mercantile, the manufacturing, the agricultural classes were involved in a common distress, elements of political excitement, scarcely ever before combined, were united in a vague longing for a great political change. Then were to be seen the highest statesmen discussing before huge masses of the people the most profound questions of public finance and constitutional construction, and stump orators of all degrees, sounding the depths of popular agitation. The songs, the mottoes, the cries, the emblems of the party which had adopted the name of Whigs, a name which, both in English history and in our own, had represented popular interests against the prerogatives of government, were at once puerile and effective. They convey a scarcely intelligible meaning to the present generation, but to those who listened to and looked upon them, they expressed feelings and passions which 451stirred the popular heart.[61] For once, the Whigs had laid hold of a string, coarse indeed and rude, but which vibrated to every touch throughout the land with singular force. The divorce of the Government from all connection with the currency, the disclaimer of all responsibility about the circulating medium which must be used by the people, the exclusive regard for the monetary concerns of the Government as distinguished from the monetary interests of the community, were arrayed by the Whigs as the favorite and pernicious doctrines of the party in power. In all this there was some injustice, but when does not popular suffering produce injustice?

The result of this upheaving of society was the election of General William Henry Harrison, of Ohio, as President, and of John Tyler, of Virginia, as Vice President, by a majority of 114 electoral votes. Never was a political defeat more overwhelming than the defeat of Mr. Van Buren. He obtained but 60 out of the 234 electoral votes. Of the larger States, he held only Virginia.[62]

Mr. Buchanan's personal position was unaffected by this political change. He had been re-elected to the Senate in January, 1837, by a very large vote, and for a full term, which would not terminate until the 3d of March, 1843.[63] When the political "campaign" of 1840 came on, he did his part, and did it valiantly, for the success of his party and the re-election of Mr. Van Buren. The detail of his exertions would not be interesting now. It is enough to say that in the arrangements of the public meetings held by his political associates in various States, he was much relied upon as an antagonist to the great Whig leaders, and was often in one sense pitted against Mr. Webster and Mr. Clay, although it was not the habit of the time for public men on opposite sides to encounter each other on the same platform. As a popular orator, there was no one on the Democratic side who was listened to with more respect than Mr. Buchanan. But popular eloquence was not his forte. On the platform, as in the Senate, he was grave, earnest, perspicuous and impressive: but he did not kindle the passions or arouse the enthusiasm of audiences: nor indeed was there much enthusiasm to be evoked in the defence of a cause against which almost all the elements of ardent popular feeling were at the command of its adversaries. Mr. Buchanan might have escaped from the Senate into the Cabinet of Mr. Van Buren, if he had wished to do so. It was Mr. Van Buren's desire, in 1839, that Mr. Buchanan should become Attorney-General in his administration, to fill the vacancy caused by the resignation of Mr. Grundy. The correspondence between them discloses that Mr. Buchanan preferred to remain in the Senate.

[MR. VAN BUREN TO MR. BUCHANAN.]
Washington, Dec. 27th, 1839.
Dear Sir:—

The office of Attorney-General of the United States has become vacant by the resignation of Mr. Grundy. Although I have no reason to suppose that it would be desirable to you to change your present position in the public service, I have nevertheless felt it to be my duty to offer the seat in my cabinet, which has thus been placed at my disposal, for your acceptance, and to assure you that it will afford me sincere pleasure to hear that it will be agreeable to you to accept it, a sentiment in which those who would be your associates, will, I am confident, cordially participate.

Should you decide otherwise, the occasion will have been presented, and cheerfully embraced, to express the high sense I entertain of your talents, and also my confidence in your patriotism and friendship for the administration.

Please to let me hear from you at your earliest convenience, and believe me to be very respectfully and truly your friend and obedient servant,
M. Van Buren.

[MR. BUCHANAN TO MR. VAN BUREN.]
Washington, Dec. 28th, 1839.
Dear Sir:—

I have received your note of yesterday evening, tendering to me the office of Attorney-General. Whilst I regard it, with grateful sensibility, as a distinguished mark of your kindness and confidence, yet I prefer my position as a Senator from Pennsylvania to the Attorney-Generalship, high and honorable as it is justly considered. Nothing could induce me to waive this preference, except a sense of public duty; and happily upon the present occasion, this presents no obstacle to the indulgence of my own inclination. Devotedly attached, as I am, to the great principles upon which your administration has been conducted, I feel that I can render a more efficient support to these principles on the floor of the Senate than I could in an executive office, which, from its nature, would necessarily withdraw me, in a great degree, from the general politics of the country, and again subject me to the labors of the profession.

Permit me to embrace this occasion of again respectfully reiterating my earnest desire that you would confer this appointment upon Judge Porter. I believe him to be eminently qualified to discharge the duties of the station; and that it would be highly gratifying to the Democracy of Pennsylvania to be represented in your cabinet by a gentleman who enjoys so large a portion of their confidence.

With the highest esteem, I remain very respectfully your friend,
James Buchanan.

[TO GENERAL PORTER.]
Washington, May 30th, 1840.
My Dear Sir:—

I have received yours of the 28th inst., and it afforded me much pleasure.

I have had a long and free conversation with Mr. Van Buren this morning on the subject of Pennsylvania politics. It was the first of the kind for some time. In the course of it I took occasion to read your letter to him, with which he was much gratified.

I impressed upon him, in the same terms I used to yourself, the absolute necessity of union and harmony between the State and national administration. I told him that if one portion of the party in Pennsylvania said they were for Paul, and another for Apollos, the great cause with which both Paul and Apollos were identified might be ruined. He expressed, as he ever has done, a great regard for you, and said he had given conclusive evidence of it by the appointment of Judge Blythe, and that he never had concealed the fact that this appointment was made to gratify your wishes. Upon a suggestion of mine, that an opportunity might probably be presented, on the 4th of July, to manifest his regard for you by giving a toast in your favor, he said he doubted the policy of that course, both in regard to you and himself. That the better mode was for both to evince their feelings by their conduct. He spoke freely of certain politicians in Philadelphia, and I have no doubt from what he said, that he will exert his influence in some manner to prevent them from any longer treating you unfairly. Upon the whole, I left him more convinced than I ever was before, that he is your friend. He made the very observation to me which I had made to you, that in the progress of the Presidential canvass, when the party became excited, the feeling which now existed against you in a few places would be entirely forgotten. Of this I am perfectly convinced, especially if the bill should pass imposing the restrictions on the banks recommended in your January message. There is no man in the State who more ardently desires this result than myself, and none who will more endeavor to accomplish it. Devoted as I am to bank reform, from a conviction of its absolute necessity, and having always expressed the same opinion on this subject, publicly and privately, this bill would place a powerful weapon in my hand. I shall have to visit Westmoreland County, on the business of my late brother-in-law's estate, very soon after the adjournment of Congress, and I am under the impression that I can do much good there. I shall be very much rejoiced indeed to hear of the passage of this bill.

I have had a long and a strong talk with —— ——. I am confident his feelings towards you are not unkind.

The resolution of the Senate, expressing their opinion in favor of the bankrupt system will place me in an embarrassing position, should it pass the House. Had the legislature instructed me, I should obey with pleasure, because all my sympathies are in favor of the suffering debtors. If left to myself, my judgment is so much opposed to my feelings, that I believe I should vote against the bill without making any speech. The expression of a legislative opinion would probably compel me to give my reasons for dissenting from their opinion. If there be a majority of the House in favor of the measure, why not change the expression of their opinion into instructions, and then I shall be relieved from all responsibility on the subject. I made a long speech in opposition to the bankrupt bill during the first session of my service in Congress, 1821–2; and I have yet heard nothing materially to shake my ancient opinions, though I am still open to conviction. I have not yet heard from Mr. Espy.

Ever your friend,
Very respectfully,
James Buchanan.

[TO GENERAL PORTER.]
Senate Chamber, Washington, February 9, 1841.
My Dear Sir:—

The third crash of the Bank of the United States so soon after its resumption has taken us all by surprise. I sincerely hope that it has made its last struggle, and may now go into final liquidation. Whilst I regret the sufferings to which its stockholders may be exposed, I yet believe that its dissolution is necessary to the prosperity of the country. As long as it shall continue to exist, it will continue to derange the business of the country, and produce again and again those revulsions to which we have been subjected. It has ever been a lawless institution, and has done what it pleased, knowing that to destroy it would subject the people to evils which they would be unwilling to encounter. We ought to rejoice that it has now destroyed itself. I most sincerely hope that you may take this view of the subject; and adhere strictly, as I have no doubt you will, to your opposition to permitting the banks to issue notes under five dollars.

As a sincere friend, both personally and politically, I have deemed it to be my duty to make these suggestions, and I have no doubt you will receive them as they are intended.

From your friend, sincerely,
James Buchanan.

[TO GENERAL PORTER.]
Washington, February 17, 1841.
My Dear Sir:—

Sitting "solitary and alone" in my private room, the thought has just struck me that I would address you a few lines. If I were capable of envying any man, I should envy the position in which you are now placed. The eyes of the Democracy of the whole Union are now directed towards you with intense anxiety; and all you have to do to render yourself an object of their respect and admiration is to adhere firmly to your avowed principles. That you will adopt this course, I have not the shadow of a doubt.

To put down the Bank of the United States will be a measure of the greatest relief to the State. It has not strength enough to assist the people; but must exist by borrowing money and crippling other institutions. If it were out of the way, the other State institutions might safely be left to the people of the State. And I firmly believe there would be no serious attempt to forfeit their charters. The Bank of the United States makes a merit of having loaned large sums to the State government, when, by this means, it has preserved its existence this long. It exchanged its own paper for what would command specie, and enable it to raise money abroad. Whilst, therefore, I feel for the distress of those whom it has ruined, I believe its going into liquidation would be the best relief measure which could be adopted. It may occasion much suffering for the present; but this will soon be over, and all may then again hope to see settled times.

When I sat down, I wanted to say a word against small notes; but I am interrupted and must stop.

Ever sincerely your friend,
James Buchanan.

[MR. BUCHANAN TO GEORGE G. LEIPER, ESQ.]
Lancaster, October 23, 1841.
My Dear Sir:—

I most sincerely sympathize with you in your domestic afflictions, and trust that He who tempers the wind to the shorn lamb may comfort and sustain your daughter in her distress.

456I reciprocate your congratulations on our recent victory with all my heart. It is a great moral triumph. After the late Presidential election many, who had formerly felt an abiding confidence in the integrity and intelligence of the people, began to waver. The ridiculous mummeries which apparently had an effect upon them were insults to their understanding. But nobly have they redeemed themselves, and have proved to the world that if they can be made to slumber over their rights for a moment, they are certain to awake with a firmer determination than ever to maintain them. Governor Porter has now a fine opportunity of distinguishing himself; and most ardently do I hope that he may embrace it. By doing his duty fearlessly, he will make a name for himself, which no other governor of Pennsylvania has ever yet enjoyed. On the other hand, should he falter, we shall lose the State, if not at the next election, at the next gubernatorial contest. He must devote himself to reforming the administration of our internal improvements, and rendering them productive; he must firmly resist any increase of the State debt. And if he does no more, he must veto every bill to create a new bank or renew the charter of an old one. These are principles on which the Democracy will insist. Besides, he ought to recommend and urge a thorough investigation of the Bank of the United States, and the Pennsylvania and other banks. The time has passed for consulting mere expediency; and the Democratic party has risen again upon its principles, and it will continue to stand no longer than it maintains them. I do not think that the Presidential question to which you allude will occasion any serious embarrassment to the party. Throughout the Union, with the exception of Philadelphia, they all appear to be alive to the necessity of forbearance. When the proper time shall arrive, the choice of a candidate will be made without serious difficulty; because I believe that the candidates who will be the most prominent are all willing to yield their pretensions, if that should be found necessary to promote the success of the great causes.

Please to remember me, in the kindest terms, to your family, and believe me to be your friend sincerely,
James Buchanan.

[TO MR. WILLIAM FLINN, JR.]
Washington, September 5th, 1841.
My Dear Sir:—

I thank you for your kind and acceptable letter, and feel much gratified that the honest and incorruptible farmers of your county have expressed their approbation of my political course. To live in their esteem would be a high reward.

The second bank bill, or "kite-flying fiscality," is now before President Tyler, and I have no doubt but that it will share the fate of its predecessor. Should the second veto be of a firm and manly character, precluding all hope of the establishment of a national bank during the present Presidential term, 457it will be, as it ought to be, hailed with enthusiasm by the Democratic party. In Congress we shall pursue the straight line of political duty, and shall yield the measures of the President, so far as they may be in accordance with our principles, a cheerful and hearty support. As to President-making, we shall leave that to the people, where it ought to be left.

I should be pleased to see you established as the editor of a Democratic paper. That is a much more honorable and independent vocation than to be hanging about the public offices here as a subordinate clerk. Should you become the editor of the Mercury, however, whilst I am deeply sensible of your kindness, I would not wish you to bring out my name as a candidate for the Presidency. It is yet too soon to agitate this question in the public journals; and any premature movement would only injure the individual it was intended to benefit. Besides, I have no ambitious longings on this subject. Let events take their course; and my only desire is, that at the proper time, the individual may be selected as our candidate, who will best promote the success of the party and its principles.

I am rejoiced at our flattering prospects in Pennsylvania. Should the Keystone State come "booming" into the Democratic line in October next, by a handsome majority, this auspicious event will do much to prostrate the present Whig party.

With sentiments of regard, I remain your friend,
James Buchanan.
458

CHAPTER XVI.
1841–1842.

DEATH OF PRESIDENT HARRISON—BREACH BETWEEN PRESIDENT TYLER AND THE WHIGS—TYLER'S VETOES—BUCHANAN'S REPLY TO CLAY ON THE VETO POWER—HIS OPPOSITION TO THE BANKRUPT ACT OF 1841.

Rarely has a party in a constitutional government come into power with apparently a better prospect of doing good to their country, and retaining their hold upon it, than did the Whigs under President Harrison. This worthy man, who was by no means a statesman of the first or even of the second order, was a person of fair intelligence, of entire honesty of character, and was moderately well taught in the principles of the Constitution. Almost his first act, after his election, was to tender the chief place in his cabinet to Mr. Webster. This was done with the concurrence of Mr. Clay, whom it suited to remain in the Senate, as its leader, and who expected to carry a new national bank, as a remedy for the existing disordered condition of the currency.

But General Harrison died on the day which completed the first month of his official term.[64] His successor, John Tyler, of Virginia, had been chosen as Vice President, with very little attention to his political opinions on the part of those who selected him for that position, or of those who voted for him. When he assumed the duties of the Presidency, he requested the members of General Harrison's cabinet to remain in office. They were all of that political school which regarded a national bank of some kind as a necessity, and held it to be an instrument of Government which Congress might constitutionally create.[65] President Harrison and his official advisers had 459deemed it necessary to convene an extra session of Congress; and his proclamation had summoned it for the 31st of May. When that day arrived, it began to be remembered that Mr. Tyler had theretofore been among those who denied the power of Congress to establish a national bank, and that as a Senator he had voted against one. Here, then, the long-cherished policy of the leading Whigs, which they claimed had been affirmed by the people in the late election, was in peril of encountering the opposition of the President. In July, a bill for a bank, with power to establish offices of discount and deposit in the several States, either with or without their consent, was passed by both Houses and sent to the President. He returned it on the 16th of August, with his objections, from which it appeared that he held such a bank to be unconstitutional. In the Senate, Mr. Clay made a bitter attack upon the President; the Whigs in the House of Representatives burst into a fury of indignation. But the Whig majority was not large enough to pass the bill over the President's "veto." A new bill to create a "Fiscal Corporation of the United States" was brought in. In the mean time the President was denounced in the press by persons who stood in close relations with Mr. Clay, as a man faithless to the party which had made him Vice President. In the debate on the new bill, Mr. Clay again assailed the President with great violence, expecting by that means to prevent a second "veto." Mr. Tyler remained firm to his own convictions; the second "veto" came; an irreparable breach between the Whigs and the President ensued; four of the members of the cabinet appointed by President Harrison resigned their places, without previous conference with Mr. Webster, who remained in office.[66] Thus within six months after the death of General Harrison, the Whigs lost the power of shaping the financial legislation of the country, which their triumphant success in the late election appeared to have given them.

Mr. Buchanan, if not now the leader of the opposition in the Senate, was one of its most prominent debaters. It has already been said that he was not an orator, in the highest 460sense of that term. But in all the polemics of debate he was exceedingly efficient. He could mingle logic with humor; and although in discussions which were largely occupied with party topics and with grave constitutional questions, he was not sparing in his thrusts, there was a gentleman-like manner in his wielding of the rapier, as well as force in handling the weightier weapon of argument. On both of the bills which were prepared with a good deal of design to encounter the anticipated opposition of Mr. Tyler, and the last of which was almost avowedly gotten up as a means of "heading him off" from a union with the democratic opposition, Mr. Buchanan spoke at the extra session with remarkable energy and effect. His most elaborate speech on the first bill was delivered on the 7th of July. It related partly to the old question of the constitutional power of Congress to create a national bank of any kind; and in the course of this discussion he treated the topic of the binding authority of the Supreme Court of the United States, in reference to the legislative department, with new and forcible illustrations, contending that upon any new bank, Senators were bound to follow their conscientious convictions. The residue of the speech was a severe criticism upon the details of the bill, which he contended would establish a dangerous connection between a moneyed institution and the executive of the United States, far worse than that which had existed in the case of either of the former banks. Such a speech was well calculated to produce a strong impression at once upon the mind of the President before whom the bill was likely to come, and upon the country. Mr. Buchanan looked forward to the time when all question about a national bank, as a fiscal agent of the Government in the collection and disbursement of its revenues, would be at an end, and the "Independent Treasury" system would be resorted to as the substitute.[67]

Upon the second bill he spoke on the 2d of September, in reply to Mr. Clay. This scheme of a "Fiscal Corporation of the United States," which was to have the power of dealing in 461bills of exchange drawn between different States, or on foreign countries, but was not to be allowed to discount promissory notes, was assailed by Mr. Buchanan with great vigor. His speech placed the advocates of the bill in a somewhat ridiculous position, for it did not appear whether they concurred in founding it on the power to regulate commerce, or on the power to collect and disburse the public revenue: and in the practical operation of the scheme, he made it very plain that it would become a mere "kite-flying" machine. Mr. Clay thought that Mr. Buchanan did not succeed in "attempts at wit." Buchanan retorted that this was true, and that his opponent as rarely succeeded in argument. An impartial reader would now say that Buchanan had the argument on his side, and a very respectable share of what was certainly a telling species of humor, if it was not wit. His description of the heterogeneous political materials that made up the famous "Harrisburg Convention,"—the body which nominated Harrison and Tyler, with such an entire disregard of the opinions of the candidates that it became afterwards a disputed question whether they were "bank" or "anti-bank" men,—was not an unhappy hit.[68]

Under the advice of Mr. Webster, the Whigs postponed the subject of a bank to the next regular session of Congress. But some important measures were passed at the extra session, and approved by the President, among which was a Bankrupt Act. Mr. Buchanan opposed it in the following speech, delivered on the 24th of July, 1841:

The question being on the passage of the bill—

Mr. Buchanan said, that when he entered the Senate chamber this morning, he had not intended to say one word on the subject of the bankrupt bill. He was content that the question should have been taken silently on its final passage, and decided in its favor, as all knew it would be, from the vote yesterday upon its engrossment. The able remarks of the Senator from New York (Mr. Tallmadge) had induced him to change his purpose, and endeavor to place himself in a proper position before the public in relation to this important measure.

He trusted that he felt as much sympathy for the unfortunate as any Senator on this floor. It would, therefore, have afforded him heartfelt pleasure to be able to vote for this bill. He was sorry, very sorry, that from a 462deep sense of public duty, he should be compelled to vote against it. Would to Heaven that this were not the case!

It had been asserted over and over again, that there were five hundred thousand bankrupts in the United States anxiously awaiting relief from the passage of this bill. Now, from the very nature of the case, this must be a monstrous exaggeration of the number of these unfortunate men. Less than two millions and a half of votes had been given at the late Presidential election; and, if you add to this number five hundred thousand, the aggregate of three millions would exceed the number of all the male inhabitants of the United States who could by possibility become bankrupts. Could any man believe that half a million of this number were in a state of bankruptcy? That every sixth man in the United States was in this wretched condition? The experience of us all must demonstrate that this was impossible. There were several States in the Union where this bill would be almost a dead letter for want of subjects on which it could operate. Although we had suffered much from the spirit of wild speculation, which had been excited to madness by our unrestricted banking system, yet he did not believe there were more than one hundred thousand bankrupts in the United States who would apply for relief under this bill.

Now, sir, what was the nature of this bill? Whom did it embrace in its provisions? He would answer, every individual in the United States who was an insolvent debtor. There was no limitation, no restriction whatever. It would discharge all the insolvent debtors now in existence throughout the Union, from all the debts which they had ever contracted, on the easiest terms possible. It was said that the bill contained provisions both for voluntary and involuntary bankruptcy; and so it did nominally: but in truth and in fact, it would prove to be almost exclusively a voluntary bankrupt bill.

The involuntary clause would scarcely ever be resorted to, unless it might be by a severe and vindictive creditor, for the purpose of unjustly oppressing his unfortunate debtor. And why would this prove in practice to be a voluntary bankrupt bill, and that alone? The compulsory clause applied only to merchants—wholesale and retail, to bankers, factors, brokers, underwriters, and marine insurers. These were objects of compulsory bankruptcy, provided they owed debts to the amount of two thousand dollars. In order to enable their creditors to prosecute petitions against them, for the purpose of having them declared bankrupt, they must have committed one of the acts of bankruptcy specified by the bill. What were they? The debtor must either have departed from the State of his residence, with intent to defraud his creditors;—or concealed himself to avoid being arrested;—or fraudulently procured himself to be arrested or his goods or lands to be attached, distrained, sequestered, or taken in execution;—or removed and concealed his goods and chattels to prevent them from being levied upon or taken in execution;—or made a fraudulent conveyance or assignment of his lands, goods, or credits. These were the five acts of bankruptcy specified in the bill; and could it be supposed that any merchant or man of business, in insolvent circumstances, 463would wait and subject himself to this compulsory process by committing any of these acts; whilst the bill threw the door wide open to him, in common with all other persons, to become a voluntary bankrupt, at any time he might think proper? He would select the most convenient time for himself to be discharged from his debts; and would cautiously avoid any one of these acts of bankruptcy, which might restrain the freedom of his own will, and place him in some degree within the power of his creditors. He would "swear out" when it suited him best, and would not subject himself to their pleasure. This bill, then, although in name compulsory as well as voluntary, was in fact, from the beginning to end, neither more nor less than a voluntary bankrupt law.

Now it might be wise, on a subject of such great importance, to consult the experience of the past. In 1817, the British Parliament had appointed a commission on the subject of their bankrupt laws. The testimony taken by the commissioners was decidedly against these laws; and the Lord Chancellor declared that the abuses under them were a disgrace to the country; that it would be better to repeal them at once than to submit to such abuses; and that there was no mercy to the bankrupt's estate nor to the creditors. Mr. B. spoke from memory; but he felt confident he was substantially correct in the facts stated. This was the experience of England, and that, too, notwithstanding their bankrupt laws had interposed many more guards against fraud than the present bill contained, and were executed with an arbitrary severity, wholly unsuited to the genius of our institutions. In that country, however, these laws had existed for so long a period of time, and were so interwoven with the business habits of the people, that it was found impossible to abolish them altogether.

We have had some experience on this subject in our own country. Congress passed a bankrupt law in April, 1800. It was confined to traders, and was exclusively compulsory in its character. The period of its existence was limited to five years and until the end of the next session of Congress thereafter. It so entirely failed to accomplish the objects for which it was created, and was the source of so many frauds, that it was permitted to live out but little more than half its appointed days. It was repealed in December, 1803; and a previous resolution, declaring that it ought to be repealed, passed the House of Representatives by a vote of 77 to 12.

The State of Pennsylvania had furnished another important lesson on this subject. In March, 1812, the legislature of that State passed a bankrupt or insolvent law absolving all those who chose to take advantage of it from the payment of their debts. It was confined to the city and county of Philadelphia; but within these limits, like the present bill, it offered relief to everybody who desired to be relieved. This act was repealed, almost by acclamation, at the commencement of the very next session after its passage. Its baneful effects were so fully demonstrated during this short intervening period, that the representatives from the city and county who had, but a few months before, strained every nerve to procure its passage, were the most active and zealous in urging its repeal. 464During the first session of his service in the House of Representatives (that of 1821–2), powerful efforts were made to pass a bankrupt law. There was then a greater and more general necessity for such a measure than had ever existed since. The extravagant expansion of the Bank of the United States in 1816, '17 and '18 had reduced it to the very brink of insolvency. In order to save itself from ruin, it was compelled to contract its loans and issues with a rapidity beyond all former example. The consequence was, that the years 1819, '20 and '21 were the most disastrous which the country had ever experienced since the adoption of the federal Constitution. Not only merchants and speculators were then involved in ruin; but the rage for speculation had extended to the farmers and mechanics throughout the country, and had rendered vast numbers of them insolvent. The cry for relief, by the passage of a bankrupt bill, therefore, came to Congress from all classes of society, and from almost every portion of the Union.

The best speech which he (Mr. B.) had ever made in Congress was in opposition to that bill. The reason was, that he had derived much assistance from conversations with Mr. Lowndes upon the subject. That great and good statesman was then suffering under the disease which proved fatal to him soon after. He attempted to make a speech against the bill, but was compelled to desist by physical exhaustion before he had fairly entered on his subject. It was his decided conviction, that no bankrupt law, of which the English system was the model, could ever be adopted by Congress without great injury to the country. He (Mr. B.) had attempted to demonstrate this proposition, at that period, and he should now again, after the lapse of nearly twenty years, make a very few observations on the same subject.

And in the first place, it would be physically impossible for the district courts of the United States to carry this law into execution; and if it were even possible, it would be extremely burdensome and oppressive to the people generally.

The bill prescribes that all applicants for its benefit shall file their petitions in the district court of the district in which they reside. Twenty days' notice only is required, and that not to be served personally on the creditors, but merely by newspaper publication. At the time and place appointed, the creditors of the applicant may appear and show cause why the prayer of his petition should not be granted. If there be no appearance on the part of the creditors, or sufficient cause be not shown to the contrary, then the court decree the applicant to be a bankrupt; and thus ends the first stage of the proceedings, so far as he is personally concerned.

After such applicant has been thus declared a bankrupt, and has complied with all the provisions of the act, he may then file another petition to be discharged from his debts, which may be granted at any time after ninety days from the date of the decree declaring him a bankrupt. Seventy days' notice is to be given to his creditors to appear in court, and oppose his discharge, if they think proper.

It thus appeared that there might be two formal hearings in each case 465before the district court upon every application; and that there would be, in many of the cases, was beyond a doubt. Besides, from the very nature of the proceedings in bankruptcy, and from the provisions of the bill, the interlocutory applications, and the examinations of the bankrupt before the court, must be very numerous. At every stage of the proceedings a large portion of the time of the court must necessarily be devoted to the subject.

Should the district court decide that the bankrupt shall not be discharged, he might then demand a trial by jury, or appeal from this decision to the circuit court. This would be another prolific fountain of business for the district and circuit courts of the United States.

Thus far the proceeding was confined to the bankrupt personally. But before what court was his estate to be settled? By the terms of the bill, the demands of all creditors of the bankrupt, if disputed, must be tried in the district court; the controversies which might arise between the creditors and the assignees of the bankrupt, and also between the bankrupt himself and his assignees, must be settled in the district court; and, to use the comprehensive terms of the bill, the jurisdiction of that court was extended "to all acts, matters, and things to be done under and in virtue of the bankruptcy, until the final distribution and settlement of the estate of the bankrupt, and the close of the proceedings in bankruptcy."

There were also several criminal offences created by the bill; all of which must be tried in the district courts of the United States.

From the nature of the federal Constitution, all the business which he had enumerated must necessarily be transacted in the courts of the United States. It could not be transferred to the State courts.

Now, sir, said Mr. B., this bill will prove to be a felo de se. It can never be carried into effect, for want of the necessary judicial machinery. Another midnight judiciary must be established, to aid bankruptcy. The number of these midnight judges which were added to the federal judiciary in February, 1801, was eighteen; and if these were necessary at that time, three times the number would not be sufficient at present.

He had just examined McCullough's Commercial Dictionary, under the title Bankruptcy. He there found that the annual number of commissions of bankruptcy opened in England on an average of nine years, ending with the year 1830, was a little below seventeen hundred. The average annual number of all the commissions which issued during the same period, was about two thousand one hundred. One-half of these seventeen hundred cases were what are called town cases, and the other half country cases. To transact the town business alone, consisting of eight hundred and fifty cases annually, it had been found necessary to establish a new court of bankruptcy, similar to the ancient courts at Westminster Hall, consisting of one chief judge, and three puisne judges. To this court there were attached six commissioners, two principal registrars, and eight deputy registrars. Such was the judicial force found necessary in England to examine and decide upon the cases of seven hundred and fifty bankrupts in each year.

466Then what provision had the present bill made to discharge half a million of bankrupts, the number which its friends assert exist at present in the United States? None whatever, except to cast this burden upon the district courts of the United States, which, in the large commercial cities, where the cases of bankruptcy must chiefly be heard, had already as much business as they could conveniently transact. The courts could not transact all this business, if there were half a million of bankrupts to be discharged, within the next twenty years. Sir, unless you establish new courts, and increase your judicial force at least ten fold, it is vain for you to pass the present bill. Without this, the law can never be carried into effect. The moment it goes into operation, these unfortunate bankrupts will rush eagerly to the district courts in such numbers as to arrest all other judicial business. This bill provides that these courts shall be considered open every day in the year, for the purpose of hearing bankrupt cases.

The district courts of the United States were scattered over the Union at great distances from each other. For example, there were in the State of New York, he believed, but two of these courts. In Pennsylvania, one was held in Philadelphia, another in Pittsburg, and a third in Williamsport. Pittsburg and Philadelphia were three hundred miles apart; and parties, jurors, and witnesses must constantly be in attendance from great distances at these two places, on the hearing of the different bankrupts, and on the trial of all the causes which might arise out of the settlement of their estates. By the operation of this bill, all these causes would and must be transferred from the State to the Federal courts. This would be an intolerable oppression to the people.

Without entering into any detail of the frauds to which this bill would give birth, he must be permitted to advert to the effect which it would have upon the rights of creditors in States distant from the court where the debtor might make his application. It would speedily sponge away all the indebtedness, now very great, of the Southwestern portion of the Union to the Eastern cities. Our merchants in those cities, should the bill pass, would have no difficulty in balancing their books. This would be done for them by the bill in the easiest possible manner.

Under all other bankrupt laws which had ever existed, or ever been proposed, either in this country or in England, or anywhere else, as he believed, the debtor could not obtain his certificate of discharge without the express written assent of a certain proportion of his creditors in number and value. This rule had never been found to operate severely in practice on honest debtors, whilst it afforded some security to the creditors. Under the present bankrupt laws of England, the certificate of discharge must be signed by four-fifths in number and value of the creditors of the bankrupt; and under our old bankrupt law of 1800, two-thirds in number and value of the creditors were required to sign. Without this express assent, no bankrupt could receive his certificate of discharge. But the present bill had completely reversed this rule. Under it the debtor must be discharged, "unless a majority 467in number and value of his creditors, who have proved their debts, shall file their written dissent thereto." Now he should put a case; and many such would occur under the present bill. A merchant in Philadelphia had a debtor in Mississippi, who owed him $20,000. This debtor applies to the district court of that State for the benefit of the act. The merchant believes he has been guilty of fraud, and determines to oppose his discharge. He goes or sends to Mississippi for this purpose. I ask you, sir, what chance he would have to obtain the necessary proof, in a country where thousands were at the same time applying for the benefit of the bankrupt law. The task would be hopeless; and consequently the attempt would be made in very few cases. Had the law required the express assent of two-thirds or even a majority in number and value of the bankrupt's creditors, the merchant would have had one security left. The debtor must have satisfied him that he had acted honestly before he could have obtained his assent. Now the debtor would be discharged unless a majority expressly dissent. The ancient rule had been reversed; and instead of an express assent being required to produce his discharge, there must now be an express dissent to prevent it. And if the majority did dissent, what would be the consequence? Was this conclusive, and would the debtor still remain liable? No, sir, no. The Philadelphia merchant would then have to enter upon a new law suit. Notwithstanding this express dissent, the question would, under the bill, be referred to a jury, and if they decided in the bankrupt's favor, he was discharged from his debts forever, even against the dissent of all his creditors. This jury would necessarily be composed of his own neighbors, all having a sympathetic feeling with him, and looking upon the distant Philadelphia creditor as an unjust and an unfeeling man. This was a natural feeling, and common to almost all men in similar circumstances. It implied no imputations upon their honesty. Truly this bill was a measure to relieve all debtors who might desire to cut loose from their debts, without any adequate provision for the security of creditors.

But all these evils were nothing when compared with the baneful effects which the bill would have upon the morals of the people of this country. Our people were already too much addicted to speculation, and too anxious to become suddenly rich. As a nation, we required the rein and the bit much more than the spur. The present bill would stimulate the spirit of speculation almost to madness. Men would be tempted by the hope of realizing rapid fortunes, and living in affluence the remainder of their days, to embark in every wild undertaking, knowing that they had everything to gain and nothing to lose. This bill proclaimed not merely to merchants and insurers, whose business was from its nature hazardous; but to every citizen of the United States, "you may be as wild and extravagant in your speculations as you please—you may attempt to seize the golden prize in any manner you choose: if you succeed you will then possess what your heart most desires; if not, your debts shall be blotted out in the easiest manner possible, and you may begin the world again." This was in effect the language of the bill. 468The consequence must be that the faith of contracts would soon become an idle word. Our former bankrupt law was wholly compulsory in its character, and was confined to traders. The present English bankrupt law expressly excludes farmers and graziers from its provisions. We went a long distance in advance of both. The present bill would be in effect wholly voluntary, and it embraced everybody under the sun, and all debts which had been, or might be, contracted.

He would venture to predict, that when this bill should go into operation the people of the United States would soon become astonished and alarmed at its consequence: and it would be blotted out of existence in less time than had elapsed between the passage and repeal of the act of 1800.

He might be asked if he were opposed to a bankrupt law in any form. He could answer that he was not. He would most cheerfully vote for any safe measure of this nature which could be carried into execution by the courts of the United States, and he did not believe that it would be very difficult to frame such a measure. The judicial system of the Federal Government was of such a character, that it could never execute a bankrupt law, modelled after the English system, without producing great fraud, delay, and injustice. If you changed this system, and increased the number of courts and judges, so as to enable them to transact the business under this bill, with proper deliberation and within a reasonable time, you would go far towards producing a judicial consolidation of the Union. It was the opinion of Mr. Lowndes, that we should be compelled to abandon the idea of framing a bill upon the English model, and adopt the system which prevailed in countries subject to the civil law. For example, he (Mr. B.) would permit a debtor in failing circumstances to make any composition he could obtain from a majority or two-thirds in number and value of his creditors. In that event, he would discharge him from his debts as against the remainder, unless they could prove that he had been guilty of fraud. He would never place any unfortunate, but honest debtor, in the power of a few vindictive creditors against the will of the majority. Such a law would, in a great degree, execute itself, and dispense with nearly all the machinery of this bill. The composition between the debtor and his creditors, and his assignment of his property for the benefit of them all, which he should consider indispensable, might be filed in the district court, and receive its sanction. He would not take time at present to do more than hint at the nature of the bankrupt law, which he thought would be applicable to this country. It would very much resemble the cessio bonorum which now prevailed in Louisiana, where the civil and not the common law governed the proceedings of the courts.

But what great and overruling necessity existed for Congress to pass any bankrupt law? Each State could now pass bankrupt laws, which would relieve their citizens from the obligation of debts contracted with other citizens of the same State subsequent to the passage of such laws. This point had been solemnly adjudged by the Supreme Court of the United States, in the case of Ogden vs. Saunders, reported in 12th Wheaton, 213; and its authority was confirmed in the case of Boyle vs. Zacharie, reported in 6 Peters, 635.

This discharge, however, would be confined to debts contracted between citizens of the same State where the discharge was granted. The decision rested on the principle, that the State law under which the discharge would take place, had become a part of the original contract, in the contemplation of the parties. But if a citizen of Pennsylvania had loaned money to a citizen of New York, who should afterwards take the benefit of a bankrupt law existing in the latter State, this would not discharge the debt; but the Pennsylvanian might, notwithstanding, recover the amount due from the New Yorker, in either the federal or State courts. But, even in such a case, if the Pennsylvania creditor should accept his dividend of the estate of the New York debtor, he would then be bound for ever, and the debt would be discharged. [Vide the case of Clay vs. Smith, 3 Peters, 411.] Foreign creditors would, in almost every instance, accept such dividends, if they amounted to anything considerable; and this would be an encouragement for debtors, in failing circumstances, not to struggle on till all their property was gone, but to surrender it while something remained for the general creditors. Thus, then, it was clear that the States could provide for all prospective cases, and could enact bankrupt laws which would have the same force and effect between their own citizens as though they had been passed by Congress. Besides, the State courts, established in every county, could carry those laws into effect with promptitude, and without inconvenience to the people.

A thought had struck him at the moment. Why might not Congress declare by law that a discharge under all State bankrupt laws should be as effectual against citizens of other States as they could be against citizens of the same State? This would render the system complete in regard to future debts, without any further interposition of Congress. He would not say that we possessed the power, under the Constitution, to pass such a law, because he had never considered the subject; but, if we did, it would be the best mode in which we could exercise our power over bankruptcy. Every State would then be left at liberty to adopt the policy in relation to bankrupts required by its own peculiar circumstances, and to execute the laws which operated chiefly upon the domestic concerns of its own citizens according to its own discretion.

Mr. B. said, as he had referred to the speech which he had made in the House of Representatives on this subject, nearly twenty years ago, he felt bound to acknowledge that, upon one point, he had fallen into a then prevailing error. Of this he had been fully convinced by the debate in the Senate at the last session. In 1822, it was his opinion that the constitutional power of Congress was confined to traders, or that class of persons which were embraced by the bankrupt laws of England at the time of the adoption of the Federal Constitution. This he now believed was too narrow a construction. The Constitution declared that "Congress shall have power to establish uniform laws on the subject of bankruptcies, throughout the United States." The subject of bankruptcies was thus placed generally under our control; and wherever bankruptcy existed, no matter what might have been the pursuits of the bankrupt, whether he had been a trader or not, our power extended over him. It also, in his opinion, embraced artificial as well as natural persons. Was it not absurd to say, that an individual manufacturer on one side of the street at Lowell might be subjected to the compulsory operation of a bankrupt law; whilst two or three individual manufacturers on the other side of the same street, who had obtained a charter of incorporation from the legislature of Massachusetts, could thus withdraw themselves in their corporate capacity from the power conferred upon Congress over bankruptcies? He, therefore, entertained no doubt of the power of Congress to pass a compulsory bankrupt law against banks. If it could not pass such a law, a firm of individual bankers would be embraced by our power; but if these very individuals obtained a charter of incorporation, they might then place that power at defiance. He entertained as little doubt of the policy of such a law as applied to banks. The knowledge of its existence would of itself, in almost every instance, prevent the necessity of its application. Banks, then, in order to save themselves from destruction, would take care to conduct their business in such a manner as always to be able to pay their liabilities in specie. He indulged no hope of a permanently sound convertible paper currency except what arose from the power of Congress to subject banks to a bankrupt law. This was the only practicable method which could be devised of securing to the people this great blessing.

Mr. B. thought it might be shown that this bill was deficient in its details. He would now only refer to one particular. It dispensed with the use of commissioners of bankruptcy altogether. In this respect it was a departure from the English statute of bankruptcy, and from our own act of 1800. Now whilst he admitted that compulsory bankruptcy would rarely occur under this bill, unless it might be to gratify the malignity of a severe creditor; yet he asked the chairman of the committee (Mr. Berrien) to say what would become of the debtor's property between the time which would intervene between filing the petition against him by the creditor, and the final decree of the court declaring him a bankrupt. The debtor might require a trial by jury before the court to ascertain the fact whether or not he had committed an act of bankruptcy. This trial might, and probably would, often be delayed for years, whilst it ought to proceed immediately. What was to become of the debtor's property in the mean time, without commissioners? Was he to be left to squander it at pleasure? On the other hand, if the petitioning creditor should proceed without sufficient cause, the act of 1800 gave the debtor a remedy against him. He was bound, before the commission was sued out, to give bond, with such surety as the court might direct, conditioned that the obligor should prove the debtor to be a bankrupt. In case of failure, the debtor had his remedy on the bond to the amount of the injury he might have sustained, in case the condition of it had been violated. Surely this was no more than justice. After the debtor had been arrested in the pursuit of his business by a charge of bankruptcy—after his prospects in life had been blasted—after his credit had been destroyed—and after he had been pursued for years in a course of litigation which eventually terminated in his favor, justice required that he should have some remedy. He asked, therefore, why these provisions of the act of 1800 had been left out of the present bill?

It had been contended that as the Constitution had conferred upon Congress the power to pass a bankrupt law, it was therefore their duty to exercise this power. But power was one thing and duty another. The language of power was that you may—of duty that you must. The Constitution had also conferred upon Congress the power of declaring war, of imposing taxes, and of raising and supporting armies; but would any Senator contend that it was our duty to give life and energy to these powers by calling them into action, unless the interest or honor of the country demanded it at our hands? These sovereign powers were to be exercised or not, according to the dictates of a sound discretion; and we were under no obligation whatever to pass a bankrupt law, unless we believed that under all the circumstances of the country, such a law would promote the best interests of the people. Upon the whole, he could declare that such was his sympathy for these unfortunate debtors, that he had never given a vote in his life more disagreeable to his feelings than the vote which he should be compelled to give upon the present occasion. He was convinced, however, that the bill, in its effects, would prove disastrous to the people; and, therefore, although reluctantly, he should record his vote against its passage.

At the session which commenced in December, 1841, a measure in which President Tyler and his cabinet had united was recommended to Congress. It proposed the establishment of an "Exchequer Board," to consist of certain Government officers and other commissioners, with branch agencies in the different States. As it never took effect, it is only needful to refer to Mr. Buchanan's description of it in a speech made on the 29th of December, from which it appears that he regarded it as only another form of a Government bank. He professed his readiness to concur with the President in any unobjectionable measure confined to the collection, safe-keeping, and disbursement of the public money, "in the hope that, after all experiments should have been tried, and reason should have time to prevail, the people and the Government would at length return to and re-establish the Independent Treasury."[69] But as the Senate continued to be occupied through the winter of 1841–2 472with the discussion of these subjects of finance, Mr. Clay kept on in his bitter criticisms of the President's "vetoes" of bills which had been passed by those who had, as he claimed, bestowed on Mr. Tyler the office that had made him the successor of General Harrison. Mr. Clay went so far as to propose a joint resolution for an amendment of the Constitution, so as to require but a bare majority of all the members of each house to pass any bill into a law, notwithstanding the objections of the President. That he really expected to bring about such a change in the fundamental rule which had alone made the President's negative of any practical value, may be doubtful. He was then looking for a nomination to the Presidency by the next national convention of the Whigs, and this proposal to curtail the "veto" power would probably be, under the circumstances of the times, a popular topic on which to make his canvass against the Democratic party. It is, perhaps, to be regretted that Mr. Webster was not in the Senate at this time; but as he was not, it is fortunate that Mr. Buchanan was.[70] Notwithstanding the many differences of opinion between these two statesmen, on the scope of the legislative powers of Congress, I regard it as certain that they would not have differed in their views of the fundamental purpose of the Constitution in requiring two-thirds of each House to pass a bill over the President's objections. Great and eminent as were Mr. Webster's powers of understanding and enforcing the principles of the Constitution, and commanding as was his reputation, Mr. Buchanan was an equally conscientious and careful student of that instrument, and equally faithful to its great purposes. His speech on the veto power, in reply to Mr. Clay, delivered on the 2d of February, 1842, may be ranked very high as an exposition of one of the most important parts of our political system. There is a good deal in it of the temporary and party controversies of that period; and there is also a great deal of sound and comprehensive reasoning, valuable now and hereafter.

Mr. President: I am now sorry that I ever committed myself to make a speech upon this subject. I assure you that it has become extremely cold; 473and I think I never shall again pledge myself to address the Senate at the end of a week or ten days, to be occupied in the discussion of an intervening and different question. Cold as the subject had become, it is now still colder, after having waited for an hour to hear a debate on the mere reference of a memorial to the Committee on Commerce. But although the subject may have lost its freshness to my mind, and I may not be able to reply to the Senator from Kentucky (Mr. Clay) with as much effect as if the discussion on the bankrupt bill had not intervened, yet it has lost none of its intrinsic importance.

Before I commence the discussion, however, let me clearly and distinctly state the question to be decided by the Senate.

Under the Constitution of the United States, as it now exists—

"Every bill which shall have passed the House of Representatives and the Senate, shall, before it become a law, be presented to the President of the United States; if he approve he shall sign it, but if not he shall return it, with his objections, to that House in which it shall have originated, who shall enter the objections at large on their journal and proceed to reconsider it. If after such reconsideration two-thirds of that House shall agree to pass the bill, it shall be sent, together with the objections, to the other House, by which it shall likewise be reconsidered, and if approved by two-thirds of that House, it shall become a law. But, in all such cases, the votes of both Houses shall be determined by yeas and nays, and the names of the persons voting for and against the bill, shall be entered on the journal of each House respectively. If any bill shall not be returned by the President within ten days (Sundays excepted) after it shall have been presented to him, the same shall be a law, in like manner as if he had signed it, unless the Congress, by their adjournment, prevent its return, in which case it shall not be a law."

The same constitutional rule is applicable to "every order, resolution or vote to which the concurrence of the Senate and House of Representatives may be necessary, except on a question of adjournment."

The joint resolution offered by the Senator, proposes to change the existing Constitution, so as to require but a bare majority of all the members belonging to each House to pass any bill into a law, notwithstanding the President's objections.

The question then is, whether the Constitution ought to be so amended as to require but a bare majority of all the members of each House, instead of two-thirds of each House, to overrule the President's veto; and, in my opinion, there never was a more important question presented to the Senate. Is it wise, or is it republican, to make this fundamental change in our institutions?

The great Whig party of the country have identified themselves, in the most solemn manner, with this proposed amendment. Feeling sensibly, by sad experience, that they had suffered since the late Presidential election, from not having previously presented a clear exposition of their principles "to the public eye," they determined no longer to suffer from this cause. Accordingly, the conscript fathers of the church assembled in convention at the city 474of Washington, on the 13th September last—at the close of the ever memorable extra session—and adopted an address to the people of the United States. This manifesto contains a distinct avowal of the articles of their creed; and, first and foremost among them all, is a denunciation of the veto power. I shall refer very briefly to this address; although to use the language of my friend, the present Governor of Kentucky, it contains much good reading. So exasperated were the feelings of the party then, and so deeply were they pledged to the abolition of the veto power, that they solemnly and formally read John Tyler out of the Whig church, because he had exercised it against the bills to establish "a fiscal agent" and a "fiscal corporation" of the United States. The form of excommunication bears a resemblance to the Declaration of Independence which severed this country forever from Great Britain. I shall give it in their own emphatic language. They declare that John Tyler—

"By the course he has adopted in respect to the application of the veto power to two successive bank charters, each of which there was just reason to believe would meet his approbation; by the withdrawal of confidence from his real friends in Congress and from the members of his Cabinet; by the bestowal of it upon others notwithstanding their notorious opposition to leading measures of his administration, has voluntarily separated himself from those by whose exertions and suffrages he was elevated to that office through which he reached his present exalted station," etc.

After a long preamble, they proceed to specify the duties which the Whig party are bound to perform to the country, and at the head of these duties, the destruction of the veto power contained in the Constitution stands prominently conspicuous. The following is the language which they have employed:

"First. A reduction of the executive power, by a further limitation of the veto, so as to secure obedience to the public will, as that shall be expressed by the immediate Representatives of the people and the States, with no other control than that which is indispensable to avert hasty or unconstitutional legislation."

Mark me, sir, the object is not to secure obedience to the public will as expressed by the people themselves, the source of all political power; but as expounded by their Senators and Representatives in Congress.

After enumerating other duties, they declare that "to the effectuation of these objects ought the exertions of the Whigs to be hereafter directed." And they make a direct appeal to the people by announcing that "those only should be chosen members of Congress who are willing cordially to co-operate in the accomplishment of them." Twenty thousand copies of this manifesto were ordered to be printed and circulated among the people of the United States.

This appeal to the people, sir, was a vain one. The avowal of their principles destroyed them. The people did not come to the rescue. Never was there a more disastrous defeat than theirs, at the last fall elections, so immediately after their triumphant victory. Thank Heaven! the people have not thus far responded to this appeal, and I trust they may never consent to abolish the veto power. Sir, the Democratic party, in regard to this power, in the language of the doughty barons of England, centuries ago, are not willing that the charter of their liberties shall be changed. We shall hold on to this veto power as one of the most effectual safeguards of the Union, and one of the surest means of carrying into effect the will of the people.

In my humble judgment, the wise statesman ought equally to avoid a foolish veneration for ancient institutions on the one hand, and a restless desire for change on the other. In this respect, the middle is the safer course. Too great a veneration for antiquity would have kept mankind in bondage; and the plea of despots and tyrants, in every age, has been that the wisdom of past generations has established institutions which the people ought not to touch with a sacrilegious hand. Our ancestors were great innovators; and had they not been so, the darkness and despotism which existed a thousand years ago would have continued until the present moment. For my own part, I believe that the human race, from generation to generation, has in the main been advancing, and will continue to advance, in wisdom and knowledge; and whenever experience shall demonstrate that a change, even in the Federal Constitution, will promote the happiness and prosperity of the people, I shall not hesitate to vote in favor of such a change. Still, there are circumstances which surround this instrument with peculiar sanctity. It was framed by as wise men and as pure patriots as the sun of heaven ever shone upon. We have every reason to believe that Providence smiled upon their labors, and predestined them to bless mankind. Immediately after the adoption of the Constitution, order arose out of confusion; and a settled Government, capable of performing all its duties to its constituents with energy and effect, succeeded to the chaos and disorder which had previously existed under the Articles of Confederation. For more than half a century, under this Constitution, we have enjoyed a greater degree of liberty and happiness than has ever fallen to the lot of any other nation on earth. Under such circumstances, the Senator from Kentucky, before he can rightfully demand our votes in favor of a radical change of this Constitution, in one of its fundamental articles, ought to make out a clear case. He ought not only to point out the evils which the country has suffered from the existence of the veto power, but ought to convince us they have been of such magnitude, that it is not better "to bear the ills we have, than fly to others that we know not of." For my own part, I believe that the veto power is one of the strongest and stateliest columns of that fair temple which our ancestors have dedicated to liberty; and that if you remove it from this time-honored edifice, you will essentially impair its strength and mar its beauty. Indeed there will then be great danger that in time it may tumble into ruins.

Sir, in regard to this veto power, as it at present exists, the convention which framed the Constitution, although much divided on other subjects, were unanimous. It is true that in the earlier stages of their proceedings, it was considerably discussed, and presented in different aspects. Some members 476were in favor of an absolute veto, and others were opposed to any veto, however qualified; but they at length unanimously adopted the happy mean, and framed the article as it now stands in the Constitution. According to Mr. Madison's report of the debates and proceedings in the convention, we find that on Saturday the 21st July, 1787, "the tenth resolution giving the executive a qualified veto, requiring two-thirds of each branch of the legislature to overrule it, was then agreed to nem. con." The convention continued in session for nearly two months after this decision; but so far as I can discover, no member ever attempted to disturb this unanimous decision.

A principle thus settled ought never to be rashly assailed under the excitement of disappointed feelings occasioned by the veto of two favorite measures at the extra session, on which Senators had fixed their hearts. There ought to have been time for passion to cool and reason to resume her empire. I know very well that the Senator from Kentucky had announced his opposition to the veto power so far back as June, 1840, in his Hanover speech; but that speech may fairly be considered as a declaration of his own individual opinion on this subject. The great Whig party never adopted it as one of the cardinal articles of their faith, until, smarting under disappointment, they saw their two favorite measures of the extra session fall beneath this power. It was then, and not till then, that the resolution, in effect to abolish it, was adopted by them as a party, in their manifesto. The present amendment proposes to carry this resolution into execution.

I should rather rely upon the judgment of the Senator from Kentucky on any other question, than in regard to the veto power. He has suffered so much from its exercise as to render it almost impossible that he can be an impartial judge. History will record the long and memorable struggle between himself and a distinguished ex-President, now in retirement. This was no common party strife. Their mighty war shook the whole Republic to its centre. The one swayed the majority in both Houses of Congress; whilst the other was sustained by a majority of the people. Under the lead of the one, Congress passed bills to establish a Bank of the United States;—to commence a system of internal improvements;—and to distribute the proceeds of the public lands among the several States; whilst the other, strong in his convictions of duty, and strong in his belief that the voice of the sovereign people would condemn these measures of their representatives, vetoed them every one. And what was the result? Without, upon the present occasion, expressing an opinion on any one of these questions, was it not rendered manifest that the President elected by the mass of the people, and directly responsible to them for his conduct, understood their will and their wishes better than the majority in the Senate and House of Representatives? No wonder then that the Senator from Kentucky should detest the veto power. It ought never to be torn from its foundation in the Constitution by the rash hands of a political party, impelled to the deed under the influence of defeated hopes and disappointed ambition.

I trust now that I shall be able to prove that the Senator from Kentucky 477has entirely mistaken the character of the veto power; that in its origin and nature it is peculiarly democratic; that in the qualified form in which it exists in our Constitution, it is but a mere appeal by the President of the people's choice from the decision of Congress to the people themselves; and that whilst the exercise of this power has done much good, it never has been, and never can be, dangerous to the rights and liberties of the people. This is not "an arbitrary and monarchical power;" it is not "a monarchical prerogative," as it has been designated by the Senator. If it were, I should go with him, heart and hand, for its abolition. What is a monarchical prerogative? It is a power vested in an emperor or king, neither elected by, nor responsible to, the people, to maintain and preserve the privileges of his throne. The veto power in the hands of such a sovereign has never been exerted, and never will be exerted, except to arrest the progress of popular liberty, or what he may term popular encroachment. It is the character of the public agent on whom this power is conferred, and not the nature of the power itself, which stamps it either as democratic or arbitrary. In its origin we all know that it was purely democratic. It owes its existence to a revolt of the people of Rome against the tyrannical decrees of the Senate. They retired from the city to the Sacred Mount, and demanded the rights of freemen. They thus extorted from the aristocratic Senate a decree authorizing them annually to elect tribunes of the people. On these tribunes was conferred the power of annulling any decree of the Senate, by simply pronouncing the word "veto." This very power was the only one by means of which the Democracy of Rome exercised any control over the government of the republic. It was their only safeguard against the oppression and encroachments of the aristocracy. It is true that it did not enable the people, through their tribunes, to originate laws; but it saved them from all laws of the Senate which encroached on their rights and liberties.

Now, sir, let me ask the Senator from Kentucky, was this an arbitrary and monarchical power? No, sir; it was strictly democratic. And why? Because it was exercised by tribunes elected by the people, and responsible annually to the people; and I shall now attempt to prove that the veto power, under our Constitution, is of a similar character.

Who is the President of the United States, by whom this power is to be exercised? He is a citizen, elected by his fellow-citizens to the highest official trust in the country, and directly responsible to them for the manner in which he shall discharge his duties. From the manner in which he is elected, he more nearly represents a majority of the whole people of the United States than any other branch of the Government. Sir, one-fourth of the people may elect a decided majority of the Senate. Under the Constitution, we are the representatives of sovereign States, and little Delaware has an equal voice in this body with the Empire State. How is it in regard to the House of Representatives? Without a resort to the gerrymandering process which of late years has become so common, it may often happen, from the arrangement of the Congressional districts, that a minority of the 478people of a State will elect a majority of representatives to Congress. Not so in regard to the President of the United States. From necessity, he must be elected by the mass of the people in the several States. He is the creature of the people—the mere breath of their nostrils—and on him, as the tribune of the people, have they conferred the veto power. Is there any serious danger that such a magistrate will ever abuse this power? What earthly inducement can he have to pursue such a course? In the first place, during his first term, he will necessarily feel anxious to obtain the stamp of public approbation on his conduct, by a re-election. For this reason, if no other existed, he will not array himself, by the exercise of the veto power, against a majority in both Houses of Congress, unless in extreme cases, where, from strong convictions of public duty, he may be willing to draw down upon himself their hostile influence.

In the second place, the Constitution leaves him in a state of dependence on Congress. Without their support, no measure recommended by him can become a law, and no system of policy which he may have devised can be carried into execution. Deprived of their aid, he can do nothing. Upon their cordial co-operation the success and glory of his administration must, in a great degree, depend. Is it, then, at all probable that he would make war upon Congress, by refusing to sanction any one of their favorite measures, unless he felt deeply conscious that he was acting in obedience to the will of the people, and could appeal to them for support? Nothing short of such a conviction, unless it be to preserve his oath inviolate to support the Constitution, will ever induce him to exercise a power always odious in the eyes of the majority in Congress, against which it is exerted. But there is still another powerful influence which will prevent his abuse of the veto power. The man who has been elevated by his fellow-citizens to the highest office of trust and dignity which a great nation can bestow, must necessarily feel a strong desire to have his name recorded in untarnished characters on the page of his country's history, and to live after death in the hearts of his countrymen. This consideration would forbid the abuse of the veto power. What is posthumous fame in almost every instance? Is it not the voice of posterity re-echoing the opinion of the present generation? And what body on the earth can give so powerful an impulse to public opinion, at least in this country, as the Congress of the United States? Under all these circumstances, we must admit that the opinion expressed by the Federalist is sound, and that "it is evident that there would be greater danger of his not using his power when necessary, than of his using it too often or too much." Such must also have been Mr. Jefferson's opinion. When consulted by General Washington in April, 1792, as to the propriety of vetoing "the act for an apportionment of Representatives among the several States, according to the first enumeration," what was his first reason in favor of the exercise of this power upon that occasion? "Viewing the bill," says he, "either as a violation of the Constitution, or as giving an inconvenient exposition to its words, is it a case wherein the President ought to interpose his negative?" 479"I think it is." "The non user of his negative power begins already to excite a belief that no President will ever venture to use it; and consequently, has begotten a desire to raise up barriers in the State legislatures against Congress throwing off the control of the Constitution." I shall not read the other reasons he has assigned, none of them being necessary for my present purpose. Perilous, indeed, I repeat, is the exercise of the veto power, and "no President will ever venture to use it," unless from the strongest sense of duty, and the strongest conviction that it will receive the public approbation.

But, after all, what is the nature of this qualified veto under the Constitution? It is, in fact, but an appeal taken by the President from the decision of Congress, in a particular case, to the tribunal of the sovereign people of the several States, who are equally the masters of both. If they decide against the President, their decision must finally prevail, by the admission of the Senator himself. The same President must either carry it into execution himself, or the next President whom they elect, will do so. The veto never can do more than postpone legislative action on the measure of which it is the subject, until the will of the people can be fairly expressed. This suspension of action, if the people should not sustain the President, will not generally continue longer than two years, and it cannot continue longer than four. If the people, at the next elections, should return a majority to Congress hostile to the veto, and the same measure should be passed a second time, he must indeed be a bold man, and intent upon his own destruction, who would, a second time, arrest it by his veto. After the popular voice has determined the question, the President would always submit, unless, by so doing, he clearly believed he would involve himself in the guilt of perjury, by violating his oath to support the Constitution. At the end of four years, however, in any and every event, the popular will must and would be obeyed by the election of another President.

Sir, the Senator from Kentucky, in one of those beautiful passages which always abound in his speeches, has drawn a glowing picture of the isolated condition of kings, whose ears the voice of public opinion is never permitted to reach; and he has compared their condition in this particular, with that of the President of the United States. Here too, he said, the Chief Magistrate occupied an isolated station, where the voice of his country and the cries of its distress could not reach his ear. But is there any justice in this comparison? Such a picture may be true to the life when drawn for an European monarch; but it has no application whatever to a President of the United States. He, sir, is no more than the first citizen of this free Republic. No form is required in approaching his person, which can prevent the humblest of his fellow-citizens from communicating with him. In approaching him, a freeman of this land is not compelled to decorate himself in fantastic robes, or adopt any particular form of dress, such as the court etiquette of Europe requires. The President, intermingles freely with his fellow-citizens, and hears the opinions of all. The public press attacks him—political parties, in and out of Congress, assail him, and the thunders of the Senator's own 480denunciatory eloquence are reverberated from the Capitol, and reach the White House before its incumbent can lay his head upon his pillow. His every act is subjected to the severest scrutiny, and he reads in the newspapers of the day the decrees of public opinion. Indeed, it is the privilege of everybody to assail him. To contend that such a Chief Magistrate is isolated from the people, is to base an argument upon mere fancy, and not upon facts. No, sir; the President of the United States is more directly before the people, and more immediately responsible, than any other department of our Government: and woe be to that President who shall ever affect to withdraw from the public eye, and seclude himself in the recesses of the Executive mansion!

The Senator has said, and with truth, that no veto of the President has ever been overruled, since the origin of the Government. Not one. Although he introduced this fact for another purpose than that which now induces me to advert to it, yet it is not the less true on that account. Is not this the strongest possible argument to prove that there never yet has been a veto, in violation of the public will?

[Here Mr. Clay observed that there had been repeated instances of majorities in Congress deciding against vetoes.]

Mr. Buchanan resumed. I am now speaking of majorities, not of Congress, but of the people. I shall speak of majorities in Congress presently.

Why, sir, has no veto been ever overruled? Simply because the President has never exercised, and never will exercise, this perilous power on any important occasion, unless firmly convinced that he is right, and that he will be sustained by the people. Standing alone, with the whole responsibility of his high official duties pressing upon him, he will never brave the enormous power and influence of Congress, unless he feels a moral certainty that the people will come to the rescue. When he ventures to differ from Congress and appeal to the people, the chances are all against him. The members of the Senate and the House are numerous, and are scattered over the whole country, whilst the President is but an individual confined to the city of Washington. Their personal influence with their constituents is, and must be, great. In such a struggle, he must mainly rely upon the palpable justice of his cause. Under these circumstances, does it not speak volumes in favor of the discretion with which the veto power has been exercised, that it has never once been overruled, in a single instance, since the origin of the Government, either by a majority of the people in the several States, or by the constitutional majority in Congress. It is truly astonishing how rarely this power has ever been exercised. During the period of more than half a century which has elapsed since the meeting of the first Congress under the Constitution, about six thousand legislative acts have been passed. How many of these, sir, do you suppose have been disapproved by the President? Twenty, sir; twenty is the whole number. I speak from a list now in my hand prepared by one of the clerks of the Senate. And this number embraces not merely those bills which have been actually vetoed; but all such as were retained by him under the Constitution, in consequence of having been presented at so late a period of the session that he could not prepare his objections previous to the adjournment. Twenty is the sum total of all!

Let us analyze these vetoes (for I shall call them all by that name) for a few moments. Of the twenty, eight were on bills of small comparative importance, and excited no public attention. Congress at once yielded to the President's objections, and in one remarkable instance, a veto of General Jackson was laid upon the table on the motion of the Senator from Kentucky himself. No attempt was even made to pass the bill in opposition to this veto, and no one Senator contested its propriety. Eleven of the twelve remaining vetoes upon this list, relate to only three subjects. These are, a Bank of the United States; internal improvements in different forms; and the distribution of the proceeds of the public lands among the several States. There have been four vetoes of a Bank of the United States; one by Mr. Madison, one by General Jackson, and two by Mr. Tyler. There have been six vetoes on internal improvements, in different forms; one by Mr. Madison, one by Mr. Monroe, and four by General Jackson. And General Jackson vetoed the bill to distribute the proceeds of the sales of the public lands among the several States. These make the eleven.

The remaining veto was by General Washington; and it is remarkable that it should be the most questionable exercise of this power which has ever occurred. I refer to his second and last veto, on the first of March, 1797, and but three days before he retired from office, on the "Act to alter and amend an act, entitled an act to ascertain and fix the military establishment of the United States." In this instance, there was a majority of nearly two-thirds in the House of Representatives, where it originated, in favor of passing the act, notwithstanding the objections of the Father of his Country. The vote was fifty-five in the affirmative to thirty-six in the negative. This act provided for the reduction of the military establishment of the country; and the day will probably never again arrive when any President will venture to veto an act reducing the standing army of the United States.

Then in the range of time since the year 1789, there have been but twenty vetoes; and eleven of these related to only three subjects which have radically divided the two great political parties of the country. With the exception of twenty, all of the acts which have ever passed Congress, have been allowed to take their course without any executive interference.

That this power has never been abused, is as clear as the light of the sun. I ask Senators, and I appeal to you, sir, whether the American people have not sanctioned every one of the vetoes on the three great subjects to which I have referred. Yes, sir, every one, not excepting those on the Fiscal Bank and Fiscal Corporation—the leading measures of the extra session. Notwithstanding the solemn denunciation against the President, made by the Whig party, and their appeal to the people, there has been no election held since that session in which the people have not declared, in a voice of thunder, their approbation of the two vetoes of President Tyler. I shall not, upon the present occasion, discuss the question whether all or any of these vetoes were right or wrong. I merely state the incontrovertible fact that they have all been approved by the American people.

The character of the bills vetoed shows conclusively the striking contrast between the veto power when entrusted to an elective and responsible chief magistrate, and when conferred upon a European sovereign as a royal prerogative. All the vetoes which an American President has imposed on any important act of Congress, except the one by General Washington, to which I have alluded, have been so many instances of self-denial. These acts have all been returned, accompanied by messages remonstrating against the extension of executive power, which they proposed to grant. Exerting the influence which these acts proposed to confer upon him, the President might, indeed, have made long strides towards the attainment of monarchical power. Had a national bank been established under his control, uniting the moneyed with the political power of the country; had a splendid system of internal improvements been adopted and placed under his direction, presenting prospects of pecuniary advantage to almost every individual throughout the land; and in addition to all this, had the States become pensioners on the bounty of the Federal Government for the amount of the proceeds of the sales of the public lands, we might soon have witnessed a powerful consolidated Government, with a chief at its head, far different from the plain and unpretending President recognized by the Constitution. The General Government might then have become everything, whilst the State governments would have sunk to nothing. Thanks to the vetoes of our Presidents, and not to Congress, that most of these evils have been averted. Had these acts been all approved by the President, it is my firm conviction that the Senator himself would as deeply have deplored the consequences as any other true patriot, and that he would forever have regretted his own agency in substantially changing the form of our Government. Had these bills become laws, the executive power would then have strode over all the other powers of the Constitution; and then, indeed, the Senator might have justly compared the President of the United States with the monarchs of Europe. Our Presidents have had the self-denying firmness to render all these attempts abortive to bestow on themselves extraordinary powers, and have been content to confine themselves to those powers conferred on them by the Constitution. They have protected the rights of the States and of the people from the unconstitutional means of influence which Congress had placed within their grasp. Such have been the consequences of the veto power in the hands of our elective chief magistrate.

For what purposes has this power been exerted by European monarchs, with whom our President has been compared? When exercised at all, it has always been for the purpose of maintaining the royal prerogative and arresting the march of popular liberty. There have been but two instances of its exercise in England since the Revolution of 1688. The first was in 1692, by William the Third, the rival of Louis the Fourteenth, and beyond question the ablest man who has sat upon the throne of Great Britain for the last century and a half. He had the hardihood to veto the Earl of Shrewsbury's bill, which had passed both houses, limiting the duration of Parliaments to three, instead of seven years, and requiring annual sessions to be held. He dreaded the influence which members of the House of Commons, responsible to their constituents at the end of each period of three years, might exert against his royal power and prerogatives; and, therefore, held on by means of the veto to septennial Parliaments. And what did George the Third? In 1806 he vetoed the Catholic Emancipation bill, and thus continued to hold in political bondage millions of his fellow-men, because they insisted upon worshipping their God according to the dictates of their own consciences.

[Here Mr. Clay observed that this was a mistake, and expressed his belief that, upon the occasion alluded to, the matter had gone no further than the resignation of the Grenville administration.]

Mr. Buchanan. I shall then read my authority. It is to be found in "Random Recollections of the House of Lords, by Mr. Grant," page 25. The author says:

"But if the king refuses his signature to it, [a bill] as George the Third did in the case of the Catholic Emancipation bill of 1806, it necessarily falls to the ground. The way in which the king intimates his determination not to give his assent to the measure, is not by a positive refusal in so many words; he simply observes, in answer to the application made to him for that purpose, 'Le roi s'avisera,' namely, 'The king will consider of it,' which is understood to be a final determination not to sanction the measure."

But, sir, be this author correct or incorrect, as to the existence of a veto in 1806, it is a matter of trifling importance in the present argument.[71] I admit that the exercise of the veto power has fallen into disuse in England since the revolution. And what are the reasons? First, because its exercise by a hereditary sovereign to preserve unimpaired the prerogatives of the crown against the voice of the people, is always an odious exertion of the royal prerogative. It is far different from its exercise by an elective magistrate, acting in the character of a tribune of the people, to preserve their rights and liberties unimpaired. And secondly, because this veto power is no longer necessary to secure the prerogatives of the crown against the assaults of popular liberty.

Two centuries ago, the people of England asserted their rights by the sword against their sovereign. They dethroned and beheaded him. Since that 484time, the kings of England have changed their course. They have discovered from experience that it was much easier to govern Parliament by means of the patronage and money at the command of the crown, than openly to resist it by the veto power. This system has succeeded admirably. Influence has taken the place of prerogative; and since the days of Walpole, when the votes of members were purchased almost without disguise, corruption has nearly destroyed the independent action of Parliament. It has now descended into the ranks of the people, and threatens destruction to the institutions of that country. In the recent contest for power between the Whigs and the Tories, the bargain and sale of the votes of the electors was open and notorious. The bribery and corruption of both parties sought no disguise. In many places the price of a vote was fixed, like any other commodity in the market. These things have been proclaimed without contradiction on the floor of Parliament. The Tories had the most money to expend; and the cause of dear bread, with a starving population, prevailed over the modification or repeal of the corn laws. In a country so venal, it is easy for the crown, by a politic distribution of its honors, offices and emoluments, and if these should all fail, by a direct application of money, to preserve its prerogatives without the use of the veto power.

Besides, the principal ministers of the crown are always members of the House of Lords or the House of Commons. It is they who originate the important laws; and they, and they alone, are responsible, because it is a maxim of the British government, that the king can do no wrong. If they cannot maintain a majority in Parliament by the use of the patronage and influence of the crown, they must yield their places to their successful rivals; and the king, without the least hesitation, will receive as his confidential advisers tomorrow, the very men whose principles he had condemned but yesterday. Such is a king of England. He can do no wrong.

On one memorable occasion, when the ministers of the crown themselves—I refer to the coalition administration of Mr. Fox and Lord North—had passed their East India Bill through the House of Commons, it was defeated in the House of Lords by the direct personal influence of the sovereign. George the Third, it is known, would have vetoed that bill, had it passed the House of Lords; and well he might. It was an attempt by his own ministers to obtain possession of the wealth and the power of India, and to use them for the purpose of controlling both the sovereign and the people of England. This was not the common case of a mere struggle between opposite parties as to which should administer the government, about which the sovereign of England might be perfectly indifferent; but it was an attempt to deprive the crown of its power and prerogatives. Under such circumstances, can the Senator seriously contend that, because the veto power has been disused by the kings of England, therefore, it ought to be taken from the President of the United States? The king is a hereditary sovereign—the President an elective magistrate. The king is not responsible to the people for the administration of the executive government—the President is alone responsible. The king could feel no interest in using the veto power, except to maintain the prerogatives of the crown; and it has been shown to be wholly unnecessary for this purpose; whilst the President has never exerted it on any important occasion, but in obedience to the public will, and then only for the purpose of preventing encroachment by Congress on the Constitution of the country, on the rights of the States, and on the liberties of the people.

The Senator is mistaken in supposing that the veto power has never been exercised in France. It is true, I believe, that it has never been exerted by the government of Louis Philippe; but his government is as yet nothing but a mere experiment. It has now existed less than twelve years, and during this short period there have been nineteen different cabinets. I saw a list of them a few days ago, in one of the public journals. To cite the example of such a government as authority here, is to prove that a Senator is hard run for arguments. The unfortunate Louis the Sixteenth, used the suspensive veto power conferred upon him by the first French Constitution, upon more than one occasion; but he used it not to enforce the will of the people as our Presidents have done, but against public opinion, which was at that time omnipotent in France. These vetoes proved but a feeble barrier against the tremendous torrent of the Revolution, which was at that time overwhelming all the corrupt and tyrannical institutions of the ancient monarchy.

The Senator has referred to the Declaration of Independence, to show that the exercise of this veto power by the king on the acts of the colonial legislature was one of the causes of the Revolution. In that instrument he is charged with having "refused his assent to laws the most wholesome and necessary for the public good." In those days a douceur was presented, in Pennsylvania, to the proprietary governor, with every act of assembly in which the people felt a deep interest. I state this fact on the authority of Dr. Franklin. After the act was approved by the governor, it had then to be sent three thousand miles across the Atlantic for the approbation of a hereditary sovereign, in no manner responsible to the people of this country. It would have been strange, indeed, had not this power been abused under such circumstances. This was like the veto of Augustus after he had usurped the liberties of the Roman people, and made himself sole tribune—not like that of the tribunes annually elected by the Roman people. This was not the veto of James Madison, Andrew Jackson, or John Tyler—not the veto of a freeman, responsible to his fellow-freemen for the faithful and honest exercise of his important trust. This power is either democratic or arbitrary, as the authority exercising it may be dependent on the people or independent of them.

But, sir, this veto power, which I humbly apprehend to be useful in every State government, becomes absolutely necessary under the peculiar and complex form of the Federal Government. To this point I desire especially to direct the attention of the Senate. The Federal Constitution was a work of mutual compromise and concession; and the States which became parties to it, must take the evil with the good. A majority of the people within each of the several States have the inherent right to change, modify, and amend their Constitution at pleasure. Not so with respect to the Federal Constitution. In regard to it, a majority of the people of the United States can exercise no such power. And why? Simply because they have solemnly surrendered it, in consideration of obtaining by this surrender all the blessings and benefits of our glorious Union. It requires two-thirds of the representatives of the States in the Senate, and two-thirds of the representatives of the people in the House, even to propose an amendment to the Constitution; and this must be ratified by three-fourths of the States before it can take effect. Even if twenty-five of the twenty-six States of which the Union is composed should determine to deprive "little Delaware" of her equal representation in the Senate, she could defy them all, whilst this Constitution shall endure. It declares that "no State, without its consent, shall be deprived of its equal suffrage in the Senate."

As the Constitution could not have been adopted except by a majority of the people in every State of the Union, the members of the convention believed that it would be reasonable and just to require that three-fourths of the States should concur in changing that which all had adopted, and to which all had become parties. To give it a binding force upon the conscience of every public functionary, each Senator and Representative, whether in Congress or the several State legislatures, and every executive and judicial officer, whether State or Federal, is bound solemnly to swear or affirm that he will support the Constitution.

Now, sir, it has been said, and said truly by the Senator, that the will of the majority ought to prevail. This is an axiom in the science of liberty, which nobody at the present day will dispute. Under the Federal Constitution, this will must be declared in the manner which it has prescribed; and sooner or later, the majority must and will be obeyed in the enactment of laws. But what is this majority to which we are all bound to yield? Is it the majority of Senators and Representatives in Congress, or a majority of the people themselves? The fallacy of the Senator's argument, from beginning to end, consists in the assumption that Congress, in every situation and under every circumstance, truly represents the deliberate will of the people. The framers of the Constitution believed it might be otherwise, and therefore they imposed the restriction of the qualified veto of the President upon the legislative action of Congress.

What is the most glorious and useful invention of modern times in the science of free government? Undoubtedly, written constitutions. For want of these, the ancient republics were scenes of turbulence, violence and disorder, and ended in self-destruction. And what are all our constitutions, but restraints imposed, not by arbitrary authority, but by the people upon themselves and their own representatives? Such throughout is the character of the Federal Constitution. And it is this Constitution thus restricted, which has so long secured our liberty and prosperity, and has endeared itself to the heart of every good citizen.

This system of self-imposed restraints is a necessary element of our social condition. Every wise and virtuous man adopts resolutions by which he regulates his conduct, for the purpose of counteracting the evil propensities of his nature, and preventing him from yielding under the impulses of sudden and strong temptation. Is such a man the less free—the less independent, because he chooses to submit to these self-imposed restraints? In like manner, is the majority of the people less free and less independent, because it has chosen to impose constitutional restrictions upon itself and its representatives? Is this any abridgment of popular liberty? The true philosophy of republican government, as the history of the world has demonstrated, consists in the establishment of such counteracting powers,—powers always created by the people themselves,—as shall render it morally certain that no law can be passed by their servants which shall not be in accordance with their will, and calculated to promote their good. It is for this reason that a senate has been established in every State of the Union to control the House of Representatives: and I presume there is scarcely an individual in the country who is not convinced of its necessity. Fifty years ago, opinions were much divided upon this subject, and nothing but experience has settled the question. In France, the National Assembly, although they retained the king, rejected a senate as aristocratic, and our own Franklin was opposed to it. He thought that the popular branch was alone necessary to reflect the will of the people, and that a senate would be but a mere incumbrance. His influence prevailed in the convention which framed the first constitution for Pennsylvania, and we had no senate. The Doctor's argument against it was contained in one of his homely but striking illustrations. Why, said he, will you place a horse in front of a cart to draw it forward, and another behind to draw it back? Experience, which is the wisest teacher, has demonstrated the fallacy of this and all other similar arguments, and public opinion is now unanimous on the subject. Where is the man who does not now feel that the control of a senate is necessary to restrain and modify the action of the popular branch?

And how is our own Senate composed? One-fourth of the people of this Union, through the agency of the State legislatures, can send a majority into this chamber. A bill may pass the House of Representatives by a unanimous vote, and yet be defeated here by a majority of Senators representing but one-fourth of the people of the United States. Why does not the Senator from Kentucky propose to abolish the Senate? His argument would be much stronger against its existence than against that of the veto power in the hands of a Chief Magistrate, who, in this particular, is the true representative of the majority of the whole people.

All the beauty, and harmony, and order of the universe arise from counteracting influences. When its great Author, in the beginning, gave the planets their projective impulse, they would have rushed in a straight line through 488the realms of boundless space, had he not restrained them within their prescribed orbits by the counteracting influence of gravitation. All the valuable inventions in mechanics consist in blending simple powers together so as to restrain and regulate the action of each other. Restraint—restraint—not that imposed by arbitrary and irresponsible power, but by the people themselves, in their own written constitutions, is the great law which has rendered Democratic Representative Government so successful in these latter times. The best security which the people can have against abuses of trust by their public servants, is to ordain that it shall be the duty of one class of them to watch and restrain another. Sir, this Federal Government, in its legislative attributes, is nothing but a system of restraints from beginning to end. In order to enact any bill into a law, it must be passed by the representatives of the people in the House, and also by the representatives of the sovereign States in the Senate, where, as I have observed before, it may be defeated by Senators from States containing but one-fourth of the population of the country. After it has undergone these two ordeals, it must yet be subjected to that of the Executive, as the tribune of the whole people, for his approbation. If he should exercise his veto power, it cannot become a law unless it be passed by a majority of two-thirds of both Houses. These are the mutual restraints which the people have imposed on their public servants, to preserve their own rights and those of the States from rash, hasty, and impolitic legislation. No treaty with a foreign power can be binding upon the people of this country unless it shall receive the assent of the President and two-thirds of the Senate; and this is the restraint which the people have imposed on the treaty-making power.

All these restraints are peculiarly necessary to protect the rights and preserve the harmony of the different States which compose our Union. It now consists of twenty-six distinct and independent States, and this number may yet be considerably increased. These States differ essentially from each other in their domestic institutions, in the character of their population, and even, to some extent, in their language. They embrace every variety of soil, climate, and productions. In an enlarged view, I believe their interests to be all identical; although, to the eye of local and sectional prejudice, they always appear to be conflicting. In such a condition, mutual jealousies must arise, which can only be repressed by that mutual forbearance which pervades the Constitution. To legislate wisely for such a people is a task of extreme delicacy, and requires much self-restraining prudence and caution. In this point of view, I firmly believe that the veto power is one of the best safeguards of the Union. By this power, the majority of the people in every State have decreed that the existing laws shall remain unchanged, unless not only a majority in each House of Congress, but the President also, shall sanction the change. By these wise and wholesome restrictions, they have secured themselves, so far as human prudence can, against hasty, oppressive, and dangerous legislation.

The rights of the weaker portions of the Union will find one of their greatest securities in the veto power. It would be easy to imagine interests of the deepest importance to particular sections which might be seriously endangered by its destruction. For example, not more than one-third of the States have any direct interest in the coasting trade. This trade is now secured to American vessels, not merely by a protective duty, but by an absolute prohibition of all foreign competition. Suppose the advocates of free trade run mad should excite the jealousy of the Senators and Representatives from the other two-thirds of the States against this comparatively local interest, and convince them that this trade ought to be thrown open to foreign navigation. By such a competition, they might contend that the price of freight would be reduced, and that the producers of cotton, wheat, and other articles ought not to be taxed in order to sustain such a monopoly in favor of their own ship building and navigating interest. Should Congress, influenced by these or any other consideration, ever pass an act to open this trade to the competition of foreigners, there is no man fit to fill the executive chair who would not place his veto upon it, and thus refer the subject to the sober determination of the American people. To deprive the navigating States of this privilege, would be to aim a deadly blow at the very existence of the Union.

Let me suppose another case of a much more dangerous character. In the Southern States, which compose the weaker portion of the Union, a species of property exists which is now attracting the attention of the whole civilized world. These States never would have become parties to the Union, had not their rights in this property been secured by the Federal Constitution. Foreign and domestic fanatics—some from the belief that they are doing God's service, and others from a desire to divide and destroy this glorious Republic—have conspired to emancipate the Southern slaves. On this question, the people of the South, beyond the limits of their own States, stand alone and unsupported by any power on earth, except that of the Northern Democracy. These fanatical philanthropists are now conducting a crusade over the whole world, and are endeavoring to concentrate the public opinion of all mankind against this right of property. Suppose they should ever influence a majority in both Houses of Congress to pass a law, not to abolish this property—for that would be too palpable a violation of the Constitution—but to render it of no value, under the letter, but against the spirit of some one of the powers granted; will any lover of his country say that the President ought not to possess the power of arresting such an act by his veto, until the solemn decision of the people should be known on this question, involving the life or death of the Union? We, sir, of the non-slaveholding States, entered the Union upon the express condition that this property should be protected. Whatever may be our own private opinions in regard to slavery in the abstract, ought we to hazard all the blessings of our free institutions—our Union and our strength—in such a crusade against our brethren of the South? Ought we to jeopard every political right we hold dear, for the sake of enabling these fanatics to invade Southern rights, and render that fair portion of our common inheritance a scene of servile war, rapine, and murder? 490Shall we apply the torch to the magnificent temple of human liberty which our forefathers reared at the price of their blood and treasure, and permit all we hold dear to perish in the conflagration? I trust not.

It is possible that at some future day the majority in Congress may attempt, by indirect means, to emancipate the slaves of the South. There is no knowing through what channel the ever active spirit of fanaticism may seek to accomplish its object. The attempt may be made through the taxing power, or some other express power granted by the Constitution. God only knows how it may be made. It is hard to say what means fanaticism may not adopt to accomplish its purpose. Do we feel so secure, in this hour of peril from abroad and peril at home, as to be willing to prostrate any of the barriers which the Constitution has reared against hasty and dangerous legislation? No, sir, never was the value of the veto power more manifest than at the present moment. For the weaker portion of the Union, whose constitutional rights are now assailed with such violence, to think of abandoning this safeguard, would be almost suicidal. It is my solemn conviction, that there never was a wiser or more beautiful adaptation of theory to practice in any government than that which requires a majority of two-thirds in both Houses of Congress to pass an act returned by the President with his objections, under all the high responsibilities which he owes to his country.

Sir, ours is a glorious Constitution. Let us venerate it—let us stand by it as the work of great and good men, unsurpassed in the history of any age or nation. Let us not assail it rashly with our invading hands, but honor it as the fountain of our prosperity and power. Let us protect it as the only system of government which could have rendered us what we are in half a century, and enabled us to take the front rank among the nations of the earth. In my opinion, it is the only form of government which can preserve the blessings of liberty and prosperity to the people, and at the same time secure the rights and sovereignty of the States. Sir, the great mass of the people are unwilling that it shall be changed. Although the Senator from Kentucky, to whom I cannot and do not attribute any but patriotic motives, has brought himself to believe that a change is necessary, especially in the veto power, I must differ from him entirely, convinced that his opinions on this subject are based upon fallacious theories of the nature of our institutions. This view of his opinions is strengthened by his declarations the other day as to the illimitable rights of the majority in Congress. On that point he differs essentially from the framers of the Constitution. They believed that the people of the different States had rights which might be violated by such a majority; and the veto power was one of the modes which they devised for preventing these rights from being invaded.

The Senator, in support of his objections to the veto power, has used what he denominates a numerical argument, and asks, can it be supposed that any President will possess more wisdom than nine Senators and forty Representatives. (This is the number more than a bare majority of each body which would at present be required to pass a bill by a majority of two-thirds.) To this question, my answer is, no, it is not to be so supposed at all. All that we have to suppose is, what our ancestors, in their acknowledged wisdom, did suppose; that Senators and Representatives are but mortal men, endowed with mortal passions and subject to mortal infirmities; that they are susceptible of selfish and unwise impulses, and that they do not always and under all circumstances, truly reflect the will of their constituents. These founders of our Government, therefore, supposed the possibility that Congress might pass an act through the influence of unwise or improper motives; and that the best mode of saving the country from the evil effects of such legislation was to place a qualified veto in the hands of the people's own representative, the President of the United States, by means of which, unless two-thirds of each House of Congress should repass the bill, the question must be brought directly before the people themselves. These wise men had made the President so dependent on Congress that they knew he would never abuse this power, nor exert it unless from the highest and most solemn convictions of duty; and experience has established their wisdom and foresight. As to the Senator's numerical argument, I might as well ask him, is it to be supposed that we are so superior in wisdom to the members of the House that the vote of one Senator ought to annul the votes of thirty-two Representatives? And yet the bill to repeal the bankrupt law has just been defeated in this body by a majority of one, although it had passed the House by a majority of thirty-two. The Senator's numerical argument, if it be good for anything at all, would be good for the abolition of the Senate as well as of the veto; and would lead at once to the investment of all the powers of legislation in the popular branch alone. But experience has long exploded this theory throughout the world. The framers of the Constitution, in consummate wisdom, thought proper to impose checks, and balances, and restrictions on their Governmental agents; and woe betide us, if the day should ever arrive when they shall be removed.

But I must admit that another of the Senator's arguments is perhaps not quite so easily refuted, though, I think, it is not very difficult to demonstrate its fallacy. It is undoubtedly his strongest position. He says that the tendency of the veto power is to draw after it all the powers of legislation; and that Congress, in passing laws, will be compelled to consult, not the good of the country alone, but to ascertain, in the first instance, what the President will approve, and then regulate their conduct according to his predetermined will.

This argument presupposes the existence of two facts, which must be established before it can have the least force. First, that the President would depart from his proper sphere, and attempt to influence the initiatory legislation of Congress: and, second, that Congress would be so subservient as to originate and pass laws, not according to the dictates of their own judgment, but in obedience to his expressed wishes. Now, sir, does not the Senator perceive that his argument proves too much? Would not the President have precisely the same influence over Congress, so far as his patronage extends, as if the veto had never existed at all? He would then resemble the King of England, whose veto power has been almost abandoned for the last hundred and fifty years. If the President's power and patronage were coextensive with that of the king, he could exercise an influence over Congress similar to that which is now exerted over the British Parliament, and might control legislation in the same manner.

Thus, sir, you perceive that to deprive the President of the veto power, would afford no remedy against executive influence in Congress, if the President were disposed to exert it. Nay, more—it would encourage him to interfere secretly with our legislative functions, because, deprived of the veto power, his only resource would be to intrigue with members of Congress for the purpose of preventing the passage of measures which he might disapprove. At present this power enables him to act openly and boldly, and to state his reasons to the country for refusing his assent to any act passed by Congress.

Again: does not the Senator perceive that this argument is a direct attack upon the character of Congress? Does he not feel that the whole weight of his argument in favor of abolishing the veto power, rests upon the wisdom, integrity, and independence of that body? And yet we are told that in order to prevent the application of the veto, we shall become so subservient to the Executive, that in the passage of laws we will consult his wishes rather than our own independent judgment. The venality and baseness of Congress are the only foundations on which such an argument can rest; and yet it is the presumption of their integrity and wisdom on which the Senator relies for the purpose of proving that the veto power is wholly unnecessary, and ought to be abolished.

In regard to this thing of executive influence over Congress, I have a few words to say. Sir, I have been an attentive observer of Congressional proceedings for the last twenty years, and have watched its operations with an observing eye. I shall not pretend to say that it does not exist to some extent; but its power has been greatly overrated. It can never become dangerous to liberty, unless the patronage of the Government should be enormously increased by the passage of such unconstitutional and encroaching laws as have hitherto fallen under the blow of the veto power.

The Executive, indeed, will always have personal friends, as well as ardent political supporters of his administration in Congress, who will strongly incline to view his measures with a favorable eye. He will also have, both in and out of Congress, expectants who look to him for a share of the patronage at his disposal. But, after all, to what does this amount?

Whilst the canvass is proceeding previous to his election, the expectations of candidates for office will array around him a host of ardent and active friends. But what is his condition after the election has passed, and the patronage has been distributed? Let me appeal to the scene which we all witnessed in this city, at and after the inauguration of the late lamented President. It is almost impossible that one office seeker in fifty could have been gratified. What is the natural and necessary result of such numerous disappointments? It is to irritate the feelings and sour the minds of the unsuccessful applicants. They make comparisons between themselves and those who have been successful, and self-love always exaggerates their own merits and depreciates those of their successful rivals, to such an extent, that they believe themselves to have been injured. The President thus often makes one inactive friend, because he feels himself secure in office, and twenty secret enemies awaiting the opportunity to give him a stab whenever a favorable occasion may offer. The Senator greatly overrates the power of executive influence either among the people or in Congress. By the time the offices have been all distributed, which is usually done between the inauguration and the first regular meeting of Congress thereafter, the President has but few boons to offer.

Again: it is always an odious exercise of executive power to confer offices on members of Congress, unless under peculiar circumstances, where the office seeks the man rather than the man the office. In point of fact, but few members can receive appointments; and those soliciting them are always detected by their conduct. They are immediately noted for their subserviency; and from that moment, their influence with their fellow members is gone.

By far the greatest influence which a President can acquire over Congress, is a reflected influence from the people upon their representatives. This is dependent upon the personal popularity of the President, and can never be powerful, unless, from the force of his character, and the value of his past services, he has inspired the people with an enthusiastic attachment. A remarkable example of this reflected influence was presented in the case of General Jackson; and yet it is a high compliment to the independence, if not to the wisdom of Congress, that even he could rarely command a majority in both its branches. Still it is certain, notwithstanding, that he presented a most striking example of a powerful executive; and this chiefly because he was deservedly strong in the affections of the people.

In the vicissitude of human events, we shall sometimes have Presidents who can, if they please, exercise too much, and those who possess too little, influence over Congress. If we witnessed the one extreme during General Jackson's administration, we now have the other before our eyes. For the sake of the contrast, and without the slightest disrespect towards the worthy and amiable individual who now occupies the Presidential chair, I would say that if General Jackson presented an example of the strength, the present President presents an equally striking example of the feebleness, of executive influence. I ask what has all the patronage of his high office done for him? How many friends has it secured? I most sincerely wish, for the good of the country, and for the success of his administration, that he had a much greater degree of influence in Congress than he possesses. It is for this reason that I was glad to observe, a few days ago, some symptoms of returning favor on this (the Whig) side of the house towards John Tyler. It is better, much better, even thus late, that they should come forward and extend to him a helping hand, than, wishing to do so, still keep at a distance merely to preserve an appearance of consistency. I am sorry to see that from this mere affectation, they should appear so coy, and leave the country to suffer all the embarrassments which result from a weak administration. [Here several of the Whig Senators asked jocosely why the Democrats did not volunteer their services to strengthen the Government.] Oh! said Mr. B., we cannot do that. What is merely an apparent inconsistency in the Whigs, would be a real inconsistency in us. We cannot go for the Whig measures which were approved by President Tyler at the extra session. We cannot support the great Government Exchequer Bank of discount and exchange, with its three for one paper currency. I think, however, with all deference, that my Whig friends on this side of the House ought not to be squeamish on that subject. I think my friend from Georgia (Mr. Berrien) ought to go heart and hand for the Exchequer Bank. It is in substance his own scheme of a "Fiscal Corporation," transferred into the Treasury of the United States, and divested of private stockholders. Let me assure gentlemen that their character for consistency will not suffer by supporting this measure.

And yet, with the example of this administration before their eyes, the Whigs dread executive influence so much that they wish to abolish the veto power, lest the President may be able to draw within its vortex all the legislative powers of Congress! What a world we live in!

This authentic history is the best answer to another position of the Senator. Whilst he believes that there have been no encroachments of the General Government on the rights of the States, but on the contrary that it is fast sinking into the weakness and imbecility of the Confederation, he complains of the encroachments which he alleges to have been made by the President on the legitimate powers of Congress. I differ from him entirely in both these propositions, and am only sorry that the subject of the veto power is one so vast that time will not permit me to discuss them at present. This I shall, however, say, that the strong tendency of the Federal Government has, in my opinion, ever been to encroach upon the rights of the States and their people; and I might appeal to its history to establish the position. Every violent struggle, threatening the existence of the Union, which has existed in this country from the beginning, has arisen from the exercise of constructive and doubtful powers, not by the President, but by Congress. But enough of this for the present.

The Senator from Kentucky contends that, whether the executive be strong or weak, Congress must conform its action to his wishes, and if they cannot obtain what they desire, they must take what they can get. Such a principle of action is always wrong in itself, and must always lead to the destruction of the party which adopts it. This was the fatal error of the Senator and his friends at the extra session. He has informed us that neither "the Fiscal Bank" nor "the Fiscal Corporation" of that never to be forgotten session would have received twenty votes in either House, had the minds of members been left uninfluenced by the expected action of the Executive.

This was the most severe censure which he could have passed on his party in Congress. It is now admitted that the Whig party earnestly advocated and adopted two most important measures, not because they approved them in the form in which they were presented, but for the sake of conciliating Mr. Tyler. Never was there a more striking example of retributive justice than the veto of both these measures. Whether it be the fact, as the Senator alleges, that the Whigs in Congress took the Fiscal Corporation bill, letter for letter, as it came from the President to them, I shall not pretend to decide. It is not for me to compose such strifes. I leave this to their own file leaders. Without entering upon this question, I shall never fail, when a fit opportunity offers, to express the gratitude which I feel, in common with the whole country, to the President for having vetoed those bills, which it now appears never received the approbation of any person. It does astonish me, however, that this proceeding between the President and his party in Congress should ever have been made an argument in favor of abolishing the veto power. This argument, if it prove anything at all, sets the seal of condemnation to the measures of the late extra session, and to the extra session itself. It is a demonstration of the hasty, inconsiderate, and immature legislation of that session. In the flush of party triumph, the Whigs rushed it, before passion had time to cool down into that calm deliberation, so essential to the wise and harmonious co-operation of the different branches of the Government. They took so little time to consult and to deliberate, to reconcile their conflicting opinions and interests, and above all to ascertain and fix their real political principles which they had so sedulously concealed from the public eye throughout the contest, that none but those who were heated and excited beyond the bounds of reason ever anticipated any result but division, disaster, and defeat, from the extra session. The party first pursued a course which must have inevitably led to the defeat which they have experienced; and would then revenge themselves for their own misdeeds by assailing the veto power.

The lesson which we have received will teach Congress hereafter not to sacrifice its independence by consulting the executive will. Let them honestly and firmly pass such acts as they believe the public good requires. They will then have done their duty. Afterwards let the Executive exercise the same honesty and firmness in approving these acts. If he vetoes any one of them, he is responsible to the people, and there he ought to be left.

Had this course been pursued at the extra session, Congress would have passed an act to establish an old-fashioned Bank of the United States, which would have been vetoed by the President. A fair issue would thus have been made for the decision of their common constituents. There would then have been no necessity for my friends on this side of the house to submit to the humiliation of justifying themselves before the people, on the principle that they were willing to accept something which they knew to be very bad, because they could not obtain that which they thought the public good demanded. 496This whole proceeding, sir, presents no argument against the veto power; although it does present, in a striking light, the subserviency of the Whig party in Congress to executive dictation. We may, indeed, if insensible to our own rights and independence, give an undue influence to the veto power; but we shall never produce this effect if we confine ourselves to our own appropriate duties, and leave the Executive to perform his. This example will never, I think, be imitated by any party in the country, and we shall then never again be tempted to make war on the veto power.

To show that this power ought to be abolished, the Senator has referred to intimations given on this floor, during the administration of General Jackson, that such and such acts then pending would be vetoed, if passed. Such intimations may have been in bad taste; but what do they prove? The Senator does not and cannot say that they ever changed a single vote. In the instances to which he refers, they were the declaration of a fact which was known, or might have been known, to the whole world. A President can only be elected by a majority of the people of the several States. Throughout the canvass, his opinions and sentiments on every leading measure of public policy, are known and discussed. The last election was an exception to this rule; but another like it will never again occur in our day. If, under such circumstances, an act should pass Congress, notoriously in violation of some principle of vital importance, which was decided by the people at his election, the President would be faithless to the duty which he owed both to them and himself, if he did not disapprove the measure. Any person might then declare, in advance, that the President would veto such a bill. Let me imagine one or two cases which may readily occur. Is it not known from one end of the Union to the other, and even in every log cabin throughout its extent, that the Senator from Missouri [Mr. Benton] has an unconquerable antipathy to a paper currency, and an equally unconquerable predilection for hard money? Now, if he should be a candidate for the Presidency,—and much more unlikely events have happened than that he should be a successful candidate—would not his election be conclusive evidence that the people were in favor of gold and silver, and against paper? Under such circumstances, what else could Congress anticipate whilst concocting an old-fashioned Bank of the United States, but that he would instantly veto the bill on the day it was presented to him, without even taking time to sit down in his Presidential chair? (Great laughter, in which Mr. Benton and Mr. Clay both joined heartily.) Let me present a reverse case. Suppose the distinguished Senator from Kentucky should be elected President, would he hesitate, or, with his opinions, ought he to hesitate, a moment in vetoing an Independent Treasury bill, should Congress present him such a measure? And if I, as a member of the Senate, were to assert, in the first case which I have supposed, whilst the bank bill was pending, that it would most certainly be vetoed, to what would this amount? Would it be an attempt to bring executive influence to bear on Congress? Certainly not. It would only be the mere assertion of a well known fact. Would it prove anything against the veto power? 497Certainly not; but directly the reverse. It would prove that it ought to be exercised—that the people had willed, by the Presidential election, that it should be exercised—and that it was one of the very cases which demanded its exercise.

An anticipation of the exercise of the veto power, in cases which had already been decided by the people, ought to exercise a restraining influence over Congress. It should admonish them that they ought not to place themselves in hostile array against the Executive, and thus embarrass the administration of the Government by the adoption of a measure which had been previously condemned by the people. If the measure be right in itself, the people will, at the subsequent elections, reverse their own decision, and then, and not till then, ought Congress to act. No, sir; when we elect a President, we do it in view of his future course of action, inferred from his known opinions; and we calculate, with great accuracy, what he will and what he will not do. The people have never yet been deceived in relation to this matter, as has been abundantly shown by their approbation of every important veto since the origin of the Government.

This veto power was conferred upon the President to arrest unconstitutional, improvident, and hasty legislation. Its intention (if I may use a word not much according to my taste) was purely conservative. To adopt the language of the Federalist, "it establishes a salutary check upon the legislative body, calculated to guard the community against the effects of faction, precipitancy, or of any impulse unfriendly to the public good, which may happen to influence a majority of that body" (Congress). Throughout the whole book, whenever the occasion offers, a feeling of dread is expressed, lest the legislative power might transcend the limits prescribed to it by the Constitution, and ultimately absorb the other powers of the Government. From first to last, this fear is manifested. We ought never to forget that the representatives of the people are not the people themselves. The practical neglect of this distinction has often led to the overthrow of republican institutions. Eternal vigilance is the price of liberty; and the people should regard with a jealous eye, not only their Executive, but their legislative servants. The representative body, proceeding from the people, and clothed with their confidence, naturally lulls suspicion to sleep; and, when disposed to betray its trust, can execute its purpose almost before their constituents take the alarm.

It must have been well founded apprehensions of such a result which induced Mirabeau to declare, that, without a veto power in the king, who was no more, under the first constitution of France, than the hereditary chief executive magistrate of a republic, he would rather live in Constantinople than in Paris. The catastrophe proved his wisdom; but it also proved that the veto was no barrier against the encroachment of the Legislative Assembly; nor would it have saved his own head from the block, had he not died at the most propitious moment for his fame.

I might appeal to many passages in the history of the world to prove that 498the natural tendency of legislative power has always been to increase itself; and the accumulation of this power has, in many instances, overthrown republican institutions.

Our system of representative Democracy, Heaven's last and best political gift to man, when perverted from its destined purpose, has become the instrument of the most cruel tyranny which the world has ever witnessed. Thus it is that the best things, when perverted, become the worst. Witness the scenes of anarchy, confusion, and blood, from which humanity and reason equally revolt, which attended the French Revolution, during the period of the Legislative Assembly and National Convention. So dreadful were these scenes, all enacted in the name of the people, and by the people's own representatives, that they stand out in bold relief, from all the records of time, and are, by the universal consent of mankind, denominated "the reign of terror." Under the government of the Committee of Public Safety—a committee of the National Convention—more blood was shed and more atrocities committed, than mankind had ever beheld within the same space of time. And yet all this was done in the name of liberty and equality. And what was the result? All this only paved the way for the usurpation of Napoleon Bonaparte; and the people sought protection in the arms of despotism from the tyranny and corruption of their own representatives. This has ever been the course in which republics have degenerated into military despotisms. Let these sacred truths be ever kept in mind: that sovereignty belongs to the people alone, and that all their servants should be watched with the eyes of sleepless jealousy. The Legislative Assembly and the National Convention of France had usurped all the powers of the government. They each, in their turn, constituted the sole representative body of the nation, and no wise checks and barriers were interposed to moderate and restrain their action. The example which they presented has convinced all mankind of the necessity of a senate in a republic; and similar reasons ought to convince them of the necessity of such a qualified veto as exists under our Constitution. The people cannot interpose too many barriers against unwise and wicked legislation, provided they do not thereby impair the necessary powers of the Government. I know full well that such scenes as I have just described cannot occur in America; but still we may learn lessons of wisdom from them to guide our own conduct.

Legislative bodies of any considerable number are more liable to sudden and violent excitements than individuals. This we have all often witnessed; and it results from a well known principle of human nature. In the midst of such excitements, nothing is more natural than hasty, rash, and dangerous legislation. Individual responsibility is, also, diminished, in proportion to the increase of the number. Each person, constituting but a small fractional part of the whole mass, thinks he can escape responsibility in the midst of the crowd. The restraint of the popular will upon his conduct is thus greatly diminished, and as one of a number he is ready to perform acts which he would not attempt upon his own individual responsibility. In order to check such excesses, the Federalist tells us that this veto power, or reference of the subject to the people, was granted.

Again, sir, highly excited political parties may exist in legislative assemblies, so intent upon grasping or retaining power, that in the struggle they will forget the wishes and the interests of the people. I might cite several examples of this kind in the history of our own legislation; but I merely refer to the odious and unconstitutional alien and sedition laws. Led on by ambitious and eloquent men who have become highly excited in the contest, the triumph of party may become paramount to the good of the country, and unconstitutional and dangerous laws may be the consequence. The veto power is necessary to arrest such encroachments on the rights of the States and of the people.

But worst of all is the system of "log-rolling," so prevalent in Congress and the State legislatures, which the authors of the Federalist do not seem to have foreseen. This is not a name, to be sure, for ears polite; yet, though homely, it is so significant of the thing, that I shall be pardoned for its use. Now, sir, this very system of log-rolling in legislative bodies is that which has involved several of the States in debts for internal improvements, which I fear some of them may never be able to pay. In order to carry improvements which were useful and might have been productive, it was necessary to attach to them works of an opposite character. To obtain money to meet these extravagant expenditures, indulgence was granted to the banks at the expense of the people. Indeed, it has been a fruitful source of that whole system of ruinous and disastrous measures against which the Democracy have been warring for years. It has produced more distress in the country than can be repaired by industry and economy for many days to come. And yet how rarely has any Executive had the courage to apply the remedy which the veto power presents? Let us, for a moment, examine the workings of this system. It is the more dangerous, because it presents itself to individual members under the garb of devotion to their constituents. One has a measure of mere local advantage to carry, which ought, if at all, to be accomplished by individual enterprise, and which could not pass if it stood alone. He finds that he cannot accomplish his object, if he relies only upon its merits. He finds that other members have other local objects at heart, none of which would receive the support of a majority if separately considered. These members, then, form a combination sufficiently powerful to carry the whole; and thus twenty measures may be adopted, not one of which separately could have obtained a respectable vote. Thanks to the wisdom and energy of General Jackson, this system of local internal improvements which threatened to extend itself into every neighborhood of the nation, and overspread the land, was arrested by the veto power. Had not this been done, the General Government might, at the present day, have been in the same wretched condition with the most indebted States.

But this system of "log-rolling" has not been confined to mere local affairs, as the history of the extra session will testify. It was then adopted in regard to important party objects, and was called the "great system of measures of the Whig party." It was openly avowed that the majority must take the system in mass, although it is well known that several of the measures, had they stood alone, would have been rejected in detail. We are all perfectly aware that this was the vital principle of the extra session. By means of "log-rolling" the system was adopted. That the passage of the Distribution bill was the price paid for the Bankrupt bill, was openly avowed on this floor. By what mutual compensations the other measures were carried we are left to infer, and therefore I shall not hazard the expression of any opinion in this place on the subject. The ingredient, which one member could not swallow alone, went down easily as a component part of the healing dose. And what has been the consequence? The extravagant appropriations and enormous expenses of the extra session have beggared the Treasury.

It is to check this system, that the veto power can be most usefully and properly applied. The President of the United States stands "solitary and alone," in his responsibility to the people. In the exercise of this power, he is emphatically the representative of the whole people. He has the same feeling of responsibility towards the people at large, which actuates us towards our immediate constituents. To him the mass of the people must look as their especial agent; and human ingenuity cannot devise a better mode of giving them the necessary control than by enabling him to appeal to themselves in such cases, by means of the veto power, for the purpose of ascertaining whether they will sanction the acts of their representatives. He can bring each of those measures distinctly before the people for their separate consideration, which may have been adopted by log-rolling as parts of a great system.

The veto power has long been in existence in Pennsylvania, and has been often exercised, and yet, to my knowledge, it has never been exerted in any important case, except in obedience to the public will, or in promotion of the interests of the people. Simon Snyder, whose far-seeing sagacity detected the evils of our present banking system, whilst they were yet comparatively in embryo, has rendered himself immortal by his veto of the forty banks. The system, however, was only arrested, not destroyed, and we are now suffering the evils. The present governor has had the wisdom and courage repeatedly to exercise the veto power, and always, I believe, with public approbation. In a late signal instance, his veto was overruled, and the law passed by a majority of two-thirds in both Houses, although I am convinced that at least three-fourths of the people of the State are opposed to the measure.

In the State of Pennsylvania, we regard the veto power with peculiar favor. In the convention of 1837, which was held for the purpose of proposing amendments to our Constitution, the identical proposition now made by the Senator from Kentucky was brought forward, and was repudiated by a vote of 103 to 14. This convention was composed of the ablest and most practical men in the State, and was almost divided between the two great rival parties of the country; and yet, in that body, but fourteen individuals could be found who were willing to change the Constitution in this particular. Whilst the framers of the Constitution thought, and thought wisely, that in order to give this power the practical effect they designed, it was necessary that any bill which was vetoed should be arrested, notwithstanding a majority of Congress might afterwards approve the measure; on the other hand, they restrained the power, by conferring on two-thirds of each House the authority to enact the bill into a law, notwithstanding the veto of the President. Thus the existence, the exercise, and the restraint of the power are all harmoniously blended, and afford a striking example of all the mutual checks and balances of the Constitution, so admirably adapted to preserve the rights of the States and of the people.

The last reason to which I shall advert why the veto power was adopted, and ought to be preserved, I shall state in the language of the seventy-third number of the Federalist: "This propensity (says the author) of the legislative department to intrude upon the rights, and to absorb the powers of the other departments, has been more than once suggested. The insufficiency of a mere parchment delineation of the boundaries of each, has also been remarked upon, and the necessity of furnishing each with constitutional arms for its own defence, has been inferred and proved. From these clear and indubitable principles results the propriety of a negative, either absolute or qualified, in the Executive, upon the acts of the legislative branches."

The Executive, which is the weaker branch, in the opinion of the Federalist, ought not be left at the mercy of Congress, "but ought to possess a constitutional and effectual power of self-defence." It ought to be able to resist encroachments on its constitutional rights. I admit that no necessity has ever existed to use the veto power for the protection of the Executive, unless it may possibly have been in a single instance; and in it there was evidently no intention to invade his rightful powers. I refer to the "Act to appoint a day for the annual meeting of Congress." This act had passed the Senate by a majority of 34 to 8; but when it was returned to this body by General Jackson with his objections, the majority was reversed, and the vote stood but 16 in favor to 23 against its passage.

The knowledge of the existence of this veto power, as the framers of the Constitution foresaw, has doubtless exerted a restraining influence on Congress. That body have never attempted to invade any of the high Executive powers. Whilst such attempts have been made by them to violate the rights of the States and of the people, and have been vetoed, a sense of justice, as well as the silent restraining influence which proceeds from a knowledge that the President possesses the means of self-protection, has relieved him from the necessity of using the veto for this purpose.

Mr. President, I did not think, at the time of its delivery, that the speech of the distinguished Senator from Kentucky was one of great power; though we all know that nothing he can utter is devoid of eloquence and interest. I mean only to say that I did not then believe his speech was characterized by his usual ability; and I was disposed to attribute this to the feeble state of his health and consequent want of his usual buoyancy of spirit. Since I have seen it in print, I have changed my opinion; and for the first time in my life I have believed that a speech of his could appear better and more effective in the reading than in the delivery. I do not mean to insinuate that anything was added in the report of it; for I believe it contains all the arguments used by the Senator and no more; but I was astonished to find, upon a careful examination, that every possible argument had been urged which could be used in a cause so hopeless. This is my apology for having detained the Senate so long in attempting to answer it.

[Mr. Clay observed that he never saw the speech, as written out by the reporter, till he read it in print the next morning; and, although he found some errors and misconceptions, yet, on the whole, it was very correct, and, as well as he could recollect, contained all the arguments he did make use of, and no more.]

Mr. Buchanan. I did not intend, as must have been evident to the Senator, to produce the impression that anything had been added. My only purpose was to say that it was a better speech than I had supposed, and thus to apologize to the Senate for the time I had consumed in answering it.

I shall briefly refer to two other arguments urged by the Senator, and shall then take my seat. Why, says he, should the President possess the veto power for his protection, whilst it is not accorded to the judiciary? The answer is very easy. It is true that this power has not been granted to the judiciary in form; but they possess it in fact to a much greater extent than the President. The Chief Justice of the United States and his associates, sitting in the gloomy chamber beneath, exercise the tremendous and irresponsible power of saying to all the departments of the Government, "hitherto shalt thou go, and no further." They exercise the prerogative of annulling laws passed by Congress, and approved by the President, whenever in their opinion, the legislative authority has transcended its constitutional limits. Is not this a self-protecting power, much more formidable than the veto of the President? Two-thirds of Congress may overrule the Executive veto; but the whole of Congress and the President united, cannot overrule the decisions of the Supreme Court. Theirs is a veto on the action of the whole Government. I do not say that this power, formidable as it may be, ought not to exist: on the contrary, I consider it to be one of the wise checks which the framers of the Constitution have provided against hasty and unconstitutional legislation, and is a part of the great system of mutual restraints which the people have imposed on their servants for their own protection. This, however, I will say, and that with the most sincere respect for the individual judges; that in my own opinion, the whole train of their decisions from the beginning favors the power of the General Government at the expense of State rights and State sovereignty. Where, I ask, is the case to be found upon their records, in which they have ever decided that any act of Congress, from the alien and sedition laws until the present day, was unconstitutional, provided it extended the powers of the Federal Government? Truly they are abundantly able to protect their own rights and jurisdiction against either Congress or the Executive, or both united.

Again: the Senator asks, why has not the veto been given to the President on the acts of conventions held for the purpose of amending our Constitutions? If it be necessary to restrain Congress, it is equally necessary, says he, to restrain conventions. The answer to this argument is equally easy. It would be absurd to grant an appeal, through the intervention of a veto, to the people themselves, against their own acts. They create conventions by virtue of their own undelegated and inalienable sovereignty; and when they speak, their servants, whether legislative, executive, or judicial, must be silent. Besides, when they proceed to exercise their sovereign power in changing the forms of their Government, they are peculiarly careful in the selection of their delegates—they watch over the proceedings with vigilant care, and the Constitution proposed, by such a convention, is never adopted until after it has been submitted to the vote of the people. It is a mere proposition to the people themselves, and leaves no room for the action of the veto power.

[Here Mr. Clay observed, that Constitutions, thus formed, were not afterwards submitted to the people.]

Mr. Buchanan. For many years past, I believe that this has always been done, as it always ought to be done, in the States: and the Federal Constitution was not adopted until after it had been submitted to a convention of the people of every State in the Union.

So much in regard to the States. The Senator's argument has no application whatever to the Federal Constitution, which has provided the mode of its own amendment. It requires two-thirds of both Houses, the very majority required to overrule a Presidential veto, even to propose any amendment; and before such an amendment can be adopted, it must be ratified by the legislatures, or by conventions, in three-fourths of the several States. To state this proposition, is to manifest the absurdity, nay, the impossibility of applying the veto power of the President to amendments, which have thus been previously ratified by such an overwhelming expression of the public will. This Constitution of ours, with all its checks and balances, is a wonderful invention of human wisdom. Founded upon the most just philosophical principles, and the deepest knowledge of the nature of man, it produces harmony, happiness, and order, from elements which, to the superficial observer, might appear to be discordant.

On the whole, I trust not only that this veto power may not be destroyed, but that the vote on the Senator's amendment may be of such a character as to settle the question, at least during the present generation. Sir, of all the executive powers, it is the one least to be dreaded. It cannot create; it can originate no measure; it can change no existing law; it can destroy no existing institution. It is a mere power to arrest hasty and inconsiderate changes, until the voice of the people, who are alike the masters of Senators, Representatives 504and President, shall be heard. When it speaks, we must all bow with deference to the decree. Public opinion is irresistible in this country. It will accomplish its purpose by the removal of Senators, Representatives, or President, who may stand in its way. The President might as well attempt to stay the tides of the ocean by erecting mounds of sand, as to think of controlling the will of the people by the veto power. The mounting waves of popular opinion would soon prostrate such a feeble barrier. The veto power is everything when sustained by public opinion; but nothing without it.

What is this Constitution under which we live, and what are we? Are we not the most prosperous, the most free, and amongst the most powerful nations on the face of the earth? Have we not attained this pre-eminence, in a period brief beyond any example recorded in history, under the benign influence of this Constitution, and the laws which have been passed under its authority? Why, then, should we, with rude hands, tear away one of the cords from this wisely balanced instrument, and thus incur the danger of impairing or destroying the harmony and vigorous action of the whole? The Senator from Kentucky has not, in my opinion, furnished us with any sufficient reasons.

And after all, what harm can this veto power ever do? It can never delay the passage of a great public measure, demanded by the people, more than two, or at the most, four years. Is it not better, then, to submit to this possible inconvenience, (for it has never yet occurred,) than to destroy the power altogether? It is not probable that it ever will occur; because if the President should disregard the will of the people on any important constitutional measure which they desired, he would sign his own political death warrant. No President will ever knowingly attempt to do it; and his means of knowledge, from the ordeal through which he must have passed previous to his election, are superior to those of any other individual. He will never, unless in cases scarcely to be imagined, resist the public will when fairly expressed. It is beyond the nature of things to believe otherwise.

The veto power is that feature of our Constitution which is most conservative of the rights of the States and the rights of the people. May it be perpetual!

It was during the summer of 1842 that the treaty negotiated at Washington, between Mr. Webster and Lord Ashburton, settled various long standing and somewhat perilous controversies between the United States and England, for which Mr. Webster had remained in office under President Tyler. Mr. Buchanan was one of those who opposed the ratification of this treaty when it came before the Senate, in August, 1842. His speech in the secret session was very elaborate in its criticisms upon the whole negotiation, but it does not need to be reproduced now.

The debates on the treaty were not published until the following session of Congress, which began in December, 1842. In February, 1843, Mr. Buchanan received the following letter from Mr. Jared Sparks, the distinguished historian:[72]

[JARED SPARKS TO MR. BUCHANAN.]

Cambridge, Feb. 11th, 1843.

My Dear Sir:—

I have received the copy of your speech, which you were so kind as to send me, and for which I beg you will accept my thanks. I have read it with much interest, for although I am, on the whole, a treaty man, yet there are two sides, and you have presented one of them in a striking and forcible light. I am not well satisfied with the way in which the Caroline affair is allowed to subside. It was a gross outrage, in spite of all the soft words about it, and it demanded a round apology. I could wish also that there had been some express declaration of the sense of the Government against the pretended right of search. It is idle to dally on such a subject. There is no such right, there never was and there never ought to be; and I should be glad to have the point settled, in regard to the United States, by a positive declaration, in a formal manner, that it can in no case be admitted.

I observe that you deal out heavy blows upon my poor Paris map. I can assure you that it has not been by my knowledge or good will that it has fallen into the hands of the Senate. The information came accidentally into my possession, and, after much reflection, I thought it a duty to communicate it to the Department of State; but I never anticipated for a moment that I was thus running the hazard of having my name bandied about in the Senate; nor did it occur to me that any public use could be made of it. I do not complain of the result, but I consider it unfortunate to me personally, and I wish it could have been avoided.

You have made a slight mistake in regard to the character of this map. You represent it as an old map, with old boundary lines marked upon it. This is not a true description. It is a map of "North America," with no boundary line marked upon it between Canada and the English colonies. The red mark is drawn by hand,—manuscript mark,—not following any engraved line. It is drawn with remarkable precision and distinctness, around the United States, even running out to sea and following the windings of the coast from the St. Mary's to the St. Croix. There are no other colored lines on the map. It carries with it the evidence of having been drawn with great care; and from the head of the St. Croix to the mountains north of the sources of the Penobscot it winds along with an evident caution to separate the head waters of the streams which flow into the St. John's from those which run to the south. I am here only stating facts, having no theory on the subject, nor, least of all, any desire to weaken our claim, which, till lately, has seemed to me unassailable. This map answers fully to that described in Franklin's letter; and if he actually drew the line, it does seem to settle the question, for he could not be mistaken, at that time, as to the meaning of the commissioners.

The copy of Mitchell's map, obtained from Baron Steuben's library, has a manuscript boundary line drawn in exact accordance with this supposed line of Franklin. But I do not see any allusion to this map in the debates. There is a tradition that it once belonged to Mr. Jay, but I believe no evidence of this fact has been adduced.

But, after all, the thing which has weighed the most heavily on my mind as adverse to our claim, is the perfect silence of Mr. Jay and Mr. John Adams on the subject. Both these commissioners lived many years after the treaty of Ghent. Why should they not have declared, by some formal and public instrument, the facts of the case, and confirmed our claim, if they knew it to be just? Such a declaration would have been conclusive, even with an arbiter; and it would almost seem to have been a duty to their country to make it, of their own accord, when they saw such vast interests at stake. But no record of their opinion has ever been brought to light.

Mr. Woodbury has fallen into the same mistake as yourself, in regard to my unfortunate Paris map. Will you have the goodness to show him this letter; and believe me, with sincere respect and regard,

Your friend and most obedient servant,

Jared Sparks.

On the 7th of April, 1842, Mr. Buchanan addressed the Senate in opposition to a measure advocated by the Whigs, which proposed to pledge and appropriate the proceeds of the public lands to the payment of the interest and principal of the public debt. It must be remembered that this speech was made under very peculiar circumstances, and it is not necessary to reproduce it.

In the spring of the year 1844, it seemed that the old story of "bargain and corruption" in the election of John Quincy Adams in 1825 was about to be revived. General Jackson had again become excited on this subject by persons who wished at once to injure Mr. Clay and Mr. Buchanan. The following letter from Governor Letcher of Kentucky, an ardent admirer of Mr. Clay, informed Mr. Buchanan of what was impending:

507[GOVERNOR LETCHER TO MR. BUCHANAN.]

(Private.) Frankfort, June 20, 1844.

My Dear Sir:—

Mr. Clay is very much provoked with General Jackson and other malicious persons for attempting to revive against him that old vile, miserable calumny of "bargain and sale." It is, I must confess, as you and I both know, a most villanous outrage, and well calculated to excite the ire of any man upon earth. I am not at all surprised that he should feel indignant upon the occasion.

I am told he is resolved upon "carrying the war into Africa." Indeed I saw him for a few minutes shortly after he returned from Washington, when he alluded in some such terms to the subject. He was quite unwell at the time, and the conversation was very brief. It seems now (I was so informed an evening or two ago) he threatens to make a publication in vindication of his own character. What else he may do or say, I do not know. This much I learn, he will call upon me to give a statement of the conversation which took place between you and himself in my room in reference to the contest then pending between Adams and Jackson.

I shall regret exceedingly if any such call is made upon me. Many years ago, as you remember, a similar call was made, and on my part refused. I do not at present perceive any good reason why I should change my opinion. The truth is, if my recollection serves me, after several interviews with you in regard to the matter, I told you explicitly I did not

feel at liberty to give the conversation alluded to, and would not do so under any circumstances, without your express permission. Am I not right in my recollection? I do not think I shall or can be convinced that my decision as heretofore made is not perfectly correct.
With great regard,
R. P. Letcher.

How Mr. Clay proposed "to carry the war into Africa," is to be explained by an occurrence which took place in January, 1825, at the lodgings of Mr. Letcher in Washington, he being then a member of Congress from Kentucky. The persons present were Mr. Clay, Mr. Letcher, Mr. Buchanan, and Mr. Sloan of Ohio. The subject of the election of a President by the House of Representatives was talked of jocosely; but in the course of the conversation Mr. Buchanan expressed his conviction that General Jackson would be chosen, adding, that "he would form the most splendid cabinet the country has ever had." Mr. Letcher asked: "How could he have one more distinguished than that of Mr. Jefferson, in which were both 508Madison and Gallatin? Where would he be able to find equally eminent men?" Buchanan replied, looking at Mr. Clay, "I would not go out of this room for a Secretary of State." Clay playfully retorted that he "thought there was not timber there fit for a Cabinet office, unless it were Mr. Buchanan himself."[73] This familiar, private conversation, held in the unrestrained intercourse of a casual meeting, could have been of no use to Mr. Clay, even if divulged, in "carrying the war into Africa," unless he should treat it as an occurrence having some connection with the conversation between Mr. Buchanan and General Jackson, which is referred to in a previous chapter. The result would be that Mr. Buchanan would stand charged by Mr. Clay on the one hand, as an emissary of General Jackson to open a negotiation for Mr. Clay's vote in the House, as he had some years before been charged with being an emissary of Mr. Clay to approach General Jackson with a proposal to sell his vote for the office of Secretary of State. The truth manifestly is, that Buchanan would have been very glad to have had Mr. Clay appointed Secretary of State under General Jackson, not only because he had great admiration for Mr. Clay's splendid abilities, but for public and patriotic reasons; and there were no such strict party relations at that time as would have rendered a union between Jackson and Clay in any degree objectionable. But neither in the conversation between General Jackson and Mr. Buchanan, in December, 1824, nor in the conversation between Mr. Clay and Mr. Buchanan, at the lodgings of Mr. Letcher, in January, 1825, could either Jackson on the one hand, or Clay on the other, have had the slightest reason for claiming that on the former occasion Buchanan was acting as an agent of Clay, or that on the latter occasion he was acting as an agent of Jackson. In that scene of excitement, there were persons in Washington who stood in much closer relations with Jackson than Buchanan did at that time, in whose efforts to secure the votes of different delegations there were conversations which, construed in one way, approached pretty nearly to a tender of office to Mr. Clay. But they were the unauthorized, irresponsible and voluntary expressions by partisans of what 509they believed might take place, in case Jackson should become President; and if they were ever understood in any other sense by those to whom they were addressed, it is apparent that they were misunderstood.

Governor Letcher, as soon as he learned that Mr. Clay threatened to make use of the conversation at his lodgings, resolutely refused to be a party to the disclosure. Mr. Buchanan's answer to his letter of the 20th of June, and the further correspondence between them, are all that it is needful to add:
[MR. BUCHANAN TO GOV. LETCHER.]
(Private.) Lancaster, June 27, 1844.

Mr Dear Sir:—

I have this moment received your very kind letter, and hasten to give it an answer. I cannot perceive what good purpose it would subserve Mr. Clay to publish the private and unreserved conversation to which you refer. I was then his ardent friend and admirer; and much of this ancient feeling still survives, notwithstanding our political differences since. I did him ample justice, but no more than justice, both in my speech on Chilton's resolutions and in my letter in answer to General Jackson.

I have not myself any very distinct recollection of what transpired in your room nearly twenty years ago, but doubtless I expressed a strong wish to himself, as I had done a hundred times to others, that he might vote for General Jackson, and if he desired, become his Secretary of State. Had he voted for the General, in case of his election I should most certainly have exercised any influence which I might have possessed to accomplish this result; and this I should have done from the most disinterested, friendly and patriotic motives. This conversation of mine, whatever it may have been, can never be brought home to General Jackson. I never had but one conversation with him on the subject of the then pending election, and that upon the street, and the whole of it, verbatim et literatim, when comparatively fresh upon my memory, was given to the public in my letter of August, 1827.

The publication then of this private conversation could serve no other purpose than to embarrass me, and bring me prominently into the pending contest,—which I desire to avoid.

You are certainly correct in your recollection. You told me explicitly that you did not feel at liberty to give the conversation alluded to, and would not do so, under any circumstances, without my express permission. In this you acted, as you have ever done, like a man of honor and principle.

With every sentiment of regard, I remain sincerely,
Your friend,
James Buchanan.
510[GOV. LETCHER TO MR. BUCHANAN.]
(Private.) Frankfort, July 7, 1844.
My Dear Sir:—

I have received your answer to my letters. I am glad your recollection of what took place between us corresponds so exactly with mine.

I will not in any event violate my promise, and shall, indeed did, say as much to my distinguished friend. My resolution upon this point is firm and decided; and I do not think it can be changed.

Polk! Great God, what a nomination! I do really think the Democratic Convention ought to be damned to all eternity for this villanous business. Has Polk any chance to carry Pennsylvania?

I write you very hastily to get my letter in to-day's mail. More hereafter.
Your sincere friend,
R. P. Letcher.
[GOV. LETCHER TO MR. BUCHANAN.]
(Private.) Frankfort, July 19th, 1844.
My Dear Sir:—

I have not seen Mr. Clay since I wrote you, nor have I heard a single word more about that threatened publication. I hope he has thought better of it. I told him when I did see him, not to expect from me any statement of what took place in my room between you and him, and that I had made up my mind upon that subject years ago, and did not now see any good reason for changing it.

I hardly think he will make a publication without submitting it to me; indeed, I believe he said so expressly. As I can perceive no earthly good growing out of such a movement, of course I shall continue to oppose it in every possible manner. He has a great many facts now in his possession, and some much stronger than I had supposed to exist, and, no doubt, could put forth a powerful document, but he shall not do it with my consent.

I had a short chat with Colonel Benton a few days ago. If you remember, he was always a good friend of mine, and having the fullest confidence in my discretion, he talked very freely. It was "Multum in parvo" literally. Well, the truth is, your party, speaking classically, have come to a poor pass. Polk for your leader! and then to think of such villanous intrigues to get him on the track, and such old warriors as Van Buren, Buchanan, both the very fellows who were so rascally cheated, being compelled to support the "cretur." Why, I had rather die.

The fact is, both Benton and yourself are hunted down daily by your own dogs. No two men are more constantly the subjects of vituperation by your own party, and I would see them at the devil before I would act a part in such a miserable play as they are now getting up. Besides, you owe it to your own true principles, to your State, to your country, to your own character, 511not to engage in the dirty job of trying to elect such an —— as Polk to the greatest office in the world.

Our Whig candidate for Governor is a death slow nag, as they tell me; still he is a very worthy gentleman, and, I presume, will be elected very easily, though he is twelve or fifteen thousand votes weaker than Clay. I go to no public gatherings, but shall soon be let loose, thank God.

R. P. Letcher.

[BUCHANAN TO LETCHER.]

Lancaster, July 27th, 1844.

My Dear Sir:—

I have received your kind favors of the 7th and 19th instant, and am rejoiced to learn that your distinguished friend has probably thought better of the publication. You have ever been a sagacious man, and doubtless think that James K. Polk is not quite as strong an antagonist as Andrew Jackson, and therefore that it would not be very wise to drop the former and make up an issue with the latter. If this had been done, it would not be difficult to predict the result, at least in Pennsylvania.

The whole affair has worried me much from first to last; and yet I have been as innocent as a sucking dove of any improper intention. First to have been called on by Jackson as his witness against Clay, and then to be vouched as Clay's witness against Jackson, when, before Heaven, I can say nothing against either, is a little too much to bear patiently. I have got myself into this scrape, from the desire which I often expressed and never concealed, that Jackson, first of all things, might be elected President by the House, and that Clay might next be his Secretary of State.

It was a most unfortunate day for the country, Mr. Clay, and all of us, when he accepted the office of Secretary of State (under J. Q. Adams). To be sure, there was nothing criminal in it, but it was worse, as Talleyrand would have said, it was a great blunder. Had it not been for this, he would, in all probability, now have been in retirement, after having been President for eight years; and friends like you and myself, who ought to have stood together through life, would not have been separated. But, as the hymn says, I trust "there's better days a coming."

You ask:—Has Polk any chance to carry Pennsylvania? and I answer, I think he has. Pennsylvania is a Democratic State by a majority of at least 20,000; and there is no population more steady on the face of the earth. Under all the excitement of 1840, and Mr. Van Buren's want of popularity, we were beaten but 343; and ever since we have carried our State elections by large majorities. Besides, Muhlenburg, our candidate for Governor, is a fast horse, and will certainly be elected; and the Governor's election will exercise much influence on the Presidential. But your people, notwithstanding, are in high hopes; and, after my mistake in 1840, I shall not prophesy positively.

I was ignorant of the fact that any portion of the Democratic party were 512playing the part of Acteon's dogs towards me. I stood in no man's way. After my withdrawal, I never thought of the Presidency, and the few scattering votes which I received at Baltimore were given to me against my express instructions, at least so far as the Pennsylvania delegation were concerned. The very last thing I desired was to be the candidate. If they desire to hunt me down for anything, it must be because I have refused to join in the hue and cry against Colonel Benton, who has been for many years the sword and shield of Democracy. Although I differed from him on the Texas question, I believe him to be a much better man than most of his assailants. I sincerely hope that they may not be able to defeat his re-election to the Senate. I have delayed the publication of my Texas speech to prevent its use against him in the approaching Missouri elections.

It is neither according to my taste, nor sense of propriety as a Senator of the United States, to take the stump, and I have yet resisted all importunities for that purpose. Whether I shall be able to hold out to the end, I do not know. It is sincerely my desire, and I owe Muhlenburg much kindness, and if he should request it, I could not well refuse. Should I enter the lists, I shall never say, as I never have said, anything which could give the most fastidious friend of Mr. Clay just cause of offence. I shall go to the Bedford Springs on Monday, where I expect to remain for a fortnight.

As I grow older, I look back with a mournful pleasure to the days of "auld lang syne." There was far more heart and soul and fun in our social intercourse than exists "in these degenerate days." But, perhaps, to think so is an evidence of approaching old age. Poor Governor Kent! I was forcibly reminded of him a few days ago, when, at the funeral of a friend, I examined his son's gravestone, who was a student of mine. To keep it in repair has been for me a matter of pious duty. I loved his father to the last......

I wish I could have you with me for a few days. I have better wine than any man between this and Frankfort, and no man in the world would hail you with a heartier welcome. When shall we meet again?

Ever your sincere friend,

James Buchanan.

[LETCHER TO BUCHANAN.]

Frankfort, August 3d, 1844.

My Dear Sir:—

Your very interesting favor of the 27th ultimo has reached me and I have just read it with a great deal of pleasure.

I have not seen Mr. Clay since I wrote you, nor have I heard one single word further in regard to the threatened publication. When I saw him, as I believe I told you, he had the full benefit of my opinion upon the subject, expressed in terms by no means equivocal.

You know my warm, and strong, and long attachment to the man. A 513better and a greater man, take him altogether, in my view, has never lived in any age or country. He is a little excitable, and under that state of feeling seems to raise the imperial colors, but it's mere manner, growing out of his peculiar organization. He is not a malice bearing man, and never was. He never disliked you in his life, though I think you had always perhaps an impression to the contrary. But with all my regard for the man personally, and unbounded confidence in his political worth, I cannot be prevailed upon to advise him to make a publication, however strongly his feelings may be interested in the matter, of the character of the one alluded to, nor am I at all willing to be referred to as a witness to anything that occurred under the sanctity of my hospitality. Unless my mind undergoes a most radical change, I never will consent. And although I flatter myself I am an exceedingly amiable man, yet I am as firm, and as decided, and as unyielding in matters of judgment as any man living.

Our election comes off Monday next. The Whig candidate for governor is not considered by any means a popular man. He will not carry the entire Whig vote, according to the estimate of the knowing ones, by 10,000 votes. On the other side they are running a very popular man, and a "war horse at that." The party lines will be better drawn between the candidates for lieutenant-governor, as I am told. My position places it very much out of my power to see exactly the progress of the campaign.

One word as to yourself. Were I in your place, I would not take the stump, mark that. "I know a thing or two," and if I know anything, it is judging accurately "men and things." My opinion upon this point is correct. Polk has no more chance to be elected than if he were now dead, and buried, and damned, as he will be in due time. The idea of his being a tariff man is very provoking.

I would pay Muhlenberg at a more convenient season. He is at best, a tricky old fellow; I know him "like a book." We shall probably meet during the next spring, if we live. I may possibly make a visit to Washington after Clay gets under way. As this is rather an interesting topic (and as you pay no postage), I will explain myself to you more fully.

Mr. Clay's attachment to me, I have no doubt about. I am fully aware that he has the most entire confidence in my integrity and (to the full extent of my merits) every reasonable confidence in my judgment. When he comes into power, he will be surrounded by a set of flatterers, artful, designing, and cunning. Of course a man in that condition, will at once, or in due time, form a new set of feelings and a new set of friends. It is the true course of human nature, and all history proves it. He may offer me something, but that may not be at all agreeable to my feelings. On this subject I have never had the first word with him or anybody else, and I don't intend to have. My impression has been all along, he would take Crittenden into the cabinet, should he be inclined to take a place. Oh no, when my friends are in trouble, I am a first rate doctor, but when restored, I doubt whether there will be use for me. The impression prevails in this country, that I can get 514any place that I select. Not so. I tell you this confidentially, that in case we live, we may see how accurately we understand the business. But in fact there is no place I have set my heart upon in the slightest degree, and I do assure you now that I am not expecting, and hope that I shall never apply for any directly or indirectly. Upon a moment's reflection I doubt whether I shall go East in the spring, lest it might be supposed I was seeking place. My time is almost out as governor, and how to dispose of myself, I confess I know not, but I would rather fly to a saltpetre cave, and work for a living, than to solicit office from friends to whom I have adhered for upwards of a quarter of a century. True, my services were rendered without the hopes of personal reward. They were given purely for what I deemed the good of the country. This is a strange world, I can tell you. I often hear of its

being said, if Letcher was out of the way, Mr. Adams, Mr. Buchanan, and Mr. Clay could be provided for, but Letcher will have a controlling influence, etc., etc. What miserable stuff. The truth is I shall not try to have a controlling influence, and do not wish it, and will not have it if I could get it. But I could not have it if I wanted it. Now give me just as long a love-letter as this. Don't drink up all that good wine, but wait till I come.
Ever yours,
R. P. Letcher.

The whole substance of what Mr. Clay meant about "carrying the war into Africa" was probably this: that the familiar conversation at Mr. Letcher's room in January, 1825, was as good evidence of Jackson's effort to corrupt him as the conversation between Jackson and Buchanan in the previous December was, of a purpose on his (Clay's) part, to induce Jackson to buy his vote in the House of Representatives by promising to make him (Clay) Secretary of State.[74]

CHAPTER XVII.
1843–1844.

BUCHANAN ELECTED TO THE SENATE FOR A THIRD TERM—EFFORTS OF HIS PENNSYLVANIA FRIENDS TO HAVE HIM NOMINATED FOR THE PRESIDENCY—MOTIVES OF HIS WITHDRAWAL FROM THE CANVASS—THE BALTIMORE DEMOCRATIC CONVENTION OF 1844 NOMINATES MR. POLK—THE OLD STORY OF "BARGAIN AND CORRUPTION"—PRIVATE CORRESPONDENCE.

It was a natural consequence of so much distinction in public life, not only that Mr. Buchanan should be a third time elected to the Senate, but that his political and personal friends in Pennsylvania should be anxious to have him made the Democratic candidate for the Presidency by the next national convention of that party. In that organization there was no man whose party and public services and personal qualifications could give him greater claims than Buchanan's to the consideration of his political associates. It does not appear to me, judging from his private correspondence at this period, which lies before me in great masses, and which I have carefully examined, that he was specially anxious at this period of his life to become President of the United States. His ambition, if it led him to aim at that position, was regulated by great prudence, and it is quite apparent that he was just and considerate towards others whose names were in men's mouths or thoughts as well as his own. There can be no doubt of the entire sincerity with which he addressed the following letter to the Democratic members of the legislature, who, in communicating to him his re-election to the Senate, also expressed their desire to present his name to the nominating convention of their party as the favorite candidate of Pennsylvania for the Presidency.

[TO B. CRISPEN, AND H. B. WRIGHT, ESQUIRES, AND OTHER MEMBERS OF
THE DEMOCRATIC PARTY IN THE LEGISLATURE OF PENNSYLVANIA.]
Washington, February 2d, 1843.
Gentlemen:—

Your letter of congratulation on my recent re-election to the Senate of the United States has inspired me with feelings of profound gratitude. To have been thrice elected to this eminent station by the Democratic senators and representatives of my native State is an honor which ought to satisfy the ambition of any man: and its value is greatly enhanced by your assurance that in selecting me for another term, you but acted in accordance with the united voice of the Democratic party of Pennsylvania. So highly do I prize their good opinion that I can declare with heart-felt sincerity I would not forfeit this for all the political honors which my country could bestow. Their unsolicited and continued support have conferred upon me whatever of distinction in public life I may enjoy; and if it were possible for me now to desert their principles, I should feel that I deserved a traitor's doom. Instead of being elated, I am humbled by the consciousness of how little I have ever done to merit all their unexampled kindness.

Of all the political parties which have ever existed, the Democratic party are the most indulgent and confiding masters. All they demand of any public servant is honestly and faithfully to represent their principles in the station where they have placed him; and this I feel proudly conscious that I have done in the Senate of the United States, according to my best ability. I can, therefore, offer you no pledge for my future conduct except the guarantee of the past.

You have been further pleased to say that as Pennsylvanians you desire to see me "elevated to the highest office in the gift of the people," and you tender me "to the Union as Pennsylvania's favorite candidate for the next Presidency." I can solemnly declare that I was wholly unprepared for such an enunciation from the Democratic members of the legislature, having never received the slightest intimation of their intention until after their letter had been actually signed.

Both principle and a becoming sense of the merit of others have hitherto prevented me from taking any, even the least part in promoting my own elevation to the Presidency. I have no ambitious longings to gratify, conscious as I am that I have already received more of the offices and honors of my country than I have ever deserved. If I know my own heart, I should most freely resign any pretensions which the partiality of friends has set up for me, if by this I could purchase harmony and unanimity in the selection of a Democratic candidate. Besides, however proper it may be that candidates for inferior offices should make personal efforts to secure success, I am deeply convinced that the highest office under heaven ought to be the voluntary gift of the only free people upon earth. It ought to be their own spontaneous gift to the most worthy; and this alone can render it the crowning glory of a well spent public life. This alone can prevent the danger to our institutions which must result from the violent struggles of personal and interested partisans. The principles of the man, whom the people may thus delight to honor, ought to have borne the test of long and severe service, and ought to stand out in such bold relief before his country as to place all doubt in regard to them at defiance. In my opinion, the candidate who would either intrigue or personally electioneer for the Presidency raises a strong presumption that he is unworthy of it. Whether it be probable that a man resolved, under the blessing of Providence, to act upon these principles, will ever reach the Presidency, you can judge better than myself. I ought however in justice to myself to observe, that whilst this is my fixed purpose, I do not feel the less grateful to those kind and partial friends who have deemed me worthy of the highest office, because I have never attempted to enlist them in my support.

With these views plainly presented before the Democracy of Pennsylvania, if they should resolve to offer my name to the National Convention as a candidate for the Presidency with that degree of unanimity which can alone give moral force to their recommendation, I feel that I ought not to counteract their wishes. Should they determine differently, this will not be to me a cause of the slightest mortification.

One remark I am impelled to make before closing this letter. The principles and the success of the party so immeasurably transcend in importance the elevation of any individual that they ought not to be jeopardized in the slightest degree by personal partiality for either of the candidates. Every candidate who has been named, and hundreds of individuals whose names have never been mentioned, would ably and faithfully administer the Government according to these principles. No good Democrat, therefore, ought to suffer his feelings to become so enlisted in favor of any one candidate, that he could not yield his cheerful and cordial support to any other who may be nominated by the National Convention.

With sentiments of grateful regard, I remain yours sincerely,
James Buchanan.

It soon became apparent to Mr. Buchanan that if he permitted his Pennsylvania friends to make him a candidate for the nomination, he would encounter the pretensions of Mr. Van Buren, of Colonel Benton, and of other prominent men in the party. By the species of management common on such occasions, many of the delegates to the national Democratic convention, which was to assemble at Baltimore, on the 27th of May (1844), were instructed or pledged to support Mr. Van Buren. Mr. Buchanan promptly withdrew his name from the canvass, in a public letter. His private feelings on the whole matter of this nomination were expressed freely in the following letter to one of his lady friends, who had just gone to Europe:

[MR. BUCHANAN TO MRS. ROOSEVELT.[75]]
Washington, May 13th, 1844.
My Dear Madam:—

I shall make Colonel King the bearer of this despatch. He and Doctor Martin will be able to give you all the news from your native land. I fear that his appointment to the French mission may induce you to remain longer abroad than you would otherwise have done, or than your friends would willingly tolerate. Whilst I was delighted to learn the attentions which you had received, and which you can everywhere attract, I was sorry to entertain the apprehension that your affections might be alienated from your own country and fixed upon the aristocratic society of Europe. Do not suffer such a feeling to gain possession of your heart. It will banish content from your bosom and render you unhappy in the land where Providence has cast your lot.

I can give you but little news of the gay world of Washington. I have been incessantly occupied during the session, and have gone very little into society. How changed for me the gay world has been since you left us; and I might add that Mr. Ingersoll is nearly as great an admirer as myself. I have not seen your neighbor, the divine Julia, for many weeks, nor attended any of her soirées except one. With all her follies and foibles, she is a lady, and this implies much. When we meet she always talks about you, and no subject could be more agreeable to me.

As you doubtless receive all the gossip of this city from your lady correspondents, and as Colonel King and Doctor Martin will be able to supply any deficiencies, I shall communicate the political intelligence.

The Whigs have held their national convention at Baltimore, and consider Mr. Clay as good as elected. They are high in hope and burning with enthusiasm. Nevertheless, they may yet have cause to realize the truth of the saying in Scripture, "Let not him that putteth on his armor boast as he who taketh it off." It cannot be denied, however, that the Democratic party are at present in a sad condition. Our national convention will meet at Baltimore on this day two weeks, and a large majority of the delegates have been instructed or pledged to vote for Mr. Van Buren; whilst many and perhaps most of the delegates believe that if nominated he will be defeated. His letter against the immediate annexation of Texas to the Union has mainly produced this effect, though he was not popular before. Had he seized the occasion which was presented to him, and followed in the footsteps of his illustrious predecessor, by coming out boldly for Texas, he might, and most probably would, have been elected President; but his chances of ever again reaching this elevated station are now gone forever. I know you will not break your heart on that account, and, personally, I should not; but, politically, I prefer him to Mr. Clay, as much as I prefer political good to political evil, though I like the Kentuckian.

If Mr. Van Buren should withdraw, and the Democratic party could unite on any man, (and I think they could) we might yet elect our candidate. I fear, however, that he will not pursue this course; and should another be nominated in opposition to him, this will only make confusion worse confounded, for such a nomination would involve the violation of instructions,—a doctrine always odious to the Democracy. It is true that the new question of Texas has arisen since the instructions were voted, and this would be the pretext or the apology for his abandonment; but many would not consider this a sufficient cause. Colonel Benton, Mr. Wright, Mr. Allen, Mr. Tappan, Mr. Atherton, and probably Mr. Fairfield, agree with Mr. Van Buren on the Texas question. The remainder of the Democratic Senators will go with "Old Hickory" for immediate annexation.

You regret my withdrawal, and to me it is a source of sincere pleasure to believe that you feel an interest in my fate; but I confess I am yet fully convinced that I pursued the wise and proper course. I withdrew because a large majority of the delegates had been instructed to support Mr. Van Buren, and I wished to banish discord and promote harmony in our ranks. Should he now withdraw, I might, with honor, resume my old position; but, should he persist, if nominated, I should be defeated. A very strong party in the South would now favor my nomination, because the Texas question has absorbed the anti-tariff feeling there, and in all other respects I should be acceptable to that portion of the Union; but, I confess that if I should ever run for the Presidency, I would like to have an open field and a fair start. The battle has already been more than half fought between Clay and Van Buren; and it would be difficult for any new man to recall the forces which have already gone over to the enemy. I thus manifest the unbounded confidence which I have in your discretion and friendship, by writing to you opinions which I have never mentioned freely in conversation to any other person. Should little Van be again nominated, he shall receive my active support.

I envy Colonel King the pleasure of meeting you, and would give anything in reason to be of the party for a single week. I am now "solitary and alone," having no companion in the house with me. I have gone a wooing to several gentlemen, but have not succeeded with any one of them. I feel that it is not good for man to be alone; and should not be astonished to find myself married to some old maid who can nurse me when I am sick, provide good dinners for me when I am well, and not expect from me any very ardent or romantic affection.

Colonel King takes out with him Mrs. Ellis, his niece. I was acquainted with her some years ago, and liked her very much. I hope you will be of the same opinion.

Please to remember me in the kindest terms to Mr. Roosevelt and to Jemmy, who will remember me as long as he shall remember hickory oil.

Believe me that wherever you roam my kindest regards will follow you, and no friend on earth will greet your arrival in your native land with more joy than myself.

Ever your friend, most sincerely and respectfully,
James Buchanan.

On the eve of the assembling of the Baltimore Convention, Mr. Buchanan addressed the following letter to two of the Pennsylvania delegates:

[TO MESSRS. FOSTER AND BREWSTER.]
Washington, May 25th, 1844.
Gentlemen:—

I feel no hesitation in giving your questions a frank and explicit answer.
And first. Against Mr. Van Buren, I cannot be a candidate before the National Convention. After a large majority of the delegates to that convention had either been instructed or pledged to support him, I voluntarily withdrew my name as a candidate for the purpose of concentrating the strength, and thus securing the triumph of the party. In consequence of this act of mine, the delegates from my own State have been instructed to support him, and I am thus placed in such a position that I feel myself bound both in honor and principle not to become his competitor.
Second. Should Mr. Van Buren, after a fair trial, either be withdrawn by his friends, or should they be satisfied that he cannot obtain the nomination, and the delegates from Pennsylvania be thus left at liberty to make a second choice, in that event I should feel myself restored to my original position, and they would then have my consent to present my name, if they thought proper, as a candidate to the convention.
From your friend, very respectfully,
James Buchanan.
The Baltimore Convention nominated James K. Polk of Tennessee as the Democratic candidate for the Presidency. The Whig candidate was Mr. Clay. At the election, which took place in the autumn of 1844, Mr. Polk received 170 electoral votes, while Mr. Clay obtained but 105. No one of the leading Democratic statesmen in the country was more conspicuous, or exerted greater influence in bringing about this result, than Mr. Buchanan.
The following selections from his private correspondence at this exciting period, before and during the election of Mr. Polk, are all that can find space in this chapter:
521[TO THE REV. EDWARD Y. BUCHANAN.]
Washington, February 29, 1844.
Dear Edward:—

I have received your very acceptable letter, and rejoice to learn that you and the family have enjoyed uninterrupted health since we parted. I now begin to entertain strong hopes that Charlotte may outgrow her disease.
This city is now covered with mourning. Ere this can reach you, you will doubtless have heard of the dreadful accident which occurred on board the Princeton yesterday. Among the killed was Governor Gilmer, the recently appointed Secretary of the Navy. He and I were bound together by strong ties of friendship. He was an able, honest, clear-headed, shrewd and patriotic man, who, had he lived, would, at no distant day, have become still more distinguished. He accepted the office in which he died from the purest and most disinterested motives, and the country has lost much by his death. His wife was on board the Princeton, and—how mysterious are the ways of Providence!—urged her husband to have the fatal cannon fired once more. She is almost frantic. She is an excellent woman, and is now left with nine children, and in no affluent circumstances. Colonel Benton was at the breech of the gun and looking along the barrel, so that he might observe the course of the shot when the explosion took place, and received no bodily injury, except from the concussion.
I was not on board myself, and am disposed to consider it almost providential. I received no invitation, although I have been on terms of intimate friendship with Capt. Stockton

and all his family for more than a quarter of a century. If invited, the invitation never reached me: if not, it is perhaps still more remarkable. Had I been on board, the probability is I should have been with those who were around the gun at the time of the explosion.

Although with a straitened income, yet you must be a happy man, if you sincerely believe the doctrines which you preach and honestly practise them: and I have no reason to doubt either. If the fleeting life of man be but a state of trial for another world, he surely acts most wisely who spends his time in securing the things which pertain to his everlasting peace. I am a believer; but not with that degree of firmness of faith calculated to exercise a controlling influence over my conduct. I ought constantly to pray "help thou my unbelief." I think often and I think seriously of my latter end; but when I pray (and I have preserved, and with the blessing of God shall preserve, this good habit from my parents), I can rarely keep my mind from wandering. I trust that the Almighty Father, through the merits and atonement of his Son, will yet vouchsafe to me a clearer and stronger faith than I possess. In the mean time, I shall endeavor to do my duty in all the relations of life. This was to have been a week of great gayety here. There was to have been a party and ball at the President's on Friday evening, a grand dinner at Mr. Blair's on Saturday, a grand diplomatic dinner at the French minister's on Sunday, another at Mr. Upshur's on Tuesday, and a grand ball by Mr. Wilkins on Thursday. I was invited to them all; but promptly declined the invitation for Sunday, having too much regard for the Sabbath to partake of such a festivity on that day. Still I did not assign this as my reason, because my life would not justify me in taking such ground. God willing, I expect to visit Lancaster about the 1st of April, and pass a few days there. I then hope to enjoy the pleasure of seeing you all in good health. Give my love to Ann Eliza and the family; and remember me kindly to Dr. Sample, Joel Leighton, W. Conyngham and Mr. Mussleman, and believe me ever to be your affectionate brother,
James Buchanan.
[FROM THE HON. SILAS WRIGHT.]
Canton, September 23, 1844.
My Dear Sir:—

...... I see you are in the field, and take it for granted that you can have no more peace nor rest until after your State election, if until after the Presidential election. You will have noticed that I have been forcibly taken from the stump for promotion. Never has any incident in the course of my public life been so much against my interests, and feelings, and judgment as this proposed change, but it is too late now to complain of it; the people may release me from any other evil to result than a defeat at the election, which personally would cause the least apprehension or anxiety, but politically is most dreaded. I do not think, however, we shall be beaten in this State though I very confidently apprehend that success will most effectually beat me.

It is not my purpose, however, to trouble you with my griefs, but to tell you that all the information I receive, and my correspondents are very numerous, induces the very confident belief that we shall give Polk and Dallas the thirty-six electoral votes of this State. Never have I witnessed an equal degree of enthusiasm among our Democracy, not even in the days of General Jackson, nor have I, at any time, known greater harmony, activity or confidence.

I rejoice to say that your State seems to be surrendered by the Whigs themselves, and to be considered perfectly safe by our friends in all quarters of the Union.

Mrs. Wright joins me in kindest regards and bids me tell you she sincerely hopes the Whig governor of this State will be elected.
In much haste, I am respectfully and truly yours,
Silas Wright.
[FROM THE HON. JAMES K. POLK.]
(Private.) Columbia, Tenn., August 3, 1844.
My Dear Sir:—

I thank you for the information which you give me in your esteemed favor of the 23d ultimo. The account which you give of the political prospect in Pennsylvania, accords with all the information which I have received from other sources. The great "Key Stone State" will, I have no doubt, continue to be, as she has ever been, Democratic to the core. I was glad to hear your opinion of the probable result in New York as well as in Pennsylvania, because I have great confidence in your sober judgment, and know the caution with which you would express an opinion. I received a letter from Governor Lumpkin, of Georgia, yesterday, giving me strong assurances that that State is safe. We may not carry a majority of the members of Congress at the election which takes place next week, because of the peculiar arrangements of the districts, which were laid off by a Whig legislature, but that we will have a decided majority of the popular vote he has no doubt. In this State our whole Democracy were never more confident of success. It is true we have a most exciting and violent contest, but I think there is no reason to doubt that the State will be Democratic in November. A few weeks, however, will put an end to all speculation in the State, and in the Union.
The State elections in Pennsylvania and New Jersey will be over before this letter can reach you. Will you do me the favor to give me your opinion whether the vote in these elections may be regarded as a fair and full test of the strength of parties in November? Thanking you for your very acceptable letter, I am, very sincerely,
Your friend,
James K. Polk.
[TO THE HON. JAMES K. POLK.]
Lancaster, September 23, 1844.
My Dear Sir:—

I have delayed to write to you on purpose until I could express a decided opinion in regard to the vote of Pennsylvania. I was so much deceived in the result of our State election in 1840, that this has made me cautious. We have had much to contend against, especially the strong general feeling in favor of the tariff of 1842, but notwithstanding all, I am now firmly convinced that you will carry the Keystone by a fair majority. Your discreet and well advised letter to Mr. Kane on the subject of the tariff has been used by us with great effect.
There may, I fear, be some falling off in the city and county of Philadelphia, both on account of the Native American feelings and for some other causes. We have been much at a loss for an able and influential Democratic paper there, devoted to the cause rather than to men. The Pennsylvania is owned by a clique of the exclusive friends and officeholders of Mr. Van Buren, most of whom are obnoxious to the mass of the Democrats. It now does pretty well; but it harped too long on the two-thirds rule.
I have had several times to assure influential individuals in that city, without pretensions, however, to know your sentiments, that as you were a new man yourself, and would be anxious to illustrate your administration by popular favor as well as sound principle,

you would not select old party hacks for office, merely because they had already held office under Mr. Van Buren. By the by, this gentleman's conduct since your nomination deserves all commendation.

In my late political tour through the northern counties of Pennsylvania, I met many New Yorkers at Towanda. Among the rest were some of the members of the late Syracuse convention. They assured me, that after canvassing the information brought by the delegates from all parts of the State, they had arrived at the confident conclusion it would vote for Polk and Dallas. I have this moment received a letter from the Hon. Mr. Hubbard of Bath, in that State, a member of the present Congress, which assures me that we shall carry it by a majority of from 15,000 to 20,000, and so mote it be!

Please to remember me in the very kindest and most respectful terms to Mrs. Polk. Tell her that although I have nothing to ask from the President, I shall expect much from the President's lady. During her administration, I intend to make one more attempt to change my wretched condition, and should I fail under her auspices, I shall then surrender in despair.

With sentiments of the highest regard, I remain your friend sincerely,
James Buchanan.

[TO THE HON. JNO. B. STERIGERE.]
Lancaster, July 17, 1844.
My Dear Sir:—

It was both pleasant and refreshing to receive a letter under your well known hand. It is so long since I have enjoyed such a treat, that I consider it a "bonne bouche." I hope it may never again be such a rarity.

Nearly half my time is now occupied in writing answers to mass, county, township and association meetings; and many of them are not satisfied with a single answer. I scarcely know what to do. If I once begin, to which I am very reluctant, I must continue. A public man cannot make selections. Besides, I have not been well since the adjournment of Congress, and must go to Bedford or have a bilious fever. I have never been in the Northern counties of the State; and if I make a start at all, I shall visit there in September. Should I commence earlier, I would be broken down long before the election. I would thank you, therefore, not to have me invited to address your meeting. Indeed, it is very uncertain whether I can attend.

When you and I served with Mr. Polk in Congress, neither of us probably supposed that he would ever be President. He has since greatly improved. The last time he was in Washington he dined and passed the afternoon with me; and the change forcibly impressed itself on me. Under all the circumstances, I believe no better selection could have been made. I think there is but little doubt that he will carry Pennsylvania and be elected, even without New York or Ohio, unless we have been greatly deceived by our Democratic friends in the strength of the Texas question in the South. The returns from Louisiana do not please me.

525I am much urged to attend the Nashville meeting on the 15th August; but the thing is impossible. I fear that the "hot bloods" of the South may say or do something there to injure us in the North. They are becoming rabid again on the subject of the tariff. I have written to Donelson this day, strongly urging caution and discretion in their proceedings. Please to remember me very kindly to my friend Slemmer, and believe me ever to be, sincerely and respectfully,
Your friend,
James Buchanan.

[TO THE HON. JAMES K. POLK.]
Lancaster, November 4, 1844.
My Dear Sir:—

I think I may now congratulate both yourself and the country on your election to the highest and most responsible office in the world. After our glorious victory on Friday last, I can entertain no doubt of the final result. I feel confident that New York will follow in our footsteps, notwithstanding their majority may be greatly reduced, as ours has been, by an unholy union of the Native Americans with the Whigs.

Never have there been such exertions made by any party in any State as the Whigs have made since our Governor's election to carry the Keystone. They have poured out their money like water; but our Democracy has stood firm everywhere, except the comparatively few who have been seduced on the tariff question, and those whom the Native American humbug has led away. Immediately after the first election, we requested our honest and excellent Governor elect to come East of the mountains and take the stump in your favor; and this was no sooner said than done. He produced a powerful impression wherever he went. I attended two mass meetings with him, and he made speeches at several other places. In "Old Bucks," he gave it to them both in Dutch and English much to their satisfaction.

Whoever has observed with a reflecting eye the progress of parties in this country, must have arrived at the conclusion that there is but one mode of reuniting and invigorating the Democratic party of the Union and securing its future triumph, and that is, whilst adhering strictly to the ancient landmarks of principle, to rely chiefly on the young and efficient Democrats who have fought the present battle. These ought not to be forgotten in the distribution of offices. The old officeholders generally have had their day, and ought to be content. Had Mr. Van Buren been our candidate, worthy as he is, this feeling, which everywhere pervades the Democratic ranks, would have made his defeat as signal as it was in 1840. Clay would most certainly have carried this State against him by thousands; and I firmly believe the result would have been similar, even in New York. The Native American party in Philadelphia never could have become so strong had it not been for the impression which, to some extent, prevailed there, that your patronage would be distributed in that city amongst those called the Old Hunkers by the Democratic masses.

526Yours is a grand mission; and I most devoutly trust and believe that you will fulfil it with glory to yourself and permanent advantage to the country. Democrats have been dropping off from their party from year to year on questions not essentially of a party character. It will be your destiny to call home the wanderers and marshal them again under the ample folds of the Democratic flag. It is thus that the dangerous Whig party will be forever prostrated, and we shall commence a new career of glory, guided under the old banner of our principles.

From the violence of the Southern papers and some of the Southern statesmen, I apprehend that your chief difficulty will be on the question of the tariff. They seem to cling with great tenacity to the horizontal ad valorem duty of the compromise act, which would in practice prostrate the Democracy of the Middle and Northern States in a single year, because it would destroy all our mechanics who work up foreign materials. If the duty on cloth and ready-made clothing were both 20 per cent. ad valorem, we should soon have no use for tailors in our large towns and cities. So of shoemakers, hatters, etc. Foreigners would perform the mechanical labor.

The tariff ought to have been permanently settled in 1842. That was the propitious moment. With much difficulty I have prevented myself from being instructed that I might be free to act according to my own discretion. I then proposed to our Southern friends to adopt the compromise act as it stood in 1839. The Treasury required fully that amount of duties; whilst such a measure would have saved their constituency. For some time I thought they would have gladly embraced this proposition which was presented by Mr. Ingersoll in the House; but at a great caucus of the party several of the ultras opposed the measure, and the consequence has been the extravagant tariff of 1842. Had my proposition been adopted the country would have been just as prosperous as it is at present, and this would have been attributed in the North to that measure, as it now is to the tariff of 1842; you would then have received a majority of 25,000 in Pennsylvania. With sentiments of the highest respect, I remain
Sincerely your friend,
James Buchanan.
[TO GOVERNOR SHUNK.]
Washington, December 18, 1844.
My Dear Sir:—

I do most heartily rejoice that those who communicated to me expressions used by our friend Magraw must have been mistaken in the inferences which they deduced from his language. He was much in the company of my deadly enemy —— who is ——'s most unscrupulous tool, and of ——. That he did use some unguarded language is beyond a doubt; but all this shall be as if it never had been. I venerated his deceased father, and have always been so much attached to him, that it almost unmanned me, when I learned that he had spoken unkindly of myself. Please to say nothing to him of what my former letter contained.

The income tax of England has never been resorted to except in cases of extreme necessity. That tax at present in existence imposes seven pence per pound upon the annual rent of land and houses, upon the income from titles, railways and canals, mines and iron-works; also upon the income of tenants or renters of land, upon public lands and securities, dividends on bank stock, Indian stock, and foreign stock payable in England, upon the profits of trades and professions, upon the income of public officers, salaries, etc. All incomes under £150 sterling per annum are exempt from this tax. Under the British government, they have adopted the means necessary to secure a just return of all incomes; under ours, this, in many cases, would prove almost impossible, without resorting to an inquisition unknown to our form of government. Indeed, as far as I know, our present taxes on income are eluded to a most shameful extent. The income tax has always been odious in England; and it would prove to be so, if carried to anything like the same extent, in this country. The more I reflect upon the subject the more I am convinced that your "inaugural" should not specifically recommend any new mode of taxation. I know that, in common with myself, you entertain a horror of repudiation, either express or implied, and this might be expressed in the strongest terms, together with a willingness on your part to concur with the legislature in adopting any measures necessary to prevent so disgraceful a catastrophe; leaving to your administration, after it shall get fairly under way, to adopt the necessary measures to redeem the faith of the State.

In regard to your selection for secretary of state, I entertain the same opinion, more strongly now than ever, which I have held from the beginning. Your attorney-general ought to be a Muhlenberg man, and such an one as will be satisfactory to that branch of the party. After his appointment, I hope to hear no more of these distractions; and I trust that then we shall all be united under the broad banner of Democracy in support of your administration.

I know John M. Read well; and I also know, that he enjoyed and deserved the confidence of Mr. Muhlenberg and his friends in an eminent degree. After his death, Mr. Read's conduct towards you was worthy of all praise. There are few lawyers, if any, in Philadelphia, his superiors; and he is a man of such firmness, energy, and industry, that he will always be found an efficient supporter in the hour of need. He holds a ready and powerful political pen, and is a gentleman of the strictest honor and integrity. I know you would be safe with him. Of both Mr. Brewster and Mr. Barr, I also entertain a high opinion; and I think the appointment of either would give satisfaction to the friends of Muhlenberg. I confess I do not like Mr. Kane's political associations; but he is a gentleman and a man of honor.

There is one subject to which I desire to direct your attention. I know, from various quarters, that Porter is making a desperate effort to be elected United States Senator. He calculates upon seducing a sufficient number of Democrats from their allegiance to the party, which, when united with the Whigs, would constitute a majority. —— and —— have both been here, and, on several occasions, expressed their confident belief in his success. From the conversation of the Whigs here and elsewhere, I think they will be mistaken as to the votes of their members; but this I know, that it is of the last importance to you to maintain the caucus system. Should it be broken down at the commencement of your administration, it is easy to predict the consequences which may follow. I would, therefore, most respectfully advise that you should be at Harrisburg at the commencement of the session, not to take any part in favor of any candidate for the Senate, but to express your opinion strongly and decidedly in favor of an adherence to caucus nominations.

We have no authentic news here from President Polk; all is as yet conjecture. His path will be beset by many difficulties. The first which will present itself, is Mr. Calhoun. To remove him will give great offence to many of the Southern gentlemen, who were mainly influential in procuring the nomination of Mr. Polk; to retain him, will exasperate Colonel Benton and that wing of the party.[76] It is hoped that he may retire, or consent to accept the mission to England. Then there are the Texas and tariff questions, which it will be difficult to settle to the satisfaction of the party. Colonel Polk has a cool and discreet head himself, and he will be surrounded by cool and discreet friends.

Philadelphia is now in a state of office-hunting excitement, never known before. The office-hunters have taken it into their heads that Mr. Dallas, because he has been elected Vice President, can procure them all offices, and they are turning his head with their incense. I venture to predict that they will prove to be greatly mistaken. The moment they discover this, their plans will be directed to some other divinity.

You ask my advice in regard to recommendations from you to President Polk. I think you ought to be cautious in giving them, if you desire that they shall produce the effect your recommendations well deserve. I hope, however, to meet you at the inauguration.

I have sat up until a late hour to write you this long letter. I receive at the rate of about thirty letters a day; and between important private calls and public business, I have found time to answer very few of them.

Please remember me most kindly and respectfully to Mrs. Shunk and the young ladies, and believe me to be sincerely and devotedly
Your friend,
James Buchanan.

Before the following letters were written, Mr. Polk's nomination to the Presidency had occurred.

[FROM MRS. CATRON.[77]]
Nashville, July 4, 1844.
Dear Sir:—

I have received your kind letter of the 23d of June, and I feel a just appreciation of the compliment, in being selected from the number of your many fair and accomplished friends, as the companion of your solitude. I know "it is not good for man to be alone," and if you could but take time to remember the sage advice I have often given you to the contrary of such an unchristian and vain attempt, you would now be basking in the charms of some blooming widow, and not be driven to the humble necessity of seeking stray rays of comfort from the "old head on young shoulders" of other men's wives. As, however, you are brought to the sad predicament—and strange to say, I am but little better off during the court,—and as nothing I just now think of affords me more pleasure than to add a crumb of support to your forlorn condition by boarding with you next session of Congress, and as Mr. Catron is the most generous of husbands to risk such dangerous associations, he will write to Mr. Carroll to engage us a house.

N. B.—The court and Congress now meet at the same time, and Polk runs for President only once—positively only once—and all anti-annexation men are dead and buried. So I think, and that you know is law to you, as in Miss Gardiner's case, of whose ambitious aspirations I don't believe one word. In conclusion, permit me to say that on this occasion I have availed myself of your once offered kindness of the liberty of speech.
Most truly your friend,
M. Catron.
The Hon. James Buchanan.

[TO MRS. CATRON.]
My Dear Madam:—

I sincerely thank you for having taken compassion on my forlorn and destitute condition. I can assure you that I greatly prefer the stray rays of comfort from yourself to "basking in the charms of any blooming widow" in the land. I do not like everlasting sunshine, or too much of a good thing:—and as to widows, "I'll none of them. Comparisons are odoriferous," as Dogberry says.

Ere this you have learned that with all your shrewdness you were mistaken. The President is the most lucky man that ever lived. Both a belle and a fortune to crown and to close his Presidential career.[78]

I hope you will be able to give Polk Tennessee. All appearances indicate his signal triumph in the Keystone State. His tariff letter to Kane was a good thing for us. Under the circumstances, I do not think a better nomination could have been made; and as I had the honor of being Mrs. Polk's candidate I feel myself bound both in gallantry and in gratitude to do my best for the election of her husband.

When she becomes the lady of the White House, as I believe she will be, I shall both expect and desire to be a favorite. As to yourself you stand fair under all administrations. Remember me most kindly to the judge, and believe me ever to be sincerely and respectfully
Your friend,
James Buchanan.

CHAPTER XVIII.
1842–1849.

HARRIET LANE.

From all "the heady currents of a fight" of politics, from the toils of statesmanship and the objects of ambition, the reader can now turn to the sweet charities of domestic and social life; for these, notwithstanding his bachelor state, were not wanting to the public man whose life is traced in these volumes. A biography of Mr. Buchanan would be exceedingly imperfect without mention of that member of his family who, for the last twenty-five years of his life, stood in a very intimate domestic relation with him. It is a delicate matter to write of a living lady; but the name of Harriet Lane will recall to many readers one who occupied with singular grace positions in her uncle's household that were almost public, and whose domestic connection with him formed a most important element in his private happiness. Mr. Buchanan discharged with great fidelity all his duties to the various members of his family who could be said to have any claims upon him. Of that family he was always regarded as the head; and when, in consequence of the death of one of his sisters and her husband, the care of four orphans devolved upon him, the youngest was at such an age that he could form her as he wished, and his wish was guided by the nicest sense of what belongs to the highest female excellence.

His sister, Mrs. Lane, wife of Elliott T. Lane, died at Mercersburg, in the year 1839. Her husband survived her for only two years. They left four children: James Buchanan, Elliott Eskridge, Mary Elizabeth Speer, and Harriet Rebecca.[79] They each inherited from their parents a moderate property. After the death of her father, Harriet, the youngest of the four orphans, was brought to Lancaster, and resided in her uncle's house, when he was at home in that city. During his absences in Washington, she occasionally lived with two ladies in Lancaster, friends of her uncle,—the Misses Crawford. For a few years she attended a school in Lancaster, and also had private teachers. She and her sister Mary were then placed at a boarding-school in Charlestown, Virginia, in the neighborhood of some of their father's relatives. Harriet's education was finished at the well-known Roman Catholic convent at Georgetown, in the District of Columbia. The present superintendent of that institution was one of her school-mates.

To direct the education of this young girl, to form her religious and moral principles, to guard her against the temptations that beset an impulsive temperament, and to develop her into the character of a true woman, became one of the chief objects of Mr. Buchanan's busy life. At first there was danger that the hoyden might become a "fast" and dashing young lady. There was an exuberance of animal spirits, the accompaniment of a fine physical organization and a healthy youth. There was an abundance of the generous, frank and joyous qualities of the female heart, along with its delicacy and purity. Such a nature required much discipline and a careful training; and it might, perhaps, be thought that an old-bachelor uncle, absorbed in public life, was not exactly the person to undertake this duty; that, after spoiling the child as a pet, he would leave her to take her chances as a woman. But Mr. Buchanan was a man in whom authority and affection could be most happily blended. He knew just how to exercise the one and to bestow the other. He knew the girl whom he had to influence, and he had a perfectly true sense of what a woman and a lady should be.

It is not my purpose, or according to my taste, to enlarge on my own estimate of the results which he produced. The methods by which they were attained will sufficiently exhibit themselves in what I am to give to the reader; and what is widely known of the lady who is unavoidably the subject of these observations, attests that a beautiful woman, whom flattery and adulation 533could not injure, and who became alike an ornament to society and a model of the domestic virtues, was formed by one of the busiest statesmen of our time, without a mother's aid and a mother's love. There is rarely to be met, in any literature of real life with which I am acquainted, a more interesting and instructive picture of a wise man's care for a woman's education, manners, deportment, and inner character, than is to be traced in Mr. Buchanan's charming letters to his niece. They began when she was a school-girl, were continued when she became the companion of his age and the friend of his declining years; and they did not cease when he gave her to the husband of her choice. They are so numerous that it is difficult to make the selections to which my space confines me. After Miss Lane had grown up, whenever she was absent from her uncle, he wrote to her almost daily. But his affection for her was unselfish. He never failed to let her know how welcome would be her return, but he never exacted from her an abridgment of her pleasures, unless it was for her good that they should be interrupted. He could guide her, when she was away from him, by a dozen written words, just as infallibly as if she were under his eye and within the sound of his voice. One of her letters to him, which has come into my hands among the great mass of his papers, shall be given in its proper place, as an artless proof that he had his reward, and knew that he had it. I shall make many extracts from this correspondence, because nothing that has come within my reach can so well reveal a beautiful side of Mr. Buchanan's character, of which the world, as yet, knows very little. One is reminded by these letters of many well-known instances of such a tender care for a young relative, evinced by a series of letters. Lord Eldon's letters to his grandson and heir will occur to the reader; but the chancellor was always a stiff and formal writer, although his letters to his young kinsman are admirably wise. Lord Chatham's letters to his son William afford delightful reading; but even in his expressions of affection, the "Great Commoner" could not be otherwise than stately, classical, and a little dramatic. Lord Chesterfield's letters to his son, although written, like everything that came from his pen, with the utmost correctness of a marvellous grace, lack, of course, the religious 534and moral basis of all sound philosophy of life. Madame De Sévigné's lively letters to her adored daughter, Burke's to the son whom he strangely over-estimated, are among the treasures that the world would not willingly lose. But I should omit a very interesting part of my duty in this work, if I did not place before the reader as many of the letters of President Buchanan to his niece as I can find room for; and although they are not to be ranked in all respects side by side with the most renowned specimens of the class to which they belong, they seem to me to exhibit a happy union of the tenderest affection, deep religious principle, sound inculcation, minute direction of conduct, playfulness, vivacity, and an abounding confidence in the person to whom they were written. They are unique also in this—that they were written to a female relative, whom Providence had cast upon the care of an unmarried uncle, intensely occupied with the pursuits and interests of a statesman.

But by way of preface to such of these letters as can be quoted, it will be well to inform the reader that until the year 1848, Mr. Buchanan, when at home in Lancaster, resided in a bachelor establishment, at the head of which, as housekeeper, was a lady who was always called "Miss Hetty." I am indebted to his nephew, Mr. James Buchanan Henry, for the following description of their domestic circle:

In consequence of the death, in 1840, of my surviving parent, the youngest sister of Mr. Buchanan, I became a member of his immediate family. He was executor of my mother's will, and by it he was appointed my guardian. I was then seven years old. Mr. Buchanan at that time lived in a spacious brick house in the quiet inland city of Lancaster, on the principal street, called East King Street. This ancient town—one of the oldest in

Pennsylvania, still retained the loyal names of colonial times, its best streets being named King, Queen, Duke, Orange, etc. At that date, Mr. Buchanan was in the Senate, and of course much of his time was passed in Washington; but during the recess of Congress he resided in Lancaster, where he was much honored and beloved by its citizens; and this personal attachment continued in a marked degree until his death. At the time of which I speak, his family consisted of a housekeeper, Miss Parker, always called "Miss Hetty," myself and his servants. At a little later period, my cousin, Harriet Lane, after the death of her parents, also became a member of our uncle's household. This little family circle continued unbroken, excepting during the temporary absences 535of my uncle in Washington, or on other public duty, or when my cousin and I were at boarding school or college, until my marriage in 1860, and until my cousin's departure for her new home in Baltimore, after her marriage. No father could have bestowed a more faithful and judicious care upon his own children, than this somewhat stern but devoted bachelor uncle of ours bestowed upon us. While I was at school, in the little Moravian town of Litiz near by, when I was eleven years old, he required me to write to him once every month with great exactitude, and to each boyish letter he would write a prompt reply, carefully but kindly criticizing every part of it; and if I had been careless in either penmanship or spelling, he would give me sharp reproof, which, coming from the hero of my youthful worship, made an impression which I remember to this day.

Miss Hetty Parker, now a venerable lady of seventy-eight, residing in Lancaster in a comfortable house provided for her by my uncle's will, belonged to a respectable and quite "well-to-do" family in Philadelphia. She became his housekeeper, I think, in 1834, or soon after, and was, by him and all of us, treated as a valued member of the family, and as a friend. She was always present at the table, and dispensed the hospitalities of my uncle's house until my cousin had grown to womanhood, and assumed a part of such duties. "Miss Hetty" continued to be one of the family circle, and to perform her duties most acceptably to Mr. Buchanan through the remainder of his life. I do not hesitate to say that, it was largely owing to her vigilant care of his interests, and her wise economy, that his moderate private fortune, mainly earned by him in the practice of the law, and before he entered public life, not only proved sufficient for his wants, but slowly increased, amounting, at his death, to about $300,000.[80] Miss Hetty was for nearly forty years his faithful attendant in health and nurse in sickness; and he was so much attached to her, that I have often heard him say that nothing should ever part her from him while he lived. He would let her do what she pleased, and say to him what she pleased, and even scold him, without rebuke;—a privilege I never knew him to accord to any one else. No biography of Mr. Buchanan would be complete that did not mention this humble, unselfish and most faithful companion, who was so well known to the frequenters of Wheatland, and to the whole circle of Mr. Buchanan's friends.

Although the dates of the following letters run somewhat beyond the period at which the last chapter terminated, they embrace the six years of Miss Lane's school-girl life and her 536entrance into society, and I therefore do not separate them. The foot-notes explain the public positions held by Mr. Buchanan at the respective dates, and some of the allusions to persons.

[LETTERS TO MISS LANE.]

Washington, February 16th, 1842.

My Dear Harriet:—

Your letter afforded me very great pleasure. There is no wish nearer my heart than that you should become an amiable and intelligent woman: and I am rejoiced to learn that you still continue at the head of your class. You can render yourself very dear to me by your conduct; and I anticipate with pleasure the months which, I trust in Heaven, we may pass together after the adjournment of Congress. I expect to be in Lancaster for a week or ten days about the 1st of April, when I hope to see you in good health, and receive the most favorable reports of your behavior.

Buck Yates is now a midshipman in the navy.[81] He is now at Boston, on board of the John Adams, and will sail in a few days for the Brazilian station. He may probably be absent for two or three years. He is much pleased with his situation, and I trust that his conduct may do both himself and his friends honor. When he left Meadville they were all well, except your aunt Maria, who still complains of a cough. Elizabeth is better than she has been for years.

I send you $———, the remains of poor Buck's money when he arrived here. It was of no use to him and would be of no use to me here. Please to hand it to your brother James, and tell him to place it to my credit for what it is worth.

When you write to your sister Mary, give her my kindest and best love.

Remember me affectionately to your brother James, Miss Hetty and the Miss Crawfords, and believe me to be ever your affectionate uncle. May Heaven bless you.

James Buchanan.

Lancaster, March 20, 1843.

My Dear Harriet:—

It affords me sincere pleasure to receive your letter. It is one of the first desires of my heart that you should become an amiable and a good girl. Education and accomplishments are very important; but they sink into insignificance when compared with the proper government of the heart and temper. How all your relatives and friends would love you,—how proud and happy I should be to acknowledge and cherish you as an object of deep affection, could I say, she is kind in heart, amiable in temper, and behaves in such a manner as to secure the affection and esteem of all around her! I now cherish the hope that ere long this may be the case. Endeavor to realize this ardent hope. What a long list of studies you are engaged upon! The number would be too great for any common intellect; but it would seem that you manage them all without difficulty. As mythology and history seem to be your favorites, I shall expect, when we meet, that you will have all the gods and heroes of Greece and Rome at your fingers' ends. At a dinner table at Washington, during the last session, a wager was made that no person at the table could name all the Muses; and the wager was won. Had you been one of the company, the result would doubtless have been different. I presume that the Muses and Graces are great favorites with you. Attend diligently to your studies; but above all, govern your heart and your conduct.

Your friends, the Miss Crawfords, are about to move to a much more comfortable house; so that should you return to school in Lancaster, you may be better accommodated. I presume your partiality still continues for these good ladies; but to be serious, you must acknowledge that you did not treat them as they deserve.

Our recent news from poor Elizabeth is very discouraging. Dr. Yates, who has been to see her, considers her case hopeless. Poor thing! She seems destined to tread the path that so many of our family have already trodden. Her husband is kind, affectionate and attentive, and she is surrounded by every comfort. She is in full communion with the Episcopal church.

I know of no news here which would interest you. Lancaster has been very dull; and is likely so to continue. Your music mistress, Miss Bryan, was married a few evenings since

to a Mr. Sterrett of Pittsburg. Annie Reigart and Kate Reynolds will take their degrees in a fortnight, and enter the world as young ladies. Judge Hayes has removed into town.
Miss Hetty says that both Mary and yourself promised to write to her, but that neither of you has written. She desires me to give her love to you both. Your brother James is well. Had Mary written to me that you were a good girl, and had behaved yourself entirely well, I should have visited you during the Christmas holidays. Tell her, I shall expect her to write soon; and as I rely confidently that she will not deceive me, I shall most heartily rejoice should her account of you be favorable. In that event, God willing, I intend to pay you a visit.
Remember me most kindly to Mrs. Kennedy, whom I remember with much of "auld lang syne;" also to Miss Annie.
Give my kindest love to Mary, and believe me to be yours,
Most affectionately,
James Buchanan.
P. S.—Your uncle Edward and the family are well except your aunt. 538She has been in delicate health all winter, but is now much better. Jessie Magaw is in Baltimore, but will return home to Meadville soon. Your letter is without date, and does not purport to come from any particular place.
Lancaster, July 25th, 1843.
My Dear Harriet:—

I enclose you a letter which I have received from Buck Yates, as your name is honorably mentioned in it. I wrote to him that it was ungallant for a young naval officer to inform a "lady faire" that he would answer her letters should she write, and that he should himself commence the correspondence.
I intend to leave for Bedford Springs in a day or two, and it is my purpose to return by Charleston, after two or three weeks, and pass a day with Mary and yourself. Give my kindest love to Mary, and believe me to be
Yours affectionately,
James Buchanan.
Washington, July 17th, 1845.[82]
My Dear Harriet:—

Although I should most gladly have you with me, yet I can not ask you to come here in this excessive heat. I have never felt the heat so oppressive as it has been for some time past; and I should fear you might become sick were you to visit Washington. Besides, you could not have any enjoyment.
I entertain a hope that I may be able to visit Bedford about the first of August. In that event, I should be willing to take you along with me. But whether it will be in my power to leave this city is still uncertain. Please to write to me how you intend to spend your vacation, and where a letter would reach you. Should the heat moderate, I still hope to see you in Washington.
Yours affectionately,
James Buchanan.
Washington, July 27th, 1845.
My Dear Harriet:—

I believe, although I am not yet quite certain, that I shall be able to leave here for the Bedford Springs on Thursday next. I shall be glad if you will accompany me. Unless you

hear from me in the meantime, you may be at Harper's Ferry on Thursday, before the cars pass from Baltimore to Cumberland. If I should not be able to go on that day, you may still be there. Mrs. Pleasonton,[83] Miss Pleasonton and Mrs. Bancroft will take charge of you to Bedford; and there you will find Mr. and Mrs. Plitt, under whose care I will place you until I can reach the Springs myself. Still, I hope to be able to go on Thursday. Of course you will get some one of your friends to accompany you from Charleston to Harper's Ferry. Please to write to me immediately on the receipt of this.
Yours affectionately,
James Buchanan.
Washington, July 6th, 1846.
My Dear Harriet:—

Your welcome letter has been received, and I rejoice to learn...... I trust you will soon be well enough...... I think of all places for you the nunnery at Georgetown would be the best. Your religious principles are doubtless so well settled that you will not become a nun.
My labors are great; but they do not "way" me down, as you write the word. Now I would say "weigh;" but doctors may differ on this point.
I hope Mary has recovered ere this from her bruises. Give my love to her, and tell her to have her saddle girthed tighter the next time she rides.
It will be easy for you to find Dr. Jackson's remedy in any hay-field near Lancaster at this season. It would be quite romantic and interesting to witness your exploits on such a theatre.
Your friends, Mrs. Bancroft and the Pleasontons, often inquire for you with kindness. They have given you somewhat of a name here; and Mrs. Polk and Miss Rucker, her niece, have several times urged me to permit you to come and pass some time with them. I have been as deaf as the adder to their request, knowing, to use a word of your grandmother, that you are too "outsetting" already. There is a time for all things under the sun, as the wise man says, and your time will yet come.
I intend to go to the Bedford Springs this summer, if possible; but as Congress may not adjourn until the 10th August, the fashionable season will then be over. I had thought of giving Mary and yourself a polite invitation to accompany me there; but I fear it will be too late in the season for Mary to enact the character of a belle, and you are quite too young to make the attempt.
Miss Hetty requests me to send her love to you, and to say that she would be very glad to see you in Washington...... I fear she might be twice glad, once on your arrival, and still more so on your departure. She will be in Lancaster in September.
James Henry is here.[84] I intend to commence with him to-morrow and make him eat vegetables, or he shall have no meat. I have not yet determined upon a school for him.
I wish you to embrace the first opportunity to remember me very kindly to Mrs. Franklin. I never lived beside a better or more agreeable neighbor. Give my love to Mary, though I perceive this is the second time, and Patt, and believe me ever to be
Yours affectionately,
James Buchanan.
Washington, July 19, 1847.
My Dear Harriet:—

The Secretary of the Treasury,[85] with his mother-in-law, Mrs. Bache, and Miss Bache, will leave here for Rockaway, to enjoy the benefit of sea-bathing, on Thursday morning next. I know of no other opportunity of sending you, and this will be an excellent one. It is impossible for me to accompany you myself. I hope that the good sister Cecilia may permit you to leave with them. You will lose but a few days by this arrangement. Your clothes, if they should not be ready, can be placed in order at Rockaway under the direction of Mrs. Bache. Besides, it is uncertain how long our friends, the Pleasontons, may remain at Oyster Bay, and whether they will like it. Mr. Walker has hired a cottage at Rockaway, and you may remain with his family as long as you please.

I am extremely anxious that this arrangement should be made, because I know of no other means by which you can reach the sea-shore. If possible, please to send me an answer by the bearer.

Yours affectionately,
James Buchanan.
Washington, July 8, 1848.
My Dear Harriet:—

I suppose you will now, within a week or ten days, return to the exhibition, and we shall all be happy to see you. If you should not have good company all the way through, I could meet you in Baltimore without inconvenience almost any evening, leaving here in the cars at 5 o'clock P. M. You would arrive in Baltimore, probably, a little before my arrival; but whoever might accompany you to Baltimore could take you to Barnum's until my arrival. If you should adopt this course, inform me certainly of the day you will leave Lancaster, so that there may be no mistake.

We have no news here which would interest you. Everything has been quiet since you left. The Pleasontons and others often inquire of your health.

I am glad to learn that Mary has turned out to be "a grand housekeeper." You could not have given me any more agreeable information. If she had proved to be idle and extravagant in youth, the promise of her age would have been poverty and dependence. There is no spectacle more agreeable to me than that of a young married woman properly sensible of the important duties of her station, and acting upon those high principles which add lustre to the female character. Give her my kindest love, with my best respect to Mr. Baker.

Remember me affectionately to James, and the family, and believe me to be

Yours, as ever,
James Buchanan.
541Washington, August 2, 1848.
My Dear Harriet:—

I have this moment received your letter of the 30th ultimo, and hasten to give it an answer. I regret very much that you are not pleased with Rockaway. You went there for the benefit of your health, under the advice of physicians, and I should be very sorry you should leave it without giving sea-bathing a fair trial.

It is certainly out of the question for me to accompany you on a tour to West Point, Niagara, Boston, etc. If I should be able to leave Washington at all, I cannot go to any place from which I could not immediately return in case of necessity. I require rest and quiet. Besides, under existing circumstances, which I need not explain, I could not visit the States of New York and Massachusetts, unless it might be to pass through them quietly and rapidly. It is possible, if the weather should be suitable towards the close of August, that I may go to Saratoga for a few days; but my movements are altogether uncertain.

I am much gratified that you have acquitted yourself so handsomely as to obtain medals and premiums; and under other circumstances, I should cheerfully accompany you on your travels. It is possible that I may take you to West Point.
Miss Hetty is gradually, but slowly, recovering. Please to remember me very kindly to Mrs. Bache, Mrs. Walker, and the ladies, and believe me to be
Yours affectionately,
James Buchanan.
Washington, August 22, 1848.
My Dear Harriet:—

I have this moment received your letter of the 20th instant. I answered your former letter very soon after it was received, and am sorry that my answer miscarried.
I expect sister Maria here to-day or to-morrow, and of course ———.[86] At this moment I was interrupted by the agreeable information that she had arrived, and I have just seen her. It is now four years since I enjoyed that pleasure. How long she will remain I do not know; but it will be impossible to leave before her departure. She will remain until James[87] shall receive his appointment in the revenue cutter service, which was kindly promised him by Mr. Walker, but which cannot be conferred until after the President's return, who is not expected until this day week, the 29th instant. From present appearances I shall not be able to leave Washington before the first of September. I cannot, therefore, promise positively to visit Rockaway.
I hope you are enjoying yourself, and may be benefited in your health by the sea-bathing. 542Should I go to New York, I may take you as far as West Point. I presume the season will be too late for the Saratoga Springs.
Give my kindest regards to Mrs. Bache and the ladies, and believe me to be
Yours affectionately,
James Buchanan.
Washington, January 8, 1849.
My Dear Harriet:—

You have acted wisely in controlling your inclinations and remaining at home. This act of self-restraint has raised you in my estimation. Let nothing divert you from your purpose. Washington now begins to be gay. Mrs. Walker is at home to-night,—the first assembly will be held to-morrow evening. Mrs. Polk gives a drawing-room on Wednesday evening; and on Thursday evening Miss Harris will be married, and there will be a party at Captain McCauley's at the Navy Yard. I now give dinners myself once a week. I rarely go out to evening parties. I have had my day of such amusement, and have enjoyed it. Yours is just commencing, and I hope it may be a happy one. I dare say Mr. Sullivan[88] will be inconsolable when he learns that you will not be here during the present winter.
I wish now to give you a caution. Never allow your affections to become interested or engage yourself to any person without my previous advice. You ought never to marry any man to whom you are not attached; but you ought never to marry any person who is not able to afford you a decent and immediate support. In my experience, I have witnessed the long years of patient misery and dependence which fine women have endured from rushing precipitately into matrimonial connections without sufficient reflection. Look ahead, and consider the future, and act wisely in this particular.
Mrs. Pleasonton of Philadelphia left here on Saturday morning last. I saw her and her two daughters on Friday evening. They all inquired for you very affectionately; and the

Pleasontons of this city are, I believe, sincerely anxious that you should pass some time with them. At a proper period you may enjoy this pleasure.

It may be that I shall not reach Lancaster until the first of April, as I have some business to attend to here which may require a fortnight or three weeks after I shall be relieved from office. When I reach there, I shall be happy to have you with me.

Yours affectionately,

James Buchanan.

P. S.—Give my love to Mary and all the rest.

CHAPTER XIX.
1844–1845.

ANNEXATION OF TEXAS—ELECTION OF PRESIDENT POLK—THE DEPARTMENT OF STATE ACCEPTED BY MR. BUCHANAN.

In the Presidential election of 1844, there was a third party in the field. By this time, the anti-slavery sentiment in some of the Northern States had taken the form of a political organization, which called itself the "Liberty" party, and was called by the others the party of the "Abolitionists." Their candidate for the Presidency was Mr. James G. Birney, of Ohio, a gentleman who had taken a leading part in organizing "The American Anti-Slavery Society," and was at this time its secretary. He had never held a public office. Texas, which had in 1836 made itself independent of Mexico, had been for more than nine years a slaveholding country, with a republican form of government. Between that government and the United States a secret treaty was negotiated, after Mr. Tyler became President, for the annexation of Texas to this Union. It had been submitted to the Senate, and had been rejected, chiefly because Texas claimed to carry her western boundary to the Rio Grande; and to incorporate her with the United States and to adopt that claim would, it was supposed, give Mexico a just cause for war. After the sudden death of Mr. Upshur,[89] who became Secretary of State when Mr. Webster retired from President Tyler's cabinet, Mr. Calhoun, who succeeded him, took up and carried out a new negotiation, which Mr. Upshur had begun, for making Texas a part of the United States by the action of Congress. This project was pending, and more or less suspected, or believed not to have been relinquished, when the three parties made their nominations for the Presidency. The Democratic party, by the nomination of Mr. Polk, and by their avowed declarations, made the annexation of Texas distinctly one of their party measures. The Whigs, in nominating Mr. Clay, selected a candidate who was understood to oppose the annexation, not because Texas was a slaveholding country, but because it might lead to a war with Mexico. They did not proclaim it as a part of the policy of their party to prevent the annexation of any more slave territory. This was one of the principal reasons why Mr. Birney drew many votes away from Mr. Clay. As Mr. Polk obtained a majority of sixty-five electoral votes over Mr. Clay, and as six of the States which voted for him were Northern and non-slaveholding States, including both Pennsylvania and New York, the Democratic party claimed a right to say that the country had pronounced for the annexation of Texas, its slavery notwithstanding. The correspondence between the Government of the United States and Texas was submitted to Congress by President Tyler, in December, 1844. Joint resolutions for the annexation of Texas were finally adopted by Congress on the 1st of March, 1845. They admitted Texas into the Union, as a State whose constitution recognized slavery, and they also pledged the faith of the United States to allow of the future formation of four more States out of Texas, and to admit them into the Union, either with or without slavery, as their constitutions might require, if formed below the Missouri compromise line of 36° 30′ , but if formed above that line, slavery was to be excluded. In the Senate, there were twenty-seven votes for the admission of Texas on these conditions, and twenty-five votes against it; of the affirmative votes, thirteen were from free States, and four of these were from New England. The Missouri compromise line was extended through Texas; the "Wilmot Proviso," which aimed to exclude slavery from the whole of this newly acquired region, came up a year later.

Mr. Buchanan's course as a Senator, on these resolutions, can easily be inferred from what has already appeared in regard to his sentiments on the whole subject of Texan independence, and the relations of that country to the United States. But the official record shows, with entire distinctness, that against the constitutional objection which maintained that new States could not be admitted into the Union unless they had lawfully arisen within the United States, he held with those who rejected this restriction, and who maintained that a foreign State could be made a member of the Union. After the joint resolutions had come before the Senate from the House of Representatives, the Senate Committee on Foreign Relations, by a majority report, recommended their rejection. Mr. Buchanan, who was a member of that committee, did not make a minority report, but on the 27th of February (1845), he said:

He did not rise to debate the question. He had heard some of his respected friends on this side of the Senate, in whose sincerity he had the most entire confidence, observe that if these resolutions should pass the Senate, the Constitution would receive a mortal stab. If Mr. B. thought so, great as was the acquisition we were about to make, he should be the last man in existence to acquire the richest benefit the world could hold out to our grasp at such a price.

Mr. B. said he might have assumed the privilege of reply which belonged to him from the position he occupied on the Committee on Foreign Relations; but he waived it. Not because the arguments on the other side had not been exceedingly ingenious and plausible, and urged with great ability; but because all the reasoning in the world could not abolish the plain language of the Constitution, which declared that "new States might be admitted by Congress into the Union." But what new States? The convention had answered that question in letters of light, by rejecting the proposed limitation of this grant, which would have confined it to States lawfully arising within the United States. The clause was introduced with this limitation, and, after full discussion, it ended in the shape it now held, without limitation or restriction of any kind. This was a historical fact. It could not be denied. Planting himself upon that fact, and having heard no argument which shook the position—believing, as he most conscientiously did believe, that the Constitution would not be violated in the least by the adoption of the pending resolutions, he here entered his solemn protest against the solemn protests which had been made on the other side, and which went almost the length of implying that he, and the advocates of these resolutions, were knowingly and of design violating the Constitution and their oaths, to secure a favorite political measure. This was the greatest public act in which Mr. Buchanan had ever had the honor of taking an humble part; he should do it cheerfully, gladly, gloriously, because he believed that his vote would confer blessings innumerable upon his fellow-men. now, henceforward, and forever.

Mr. Berrien said he would not consent that this debate should close with the declaration of the Senator from Pennsylvania (Mr. Buchanan), that the convention had not determined the sense of the term "new States."

Mr. Buchanan rose to explain. What the Senator from Pennsylvania did say was, that at first the clause granting power to Congress to admit new States into the Union had been confined to States arising within the United States; but that after debate and a full discussion, the Constitution was adopted with the clause in its present clear unrestricted form, written as in letters of light.

After some further remarks from other Senators, and some attempts to amend the resolutions, they were passed and engrossed on the same day. President Tyler, on the 3d of March, announced by special message to the Senate, that he had approved and signed them.[90]

The electoral college of Pennsylvania, when the votes of that State were given to Mr. Polk, united in a strong recommendation to him to make Mr. Buchanan Secretary of State. Mr. Buchanan took no steps to influence the newly-elected President in regard to this or any other cabinet appointment. He maintained a dignified reserve in his personal relations to Mr. Polk, both during and after the election. Certainly there were very strong reasons of fitness, which should have led Mr. Polk to desire that Mr. Buchanan would accept the Department of State. His qualifications for it were far greater than those of any other public man in the Democratic party; and, if such a consideration could have any weight, he personally deserved at the hands of Mr. Polk all that a President could bestow of opportunity to render further service to the country. In looking back over Mr. Buchanan's public life, now covering a period of nearly twenty-five years, one can perceive the intellectual growth of an American statesman, who had not been taken suddenly from private pursuits to fill an important public position, but who had been trained by the regular gradations of office for the affairs of government. To have a constituency who can appreciate the value of such a training, and can support a public servant in the devotion of his time and abilities to the public service, is a great advantage. This advantage Mr. Buchanan had enjoyed for twenty-five years, and he had well repaid the devotion of his friends. The people of Pennsylvania had but once in twenty years swerved from the 547party in which Mr. Buchanan was a distinguished leader, and they had now returned to it. His experience, his aptitude for public life, his solid, though not brilliant abilities, and the weight of the great State which had kept him in the Senate, marked him as the fittest person to be at the head of Mr. Polk's cabinet. Mr. Polk, however, while conscious of the propriety of offering this position to Mr. Buchanan, and while he felt the need of his services, seems to have had a fear lest his administration might be disturbed by Mr. Buchanan's ambition to become his successor. He took the somewhat singular step of asking from Mr. Buchanan a promise that he would retire from the cabinet, if he should be a candidate for the Presidency in 1848. There is no good reason for attributing this to personal jealousy of Buchanan, for Mr. Polk did not expect to become a candidate for re-election. He was a sagacious man, who took a just view of his own situation, he knew quite well that he had become President because the conflicting claims of others had rendered it necessary to compromise upon an unexpected and far from conspicuous candidate. But he desired, and wisely desired, to avoid all internal difficulties, by freeing his administration from complications about the succession. Every one will commend the spirit of the following letter, and every one, it should seem, will commend the manner in which it was met by Mr. Buchanan, who could hardly be expected to say that he would renounce all idea of becoming a candidate for the Presidency in 1848, since he could not tell what his public duty might require of him.

[MR. POLK TO MR. BUCHANAN.]

Washington City, February 17, 1845.

Sir:—

The principles and policy which will be observed and maintained during my administration are embodied in the resolutions adopted by the Democratic National Convention of delegates, assembled at Baltimore in Maryland, and in the inaugural address which I propose to deliver to my fellow-citizens on assuming the duties of President of the United States, and which is herewith handed to you for your perusal. In making up my cabinet, I desire to select gentlemen who will agree with me in opinion, and who will cordially co-operate with me in carrying out these principles and policy.

In my official action I will take no part between gentlemen of the Democratic party who may become aspirants or candidates to succeed me in the Presidential office, and desire that no member of my cabinet shall do so. Individual preferences it is not expected or desired to limit or restrain. It is official interference by the dispensation of public patronage or otherwise that I desire to guard against. Should any member of my cabinet become a candidate for the Presidency or Vice Presidency of the United States, it will be expected upon the happening of such an event, that he will retire from the cabinet.

I disapprove the practice which has sometimes prevailed, of cabinet officers absenting themselves for long periods of time from the seat of Government and leaving the management of their department to chief clerks; or other less responsible persons than themselves. I expect myself to remain constantly at Washington, unless it may be that no public duty requires my presence, when I may be occasionally absent, but then only for a short time. It is by conforming to this rule that the President and his cabinet can have any assurance that absences will be prevented, and that the subordinate executive officers connected with them respectively will faithfully perform their duty.

If sir, you concur with me in these opinions and views, I shall be pleased to have your assistance in my administration, as a member of my cabinet, and now tender to you the office of Secretary of State, and invite you to take charge of that department.

I am, with great respect, your obedient servant,
James K. Polk.

[MR. BUCHANAN TO MR. POLK.]
Washington, February 18, 1845.
My Dear Sir:—

I feel greatly honored by your kind invitation to accept the station of Secretary of State in your cabinet; and I cheerfully and cordially approve the terms on which this offer has been made, as they have been presented in your note of yesterday. To prevent, however, any possible misunderstanding between us hereafter, I desire to make an explanation in regard to that portion of your letter which requires that any member of your cabinet shall retire upon becoming a candidate for the Presidency.

Before I had anticipated that you would do me the honor of inviting me to a seat in your cabinet, I had publicly presented my views on the subject of agitating the question of the next Presidency in the strongest colors. Both patriotism and policy, the success of the party as well as that of your administration, require that we should have repose from the strife of making Presidents. I am, therefore, utterly opposed to the agitation of this question in any shape or form, and shall exercise any influence which I may possess to prevent it, both in regard to myself and others. Nay, more, I think the welfare of your administration requires that in every prudent and appropriate manner this principle should be maintained by it; and the patronage of the Government ought to be dispensed, not to favor any individual aspirant, but solely for the good of the country and the Democratic party.

I do not know that I shall ever desire to be a candidate for the Presidency. Most certainly I never yet strongly felt such an inclination; and I have been willing, and should at this moment be willing, to accept a station which would, in my estimation of what is proper, deprive me of any prospect of reaching that office. Still, I could not, and would not, accept the high and honorable office to which you have called me, at the expense of self-ostracism. My friends would unanimously condemn me were I to pursue this course. I cannot proclaim to the world that in no contingency shall I be a candidate for the Presidency in 1848; nor in the meantime can I be held responsible for the action of occasional county meetings, in my own or other States, preceding general elections, which, without my previous knowledge or consent, might present my name in connection with this office. I can answer for myself that as I have never yet raised a finger or stirred a step, towards the attainment of this station; so I never shall make any personal exertions for that purpose without your express permission, so long as I remain a member of your cabinet. If, however, unexpectedly to myself, the people should by a State or national convention present me as their candidate, I cannot declare in advance that I would not accede to their wishes; but in that event I would retire from your cabinet, unless you should desire me to remain.

I do not deny that I would be as much pleased to accept the station of Secretary of State from yourself as from any man living. I entertain a strong conviction that under the controlling direction of your wisdom, prudence and firmness, I might be useful to you in conducting the Department of State, and I know from your established character, so far as it is given to mortals to know anything, that our social and personal intercourse would be of the most friendly and agreeable character.

If under these explanations, you are willing to confer upon me the office of Secretary of State, I shall accept it with gratitude, and exert my best efforts to do my duty to the country and to yourself.

With sentiments of the highest and most sincere respect, I remain.

Your friend,

James Buchanan.

In 1858, there again came about rumors of General Jackson's hostility to Mr. Buchanan. The following letter written by a citizen of Nashville to a friend, gives decisive evidence on General Jackson's feelings towards Mr. Buchanan, at the time when the latter became Secretary of State.

550[MR. JOHNSON TO GENERAL ANDERSON.]

Nashville, Oct. 6th, 1858.

Dear Sir:—

I received your letter of the 5th inst., making inquiries of my recollection as to the feelings entertained by General Jackson towards Mr. Buchanan at the time of the nomination of Mr. Polk and the appointment of Mr. Buchanan as Secretary. I do not remember to have met General Jackson after the election of Mr. Polk, but was upon the most intimate terms with President Polk, both before and after his election. General Jackson was the avowed and open friend of Mr. Van Buren, and when it was ascertained that Mr. Van Buren could not get the nomination, he expressed himself to many friends favorable to the nomination of Mr. Buchanan, as the true and proper course of the Democratic party, before Mr. Polk's name was known to be before the convention for the Presidency. This I have heard from so many sources as to entertain no doubt of the fact. Mr. Polk, it is well known, consulted with him freely as to the individuals who should compose his cabinet, and the appointment of Mr. Buchanan as Secretary of State met his decided approbation, as did all the other individuals composing the cabinet, excepting the Secretary of the Treasury. He had some misgivings and apprehensions as to the propriety of the selection, as did many others of the friends of President Polk.

These are my recollections from the most free and unreserved intercourse with President Polk, and my recollection now is that I have seen letters from General Jackson to President Polk confirming substantially the above statement.

General Jackson was known to have strong feelings—warm towards his friends, bitter towards his enemies—and in the exciting canvasses for the Presidency may have used, and even written, harsh expressions about many prominent friends of his own, founded upon perversions and misrepresentations of their conduct by those toadies with whom he was beset, and often deceived by them as to the conduct and expressions of leading and prominent men in the Democratic party, and by none of them so often as by —— and ——, who never deserved his confidence or merited the favors bestowed on them.

The General, however, never hesitated to do justice to any man when the truth was ascertained as to his conduct.

From the whole of my intercourse with General Jackson and Mr. Polk, after the second election of General Jackson, I never had reason to suppose that he ever had any unkind feelings toward Mr. Buchanan. On the contrary, Mr. Buchanan was considered in the Senate one among his most active and confidential friends, as President Polk was in the House of Representatives.

Mr. Polk, or Buchanan, could neither be used nor controlled by such men as —— and ——, and hence their hostility to them after the second election of General Jackson, which was manifested in various ways which I could specify.

I am, very respectfully, your friend,
E. Johnson.
551

CHAPTER XX.
1845–1846.

THE OREGON CONTROVERSY—DANGER OF A WAR WITH ENGLAND—NEGOTIATION FOR A SETTLEMENT OF THE BOUNDARY—PRIVATE CORRESPONDENCE.

Among the subjects involved in the foreign relations of the country, when Mr. Buchanan became Secretary of State, and which demanded his immediate attention, one of the most important and critical was the title to the territory of Oregon, that had long been in dispute between Great Britain and the United States. The northern boundary of this region of country, which should have separated British America west of the Rocky Mountains from the dominion of the United States, had not been settled by the treaty negotiated at Washington between the two powers in 1842, because Lord Ashburton had no instructions to deal with it. As far back as the administration of President Monroe, an extension of the 49th parallel of latitude to the Pacific, as the boundary, was offered by the United States to England, but it was declined. The British claim was founded on the assertion that the title of the United States, which was derived through the Louisiana and Florida treaties, was not exclusive as to any part of the territory; and since it was for the interest of the Hudson Bay Company to follow the Columbia River to the ocean, and since the English asserted an actual and previous occupation as well as the Americans, it became desirable for England to have a right of joint occupation established, until the boundary between the two national possessions should be finally settled. A convention was entered into in 1827, establishing such a joint occupation until notice of its termination should be given by either of the two powers. This concession on the part of the United States, made in the 552interest of peace, left an open question between the two governments, both claiming the whole territory. But what was "the whole" of Oregon? On the American side of the controversy, the region claimed extended to a line that would be marked by the parallel of 54° 40′ north latitude. This would have carried the American title on the Pacific coast far above the Strait of Fuca and Vancouver's Island, and would have made an irregular boundary, not coinciding in latitude with the northern boundary of the United States east of the Rocky Mountains. On the other hand, the claim of England brought her down to the mouth of the Columbia River, which has its source nearly at the 50th parallel, and flows in a circuitous course of about eight hundred miles, first to the south, and then to the west, until it reaches the Pacific. The joint occupation agreed upon in 1827, had become inconvenient, and indeed dangerous for both nations. A very uneasy feeling sprang up in our Western States and among the settlers who were pushing into this territory, and who looked to the United States for titles to the land, and for the protection due from the sovereign power. Popular opinion about our right was not likely to be founded in intelligent investigation, but it was sure to find its way into the political action of the Democratic party. The political body which nominated Mr. Polk as its candidate for the Presidency, proclaimed our title to be "clear and unquestionable." Mr. Polk considered himself as elected under an imperative popular instruction to assert this claim, and in his inaugural address he put it forth in very strong terms as extending to the parallel of 54° 40′ . This was the attitude of the matter when Mr. Buchanan became Secretary of State.

Notwithstanding the strong personal convictions of the President and the Secretary of State of the validity of this claim as it was asserted in Mr. Polk's inaugural address, deference for the action of former administrations and a desire to avoid a rupture with England, led the President to authorize Mr. Buchanan to offer the 49th parallel as the boundary. This offer was made to Mr. Pakenham, the British Minister at Washington, on the 10th of July, 1845. Without referring this offer to his own government and awaiting instructions, Mr. Pakenham replied on the 30th of July, that "after this exposition 553of the views entertained by the British government respecting the relative value and importance of the British and American claims, the American Plenipotentiary will not be surprised to hear that the undersigned does not feel at liberty to accept the proposal offered by the American Plenipotentiary for the settlement of the question." He closed his note by expressing his "trust that the American Plenipotentiary will be prepared to offer some further proposal for the settlement of the Oregon question, more consistent with fairness and equity, and with the reasonable expectations of the British government." These were very unfortunate expressions, since they implied, under the circumstances, that the American Government had begun the negotiation by asserting a claim that was untenable, and had followed its assertion with an unfair and inequitable offer. Had this language of the British plenipotentiary become public at that moment, the consequences would have been an uncontrollable excitement throughout this country. Careful, however, to keep open the door for mutual concessions, Mr. Buchanan, before he answered Mr. Pakenham's note, wrote to Mr. McLane, who had succeeded Mr. Everett as United States Minister in London, an elaborate despatch, tracing the diplomatic history of the Oregon question, and suggesting, with much skill, the modes in which an unfortunate result might be avoided. Indefatigably industrious, and employing no pen but his own, he gave to his official papers a polish, the marks of which remain on the original drafts, attesting the extreme care that he bestowed upon them. Mr. McLane was instructed to make known the contents of this despatch to the British ministry, in case they made inquiries of him.

The offer of the 49th parallel having been withdrawn, Mr. Buchanan, on the 30th of August, addressed a note to Mr. Pakenham, in which he reasserted the American claim to what he regarded as "the whole of Oregon," and made an elaborate and exhaustive exposition of its grounds. There are few papers on the diplomatic records of our Government more able and searching than this exposition of the American claim to the territory of Oregon. Thoroughly master of his subject, and fully convinced of the validity of the claim which he was asserting, Mr. Buchanan wrote this paper with a dignified force that was not unlikely to command the assent of impartial persons, when the document should become public. Writing to Mr. McLane afterwards, he said: "this note of Mr. Pakenham (July 30th) became the subject of grave deliberation by the President. Upon a full consideration of the whole question, and after waiting a month, he deemed it to be a duty which he owed to his country to withdraw his proposition (of the 49th parallel), which he had submitted, and to maintain the right of the United States to the whole of Oregon. This was done by my note to Mr. Pakenham of the 30th of August last."

But the note of August 30th could not become public while the negotiation was pending, or before the meeting of Congress in December. In the mean time, Mr. Pakenham endeavored to have the American offer of the 49th parallel restored. "Judging from late conversations with Mr. Pakenham," Mr. Buchanan again writes to Mr. McLane, "he is now anxious that this withdrawal should be withdrawn, and that the negotiation might proceed as if our offer were still in force. But the President will not consent to change his position and to recall what has already been done. He will not renew his former offer, nor submit any new proposition; and it must remain for the British government to decide what other or further steps, if any, they may think proper to take in the negotiation. The President has adopted this determination after two cabinet councils, and he deems it necessary that this should be communicated to you, in order that you may clearly understand his purpose."

The correspondence was submitted by the President to Congress, in December (1845), and its publication was immediately followed in this country by a considerable change of feeling in those quarters where the course of the administration was watched with most jealousy, and where war was most dreaded. In the House of Representatives, where the war feeling of the Northwest found expression, some violent speeches were made. In the Senate there was a moderate tone, but steps were taken looking to the termination of the joint occupation, and to an inquiry into the state of the national defences. These movements had an ominous appearance. In the diplomatic department, however, the negotiation went on quietly.

On the 23d of December, Mr. Buchanan made the following brief minute of a cabinet consultation held on that day, at which the President said:

If Mr. Pakenham inquires if a new proposition made by them would be respectfully considered, I would refer him to the correspondence—your last note of the 30th August, and say it has been at your option, with a perfect liberty to propose any proposition you thought proper, and you had no reason to conclude from what had occurred here that the Government would not have treated such a proposition with respectful consideration when made. You have made no new proposition, and the question, therefore, stands on its present attitude.

December 23, 1845.—I took down the foregoing from the lips of the President, in the presence of the cabinet.

Four days afterward an interview took place at the State Department, of which I find the following account in Mr. Buchanan's hand-writing:

On Saturday afternoon, 27th of December, 1845, Mr. Pakenham called at the Department of State. After some brief preliminary conversation on other topics, he informed me that he had received instructions from his government relative to the Oregon question; without at the time informing me what they were. He then proceeded to express his desire that I should recall the withdrawal of our offer to settle the Oregon question by the 49th parallel of latitude, and suffer the negotiation to proceed on that basis, expressing the belief that it might then result in a satisfactory manner. I informed him that he had made one proposition to Mr. Calhoun, which had been rejected; that I had made a proposition which had been rejected by him and then withdrawn; that the whole negotiation had been submitted to Congress with the President's message; and after all this, it was too late to expect that the President would now retrace his steps. That what had been done must be considered as done.

He then said that if he were now to make a new proposition, he had no means of knowing whether it would be accepted: if he made a proposition it might be rejected. I replied that the whole field was open to him, as it had been in the beginning; that it was as free to him as it had been to him at first, or was to me afterwards, to make any proposition he thought proper; that all I could say was that any proposition he might make would be respectfully considered by the President; but I said no more.

He then observed that as I was not willing to go further (as I understood him), he would, under his instructions, present me the offer of the British government to arbitrate the question. He said it was drawn up chiefly in the very language of Lord Aberdeen.

556I then received the communication from him, and read it over carefully. As soon as I had completed its perusal, he urged its acceptance strongly; expressed his great desire for the preservation of peace between the two countries, and said that it was impossible that war should grow out of such a question between two great nations. He said he was not worth much in the world; but would give half what he was worth to see the question honorably and amicably adjusted between the two nations.

I stated the strong desire, both on the part of the President and myself, that the question might be amicably and honorably adjusted. That we had every disposition that this result might be attained. I observed, however, that if ever this was accomplished, I thought it must be by negotiation, and not by arbitration; and especially such an arbitration as he proposed. That both the President and myself were firmly convinced of the validity of our title up to 54° 40′; and yet his proposition to arbitrate assumed the right to a portion of the territory on the part of Great Britain, and left it to the arbitrator alone to decide in what manner the territory should be divided between the parties. That this alone, I thought, would be a sufficient reason for the rejection of his proposition, even if others did not exist, of which he must be aware from our previous conversations on the subject; but I would consult the President, and give him an answer with as little delay as possible. He intimated rather than expressed a wish that his answer might be communicated to him in time for the packet (Monday). I told him that a proper respect for the British government required that the answer should be well considered; that the cabinet would not meet again before Tuesday, and I could not encourage him to expect the answer before Saturday next. He said he had no doubt my answer would be well considered. He hoped that in it I would not assert a claim to the whole territory, and Saturday next would be in time.

He then branched off, and said that the proposition was to refer the question to a state as well as a sovereign; he said that this had been done on purpose to get clear of the objection to crowned heads. I asked him to whom he thought it might be referred if not to a sovereign. He suggested the Republic of Switzerland, or the government of Hamburg or Bremen. I told him that whilst my own inclinations were strongly against arbitration; if I were compelled to select an arbitrator, it would be the Pope. That both nations were heretics, and the Pope would be impartial. This he appeared at first to take seriously,—he said the Pope was a temporal sovereign; but I thought he was disinclined to select him as an arbitrator. He perceived, however, that I was not in earnest, and suggested that the reference might be made to commissioners from both countries. I told him I thought it was vain to think of arbitration; because, even if the President were agreed to it, which I felt pretty certain he was not, no such treaty could pass the Senate. That the pursuit of arbitration would only involve the question in new difficulties. He then suggested the mediation of a third power in the adjustment of the question. I told him that was an idea which he had never suggested before, and on which I could say nothing. He observed that this, together with his suggestion of commissioners, came from himself and had not been embraced in his instructions. He said that a mediator who would interfere might share the fate of the man who interfered between two other men who were fighting, when both fell upon him and gave him a sound drubbing.

He remarked that the affair might remain just where it was, and the British government would not disturb it. He did not entertain serious apprehensions of war.

He then told me that he had met Judge Douglas at Mr. Cox's party the other evening, and had a good deal of conversation with him about his bill.

He objected to a promise of a grant of lands to actual settlers in Oregon, and to the erection of forts by the Government within it, as violations of the treaty. I told him I had formed no decided opinion as to the promise of grants of land; but as to the forts, it was very clear, in my opinion, that we had a right to erect them. We did not purpose to erect fortifications capable of enduring a siege in civilized warfare; but merely stockade forts to protect our emigrants from the savages. That the Hudson's Bay Company had erected many such forts, and we surely had the right under the treaty to do what they had done. He observed that the settlers might do this themselves as the Company had done. I replied that they were too poor; that this Company had the entire government in its hands; and surely we might do what they had done. I observed that this was ever the way with Great Britain, she was always fettered by monopolies; and if it were not for the Company they would at once give us our rights to the whole country up to $54°\ 40'$. He said that the Hudson's Bay Company had rights in Oregon which must be protected; but I understood him to admit that they did interpose an obstacle in the way of the settlement of the question. He said the British government would be glad to get clear of the question on almost any terms; that they did not care if the arbitrator should award the whole territory to us. They would yield it without a murmur. I said I had no doubt of this. They never played the part of the fox: but always of the lion. They would preserve their faith inviolate. He said they wished for peace; but intimated that this was not our wish. I asked him why we should desire war. Would not their superiority at sea give them command of the coasts of Oregon. Yes, he said, that was true, but the war would not be confined to that region. That he would willingly make a bargain to fight it out with us there, if we would agree to that.

On the 26th of February (1846), Mr. Buchanan addressed an elaborate official despatch to Mr. McLane, explaining fully the reasons which had led the President to decline to make the boundary of Oregon a subject of arbitration, and suggesting what it would be practicable for the President to agree upon, if proposed by the British government. Mr. McLane was authorized to make known to Lord Aberdeen the contents of this despatch; and between its date and the 1st of June, Sir Robert Peel's government determined to send to Washington the project of a convention which is described in a despatch addressed to Mr. J. Randolph Clay on the 13th of June, and which is given below. The despatch of February 26th, to Mr. McLane, was accompanied by a private letter of the same date. On the 6th of June, another private letter to Mr. McLane informed him of the President's purpose to submit Lord Aberdeen's project to the Senate, and the despatch of June 13th to Mr. Clay gives the result.

[MR. BUCHANAN TO HON. LOUIS McLANE.]
Washington, Feb. 26, 1845.
My Dear Sir:—

The brief space left to me before the departure of our messenger to Boston shall be devoted to writing you a private letter...... By my despatch you will be made distinctly acquainted with the ground which the President has determined to maintain on the Oregon question; and I do not perceive, after what has passed, how he could do more than submit a British proposition, based on the parallel of 49°, to the Senate. From all I can learn, there is not the least doubt but that either of the two propositions specified in my despatch would receive the previous sanction of a constitutional majority of that body. I say the previous sanction, for reasons which I have not the time to give you. All that I apprehend is, that the British government, in their offer, may insist on the perpetual free navigation of the Columbia. This would indeed be truly embarrassing; and all your diplomacy should be exerted to prevent it. The President would not present such a proposition to the Senate, unless he should greatly change his mind; and if he should, I do not believe that two-thirds of that body would give it their sanction.

I am convinced that the Oregon question is rapidly reaching that point when it must, if ever, be peaceably settled. Although what I have said to you of the present disposition of the Senate is strictly true, it is uncertain how long this may continue. Public opinion on this subject is far in advance of Congress. I am convinced that if the question should remain open until the Congressional elections next fall, this would be clearly evinced...... In Great Britain they form their judgment of popular opinion from what they read in the newspapers, chiefly Whig, of our large commercial cities. This you know to be a mistake. The commercial interest which, in a great degree controls these papers, has a direct interest in the preservation of peace, and especially with Great Britain. The strong and irresistible public opinion throughout the vast interior of our country, which controls the action of the Government, is but little, if at all, affected by the considerations which influence the mercantile community. General Cass and Mr. Allen, who are both candidates for popular favor, the one immediately and the other prospectively, will not consent to accept the parallel of 49°. The two Senators from Indiana, the two from Illinois, and one from Missouri (not Colonel Benton), occupy the same ground.

Mr. Calhoun, from a variety of circumstances, came to the Senate with a flush of popularity, which might have rendered him highly useful, both to himself and to his country; but, already, it is nearly all gone. He at once took open and bold ground against the notice, and propagated his opinions with that degree of zeal which belongs to his character. He succeeded in inducing a small number of Democrats in the House, chiefly Virginians, to vote against the notice; and such is now the weight of public opinion in its favor, that it is said he would vote for it himself, but for the awkward dilemma in which this would place his friends in the House. The truth is, that the discreet friends of peace clearly perceive that the question must be settled peaceably within the year, or war may be the consequence. In some form or other it will pass the Senate by a large majority; and many anticipate an almost unanimous vote. I do not believe this. I have always liked Mr. Calhoun very much, and am truly sorry that he did not adopt a wiser course. He must have been the great man of our party in the Senate. Colonel Benton's conduct and speech on the Oregon question are entitled to warm commendation. Your son Robert is winning laurels for himself in the Maryland legislature. He is indeed a fine fellow, and a worthy chip of the old block.

I have for years been anxious to obtain a seat on the bench of the Supreme Court. This has been several times within my power; but circumstances have always prevented me from accepting the offered boon. I cannot desert the President, at the present moment, against his protestations. If the Oregon question should not be speedily settled, the vacancy must be filled; and then farewell to my wishes.

...... Please to remember me in the kindest terms to Mrs. McLane, and believe me, as ever, to be, sincerely and respectfully,
Your friend,
James Buchanan.
[BUCHANAN TO McLANE.]
(Private and Confidential.) Washington, June 6, 1846.
My Dear Sir:—

I have but little time to scribble you a private letter before the closing of the mail to go by the Great Britain.

The President has determined to submit Lord Aberdeen's project to the Senate. He had no alternative, as you know, between this and its absolute rejection.

560The proviso to the first article would seem to render it questionable whether both parties would have the right to navigate the Strait of Fuca, as an arm of the sea, north of the parallel of 49°; neither does it provide that the line shall pass through the Canal de Arro, as stated in your despatch. This would probably be the fair construction.

The article relating to the possessions of British occupants south of 49° is vague and indefinite; and in order to prevent disputes between the two governments hereafter, as to the extent of these possessions, it would seem to be a prudent precaution to provide some means of ascertaining the rights of these occupants respectively. There is no reciprocal provision in the treaty for American settlers north of 49°. There may be none there; but yet such a provision would give the convention a fairer appearance.

The right of the Hudson's Bay Company to the navigation of the Columbia presents the important difficulty. It is considered doubtful by the President and several members of the cabinet whether under the terms of the projet this right would not expire upon the termination of the existing charter of that company in 1859.

The President's message will reiterate the opinions expressed in his annual message in favor of our title to 54° 40´; but in consideration of and in deference to the contrary opinions expressed by the Senate, his constitutional advisers, he submits the projet to them for their previous advice. He may probably suggest some modifications.

What the Senate may do in the premises is uncertain. There undoubtedly is in that body a constitutional majority in favor of settling the question on the parallel of 49° to the Straits of Fuca. The question of the perpetual navigation of the Columbia is and ought to be the point of difficulty. Should the Senate modify this article so as to limit the right to the termination of the existing charter of the Hudson's Bay Company, I can scarcely suppose that the modification would be rejected by the British government.

I sincerely hope that you may not think of leaving London until the question shall be finally settled; and I am happy to learn from Robert that your continuance in London will not be prejudicial to your private interest at home.

With my kindest respects to Mrs. McLane, I remain sincerely and respectfully your friend,

James Buchanan.
[MR. BUCHANAN TO JOHN RANDOLPH CLAY, ESQ.]
No. 2.   Department of State,
Washington, June 13, 1846. }
Sir:—

The Oregon question may now be considered as settled. On the 6th instant Mr. Pakenham presented to me the project of a convention for its adjustment: and the President, after mature deliberation, determined, in pursuance of several precedents adopted in the early history of our Government, 561to submit it to the Senate for their previous advice. This was done by a confidential message on the 10th instant, of which I transmit you a copy.

On the 12th instant the Senate adopted a resolution by a vote of 37 to 12, of which the following is a copy:

"Resolved (two-thirds of the Senators present concurring) that the President of the United States be, and he is hereby, advised to accept the proposal of the British government accompanying his message to the Senate, dated 10th June, 1846, for a convention to settle boundaries, etc., between the United States and Great Britain, west of the Rocky or Stony Mountains."

The convention will be signed by the plenipotentiaries on Monday next: and in the course of the next week will doubtless be ratified by and with the advice and consent of the Senate.

The terms are, an extension of the 49th parallel of latitude to the middle of the channel which separates the continent from Vancouver's Island, thence along the middle of this channel and the Strait of Fuca, so as to surrender the whole of that island to Great Britain.

The navigation of the Columbia is conceded, not to British subjects generally, but to the Hudson's Bay Company and those trading with it. To this concession there is no express limitation of time; but it was believed by the Senate, that under the true construction of the projet this grant will expire on the 30th May, 1859, the date of the termination of the existing license to that Company, to trade with the Indians, etc., on the North-west Coast of America.

I need not enumerate the other less important particulars.

I am, sir, respectfully, your obedient servant,

James Buchanan.

While in December 1845 many political friends and opponents in all parts of the country were reading with approbation the correspondence on the Oregon question, so far as it had been published, an approbation which appears from a great multitude of private letters addressed to Mr. Buchanan, he thus wrote confidentially to Mr. McLane:

"I should this day [December 13th] have been on the bench of the Supreme Court, had it not been for the critical state of our foreign relations. I very much desired the position, because it would have enabled me to spend the remainder of my days in peace. I have now been on the stormy deep nearly a quarter of a century. Besides, I sincerely wished, if possible, to prevent my name being even mentioned in connection with the next Presidency."

The vacancy on the bench of the Supreme Court of the United States was occasioned by the death of Mr. Justice 562Baldwin. According to an invariable custom the appointment should be made from the Pennsylvania circuit. There were persons who desired, not without a mixture of motives, that Mr. Buchanan might receive it; for his transfer to the bench would, it was assumed, bring into the Department of State a gentleman whose friends were exceedingly anxious to have him in that position. Others wished Buchanan to be out of the cabinet, without much reference to the question of who was to be his successor. There came about a kind of intrigue, to produce a public belief that he was to be appointed a judge, in order that it might be considered as a foregone conclusion and appear to be called for by the general voice. Some of Mr. Buchanan's friends, of both political parties, believing that he had eminent qualifications for the judicial office, urged him to accept the offer, if it should be made to him; others, who had just as strong convictions that he would be a great acquisition to the bench, were not willing to have him retire from political life, and were earnestly opposed to his leaving the Department of State at that time. The great body of the discreet friends of the administration took the same view. The matter was kept open for a long time, and meanwhile Mr. Buchanan, uncertain of his own future, had to go on and manage the foreign relations of the country, in which, besides the Oregon question, the state of things consequent upon the proposed annexation of Texas and the other difficulties with Mexico, of which I shall treat hereafter, became extremely perplexing. That he would have preferred the safe retirement of the bench to anything that political office could give him, and that he would have renounced all further connection with politics if he had received this appointment, cannot be doubted. Having had occasion thus far to estimate the qualities of his mind and character, I may here express the opinion, that he would have been a highly useful and distinguished judge. If this change in the course of his life had taken place, he would never have become President of the United States, and his biography, if written, would have been only that of a man who had been very eminent in political life to the age of forty-six, and had then passed the remainder of his days in the tranquillity of a judicial career, giving more or less proof of the versatility of his powers. He 563believed that it would be a gain of happiness to escape from the stormy conflicts of the political sphere. But public men can rarely do more than "rough-hew their ends;" to entirely "shape" them is not given to mortals. The following interesting letters from his friend King give, by reflex, all that can now be known concerning his feelings in regard to this disappointment:[91]

[HON. WM. R. KING TO MR. BUCHANAN.]
Paris, January 25, 1846.
Dear Buchanan:—

Your friendly letter gave me both pleasure and pain. Pleasure, in the renewed assurance of your friendship; and pain, to perceive that the course of the President towards you has not been entirely characterized by that delicacy and confidence which is certainly due to your position, and to the important services you have rendered to him and the country. Let me entreat you, however, to act with great deliberation and prudence. Do not suffer yourself to be operated upon by professing, or even by real friends, to act hastily. I am not of the opinion that any slight was intended by the President. He no doubt gave the true reason for having nominated Judge —— without consulting you, as he knew you were opposed to his selection.[92] It is not, I think, of sufficient importance to produce a quarrel; and the President must be too well aware of the strength you give to his administration to desire your withdrawal. Your doing so at this most important juncture would be to give the staff into the hands of your enemies; who would desire nothing better to prostrate you with. Your able correspondence with Pakenham has justly turned the eyes of the country towards you as a talented and safe helmsman to guide the ship of State. This your enemies know and feel. Do not, I again entreat you, by your own act, aid them to defeat your future prospects. Probably I have dwelt more on this matter than it merits; if so, I feel assured you will attribute it to the true motive, my anxiety to see you elevated to a station you are so well qualified to fill, with honor to yourself and advantage to the country....

564[KING TO BUCHANAN.]
Paris, February 28, 1846.
My Dear Friend:—

I read your kind letter attentively, and then committed it to the flames, as you requested. The refusal of the President to place you on the Bench of the Supreme Court, after you had manifested a willingness to accept of the situation, surprises me greatly. I had supposed, independent of a desire to gratify you, to whom he owes so much, he would have seized with avidity on the opportunity thus afforded him to get freed from the importunities of persons of doubtful qualification, none of whom could venture to complain of your being preferred to him. I have turned it over and over in my mind, to see if I could discover any motive for his refusal other than that assigned by himself, viz., that you were too important to his administration in the post you now occupy to enable him to dispense with your services. If this was in truth his sole reason, he should have frankly and unreservedly placed before you the difficulties and embarrassments your abandonment of the State Department would involve him in; how necessary you were to enable him to carry on the Government successfully, and at the same time have expressed his willingness to meet your wishes if persisted in. If such had been his course, I know you too well to doubt for a moment but that you would have relinquished the judgeship, and continued your invaluable services as a member of the administration. This, however, you must still do; you owe it to the country; you owe it to yourself. You can form no idea of the reputation you have acquired, even in Europe, by the able and masterly manner in which you have presented our claim to Oregon, never before perfectly understood, either in Europe or America. You certainly occupy at this moment, in public estimation, a more enviable position than any other distinguished man of our country, and your prospects for the future are brighter than those of any one I know. Do not, I beg you, mar those prospects by abandoning your place at this critical period of our foreign relations. Finish the work you have so ably begun. Settle the Oregon question by an equitable compromise, and whatever a few hot heads or selfish aspirants may say, your reputation will rest upon a foundation broad and strong, the approval of a virtuous and intelligent people at home, and the wise and good of every land. You know I am no flatterer. I speak in all sincerity, and say nothing but what is strictly true.

[KING TO BUCHANAN.]
Paris, March 28th, 1846.
Dear Buchanan:—

The last steamer brought me your very acceptable letter of the 26th February. The publication of my correspondence with M. Guizot has been well received by all parties in Paris, and has put at rest forever all speculation as to the correctness of my despatch. Even M. Guizot himself manifests a 565greater degree of cordiality than formerly, and made it a point to attend a ball I gave on the 22d February, although he is not in the habit of going to parties. I knew the course I pursued would, so far from committing me with any one here, produce a salutary result; and it was not taken in passion, or because I am "thin skinned." My position was never better than at this time with all in power here, from the king down to the lowest official. Present me kindly to my friend, Mr. Trist, and tender him my thanks for the interest he has manifested for me. The postponement of the election of Senator for Alabama will, as you say, enable me to enter the field with a fair prospect of success, and I am free to declare that I should be truly gratified to be reinstated in the Senate. It is possible, however, that the Governor may be operated upon by those on the spot, who aspire to the situation, and dread my return, to call the legislature together this spring, and before I can possibly be present. This my friends Bagby and others should prevent. A called session would involve unnecessary expense, without an adequate advantage, or, in fact, any advantage whatever, so far as the public is concerned. My arrangements are such that I cannot, with convenience, return to the United States before the last of July. I am anxious, however, to conform to the wishes of the President in the appointment of my successor, and will either hasten or retard my surrender of my place, as to him may seem best. Should he prefer to delay the appointment of my successor until after the adjournment of Congress, I could return on leave of absence, as he once kindly permitted me to do, and leave my Secretary, Mr. Martin, as chargé des affaires. He is, as you know, well qualified to discharge the duties, and on his account I should be pleased to give to him the advantages of the position. You will confer with the President and let me know what course will be most acceptable to him, and I will then make my request accordingly. If a vacancy occurs at Turin by the resignation of Wickliff, could you not lend a helping hand to Dr. Martin? The place will not, I presume, be sought for by any of the prominent politicians, and Martin's information and experience peculiarly fits him to be useful. He is, withal, very poor; and even if my successor consented to retain him here, his condition would be greatly altered for the worse, as with me he lives without expense. Serve him if you can; at any rate, save us from that miserable toady ———.

I altogether approve of the President's refusal to submit the Oregon question to arbitration, as proposed by the British government. The objections enumerated by you are all sufficient, but, in addition, it could not escape your observation that, by the terms of submission, whether referred to a crowned head or to private individuals, the result would, in all probability, have been to deprive us of all the country north of the Columbia, simply upon the ground that actual possession should not be disturbed. Information on which I can rely convinces me that Lord Aberdeen, when he directed the offer to be made, did not expect it to be accepted. His object was, first, to induce the European governments to believe that they were anxious to settle the question upon just terms, and, secondly, to gain time, as they calculated on Sir Robert Peel's measure inducing the American people to force their Government to give way on the Oregon question that they may receive the advantages it holds out to them.[93] I know the calculation is altogether erroneous, and that, as you say, the people are ahead of the Government on the question. Still, such is the impression made in England by Pakenham's despatches, the speeches of some of our prominent men, and the tone of our opposition press generally. I have my doubts whether Pakenham is as yet instructed to make a proposition for a compromise, but it will be made; and will, I think, be such as we should not hesitate to accept, unless the perpetual navigation of the Columbia is insisted upon. This I would not grant without an equivalent in the navigation of the St. Lawrence; but there seems to be a propriety in allowing the use of the river for a term of years, not to exceed ten, to enable the Northwest Fur Company gradually to withdraw an interest which has grown up under the treaty of joint occupancy. The President will certainly act with prudence by submitting the proposition, whatever it may be (unless altogether inadmissible), to the Senate, for the advice in advance of that body. Cass, Allen and Company will find that no political capital can be made by arraying themselves against an arrangement which makes the 49th parallel the boundary, but yielding the whole of Vancouver's Island, and the use for a few years of the Columbia River. The good sense of the whole country will approve of such a settlement. I am not at all surprised to hear that Calhoun is anxious to free himself from the odium of voting against the notice, regardless of the dilemma in which he has involved his devoted adherents in the House. If the Senate amends the House resolutions, my life upon it, they will receive Calhoun's vote; and all chivalry will exclaim: Behold the great statesman, whose wise and prudent course has alone saved the nation from the horrors of war. The speech of Colonel Benton was excellent, and proves him to be a statesman indeed. Still, I do not, I am sorry to say, approve of his opposition to an increase of our navy. If we hope to command the respect of the powers of Europe, we must put ourselves in a position not only to repel all aggression, but, if needs be, to act on the offensive. They are all jealous of our rapid growth and prosperity, and would, if they dared, unite to retard or destroy it. We should hasten to repair our forts, build some new ones, and add to our little navy ten or twelve war steamers.

Such preparation, although it involves expense, would in all probability save us millions, as it would effectually put down all attempts to wrest the Island of Cuba from Spain, or to establish a monarchy in Mexico. I highly approve of the views taken by Bancroft; he promises to make an able and efficient Secretary of the Navy, and I hope he will retain his place and give up, if he has thought of it, all idea of a foreign mission. —— —— is here on his return home; he is no doubt an amiable man, but weak beyond description. Such a representative at such a court was calculated to do us a positive injury; we require to have there one of our ablest men. Berlin is of much less importance; in truth, to keep a minister there is scarcely worth the expense. Donalson is a good appointment; I wish it had been for St. Petersburg. I am fully aware that diplomatic situations are in great demand, and that the President is worried with applications from second and even third-rate men for the most important stations. I trust, however, that no commonplace men may be sent to London, Paris or St. Petersburg. My residence abroad has convinced me that the respect in which our country is held very much depends on the character and standing of its representative; and I greatly doubt the policy of making removals when the incumbent possesses talent and information, and from a long residence has acquired facilities for obtaining useful information which a new man, whatever his ability, it may be will require years to obtain. This I know runs counter to your theory of rotation in office; which may be correct as respects office at home, but should not, I think, apply to those held abroad. I once gave you my opinion of Wheaton. I see no reason to change that opinion. He is peculiarly well qualified to represent his country with advantage. Could he not be sent to St. Petersburg? He has grown old in diplomacy without growing rich, and at his period of life will find it exceedingly difficult to engage in any pursuit, other than that he has so long followed, with a prospect of securing to his family a decent support. I should feel truly gratified if you would bring him to the attention of the President. I am much gratified to learn that harmony prevails in the Cabinet; a break up would do much mischief. Retain your place regardless of all minor annoyances. The country requires your services to bring to a successful termination the important and delicate question of Oregon. You have the confidence of all parties; and I heartily believe that in the present state of things the President could not find a man capable of supplying your place. Stay where you are, settle the Oregon question, and great shall be your reward. Tender my respects to my friends Sturgeon and General Cameron, also to Walker, Mason and Benton.

Your friend sincerely,
William R. King.

P.S.—Present me most respectfully to the President and his accomplished lady.
W. R. K.
[KING TO BUCHANAN.]
Paris, April 30, 1846.
Dear Buchanan:—

I thank you for your long and friendly letter. Engrossed as your time must be by cares of State, official duties and social intercourse, I feel flattered in having engaged so much of your attention. On the 16th of this month Paris was thrown into a state of great excitement by an attempt made to assassinate the king at Fontainebleau, where he had been spending a few days with his family. Two shots were actually fired into the char à banc (an open carriage), in which he was returning from a hunting party, in company with the queen, Madame Adelaide, and several other members of the royal family. Fortunately, no one received the slightest injury. The ladies were terribly frightened, but the king showed his usual coolness and disregard of danger. The wretched assassin was instantly seized by the attendants. He turned out to be a former employé of the government, who, having lost his place, had brooded over the injustice he conceived had been done him until he determined to kill the king to revenge himself. Lecomt, for that is the name of the miserable man, has been subjected to several examinations, but nothing has transpired to connect him in any manner with any of the political parties of the country. Although the Journal des Debats, the semi-official paper, whatever disclosures Mr. Guizot may make, has, and as I think, most imprudently, contended that it was political. Be that as it may, it has certainly called forth the better feelings of the French generally in favor of their wise, prudent and pacific old monarch, which will add strength to his government and give permanency to his dynasty. I hastened on his return to Paris to tender him my congratulations on his extraordinary and most providential escape; for Lecomt is said to be one of the best shots in France. The old man bears a charmed life. Would it not be well for the President to address him with his own hand a letter of congratulation at his fortunate escape from the hands of the base assassin? It would, I know, be well received, and in the present state of our relations with England, we should treat France with marked courtesy. Trifles in themselves are of great importance here. I am somewhat surprised at Lord Aberdeen's course on the Oregon question, especially as he has openly expressed a desire to settle it on amicable terms. That arbitration would be rejected, he must have known when he instructed Pakenham to make the proposition; and it strikes me that the motive for making it was to gain time, pass their free trade measures, and avail themselves of the effects it would have in the United States, to obtain more favorable terms than had been offered by us—or should negotiation fail and war ensue, they would be able to prejudice the European governments against us by showing that they had tendered arbitration, which was rejected. I must think, however, that as soon as the resolutions, to give the notice to put an end to the existing treaty, shall have passed the Senate, a proposition for a compromise will be made; but whether it will be such as ought to be accepted by us, is more than doubtful. My information leads me to believe it will not be. Still it will open the door for negotiation, and however extravagant, should not be promptly rejected, but with proposed modifications. If Pakenham has common sense, he must long before this have well understood that a proposition to fix the line at 49° to the Straits; the whole of Vancouver's Island; part of Puget Sound; the navigation of the Columbia; with indemnity to the North West Fur Company, would never be acceded to by us, be the consequences what they may. Should such an extravagant offer be made, be assured Mr. P. will have a wide margin given him for

modifications; and in the end he will settle down on Vancouver's Island and the navigation of the Columbia for a term of years. You already know my opinions on this subject, and further I would not go, war or no war. Be not surprised, if the conducting of this negotiation falls into the hands of the Whigs, unless speedily settled. I do not think many months will pass over before Lord John Russell will be at the head of affairs in England, and Lord Palmerston in the Foreign Office. Now, I am not of the number who believe that the return of the Whigs to power will throw additional obstacles in the way of the adjustment of our difficulties, and I trust, should the change take place, we shall have no alarm speeches from those Senators who recently expressed such heart-felt pleasure that Lord John had failed to form a ministry. When shall we learn prudence in our national councils? You are, I am sorry to see, dissatisfied with your position; and I am no less wearied with mine. Most sincerely do I wish that we had both remained in the Senate. You, however, have much to reconcile you to the change; having acquired increased reputation by your able correspondence with Pakenham; nor must you on any account abandon your post, until that affair is finally settled. The war spirit of Cass, Allen, etc., must not deter the President from making, if practicable, a fair compromise. In such a course he will be sustained by the good sense of the country. When I wrote you to consult the President relative to my return home, it was simply because I was desirous to subject him to no inconvenience in the selection of my successor. The state of my private affairs renders it imperative that I should be at home in September. I can remain here until the first of that month, but not longer; and I wish you so to inform the President. Any mode he chooses to adopt to enable me to execute my purposes, will be perfectly satisfactory, and my object in writing thus early, is to know what course will be adopted, that I may make my arrangements accordingly. I shall not fail to procure a breast-pin, or ring, or something of the kind, and present it Mrs. Walsh in your name. It should have been done before this, but I have been suffering from lumbago, which has confined me to the house. I am now, however, nearly well. Poor McLane has for many weeks been suffering severely from some affection...... He is still in the hands of his physician, but much better. He stands deservedly high in England, with both Whig and Tory. Lord Landsdown, who will be the president of the council, if the Whigs get into power, was in Paris a few days past, and spoke to me of McLane in the most exalted terms. Catlin has, I understand, applied to Congress, to purchase his Indian gallery. It should not be lost to our country, as it will be if Congress refuses the purchase, for he has offers from England, which he is only prevented from accepting by his anxious desire that his own country should possess it. It is richly worth what he asks for it, and you would be doing a service to a most estimable man if you would take the trouble to enlist some of your friends in favor of the purchase. As Grund gives up the consulate at Antwerp, why not appoint Vesey? He is honest and capable, and withal a good and true American in all his principles. Mrs. Ellis thanks you for your kind remembrance of her. Present my kindest regards to the Bentons, Bagbys, Pleasontons and Beans.
Your friend sincerely,
William R. King.
P. S.—Say to my friend, Col. Benton, that exalted as was my opinion of his statesmanlike qualities, his courage on the Oregon question has raised him still higher in my estimation. Richly does he deserve his well earned popularity. But for my stiff fingers, which almost disable me from holding my pen, I would write to him and express more fully the respect and regard I entertain for him. I wish you would call his attention to Catlin's proposition to dispose of his gallery of Indian portraits and curiosities. I do not think it should be lost to our country.

W. R. K.
[KING TO BUCHANAN.]
Paris, July 15th, 1845.
Dear Buchanan:—

I have this moment received your letter of the 23d June, brought out by the Great Western. I have at once availed myself of your suggestion, and asked officially for my recall. I hope to embark for the United States on the 15th of September, or, at farthest, by the first of October. I am most anxious to see you, and, as far as I have any influence, to prevail on you to abandon all idea of the judgeship, and to continue in your present position, where you have rendered such important services to our country, and justly elevated yourself in the estimation of all whose good opinion is worth having.

As for ——, envy and vanity are his controlling passions, his praise or his censure are alike worthless, and you should treat them with contempt. You speak of three sections of the Democratic party in the Senate, headed by Cass, Benton and Calhoun. Cass may have a small party composed almost exclusively of the old followers of Benton; but I am at a loss to understand who they are who now constitute the late Colonel's party. It seems to me, able general as I admit he is, that all his men have deserted, and unless he can enlist recruits from the Whig ranks, he must be his own standard-bearer. Calhoun's followers are beginning to look over the left shoulder, and even his fidus Achates, D. H. Lewis, will very soon turn his back on him. Calhoun is politically dead. The Oregon question and the Mexican war have already proved fatal to many distinguished leaders, Democrat and Whig, so that you will find the field open for the Presidency, unless you place yourself on the shelf by accepting of the judgeship. I am much pleased to learn that the best possible relations exist between you and the President. Use your influence to prevent him from selecting improper persons to fill the missions to London, Paris and St. Petersburg. They are most important positions, and should be filled by the first men of our country, and not by mere seekers of office, or by those who erroneously suppose that they can enrich themselves by the outfit and salary. I speak from my own experience when I say that no American minister can live even respectably in Paris for less than fifteen thousand dollars a year. Congress should look to this, and give such compensation as will enable the country to avail itself of the services of the best qualified, who are but too often destitute of private fortune. Mrs. Ellis still continues to be your warm advocate for the Presidency. She requests me to present her best respects. Mr. Martin is much pleased with diplomacy, but has great apprehension lest he should not find his position as Secretary altogether as desirable with my successor; and he is looking forward with hope to an appointment as chargé des affaires, either at Turin, or some other place. Could you not aid him? He is, as you know, exceedingly poor, and not very provident, and an increase of salary would be important to him. Present my best respects to my friends, the Pleasontons, Taylors, and old associates in the Senate.

Faithfully your friend,
William R. King.

[KING TO BUCHANAN.]
Liverpool, Oct. 1, 1847.
Dear Buchanan:—

On the 15th of September, I presented my letters of recall, and took leave of his Majesty, the King of the French. He was pleased to express great regret at parting with me, and a hope that nothing had occurred during my residence at his court which had given me dissatisfaction. I assured him such was not the case, and that I should ever cherish towards him and his amiable family the kindest feelings for the uniform courtesy and cordiality he and they had manifested towards me. He abounded in professions of friendship for myself personally, and for my country; but Louis Philippe is full of duplicity, and professions cost him but little. I left Paris on the 16th, and hastened to Liverpool to embark on board the splendid iron steamer, the Great Britain. On the 22d we took our departure. The day was fine, the wind fair, and we proceeded on our voyage at the rate of twelve miles an hour. The passengers, 180 persons, were all in high spirits, and flattered themselves with a short and agreeable voyage. Most lamentably were our hopes blasted. In an evil hour the captain determined to take the dangerous northern passage. Why, it would be difficult to tell, as the wind was equally fair for the southern. Night came on dark and gloomy. The breeze freshened, almost approaching to a gale; still he kept on his way at the same rapid rate, although he now acknowledges that he had mistaken his reckoning and was, in fact, ignorant of his situation. A little before eleven the ship struck on the ledge of rocks which surround Dundee Bay, north of Ireland. The shock was indeed terrific, and the ladies, many of whom had retired for the night, rushed from their rooms, frantic with alarm. Among them was Mrs. Ellis. Believing that the ship must go to pieces in a few minutes, I frankly told her her danger. To my astonishment, she became calm and composed, and during the whole trying scene displayed extraordinary composure. To our extraordinary speed we probably, under Providence, owe our escape from a watery grave. The good ship cleared the reefs and imbedded herself in the sand, where as the tide was receding, she sunk deeper and deeper, maintaining an upright position. Our hope now was that her great strength would enable her to resist the waves, which thundered against her side and dashed over her lofty decks, until the dawn of day; for should she break up in the darkness of the night, on a rocky shore, with a heavy sea, all were convinced that few, if any, could be saved. Long indeed appeared that terrible night, but day at length dawned, and the tide being out, we found we were but a short distance from the dry land. The boats were lowered. I placed Mrs. Ellis in the first that left the ship, and saw her make the shore in safety. My nephew and myself followed as soon as all the ladies were landed, and joined her in a miserable cabin where she had taken refuge from the rain. No lives were lost. I procured a conveyance for Down Patrick, where we rested for the night. The next day we arrived at Belfast and took the steamer for Liverpool. Being unable to procure a passage in any of the steamships which leave in this month, I shall sail to-morrow in the packet ship New York, with the prospect of a passage of at least thirty days, but I trust it will be a safe one.

Your friend sincerely,

William R. King.

[HON. RICHARD RUSH TO MR. BUCHANAN.]
Sydenham, near Philadelphia, December 16, 1845.
My Dear Sir:—

...... I have this morning been turning once more to your note of the 30th of August on the Oregon question, in answer to the British minister's of the 29th of July. I had, to be sure, read it on its first appearance with the greatest attention; and it would be unjust to withhold longer from you my poor tribute to its value. Its demonstration of our title is so full, as to leave nothing further to be said; so clear that our whole country can now fortunately understand it; and it is in a spirit so fair, and in a tone of patriotism so high and just, that every American has solid ground to feel proud of it. I rejoice that the country has found so powerful an exponent of her rights as is recorded in this most able state paper; and, as one of her sons formerly striving to defend those rights abroad, gladly award to you both my tribute and my share of the public thanks, for this comprehensive, final and triumphant vindication of them which your pen has accomplished.

Perhaps, in propriety and prudence, I ought here to stop. I know how rash it generally is, in those not behind the curtain, to be venturing opinions before those who are; yet while writing I cannot avoid adding my belief, founded upon as much only as is known to the public, that war is at hand. I rest on the courageous spirit of Britain, which we must not undervalue, as it is the root of our own: and from a belief in the stability of her resources—more than is entertained by all of our friends. These are no reasons why we should fear her, but only for being on the look out; and we shall all, when the extremity comes, owe you, my dear sir, a heavy debt for making our right so manifest in the eyes of this great nation. But Britain, I believe, has a firm conviction (such are the different eyes with which nations look) that she has rights in that country; and, by my estimate, she will not, as things stand, yield them north of the Columbia, but appeal to the sword, and very soon—unless an arbitration, or a mediation should arrest the appeal.

I pray you to excuse these presumptuous forebodings, in which I truly hope I may be wrong, but in the faith of which I am at present deeply imbued; and to believe me to be, with the most unfeigned and friendly respect,

Yours most faithfully,
Richard Rush.

[RUSH TO BUCHANAN.]
Sydenham, near Philadelphia, August 26, 1846.
My Dear Sir:—

I hardly know how to thank you sufficiently for your obliging favor of the 22d instant and the documents you have so kindly sent me respecting the Oregon negotiation. All have arrived safely, as well those by Mr. Sword as the separate one from you by mail; and now I have in hand everything I could wish.

My attention was specially directed to the protocol of the 24th of September, 1844, recording the break-up between Mr. Calhoun and Mr. Pakenham, and I can understand the hopeless prospect it seemed to leave to the new administration. When I used to brood over that protocol last winter, and recall what passed in Mr. Gallatin's negotiation in '26 and in mine of '24, and weighed the long inflexibility with which England had adhered to the Columbia as her basis; and remembered also, as I freshly could and did, the solemnity—I have no doubt sincerity too at that time—with which Huskisson used to tell me that he and their whole cabinet thought even that line a great concession to us, I did not see how war was to be avoided after the President's bold and brilliant message when Congress opened. One of the Paris papers, the Constitutionnel, speaking of the settlement of the dispute, said that the English journals pretended that England had given to the United States a lesson of wisdom and moderation; but they might add, said the same paper, that "the Government of the United States, on its part, has given to all powers in relation with England a lesson of firmness." This is the truth. I again own, that I did not think England would have yielded as much as she has; and although it appears from Mr. McLane's communications that terms something better might have been finally obtained, but for the Senate, history will be justified in pronouncing the President's course under the complications of the occasion (Mexico and everything else) wise and advantageous for the country, and one to draw a just fame to himself and the administration. England had got very near to her fighting point, and the settlement marks a great epoch in our annals—one not unlike, under some parallels that might be drawn, the war of 1812 in its acceleration of our national character.

The last article in the last Edinburgh Review, headed "Colonial Protection," is an argument for us touching the West India trade with England, its principle covering full reciprocity as to our shipping as well as traffic, though the Reviewers do not utter the former word; and now that the Whigs are in, it may be hoped that they will think so, and that Sir Robert Peel will co-operate with them, as on the sugar question. Sir Robert having done so much already, might now set about pushing Lord John Russell into farther liberality! What a curious spectacle this would present in the British parliament; yet things more remarkable have been happening there lately, and much more so than if they were at length to admit our tobacco almost duty free.

I am gratefully sensible to the friendly invitation you give me to your hospitable roof while going on with the investigation I spoke of, though am now through your kindness supplied with sufficient materials. Whether I shall venture upon another volume or not, I am quite undetermined. Sometimes I feel half inclined; then again the other scale kicks the beam. The latter is the case whenever I think of Hannah More's comment upon Pope, who when quoting the line from him which says the greatest art in writing is "to blot," says there is a greater—"the art to stop."

If I live as long as my mother, who was out here this week at 86, in good health, I shall have time to make up my mind. Excuse this flight, as well as so long a letter, and pray believe in the friendly and perfect respect and esteem with which I am, my dear sir,
Sincerely yours,
Richard Rush.

Mr. McLane, at his own request, was recalled from London after the settlement of the Oregon question, and Mr. Bancroft, who had been Secretary of the Navy, in October, 1846, became Mr. McLane's successor. The following private letters may fitly close the present chapter:

[MR. BUCHANAN TO HON. GEO. BANCROFT.]
Washington, October 6, 1846.
My Dear Sir:—

I cannot suffer you to depart from the country without saying from the heart, God bless you! May your mission be prosperous, and Mrs. Bancroft and yourself happy! I sorely regret that we have lost your services in the Navy Department, and still more that we have lost your society; and this I do, without any disparagement to your successor, whom I highly esteem. My feelings, both in regard to Mrs. Bancroft and yourself, are warmly entertained by Mrs. Polk, with whom I have recently held a conversation on the subject. The two most important objects of your mission will be to have the duties on tobacco diminished, and to obtain a relaxation of the present arrangement regulating our trade with the British West Indies and American provinces. Free trade is now the order of the day, and I am not without hope that these objects may be accomplished. I have omitted to instruct you on the former subject on your own suggestion. I desire that you should enjoy all the credit of the movement. I think a despatch embracing all the statistical and other information on the subject, with your own views, might do both the country and yourself much good.[94] In regard to the latter subject, I have not had sufficient time to give it a thorough investigation.

There is still much sickness in Washington, though not of a dangerous character. The centre of the city, F Street and the avenue, is comparatively healthy. Both Marcy and Mason have had intermittents,—they were, however, at the cabinet to-day. Miss

Annie[95] appears to be entirely well, and is again as gay as a lark. Miss Clem.[96] is still very weak, and has not yet left her chamber, unless she has done so to-day.
With my kindest regards for Mrs. Bancroft, I remain, as ever, sincerely and respectfully,
Your friend,
James Buchanan.
[BANCROFT TO BUCHANAN.]
October 8, 1846.
My Dear Mr. Buchanan:—

My heart sunk within me as I read your letter containing new evidences of your friendship and regard; because it made me feel more sensibly how much I lose in parting from immediate co-operation with you. Your hint about tobacco I shall adopt, and will make it my special business to collect all the details. On the other subject also, which is of less immediate necessity, I propose to enter upon its consideration fully, first, however, submitting to you the paper which I may prepare. You must always deal with me frankly, giving me advice as freely as you would to a younger brother. You may be sure of my acting with caution; and I shall always aim to carry out your views in the manner that I think will be most satisfactory to you. I shall hope to hear from you very often privately, as well as officially.
Your parcels came yesterday safely to me, about an hour after I wrote to you.
Mrs. Bancroft joins me in expression of the most cordial regard.
Ever most truly yours,
George Bancroft.
576[BANCROFT TO BUCHANAN.]
London, November 3, 1846.
My Dear Mr. Buchanan:—

I must add a line to you if it be but to remind you personally of me. To-night I shall see a good deal of Lord Palmerston. The tone in England is, towards us, one of respect. Public opinion is in favor of letting us alone, and people are beginning to say that it would be a blessing to the world if the United States would assume the tutelage of Mexico. This country is neither in the disposition, nor in the ability, to interrupt its friendly relations with us. The good understanding between the British cabinet and the French is quite broken up, and they use in the newspapers and in private very harsh language towards each other. But by the next steamer I shall know more.
The paper at Springfield, Mass., which I named to you for the publication of the laws was the "Hampden Post," the old Democratic newspaper with which I fought many a hard battle against the worst sort of malignant Whigs.
"Give my love to Mr. Buchanan," says Mrs. Bancroft. So give my love to Clementina and Annie, say I, and wish them all happiness and abundant health. I wish them good husbands and you a good wife.
Ever faithfully yours,
G. Bancroft.
[FROM MR. CALHOUN.]
Fort Hill, August 30, 1845.
My Dear Sir:—

I enclose a letter to ——, the minister appointed by the Dominican Republic to our Government, which I will thank you to have forwarded to his address.

He informs me that Mr. Hogan's report will shortly be made. I hope if it should be favorable, the administration will not fail to recognize the independence of the republic, as soon as it can be done according to what has been usual in such cases. St. Domingo is, perhaps, the most fertile and best of all the West India Islands. It was lost to civilization and commerce through the insane movements of France during her revolution. Should the Dominican Republic sustain itself, it opens a prospect of restoring the island again to the domains of commerce and civilization. It may one day or another be one of the great marts for our products. It can sustain a population of many millions. It belongs to us to take the lead in its recognition.

I have good reason to believe that our recognition would be acceptable to both France and Spain......

I regret to learn that the prospect is so discouraging in reference to the settlement of the Oregon question by the parties. I regard it as very important that it should be settled. If it should not be, there is great danger of its leading 577to a rupture between the two countries, which would be equally disastrous to both. It is beyond the power of man to trace the consequences of a war between us and England on the subject of Oregon. All that is certain is, that she can take it and hold it against us, as long as she has the supremacy on the ocean, and retains her Eastern dominions. The rest is left in mystery. As to my going again into the Senate, I do not contemplate to return ever again to public life. I am entirely content with the portion of the public honors which have fallen to my share, and expect to spend the rest of my days in retirement, in my quiet retreat near the foot of the mountains. I find ample and agreeable occupation both of mind and body. With great respect, yours truly,

J. C. Calhoun.

NOTE ON THE OREGON QUESTION.

Mr. Justin McCarthy, in his "History of our own Times," passes very lightly over the Oregon controversy, leaving his readers to infer that the only element of danger was the popularity which any President would have gained by forcing England into a war. Nearly the whole of his "history" of this question is condensed into the following sentences: "The joint occupancy was renewed for an indefinite time; but in 1843 the President of the United States somewhat peremptorily called for a final settlement of the boundary. The question was eagerly taken up by excitable politicians in the American House of Representatives. For more than two years the Oregon question became a party cry in America. With a large proportion of the American public, including, of course, nearly all citizens of Irish birth or extraction, any President would have been popular beyond measure who had forced a war on England. Calmer and wiser counsels prevailed, however, on both sides. Lord Aberdeen, our foreign secretary, was especially moderate and conciliatory. He offered a compromise which was at last accepted."

A true understanding of any past controversy between England and the United States is of importance in the future, not only that justice may be done to individual statesmen, but that the methods by which war has been averted and mutual respect and good feeling have been preserved, may have a salutary influence in all time to come. This is the chief value of the history of such international controversies. The truth is, that in this Oregon matter there were undoubtedly popular tendencies in this country, which, if they had been yielded to, might have enabled any President to force a war upon England, if he had been disposed to have one. But it is not true that there was anything precipitate or peremptory in the call for a final settlement of the boundary, or that the American Government was disposed at any time to go further in compliance with the popular demand than it was bound to go, by a proper regard for the rights of the country and the interests of the settlers in the national domain, who looked to it for protection. Moreover there was at one time quite as great a probability that a war on this question of Oregon would find backers in England, as there was that it would be popular in America. There were interests and passions in both countries that had strong tendencies to provoke a war: and the war would have occurred at a time when, to repeat the words of Mr. Webster, it "would have kindled flames that would have burned over the whole globe."

When the President's message of December, 1845, communicating to Congress the correspondence down to that period reached England, the British press became excessively violent and even abusive. Worse things could not have been said of any government or people than were said of the American nation and their rulers; and it is just as true, historically, that a war would have been popular in England, as it was that it would have been popular in America. In the House of Commons there were by no means wanting strong proofs of an unnecessary excitement.

In estimating the causes which produced the real peril of a war, it would not be just to overlook the loose, not to say careless, manner, in which the negotiation was at first conducted by and through the British minister in Washington. His rejection of Mr. Buchanan's 578offer of the 49th parallel, without a reference to his own government, made in terms that were not well considered—that were in fact scarcely respectful—put it out of the power of the President to do anything but to reassert the American claim, and to leave the British government to renew the negotiation by other steps, or to take the consequences of a termination of the joint occupancy. It is not to be questioned that Lord Aberdeen's subsequent course became moderate and conciliatory. But in the earlier stages of this business, Sir Robert Peel's ministry had on hand a most serious domestic question. To borrow the pithy words of Mr. McCarthy himself, used in reference to that question: "Peel came into office in 1841 to maintain the corn laws, and in 1843 he repealed them." It was in fact with Peel one long struggle between his former connections and the new opinions forced upon him by the circumstances in which he was placed; and although, in dealing with the relations between England and this country, in the earlier part of his ministry, there were manifested great care, prudence, and conciliation, it is quite certain that in the later controversy about Oregon, which had not been settled by the treaty of 1842, the British foreign office did not act at first with the same attentive circumspection, and was not represented at Washington with anything like the same ability and wisdom, as it was in the time of Lord Ashburton's special mission. And how was it that public opinion and official persons in England were brought to a sense of the peril in which both nations stood in 1845–6? So far as salutary influences could be exerted on this side of the Atlantic and be felt in either country, great merit is due to two of our statesmen, Mr. Buchanan and Mr. Webster; the one having the duty of conducting the negotiation to a peaceful issue; the other the duty of watching it, and of using all his influence at home and abroad to produce caution, moderation, and a just sense of the responsibility that would rest upon those in either country who should unnecessarily lead the two nations into a war.

To Mr. Buchanan the praise is due, that he conducted the negotiation throughout with skill and firmness, with entire good temper, and without any wish to gain for the President or himself the cheap popularity that might have followed their propitiation of the war spirit among their countrymen. Mr. Webster's admonitions, uttered with his accustomed solemnity, both on the popular platform and in the Senate, were addressed alike to both governments and both nations; but they were chiefly designed to affect opinion and feeling in England, and this design was, in a considerable degree, accomplished.

CHAPTER XXI.
1845–1848.

ORIGIN OF THE WAR WITH MEXICO—EFFORTS OF MR. POLK'S ADMINISTRATION TO PREVENT IT.

The administration of President Polk inherited the Texas question from the preceding administration of President Tyler. The mode in which it was finally proposed to bring the republic of Texas into the American Union has been already described. When Mr. Polk became President of the United States, Texas had been for nine years practically an independent power, with a form of government modelled on that of the United States, with the exception of the fact that Texas consisted of a single State. The emigration which had flowed into it from the south-western region of the United States had made it a slaveholding country. From the time when its independence was acknowledged by the American Government, the question whether it should remain a separate nation, or be absorbed into the American Union, became a very serious one. The leading men who had gone thither, had made the revolution which claimed to have expelled, and had practically expelled, the Mexican power; and together with the great bulk of the inhabitants, they looked upon the United States as their mother country. There were great difficulties attending either of the two courses that remained open for the American Government. On the one hand, if Texas should be left as a separate nationality, to continue her war with Mexico, which still lingered after the battle of San Jacinto, that war was quite certain to end in efforts of the Texans to invade and conquer Mexico. This would have been resisted by England, and with her aid Mexico would in turn have invaded Texas. The power of England once introduced into Mexico, she would in all probability have shared the fate of India. On the other hand, the introduction of Texas into the American Union was proposed at a time when the "Abolitionists" of the North had long been pressing forward the immediate and unconditional abolition of slavery everywhere, by what they regarded as "moral means," without any consideration for the feelings or apprehensions of the Southern people. To make a large addition to the area of slavery by the annexation of Texas, a slaveholding State, was regarded in the South as a necessary means of strengthening the political power of that section against the control of the General Government, which, it was feared, might eventually be obtained by a sectional combination of the Northern States on questions relating to the whole subject of slavery. It was a hazardous mode of meeting the dangers arising from the Northern anti-slavery agitation, because it placed the people of the South in the attitude of seeking a preponderance of political power upon a sectional issue, at a time when the people of the North were not seeking to obtain such a sectional preponderance, and when there was only an apprehension that they might do so. But at the time when President Polk succeeded to the management of this delicate matter, it was believed by him and by many of his most considerate Southern supporters, that the repose of both North and South could be, and required to be, secured by an arrangement with the executive government of Texas, before her admission into the Union, fixing the northern boundary of slavery at the Missouri compromise line of 36° 30′ north latitude, by extending that line westward. North of that line and west of Missouri, it was believed that negro labor could not be valuable, and that the negro could not encounter the climate. These were the views entertained by Mr. Buchanan when he accepted the position of Secretary of State; and he had reason to know that they were the views of Mr. Polk before his election. To Mr. Buchanan the Missouri compromise line recommended itself as a practicable mode of giving effect to the principle of equality among the States in regard to the common territories of the United States.

The precise attitude of the Texas negotiation, and the relations of the United States with Mexico, at the time when Mr. Buchanan took charge of the State Department, must now be stated, together with some reference to the previous history of 581the project of annexation. The first formal overture of annexation came from the government of Texas, in the time of President Van Buren, after the independence of Texas had been recognized by the United States. Mr. Van Buren declined the proposal, because he considered it inexpedient to open the constitutional questions involved, and because of our friendly relations with Mexico under existing treaties of amity and commerce. The secret treaty of annexation negotiated by Mr. Upshur under President Tyler was rejected by the Senate. Mr. Calhoun's plan for bringing Texas into the Union as a State, through the action of Congress, was arranged by him with the government of Texas, after he became Secretary of State in March, 1844, and in the following December this plan and the correspondence with the executive government of Texas were submitted to Congress by President Tyler at the opening of the session. The motive was fully disclosed. It was plainly made known that the American executive believed that the British government was about to interpose to cause the people of Texas to abolish slavery in their country. This it was considered would leave the Southwestern States of this Union on what Mr. Calhoun described as the "exposed frontier" of a free state, into which their slaves would be induced to escape, and from which the foreign and the American abolitionists would be able to operate upon slavery in the domains of those States.[97]

The objections urged against this measure, when the resolutions for accomplishing it were finally adopted, three days before Mr. Polk became President, were the great extent of territory which it would add to our dominions, the increase of slavery and 582slave representation, and its tendency to produce a war with Mexico. It could not be said, however, that under the circumstances Mexico would have a clearly just cause for war if the annexation should be accomplished, whatever she might have had at an earlier period. Texas was now actually independent of Mexico. The United States had not only recognized her independence, but had made treaties and carried on commerce with her, in entire disregard of the claim of Mexico to the sovereignty of this revolted province. And Mexico had during all this period made no attempt at reconquest. She had practically acquiesced in the recognition of Texan independence by the United States and other powers; and therefore it could not be said, after such a lapse of time, that a new and just cause for war would arise if Texas should be annexed to the American Union.[98] There was undoubtedly much danger that Mexico would not regard the annexation in this light; and, therefore, what the new Secretary of State had to do was to conduct the whole matter, under the resolutions of Congress, so as to preserve peace, if possible.

His first official duty was to answer a protest addressed to the Government of the United States by General Almonte, the Mexican minister at Washington. Mr. Buchanan's answer was regarded by Mr. Webster as "mild and conciliatory." It was, in substance, that Mexico had no right to complain of such a transaction between independent states; that the Government of the United States would respect all the just rights of Mexico, and hoped to bring all pending questions with her to a fair and friendly settlement; but that the annexation of Texas must 583now be considered as a thing done. Still, a period of sixty or seventy days must elapse before it could be known how the government of Texas had taken the passage of the joint resolutions. At that time, there were instalments of money due from Mexico to the United States, under an existing treaty, to meet claims of citizens of the United States to a large amount. These Mexico might choose to withhold; perhaps

she might decree non-intercourse with the United States; but that she would go to war was not regarded as probable by the best informed persons at Washington. In the meantime, Mr. Buchanan had not only to manage the relations between the United States and Mexico, under circumstances of great delicacy, with firmness, as well as conciliation, but also to keep a watchful eye upon the course of England and France in reference to this measure. It must be remembered that Mr. Buchanan had succeeded, as Secretary of State, to the management of the Oregon question with England, as well as to the completion of the arrangements for annexing Texas to the United States. He was informed, both privately and officially, by the ministers of the United States at London and Paris, of the danger of an intervention by England and France in the affairs of Mexico; and soon after he became Secretary of State, he had some reason to apprehend that the settlement of the Oregon difficulty might be delayed for the purpose of keeping open the unsettled questions in regard to the final disposal of Texas. Mexico was at this time about to undergo one of its many revolutions, and it might become difficult to find an executive government with which to establish diplomatic relations. In this posture of affairs, an interference by either France or England, or both, might render it impracticable to carry out the annexation of Texas to the United States, and might lead to very serious complications. Writing from London on the 3d of March, at the moment when the resolutions providing for the annexation of Texas had just passed, but before they could have become known in London, Mr. McLane said, in a private letter to Mr. Buchanan: "Allow me to add a word in regard to Mexico. I stated in an early despatch that the policy here would be to keep open our difficulties there, to 584await the issue of the Oregon question; and of that I have very little doubt. But why not disappoint such calculation? Even if our affairs with Great Britain are to end in a rupture, that result, with proper precaution, may be postponed until the expiration of the year's notice. Then why not act promptly and decisively in regard to Mexico? ...... Every day is leading to machinations in Europe to interfere with the settlement of the Mexican government."
On the 25th of March (1845,) Mr. Buchanan sent the following official despatch to Mr. King, the Minister of the United States at Paris:
[BUCHANAN TO KING.]
Department of State,
Washington, March 25, 1845.

}
Sir:—

Your Despatch, No. 11, under date of the 27th ultimo, has been received and submitted to the President. In commencing his administration, he had confidently hoped, that the government of France was animated by the same kind spirit towards the United States which inspires the Government and people of this country in all their conduct towards their ancient Revolutionary ally. This agreeable impression was made upon his mind by the emphatic declaration of his Majesty to yourself on the 4th July last, when speaking on the subject of the annexation of Texas to our Union, "that in any event no steps would be taken by his government, in the slightest degree hostile or which would give to the United States just cause of complaint." The President was also gratified with the subsequent assurance of M. Guizot, given to yourself, that France had not acted and would not act in concert with Great Britain for the purpose of preventing annexation, but that in any course she might pursue she would proceed independently of that power. You may then judge of the surprise and regret of the President, when he discovered from your last despatch, that the governments of France and Great Britain were now acting in concert and endeavoring by a joint effort to dissuade the government and people of Texas from giving their consent to annexation. Nay, more, that so intimate has been their alliance to accomplish this purpose, that even "the instructions of the French government to its representative in Texas had been communicated to Lord Aberdeen."

The people of Texas are sovereign and independent. Under Providence they hold their destiny in their own hands. Justice to them requires that they should have been left free to decide the question of annexation for themselves without foreign interference and without being biassed by foreign influence. Not a doubt exists but that the people of the two Republics are anxious to form a re-union. Indeed, the enthusiastic unanimity which has been displayed by the citizens of Texas in favor of annexation is unexampled in the history of nations. Little reason then had we to anticipate that whilst the two Republics were proceeding to adjust the terms for accomplishing this re-union that France in concert with Great Britain, and under the lead of that power, should interpose her efforts and influence to paralyze and obstruct the free action of the people of Texas, and thus place herself in an unfriendly attitude towards the United States.

The President leaves it to your sound discretion to decide whether you ought not to embrace a favorable opportunity to communicate, formally or informally, to the government of France, the painful disappointment which he has experienced from a review of these circumstances.

I am, sir, respectfully, your obedient servant,
James Buchanan.

At the time when this despatch was written, the British and French agents in Texas, in conjunction with certain of the principal officials of that country, were making efforts to produce dissatisfaction with the terms of annexation proposed by the American Government. The people of Texas were by a very large proportion in favor of the annexation. The terms offered by the United States could be made the means of preventing it. Writing privately to Mr. Buchanan, on the 25th of April, Mr. King said:

...... There is scarcely any sacrifice which England would not make to prevent Texas from coming into our possession. France is acting in concert with her, so far as influence goes, but will stop there. She will make no pecuniary sacrifices. I have weighed well the contents of your last despatch, and as you give me full discretion in the matter, I have come to the conclusion that in the present threatening state of our relations with England, no good purpose could be effected by convicting M. Guizot of the gross duplicity of which he has been guilty; and especially as it is to be hoped that the question of annexation has before this been definitely settled. The notice taken of the President's inaugural on the Oregon question in both Houses of Parliament has roused up a war spirit in that country which pervades all classes, and caused the detention of the steamer which should have left on the 4th, to take out despatches to Mr. Pakenham. As the excitement was then at its height, it was supposed that their instructions contained an ultimatum which was to yield nothing beyond the Canning proposition. Should this be the determination of that government, negotiation must cease, for to such terms we can never accede. I am induced, however, to believe, from conversations I have held with Mr. Ellis, now in Paris, who is connected with the ministry, being a brother-in-law of Lord Ripon, and himself a privy councillor, that Mr. Pakenham's instructions will be of a conciliatory character; and that they have great hopes of being able to settle the matter upon fair and liberal terms. But of this you are probably much better informed than he is. I am still of the opinion that we should not hesitate to divide the Territory [Oregon] by fixing our northern boundary at latitude 49°. To settle the question, I would yield something more and take the southern shore of the Strait of Fuca, and thus give to England the whole of Vancouver's Island. Such a variation of the proposition, which was rejected by Mr. Canning, would afford Sir Robert Peel ground to stand on, and might facilitate an arrangement. I fully understand the difficult position you occupy as regards this question, looking to the generally received opinion that our title to the whole of the Territory is unquestionable.

As Mr. King, under the discretion given to him, did not think it best at that moment to make a formal complaint of the conduct of the French government, it became necessary for Mr. Buchanan to encounter the intrigues of the British and French diplomatic agents in Texas to prevent the government of that country from acceding to the proposal of annexation. Satisfied that the people of Texas, with a very near approach to unanimity, desired the annexation, Mr. Buchanan, with the approbation of the President, instructed the representative of the United States in Texas, Major Donaldson, to assure the government and people of that republic that if they accepted the terms of annexation offered by the joint resolutions of the American Congress, they might rely on the United States to make fair and equitable arrangements with them on all points not covered by those resolutions. He also despatched to Texas other trustworthy persons, on whom he could rely, in an unofficial character, to watch the movements of the British and French agents, and to aid Major Donaldson in counteracting them. The Texan Congress was not in session when the resolutions of our Congress were received there. Whether action would be taken upon them with sufficient promptness to prevent foreign interference from encouraging Mexico to invade Texas, depended upon the willingness of the executive of Texas to call that body together before its usual time of assembling. That interference would be attempted by the English and French agents, the American Government was well assured. That England would take the lead in efforts to make the government and people of Texas prefer independence to annexation to the United States, and that France would second these efforts, there could be no doubt. There could be as little doubt that, whatever might be the motive of either power, there could be no solid justification for their interference between the United States and a country which had been practically independent of Mexico for nine years. There was no just ground on which any European power could assume that the United States was dealing unfairly with Mexico; and it should have been remembered that there were then pending questions between the United States and Mexico, quite independent of this matter of Texas, with which no foreign power could have the least right to interfere, and which the Government of the United States might find it necessary to settle along with the questions of Texas. Nevertheless, an intrigue was now set on foot in Texas, by the British agent, Captain Elliott, seconded by the French agent, M. Saligny, to induce the executive government of Texas to accept the guarantee of England and France that Mexico should be made to acknowledge the independence of Texas, provided that her annexation to the United States should be refused. An offer to make Texas independent was actually obtained from the power then ruling in Mexico. That this was done with the knowledge and consent of the President of Texas is true. He was, as he afterwards said, willing to have such an offer drawn from Mexico, because he believed that it would strengthen the cause of annexation and place it on higher grounds with the world. The truth is that the executive government of Texas and leading persons in that country hesitated for some time in regard to the best course to be pursued. They listened to the representations of Captain Elliott and postponed the call for the meeting of their Congress at his instigation. Elliott believed that if the Texan authorities should delay action, or even if the terms of annexation offered by the United States should now be accepted, the consummation would be defeated in the next session of the American Congress, and that in the meantime England and France would come forward and guarantee the independence of Texas. He made these representations to the President of Texas early in May, and he and M. Saligny then left the country, without making known whither they were going; and at about the same time it became known that the Texan secretary of state had suddenly departed for Europe. It was believed in Texas that Elliott had gone to the United States to confer with some of the prominent opponents of annexation, and to bring back proofs that the whole measure would be finally rejected by the Congress and people of the United States. These occurrences aroused the people of Texas to such a degree of earnestness and determination, that their executive was compelled to call the Congress together, for the purpose of summoning a convention to ratify the annexation and to form a State constitution. The meeting of the Congress was fixed for the 16th of June. When this was announced, the people of Texas in general regarded the annexation as settled, and they turned their attention to the subject of their new constitution.[99]

The Texan Congress, when assembled, adopted the basis of annexation proposed by the United States, and made provision for a convention to be held at Austin on the 4th of July. Captain Elliott was then convinced that further opposition would be useless. He was reported to have said: "The hunt is up. I retire and await orders from Her Majesty." The annexation was ratified by the convention in the month of July.

There were of course no United States troops in Texas at the time of this action of its convention; but after this event it was thought best to place a small force there, and this force was to arrive in the early part of July. But before the convention had assembled, namely, in the last week in June, Mexican troops were put in motion towards the Rio Del Norte. A new election of a President was to take place in Mexico before the close of the year. Whoever might aspire to that position would find his chief means of success in stimulating the war feeling of the nation. In the latter part of July, Mr. Buchanan had left Washington for a short absence in Pennsylvania. He was recalled by the following letter from the President, inclosing one from Mr. Bancroft, the Secretary of the Navy:

[PRESIDENT POLK TO MR. BUCHANAN.]

Washington City, August 7, 1845.

My Dear Sir:—

I enclose to you a letter from Mr. Bancroft, and will add to what he has said, that the information from Mexico comes in so authentic a shape as to entitle it to entire credit. The strong probability is that a Mexican army of eight or ten thousand men are now on the western borders of Texas. Should they cross the Del Norte, as no doubt they will, our forces at present in the country will be inadequate to resist them in their march upon Texas. Orders will be issued to-day to increase our forces as far as our disposable troops will enable us to do so. The necessary despatches from your department to Major Donaldson, or (in the event that he has left the country), to the United States Consul at Galveston, will of course be prepared by Mr. Mason. I wish it were so, that while these important steps were being taken, we could have the benefit of your advice.

Before you left you requested me to inform you, if anything should occur which in my judgment would make it necessary for you to return earlier than you intended. We are in daily expectation of receiving further information from Mexico, which may, and probably will, confirm the statement given you by Mr. Bancroft. The news of the action of the convention of Texas was despatched from New Orleans to Vera Cruz by the Mexican Consul on the 15th ult., and would probably be conveyed to the city of Mexico by the 21st or 22d. Upon receiving this information, some decisive action no doubt took place.

In addition to these reasons, which make it very desirable to have the benefit of your counsel, I must confess that the developments which are taking place, as well as my daily reflections, make it, in my opinion, more and more important that we should progress without delay in the Oregon negotiation. You may consider me impatient on this subject. I do not consider that I am so, but still I have a great desire, that what is contemplated should be done as soon as it may suit your convenience. I have felt great reluctance in saying this much, because I desired not to interfere with your arrangements during the short recreation which you have taken from your arduous labors.
I am, very faithfully and truly, your friend,
James K. Polk.
P. S.—If you determine to anticipate the period of your return to Washington, you will see the propriety of leaving Bedford in a way to produce no public sensation as to the cause of your departure. That it may not be known that you leave on receiving a letter from me, I will not place my frank on this letter.
Yours, &c.,
J. K. P.
590[MR. BANCROFT TO MR. BUCHANAN.]
Washington, August 7, 1845.
My Dear Mr. Buchanan:—

You remember I told you, before you left, that Baron Gerolt[100] predicted war on the part of Mexico. Yesterday morning, at the President's request, I went to see him, and found him very ready to communicate all his intelligence, concealing only the name of his informant, and desiring that his own name may not be used.
His letters came by way of Havana, and Charleston, S. C., and are from Mexico city, of the date of June 28th. He vouches for the entire authenticity and good opportunities of information on the part of his correspondent.
General Arista, with three thousand men, chiefly cavalry, himself the best cavalry officer in Mexico, had been directed to move forward towards the Del Norte; but whether he had orders to cross the Del Norte was not said.
At San Louis Potosi, General Paredes, the commander-in-chief, had his general quarters, with an army of seven thousand men. These also were directed to move forward, in small divisions, towards the Del Norte.
From Mexico City, General Felisola, the old woman who was with Santa Anna in Texas, was soon to leave with three thousand men to join the army of Paredes.
Thus far positive information. It was stated by the baron as his opinion that Mexico would certainly consider the armistice with Texas broken by the action of the Texas convention; that she would shun battles and carry on an annoying guerilla warfare; that she would protract the war into a very expensive length; that she would agree to no settlement of boundary with us, but under the guarantee of European powers.
On these opinions I make no comment. The seemingly authentic news of hostile intentions has led Governor Marcy,[101] under proper sanctions, to increase his little army in Texas, and Mr. Mason has written all the necessary letters. I do not see but that the sun rises this morning much as usual. The President, too, is in excellent spirits, and will grow fat in your absence, he sleeps so well now, and sees nothing before him but the plain, though steep and arduous path of duty.
So wishing you well,
Your faithful friend,
George Bancroft.

Mr. Buchanan had already determined what course to advise the President to pursue in regard to Mexico. This was to re-establish diplomatic relations with her, by sending a minister with special instructions and authority to negotiate a settlement 591of all questions between the two countries, including the western boundary of Texas. To select a suitable person for this mission and send him into Mexico with an uncertainty of his being received, or of his being received and treated with, was a delicate matter. The appointment had to be made, and to be kept a profound secret, until it could be known what reception the minister would meet with. It was settled early in the autumn that this appointment should be offered to Mr. John Slidell of Louisiana. His acceptance of the position was made known to the President in September. The following private letter to Mr. Buchanan is somewhat amusing in its earnestness respecting the secrecy which had been enjoined upon the writer:[102]

[MR. SLIDELL TO MR. BUCHANAN.]

New Orleans, Sept. 25, 1845.

My Dear Sir:—

You can scarcely imagine how much I was surprised to-day by receiving your most kind and friendly letter of the 17th inst.

I have never at any time believed that we should have war with Mexico. I have looked upon the rhodomontades of the press and the manifestoes of secretaries, as alike having but one object in view, the presidential contest; and in this point of view I consider it of little consequence who shall be elected. He who had been most strenuous in proclaiming war as indispensable to the vindication of Mexican honor, would, when installed in the presidential chair, "roar you an 'twere any nightingale." The truth is that although I have no very exalted idea of ...... yet I cannot imagine that any one who could possibly be elected president, could have so small a modicum of sense as to think seriously of going to war with the United States. But strong as I have been in this belief, I had not thought that the government would have been prepared so soon to receive from us an accredited agent. I think with you that they desire to settle amicably all the questions in dispute between us. But will they dare in the present distracted state of the country, to give so great a shock to what is their settled public opinion. They have stimulated popular prejudice to a degree that it may, under any appearance of disposition to treat with us, be fatal to the new administration. But of this you have infinitely the best means of judging, and I shall hold myself in readiness to receive your instructions. I feel most deeply the 592importance of the mission, and I confess, now that it is probable I shall soon enter upon it, I have some misgivings about it. I hope that you will not consider this as an affectation of modesty and humility. I assure you I am perfectly sincere, but will probably grow in better favor with myself when the work is fairly commenced. I am truly grateful to you for the proof of your friendship and esteem, and am flattered by the confidence reposed in me by the President. I shall endeavor to justify them. The President has enjoined on me the strictest secrecy; he even goes so far as to say that I should not communicate what he had said to me to a single human being. I have told him that I was obliged to make an exception in favor of Mrs. S., but as I could not well enter into particulars with him on this subject, pray let me explain it to you. If I had made an unreserved pledge to the President, I could not have felt myself at liberty to hint it even to my wife. I could have made no preparations for my voyage without her knowing it. We were making our arrangements to proceed shortly to Washington. If I were mysterious with her, she would be shrewd enough to guess what was in the wind. She would have some theory to guide her, because you may recollect that when you first broached this subject with me, I told you that I had no secrets for her. Now I am not one of those who believe that a woman cannot keep a secret. I know she can, for I am sure that she has never breathed a word, respecting it, to any one, not even to her mother. Besides she is living in the country, where we seldom see any one, and where there is little gossiping. Pray, explain this to the President, who might perhaps consider my disobedience of his injunction as an inauspicious omen in the opening of my diplomatic career. It is a matter of great regret to me not to have the opportunity of full personal communication with you before going to Mexico. I feel that it will be a great disadvantage, but I must rely upon your alleviating it as far as possible by your communications and instructions.... I will not fail to convey your very flattering message to Mrs. S. I think I must get her to write to you to remove an impression which I fear you have taken up. She will tell you that I am one of the best tempered men living. I have written in great haste, having barely had time to save the mail.

Believe me, my dear sir, most truly and respectfully,

Your friend and servant,

John Slidell.

Mr. Slidell was at Pensacola in the middle of November (1845), prepared to embark for Vera Cruz, on his way to the City of Mexico. He was somewhat disturbed by a rumor that Mr. Buchanan was about to retire from the State Department, but this proved to be unfounded. His instructions came from Mr. Buchanan, and were received before he reached the capital of Mexico, where he arrived in the early part of December. At this time there were two unpaid instalments of money which 593became due from Mexico to the United States in April and September, 1844, under a convention of April 11th, 1839, and a large amount of claims of citizens of the United States against Mexico which had arisen subsequent to that convention. Mr. Slidell was now authorized to make an offer that the Government of the United States would assume the payment of all just claims of citizens of the United States against Mexico down to that time, which could be established by proofs according to the principles of right and justice, the law of nations, and the existing treaties between the two countries. He was further authorized to include in the new treaty which he was to negotiate an adjustment of the western boundary of Texas; to stipulate for the payment by the United States, in cash, of an ample equivalent for such a settlement of the boundary as the United States desired, and to agree to make the payment on the exchange of ratifications. By such a settlement, while the United States would secure incalculable advantages, Mr. Buchanan believed that Mexico would be more than indemnified for the surrender of her doubtful right to reconquer Texas, and for the establishment of the boundary which the Government of the United States intended to claim.

In the latter part of the year (1845), General Paredes procured himself to be declared President of Mexico, by a process which is described in the following private letter to Mr. Buchanan, written by Mr. Slidell from the City of Mexico:

[SLIDELL TO BUCHANAN.]

Mexico, January 10, 1846.

Mr Dear Sir:—

I am sending to Vera Cruz, to be forwarded by the first merchant vessel my despatch respecting the instalments of April and September, 1844.

The facts are not as completely developed as I could have wished, but it is impossible to obtain any further information at present...... Paredes, notwithstanding his solemn protestation that he would accept no place in the government, has been elected president by a junta of notables of his own choice, and, as you may readily imagine, unanimously. The government is now really, although not in form, a military despotism. Many of the states have already given in their adhesion, and from present appearances, Paredes is likely to establish his authority throughout the republic. He seems to possess considerable energy, and he is believed to have pecuniary honesty. He will probably maintain himself for some time, if he can arrange the difficulties with the United States. Unless he does this, he will soon find himself without means to pay his troops, for the capitalists will not advance him a dollar in the present state of our relations. So soon as he was elected, I applied wholly through the consul, to the military commandant, for an escort—the cabinet was not appointed for some days after his election. The commandant replied that while Paredes was in opposition to the government, he could not furnish the escort. On the 7th inst. the Minister of Foreign Relations was appointed, when Mr. Black applied in writing for an escort, and received yesterday a reply "that public order not having been yet completely restored, the president could not spare the force necessary for an escort." Now Puebla has submitted to the government, and nearly the whole of the army is in the capital and on the road to Vera Cruz, this answer looks very much as if the government did not wish him to leave the city, and I should not be at all surprised to receive very soon an intimation of a disposition to receive me.

General Almonte is Secretary of War, and understood to be the soul of the cabinet. The Secretary of State is Mr. Castillo y Zurgas, who was for some years chargé des affaires at Washington. I met with him at Jalapa, where I saw him much, and conversed freely with him during my stay of ten days. He is an intelligent and well educated man, and seemed to have the most friendly feelings towards the United States, and spoke without reserve of the absolute necessity of a friendly settlement of our difficulties. I have not seen him since his appointment, and avoid, indeed, all intercourse with people in any way connected with public affairs, because I am well satisfied that any manifestation of a disposition to approach the new government would only tend to procrastination, if not defeat my object. I think that I shall have a better chance of succeeding than with the former government, for Paredes has the nerve to carry through any arrangement that he may consider expedient, and calculated to promote his continuance in power.

Believe me, my dear sir, faithfully,
Your obedient servant,
John Slidell.

Although at the date of this letter it appeared probable that Paredes would receive the general submission of the people of Mexico, and that he must be regarded as at least the de facto President, it could not be considered that a counter-revolution of some kind was not likely to take place. The Mexican Congress was to assemble on the 1st of January (1846). Before Mr. Buchanan had received Mr. Slidell's private letter of January 10th, he sent to Mr. Slidell the following official despatch:

[MR. BUCHANAN TO MR. SLIDELL.]
Department of State,
(No. 5.) Washington, January 20, 1846.
Sir:—

I have the honor to transmit herewith your commission as Envoy Extraordinary and Minister Plenipotentiary of the United States of America to the Mexican Republic, under the appointment made by the President, by and with the advice and consent of the Senate.

Your despatches, Nos. 2 and 3, under date respectively, the 30th November and 17th December, have been received; and I shall await the arrival of others by the Porpoise with much solicitude. Should the Mexican government, by finally refusing to receive you, consummate the act of folly and bad faith of which they have afforded such strong indications, nothing will then remain for this Government but to take the redress of the wrongs of its citizens into its own hands.

In the event of such a refusal, the course which you have determined to pursue is the proper one. You ought, in your own language, so to conduct yourself as to throw the whole odium of the failure of the negotiation upon the Mexican government; point out in the most temperate manner the inevitable consequences of so unheard of a violation of all the usages which govern the intercourse between civilized nations, and declare your intention to remain in Mexico until you can receive instructions adapted to the exigencies of the case. This sojourn will afford you an honorable opportunity to watch the course of events, and avail yourself of any favorable circumstances which, in the mean time, may occur. Should a revolution have taken place before the first of January, the day appointed for the meeting of Congress, an event which you deemed probable; or should a change of ministry have been effected, which you considered almost certain; this delay will enable you to ascertain the views and wishes of the new government or administration. The desire of the President is that you should conduct yourself with such wisdom and firmness in the crisis, that the voice of the American people shall be unanimous in favor of redressing the wrongs of our much injured and long suffering claimants.

It would seem to be the desire of the Mexican government to evade the redress of the real injuries of our citizens, by confining the negotiation to the adjustment of a pecuniary indemnity for its imaginary rights over Texas. This cannot be tolerated. The two subjects must proceed hand in hand. They can never be separated. It is evidently with the view of thus limiting the negotiation, that the Mexican authorities have been quibbling about the mere form of your credentials; without even asking whether you had instructions and full powers to adjust the Texan boundary. The advice of the Council of Government seems to have been dictated by the same spirit. They do not advise the Mexican government to refuse to receive you; but, assuming the fact that the government had agreed to receive a plenipotentiary to treat upon 596the subject of Texas alone, they infer that it is not bound to receive an envoy extraordinary and minister plenipotentiary without this limitation.

In the mean time, the President, in anticipation of the final refusal of the Mexican government to receive you, has ordered the army of Texas to advance and take a position on the left bank of the Rio Grande, and has directed that a strong fleet shall be immediately assembled in the Gulf of Mexico. He will thus be prepared to act with vigor and promptitude the moment that Congress shall give him the authority.

This despatch will not be transmitted to you by the Mississippi. That vessel will be detained at Pensacola for the purpose of conveying to you instructions with the least possible delay, after we shall have heard from you by the Porpoise; and of bringing you home in case this shall become necessary.

By your despatch No. 2, written at Vera Cruz, you ask for an explanation of my instructions relative to the claim of Texas on that portion of New Mexico east of the Del Norte; and you state the manner in which you propose to treat the subject in the absence of any such explanation. I need say nothing in relation to your inquiry; but merely to state that you have taken the proper view of the question, and that the course which you intend to pursue meets the approbation of the President.

I am, &c.,

James Buchanan.

It is now necessary to recur to the military movement referred to in this despatch. In August, 1845, General Zachary Taylor was encamped at Corpus Christi, in Texas, in command of a small American force of fifteen hundred troops. In the following November, his force was recruited to about four thousand men. On the 8th of March, 1846, acting under the President's orders, given in anticipation of a refusal of the Mexican authorities to receive or to treat with Mr. Slidell, Taylor moved towards the Rio Grande, and on the 28th his little army reached the banks of that river, opposite the town of Matamoras. In a despatch written on the 12th of March to Mr. Slidell, Mr. Buchanan said: It is not deemed necessary to modify the instructions which you have already received, except in a single particular; and this arises from the late revolution effected in the government of the Mexican Republic by General Paredes. I am directed by the President to instruct you not to leave that republic, until you shall have made a formal demand to be received by the new government. The government of Paredes came into existence not by a regular constitutional succession, but in consequence of a military revolution 597by which the subsisting constitutional authorities were subverted. It cannot be considered as a mere continuation of the government of Herrera. On the contrary, the form of government has been entirely changed, as well as all the high functionaries at the head of the administration. The two governments are certainly not so identical that the refusal of the one to receive you ought to be considered conclusive evidence that such would be the determination of the other. It would be difficult, on such a presumption, in regard to so feeble and distracted a country as Mexico, to satisfy the American people that all had been done which ought to have been done to avoid the necessity of resorting to hostilities.

On your return to the United States, energetic measures against Mexico would at once be recommended by the President; and these might fail to obtain the support of Congress, if it could be asserted that the existing government had not refused to receive our minister. It would not be a sufficient answer to such an allegation that the government of Herrera had refused to receive you, and that you were therefore justified in leaving the country after a short delay, because, in the meantime, the government of Paredes had not voluntarily offered to reverse the decision of his predecessor.

The President believes that, for the purpose of making this demand, you ought to return to the City of Mexico, if this be practicable, consistently with the national honor. It was prudent for you to leave it during the pendency of the late revolution, but this reason no longer continues. Under existing circumstances your presence there ought to be productive of the most beneficial consequences......

The time when you shall ask to be received by the government of Paredes is left to your own discretion. The President thinks this ought to be done speedily, unless good reasons exist to the contrary. Your demand ought to be couched in strong but respectful language. It can no longer be resisted on the ridiculous pretence that your appointment has not been confirmed by the Senate......

In regard to the time of your departure from the Mexican Republic, the President is willing to extend your discretion. In the present distracted condition of that republic, it is impossible for those at a distance to decide as correctly what ought to be your course, in this particular, as you can for yourself upon the spot. The intelligence which you have communicated, "that the department of Sinaloa has declared its independence;" "that the garrison of Mazatlan has pronounced against Paredes;" and "that the authorities of the departments of Nuevo Leon, Tamaulipas, Chihuahua, Michoacan, and Queretero have protested in strong terms against the usurpation of Paredes; and refusing to continue in the exercise of their functions, have dissolved," may well exercise an influence on your decision. Indeed, you suppose "that appearances justify the belief that Paredes will not be

435

able to sustain himself until the meeting of the constituent congress; that his government will perish from inanition, if from no other cause. In this critical posture of Mexican affairs, it will be for yourself to decide the question of the time of your departure according to events as they may occur. If, after you shall have fulfilled your instructions, you should indulge a reasonable hope, that by continuing in Mexico, you could thus best subserve the interests of your country, then you ought to remain, provided this can be done with honor. The President reposes entire confidence in your patriotism and discretion, and knows that no temporary inconvenience to yourself will prevent you from performing your duty. It may be that when prepared to take your departure another revolution might be impending, the result of which would enable you, by a timely interposition, to accomplish the great objects of your mission. Besides, in the present distracted condition of Mexico, it is of importance that we should have an able and discreet agent in that country to watch the progress of events, and to communicate information on which this department could rely. Jalapa is probably not so favorable a position for observation as the City of Mexico.

We have received information from different quarters, in corroboration of your statement, that there may be a design on the part of several European powers to establish a monarchy in Mexico. It is supposed that the clergy would generally favor such a project, and that a considerable party already exists among the people, which would give it their countenance and support. It is believed by many that this party will continue to increase in consequence of the successive revolutions which may afflict that country, until at length a majority of the people will be willing to throw themselves into the arms of a monarch for security and protection. Indeed, rumor has already indicated the king, in the person of the Spanish Prince Henry, the son of Francisco de Paula, the rejected suitor of Queen Isabella.

These may be, and probably are, idle speculations; but they come to us in such a shape that they ought not to be wholly disregarded. It will be your duty to exercise your utmost vigilance in detecting this plot and its ramifications, if any such exists......

This despatch will be transmitted to you by the Mississippi (which is placed at your disposal), and will be delivered to you by an officer of that vessel. There will always be a vessel of war at Vera Cruz, ready to bear your despatches or yourself to the United States. In conclusion I would remark that it is impossible, at this distance from the scene of action, to anticipate all the contingencies which may occur in a country in a state of revolution, as Mexico is at present, and to provide for cases of sudden emergency. Much must necessarily be left to the discretion of the envoy, who, on the spot, can take advantage of circumstances as they may arise: and the President is happy in believing that you possess all the qualifications necessary for the crisis.

P. S.—To provide for possible contingencies, two letters of credence are transmitted to you: the one directed to General Paredes by name, and the other to the President of the Mexican Republic.

The government of Paredes refused to receive Mr. Slidell, and he consequently retired from Mexico to New Orleans, and on the 9th of April he wrote thence to Mr. Buchanan the following private letter:

[SLIDELL TO BUCHANAN.]
New Orleans, April 9, 1846.
My Dear Sir:—

When I left here a few months since I little thought, or rather I never dreamed, that I should so soon return. Had I found a fair field in Mexico, I believe that I would have justified your good opinion and the confidence which the President, through your recommendation, reposed in me. But the fates have willed it differently, and I return an unsuccessful, and of course in the estimation of the public generally, an inefficient diplomatist. I flatter myself that such will not be your opinion and that of the discreet few, and I must console myself with that reflection. Be that as it may, I shall never cease to entertain the warmest recollections of your kindness and friendship.

I hope to hear from you in a few days; if you express any desire to see me in Washington, I shall leave immediately. I shall probably defer my departure until the end of the month. I most sincerely hope that your anticipations of embarrassment to the Oregon question from my return will not be realized, but if such be the case, the publication by the Mexican government of my correspondence rendered the mischief irreparable.

Mrs. Slidell begs me to present her to your recollection. She will soon have an opportunity of thanking you in person for your many kind remembrances.

Believe me, my dear sir, most faithfully, your friend and servant,

John Slidell.

Within a little more than a month after the date of this letter a state of war was declared by an act of Congress to exist between the United States and Mexico. This peculiar declaration came about in consequence of events which had occurred after Taylor had taken up a position on the Rio Grande opposite to Matamoras. The Mexican General Arista, commanding a large force at Matamoras, menaced Taylor with hostilities, if he did not retire to a position beyond the river Neuces. The threat was disregarded, and, in a short time, a small reconnoitering party of Taylor's troops were attacked by the Mexicans and captured. This occurrence, and the refusal of the Paredes government to receive Mr. Slidell, were regarded by President 600Polk as tantamount to actual war. By a special message sent to Congress on the 11th of May, 1846, Mr. Polk officially informed Congress of all the facts which he regarded as establishing a state of war, and asked for its recognition. On the 12th of May the act recognizing the war was passed, and provision was made for its vigorous prosecution. The main justification relied upon by the administration for the presence of an American army on the Rio Grande was, that it was encamped upon territory which had already become part of the United States, and that it was the duty of the United States Government to defend this territory from invasion, especially as the only existing executive government of Mexico had refused to receive an American envoy, through whom an adjustment of all questions of boundary and all other pending difficulties could have been negotiated.

[SLIDELL TO BUCHANAN.]

New York, July 1, 1846.

My Dear Sir:—

As I have not heard from you, and have seen no notice in the newspapers of the matter which was the subject of our last conversation, I feel happy in the belief that your application to Mr. A. has resulted in a satisfactory explanation. By this time you must have decided the question so important for the country, as well as decisive of your future political fortunes, whether you will remain in your present post or accept the vacant judgeship. You might not think me altogether a disinterested adviser were I to urge you not to leave the Department of State; and indeed I myself feel that a certain degree of selfishness may render me a somewhat unsafe counsellor; but of one thing I am sure, unless some absolute necessity exist for an immediate decision, you should not take a step which cannot be recalled, and which you may hereafter regret, until the tariff question has been definitively acted on. That stumbling block out of your way, I should most deeply regret to see you shelved upon the Supreme Bench.

There may be here and there in this part of the world, some extreme 54–40 men who disapprove of the settlement of the Oregon question, but I have not as yet met with one of them; and if we acquire California, the specimens will be equally rare in the Western States; it will soon be indeed an extinct race, and two years hence it will be as difficult to make an issue on that question as on the Mexican boundary.

Our people are essentially practical; they look ahead only; no party can be organized on matters that are past. The President has made most judicious promotions in the army and selections for the volunteers, and now that he has got rid of this source of uneasiness, he must feel himself in very smooth water. We have most shocking weather. So soon as it becomes a little more summer like, we shall go to Saratoga. Mrs. Slidell begs me to present her regards.

Believe me, very faithfully yours,
John Slidell.

War having been declared General Scott demanded of the Government, as his "right," to be appointed to lead our armies into Mexico. Whether it was because his "right" was recognized, or because he was regarded as the fittest general for the chief command, his appointment to that position was made, notwithstanding the brilliant victories gained by General Taylor as soon as the war opened.[103] The military history of the war does not come within the scope of this work. During its progress, the American Government kept a diplomatic agent in Mexico, Mr. N. P. Trist, ready to agree on terms of peace. The treaty of Guadalupe Hidalgo, negotiated between him and three plenipotentiaries on the part of the Mexican Republic was signed on the 2d of February, 1848, and was ratified by the Senate of the United States on the 16th of March. It ceded to the United States New Mexico and California, and settled the western boundary of Texas. The private letters given below are of the years 1845 and 1846, and with them the present chapter must close.

[SLIDELL TO BUCHANAN.]
New Orleans, November 5, 1846.
My Dear Sir:—

I reached home about a fortnight since, and was met by the unpleasant intelligence of our overwhelming defeat in Pennsylvania. I have persuaded myself that this can only be a temporary reverse, and that Pennsylvania must very soon retake her position in the Democratic ranks. I should feel much better satisfied, however, to have this opinion confirmed by you. I do not know what to think of Santa Anna's movements, letters, etc. It may be that he is only mystifying his countrymen, but the more reasonable solution seems to me to be that he has not found himself as strong as he expected, and has not thought it prudent to declare his real sentiments. I believe that he is fully impressed with the necessity of making peace, but whether he will be able to carry out his views is another question. When I last saw you, the course to be pursued, if Mexico refused to treat, had not been decided upon. It is time that this question should be decided. The present system of operation involves the most enormous expense. That would be a minor consideration were adequate results produced. I believe that if the Mexican Congress refuse to treat, the war may be ended in the course of the next year by the capture of the capital. This, if pursued with vigor and under a competent commander-in-chief, would be the better course. I doubt if General Taylor possesses the capacity for operations on so extended a scale; and yet, until he has committed some grave and palpable error, it would

438

be a very unsafe step to supersede him. I have seen many persons from the army; they all think Worth the most competent man. Kearney, perhaps, is equal to Worth. I do not know enough of Butler to have any fixed opinion as to his capacity. The fate of the administration depends on the successful conduct of the war.

There are but two modes of carrying it on—to march upon the capital with such a force as will ensure success, or to hold the northeastern provinces and California, with the ports of Vera Cruz and Tampico, keeping up a rigid blockade of both coasts, and requiring the enemy to supply all the provisions we may require. For this purpose we should not require more than fifteen thousand effective men. If we do not march upon Mexico, it is every way essential to take San Juan de Ulloa. The navy should have an opportunity to distinguish itself, and the people must have something to huzza about.

There is a Doctor Mesa here, just arrived from Victoria, the capital of Tamaulipas. He brings letters, stating him to be a man of character and influence, and that he is authorized to speak the sentiments of the leading men of Tamaulipas. He says that the people of that department are willing to separate from Mexico, if they can have assurances of protection from us, and that they would be joined in the movement by the neighboring departments. I of course did not pretend to say what would be done by the administration, but suggested that at present it would be indiscreet to guarantee a northern confederation, but that we would be under the strongest obligations of honor, in making a treaty of peace, to stipulate for full protection in person and property to all those who might take part in the movement. He will proceed to Washington, and I have taken the liberty of giving him a letter of introduction to you. I shall patiently await the expiration of the month of December; if by that time Mexico has not signified her wish to treat, I shall no longer continue to look forward to a renewal of my mission. I have written to the President, and I have felt it my duty to say what I have heard from almost every quarter, that General ——— (of whose qualifications I personally have no knowledge whatever), does not command the confidence of the army. Do you know General Pillow? Has not the President exaggerated views of his military talents?

Believe me, my dear sir, very faithfully and respectfully,

Your friend, etc.,

John Slidell.

603[MR. SLIDELL TO PRESIDENT POLK.]

New Orleans, January 6, 1847.

My Dear Sir:—

The tenor of all the advices from Mexico is such as to satisfy me that [the Mexican] Congress will not authorize the opening of negotiations, and that we are not to have a peace until its terms are dictated by a victorious army before the walls of the capital. The public interest may, and probably will, require that you should make, under such circumstances, other arrangements for future negotiations than those which you had heretofore proposed, and my object in now addressing you is to state, as I do with the most entire frankness, and without the slightest reservation, that I do not expect or desire that my previous mission, or any understanding that has existed in regard to its resumption, should interfere in the remotest degree with any new selection that you may consider it expedient to make. While I shall ever entertain the warmest sense of the distinguished and unsolicited mark of your good opinion in charging me with one of the most important trusts which has ever been confided to a citizen of the United States, I feel that I should be unworthy of its continuance if I permitted any claims of mine, real or supposed, to embarrass you for a single moment.

General Scott, when he passed through this place, considered himself, in consequence of my relation to Mexican affairs, at liberty to communicate in confidence to me, as he did fully, his plan of the campaign, and I was highly gratified to learn that Vera Cruz was to be attacked by a force that will insure the possession of that most important position. I am not so well satisfied, however, that the shortest road to Mexico is the best, and while I take it for granted that the topography, resources and climate of Mexico have been maturely studied, and due weight given to all the considerations which should decide the choice of routes, yet I can not but feel some misgiving as to the result. At all events, the most abundant resources of men and materials should be placed at his disposition. There is one subject connected with this, of which I have long been thinking of writing to you, but have been restrained by feelings which you can understand and appreciate. I fear that the commander of our squadron has not the qualities of energy and decision which are imperatively required for an emergency like the present. Commodore Conner is a brave man, an accomplished officer, and a good seaman, but his health is, and has been for some time past, so much impaired as, in a great degree, to neutralize these qualities; the sound mind, in military matters especially, is not sufficient without the strong body; and frequent violent attacks of a most painful nervous affliction, the tic-douloureux, cannot fail to affect the clearness of his perception and the vigor of his action. To my mind this has been abundantly demonstrated by his two abortive attempts at Alvarado. On this point there is little difference of opinion among the officers under his command. Alvarado might have been taken without difficulty on either occasion. He does not command the confidence of those who serve under him, and confidence is the vital principle of success. I make these remarks with great diffidence and still greater reluctance, for I have the highest regard for Commodore Conner, as an officer and a gentleman, and were it not for his bodily ailments, there are few men in the navy whom I consider better fitted for so important a command. I trust that you will pardon me for suggestions which may perhaps be considered misplaced, but I am sure that you will do justice to the feeling that has dictated them. Your own fame, the success of your administration, the great interests of the country are staked upon a brilliant termination of the war, and the feelings of an individual are but dust in the balance of such momentous issues. This is the scale in which I wish my own to be weighed, and be assured, my dear sir, that so far as I am concerned, I shall most cheerfully and cordially acquiesce in any decision which you may think proper to make.

Yours ever,
John Slidell.

[HON. RICHARD RUSH TO MR. BUCHANAN.]
Sydenham, near Philadelphia, October 7, 1846.
My Dear Sir:—

I am half ashamed to be again sending you little bits of my correspondence from abroad; but you, who have so much to do with heads of governments and nations, will know how to appreciate even general expressions from those who live in daily intercourse with sovereigns, and are constantly hearing them talk—yet whose discretion and training guard them against mentioning names. The enclosed letter, received by the last steamer, is from Lady Lyttleton, and I naturally am disposed to infer that the words I have pencilled, mean Queen Victoria; or that they include her—at the least. This Lady L. is the widow of the late Lord Lyttleton, and daughter of Earl Spencer, and holds the post of chief governess to the queen's children; for which she was selected from among England's highest women for virtues and accomplishments, to aid in forming their principles and conduct. Her home is chiefly Windsor Castle, but she dates now from "Osborne House," the queen's marine residence at the Isle of Wight, where she was at the time of writing, with the queen and children. The queen is understood to hold her in the greatest esteem and confidence: and the little pencilled words, dropping from such a quarter in this private letter, do seem to me to import that this little successor to Queen Elizabeth personally likes your treaty, full as much as when Lord Aberdeen writes officially that it is approved; and so may be taken as a veritable addition to all the other evidences you have on that head; and this must be my excuse for sending the letter to you—which can be returned at your perfect convenience. I need not stop to explain the little allusions it has to my family or self, as they are the mere common courtesies of an amiable lady. The "niece" in question, is the wife of Colonel Bucknall Estcourt, known to you as lately in our country under a commission from the British government.

This good lady's letter done with, I am tempted to go on and remark, as somewhat growing out of it, that if those who could doubt the President's consistency in agreeing to the Oregon treaty, or yours in supporting him in it, be not convinced by the articles now in course of publication in the Pennsylvanian (following up the powerful discussions in the Union on the same point), that there was perfect consistency, we may say of them what Hume says of the sturdy Scotch Jacobites who declared for the innocence of Mary of Scots; viz, that they are beyond the reach of reason and argument, and must be left to their prejudices......

I have just been reading my last Union. The Santa Fe army of the West appears to have done, and to be doing, nobly; but war, war, war all over Mexico, by land and sea, say I for one. All else is leather and prunella just now, and would be inhumanity to ourselves in the end. If a blow can be struck at Vera Cruz, so much the better. That would tell through the world; which, otherwise, will say, in spite of the different circumstances, that the French took the castle, whilst we, with all our naval resources so much nearer, could not. A thousand of our seamen would do the business. Let them land by night, armed to the teeth, during, or at the close of, a furious bombardment, we having bomb vessels and heavier ships perhaps than now, and they will go right into the works—nothing can stop them—carrying all before them as surely as Decatur succeeded at Tripoli, when, in the face of all their soldiers, batteries, gun-boats, and the guns of the frigate, odds twenty to one more against him than there would be against our squadron in the gulf, he and his mere handful of gallant men, so signally triumphed. There are Decaturs somewhere in our squadron now, or those who have their mantle. Nothing more certain. They would put the gulf in a blaze of glory for us, if you let them try it.

I have been writing a good deal for my little paper; ever a sort of privilege to irresponsibility, joined, if not to entire ignorance, at least to want of full knowledge. But I console myself with the reflection that it must be ever a sort of relief to a high official man with his hands full of engagements, on getting quite through a letter to him, to find at last, as you do with this, that it makes no complaints, taxes him with no business, nor even demands any answer.

And now I will conclude with begging you to accept the assurances of esteem and friendship with which I desire, my dear sir, to subscribe myself,
Very faithfully yours,
Richard Rush.
[RUSH TO BUCHANAN.]
Sydenham, near Philadelphia, June 2d, 1846.
My Dear Sir:—

A rumor catches my eye in one of the morning papers that General Scott has claimed of the administration his right to lead our army into Mexico. 606This may or may not be true. I am little inclined to believe all I see in the newspapers, or the half of it; but I know what is true, viz: That when General Brown died, Scott did claim, in the most objectionable manner, his right to succeed to the command of the army. He addressed a series of letters to the Secretary of War, then Governor Barbour,[104] to prove, as he confidently supposed that he did, his alleged right, all of them written in a highly improper tone. One of the members of the cabinet likened them, by a figure of speech, as I remember, to taking the Government by the throat, and demanding its surrender upon his own terms. Being then of the cabinet myself, invited by Mr. Adams from the English mission, where I had been some seven years, (in which country, to give the devil his due, I had observed the military to be always de facto as well as in theory, wholly subordinate to the civil power, above all the supreme executive power), I heard all his letters read, and confess that I was astounded at them. So out of place were they conceived to be as addressed to a member of the cabinet, and thus in effect to the President, that there were those of the body (I am sure there was one) who would have been in favor of striking his name from the army without more ado, and this in the face of the gallant manner in which he did his duty last war in the field, on the mere footing of the spirit of insubordination and dangerous temper for a military man which these letters bespoke. In the end, as you know, Macomb was appointed Brown's successor, over both Scott and Gaines, for the latter had put in his somewhat imperious claims too, urging it offensively, though in a less degree than Scott. I presume that Scott's letters are on file in the War Department. The whole history of the affair is curious. It would not do for me to write, or for me to make public, but if ever the opportunity happens to occur to me in conversation, you might be amused to hear some of its details. It came near to breaking Mr. Adams's cabinet to pieces at the time.

Has not the case occurred for the balancing principle we have been threatened with, and might it not be well to forestall its application? Prevention is better than cure. If we promptly get possession of the Mexican capital, and make them sign a treaty doing us full justice at last, it would be too late for Guizot and company to interfere. They would see too clearly its utter hopelessness. "The burying would have gone by," as our Judge Yates was fond of saying. It would be the a posteriori argument rather than the a priori. These are crude thoughts, occurring while I write, which, of course, you have all been more fully weighing in Washington; but one more I must indulge in, not crude, which is, that really our whole operations in regard to Mexico, compared to the ultimatum of the French Minister Deffands, which preceded the bombardment of Vera Cruz by Admiral Baudin and the Prince de Joinville, quite naturally remind us of Fontaine's fable of the beasts who accuse each other of their sins. The lions, the wolves and the bears are pardoned everything, while the lamb is devoured for nibbling a little grass.

607I had intended only to mention confidentially those letters of General Scott which, if on file, may be seen by all; but I cannot conclude without congratulating the President and yourself on General Taylor's victories as equally glorious and pure. They are the former by all the best titles that can be laid to efficient and splendid achievements in arms, with greatly inferior numbers, and the latter from having been gained on our own soil in repelling hostile aggressions, following upon "long continued and unredressed injuries." A people who have thus deliberately commenced a war upon this patient and long forbearing Republic have surely invited its vigorous recoil upon themselves, whatever the consequences to themselves. Such must be the calm voice of history, pronouncing her judgment on well authenticated facts when party spirit is forgotten.

I remain, my dear sir, very sincerely yours,
Richard Rush.
[RUSH TO BUCHANAN.]
Sydenham, near Philadelphia, August 18, 1845.
My Dear Sir:—

I have to pray your excuse for the trouble of this letter.
I wish to have all the documents respecting Oregon that accompanied the President's message to the Senate of the 21st of July. They were given in the Union, which I take, but so often miss, through one bad chance or other at the post office, that I have not these documents; and as they are generally published in the pamphlet form, I would feel greatly indebted to you if (having a copy to spare) you would have the goodness to direct it to me, as I know not where else to seek it. Sometimes I am meditating one more volume on our relations with England, the Oregon question closing the list of the historical ones growing out of our revolution; and I desire at any rate to gather up the authentic documents bearing on that question which seem to me, with the facts they furnish, to supply the materials perhaps of some reflections also, at this new and remarkable epoch in our affairs. On the whole, I think you made a wise settlement of that long pending difficulty. My own impression was ever very strong, that England was ready to appeal to the sword, unless she got territory and advantages south of 49°; and I will candidly own to you that she took up with fewer at last than I supposed she would have done. This I ascribe to the energy and whole course of our Government since Mr. Polk came in, at which I was a little startled at first; but it came out nobly, and what a fine prospect the settlement now offers to us of intercourse with England, in connection with our new tariff.
On this latter head, will not England now do something for our tobacco, and become wholly liberal in the arrangements of her West India trade with us? Our new tariff may well justify us in urging her on these and other points in which she is still much behind the liberality of our own system.
I am sincerely glad that your services are retained in the Department of 608State. If I might claim to speak, I should say that it is due both to your country and yourself, that, having accomplished so much of good in that station already, you should continue in it to do more.
How ill-judged, I would almost say criminal, in the Senate, to have refused the President the small sum he asked towards the executive plans with Mexico! Reading lately a life of Mirabeau, I was much struck with a remark quoted from Madame de Sévigné, that "there is nothing so expensive as want of money." What may be the executive plans precisely in regard to Mexico, I of course know not; but I can conceive that to have given the President those two millions in hand he asked for, might have saved the ultimate expenditure of fifty or a hundred millions.
I remain, my dear sir, with sincere respect, very faithfully yours,
Richard Rush.
[MR. PICKENS TO MR. BUCHANAN.]
Edgewood (South Carolina), July 5th, 1846.
My Dear Sir:—

I owe you a letter; but, as in your last, you said you were so much overwhelmed in business, I thought it would be wrong to inflict a letter upon you until you might have more leisure. And as I see you have disposed of the Oregon question and its difficulties, I suppose now you must be resting upon your triumphs and honors, and have some time to read a humdrum letter from a quondam friend, who assures you in advance that he is not going to beg you for any office whatever.

You wrote me you were about to give a letter of introduction to me for an English lady who was to travel South, etc. I looked a long time for this distinguished visitor, and had my household put in order to receive her, particularly as I heard she was about to write a "book," and I desired to figure largely in English history.

By the by, I see it stated by "letter-writers," who now constitute a distinguished fraternity illustrious for the intimate knowledge they possess of everything, that you are going to England yourself, and I see it also stated in the same quarter that you will take with you a very brilliant cousin of mine. Now, I will not tell you how I think you will represent us at the court of St. James, but I have no hesitation in saying that she will do us honor in any court in Europe. Is this all true? Where is King? Is he going to quit Paris? I hope if he comes home he will bring a French lady—it would suit him well. He was a little French before he went, and he must be very much so now. Tell him if he does intend to bring out a lady, for God's sake, let it be no French or Italian countess. They say you were not satisfied with the settlement of the Oregon question, but that you wanted more rocks, and ice, and muskrats. I think it all turned out right, and would have been settled much earlier if the "notice" had passed at the first of the session. I know you are satisfied. I suppose it is about like what they used to say of you in relation to the tariff, that you wanted thirty-six dollars a ton on iron and prohibition on coal, etc., and yet I always knew you did not care a fig for the tariff, except some of your people were rising about it. I think I can tell what you do desire now above all things, and that is the luxurious feeling of honest independence enjoyed in the retirement of your beautiful homestead at Lancaster. If there is one feeling sweeter to man than any other, it is, after leaving cabinets, and courts, and politicians to breathe once more the pure air of one's native hills and valleys.

What are you going to do with the Mexican war? I hope there will be no treaty without the acquisition of California. The loss of California to Mexico will be nothing, as it will aid in consolidating her government, and finally strengthen it, while its acquisition will be immense to us. In fact we have already conquered it, as there is no force between us and the North provinces to keep us out of it.

If we had California with its vast harbors, in the next fifty years we could control the commerce of the Pacific, and the wealth of China and India, and the future destiny of our glorious Republic would be to accumulate as vast wealth and power on the Pacific as we have on the Atlantic. Some people seem to have very tender consciences of late as to conquests, etc. I should like to know if half the earth is not now owned by the rights of conquests.

Some time since, when the Mexican war broke out, I wrote the President cordially approving of what had been done, etc.; but I have never heard a word. I hope he has no one to select letters for his eye, and to keep others from him, as used to be done by others who preceded him. This remark is suggested by the fact that I see lately some of his important appointments in this quarter have been made from his bitterest and most malignant opponents. I say this to you in confidence.

If you have time I should be glad to hear from you; and tell me who is to be the next President; and who I must pull off my cap to shout for, etc.

I expect to take my family North this summer, and if so may pass through Washington on my way to Saratoga and the lakes. If nothing happens, I may call to see you about the commencement of the dog-days, if you have not left Washington before that. I believe I will also go to see Van Buren, and console him for the split in the Democratic party of

New York, and the political death of Wright, etc. I always liked the stoic indifference with which Van Buren took everything, and the easy way in which he lolled in an armchair. He looked like he would make a good fisherman. The truth is, he was a very firm and sagacious man, but made very poor selections for office. If he had changed his cabinet, and selected young, talented, and ambitious men he never would have been turned out, but he had old men about him who loved ease as well as himself.

I have written you a rambling letter, as I had nothing else to write. If you had been a planter, I would have written you about cotton and our crops. You know I am engaged entirely on my estates at present, and solely occupied, thank God! in the finest and noblest pursuit, the cultivation of the soil. 610And I hope, if they reduce the tariff, as they ought to do, if there is any honesty at Washington, that I may be able next year to sell my cotton at nine cents to some Pennsylvania manufacturer, and get my iron from your iron-masters cheap enough to use more ploughs and axes for next crop.

Very truly your friend,

F. W. Pickens.[105]

The following lively letters were written by an English lady, who was a good while in this country, and who soon afterwards published a little book called "The Statesmen of America in 1846":

[FROM MRS. MAURY.]

Cincinnati, April 14, 1846.

My Dear Mr. Buchanan:—

Your letter reached me shortly after my arrival in New Orleans, and at once made Mrs. Maury a great lady at the St. Charles. I have been anxiously waiting some information from various quarters, which might decide my plans for the next few weeks, but as yet I have received none. The Unicorn can hardly have sailed at the time we have supposed. I do not wish to remove further from the seaports until I shall be assured that my husband and his anxious charge do not yet require my presence. I have, of course, no news of Dr. Hughes, and therefore have no idea when and where he will wish me to meet him. Mr. Clay is still at St. Louis, and his return to Lexington very uncertain. I have been suffering from a slight indisposition for the last few days, and am not yet ready for travelling. This is a tolerable list of perplexities for a lady. In addition, I cannot avoid feeling great interest and some degree of alarm at the scenes which have lately transpired in Congress.[106] ... Winthrop is a gallant advocate, but neither his noble spirit nor his truthful nature should be wasted thus. For Mr. Ingersoll, to whom, as you know, my personal attachment is very strong, I have felt most keenly; his temperature is warm, and his susceptibilities as exquisite and acute as those of a woman; and I, who admire his mind, and enjoy his wit, and love his worth, cannot endure to think of the abusive epithets which Mr. Webster has heaped upon him. Nevertheless, I always considered his first allusion to the affair of McLeod an indiscretion, and felt certain from the first that evil would arise from it. I can only attribute his turning back to that period, to the historical habits of his mind, which led him to take a new view of affairs subsequent to that event, from the information he had received from Governor Seward. The Governor is intrepid, and will give the unvarnished truth, nothing adding thereto, nor diminishing aught therefrom. I cannot for one 611moment conceive that Ingersoll has been instigated by personal resentment, because he was in the habit of expressing to me his private opinions of every public man in Washington, and I have never heard from his lips one vindictive word against Mr. Webster....

To proceed, however, to a less painful theme. I like Cincinnati much better than New Orleans, feeling myself here once more in America instead of in some shabby old town of Brittany, listening to patois French (vulgarly called gumbo French in New Orleans). This city presents all the interest which a growing community ever possesses, and Cincinnati is an infant Hercules. We receive from Judge McLean every attention and hospitality, and I find the Judge as attractive and estimable in private life as he is gracious and dignified on the bench. The society here, as elsewhere in America, is excellent, and confirms my preconceived opinions that good society is the same in Europe and in America. At the hands of the excellent Dr. Purcell, the Catholic bishop, I receive every indulgence; he has conducted us in person through his various institutions, which are all prospering, and intends also to accompany us to visit his Ursulines. From him I learned the striking fact that there were present in the cathedral at high mass on Easter Sunday, 600 persons who are converts to the Catholic faith. Here, as elsewhere, the Sisters of Mercy, by their devotion and virtue, afford us proof that even on earth there exist angelic natures. The cotton factories flourish in Cincinnati, and even at Madison, a small town we passed on the Ohio, I saw the black tall chimneys, indicative of the successful progress of the labor going on at its base. It seems to me, from all I have seen, that notwithstanding all the expected (may I say hoped for?) approaches to free trade, that the manufactures of this country are now too firmly established to suffer. I think you know me well enough to be assured that my zeal for the welfare of America is second only to that I feel for the prosperity of that fair and distant Isle to which I owe my birth, which has been the cradle of my children, and the happy home in which for eighteen years I have been the cherished wife of a husband to whom time has made me more dear. How ardently I wish that every feeling of affection which I shall ever preserve for the people of America were shared by my countrymen.

I hope yet to visit Mrs. Catron—instead of challenging each other for the sake of the chairman, we will take your advice, and share his esteem and regard between us. He being our Oregon territory, and each lady having determined not to give notice—of course the treaty of joint occupancy must remain in force. Moreover, on my side, I shall refuse arbitration, either by citizen or sovereign—and I think Mrs. Catron will be of my mind, viz., that the division of a lover's heart is not a proper subject for interference by foreign powers. Should we ultimately find that we cannot get along with the joint occupancy, but that we are continually shouldering one another, as you, dear sir, are friendly to us both, will you give us permission to ask your advice, as to the most satisfactory mode of dividing equitably between us the heart and head of the honorable gentleman in dispute. I presume, of course, 612that, like the Oregon territory, he will be content with being contended for by two fair dames, without putting in one word about his own ultimate destiny.

I hope, dear Mr. Buchanan, that I have not tired your patience. I am writing in bed, and still somewhat of an invalid; separated from home, it is a source of great pleasure to write to one who has expressed so much regard for me as you have done.

Believe me always, most sincerely and gratefully,

Your obliged friend,

Sarah Mytton Maury.

Will you give my love to Mrs. Plitt, and say to her that I wished for her presence much yesterday, when Judge McLean was eulogizing the talents and virtues of the Secretary of State.

[FROM MRS. MAURY.]

Washington, Friday Morning, 10 A. M., June 10, 1846.

My Dear Mr. Buchanan:—

I would have called to see you this morning, but had so much fear of too frequently intruding on your patience that I abstained.

I have had a very interesting conversation with Mr. Calhoun upon the subject of his going out to England. He urged his age, his various engagements, the allotment he had already made of the few remaining years of his life, the use that he can render to his country by staying here, and many other reasons. I replied that his age was no objection, that he is not old, and that no duties could be higher than those he would fulfil by going to England; that the effects of his mission would be not only beneficial at the present moment, but throughout all future time; and urged him by every principle of patriotism, utility and devotion, to accept the trust. He yielded at length to my entreaties, and said: "If I can be convinced that it is my imperative duty, then, as duty is above all things, I will go."

I can scarcely describe the emotions with which I heard this concession, and requested his permission, which was at once granted, to mention it publicly. Of course you are the first to whom I have named it.

On my return, Mr. Calhoun will do himself the pleasure of visiting you, and has promised me the happiness of accompanying him. He wishes to see you in friendly style at your own house, and in an evening; so I shall inquire from Mr. Plitt if you are at home. I hope to be here in less than ten days.

I have seen Mr. Winthrop and Mr. Crittenden. Both highly approve of Mr. Calhoun for the appointment to England. Also Mr. Benton, who would cordially assent; and Mr. Hannegan expressed the highest respect for Mr. C. The two first answered for their party and the country. Benton thought it would be a universally popular movement. Hannegan included his party in his own expressions of respect.

I could not, my dear Mr. Buchanan, leave Washington happily without telling you these circumstances, and confiding them to your wisdom and experience for any use you may deem them eligible.

Looking forward to seeing you shortly again, I remain always, with the highest respect, your obliged and grateful friend,
Sarah Mytton Maury.
[FROM MRS. MAURY.]
Washington, June 14, 1846.
My Dear Sir:—

I was sorry to find that you have suffered from indisposition. I went to Coleman's last night to inquire for you, but found Mr. and Mrs. Plitt absent.

Will you tell me that you are well, or at least better? and will you let me come and see you? and say how soon.

I have a letter, or rather a lecture, from the bishop this morning; not on religion, but morality. He has, however, made me a proposition so singularly flattering and unexpected that I wish to tell you of it.

If you are going to England, how delighted I should be if you were to go in the same steamer with myself and my son, the Great Britain of the first August. But perhaps you would have a ship of war.

I think you would like England and the English upon a near acquaintance, and your sincerity of purpose and warmth of heart would interest their esteem and affections most strongly. But how could you be spared from home, for there is no other Secretary of State in the Cabinet? My hopes of the Ministry to England, if you do not go, are for Calhoun, because he could set the people there right on the slave question, and also, I believe, he would do much to get the duties on tobacco reduced in England.

Though the treaty (making) is on the 49th, I shall, in writing, enforce the superior claims of America, and treat the whole arrangement as a concession on the part of the United States. Yours it will be, yours it must be; and however unpopular may be this doctrine in England, such inevitably will be the ultimate conclusion. To-morrow Mrs. Madison takes me under her wing to pay my farewell respects to Mrs. Polk. I will also call on the President for five minutes before I leave Washington.

The Emigrant Surgeon's Bill will be lost, but, thanks to the admonitions of the excellent bishop and to your expressions of praise and sympathy, I shall bear the disappointment without repining, and trust to do more for those unfortunates at a future time.

How can I ask you to read this long note, and to see me too? But you have made me bold by indulgence, for you have never refused me any one request.

Believe me, my dear Mr. Buchanan, most respectfully your sincere and grateful friend,
Sarah Mytton Maury.

614[FROM MRS. MAURY.]
Barnum's Hotel,
Baltimore, Friday, July 10, 1846

}
My Dear Mr. Buchanan:—

I received your kind and considerate note, and have laid it with the letter you wrote to me in New Orleans to carry home for my husband.

Mr. Calhoun called at eleven, and stayed some time with me. Though I assured him over and over again that I only repeated, both to the President and to you, the exact words which he himself had used, and that I mentioned at the same time distinctly that the whole responsibility was mine,—and mine alone,—still Mr. Calhoun is fearful that you should misunderstand him—I therefore said that in a few days I promised myself the pleasure of writing to you, and that I would again mention to you his scrupulous delicacy of feeling on this subject. I thought of you, dear Mr. Buchanan, on Sunday, and wished that I could have been present at your interview—the conversation of two distinguished men is the highest privilege and advantage that a woman can enjoy, and I should have derived more pleasure from listening than I ever do from talking;—though my reputation for silence is not, I fear, very well established—at least so says our playful friend Ingersoll. We have visited Emmittsburg since we left Washington, and all the institutions in Baltimore—among others the Penitentiary, where they permitted three English prisoners to come and speak with me—they were well looking men, all acknowledging the justice of their punishment, and apparently cured of their evil propensities. This evening we take the boat for Philadelphia, a cooler and pleasanter mode for travelling than the railroad, and shall arrive about four in the morning. After spending Sunday there we shall reach New York on Monday afternoon.

This hotel has many guests at present, among them are some Creole families—all very pleasant and intelligent—they are full of anecdotes of the war, and all the ladies are in love with the Captain-general La Vega. Mrs. Commodore Stewart, of somewhat eccentric character, is of the number, and informs me that the Mexican enjoys himself greatly, and is most hospitably entertained.

448

How shocked you must have been at the death of Mrs. Ogle Tayloe. I had sat an hour with her on Friday. She was then very ill, and our conversation became serious. Our acquaintance had been only general, and had entirely arisen from her hospitality towards me; but I imagine that often previous to solemn events, we become intimate and confidential, and thus it was with us, and truly she was a good and pious woman. From what I learned at Mrs. Madison's door on Saturday, there is much to fear both for her and her niece, and how sad it is to think of. Sometimes I am led to marvel at the singular favor which has been hitherto granted to me, that of perfect health to all my little ones, and restored health to myself and son during our long absence from home. When I shall arrive there and find all 615 well, I shall not fail to write and tell you, for I flatter myself that the advances which I have made in your good opinion will never be obliterated by my absence, whether temporary or permanent, and truly I shall ever hear of you either as presiding in the councils of the Republic, or adorning the ease and elegance of private life, with sincere and heartfelt interest.

I paid my respects to-day to the Chief Justice;[107] he bestowed a delightful half hour upon me, and gave me his parting benediction and kindest wishes. His health is much improved since the winter.

In Baltimore as in Washington the same perplexity exists about a Secretary of State. No one is spoken of, and it would almost seem that people do not realize your resignation. Must it be so? You know that in England we have abandoned the precedent of the minister's retiring on a change of measures. Such, if I remember right, was the course of Earl Grey, he withstood even the majorities against the Reform Bill, and continued at the helm.

To make Mr. Calhoun feel satisfied that you should understand him thoroughly, I have written the above, but you have encouraged me to speak freely with you on all matters, and therefore I shall add as my supplement to his message, that in case you should see the advantage of Mr. Calhoun's holding office, I sincerely hope that you and the President will make out a strong case, and overrule his delicacy; besides, he is very powerful. My confidence in him is as unlimited as it is in you, for you are both equally noble, finely tempered, faithful and pure.

Dear Mr. Buchanan, do not forget me, for I shall relate in England the considerate solicitude which you have exercised in my behalf. At your hands I have received all the assistance, all the protection which I had anticipated from the minister of my country, and my advice to all who like myself are alone and unattended will be, trust yourselves to the courtesy of the Americans, they will never fail you.

Always believe me, most sincerely, most gratefully,
Your English friend,
Sarah Mytton Maury.

P. S.—I think I should add in confidence to you that should any difficulties arise out of the Mexican war between the United States and England, Mr. Calhoun would consider it his duty, if requested by the President, to give his services in an official capacity;—of course I leave it to your judgment, to use this information as you think best, and I believe Mr. Calhoun would at once acquiesce, should such a case present itself.

[FROM MRS. MAURY.]
Liverpool, November 3, 1846.
My Dear Mr. Buchanan:—

I am wearying to write you a long letter, and first let me offer you my best congratulations on the recent successes in Monterey;—this Mexican war 616 must give you much anxiety, from the various difficulties which General Taylor has had to encounter in a country scarcely known, and where the climate was new and therefore trying to his troops. I was delighted to observe that the President had made offers of peace, because such a step is worthy of a great, and powerful, and magnanimous nation; thus a wise parent offers to his refractory child, or a forbearing friend to his companion, constant and kindly proposals of peace, pitying the recklessness and stupidity which continue to prompt a refusal of their proffered tenderness.

The ill-fated Great Britain carried myself and my doctor home in safety. Our passage was agreeable, and the recollection of it makes me feel much for the ship, and for her commander. Poor Captain Hawkens had taken leave of his wife, who was not expected to live many hours, just before he sailed. She has since rallied, but only for a season. In a few moments he seemed to lose everything that would render life desirable—his fortune and his fame, and the partner of his life. There is no doubt that the Great Britain had outrun her reckoning. My husband who is the chairman of the Marine Insurance Company has voted in favor of giving her a chance through the aid of a well-experienced engineer; but nothing can be done until the spring, and she will have much to suffer during the winter, besides the danger of rusting.

I have had a most pleasant chit-chat letter from Mrs. Plitt, giving me all the details of our various friends; I have also heard from the bishop who is still suffering from the refractory tooth, and still with extraordinary pertinacity refusing "to pluck it out, and cast it from him." I am going this day to write and upbraid his "holiness" with neglecting to practise what he preaches. Mr. Ingersoll tells me that he is again a candidate for Congress, and I most earnestly hope he will be successful on account of the vexatious affair which occurred in the spring. Nothing has contributed more to my happiness than your gentlemanly and considerate expressions of unabated regard for my guardian. His letter is like himself, unreserved in confidence, and always a most pleasant mingling of smiles and tears.

I called with my husband to pay our respects to Mr. and Mrs. Bancroft. They had a stormy passage, and Mrs. B. was suffering from the effects of it. The American Chamber of Commerce, of which my husband is the treasurer, waited upon the minister with their best wishes and welcome. He made a very appropriate speech, and acquitted himself extremely well. His manners are less popular than those of McLane, but I predict that he will be highly esteemed and respected here. Mrs. B. is quite a nice woman, and the American ladies have a naïveté which I hear is much admired as a contrast to the sameness of manner which necessarily exists among the aristocratic ladies of an old country. They see none but the artificial phases of society.

I have been in London a month, and have had an interview with the commissioners of the board of emigration, Mr. Elliot and Mr. Rogers. They entered fully into the subject of the Emigrant Surgeon's Bill. I told them your opinion, and gave them among other documents the report of the expenses of whaling vessels for sickness; they regard it as a very important statement 617in our favor. I believe them both to be in earnest, and the more especially as they requested me to procure for them various kinds of information relative to the supply of surgeons having taken out diplomas in Liverpool, Dublin, New York, etc. Of course I have lost no time in setting the requisite machinery to work. The commissioners frankly stated that the shipowners would make the same difficulties that Mr. Grinnell had conjured up on the other side. As the bill will have to go through parliament, of course it will be some time before I hear anything from the board; but as soon as I do, I shall hasten to inform you who have been so valuable an ally to me.

Accompanied by my husband, I had afterwards an interview with Lord Palmerston, and after showing him the letter which I wrote in January last from Washington, on the subject of Pakenham's unfitness for his position there, I fortified the report by several anecdotes. The secretary looked perplexed, heard me most patiently, and when I had ended my story, endeavored as well as he could to defend his representative. As far as respectful politeness allowed me to go, I entirely differed from him, and I said that he was quite unequal in capacity to the men he had to deal with; that he knew nothing of commerce; received neither the Americans nor the English at his house; had quarrelled with the chairman of foreign relations in the House of Representatives; and in fact that this government should send one of their foremost men to Washington with rank, wealth, good manners, and ability to carry him through.

Lord Palmerston then observed:

"Well, they have got more than they bargained for."

Mrs. M.—They will have the whole of Oregon very soon, my lord.

Lord P.—Do you really think so?

Mrs. M.—Certainly, and the Pope is doing all he can to help them. He has just divided the Oregon into an archbishopric and eight bishoprics, and the Irish and German emigrants will pour in by thousands.

Lord P.—I had not observed that. Is it so, indeed?

Mrs. M.—Undoubtedly.

Here laughing, I rose to take leave. The viscount was extremely courteous, and expressed much pleasure at having made my acquaintance. It is somewhat strange that I should have had the opportunity of expressing these sentiments to yourself and Mrs. Walker in Washington, in the presence of the British minister, and also in England to the secretary for foreign affairs.

And now, my dear Mr. Buchanan, I am going to my old trade of begging favors, and have still a long story to tell you by way of introduction. I have wished to prepare a work with the title of "An English Woman's Opinions of America," in compliance with the gratifying wishes of my friends both here and in America; but I cannot get this ready for some months, for you know I have eleven children, and found much to do for them on my return, besides I have had much to do for my husband in the way of business, and the daily congratulations of my numerous friends here to receive, and to return.

618In the meantime, however, I am trying to get ready the "Statesmen of America," that is, my own sketches of their characters, etc., with extracts from their works or speeches. While reading over to my husband the two charming letters you have written to me, it occurred to me that I would ask your permission to place them before my friends here to show that the American statesmen are as elegant in their private correspondence as they are able in their public documents. I have made a mark with a pencil through the opening of the paragraph relating to Mr. Calhoun; but I should dearly like to publish your opinion of him. Mr. Panizzi of the British Museum Library is in love with these letters, and he is head authority in all literary matters. I enclose them for your perusal, because I have thought you might wish to see them before granting me permission to publish them; but whether you grant me this permission or decline it, pray restore me the letters. I cherish with jealous care every memorial of those who made me so happy when among them. My husband begs that you will accept his most grateful and respectful thanks for all your goodness to me. Forgive me, dear Mr. Buchanan, this unconscionable letter and its long weariness, and believe me always most respectfully and affectionately your friend,

Sarah M. Maury.

[FROM MADAME CALDERON.[108]]

Newport, August 1st, 1846.
Dear Mr. Buchanan:—

As I see a letter for Calderon this morning in your handwriting, I think it as well to let you know that he has gone to New York on business, in case there should be any delay in his answer. Calderon tells us that there is some chance of your coming to New York, which I hope is the case. I am anxious to inquire into the progress of your domestic affairs, and whether I have more chance than I formerly had of finding Mrs. Buchanan when I call at your house. I think, now that you have settled Oregon and the tariff, and are in a fair way of disposing of Mexico, it is time for you to look at home, and bring about the annexation of a certain fair neighbor of ours. Newport is very cool: we have not had a single really hot day. I hope you have stood the heat of Washington better than Calderon did. We are living very quietly here as to society, but with bathing, riding, fishing, etc., pass our time very agreeably. We are at this moment nine ladies in one house, and no gentlemen.
Pray remember me to Mr. Pleasonton and his family the next time you go there, and especially to my friend Miss Clementina. My sister and nieces beg their best regards, and I remain
Yours very truly and respectfully,
Fanny Calderon de le Barca.
619
CHAPTER XXII.
1848–1849.

CENTRAL AMERICA—THE MONROE DOCTRINE, AND THE CLAYTON-BULWER TREATY.

To give an account of every public transaction with which Mr. Buchanan was connected as Secretary of State, would be impracticable within the limits of these volumes. But there remains one subject which must not be overlooked—the affairs of Central America, and the position in which they stood before the negotiation of the Clayton-Bulwer Treaty. The policy of Mr. Polk's administration towards the States of Central America and on the subject of the Monroe Doctrine was shaped by Mr. Buchanan very differently from that adopted by the succeeding administration of General Taylor, whose Secretary of State was Mr. Clayton, the American negotiator of the Clayton-Bulwer Treaty with Great Britain. In 1845, when the war between the United States and Mexico was impending, there was reason to believe that England was aiming to obtain a footing in the then Mexican province of California, by an extensive system of colonization. Acting under Mr. Buchanan's advice, President Polk, in his first annual message of December 2, 1845, not only re-asserted the Monroe Doctrine in general terms, but distinctly declared that no future European colony or dominion shall, with the consent of the United States, be planted or established on any part of the North American continent. This declaration was confined to North America, in order to make it emphatically applicable to California. The effect was that the British plan of colonization in California was given up. Two years afterward, when the Mexican war was drawing to a close, after the capture of the City of Mexico in September, 1847, Mr. Buchanan turned the attention of President Polk to the encroachments of the British 620government in Central America, under the operation of a protectorate over the king and kingdom of the Mosquito Indians. In his annual message of December 7, 1847, the President, after reiterating the Monroe Doctrine, asked for an appropriation to defray the expense of a chargé d'affaires to Guatemala, the most prosperous and important of the Central American states. The appropriation was made, and in April, 1848, the chargé was appointed. But before his departure a state of things occurred in Yucatan, which made it necessary for the President to make a fresh and solemn declaration of his purpose to maintain the Monroe Doctrine at every hazard against Great Britain and all other European powers. This was the war of extermination waged by the Indians against the white population of Yucatan in 1847–48. If not actually incited by the British authorities, the savages were known to be supplied with British muskets. The whites were reduced to such extremities that the authorities of Yucatan offered to transfer the dominion and sovereignty of the peninsula to the United States, as a consideration for defending it against the Indians, at the same time giving notice that if this offer should be declined, they would make the same proposition to England and Spain. By a special message sent to Congress on the 29th of April, 1848, President Polk recommended to Congress the appeal of Yucatan for aid and protection against the Indians, but he declined to recommend the adoption of any measure with a view to acquire the dominion and sovereignty over the peninsula. But it was necessary for him to announce what would be his policy should Great Britain or Spain accept a similar offer. Anticipating that England might take advantage of such an offer to establish over Yucatan such another protectorate as that which she claimed to exercise over the Mosquito coast, the President, at the close of his message, recommended to Congress "to adopt such measures as, in their judgment, may be expedient to prevent Yucatan from becoming a colony of any European power, which, in no event, could be permitted by the United States, and, at the same time, to rescue the white men from extermination or expulsion from their country."

It then became necessary for Mr. Buchanan to consider how the removal of the British government from their assumed protectorate 621over the Indians of the Mosquito Coast could be best accomplished. He was convinced that the best thing to be done would be to re-unite the Central States of America in a federation, so that they could aid each other and be in a condition to receive aid from the United States. Accordingly, with the approbation of the President, on the 3d of June, Mr. Buchanan instructed Mr. Hise, the new chargé to Guatemala, as follows:

"When the federation of the centre of America was formed, the Government and people of the United States entertained the highest hopes and felt the warmest desire for its success and prosperity. Its government was that of a federal republic, composed of the five states of Guatemala, Honduras, Nicaragua, St. Salvador, and Costa Rica; and its constitution nearly resembled that of the United States. This constitution unfortunately endured but a brief period, and the different states of Central America are now politically independent of each other. The consequence is that each of them is so feeble as to invite aggressions from foreign powers. Whilst it is our intention to maintain our established policy of non-intervention in the concerns of foreign nations, you are instructed, by your counsel and advice should suitable occasions offer, to promote the reunion of the states which formed the federation of Central America. In a federal union among themselves consists their strength. They will thus avoid domestic dissensions, and render themselves respected by the world. These truths you can impress upon them by the most powerful arguments.

A principal object of your mission is to cultivate the most friendly relations with Guatemala. It is now an independent sovereignty, and is by far the most populous and powerful of the states of the former federation. Whilst representing your Government at Guatemala, however, you will enjoy frequent opportunities of cultivating friendly relations between the United States and the other states of Central America, which you will not fail to embrace.

The enemies of free institutions throughout the world have been greatly encouraged by the constantly recurring revolutions and changes in the Spanish-American republics. They are thus furnished with arguments against the capacity of man for self-government. The President and people of the United States have viewed these incessant changes with the most profound regret. Both our principles and our policy make us desire that these republics should become prosperous and powerful. We feel a deep interest in their welfare; but this we know can only be promoted by free and stable governments. The enjoyment of liberty and the maintenance of private rights cannot be secured without permanent order; and this can only spring from the sacred observance of law. So long as successive military chieftains shall possess the ability and the will to subvert subsisting governments by the 622sword, the inevitable consequences must be a disregard of personal rights, weakness at home, and want of character abroad. In your intercourse with the authorities of Guatemala and other states of Central America, you will not fail to impress upon them our example, where all political controversies are decided at the ballot-box.

I have no doubt that the dissolution of the confederacy of Central America has encouraged Great Britain in her encroachments upon the territories of Honduras, Nicaragua and Costa Rica, under the mask of protecting the so-called kingdom of the Mosquitos. We learn that under this pretext she has now obtained possession of the harbor of San Juan de Nicaragua—probably the best harbor along the whole coast. Her object in this acquisition is evident from the policy which she has uniformly pursued throughout her past history—of seizing upon every valuable commercial point throughout the world, whenever circumstances have placed this in her power. Her purpose probably is to obtain the control of the route for a railroad and a canal between the Atlantic and Pacific oceans, by the way of Lake Nicaragua. In a document prepared, as it is understood, by Mr. Macgregor, and printed by order of the British Parliament, which has been furnished to me by Mr. Crampton, her Britannic Majesty's chargé d'affaires to the United States, Great Britain claims the whole of the sea-coast for the king of the Mosquitos, from Cape Honduras to Escuda de Veragua. By this means she would exclude from the Caribbean Sea the whole of Honduras south of Cape Honduras, and the entire states of Nicaragua and Costa Rica, as well as the New Granadian state of Veragua. Under the assumed title of protector of the kingdom of the Mosquitos—a miserable, degraded and insignificant tribe of Indians—she doubtless intends to acquire an absolute dominion over this vast extent of sea-coast. With what little reason she advances this pretension appears from the convention between Great Britain and Spain, signed at London on the 14th day of July, 1786. By its first article, "His Britannic Majesty's subjects, and the other colonists who have hitherto enjoyed the protection of England, shall evacuate the country of the Mosquitos, as well as the continent in general and the islands adjacent, without exception, situated beyond the line hereafter described as what ought to be the frontier of the extent of territory granted by his Catholic majesty to the English for the uses specified in the third article of the present convention, and in addition to the country already granted to them in virtue of the stipulations agreed upon by the commissioners of the two crowns in 1783."

The country granted to them under the treaties of 1783 and 1786 was altogether embraced in the present British provinces of Belize, and was remote from what is now claimed to be the Mosquito kingdom. The uses specified in the third article of the convention were merely, in addition to that of "cutting wood for dyeing," the grant of the liberty of cutting all other wood, without even excepting mahogany, as well as gathering all the fruits or produce of the earth, purely natural and uncultivated, which may, besides being carried away in their natural state, become an object of utility or of commerce, 623whether for food or for manufactures; but it is expressly agreed that this stipulation is never to be used as a pretext for establishing in that country any plantation of sugar, coffee, cocoa, or other like articles, or any fabric or manufacture, by means of mills or other machines whatsoever. (This restriction, however, does not regard the use of sawmills for cutting or otherwise preparing the wood.) Since all the lands in question being indisputably acknowledged to belong of right to the crown of Spain, no settlements of that kind, or the population that would follow, could be allowed. "The English shall be permitted to transport and convey all such wood and other produce of the place in its natural and uncultivated state down the rivers to the sea; but without ever going beyond the limits which are prescribed to them by the stipulations above granted, and without thereby taking an opportunity of ascending the said rivers beyond their bounds into the countries belonging to Spain."

And yet from this simple permission within certain limits to cut and carry away all the different kinds of wood and "the produce of the earth, uncultivated and purely natural," accompanied by the most solemn acknowledgment on the part of Great Britain that all the lands in question "belong of right to the crown of Spain," she has by successive encroachments established the British colony of the Belize.

The Government of the United States has not yet determined what course it will pursue in regard to the encroachments of the British government as protector of the king and kingdom of the Mosquitos; but you are instructed to obtain all the information within your power upon the nature and extent of these encroachments, and communicate it with the least possible delay to this department. We are also desirous to learn the number of the Mosquito tribe, the degree of civilization they have attained, and everything else concerning them.

The independence, as well as the interests of the nations on this continent, require that they should maintain an American system of policy, entirely distinct from that which prevails in Europe. To suffer any interference on the part of the European governments with the domestic concerns of the American republics, and to permit them to establish new colonies upon this continent, would be to jeopard their independence and ruin their interests. These truths ought everywhere throughout this continent to be impressed upon the public mind; but what can the United States do to resist such European interference whilst the Spanish American republics continue to weaken themselves by division and civil war, and deprive themselves of the ability of doing anything for their own protection?

Mr. Hise was prevented by illness and other causes from reaching Guatemala until a late period in Mr. Polk's administration, and before any despatches were received from him Mr. Polk had ceased to be President. The plan wisely conceived 624by Mr. Buchanan and adopted by President Polk, for uniting the States of Central America in a new federation, which, by the aid of the United States, could compel the surrender of the British protectorate, was not carried out by their successors, although it descended to them in the best possible shape. In the mean time, the British government, taking advantage of the wretched internal condition of those States, had undertaken to extend the dominions of the puppet king of the Mosquitos far beyond their former pretensions, and in February, 1848, had seized upon the port of San Juan de Nicaragua, expelled the State from it, and thus deprived her and the State of Costa Rica of the only good harbor along the coast. To counteract this encroachment and to enable the Central States, by uniting them, to demand the withdrawal of the protectorate asserted by Great Britain, was the purpose for which Mr. Hise was sent to Guatemala. Instead of taking up and carrying out this policy, the succeeding administration of General Taylor, without consulting the States of Central America, entered into the Clayton-Bulwer Treaty, concluded April 19, 1850, the ratifications being exchanged July 4, 1850.

It is necessary to make a brief analysis of this treaty, because Mr. Buchanan, when he became minister to England under President Pierce, had to do what he could to unravel the complications to which the ambiguous language of the treaty had given rise. There were two provisions in the first article of the treaty which need separate examination. By the first of them, the contracting parties stipulated that neither of them should ever exercise exclusive control over the ship-canal that was to be constructed between the Atlantic and Pacific oceans by the way of the river San Juan de Nicaragua, or erect any fortifications commanding it. The treaty then proceeded to declare that neither of the parties shall ever "occupy, or fortify, or colonize, or exercise any dominion over Nicaragua, Costa Rica, the Mosquito coast, or any part of Central America." One general objection to this provision was, that so long as it should remain in operation it would preclude the United States from ever annexing to their dominions any state of Central America, even if such state should desire to come into our Union. But the last clause of the first article of the treaty was the one which led to the subsequent controversy. Instead of a simple provision requiring Great Britain absolutely to recede from the Mosquito protectorate, and to restore to Honduras, Nicaragua, and Costa Rica their respective territories, the treaty declared as follows: "Nor will either [of the parties] make use of any protection which either affords or may afford, or any alliance which either has or may have, to or with any state or people, for the purpose of erecting or maintaining any such fortifications, or of occupying, fortifying, or colonizing Nicaragua, Costa Rica, the Mosquito Coast, or any part of Central America, or of assuming or exercising any dominion over the same."

It soon became the British construction of this clause that it recognized the existence of the Mosquito protectorate for all purposes other than those expressly prohibited. Under this construction, Great Britain claimed that she could still direct and influence the Mosquito king in the administration of his government; and down to the time when Mr. Buchanan was sent by President Pierce as minister to England, this claim was still maintained. On the other hand, taking all its provisions together and interpreting them according to the fair meaning of the stipulations as applied to the facts, the treaty was understood in this country to bind the British government not to exercise in any part of Central America any "dominion," either through the name and authority of the titular king of the Mosquitos, or otherwise; or in other words not to exercise dominion, either directly or indirectly. Manifestly the treaty was destined to be a source of discord between Great Britain and the United States; and when, as will hereafter be seen, it devolved upon the administration of President Pierce to meet the British construction, there was an imperative necessity for Mr. Buchanan's services as minister to Great Britain, in order that this and other pending questions between the two governments might be adjusted without further hazard of more serious collision.

NOTE.

On page 459 of this volume, it should have been stated that the charge of "treachery" made by Mr. Clay and the Whigs generally against President Tyler, was chiefly based on the assertions that the first Bank bill (passed August 6th, 1841), was framed by Mr. Ewing, Secretary of the Treasury, and approved by the President and his Cabinet; that it was vetoed on the ground of essential alterations; that the second bill was framed to meet his special objections, was privately submitted to him and approved before its passage, but vetoed afterwards. The central point in the Whig charge is that Mr. Tyler vetoed a bill which he had promised to approve, and which was first submitted to him in order that its terms might be altered, or that the whole might be abandoned, if he could not approve it.

It has not been my intention in this work to express any opinion upon the conduct of President Tyler in relation to the Bank bills. In the Life of Mr. Webster, the reader will find, at pages 69 to 80 of the first volume, his explanations of the whole difficulty. But since page 459 of the present volume was written and stereotyped, I have thought it proper to advert, without comment, to the precise character of the Whig charge against Mr. Tyler, lest it might be said that I have omitted to refer to an important part of the history.

1. Under the date of September 13, 1813, Mr. Buchanan's father writes to him: "Yesterday the fast day was kept here pretty unanimously. Mr. Elliot gave us an excellent sermon, and spoke of the war as a judgment, and the greatest calamity that could befall a people. He showed it to be worse than the famine or the pestilence. In the two latter cases, he said God acted as the immediate agent: in that of war he acted by subordinate agents; therefore the calamity was the greater." This was the tone of many Federalist sermons.

2. "There is extant, according to the best of my recollection in the National Intelligencer, though not in Everett's edition of his works, a speech of Mr. Webster in 1814, in the House of Representatives, on the 'Conduct of the War.' It is very severe on the military operations, especially in Canada (which no doubt, as a general thing, deserved all that was said of them), but he dwells with pride on our naval exploits. 'However,' says he, 'we may differ as to what has been done or attempted on land, our differences cease at the water's edge.'" (Note by Mr. Buchanan.)

3. I find a memorandum in Mr. Buchanan's handwriting of his professional emoluments during his years of active practice.

1813	$938	1821–2	$11,297
1814	$1,096	1823	$7,243
1815	$2,246	1825	$4,521
1816	$3,174	1826	$2,419
1817	$5,379	1827	$2,570
1818	$7,915	1828	$2,008
1819	$7,092	1829	$3,362
1820	$5,665		

4. These and other papers of importance were sent by Mr. Buchanan from Wheatland to a bank in New York during the Civil War, when Pennsylvania was threatened with an invasion by the Confederate troops.

5. Conversing once in London with an intimate friend, very much younger than himself (Mr. S. L. M. Barlow of New York), Mr. Buchanan said: "I never intended to engage in politics, but meant to follow my profession strictly. But my prospects and plans were all changed by a most sad event which happened at Lancaster when I was a young man. As a distraction from my great grief, and because I saw that through a political following I could secure the friends I then needed, I accepted a nomination."

6. Mr. Thompson, Secretary of the Navy, was appointed to the Bench of the Supreme Court in December, 1823, and Mr. Southard, of New Jersey, took his place.

7. These notes were written by Mr. Buchanan in 1867.

8. Benton's Thirty Years in the Senate, Vol. I, p. 19.

9. In the debate on Chilton's Resolutions, in 1825, Mr. Sergeant said:

"At the head of the Committee of Ways and Means in 1816, was one who could not be remembered without feelings of deep regret at the public loss occasioned by his early death. He possessed, in an uncommon degree, the confidence of this House, and he well deserved it. With so much accurate knowledge, and with powers which enabled him to delight and instruct the House, there was united so much gentleness and kindness, and such real, unaffected modesty, that you were prepared to be subdued before he exerted his commanding powers of argument. I mean William Lowndes of South Carolina."—Benton's Debates, Vol. IX, 730.

10. Art. I., § 8.—"To lay and collect taxes, duties, imposts, and excises, to pay the debts and provide for the common defence and general welfare of the United States; but all duties, imposts, and excises shall be uniform throughout the United States."

11. February 21, 1823.

12. Post.

13. Mr. Gorham's speech has not been preserved.

14. The phrase "Presidential Election" is an awkward and incorrect one. But it has been sanctioned by long usage, and I adopt it because of its convenience.

15. Mr. Crawford was regarded as out of the question, both because he had less than one-half of the electoral votes, and because a recent paralytic affection was supposed to have rendered him incapable of performing the duties of the office.

16. The person here alluded to was the Hon. Molton C. Rogers, Chairman of the State Central Committee at Harrisburg, and Secretary of the State of Pennsylvania. He was afterwards a Judge of the Supreme Court of that State.

17. At a little later period, Mr. Webster was transferred from the House to the Senate, and became there one of the strongest and most conspicuous of the friends of the administration.

18. Joint Resolutions of 13th and 24th March, 1779. See Journals, pages 335, 336, 342. 1 Smith's Laws, 487. Life of Joseph Reed, President of the Supreme Executive Council of Pennsylvania, Vol. II, p. 65.

19. The peroration of Mr. Everett's speech was as follows:

"The present year completes the half century since the Declaration of Independence; and most devoutly do I hope, that, when the silver trumpet of our political jubilee sounds, it may be with a note of comfort and joy to the withered heart of the war-worn veteran of the Revolution. Our tardy provision will, indeed, come too late to help him through the hard journey of life; it will not come too late to alleviate the sorrows of age, and smooth the pillow of decline. It is the fiftieth year of our Independence. How much shall we read, how much shall we hear, how much, perhaps, we shall say this year, about the glorious exploits of our fathers, and the debt of gratitude we owe them. I do not wish this to be all talk. I want to do something. I want a substantial tribute to be paid them. Praise is sweet music, both to old and young; but I honestly confess that my mind relucts and revolts, by anticipation, at the thought of the compliments with which we are going to fill the ears of these poor veterans, while we leave their pockets empty, and their backs cold. If we cast out this bill, I do hope that some member of this House, possessing an influence to which I cannot aspire, will introduce another, to make it penal to say a word on the fourth of July, about the debt of gratitude which we owe to the heroes of the Revolution. Let the day and the topic pass in decent silence. I hate all gag-laws; but there is one thing I am willing to gag—the vaporing tongue of a bankrupt, who has grown rich, and talks sentiment, about the obligation he feels to his needy creditor, whom he paid off at 2s. 6d. in the pound."

20. In the course of his speech on the 14th of April, Mr. Webster said: "The gentleman from Pennsylvania, with whom I have great pleasure in concurring on this part of the case, while I regret that I differ with him on others, has placed this question in a point of

view which can not be improved. These officers do indeed already exist. They are public ministers. If they were to negotiate a treaty, and the Senate should ratify it, it would become a law of the land, whether we voted their salaries or not. This shows that the Constitution never contemplated that the House of Representatives should act a part in originating negotiations or concluding treaties." Mr. Webster made further observations, in confirmation of the views expressed by Mr. Buchanan on the duty of making the appropriation. (Works of Daniel Webster, Vol. III, p. 181.)

21. The subsequent fate of this measure can be related very briefly. Mr. Anderson died at Carthagena, on his way to the isthmus of Panama. The "Congress" adjourned to meet at Tacuboya, a village near the city of Mexico. Mr. Poinsett was appointed in the place of Mr. Anderson, and Mr. Sargeant sailed for Vera Cruz on the 2d of December, 1826. He arrived in Mexico in January, 1827, and found a few fragments of the "Congress" floating about, without action or organization. Bolivar, who was supposed to have originated the project, had changed his mind. Mr. Sargeant remained for six months in Mexico, and in the summer of 1827 returned home.

22. This allusion to Mr. Everett requires some explanation. On the 9th of March, 1826, he made a speech on the proposed Constitutional Amendment, in the course of which he said:
"I am not one of those citizens of the North who think it immoral and irreligious to join in putting down a servile insurrection at the South. I am no soldier, my habits and education are very un-military; but there is no cause in which I would sooner buckle a knapsack to my back, and put a musket on my shoulder, than that. I would cede the whole continent to any one who would take it—to England, to France, to Spain; I would see it sunk in the bottom of the ocean, before I would see any part of this fair America converted into a Continental Hayti, by that awful process of bloodshed and desolation, by which alone such a catastrophe could be brought on. The great relation of servitude, in some form or other, with greater or less departures from the theoretic equality of man, is inseparable from our nature. I know no way by which the form of this servitude shall be fixed, but by political institution. Domestic slavery, though, I confess, not that form of servitude which seems to be most beneficial to the master—certainly not that which is most beneficial to the servant—is not, in my judgment, to be set down as an immoral and irreligious relation. I cannot admit that Religion has but one voice to the slave, and that this voice is, 'Rise against your master.' No, Sir, the New Testament says, 'Slaves obey your masters,' and though I know full well that, in the benignant operations of Christianity, which gathered master and slave around the same communion table, this unfortunate institution disappeared in Europe, yet I cannot admit that, while it subsists, and where it subsists, its duties are not pre-supposed and sanctioned by religion. I certainly am not called upon to meet the charges brought against this institution, yet truth obliges me to say a word more on the subject. I know the condition of the working classes in other countries, and I have no hesitation in saying that I believe the slaves of this country are better clothed and fed, and less hardly worked, than the peasantry of some of the most prosperous States of the continent of Europe."

23. Mr. Buchanan's speech extended through two sessions of the Committee of the Whole. After some amendments by the Senate, the bill was finally passed, and was approved by the President May 19, 1828. The speech may be found in Gales & Seaton's Register of Debates, Vol. IV, Part 2, page 2089, et seq.

24. Mr. Buchanan's proposal was not adopted, and on the 2d of March, 1829, the President, Mr. Adams, approved "An act for the continuation of the Cumberland Road." Mr. Buchanan voted against this bill, saying that he did so reluctantly, but that now the

House had voted to keep the Cumberland Road in repair, by erecting toll-gates upon it under the authority of the Federal Government, and so long as this pretension continued to be set up, he would not vote for the construction of any road intended, after its completion, to be thus placed under the jurisdiction of the United States, as he believed it to be entirely unconstitutional.

25. This allusion to the Secretaryship of the Russian Mission was, of course, merely playful. George Buchanan had no thought of seeking this appointment, nor would his brother have asked for it.

26. Colonel Benton, writing to Mr. Randolph on the 26th of May, said: "Your nomination came up this morning, and was acted upon with great promptness. Tyler called it, but before it was called it was understood that the opposition would support it unanimously. This they did with some degree of empressement. Several voices from their side called for the question as soon as Tyler sat down, among them Louisiana Johnston, and Webster, were most audible. There were no yeas and nays, and nothing said by any person but Tyler, and only a few words by him, and those of course complimentary; the opposition evidently wishing to be observed as supporting it. Everybody is asking me whether you will accept. I tell them what surprises many, but not those who know you, that not a word between you and me had ever passed on such a subject."

27. In this debate, it was charged that the President's Message was written by Mr. Van Buren, the Secretary of State, and that General Jackson was incapable of writing his official papers. It is very probably true that he did not write some of them. His Proclamation against the Nullifiers is generally assumed to have been written by Edward Livingston. But that General Jackson was capable of writing well, there can be no doubt. I remember, however, that in my youth, during his Presidency, it was generally believed in New England among his political opponents that he was an entirely illiterate man, who could not write an English sentence grammatically, or spell correctly. This belief was too much encouraged by persons who knew better; and it was not until many years afterwards that I learned how unfounded it was. There now lie before me autograph letters of General Jackson, written wholly with his own hand, and written and punctuated with entire correctness, and with no small power of expression. Some of them have been already quoted. These have been, and others will be, printed without the slightest correction. The handwriting is sometimes rather better, for example, than Mr. Webster's. There is not a single erasure in any one of the letters, and but one very trifling interlineation. The spelling is perfectly correct through-out. General Jackson wrote better English than Washington: and as to King George III, the General was an Addison, in comparison with his majesty.

When General Jackson visited New England as President, in the summer of 1833, the Degree of LL.D. was conferred upon him by Harvard College. This was much ridiculed at the time, in that neighborhood, on account of his supposed illiteracy.

28. Mr. Livingston became Secretary of State in May, 1831, in the place of Mr. Van Buren, who resigned in order to be made Minister to England, a post to which he was nominated by the President, but he was not confirmed by the Senate.

29. Mr. afterwards Sir William Brown, an eminent banker of extensive American connections.

30. As Vice-President.

31.

[MRS. BUCHANAN TO HER SON JAMES.]
July 3d, 1821.

My Dear James:— ... A letter from William came to hand on the 11th of June, in which he expressed considerable anxiety to return home, that he might once again see his father and receive his last benediction; but upon receiving the melancholy information of his death, his desire of coming home is subsided. I am highly gratified by the reception from him of a letter of the 18th, in which is exhibited a resignation to and acquiescence in the will of Providence, together with appropriate sentiments on that melancholy occasion, far beyond his years. For this I bless the Giver of every good and perfect gift. Hoping you may be ever the care of an indulgent Providence, and all your conduct regulated by His unerring wisdom, I subscribe myself your affectionate
Mother.

32. It should be said here that the whole course of this negotiation shows that the details of the treaty were entrusted largely to Mr. Buchanan's discretion. At that time, indeed, it was impracticable for an American minister in Europe, and especially at St. Petersburg, to be guided from day to day, or even from month to month, by the Secretary of State. The Atlantic had not then been crossed by steam. I have gone through with the minute discussions which took place between Mr. Buchanan and the Russian Foreign Office, but have not deemed it necessary to display them to my readers. They evince on his part a thorough acquaintance with the whole subject, and a remarkable power of carrying his points.

33. See post an account of Mr. Buchanan's conversation with Pozzo di Borgo in Paris.

34. General Jackson at his second election received 219 electoral votes out of 288.

35. This I believe to have been a mistake, in respect to the nullification ordinance. It was adopted by a State convention, and consequently could only be repealed by another convention. This, I believe, was not done; but the laws based upon this ordinance were probably repealed by the legislature after Mr. Clay's compromise. See the Life of Webster, by the present writer, Vol. I, p. 156.

36. Louis McLane, of Delaware, became Secretary of State in May, 1833. He was succeeded by John Forsyth, of Georgia, in June, 1834.

37. Mrs. Buchanan died on the 14th of May, 1833, at the house of her daughter, Mrs. Lane, in Greensburg, Pennsylvania. The letters of Mrs. Buchanan, of which I have seen many more than I have quoted, although rather formal in expression, show a mind of much cultivation, imbued with a fervent religious spirit, and of very decided and just opinions. In one of her letters to her son James, written in 1822, she says: "Harriet and myself, at the request of Mr. S., a clergyman, are engaged in reading Neale's History of the Puritans, in which I observe a development of Queen Elizabeth's character and management, not much to her honor; however, it appears evident, in opposition to her own intentions, she was made an instrument in the hands of Providence, of promoting the Reformation, which has certainly rendered an essential service to the world." If the good lady had read Mr. Hallam's very impartial account of Elizabeth's management of the two opposite parties among the English Protestants, she would not have had much reason for changing the opinion which she formed from reading Neale, although it would not have been correct to say that the Queen's course was in any just sense dishonorable to her. The truth probably is, that Elizabeth, in nearly everything that she did in regard to religion, was governed by motives of policy, and not by convictions or special inclinations. In many respects, she was not a Protestant, according to the Puritan standard, and in many others she was not a Catholic.

38. George IV.

39. This remarkable woman is regularly chronicled in Encyclopedias and Biographical Dictionaries as a Russian diplomatist. She certainly fulfilled that character in an

extraordinary manner for a period of about forty years. When Mr. Buchanan met her, on his passage down the Baltic, she was on her way to join her husband in London. She was then forty-nine. The children referred to both died in 1835. The princess died at Paris, January 25, 1857, at the age of 73. She is said to have been a Protestant. In her later years she was a very intimate friend of M. Guizot, who was present at her death-bed. See further mention of her, post.

40. Henry Wheaton, the learned author of "Elements of International Law," long in the diplomatic service of the United States.

41. At that time American chargé d'affaires in Paris.

42. Carlo Andrea Pozzo di Borgo was a native of Corsica, born at Ajaccio, in 1764. His efforts, along with those of Paoli, to accomplish the liberation of Corsica from the French power, and place it under the protection of England, produced in him a decided leaning against France through his whole career. In 1803 he entered the diplomatic service of Russia, in which he continued for the remainder of his long life, under both the emperors Alexander I and Nicholas I. He was Russian ambassador at Paris from 1815 to the time of his death, with temporary absences in London on special missions. He died in 1845. At the period of Mr. Buchanan's visit to Paris, di Borgo was seventy years old, with as full and varied a diplomatic experience as any man of his time. He was celebrated for the brilliancy of his conversation in the French language. In the private journal of the late Mr. George Ticknor, written at Paris in ———, I find the following passage: "I do not know how a foreigner has acquired the French genius so completely as to shine in that kind of conversation from which foreigners are supposed to be excluded, but certainly I have seen nobody yet who has the genuine French wit, with its peculiar grace and fluency, so completely in his power, as M. Pozzo di Borgo." In a note to this passage Mr. Ticknor adds: "I have learned since that he is a Corsican, and by a singular concurrence of circumstances, was born in the same town with Bonaparte, and of a family which is in an hereditary opposition to that of the emperor." It was no doubt with singular zest, that di Borgo, in 1814–15, took part in the great European settlement which dethroned Bonaparte.

43. American friends.

44. See post, in relation to this collision between France and the United States.

45. The wife of Prince Talleyrand's nephew, the Duc de Dino.

46. Joshua Bates, Esq., long the American partner of the house of Baring Brothers & Co., and for many years its head.

47. General Jackson's first term extended from March 4th, 1829, to March 4th, 1833. His second term ended March 4th, 1837.

48. Upon this vexed question of instruction there is perhaps no more important distinction than that which was drawn by Mr. Webster in his celebrated speech of March 7, 1850: namely, that where a State has an interest of her own, not adverse to the general interest of the country, a Senator is bound to follow the direction which he receives from the legislature; but if the question be one which affects her interests, and at the same time affects equally the interests of all the other States, the Senator is not bound to obey the will of the State, because he is in the position of an arbitrator or referee. The first proposition seems evident enough, but of course it embraces none but a limited class of questions. It is in the far more numerous cases which fall under the second proposition that the difficulty inherent in the doctrine of instruction arises. Mr. Buchanan, it will be seen hereafter, consistently acted upon the view with which he began his senatorial career.

49. General Jackson himself continued, during his Presidency and after his retirement, in his correspondence to apply to his party the term "Republican."

50. John Sargent of Pennsylvania was the Whig candidate for the Vice-Presidency along with Mr. Clay, and he received the same electoral vote.

51. The secret history of such collisions between governments not infrequently throws an unexpected light upon their public aspects. When General Jackson was preparing his annual message of December, 1834, some of his friends in Washington were very anxious that it should not be too peremptory on the subject of the French payment. At their request, Mr. Justice Catron, of the Supreme Court, waited upon the President, and advised a moderate tone. The President took from his drawer an autograph letter from King Louis Philippe, and handed it to the judge to read. In this letter the king represented that a war between the United States and France would be especially disastrous to the wine-growing districts, and that the interests of those provinces could be relied upon to oppose it; but that it was necessary that the alternative of war should be distinctly presented as certain to follow a final refusal of the Chambers to make the payment demanded. The king therefore urged General Jackson to adopt a very decided tone in his message, being confident that, if he did so, the opposition would give way and war would be avoided.

Another anecdote concerning this message was communicated to the writer from an entirely authentic source. After the message had been written, some of its expressions were softened by a member of the Cabinet, before the MS. was sent to the printer, without the President's knowledge. When it was in type, the confidential proof-reader of the Globe office took the proof-sheets to the President; and he afterwards, said that he never before knew what profane swearing was. General Jackson promptly restored his own language to the proof-sheets.

52. Mr. Ticknor, writing from Paris, February, 1836, said: "One thing, however, has done us much honor. General Jackson's message, as far as France is concerned,—for they know nothing about the rest of it,—has been applauded to the skies. The day it arrived I happened to dine with the Russian minister here, in a party of about thirty persons, and I assure you it seemed to me as if nine-and-twenty of them came up to me with congratulations. I was really made to feel awkward at last; but this has been the tone all over the Continent, where they have been confoundedly afraid we might begin a war which would end no prophecy could tell where." (Life, &c., of George Ticknor, I. 480.) Count Pozzo di Borgo's company would not be likely to be composed of persons sympathizing with the French opposition.

53. The writer has had occasion to treat of this occurrence more at length in his Life of Mr. Webster. He has there expressed the opinion that if the friends of the President, when they obtained a majority in the Senate, had contented themselves with adopting a resolution exonerating him from the censure passed in 1834, no one could have complained. Probably they would have done so, if the circumstances attending the adoption of Mr. Clay's resolution had not provoked them to devise what they regarded as an imposing form of stigmatizing that act. All that is of any consequence now, in relation to this proceeding, turns upon the contradiction between the constitutional requirement to "keep" a legislative journal, and a subsequent obliteration or cancellation of any part of it, by any means whatever. On this subject, see the protest read in the Senate by Mr. Webster, in his Life, by the present writer, vol. I, p. 545, et seq.

54. Dr. Parrish, Wm. Wharton, Joseph Foulke.

55. There is, perhaps, no other of the writings of Hamilton which more strikingly exhibits his marvellous powers, the perspicuity of his style, and his faculty of illustrating an intricate subject, than this report. When he made it he was at the age of thirty-three. It reads as if he had passed a long life in some country where banks had been established for

centuries, and in some official connection with them, or in mercantile pursuits that had brought him into daily experience of their operations; yet he had never been out of the United States since he came from the Island of St. Christopher, at the age of fifteen; there had been but three banks in this country when he wrote this report; and every part of his life that had not been passed in the army, in Congress, or in the proceedings to form and establish the Constitution of the United States, had been employed in the practice of the law. This master-piece of exposition may be read with delight by any person of taste, such are the grace, precision, force and completeness with which he handles his subject. We need not wonder that it carried conviction among the members of the body to which it was addressed.

56. Works of Thomas Jefferson.

57. See the history of the various bills for creating a national bank stated more in detail in the Life of Mr. Webster, by the present writer, vol. I.

58. McCullough vs. the State of Maryland, 4 Wheaton's R. 316.

59. At the time of the election of Mr. Van Buren, the whole number of electoral votes was 294, a majority being 148. There was no choice of a Vice President by the electoral colleges. Richard M. Johnson, of Kentucky, received 147 votes, and was afterwards elected Vice President by the Senate. General Harrison, the leading Whig candidate for the Presidency, received the electoral votes of Vermont, New Jersey, Delaware, Maryland, Kentucky, Ohio and Indiana, seventy-three in all. The fourteen votes of Massachusetts were given to Mr. Webster. Hugh L. White, of Tennessee, received the votes of Tennessee and of Georgia, twenty-six in all. The votes of South Carolina, eleven, were given to W. P. Mangum, of North Carolina. It is apparent, therefore, that at this time the Whigs, if we comprehend in that term all the opponents of the Democratic party, were in a decided minority in the country at large. This was partly because their leading candidate was far inferior to the important men of the opposition; but it was chiefly because the great States of New York, Pennsylvania and Virginia still adhered to the financial and other measures of General Jackson, and because so many of the smaller States were still indisposed to return to the policy of a national bank.

60. The persons here referred to as "Conservatives," were a class of Democrats or Republicans, who stood aloof for a time from their party.

61. Subsequent generations will need a key to the "log cabin" and the barrel of "hard cider," the shouts of "Tippecanoe and Tyler too," the long processions of trades, the enormous multitudes that gathered at the great open-air meetings. Omnia quæ vidi, the writer might say, and he might add with a variation, quorum pars minima fui.

62. The sixty electoral votes obtained by Mr. Van Buren were given by the States of New Hampshire, Virginia, South Carolina, Illinois, Alabama, Missouri and Arkansas.

63. In a letter from one of his friends, which lies before me, written at the time of his re-election, it is said that he was the first person who had been elected a second time to the Senate of the United States by the legislature of Pennsylvania.

64. April 4th, 1841.

65. The members of the Harrison cabinet were Daniel Webster, Secretary of State; Thomas Ewing, Secretary of the Treasury; John Bell, Secretary of War; George E. Badger, Secretary of the Navy; John J. Crittenden, Attorney General; Francis Granger, Postmaster General.

66. For the reasons which led Mr. Webster to remain in office, see his Life, by the present writer, vol. II., pp. 69 et seq. See farther, note on page 625 post.

67. Speech delivered in the Senate July 7th, 1841. Compare President Tyler's veto message.

68. See the speech of Sept. 2, 1841.
69. Speech of December 29, 1841.
70. Compare what Mr. Webster has said on the veto power.
71. Mr. Buchanan cannot discover, after careful examination, that any Catholic Emancipation bill was vetoed by George the Third in 1806, according to the statement of Mr. Grant. That gentleman, most probably, intended to refer to the bill for this purpose which was introduced by the Grenville ministry, in March, 1807, under the impression that they had obtained for it the approbation of His Majesty. Upon its second reading, notice was given of his displeasure. The ministry then agreed to drop the bill altogether; but, notwithstanding this concession, they were changed, because they would not give a written pledge to the king, that they should propose no farther concessions to the Catholics thereafter. This was an exertion of the royal prerogative beyond the veto power. (Note by Mr. Buchanan.)
72. The history of this treaty and of the controversy relating to the maps is given in the author's Life of Mr. Webster, vol. II, chap. 28.
73. This account of the conversation is taken from a memorandum in the handwriting of Mr. Sloan.
74. General Samuel Houston, an intimate friend of General Jackson, held conversations in the winter of 1824–5 with the members of the Ohio delegation, in which he took it upon him, in his efforts to persuade them to vote for Jackson, to say, that in the event of his election, "your man" (Clay) "can have anything he pleases." All this, and a great deal more of the same kind, meant only an expectation and belief on the part of some of Jackson's friends, that a political union between him and Mr. Clay would be for the good of the country, and it was their earnest wish to see it take place. Some of the friends of Mr. Clay supposed that these were advances made to him with General Jackson's knowledge and consent, and that, as they were not met by Clay, the indifference with which they were treated caused General Jackson's subsequent charge of "bargain and corruption" between Mr. Clay and Mr. Adams. This and many similar mistakes were the natural fruits of the excitement which prevailed in Washington during the winter of 1824–5.
75. Wife of the Hon. James J. Roosevelt of New York.
76. Mr. Calhoun was Secretary of State under President Tyler.
77. Wife of Mr. Justice Catron of the Supreme Court of the United States.
78. President Tyler's marriage to Miss Gardiner is the event here alluded to. The letter is without date.
79. Mary married George W. Baker, and died in San Francisco in 1855, while Mr. Buchanan was Minister to England. Eskridge died in 1857; James in 1862. Harriet dropped the name of Rebecca after she had grown up, and was always known as Miss Lane, or Miss Harriet Lane.
80. In these days of millions, such a fortune, accumulated by a man who had been in public life for about forty years, seems moderate indeed. It will appear, as we draw near the end of Mr. Buchanan's life, that he did not enrich himself out of the public, and that such fortune as he did accumulate must have been, as Mr. Henry says, the slow increase of means honorably acquired and carefully husbanded. Yet he was not a parsimonious, but, on the contrary, he was a generous man.
81. James Buchanan Yates, son of Mr. Buchanan's sister Maria, who married Dr. Yates, a physician in Meadville, Pennsylvania.
82. Mr. Buchanan became Secretary of State under President Polk in March of this year.

83. Wife of the Hon. Stephen Pleasonton, for very many years Fifth Auditor of the Treasury Department. He possessed the entire confidence of all administrations.
84. James Buchanan Henry: very averse as a boy to a vegetable diet.
85. The Hon. Robert J. Walker of Mississippi, Secretary of the Treasury under President Polk, appointed March 6, 1845.
86. Mrs. Yates.
87. James Buchanan Yates.
88. John Sullivan, Esq., an Irish gentleman of advanced years, long a resident of Washington, famous for his good dinners.
89. Mr. Upshur was killed by the explosion on board the Princeton, in February, 1844. See ante, p. 521.
90. Congressional Globe, Vol. 14, pp. 240, 271, 362. The resolutions may be found at page 332.
91. William R. King of Alabama. He was a Senator in Congress from that State for a period of nearly twenty-five years, from 1819 to 1844. He resigned his seat in the Senate and accepted the mission to France, to which he was appointed in April, 1844, by President Tyler. He was an accomplished statesman of broad and liberal views. A strong friendship had existed between him and Mr. Buchanan, from the time when the latter entered the Senate. Mr. King was at first under the impression that Mr. Buchanan had declined the judgeship, and on the 1st of January he wrote to express his gratification that the matter had taken this turn. But in fact the appointment was never offered.
92. This does not refer to Mr. Justice Grier, who became the successor of Judge Baldwin.
93. This refers to the measure for free trade in corn.
94. Mr. Bancroft informs me that he subsequently advised Mr. Buchanan not to open a negotiation for a reduction of the British taxes on tobacco, knowing that it would be a useless effort to endeavor to persuade England to change that part of her financial system.
95. The niece of Mrs. Madison.
96. Miss Clementina Pleasonton.
97. It should in justice be stated that, after it was known to Mr. Webster in the winter of 1843–44, that a project was on foot for bringing in Texas by treaty, he, not being at that time in any public position, made great efforts to arouse a popular opposition to it in New England, but without any success. It was not until after the executive Government had become committed to the government and people of Texas to promote the annexation by Mr. Calhoun's plan of legislative action, and after this plan had been submitted to Congress, that there began to be any considerable opposition to it in the North, coming from organized popular meetings. During the Presidential election of 1844, although the Democratic party made the annexation of Texas one of the measures to be expected from it in case of the election of its candidate, the Whig party, in consequence of the attitude of their candidate, Mr. Clay, on this subject, was not in a position to oppose the annexation on account of the slavery existing in that country. (Compare the detailed account of the annexation of Texas in the Life of Mr. Webster, at the passages referred to in the Index, verb. "Texas.")
98. This was not only the view entertained by President Polk and his political party, but it was the deliberate opinion of Mr. Webster, who may be said to have represented all the grounds of opposition to the measure. He re-entered the Senate on the 5th of March, 1845, four days after the passage of the joint resolutions for the annexation of Texas. On the 11th he wrote a letter to his son, in which he expressed with precision the whole of his objections to this measure, and decidedly maintained that Mexico could now have no

just cause for war, if the measure should be accomplished. He exonerated Mr. Polk and his cabinet from any desire to provoke a war with Mexico, and in regard to foreign intervention he said: "Nor do I believe that the principal nations of Europe, or any of them, will instigate Mexico to war. The policy of England is undoubtedly pacific. She cannot want Texas herself; and though her desire would be to see that country independent, yet it is not a point she would seek to carry by disturbing the peace of the world. But she will, doubtless, now take care that Mexico shall not cede California, or any part thereof, to us. You know my opinion to have been, and now is, that the port of San Francisco would be twenty times as valuable to us as all Texas." (See the entire letter, Life of Mr. Webster, II., 249.)

99. Mr. C. A. Wickliffe, who was sent by Mr. Buchanan to Texas as a confidential agent, and from whose report I have taken the principal facts above related, writing from Galveston on the 6th of May, said: "The subject of the terms of annexation, or the result of the measure when Congress meets, no longer constitutes the topic of conversation among the people. They speak of this as a subject settled. The all-engrossing topic among them is the provisions of their constitution to be adopted. Upon this subject I have been gratified to listen to the views and opinions of many intelligent men. The deep interest they feel in the work of making a constitution which shall secure to Texas and her citizens the blessings of a good government and social order, gives high hopes of their future destiny. I undertake to predict that you will be surprised when you shall see their constitution, emanating from a people of whose disorder so much has been said."

100. Prussian Minister.

101. Secretary of War.

102. John Slidell of New Orleans, at this time a Representative in Congress from Louisiana, was the same person who became famous all over the world, along with his colleague, Mr. Mason, during our civil war, after they were seized from on board the British steam-packet Trent, on their way as Confederate envoys to England, brought to the United States, imprisoned, and afterwards released. Consult the Index, verb. "Slidell."

103. Colonel Taylor was promoted to the rank of major-general soon after the first of his victories.

104. James Barbour of Virginia, Secretary of War under President John Quincy Adams.

105. Afterwards governor of South Carolina during the first period of secession.

106. This refers to the charges made by Mr. C. J. Ingersoll against Mr. Webster. See the Life of Webster, Index, verb. "Ingersoll."

107. Chief Justice Taney.

108. Wife of the Spanish Minister. She was a Scotch lady, née Inglis.